Programme for International Student Assessment

PISA™ 2006
Science Competencies for Tomorrow's World

Volume 1 – Analysis

OECD

ORGANISATION FOR ECONOMIC CO-OPERATION AND DEVELOPMENT

ORGANISATION FOR ECONOMIC CO-OPERATION AND DEVELOPMENT

The OECD is a unique forum where the governments of 30 democracies work together to address the economic, social and environmental challenges of globalisation. The OECD is also at the forefront of efforts to understand and to help governments respond to new developments and concerns, such as corporate governance, the information economy and the challenges of an ageing population. The Organisation provides a setting where governments can compare policy experiences, seek answers to common problems, identify good practice and work to co-ordinate domestic and international policies.

The OECD member countries are: Australia, Austria, Belgium, Canada, the Czech Republic, Denmark, Finland, France, Germany, Greece, Hungary, Iceland, Ireland, Italy, Japan, Korea, Luxembourg, Mexico, the Netherlands, New Zealand, Norway, Poland, Portugal, the Slovak Republic, Spain, Sweden, Switzerland, Turkey, the United Kingdom and the United States. The Commission of the European Communities takes part in the work of the OECD.

OECD Publishing disseminates widely the results of the Organisation's statistics gathering and research on economic, social and environmental issues, as well as the conventions, guidelines and standards agreed by its members.

This work is published on the responsibility of the Secretary-General of the OECD. The opinions expressed and arguments employed herein do not necessarily reflect the official views of the Organisation or of the governments of its member countries.

Also available in French under the title:
PISA 2006
Les compétences en sciences, un atout pour réussir
VOLUME 1 ANALYSE DES RÉSULTATS

Foreword

Compelling incentives for individuals, economies and societies to raise levels of education have been the driving force for governments to improve the quality of educational services. The prosperity of countries now derives to a large extent from their human capital, and to succeed in a rapidly changing world, individuals need to advance their knowledge and skills throughout their lives. Education systems need to lay strong foundations for this, by fostering learning and strengthening the capacity and motivation of young adults to continue learning beyond school.

All stakeholders – parents, students, those who teach and run education systems, and the general public – therefore need good information on how well their education systems prepare students for life. Many countries monitor students' learning in order to provide answers to this question. Comparative international assessments can extend and enrich the national picture by providing a larger context within which to interpret national performance. They can provide countries with information to judge their areas of relative strength and weakness and to monitor progress. They can also stimulate countries to raise aspirations. And they can inform national efforts to help students to learn better, teachers to teach better, and schools to become more effective.

In response to the need for cross-nationally comparable evidence on student performance, the Organisation for Economic Co-operation and Development (OECD) launched the OECD Programme for International Student Assessment (PISA™) in 1997. PISA represents a commitment by governments to monitor the outcomes of education systems in terms of student achievement on a regular basis and within an internationally agreed common framework. It aims to provide a new basis for policy dialogue and for collaboration in defining and implementing educational goals, in innovative ways that reflect judgements about the skills that are relevant to adult life.

Key features driving the development of PISA have been: its policy orientation, its innovative "literacy" concept that is concerned with the capacity of students extrapolate from what they have learned and apply their knowledge in novel settings, its relevance to lifelong learning, and its regularity. PISA has now become the most comprehensive and rigorous international programme to assess student performance and to collect data on the student, family and institutional factors that can help to explain differences in performance. The countries participating in PISA together make up close to 90% of the world economy.

The first PISA survey was conducted in 2000. Focusing on *reading literacy*, PISA 2000 revealed wide differences in the extent to which countries succeeded in enabling young adults to access, manage, integrate, evaluate and reflect on written information in order to develop their potential and further expand their horizons. For some countries, the results were disappointing, showing that their 15-year-olds' performance lagged considerably behind that of other countries, sometimes by the equivalent of several years of schooling and sometimes despite high investments in education. PISA 2000 also highlighted significant variation in the performance of schools and raised concerns about equity in the distribution of learning opportunities. However, PISA 2000 also showed that some countries were highly successful in achieving high and equitable learning outcomes, and this has sparked an unprecedented research and policy debate in many countries as to the factors that drive successful educational performance. That debate intensified when results from the PISA 2003 assessment, with its focus on mathematics competencies, were published.

PISA 2003 not only extended the range of competencies covered by PISA to the area of cross-curricular problem solving, but it also deepened analysis at both national and international levels of those policies and practises associated with high performance standards.

How have things changed since then? This report presents first results from the PISA 2006 survey and adds an important new perspective, by examining not just where countries stand but also how things have changed since 2000. While those countries with strong and equitable student performance remain important benchmarks, those where results have significantly improved will no doubt receive much attention too. But the report goes well beyond the relative standing of countries in terms of student performance. With a focus on science performance, the report also examines students' attitudes towards science, their awareness of the life opportunities that possessing science competencies may bring, and the science learning opportunities and environments offered by their schools. It also places student performance in the context of other factors, such as gender, socio-economic background and school policies and practices, providing insights into how they influence the development of knowledge and skills at home and at school and analysing what the implications are for policy development.

The PISA 2006 assessment was completed in countries between March and November 2006. Therefore, this report can only provide an initial picture of the results. It should be seen as a starting point for further research and analysis at national and international levels, much in the same way as the initial reports from the PISA 2000 and PISA 2003 surveys have been.

The report is the product of a collaborative effort between the countries participating in PISA, the experts and institutions working within the framework of the PISA Consortium, and the OECD. The report was drafted by Andreas Schleicher, John Cresswell, Miyako Ikeda and Claire Shewbridge of the OECD Directorate for Education, with advice as well as analytical and editorial support from Alla Berezner, David Baker, Roel Bosker, Rodger Bybee, Eric Charbonnier, Aletta Grisay, Heinz Gilomen, Eric Hanushek, Donald Hirsch, Kate Lancaster, Henry Levin, Elke Lüdemann, Yugo Nakamura, Harry O'Neill, Susanne Salz, Wolfram Schulz, Diana Toledo Figueroa, Ross Turner, Sophie Vayssettes, Elisabeth Villoutreix, Wendy Whitham, Ludger Woessman and Karin Zimmer. Chapter 4 also draws in significant ways on analytic work undertaken in the context of PISA 2000 by Jaap Scheerens and Douglas Willms. Administrative support was provided by Juliet Evans.

The PISA assessment instruments and the data underlying the report were prepared by the PISA Consortium, under the direction of Raymond Adams at the Australian Council for Educational Research. The expert group that guided the preparation of the science assessment framework and instruments was chaired by Rodger Bybee.

The development of the report was steered by the PISA Governing Board, which is chaired by Ryo Watanabe (Japan). Annex B of the report lists the members of the various PISA bodies as well as the individual experts and consultants who have contributed to this report and to PISA in general.

The report is published on the responsibility of the Secretary-General of the OECD.

Ryo Watanabe
Chair of the PISA Governing Board

Barbara Ischinger
Director for Education, OECD

Table of contents

FOREWORD 3

CHAPTER 1 **INTRODUCTION** 15
PISA – An overview 16
- PISA 2006 – focus on science 16
- The PISA surveys 16

What PISA measures and how 20
- Performance in PISA: what is measured 20
- The PISA instruments: how measurement takes place 22
- The PISA student population 22

What is different about the PISA 2006 survey? 25
- A detailed understanding of student performance in and attitudes to science 25
- A comparison of change over time 26
- The introduction of new background information about students 26

Organisation of the report 26

READER'S GUIDE 29

CHAPTER 2 **A PROFILE OF STUDENT PERFORMANCE IN SCIENCE** 31
Introduction 32

The PISA approach to assessing student performance in science 33
- The PISA approach to science 33
- The PISA definition of scientific literacy 34
- The PISA science framework 35
- The PISA 2006 science units 40
- How the results are reported 41
- A profile of PISA science questions 44

What students can do in science 48
- Student performance in science 48

An overview of student performance in different areas of science 62
- Student performance on the different science comptetencies 62
- Student performance in the different knowledge domains 71

A detailed analysis of student performance on the science comptetency scales 76
- Student performance in identifying scientific issues 76
- Student performance in explaining phenomena scientifically 86
- Student performance in using scientific evidence 100

Implications for policy 113
- Meeting demands for scientific excellence 113
- Securing strong baseline science competencies 113
- Strengths and weaknesses in different aspects of science 114
- Gender differences 114
- Do the results matter? 115

CHAPTER 3 **A PROFILE OF STUDENT ENGAGEMENT IN SCIENCE**...121

Introduction...122

Measuring attitudes and engagement in PISA...122
- Notes on the interpretation of the measures..125

Do students support scientific enquiry?...127
- General value of science...127
- Support for scientific enquiry...130
- Personal value of science...133

Do students believe they can succeed in science?..133
- Students' confidence in overcoming difficulties in science...134
- Students' self-concept in science..137

Are students interested in science?...139
- Interest in learning science as a subject...139
- The importance of doing well in science..145
- Motivation to learn science because it is useful...145
- Science-related activities..153

Do students feel responsible towards resources and the environment?.................................155
- Awareness of environmental issues...155
- Students' level of concern for environmental issues...158
- Optimism regarding environmental issues..158
- Responsibility for sustainable development..161
- Gender differences in responsibility towards resources and the environment................163

Overview of gender differences in science performance and in attitudes towards science.....163

Implications for policy..164

CHAPTER 4 **QUALITY AND EQUITY IN THE PERFORMANCE OF STUDENTS AND SCHOOLS**.............169

Introduction...170

**Securing consistent standards for schools: a profile of between- and within-school differences
in student performance**..170

The quality of learning outcomes and equity in the distribution of learning opportunities..........173
- Immigrant status and student performance...174
- Socio-economic background and student and school performance.................................181

**Socio-economic difference and the role that education policy can play in moderating the impact
of socio-economic disadvantage**..193

Socio-economic background and the role of parents..196

Implications for policy..198
- A concentration of low-performing students...199
- Differing slopes and strengths of socio-economic gradients..200
- Differing socio-economic profiles...202
- Differing gradients across schools..203
- Differing gradients within schools..204

CHAPTER 5 **SCHOOL AND SYSTEM CHARACTERISTICS AND STUDENT PERFORMANCE
IN SCIENCE**..........213

Introduction..........214

Admittance, selection and grouping policies..........216
- School admittance policies..........216
- Institutional differentiation and grade repetition..........220
- Ability grouping within schools..........223
- The relationship between school admittance, selection and ability grouping and
  student performance in science..........225

Public and private stakeholders in the management and financing of schools..........229
- The relationship between public and private stakeholders in the management and financing
  of schools and student performance in science..........229

The role of parents: school choice and parental influence on schools..........232
- The relationship between school choice and parental influence on schools and
  student performance in science..........236

Accountability arrangements..........237
- Nature and use of accountability systems..........240
- Feedback on student performance to parents and the public..........240
- The existence of standards-based external examinations..........242
- The relationship between accountability policies and student performance in science..........243

Approaches to school management and the involvement of stakeholders in decision making..........245
- Involvement of school staff in decision making at school..........245
- Involvement of stakeholders in decision making..........249
- The relationship between school autonomy and student performance in science..........252

School resources..........254
- Human resources reported by school principals..........254
- Material resources reported by school principals..........256
- Learning time and educational resources reported by students and school principals..........258
- The relationship between school resources and student performance in science..........262

The joint impact of school and system resources, practices, and policies on student performance..........264

**The joint impact of school and system resources, practices, and policies on the relationship
between socio-economic background and student performance in science**..........272

Implications for policy..........275

CHAPTER 6 **A PROFILE OF STUDENT PERFORMANCE IN READING AND MATHEMATICS
FROM PISA 2000 TO PISA 2006**..........283

Introduction..........284

What students can do in reading..........284
- A profile of PISA reading questions..........286

Student performance in reading..........293
- The mean performances of countries/economies in reading..........295
- How student performance in reading has changed..........301
- Gender differences in reading..........303

What students can do in mathematics..304
  ▪ A profile of PISA mathematics questions..304

Student performance in mathematics...312
  ▪ The mean performances of countries/economies in mathematics...................................315
  ▪ How student performance in mathematics has changed..319
  ▪ Gender differences in mathematics..320

Implications for policy..321
  ▪ Reading..321
  ▪ Mathematics...322
  ▪ Gender differences...323

REFERENCES...327

ANNEX A **TECHNICAL BACKGROUND**..331
Annex A1: Construction of indices and other derived measures from the student, school
              and parent context questionnaires..332
Annex A2: The PISA target population, the PISA samples and the definition of schools...........347
Annex A3: Standard errors, significance tests and subgroup comparisons..........................359
Annex A4: Quality assurance...362
Annex A5: Development of the PISA assessment instruments...363
Annex A6: Reliability of the coding of responses to open-ended items...............................367
Annex A7: Comparison of results from the PISA 2000, PISA 2003 and PISA 2006 assessments...............369
Annex A8: Technical notes on multilevel regression analysis...372
Annex A9: SPSS syntax to prepare data files for multilevel regression analysis...............372
Annex A10: Technical notes on measures of students' attitudes to science...........................372

ANNEX B **THE DEVELOPMENT AND IMPLEMENTATION OF PISA – A COLLABORATIVE EFFORT**.........377

ANNEX C **LINKS TO THE DATA UNDERLYING THIS REPORT**...383

LIST OF BOXES

Box 1.1   Key features of PISA 2006...19

Box 1.2   Population coverage and the exclusion of students...24

Box 1.3   How a PISA test is typically carried out in a school..25

Box 2.1   How skill demands in the job market have changed – trends in routine and nonroutine task input
            in the United States since 1960 33

Box 2.2.   Interpreting sample statistics 50

Box 2.3   Science performance at age 15 and countries' research intensity 51

Box 2.4.   How seriously do students take the PISA assessment?..52

Box 2.5   Interpreting differences in PISA scores: how large a gap?...55

Box 2.6   Computer-based assessment of science..100

Box 3.1   An overview of 15-year-olds' attitudes to science...124

Box 3.2   Interpreting the PISA indices..126

Box 3.3   Comparing differences in attitudes towards science by gender, socio-economic background
            and immigrant background 128

Box 3.4   Do students' beliefs about their abilities simply mirror their performance? 137

Box 4.1   How to read Figure 4.5..182

Box 5.1   Interpreting the data from schools and their relationship to student performance 215

Box 5.2   Multilevel models: Admitting, grouping and selecting...227

Box 5.3   Multilevel models: School management and funding – public or private...232

Box 5.4   Multilevel models: Parental pressure and choice...237

Box 5.5   Multilevel models: Accountability policies...244

Box 5.6   Multilevel models: School autonomy..253

Box 5.7   Multilevel models: School resources...263

Box 5.8   Combined multilevel model for student performance...265

Box 5.9   Combined multilevel model for the impact of socio-economic background..273

Box 6.1   How well does PISA performance at age 15 predict future educational success?...300

LIST OF FIGURES

Figure 1.1   A map of PISA countries and economies..18

Figure 1.2   Summary of the assessment areas in PISA 2006...21

Figure 2.1   The PISA 2006 science framework...35

Figure 2.2   PISA 2006 science context..36

Figure 2.3   PISA 2006 science competencies..37

Figure 2.4   PISA 2006 content areas for the *knowledge of science* domain...38

Figure 2.5   PISA 2006 categories for the *knowledge about science* domain...39

Figure 2.6   PISA 2006 survey of student attitudes...39

Figure 2.7   The relationship between items and students on a proficiency scale 41

Figure 2.8   Summary descriptions of the six proficiency levels on the science scale...43

Figure 2.9   A map of released science questions in PISA 2006, illustrating the proficiency levels 45

Figure 2.10   A map of selected science questions in PISA 2006, cross-referencing knowledge and competencies 46

Figure 2.11a   Percentage of students at each proficiency level on the science scale 49

Figure 2.11b   Multiple comparisons of mean performance on the science scale 56

Figure 2.11c   Range of rank of countries/economies on the science scale 58

Figure 2.12a   Student performance on the science scale and national income 59

Figure 2.12b   Student performance on the science scale and spending per student 60

Figure 2.13   Comparison of performance on the different scales in science 63

Figure 2.14a   Countries where students demonstrate relative weakness in *explaining phenomena scientifically*, but relative strength in other areas 64

Figure 2.14b   Countries/economies where students demonstrate relative strength in *explaining phenomena scientifically*, but relative weakness in other areas 65

Figure 2.14c   Countries where students demonstrate relative weakness in *using scientific evidence* 65

Figure 2.14d   Countries where students demonstrate relative strength in *using scientific evidence* 65

Figure 2.14e   Range of rank of countries/economies on the different science scales 66

Figure 2.15   Performance of males and females on the *identifying scientific issues* scale 69

Figure 2.16   Performance of males and females on the *explaining phenomena scientifically* scale 70

Figure 2.17   Performance of males and females on the *using scientific evidence* scale 70

Figure 2.18a   Mean score on the *knowledge about science* and *knowledge of science* scales 72

Figure 2.19a   Countries where students demonstrate relative strength or weakness on the "Physical systems" scale 73

Figure 2.19b   Countries/economies where students demonstrate relative strength or weakness on the "Earth and space systems" scale 74

Figure 2.19c   Countries/economies where students demonstrate relative strength or weakness on the "Living systems" scale 75

Figure 2.20   Summary descriptions of the six proficiency levels in *identifying scientific issues* 77

Figure 2.21a   Percentage of students at each proficiency level on the *identifying scientific issues* scale 79

Figure 2.22   GENETICALLY MODIFIED CROPS 80

Figure 2.23   SUNSCREENS 82

Figure 2.24   Summary descriptions of the six proficiency levels in *explaining phenomena scientifically* 86

Figure 2.25a   Percentage of students at each proficiency level on the *explaining phenomena scientifically* scale 88

Figure 2.26   CLOTHES 89

Figure 2.27   GRAND CANYON 91

Figure 2.28   MARY MONTAGU 94

Figure 2.29   PHYSICAL EXERCISE 97

Figure 2.30   Summary descriptions of the six proficiency levels in *using scientific evidence* 101

Figure 2.31a   Percentage of students at each proficiency level on the *using scientific evidence* scale 103

Figure 2.32   ACID RAIN 104

Figure 2.33   GREENHOUSE 108

Figure 3.1   PISA 2006 assessment of attitudes 123

Figure 3.2   Index of general value of science 129

Figure 3.3   Examples of students' support for scientific enquiry 131

Figure 3.4   Index of personal value of science 132

Figure 3.5   Index of self-efficacy in science 135

Figure 3.6   Performance in science and self-efficacy in science 136

Figure 3.7   Index of self-concept in science 138

Figure 3.8   Index of general interest in science 141

Figure 3.9   Examples of students' interest in learning science topics 142

Figure 3.10   Index of enjoyment of science 144

Figure 3.11   Students' perceptions of the importance of doing well in science, reading and mathematics 146

Figure 3.12   Index of instrumental motivation to learn science 147

Figure 3.13   Index of future-oriented motivation to learn science 149

Figure 3.14   Students expecting a science-related career and performance in science 151

Figure 3.15   Performance in science and proportions of students expecting a science-related career at age 30 152

Figure 3.16   Index of science-related activities 154

Figure 3.17   Index of students' awareness of environmental issues 156

Figure 3.18   Performance in science and awareness of environmental issues 157

Figure 3.19   Index of students' level of concern for environmental issues 159

Figure 3.20   Index of students' optimism regarding environmental issues 160

Figure 3.21   Index of students' responsibility for sustainable development 162

Figure 4.1   Variance in student performance between schools and within schools on the science scale 171

Figure 4.2a   Student performance on the science scale by immigrant status 177

Figure 4.2b   Percentage of second-generation versus native students scoring below Level 2 on the science scale 177

Figure 4.3   Characteristics of schools attended by native students and students with an immigrant background 179

Figure 4.4   Differences between native students and students with an immigrant background with regard to
               their personal value of science, enjoyment of science and future-oriented science motivation 181

Figure 4.5   Relationship between student performance in science and socio-economic background for
               the OECD area as a whole 183

Figure 4.6   How socio-economic background relates to student performance in science 184

Figure 4.7   Difference between the unadjusted mean score and the mean score on the science scale if the mean
               PISA index of economic, social and cultural status were equal in all OECD countries 187

Figure 4.8   Student variability in the distribution of the PISA index of economic, social and cultural status (ESCS) 188

Figure 4.9   School variability in the distribution of the PISA index of economic, social and cultural status (ESCS) 188

Figure 4.10   Performance in science and the impact of socio-economic background 189

Figure 4.11   Within-school and between school socio-economic effect 192

Figure 4.12   Effects of students' and schools' socio-economic background on student performance in science 194

Figure 4.13   Socio-economic background and the role of parents 197

Figure 4.14a   Relationship between school performance and schools' socio-economic background in Denmark, Portugal,
               Korea and the United Kingdom 200

Figure 4.14b   Relationship between school performance and schools' socio-economic background in Sweden and Mexico 202

Figure 4.14c   Relationship between school performance and schools' socio-economic background in United States,
               Germany, Spain and Norway 203

Figure 4.14d   Relationship between school performance and schools' socio-economic background in Belgium,
               Switzerland, New Zealand and Finland 204

Figure 4.14e   Relationship between school performance and schools' socio-economic background:
               school mean score 300-700 205

Figure 4.14f   Relationship between school performance and schools' socio-economic background:
               school mean score 200-600 and 100-500 210

11

Figure 5.1   School admittance policies...218

Figure 5.2   Interrelationships between institutional factors...220

Figure 5.3   Ability grouping within schools and student performance in science...224

Figure 5.4   Impact of the socio-economic background of students and schools on student performance in science,
             by tracking systems...228

Figure 5.5   Public and private schools..230

Figure 5.6   School choice...233

Figure 5.7   School principals' perceptions of parents' expectations...234

Figure 5.8   Parents' perceptions of school quality..235

Figure 5.9   Use of achievement data for accountability purposes...238

Figure 5.10   School accountability to parents...241

Figure 5.11   Involvement of schools in decision making..246

Figure 5.12   Direct influence of stakeholders on decision making at school..250

Figure 5.13   Influence of business and industry on the school curriculum...252

Figure 5.14   School principals' reports on vacant science teaching positions and their perception of the supply
             of qualified science teachers..255

Figure 5.15   Material resources – index of the quality of schools' educational resources.....................................257

Figure 5.16   Percentage of students following science courses at age 15...259

Figure 5.17   Students' time spent on learning...260

Figure 5.18   Index of school activities to promote the learning of science...261

Figure 5.19a Variance and explained variance in science performance at the student, school and system levels....266

Figure 5.19b School-level variance and explained variance in science performance, by country...........................268

Figure 5.20   Net association of school factors with student performance in science...270

Figure 5.21   Relationship between student economic, social and cultural status and student performance in science,
             by learning time at school..274

Figure 5.22   Relationship between student economic, social and cultural status and student performance in science,
             by tracking system...275

Figure 6.1   Percentage of students at each proficiency level on the reading scale...286

Figure 6.2   A map of selected items in reading...287

Figure 6.3   LABOUR..288

Figure 6.4   GRAFFITI...289

Figure 6.5   LAKE CHAD...290

Figure 6.6   RUNNERS..291

Figure 6.7   Summary descriptions for the five proficiency levels in reading...292

Figure 6.8a   Multiple comparisons of mean performance on the reading scale...296

Figure 6.8b   Range of rank of countries/economies on the reading scale...298

Figure 6.9   Differences in reading between PISA 2006 and PISA 2000...301

Figure 6.10   Performance of males and females on the reading scale...303

Figure 6.11   A map of selected items in mathematics..305

Figure 6.12   CARPENTER..306

Figure 6.13   TEST SCORE..307

Figure 6.14   EXCHANGE RATE – *QUESTION 11*..308

Figure 6.15   GROWING UP...309

Figure 6.16   STAIRCASE..310

Figure 6.17   EXCHANGE RATE – *QUESTION 9* 311

Figure 6.18   Summary descriptions of the six proficiency levels in mathematics 312

Figure 6.19   Percentage of students at each proficiency level on the mathematics scale 314

Figure 6.20a   Multiple comparisons of mean performance on the mathematics scale 316

Figure 6.20b   Range of rank of countries/economies on the mathematics scale 318

Figure 6.21   Differences in mathematics between PISA 2006 and PISA 2003 319

Figure 6.22   Performance of males and females on the mathematics scale 321

Figure A3.1   Labels used in a two-way table 360

LIST OF TABLES

Table A1.1   Levels of parental education converted into years of schooling 335

Table A1.2   A multilevel model to estimate grade effects in science performance, after accounting for selected background variables 338

Table A2.1   PISA target populations and samples 349

Table A2.2   Exclusions 352

Table A2.3   Response rates 355

Table A5.1   Distribution of items by the dimensions of the PISA framework for the assessment of science 364

Table A5.2   Distribution of items by the dimensions of the PISA framework for the assessment of reading literacy 364

Table A5.3   Distribution of items by the dimensions of the PISA framework for the assessment of mathematics 365

Table A7.1   Linking errors 369

Table A7.2   Comparison of science link items in the three PISA surveys 370

Table A10.1   Population context: proportion of students enrolled in formal education 372

Table A10.2   Psychometric quality of the PISA 2006 attitudinal measures: classical item statistics for the pooled OECD and pooled partner countries/economies 373

Table A10.3   Overview of the relationship between the attitudinal indices and science performance 374

Table A10.4   List of PISA science-related careers in ISCO-88 375

Introduction

PISA – An overview 16
- PISA 2006 – focus on science 16
- The PISA surveys 16

What PISA measures and how 20
- Performance in PISA: what is measured 20
- The PISA instruments: how measurement takes place 22
- The PISA student population 22

What is different about the PISA 2006 survey? 25
- A detailed understanding of student performance in and attitudes to science 25
- A comparison of change over time 26
- The introduction of new background information about students 26

Organisation of the report 26

PISA – AN OVERVIEW

PISA 2006 – focus on science

Are students well prepared to meet the challenges of the future? Are they able to analyse, reason and communicate their ideas effectively? Have they found the kinds of interests they can pursue throughout their lives as productive members of the economy and society? The OECD Programme for International Student Assessment (PISA) seeks to provide some answers to these questions through its surveys of key competencies of 15-year-old students. PISA surveys are administered every three years in the OECD member countries and a group of partner countries, which together make up close to 90% of the world economy.[1]

PISA assesses the extent to which students near the end of compulsory education have acquired some of the knowledge and skills that are essential for full participation in society, focusing on student competencies in the key subject areas of reading, mathematics and science. PISA seeks to assess not merely whether students can reproduce what they have learned, but also to examine how well they can extrapolate from what they have learned and apply their knowledge in novel settings, ones related to school and non-school contexts. This report presents the results of the most recent PISA survey held in 2006.

PISA 2006 focused on students' competency in science. In today's technology-based societies, understanding fundamental scientific concepts and theories and the ability to structure and solve scientific problems are more important than ever. Yet the percentage of students in some OECD countries who are studying science and technology in universities has dropped markedly over the past 15 years. The reasons for this are varied, but some research suggests that student attitudes towards science, may play an important role (OECD, 2006a). PISA 2006 therefore assessed not only science knowledge and skills, but also the attitudes which students have towards science, the extent to which they are aware of the life opportunities that possessing science competencies may open, and the science learning opportunities and environments which their schools offer.

The PISA surveys

PISA focuses on young people's ability to use their knowledge and skills to meet real-life challenges. This orientation reflects a change in the goals and objectives of curricula themselves, which are increasingly concerned with what students can do with what they learn at school and not merely with whether they have mastered specific curricular content.

Key features driving the development of PISA have been its:

- Policy orientation, which connects data on student learning outcomes with data on students' characteristics and on key factors shaping their learning inside and outside school in order to draw attention to differences in performance patterns and to identify the characteristics of schools and education systems that have high performance standards.

- Innovative "literacy" concept, which is concerned with the capacity of students to apply knowledge and skills in key subject areas and to analyse, reason and communicate effectively as they pose, solve and interpret problems in a variety of situations.

- Relevance to lifelong learning, which does not limit PISA to assessing students' curricular and cross-curricular competencies, but also asks them to report on their own motivation to learn, their beliefs about themselves and their learning strategies.

- Regularity, which enables countries to monitor their progress in meeting key learning objectives.

- Breadth of geographical coverage and collaborative nature, which in PISA 2006 encompasses the 30 OECD member countries and 27 partner countries and economies.

The relevance of the knowledge and skills measured by PISA is confirmed by recent studies tracking young people in the years after they have been assessed by PISA. Studies in Australia, Canada and Denmark display a strong relationship between the performance in reading on the PISA 2000 assessment at age 15 and the chance of a student completing secondary school and of carrying on with post-secondary studies at age 19. For example, Canadian students who had achieved reading proficiency Level 5 at age 15 were 16 times more likely to be enrolled in post-secondary studies when they were 19 years old than those who had not reached the reading proficiency Level 1 (see Box 6.1).

PISA is the most comprehensive and rigorous international programme to assess student performance and to collect data on the student, family and institutional factors that can help to explain differences in performance. Decisions about the scope and nature of the assessments and the background information to be collected are made by leading experts in participating countries and are steered jointly by governments on the basis of shared, policy-driven interests. Substantial efforts and resources are devoted to achieving cultural and linguistic breadth and balance in the assessment materials. Stringent quality assurance mechanisms are applied in translation, sampling and data collection. As a consequence, the results of PISA have a high degree of validity and reliability, and can significantly improve understanding of the outcomes of education in the world's economically most developed countries, as well as in a growing number of countries at earlier stages of economic development.

Together with the PISA 2000 and PISA 2003 surveys, PISA 2006 completes the first cycle of assessment in the three major subject areas – reading, mathematics and science. PISA is now conducting a second cycle of surveys, beginning in 2009 with reading as the major subject and continuing in 2012 (mathematics) and 2015 (science).

Although PISA was originally created by the governments of OECD countries, it has now become a major assessment tool in regions around the world. Beyond the OECD member countries, the survey has been conducted or is planned in:

- East and Southeast Asia: Shanghai-China, Hong Kong-China, Indonesia, Macao-China, Singapore, Chinese Taipei and Thailand
- Central and Eastern Europe[2] and Central Asia: Albania, Azerbaijan, Bulgaria, Croatia, Estonia, Kazakhstan, Kyrgyzstan, Latvia, Lithuania, Macedonia, Moldova, Montenegro, Romania, the Russian Federation, Serbia and Slovenia
- The Middle East: Israel, Jordan and Qatar
- Central and South America: Argentina, Brazil, Chile, Colombia, the Dominican Republic, Panama, Peru and Uruguay
- North Africa: Tunisia

Across the world, policy makers are using PISA findings to: gauge the knowledge and skills of students in their own country in comparison with those of the other participating countries; establish benchmarks for educational improvement, for example, in terms of the mean scores achieved by other countries or their capacity to provide high levels of equity in educational outcomes and opportunities; and understand relative strengths and weaknesses of their education systems. The interest in PISA is illustrated by the many reports produced in participating countries,[3] the numerous references to the results of PISA in public debates and the intense media attention shown to PISA throughout the world.

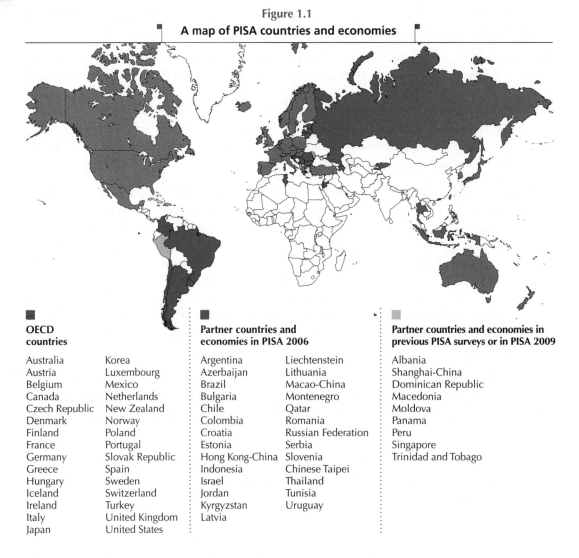

Figure 1.1
A map of PISA countries and economies

◼ **OECD countries**		◼ **Partner countries and economies in PISA 2006**		◼ **Partner countries and economies in previous PISA surveys or in PISA 2009**
Australia	Korea	Argentina	Liechtenstein	Albania
Austria	Luxembourg	Azerbaijan	Lithuania	Shanghai-China
Belgium	Mexico	Brazil	Macao-China	Dominican Republic
Canada	Netherlands	Bulgaria	Montenegro	Macedonia
Czech Republic	New Zealand	Chile	Qatar	Moldova
Denmark	Norway	Colombia	Romania	Panama
Finland	Poland	Croatia	Russian Federation	Peru
France	Portugal	Estonia	Serbia	Singapore
Germany	Slovak Republic	Hong Kong-China	Slovenia	Trinidad and Tobago
Greece	Spain	Indonesia	Chinese Taipei	
Hungary	Sweden	Israel	Thailand	
Iceland	Switzerland	Jordan	Tunisia	
Ireland	Turkey	Kyrgyzstan	Uruguay	
Italy	United Kingdom	Latvia		
Japan	United States			

The results of PISA 2006 are presented in two volumes. This is Volume 1; it summarises the performance of students in PISA 2006 and uses the information gathered to analyse what factors may relate to success in education. Volume 2 contains the data tables generated from the PISA 2006 database that have been used as a basis for the analysis included in this volume. A detailed description of the methodology employed in the implementation of PISA will be presented in the *PISA 2006 Technical Report* (OECD, forthcoming).

The remainder of this chapter looks at:

- What PISA measures (overall and within each assessment area), the methods that were employed and the target population that is involved;

- What is distinctive about PISA 2006, including the extent to which the repeat of the survey allows for comparisons across time (PISA 2000, PISA 2003 and PISA 2006);

- How the report is organised.

Box 1.1 **Key features of PISA 2006**

Content

- Although the main focus of PISA 2006 was science, the survey also covered reading and mathematics. PISA considers students' knowledge in these areas not in isolation, but in relation to their ability to reflect on their knowledge and experience and to apply them to real world issues. The emphasis is on the mastery of processes, the understanding of concepts and the ability to function in various situations within each assessment area.

- The PISA 2006 survey also, for the first time, sought information on students' attitudes to science by including questions on attitudes within the test itself, rather than only through a complementary questionnaire.

Methods

- Around 400 000 students were randomly selected to participate in PISA 2006, representing about 20 million 15-year-olds in the schools of the 57 participating countries.

- Each participating student spent two hours carrying out pencil-and-paper tasks. In three countries, some students were given additional questions via computer.

- PISA contained tasks requiring students to construct their own answers as well as multiple-choice questions. These were typically organised in units based on a written passage or graphic, of the kind that students might encounter in real life.

- Students also answered a questionnaire that took about 30 minutes to complete and focused on their personal background, their learning habits and their attitudes to science, as well as on their engagement and motivation.

- School principals completed a questionnaire about their school that included demographic characteristics as well as an assessment of the quality of the learning environment at school.

Outcomes

- A profile of knowledge and skills among 15-year-olds in 2006, consisting of a detailed profile for science, and an update for reading and mathematics.

- Contextual indicators relating performance results to student and school characteristics.

- An assessment of students' attitudes to science.

- A knowledge base for policy analysis and research.

- Trend data on changes in student knowledge and skills in reading and mathematics.

Future assessments

- The PISA 2009 survey will return to reading as the major assessment area, while PISA 2012 will focus on mathematics and PISA 2015 once again on science.

- Future tests will also assess students' capacity to read and understand electronic texts – reflecting the importance of information and computer technologies in modern societies.

WHAT PISA MEASURES AND HOW

A framework and conceptual underpinning for each assessment area in PISA was developed by international experts from participating countries and, following consultation, agreed upon by governments of the participating countries (OECD, 1999; OECD, 2003; and OECD, 2006a). The framework starts with the concept of literacy, which is concerned with the capacity of students to extrapolate from what they have learned, and to apply their knowledge in novel settings, and students' capacity to analyse, reason and communicate effectively as they pose, solve and interpret problems in a variety of situations.

The concept of literacy used in PISA is much broader than the historical notion of the ability to read and write. Furthermore, it is measured on a continuum, not as something that an individual either has or does not have. It may be necessary or desirable for some purposes to define a point on a literacy continuum below which levels of competence are considered inadequate, but the underlying continuum is important.

The acquisition of literacy is a lifelong process – taking place not just at school or through formal learning, but also through interactions with family, peers, colleagues and wider communities. Fifteen-year-olds cannot be expected to have learned everything they will need to know as adults, but they should have a solid foundation of knowledge in areas such as reading, mathematics and science. In order to continue learning in these subject areas and to apply their learning to the real world, they also need to understand fundamental processes and principles and to use these flexibly in different situations. It is for this reason that PISA measures the ability to complete tasks relating to real life, depending on a broad understanding of key concepts, rather than limiting the assessment to the understanding of subject-specific knowledge.

As well as assessing competencies in the three key subject areas, PISA aims to examine students' learning strategies, their competencies in areas such as problem-solving skills that cross disciplines and their interests in different topics. This was first done in PISA 2000 by asking students about motivation and other aspects of their attitudes towards learning, their familiarity with computers and, under the heading "self-regulated learning", aspects of their strategies for managing and monitoring their own learning. In PISA 2003, these elements were further developed and complemented with an assessment of cross-curricular problem-solving knowledge and skills. The assessment of students' motivations and attitudes continued in PISA 2006, with special attention being given to students' attitudes to and interest in science. This is further elaborated in a later section of this chapter and in detail in Chapter 3.

Performance in PISA: what is measured

PISA 2006 defines *scientific literacy* and develops its science assessment tasks and questions within a framework of four interrelated aspects, namely the:

- Knowledge or structure of knowledge that students need to acquire (*e.g.* familiarity with scientific concepts);

- Competencies that students need to apply (*e.g.* carrying out a particular scientific process);

- Contexts in which students encounter scientific problems and relevant knowledge and skills are applied (*e.g.* making decisions in relation to personal life, understanding world affairs); and

- Attitudes and dispositions of students towards science.

The frameworks for assessing science, reading and mathematical literacy in 2006 are described in full in *Assessing Scientific, Reading and Mathematical Literacy: A Framework for PISA 2006* (OECD, 2006a), and summarised in Chapters 2 and 6 of this report. Figure 1.2 below also summarises the core definition of each assessment area and how the first three of the above four dimensions are developed in each case.

Figure 1.2
Summary of the assessment areas in PISA 2006

	Science	Reading	Mathematics
Definition and its distinctive features	The extent to which an individual: • Possesses scientific knowledge and uses that knowledge to identify questions, acquire new knowledge, explain scientific phenomena and draw evidence-based conclusions about science-related issues. • Understands the characteristic features of science as a form of human knowledge and enquiry. • Shows awareness of how science and technology shape our material, intellectual and cultural environments. • Engages in science-related issues and with the ideas of science, as a reflective citizen. *Scientific literacy* requires an understanding of scientific concepts, as well as the ability to apply a scientific perspective and to think scientifically about evidence.	The capacity of an individual to understand, use and reflect on written texts in order to achieve one's goals, to develop one's knowledge and potential, and to participate in society. In addition to decoding and literal comprehension, *reading literacy* involves reading, interpretation and reflection, and the ability to use reading to fulfil one's goals in life. The focus of PISA is on reading to learn rather than learning to read, and hence students are not assessed on the most basic reading skills.	The capacity of an individual to identify and understand the role that mathematics plays in the world, to make well-founded judgements and to use and engage with mathematics in ways that meet the needs of that individual's life as a constructive, concerned and reflective citizen. *Mathematical literacy* is related to wider, functional use of mathematics; engagement includes the ability to recognise and formulate mathematical problems in various situations.
Knowledge domain	*Knowledge of science,* such as: • "Physical systems" • "Living systems" • "Earth and space systems" • "Technology systems" *Knowledge about science,* such as: • "Scientific enquiry" • "Scientific explanations"	The form of reading materials: • *Continuous texts* including different kinds of prose such as narration, exposition, argumentation • *Non-continuous texts* including graphs, forms and lists	Clusters of relevant mathematical areas and concepts: • *Quantity* • *Space and shape* • *Change and relationships* • *Uncertainty*
Competencies involved	Type of scientific task or process: • *Identifying scientific issues* • *Explaining scientific phenomena* • *Using scientific evidence*	Type of reading task or process: • Retrieving information • Interpreting texts • Reflecting and evaluating of texts	Competency clusters define skills needed for mathematics: • *Reproduction* (simple mathematical operations) • *Connections* (bringing together ideas to solve straightforward problems) • *Reflection* (wider mathematical thinking)
Context and situation	The area of application of science, focusing on uses in relation to personal, social and global settings such as: • "Health" • "Natural resources" • "Environment" • "Hazard" • "Frontiers of science and technology"	The use for which the text is constructed: • *Private* (e.g. a personal letter) • *Public* (e.g. an official document) • *Occupational* (e.g. a report) • *Educational* (e.g. school-related reading)	The area of application of mathematics, focusing on uses in relation to personal, social and global settings such as: • *Personal* • *Educational and occupational* • *Public* • *Scientific*

The PISA instruments: how measurement takes place

As in the earlier PISA surveys, the assessment instruments in PISA 2006 were developed around units of assessment. A unit consists of stimulus material including texts, tables and/or graphs, followed by questions on various aspects of the text, table or graph, with the questions constructed so that the tasks students had to undertake were as close as possible to tasks likely to be encountered in the real world.

The questions varied in format, but in each of the assessment areas of science, reading and mathematics about 40% of the questions required students to construct their own responses, either by providing a brief answer (short-response questions) or by constructing a longer response (open-constructed response questions), allowing for the possibility of divergent individual responses and an assessment of students' justification of their viewpoints. Partial credit was given for partly correct or less sophisticated answers, with questions assessed by trained specialists using detailed scoring guides which gave direction on the codes to assign to various responses. To ensure consistency in the coding process, a proportion of the questions were coded independently by four coders. In addition, a sub-sample of student responses from each country was coded by an independent panel of centrally trained expert coders in order to verify that the coding process was carried out in equivalent ways across countries. The results show that consistent coding was achieved across countries. For details on the coding process and the reliability of scores within and across countries, see Annex A6 and the *PISA 2006 Technical Report* (OECD, forthcoming).

A further 8% of the test questions required students to construct their own responses, based on a predefined set of possible responses (closed-constructed response questions), which were scored as either correct or incorrect. The remaining 52% of questions were asked in multiple-choice format, in which students made either one choice from among four or five given alternatives or a series of choices by circling one of two optional responses (for example "yes" or "no", or "agree" or "disagree") in relation to each of a number of different propositions or statements (complex multiple-choice questions).

As elaborated further below and in Chapter 2, the PISA 2006 science assessment also included 32 questions relating to students' attitudes to science. These questions generally required students to indicate their preferences or opinions. There were no right or wrong answers to these questions. Chapter 3 offers further information on how the answers to these questions were used.

The total assessment time of 390 minutes was organised in different combinations in 13 test booklets with each individual being tested for 120 minutes. The total time across all the booklets devoted to the assessment of science was 210 minutes (54% of the total), 120 minutes were devoted to mathematics (31% of the total) and 60 minutes to reading (15% of the total). Each student was randomly assigned one of the 13 test booklets.

The PISA student population

In order to ensure the comparability of the results across countries, PISA devoted great attention to assessing comparable target populations. Differences between countries in the nature and extent of pre-primary education and care, in the age of entry to formal schooling, and in the structure of the education system do not allow school grades to be defined so that they are internationally comparable. Valid international comparisons of educational performance, therefore, need to define their populations with reference to a target age. PISA covers students who are aged between 15 years 3 months and 16 years 2 months at the time of the assessment and who have completed at least 6 years of formal schooling, regardless of the type of institution in which they are enrolled and of whether they are in full-time or part-time education, of whether they attend academic or vocational programmes, and of whether they attend public or private schools or foreign schools within the country. (For an operational definition of this target population, see the *PISA 2006 Technical Report*, [OECD, forthcoming].) The use of this age in PISA, across countries and over time, allows the performance of students to be compared in a consistent manner before they complete compulsory education.

As a result, this report is able to make statements about the knowledge and skills of individuals born in the same year and still at school at 15 years of age, but having differing educational experiences, both within and outside school. The number of school grades in which these students are to be found depends on a country's policies on school entry and promotion. Furthermore, in some countries, students in the PISA target population represent different education systems, tracks or streams.

Stringent technical standards were established for the definition of national target populations and for permissible exclusions from this definition (for more information, see the PISA website *www.pisa.oecd.org*). It was also required that the overall exclusion rate within a country be kept below 5%, to ensure that under reasonable assumptions any distortions in national mean scores would remain within plus or minus 5 score points, *i.e.* typically within the order of magnitude of two standard errors of sampling (Box 1.2). Exclusion could take place at the school level or within schools. In PISA, there are several reasons why a school or a student could be excluded. Exclusions at school level might result from removing a small, remote geographical region due to inaccessibility or size, or because of organisational or operational factors. Exclusions at the student level might occur because of intellectual disability or limited proficiency in the language of the test.

In 34 out of the 57 countries participating in PISA 2006, the percentage of school-level exclusions amounted to less than 1%, and it was less than 3% in all countries except Canada (4.3%) and the United States (3.3%). When exclusions within schools of students who met the internationally established exclusion criteria (see below), are also taken into account, the exclusion rates increase slightly. However, the overall exclusion rate remains below 2% in 32 participating countries, below 4% in 51 participating countries and below 6% in all countries, except Canada (6.35%) and Denmark (6.07%).

Restrictions on the level of exclusions of various types were as follows in PISA 2006:

- School-level exclusions for inaccessibility, feasibility or other reasons were required not to exceed 0.5% of the total number of students in the international PISA target population. Schools on the school sampling frame that had only one or two eligible students were not allowed to be excluded from the frame. However, if, based on the frame, it was clear that the percentage of students in these schools would not cause a breach of the 0.5% allowable limit, then such schools could be excluded in the field, if at that time, they still only had one or two PISA eligible students.

- School-level exclusions for students with intellectual or functional disabilities, or students with limited proficiency in the language of the PISA test, were required not to exceed 2% of students.

- Within-school exclusions for students with intellectual or functional disabilities or students with limited language proficiency were required not to exceed 2.5% of students.

Within schools in PISA 2006, students who could be excluded were:

- Intellectually disabled students, defined as students who are considered in the professional opinion of the school principal, or by other qualified staff members, to be intellectually disabled, or who have been tested psychologically as such. This category includes students who are emotionally or mentally unable to follow even the general instructions of the test. Students were not to be excluded solely because of poor academic performance or normal discipline problems.

- Students with functional disabilities, defined as students who are permanently physically disabled in such a way that they cannot perform in the PISA testing situation. Students with functional disabilities who could perform were to be included in the testing.

- Students with limited proficiency in the language of the PISA test, defined as students who had received less than one year of instruction in the language(s) of the test.

Box 1.2 **Population coverage and the exclusion of students**

The PISA test aims to be as inclusive as possible. For the definition of national target populations, PISA excludes 15-year-olds not enrolled in educational institutions. In the remainder of this report the term "15-year-olds" is used as to denote the PISA student population. Coverage of the target population of 15-year-olds within education is very high compared with other international surveys: relatively few schools were excluded from participation because of, for example, geographical remoteness. Also, within schools, exclusions of students remained below 2% in most and below 6.4% in all countries.

This high level of coverage contributes to the comparability of the assessment results. For example, even assuming that the excluded students would have systematically scored worse than those who participated, and that this relationship is moderately strong, an exclusion rate in the order of 5% would likely lead to an overestimation of national mean scores of less than 5 score points. Moreover, in most cases the exclusions were inevitable. If the correlation between the propensity of exclusions and student performance is 0.3, resulting mean scores would likely be overestimated by 1 score point if the exclusion rate is 1%, by 3 score points if the exclusion rate is 5%, and by 6 score points if the exclusion rate is 10%. If the correlation between the propensity of exclusions and student performance is 0.5, resulting mean scores would be overestimated by 1 score point if the exclusion rate is 1%, by 5 score points if the exclusion rate is 5%, and by 10 score points if the exclusion rate is 10%. For this calculation, a model was employed that assumes a bivariate normal distribution for the propensity to participate and performance. For details see the *PISA 2003 Technical Report* (OECD, 2005a).

The specific sample design and size for each country was designed to maximise sampling efficiency for student-level estimates. In OECD countries, sample sizes ranged from 3 789 students in Iceland to over 30 000 students in Mexico. Countries with large samples have often implemented PISA both at national and regional/state levels (*e.g.* Australia, Belgium, Canada, Germany, Italy, Mexico, Spain, Switzerland and the United Kingdom). The selection of samples was monitored internationally and accompanied by rigorous standards for the participation rate (both among schools selected by the international contractor and among students within these schools) to ensure that the PISA results reflect the skills of the 15-year-old students in participating countries. Countries were also required to administer the test to students in identical ways to ensure that students receive the same information prior to and during the test (Box 1.3).

Box 1.3 **How a PISA test is typically carried out in a school**

When a school has been selected to participate in PISA, a School Co-ordinator is appointed. The School Co-ordinator compiles a list of all 15-year-olds in the school and sends this list to the PISA National Centre in the country, which randomly selects 35 students to participate. The School Co-ordinator then contacts the students who have been selected for the sample and obtains the necessary permissions from parents. The testing session is usually conducted by a Test Administrator who is trained and employed by the National Centre. The Test Administrator contacts the School Co-ordinator to schedule administration of the assessment. The School Co-ordinator ensures that the students attend the testing sessions – this can sometimes be difficult because students may come from different grades and different classes. The Test Administrator's primary tasks are to ensure that each test booklet is distributed to the correct student and to introduce the tests to the students. After the test is over, the Test Administrator collects the test booklets and sends them to the National Centre for coding.

In PISA 2006, 13 different booklets were developed. In each group of 35 students, no more than three students were given the same booklet. Booklets were allocated to individual students according to a random selection process. The Test Administrator's intoduction came from a prescribed text so that all students in different schools and countries received exactly the same instructions. Before starting the actual test, the students were asked to do a practice question from their booklets. The testing session was divided into two parts – the two-hour-long test and the questionnaire session. The length of the questionnaire session varied across countries, depending on the options chosen for inclusion, but generally was about 30 minutes. Students were usually given a short break half-way through the test and again before they did the questionnaire.

WHAT IS DIFFERENT ABOUT THE PISA 2006 SURVEY?

A detailed understanding of student performance in and attitudes to science

With more than one-half of the assessment time devoted to science, PISA 2006 can report in much greater detail on science performance than was the case in PISA 2000 and PISA 2003. As well as calculating overall performance scores, it is possible to report separately on different science competencies and to establish for each performance scale conceptually grounded proficiency levels that relate student performance scores to what students are able to do. Students received scores for their capacity in each of the three science competencies (*identifying scientific issues, explaining phenomena scientifically* and *using scientific evidence*). This is different from the case for mathematics in PISA 2003, where the main distinction was by content areas (*quantity, space and shape, change and relationships,* and *uncertainty*).

In keeping with the latest research and thinking on science education (*e.g.* Bybee 1997; Fensham, 2000; Law, 2002; Mayer and Kumano, 2002), PISA 2006 also asked students about their attitudes to science within the context of the science questions themselves. The aim of this is to better understand students' views on particular science issues and to generalise these results into measures of students' interest in science and for the value they place on scientific enquiry.

One further innovative element of PISA 2006, piloted in a field trial by Australia, Austria, Denmark, Iceland, Ireland, Japan, Korea, Norway, Portugal, Scotland, the Slovak Republic and Chinese Taipei, was the extension of the science assessment to include a computer-delivered element. The aim of this was to administer questions that would be difficult to deliver in a paper and pencil test – the relevant questions included video footage, simulations and animations. This also reduced the amount of reading required so that the students' science capacity was assessed more directly. To ensure international comparability the computer test was given to the students on a set of standard laptop computers that had been loaded with the test. These computers were taken from school to school by a specially trained test administrator. Results are available for the three countries that completed the main study: Denmark, Iceland and Korea.

The development of a computer-based assessment component helped with the development of PISA science questions and the creation of several procedures has already proved useful in the development of the 2009 survey, including faster translation processes and automated coding procedures. This experience has placed PISA at the forefront of comparative international computer-delivered testing and the majority of OECD countries will participate in a computer-based assessment of reading in the PISA 2009 survey.

A comparison of change over time

Above all, PISA is a monitoring instrument. Every three years, it measures student knowledge and skills in the three assessment areas, covering each of these areas once as a major focus and twice as a minor focus in the three surveys administered across a nine-year cycle. The basic survey design remains constant, to allow comparability from one PISA assessment to the next. In the long term, this will allow countries to relate policy changes to improvements in educational standards and to learn more about how their changes in educational outcomes compare to international benchmarks.

After a first glimpse of change over time from PISA 2000 to PISA 2003, PISA 2006 offers information about performance trends in reading since PISA 2000, when the first full assessment of reading took place, as well as performance trends in mathematics since PISA 2003 when the first full assessment of mathematics took place. For science, the PISA 2006 survey has been the first full science assessment and will establish the basis for monitoring future trends.

The introduction of new background information about students

Background questionnaires completed by students and school principals provide essential information for PISA's analysis. For PISA 2006, these questionnaires were further refined and deepened. In particular:

- They explored the organisation of school science teaching and provided further information on student attitudes to science.

- Students in thirty-nine countries[4] completed an optional PISA questionnaire providing information about where students have access to computers, how often they use them and for what purposes. (A similar questionnaire was administered in PISA 2003, with the results published in *Are Students Ready for a Technology Rich World?: What PISA Studies Tell Us*, [OECD, 2006b].)

- Sixteen countries implemented a parent questionnaire, which was completed by the parents of students selected to do the PISA assessment.[5] The questionnaire collected information about parents' investment in their children's education and their views on science-related issues and careers.

ORGANISATION OF THE REPORT

Chapters 2 to 5 consider the science results for PISA 2006 and use them to analyse a range of factors associated with performance. Chapter 6 extends the analysis to performance in reading and mathematics and how this has changed over time. The following outlines the function and content of each of the chapters:

- *Chapter 2 gives a profile of student performance in science.* It begins by setting the results in the context of how performance in science is defined, measured and reported, and then examines what students are able do in science. After a summary picture of performance, each of the three science competency areas is examined separately since results vary in important ways across the three. There then is further analysis of the different science content areas and a consideration of gender differences associated with the different competencies and content areas. Any comparison of the outcomes of education systems needs to account for countries' social and economic circumstances and the resources that they devote to education. To address this, the chapter also interprets the results within countries' economic and social contexts.

- *Chapter 3 builds a profile of student engagement in science.* The chapter begins with an analysis of the extent to which students support scientific inquiry and whether they value science. Next students' self-beliefs are described in terms of their perceived capacity to handle scientific tasks effectively and to overcome difficulties in solving scientific problems. This is followed by a description of students' interest in science including such aspects as their engagement in science-related issues, their willingness to acquire scientific knowledge and skills, and their consideration of science-related careers. This is followed by a discussion of students' perceptions and attitudes regarding environmental issues. Where possible, the chapter examines how these different aspects of engagement relate to student performance.

- *Chapter 4 examines the extent and ways in which student learning outcomes depend on the socio-economic context of families and schools, which is an important measure of equity in learning opportunities.* It starts by examining more closely the performance variation shown in Chapter 2, in particular the extent to which the overall variation in student performance relates to differences in the results achieved by different schools. The chapter then looks at how factors such as immigrant status and socio-economic background affect student and school performance, and the role that education policy can play in moderating the impact of these factors.

- *Chapter 5 seeks to address what schools and school policies can do to raise overall student performance and, at the same time, moderate the impact that socio-economic background has on student performance, thus promoting a more equitable distribution of learning opportunities.* The chapter looks, in turn, at school policies and practices, with respect to school admittance, school selectivity, and ability grouping; characteristics of school funding and governance; the role for parental choice and parental expectations on schools; aspects of school accountability; school autonomy in various areas; and selected human, material and educational resources and their distribution among schools. Under each of these headings, the chapter separately examines the relevant features of school policies and practices and institutional characteristics. It also considers: how the relevant factors play out in the countries attaining both an above-average level of student performance and a below-average impact of socio-economic background on learning outcomes; the relationship of the factors with student performance before and after accounting for socio-economic background factors; and the joint relationship of the factors with the impact which socio-economic background has on performance, in order to examine the contribution of each factor to equity in the distribution of educational opportunities.

- *Chapter 6 considers student performance in reading and mathematics in PISA 2006* and examines changes in reading and mathematics performance since earlier PISA assessments.

Following the chapters, a technical annex addresses the construction of the questionnaire indices, discusses sampling issues, documents quality assurance procedures and the process followed for the development of the assessment instruments, and provides data on the reliability of coding. Many of the issues covered in the technical annex will be elaborated in greater detail in the *PISA 2006 Technical Report* (OECD, forthcoming).

A Reader's Guide is also found after this chapter, to aid in the interpretation of the tables and figures accompanying the report.

Volume 2 of this report contains the data tables underlying the various chapters.

Notes

1. The GDP of the countries that took part in PISA 2006 represents 86% of the 2006 world GDP. Some of the entities represented in this report are referred to as partner economies. This is because they are not strictly national entities.

2. This report uses the terms Macedonia, Moldova, Montenegro and Serbia to refer the former Yugoslav Republic of Macedonia, the Republic of Moldova, the Republic of Montenegro and the Republic of Serbia.

3. Visit *www.pisa.oecd.org* for links to countries' national PISA websites and national PISA reports.

4. The PISA 2006 ICT familiarity questionnaire was administered in Australia, Austria, Belgium, Canada, the Czech Republic, Denmark, Finland, Creece, Hungary, Iceland, Ireland, Italy, Japan, the Netherlands, New Zealand, Norway, Poland, Portugal, Korea, the Slovak Republic, Spain, Sweden, Switzerland and Turkey, as well as in the partner countries/economies Bulgaria, Chile, Colombia, Croatia, Jordan, Latina, Lithuania, Macao-China, Montenegro, Qatar, the Russian Federation, Serbia, Slovenia, Thailand and Uruguay.

5. The PISA 2006 parent questionnaire was administered in Denmark, Germany, Iceland, Italy, Luxembourg, New Zealand, Poland, Portugal, Korea and Turkey, as well as in the partner countries/economies Bulgaria, Colombia, Croatia, Hong Kong-China, Macao-China and Qatar.

Reader's Guide

Data underlying the figures

The data referred to in Chapters 2 to 6 of this report are presented in Volume 2 and, with additional detail, on the PISA website (*www.pisa.oecd.org*). Five symbols are used to denote missing data:

a   The category does not apply in the country concerned. Data are therefore missing.

c   There are too few observations to provide reliable estimates (*i.e.* there are fewer than 30 students or less than 3% of students for this cell or too few schools for valid inferences).

m   Data are not available. These data were collected but subsequently removed from the publication for technical reasons.

w   Data have been withdrawn at the request of the country concerned.

x   Data are included in another category or column of the table.

Calculation of international averages

An OECD average was calculated for most indicators presented in this report. In the case of some indicators, a total representing the OECD area as a whole was also calculated:

- The OECD average takes the OECD countries as a single entity, to which each country contributes with equal weight. For statistics such as percentages or mean scores, the OECD average corresponds to the arithmetic mean of the respective country statistics.

- The OECD total takes the OECD countries as a single entity, to which each country contributes in proportion to the number of 15-year-olds enrolled in its schools (see Annex A3 for data). It illustrates how a country compares with the OECD area as a whole.

In this publication, the OECD total is generally used when references are made to the overall situation in the OECD area. Where the focus is on comparing performance across education systems, the OECD average is used. In the case of some countries, data may not be available for specific indicators, or specific categories may not apply. Readers should, therefore, keep in mind that the terms OECD average and OECD total refer to the OECD countries included in the respective comparisons.

Rounding of figures

Because of rounding, some figures in tables may not exactly add up to the totals. Totals, differences and averages are always calculated on the basis of exact numbers and are rounded only after calculation.

All standard errors in this publication have been rounded to two decimal places. Where the value 0.00 is shown, this does not imply that the standard error is zero, but that it is smaller than 0.005.

Reporting of student data

The report uses "15-year-olds" as shorthand for the PISA target population. PISA covers students who are aged between 15 years 3 months and 16 years 2 months at the time of the assessment and who have completed at least 6 years of formal schooling, regardless of the type of institution in which they are enrolled and of whether they are in full-time or part-time education, of whether they attend academic or vocational programmes, and of whether they attend public or private schools or foreign schools within the country.

Reporting of school data

The principals of the schools in which students were assessed provided information on their schools' characteristics by completing a school questionnaire. Where responses from school principals are presented in this publication, they are weighted so that they are proportionate to the number of 15-year-olds enrolled in the school.

Abbreviations used in this report

The following abbreviations are used in this report:

GDP   Gross Domestic Product

ISCED   International Standard Classification of Education

PPP   Purchasing power parity

SD   Standard deviation

SE   Standard error

Further documentation

For further information on the PISA assessment instruments and the methods used in PISA, see the *PISA 2006 Technical Report* (OECD, forthcoming) and the PISA website (*www.pisa.oecd.org*).

This report uses the OECD's StatLinks service. Below each table and chart is a url leading to a corresponding Excel workbook containing the underlying data. These urls are stable and will remain unchanged over time. In addition, readers of the *PISA 2006: Science Competencies for Tomorrow's World* e-book will be able to click directly on these links and the workbook will open in a separate window.

2

A profile of student performance in science

Introduction 32

The PISA approach to assessing student performance in science 33
- The PISA approach to science 33
- The PISA definition of scientific literacy 34
- The PISA science framework 35
- The PISA 2006 science units 40
- How the results are reported 41
- A profile of PISA science questions 44

What students can do in science 48
- Student performance in science 48

An overview of student performance in different areas of science 62
- Student performance on the different science comptencies 62
- Student performance in the different knowledge domains 71

A detailed analysis of student performance on the science competency scales 76
- Student performance in identifying scientific issues 76
- Student performance in explaining phenomena scientifically 86
- Student performance in using scientific evidence 100

Implications for policy 113
- Meeting demands for scientific excellence 113
- Securing strong baseline science competencies 113
- Strengths and weaknesses in different aspects of science 114
- Gender differences 114
- Do the results matter? 115

INTRODUCTION

To what extent have students learned fundamental scientific concepts and theories? How well can they identify scientific issues, explain phenomena scientifically, and use scientific evidence as they encounter, interpret, and solve real-life problems involving science and technology? In order to provide answers to these questions for policy makers and educators and to assist them with improving the teaching and learning of science, PISA provides a series of international benchmarks. These relate to:

- Students' understanding of fundamental scientific concepts and theories, as well as the extent to which they can extrapolate from what they have learned in science and apply their knowledge to real-life problems.

- Students' interest in science, the value they place on scientific approaches to understanding the world and their willingness to engage in scientific enquiry.

- Students' school contexts including the socio-economic background of school peers and other factors that research suggests are associated with student achievement.

PISA 2006 is the first international survey to consider science competency, student interests and attitudes towards science and school contexts jointly in an international context. PISA 2006 thus provides an important opportunity to assess how students' science performance varies between countries and between school contexts within countries. In comparison with earlier PISA science assessments, two important changes have been introduced: First, the PISA 2006 assessment more clearly separates *knowledge about science* as a form of human enquiry from *knowledge of science,* that is knowledge of the natural world as articulated in the different scientific disciplines. In particular, PISA 2006 gives greater emphasis to *knowledge about science* as an aspect of science performance, through the addition of elements that underscore students' knowledge about the characteristic features of science. Second, the PISA 2006 framework has been enhanced with an additional component on the relationship between science and technology. There have also been two important changes in the way science was assessed in PISA 2006, as compared with PISA 2003 and PISA 2000. First, to more clearly distinguish *scientific literacy* from *reading literacy* the PISA 2006 science test items required, on average, less reading than did the science items used in earlier PISA surveys. Second, there were 108 science items used in PISA 2006, compared with 35 in PISA 2003; of these, 22 items were common to PISA 2006 and PISA 2003 and 14 were common to PISA 2006 and PISA 2000.

As the first major assessment of science, the PISA 2006 assessment establishes the basis for analysis of trends in science performance in the future and it is therefore not possible to compare science learning outcomes from PISA 2006 with those of earlier PISA assessments as is done for reading and mathematics. Indeed, the differences in science performance that readers may observe when comparing PISA 2006 science scores with science scores from earlier PISA assessments are largely attributable to changes in the nature of the science assessment as well as changes in the test design.[1]

This chapter explains how PISA measures and reports student performance in science, illustrated by numerous examples, and then analyses what students in different countries are able to do in science.

Any comparison of the outcomes of education systems needs to account for countries' social and economic circumstances and the resources that they devote to education. To address this, the chapter interprets the results within countries' economic and social contexts. Chapter 4 takes this analysis further and examines to what extent the socio-economic background of students and schools is interrelated with learning outcomes and Chapter 5 examines individual, school and system-level factors that help to explain the observed performance differences between students, schools and countries.

THE PISA APPROACH TO ASSESSING STUDENT PERFORMANCE IN SCIENCE

The PISA approach to science

Unlike many traditional assessments of student performance in science, PISA is not limited to measuring students' mastery of specific science content. Instead, it measures the capacity of students to identify scientific issues, explain phenomena scientifically and use scientific evidence as they encounter, interpret, solve and make decisions in life situations involving science and technology.

This approach was taken to reflect the nature of the competencies valued in modern societies, which involve many aspects of life, from success at work to active citizenship. It also reflects the reality of how globalisation and computerisation are changing societies and labour markets. Work that can be done at a lower cost by computers or workers in lower wage countries can be expected to continue to disappear in OECD countries. This is particularly true for jobs in which information can be represented in forms usable by a computer and/ or in which the process follows simple, easy-to-explain rules. Box 2.1 illustrates this by analysing how skill requirements in the United States job markets have evolved over past generations. This analysis shows that the steepest decline in task input over the last decade has not been with manual tasks, as is often reported, but with routine cognitive tasks, *i.e.* those mental tasks that are well described by deductive or inductive rules, and that dominate many of today's middle-class jobs. This highlights that if students learn merely to memorise and reproduce scientific knowledge and skills, they risk being prepared mainly for jobs that are disappearing from labour markets in many countries. In order to participate fully in today's global economy, students need to be able to solve problems for which there are no clear rule-based solutions and also to communicate complex scientific ideas clearly and persuasively. PISA has responded to this by designing tasks that go beyond the simple recall of scientific knowledge.

Box 2.1 **How skill demands in the job market have changed – trends in routine and nonroutine task input in the United States since 1960**

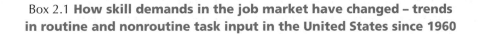

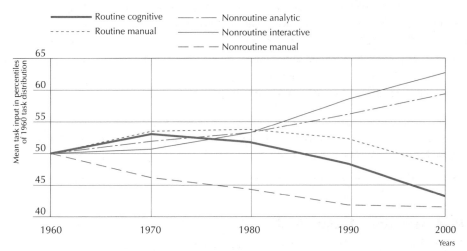

Source: Autor *et al.*, 2003; Levy and Murnane, 2006.

Note: Data are aggregated to 1 120 industry-gender-education cells by year and each cell is assigned a value corresponding to its rank in the 1960 distribution of task input (calculated across the 1 120 task cells for 1960). Plotted values depict the employment-weighted mean of each assigned percentile in the indicated year.

• • •

The figure shows a decline in labour involving physical tasks that can be well described using deductive or inductive rules. It also shows a decline in labour involving physical tasks that cannot be well described as following a set of "If-Then-Do" rules because they require optical recognition or fine muscle control that have proven extremely difficult to program computers to carry out. The decline in the demand for manual work has been widely discussed.

However, much less public attention has been devoted to the significant decline in routine cognitive task input, involving mental tasks that are well described by deductive or inductive rules. Because such tasks can be accomplished by following a set of rules, they are prime candidates for computerisation and the figure above shows that demand for this task category has seen the steepest decline over the last decade. Furthermore, rules-based tasks are also easier to offshore to foreign producers than other kinds of work: when a task can be reduced to rules – *i.e.* a standard operating procedure – the process needs to be explained only once, so the process of communicating with foreign producers is much simpler than the case of non-rules based tasks where each piece of work is a special case. By the same token, when a process can be reduced to rules, it is much easier to monitor the quality of output. This highlights the concern that if students learn merely to memorise and reproduce knowledge and skills, they risk being prepared only for jobs that are in fact increasingly disappearing from labour markets. In other words, the kind of skills that are easiest to teach and easiest to test are no longer sufficient to prepare young people for the future.

In contrast, the figure displays sharp increases in the demand for task input requiring complex communication, which involves interacting with humans to acquire information, explain it or persuade others of its implications for action. Examples include a manager motivating the people whose work she supervises, a salesperson gauging a customer's reaction to a piece of clothing, a biology teacher explaining how cells divide, an engineer describing why a new design for a DVD player is an advance over previous designs. Similar increases have occurred in the demand for expert thinking, which involves solving problems for which there are no rule-based solutions. Examples include diagnosing the illness of a patient whose symptoms seem strange, creating a delicious meal from ingredients that are fresh in the market that morning, repairing an auto that does not run well but that the computer diagnostics report says has no problem. These situations require what is referred to as pure pattern recognition – information processing that cannot now be programmed on a computer. While computers cannot substitute for humans in these tasks, they can complement human skills by making information more readily available.

This box is based on an analysis of changes in the demand for competencies in the US labour market carried out by the Massachusetts Institute of Technology and the Harvard Graduate School for Education (Levy and Murnane, 2006).

The PISA definition of scientific literacy

PISA 2006 defines *scientific literacy* in terms of an individual's:

- *Scientific knowledge and use of that knowledge to identify questions, to acquire new knowledge, to explain scientific phenomena, and to draw evidence-based conclusions about science-related issues.* For example, when individuals read about a health-related issue, can they separate scientific from non-scientific aspects of the text, and can they apply knowledge and justify personal decisions?

- *Understanding of the characteristic features of science as a form of human knowledge and enquiry.* For example, do individuals know the difference between evidence-based explanations and personal opinions?

- *Awareness of how science and technology shape our material, intellectual and cultural environments.* For example, can individuals recognise and explain the role of technologies as they influence a nation's economy, social organisation, and culture? Are individuals aware of environmental changes and the effects of those changes on economic and social stability?

- *Willingness to engage with science-related issues, and with the ideas of science, as a reflective citizen.* This addresses the value students place on science, both in terms of topics and in terms of the scientific approach to understanding the world and solving problems. Memorising and reproducing information does not necessarily mean students will select scientific careers or engage in science-related issues. Knowing about 15-year-olds' interest in science, support for scientific enquiry, and responsibility for resolving environmental issues provides policy makers with early indicators of citizens' support of science as a force for social progress.

The PISA science framework

PISA 2006 develops its science assessment tasks and questions within a framework of four interrelated aspects: the contexts in which tasks are embedded, the competencies that students need to apply, the knowledge domains involved and student attitudes (Figure 2.1).

Figure 2.1
The PISA 2006 science framework

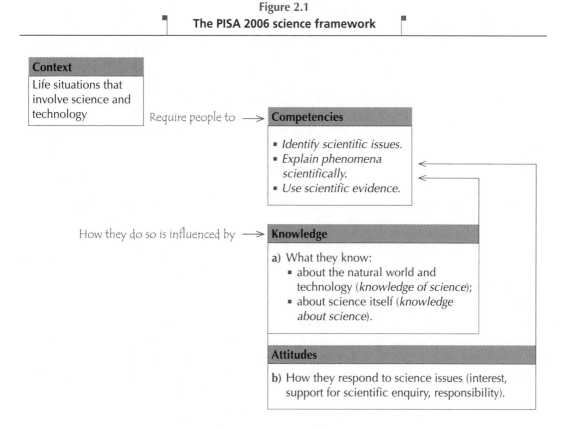

Context

Life situations that involve science and technology

Require people to ⟶ **Competencies**

- *Identify scientific issues.*
- *Explain phenomena scientifically.*
- *Use scientific evidence.*

How they do so is influenced by ⟶ **Knowledge**

a) What they know:
  - about the natural world and technology (*knowledge of science*);
  - about science itself (*knowledge about science*).

Attitudes

b) How they respond to science issues (interest, support for scientific enquiry, responsibility).

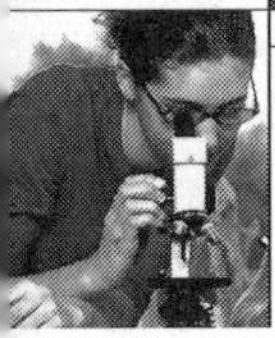

Context

In keeping with the PISA orientation of assessing students' preparation for future life, the PISA 2006 science questions were framed within a wide variety of life situations involving science and technology, namely: "Health", "Natural resources", "Environmental quality", "Hazards" and "Frontiers of science and technology". These situations were related to three major contexts: *personal* (the self, family and peer groups), *social* (community) and *global* (life across the world). The contexts used for questions were chosen in the light of relevance to students' interests and lives, representing science-related situations that adults encounter. Almost daily, adults hear about and face decisions concerning health, use of resources, environmental quality, hazard mitigation, and advances in science and technology. The science contexts also align with various issues policy makers confront. Figure 2.2 illustrates the intersection of the situations and contexts, with examples of life situations.

Figure 2.2
PISA 2006 science context

	Personal (Self, family and peer groups)	*Social* (The community)	*Global* (Life across the world)
"Health"	Maintenance of health, accidents, nutrition	Control of disease, social transmission, food choices, community health	Epidemics, spread of infectious diseases
"Natural resources"	Personal consumption of materials and energy	Maintenance of human populations, quality of life, security, production and distribution of food, energy supply	Renewable and non-renewable, natural systems, population growth, sustainable use of species
"Environment"	Environmentally friendly behaviour, use and disposal of materials	Population distribution, disposal of waste, environmental impact, local weather	Biodiversity, ecological sustainability, control of pollution, production and loss of soil
"Hazard"	Natural and human-induced, decisions about housing	Rapid changes (earthquakes, severe weather), slow and progressive changes (coastal erosion, sedimentation), risk assessment	Climate change, impact of modern warfare
"Frontiers of science and technology"	Interest in science's explanations of natural phenomena, science-based hobbies, sport and leisure, music and personal technology	New materials, devices and processes, genetic modification, transport	Extinction of species, exploration of space, origin and structure of the universe

Competencies

The PISA 2006 science questions required students to identify scientific issues, explain phenomena scientifically and use scientific evidence. These three competencies were selected because of their importance to the practice of science and their connection to key cognitive abilities such as inductive/deductive reasoning, systems-based thinking, critical decision making, transformation of information (*e.g.* creating tables or graphs out of raw data), construction and communication of arguments and explanations based on data, thinking in terms of models, and use of science. Figure 2.3 describes the essential features of each of the three science competencies.

Figure 2.3

PISA 2006 science competencies

Identifying scientific issues
- Recognising issues that are possible to investigate scientifically
- Identifying keywords to search for scientific information
- Recognising the key features of a scientific investigation

Explaining phenomena scientifically
- Applying *knowledge of science* in a given situation
- Describing or interpreting phenomena scientifically and predicting changes
- Identifying appropriate descriptions, explanations, and predictions

Using scientific evidence
- Interpreting scientific evidence and making and communicating conclusions
- Identifying the assumptions, evidence and reasoning behind conclusions
- Reflecting on the societal implications of science and technological developments

---

The competencies can be illustrated with any number of examples. Global climate change is a case in point: it is one of the most talked about global issues today and as people read or hear about climate change, they need to be able to separate out the scientific, economic and social issues at stake. It is not uncommon to hear scientists explain, for example, the origins and material consequences of releasing carbon dioxide into the Earth's atmosphere. This scientific perspective is sometimes confronted with economic arguments and citizens should recognise the difference between scientific and economic positions. Further, as people are presented with more, and sometimes conflicting, information about phenomena they need to be able to access scientific knowledge and understand the scientific assessments of various bodies. Finally, citizens should be able to use the results of scientific studies to support their conclusions about scientific issues of personal, social, and global consequence.

Knowledge

In PISA 2006, *scientific literacy* encompasses both *knowledge of science* (knowledge of the different scientific disciplines and the natural world) and *knowledge about science* as a form of human enquiry. The former includes understanding fundamental scientific concepts and theories; the latter includes understanding the nature of science. Some PISA 2006 science questions assess *knowledge of science* while others assess *knowledge about science*.

There is a vast body of scientific knowledge that could be placed into a PISA assessment, so it was necessary to structure and prioritise the content for the assessment of students' *knowledge of science*. As PISA seeks to describe the extent to which students can apply their knowledge in contexts relevant to their lives, the assessment material was selected from the major fields of physics, chemistry, biology, Earth and space science, and technology. The assessment material had to be:

- Relevant to real-life situations

- Representative of important scientific concepts and thus of enduring utility

- Appropriate to the developmental level of 15-year-olds

Figure 2.4 shows the four content areas selected for the PISA 2006 assessment by applying the above criteria to the vast range of scientific knowledge that could have been assessed. The four content areas are "Physical systems", "Living systems", "Earth and space systems", and "Technology systems". These four content areas represent important knowledge that is required by adults for understanding the natural world and for making sense of experiences in the *personal, social* and *global* contexts. PISA 2006 used the term "systems" instead of "sciences" in the descriptors of the four content areas, in order to convey the idea that people should understand varied concepts and contexts based on the components themselves and the relationships among them. Traditional science programmes of study often present science concepts emphasising a particular orientation, such as physics, chemistry or biology. This is in contrast with the manner in which most people experience science: in both professional and daily life, scientific issues often combine disciplines and interact with non-scientific considerations. For example, identifying issues associated with the use of nuclear power stations to generate electricity requires identifying the physical and biological components of Earth systems and recognising the economic and social impacts arising from this energy source. The questions in PISA reflect this combination of disciplines.

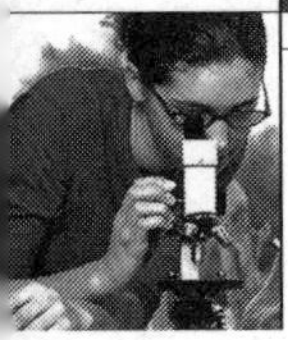

Figure 2.4
PISA 2006 content areas for the *knowledge of science* domain

"Physical systems"
- Structure of matter (*e.g.* particle model, bonds)
- Properties of matter (*e.g.* changes of state, thermal and electrical conductivity)
- Chemical changes of matter (*e.g.* reactions, energy transfer, acids/bases)
- Motions and forces (*e.g.* velocity, friction)
- Energy and its transformation (*e.g.* conservation, dissipation, chemical reactions)
- Interactions of energy and matter (*e.g.* light and radio waves, sound and seismic waves)

"Living systems"
- Cells (*e.g.* structures and function, DNA, plant and animal)
- Humans (*e.g.* health, nutrition, disease, reproduction, subsystems [such as digestion, respiration, circulation, excretion, and their relationship])
- Populations (*e.g.* species, evolution, biodiversity, genetic variation)
- Ecosystems (*e.g.* food chains, matter, and energy flow)
- Biosphere (*e.g.* ecosystem services, sustainability)

"Earth and space systems"
- Structures of the Earth systems (*e.g.* lithosphere, atmosphere, hydrosphere)
- Energy in the Earth systems (*e.g.* sources, global climate)
- Change in Earth systems (*e.g.* plate tectonics, geochemical cycles, constructive and destructive forces)
- Earth's history (*e.g.* fossils, origin and evolution)
- Earth in space (*e.g.* gravity, solar systems)

"Technology systems"
- Role of science-based technology (*e.g.* solve problems, help humans meet needs and wants, design and conduct investigations)
- Relationships between science and technology (*e.g.* technologies contribute to scientific advancement)
- Concepts (*e.g.* optimisation, trade-offs, cost, risk, benefit)
- Important principles (*e.g.* criteria, constraints, cost, innovation, invention, problem solving)

PISA identifies two categories of *knowledge about science:* the first is "scientific enquiry", which centres on enquiry as the central process of science and the various components of that process, and the second is "scientific explanations", which are the results of "scientific enquiry". One can think of enquiry as the means of science (how scientists obtain evidence) and of explanations as the goals of science (how scientists use data). The examples listed in Figure 2.5 convey the general meanings of the two categories.

Figure 2.5
PISA 2006 categories for the *knowledge about science* domain

"Scientific enquiry"
- Origin (*e.g.* curiosity, scientific questions)
- Purpose (*e.g.* to produce evidence that helps answer scientific questions, such as current ideas, models and theories to guide enquiries)
- Experiments (*e.g.* different questions suggest different scientific investigations, design)
- Data (*e.g.* quantitative [measurements], qualitative [observations])
- Measurement (*e.g.* inherent uncertainty, replicability, variation, accuracy/precision in equipment and procedures)
- Characteristics of results (*e.g.* empirical, tentative, testable, falsifiable, self-correcting)

"Scientific explanations"
- Types (*e.g.* hypothesis, theory, model, scientific law)
- Formation (*e.g.* existing knowledge and new evidence, creativity and imagination, logic)
- Rules (*e.g.* logically consistent, based on evidence, based on historical and current knowledge)
- Outcomes (*e.g.* new knowledge, new methods, new technologies, new investigations)

Attitudes

In addition to helping students gain scientific and technical knowledge, important goals of science education are to help students develop interest in science and support for scientific enquiry. Attitudes toward science play an important role in students' decisions to develop their science knowledge further, pursue careers in science, and use scientific concepts and methods productively throughout their lives. Thus, PISA's view of science competencies includes not just someone's abilities in science but also their disposition towards science. That is, a person's science competencies includes certain attitudes, beliefs, motivational orientations, self-efficacy, and values. The inclusion of attitudes and of the specific areas of attitudes selected for PISA 2006 is supported by, and builds upon, reviews of attitudinal research (OECD, 2006a).

Figure 2.6
PISA 2006 survey of student attitudes

Support for scientific enquiry
- Acknowledge the importance of considering different scientific perspectives and arguments
- Support the use of factual information and rational explanations
- Express the need for logical and careful processes in drawing conclusions

Self-belief as science learners
- Handle scientific tasks effectively
- Overcome difficulties to solve scientific problems
- Demonstrate strong scientific abilities

Interest in science
- Indicate curiosity in science and science-related issues and endeavours
- Demonstrate willingness to acquire additional scientific knowledge and skills, using a variety of resources and methods
- Demonstrate willingness to seek information and have an ongoing interest in science, including consideration of science-related careers

Responsibility towards resources and environments
- Show a sense of personal responsibility for maintaining a sustainable environment
- Demonstrate awareness of the environmental consequences of individual actions
- Demonstrate willingness to take the action to maintain natural resources

PISA 2006 gathered data on students' attitudes and engagement with science in four areas: *support for scientific enquiry, self-belief as science learners, interest in science* and *responsibility towards resources and environments* (Figure 2.6) In broad terms, these areas were selected because they provide an international portrait of students' general appreciation of science, specific attitudes and values concerning science, and sense of responsibility towards selected science-related issues that have personal, local, national and international ramifications. The measures that PISA 2006 used in this area are reported in detail in Chapter 3, together with the results.

The PISA 2006 science units

The PISA 2006 science units were constructed under the guidance of an international expert panel based on input and expertise from the participating countries to cover the various aspects of the framework described above: contexts, competencies, knowledge and attitudes. The science questions used in the assessment were developed based on material submitted by the participating countries. In PISA, a unit is made up of some type of stimulus, which is then followed by a number of questions. Each PISA test question can be characterised by its context, the competencies it elicits and the knowledge domain it represents. In each unit, the context is represented by the stimulus material – typically a brief written passage or text accompanying a table, chart, graph, photographs, or diagram. While students need to possess a certain level of reading competency in order to understand and answer the science questions, the stimulus material uses language that is as clear, simple and as brief as possible while still conveying the appropriate meaning. More importantly, each question requires students to use one or more of the science competencies as well as *knowledge of science* and/or *knowledge about science.*

As indicated in Chapter 1, the questions have a variety of formats. In many cases, students are required to construct a response in their own words. Sometimes they must write their calculations in order to demonstrate some of the methods and thought processes they used in producing an answer. Other questions require students to write an explanation of their results, which again exposes aspects of the methods and thought processes students must employ to answer the question. These open-constructed response questions require the professional judgement of trained coders to assign the observed responses to defined response categories. To ensure that the PISA 2006 coding process yielded reliable and cross-nationally comparable results, detailed guidelines and training of the coders were implemented to ensure accuracy and consistency across countries. In order to examine the consistency of this coding process in more detail within each country and to assess the consistency in the work of the coders, a subsample of questions in each country was coded independently by four coders. The reliability of these codings was then assessed and documented. Finally, to verify that the coding process was carried out in equivalent ways across countries, an inter-country reliability study was carried out on a subset of questions. In this process, independent coding of the original booklets was undertaken by trained multilingual staff and compared to the ratings by the national coders in the various countries. This process shows that very consistent coding was achieved across countries (for details see Annex A6 and the *PISA 2006 Technical Report* [OECD, forthcoming]).

For other questions in PISA 2006 requiring students to construct a response, the evaluation of their answers was restricted to the response itself rather than an explanation of how it was derived. For many of these closed-constructed response questions, the answer given was in numeric or other fixed form and could be evaluated against precisely defined criteria. Such responses generally did not require expert coders, but could be coded automatically.

PISA also uses questions that require students to select one or more responses from a number of given possible answers. This format category includes both standard multiple-choice questions, for which students are required to select one correct response from a number of given response options, and complex multiple-choice questions, for which students are required to select a response from given optional responses to each of a number of propositions or questions. Responses to these questions can be coded automatically.

Students were given credit for each question that they answered with an acceptable response. In the development of the assessment, extensive field trials were carried out in all participating countries in the year prior to the assessment to identify and anticipate the widest possible range of student responses to constructed response items. These were then assigned to distinct categories by the question developers to determine codes. In some cases, where there was clearly a correct answer, responses could be easily identified as being correct or not. In other cases a range of different responses might have been correct. In yet other cases, a range of different responses could be identified and among those some were clearly better than others. In such cases it was often possible to define three response categories that were ordered in their degree of correctness – one kind of response was clearly best, a second category was not quite as good, but was better than a third category. In these cases partial credit was given.

How the results are reported

The PISA 2006 science tasks, and also those in reading and mathematics, were arranged into half-hour clusters. Each student was given a test booklet with four clusters of questions – resulting in two hours of individual assessment time. These clusters were rotated in combinations that ensured that each cluster appeared in each of the four possible positions in the booklets and each pair of clusters appeared together in one booklet. Each item thus appeared in four test booklets, but in four different positions.

Figure 2.7
The relationship between items and students on a proficiency scale

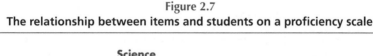
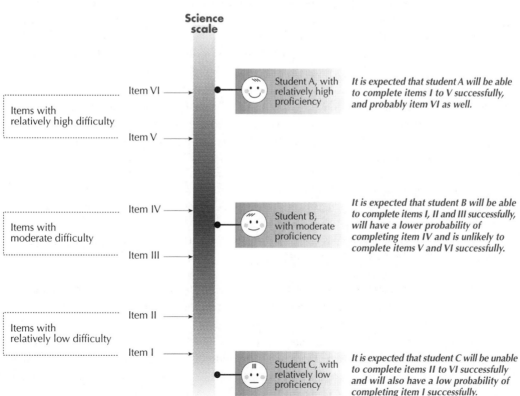

41

Such a design makes it possible to construct a scale of scientific performance, to associate each assessment question with a point score on this scale according to its difficulty and to assign each student a point score on the same scale representing his or her estimated ability. This is possible using techniques of modern item response modelling, a description of the model can be found in the *PISA 2006 Technical Report* (OECD, forthcoming).

The relative difficulty of questions in a test is estimated by considering the proportion of test takers getting each question correct.[2] The result is a set of estimates that allows the creation of a continuous scale representing science competencies. On this continuum it is possible to estimate the location of individual students, thereby seeing what degree of science competency they demonstrate, and it is possible to estimate the location of individual test questions, thereby seeing what degree of science competency each question embodies (Figure 2.7). Once the difficulty of individual questions is given a rating on the scale, student performance can be described by giving each student a score according to the hardest task that they could be predicted to perform with a certain probability.[3]

PISA 2006 constructed such scales for each of the science competencies and for each of the knowledge domains.[4] PISA 2006 also created a combined scale (referred to in this report as the science scale) that combined the questions from all scales. To facilitate the interpretation of the scores assigned to students, the science scale was constructed to have a mean score among OECD countries of 500 points, with about two-thirds of students across OECD countries scoring between 400 and 600 points.[5] (As a comparison, the 25 European Union countries[6] that participated in PISA 2006 have an average of 497 score points).

Science proficiency levels in PISA 2006

Proficiency levels are defined for the purpose of describing what science competencies students obtaining scores at each level demonstrate. Student scores in science are grouped into six proficiency levels, with Level 6 representing the highest scores (and hence the most difficult tasks) and Level 1 the lowest scores (and hence the easiest tasks). The grouping into proficiency levels was undertaken on the basis of substantive considerations relating to the nature of the underlying competencies. Students with below 334.9 score points on any of the science competencies are classified as below Level 1. That is, such students – representing 5.2% of students on average across OECD countries – are unable to demonstrate science competencies in situations required by the easiest PISA tasks. As the implied competencies shown in Figure 2.8 suggest, such a low level of science competency can be regarded as putting them at a serious disadvantage for full participation in society and the economy.

Proficiency at each of the six levels can be understood in relation to descriptions of the kind of science competency that a student needs to attain them. Later in this chapter there are three figures describing what students can typically do at each level of proficiency in each of the three competency areas. Figure 2.8 presents a synthesis of the information in those figures, providing an overview of the competencies required.

PISA applies an easy-to-understand criterion to assigning students to levels: each student is assigned to the highest level for which he or she would be expected to answer correctly the majority of assessment questions. Thus, for example, in an assessment composed of questions spread uniformly across Level 3 (with difficulty ratings of 484.1 to 558.7 scale points) all students assigned to that level would expect to get at least 50% of questions correct. However, the score points for students would vary within a level. For example, a student at the bottom of the level would be expected to get just above 50% of the questions correct. A student near the top of the level would get a higher percentage of questions correct.[7]

Figure 2.8
Summary descriptions of the six proficiency levels on the science scale

Level	Lower score limit	Percentage of students able to perform tasks at each level or above (OECD average)	What students can typically do
6	707.9	1.3% of students across the OECD can perform tasks at Level 6 on the science scale	At Level 6, students can consistently identify, explain and apply scientific knowledge and *knowledge about science* in a variety of complex life situations. They can link different information sources and explanations and use evidence from those sources to justify decisions. They clearly and consistently demonstrate advanced scientific thinking and reasoning, and they demonstrate willingness to use their scientific understanding in support of solutions to unfamiliar scientific and technological situations. Students at this level can use scientific knowledge and develop arguments in support of recommendations and decisions that centre on personal, social or global situations.
5	633.3	9.0% of students across the OECD can perform tasks at least at Level 5 on the science scale	At Level 5, students can identify the scientific components of many complex life situations, apply both scientific concepts and *knowledge about science* to these situations, and can compare, select and evaluate appropriate scientific evidence for responding to life situations. Students at this level can use well-developed inquiry abilities, link knowledge appropriately and bring critical insights to situations. They can construct explanations based on evidence and arguments based on their critical analysis.
4	558.7	29.3% of students across the OECD can perform tasks at least at Level 4 on the science scale	At Level 4, students can work effectively with situations and issues that may involve explicit phenomena requiring them to make inferences about the role of science or technology. They can select and integrate explanations from different disciplines of science or technology and link those explanations directly to aspects of life situations. Students at this level can reflect on their actions and they can communicate decisions using scientific knowledge and evidence.
3	484.1	56.7% of students across the OECD can perform tasks at least at Level 3 on the science scale	At Level 3, students can identify clearly described scientific issues in a range of contexts. They can select facts and knowledge to explain phenomena and apply simple models or inquiry strategies. Students at this level can interpret and use scientific concepts from different disciplines and can apply them directly. They can develop short statements using facts and make decisions based on scientific knowledge.
2	409.5	80.8% of students across the OECD can perform tasks at least at Level 2 on the science scale	At Level 2, students have adequate scientific knowledge to provide possible explanations in familiar contexts or draw conclusions based on simple investigations. They are capable of direct reasoning and making literal interpretations of the results of scientific inquiry or technological problem solving.
1	334.9	94.8% of students across the OECD can perform tasks at least at Level 1 on the science scale	At Level 1, students have such a limited scientific knowledge that it can only be applied to a few, familiar situations. They can present scientific explanations that are obvious and that follow explicitly from given evidence.

In PISA 2006, the six proficiency levels present a comprehensive range of achievement that PISA defines as *scientific literacy*. In 2007, following a detailed analysis of the questions from the main study, the international PISA Science Expert Group, which guided the development of the science framework and questions, identified Level 2 as the baseline proficiency level. This level does not establish a threshold for scientific illiteracy. Rather, the baseline level of proficiency defines the level of achievement on the PISA scale at which students begin to demonstrate the science competencies that will enable them to participate effectively and productively in life situations related to science and technology. To reach Level 2, for example, requires competencies such as identifying key features of a scientific investigation, recalling single scientific concepts and information relating to a situation, and using results of a scientific experiment represented in a data table as they support a personal decision. However, students at Level 1 often confuse key features of an investigation, apply incorrect scientific information, and mix personal beliefs with scientific facts in support of a decision. Figure 2.8 provides further details about what students can typically do and differentiates student achievement at Levels 1 and 2, thus showing what is needed to reach the critical baseline for PISA competencies.

Beyond the interpretation of performance differences, the proficiency scales can be used to identify skills and abilities that will contribute to higher levels of student achievement. For example, being able to select and integrate knowledge from different disciplines and using that knowledge to develop more detailed communications can make a difference between achieving at Level 3 and being proficient at Level 4.

A profile of PISA science questions

For an assessment such as PISA, which is held every three years, it is necessary to retain a sufficient number of questions from survey to survey to establish reliable trends. The remaining questions are released after the survey to illustrate the ways in which performance was measured. Later in this chapter, results for the different PISA science competencies are set alongside examples of questions used to assess each of these competencies. First, however, this section uses a selection of the released questions to illustrate broadly what is required by the different competencies and the different difficulty levels.

Figure 2.9 shows a map of these PISA 2006 science questions. For each of the three science competencies, the selected questions and scores (shown in parentheses after each question) have been ordered according to difficulty, with the most difficult at the top and the least difficult at the bottom.

The characteristics of the questions shown in the map provide the basis for a substantive interpretation of performance at different levels on the scale. Patterns emerge that make it possible to describe aspects of the science competencies that are consistently associated with different proficiency levels. It can be seen that there are a number of questions that are grouped under the heading of the unit – for example there are four questions from the unit *ACID RAIN* – so the unit can be used to assess each of the three competencies. For some questions an embedded attitude question is also included – in this question the students are asked about their attitudes to pollution and to acid rain in particular. Some questions are also labelled "partial credit" or "full credit", meaning the students are given some credit for an answer which may not be as complete as an answer which has all the required details needed to be given full credit.

The second column of the table indicates the lowest score required to achieve the relevant proficiency level. Thus the minimum score in order for a task to be regarded as at Level 6 (or for a student to achieve Level 6) is 707.9.

Near the bottom of the scale, questions are set in simple and relatively familiar contexts and require only the most limited interpretation of a situation. Essentially, they only require direct application of scientific knowledge and an understanding of well-known scientific processes of science in familiar situations.

Figure 2.9

A map of released science questions in PISA 2006, illustrating the proficiency levels

Level	Lower score limit	Competencies		
		Identifying scientific issues	Explaining phenomena scientifically	Using scientific evidence
6	707.9	**ACID RAIN** Question 5.2 (717) *(full credit)*	**GREENHOUSE** Question 5 (709)	
5	633.3			**GREENHOUSE** Question 4.2 (659) *(full credit)*
4	558.7	**SUNSCREENS** Question 4 (574) Question 2 (588) **CLOTHES** Question 1 (567)	**PHYSICAL EXERCISE** Question 5 (583)	**SUNSCREENS** Question 5.2 (629) *(full credit)* Question 5.1 (616) *(partial credit)* **GREENHOUSE** Question 4.1 (568) *(partial credit)*
3	484.1	**ACID RAIN** Question 5.1 (513) *(partial credit)* **SUNSCREENS** Question 3 (499) **GRAND CANYON** Question 7 (485)	**PHYSICAL EXERCISE** Question 1 (545) **ACID RAIN** Question 2 (506) **MARY MONTAGU** Question 4 (507)	**GREENHOUSE** Question 3 (529)
2	409.5	**GENETICALLY MODIFIED CROPS** Question 3 (421)	**GRAND CANYON** Question 3 (451) **MARY MONTAGU** Question 2 (436) Question 3 (431) **GRAND CANYON** Question 5 (411)	**ACID RAIN** Question 3 (460)
1	334.9		**PHYSICAL EXERCISE** Question 3 (386) **CLOTHES** Question 2 (399)	

Note: Numbers in brackets refer to the difficulty level of the question. Where students may receive full or partial credit is also indicated.

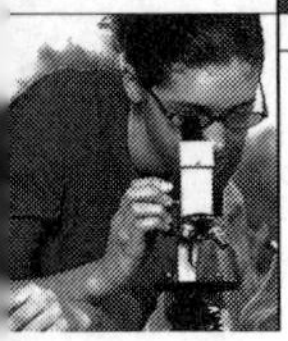

Figure 2.10 also shows the questions in terms of their knowledge categories (which will be discussed later in this chapter) and the science competencies. It also shows the questions' attitude categories (which will be discussed in Chapter 3).

The tasks *PHYSICAL EXERCISE* and *CLOTHES* (Figures 2.29 and 2.26) contain questions at Level 1 for the competency *explaining phenomena scientifically*. In *CLOTHES*, question 2, for example, the student must simply recall which piece of laboratory equipment would be used to check a fabric's conductivity. In *GRAND CANYON* (Figure 2.27), question 5, which is near the boundary between Levels 1 and 2, students are required to know that when the seas recede they may reveal fossils of organisms deposited at an earlier age. In *PHYSICAL EXERCISE,* question 3, students must have knowledge of the science fact that active muscles get an increased flow of blood and that fats are not formed when muscles are exercised.

Figure 2.10

**A map of selected science questions in PISA 2006,
cross-referencing knowledge categories and competencies**

Personal context
Social context
Global context

			Competencies		
			Identifying scientific issues	*Explaining phenomena scientifically*	*Using scientific evidence*
Knowledge	**Knowledge of science**	"Physical systems"		*ACID RAIN* Q2	*ACID RAIN* Q3
		"Living systems"		*PHYSICAL EXERCISE* Q1 *PHYSICAL EXERCISE* Q3 *PHYSICAL EXERCISE* Q5 *MARY MONTAGU* Q2 *MARY MONTAGU* Q3 *MARY MONTAGU* Q4	
		"Earth and space systems"		*GRAND CANYON* Q3 *GRAND CANYON* Q5 *GREENHOUSE* Q5	
		"Technology systems"		*CLOTHES* Q2	
	Knowledge about science	"Scientific enquiry"	*ACID RAIN* Q5 *SUNSCREENS* Q2 *SUNSCREENS* Q3 *SUNSCREENS* Q4 *CLOTHES* Q1 *GENETICALLY MODIFIED CROPS* Q3 *GRAND CANYON* Q7		
		"Scientific explanation"			*SUNSCREENS* Q5 *GREENHOUSE* Q3 *GREENHOUSE* Q4
Attitudes	**Interest in science**		*ACID RAIN* Q10 *GENETICALLY MODIFIED CROPS* Q10		
	Support for scientific enquiry		*GRAND CANYON* Q10 *MARY MONTAGU* Q10 *ACID RAIN* Q10		

StatLink ᴍ⁵ᴸ᷾ http://dx.doi.org/10.1787/141844475532

GRAND CANYON, question 3, is at Level 2, above the cut-point for the competency *explaining phenomena scientifically.* This question requires students to know the fact that freezing water expands and thus may influence the weathering of rocks. For the competency *using scientific evidence, ACID RAIN* (Figure 2.32), question 3, also provides an example for Level 2. The question asks students to use information provided to draw a conclusion about the effects of vinegar on marble, a simple model for the influence of acid rain on marble.

Still towards the bottom of the scale, a typical question for Level 2 is exemplified by question 3 in the unit *GENETICALLY MODIFIED CROPS* (Figure 2.22). This question assesses the competency *identifying scientific issues.* Question 3 asks a simple question about varying conditions in a scientific investigation and students are required to demonstrate knowledge about the design of science experiments.

Around the middle of the scale, questions require substantially more interpretation, frequently in situations that are relatively unfamiliar. Sometimes they demand the use of knowledge from different scientific disciplines including more formal scientific or technological representation, and the thoughtful linking of those different knowledge domains in order to promote understanding and facilitate analysis. Sometimes they involve a chain of reasoning or a synthesis of knowledge, and can require students to express reasoning through a simple explanation. Typical activities include interpreting aspects of a scientific investigation, explaining certain procedures used in an experiment and providing evidence-based reasons for a recommendation.

An example of a question in the middle of the scale is *ACID RAIN* (Figure 2.32), question 5. In this question, students are provided with information about the effects of vinegar on marble (*i.e.* a model for the effect of acid rain on marble) and asked to explain why some chips were placed in pure (distilled) water overnight. For partial credit and a response considered to be at Level 3, they had simply to state it was a comparison, although if a student stated that the acid (vinegar) was necessary for the reaction, the response would be considered Level 6. Both responses are linked to the competency *identifying scientific issues,* whereas *ACID RAIN,* question 2, assesses the competency *explaining phenomena scientifically.* In question 2, students are asked about the origin of certain chemicals in the air. Correct responses required students to demonstrate an understanding of the chemicals as originating from car exhaust, factory emission, and burning fossil fuels. For the competency *using scientific evidence,* the unit *GREENHOUSE* (Figure 2.33) presents a good example for Level 3. In question 3, students must interpret evidence, presented in graphical form, and deduce that the combined graphs support a conclusion that both average temperature and carbon dioxide emission are increasing. *SUNSCREENS* (Figure 2.23), question 5, is an example of Level 4 for the same competency. Here, students are given results from an experiment and asked to interpret a pattern of results and explain their conclusion.

Typical questions near the top of the scale involve interpreting complex and unfamiliar data, imposing a scientific explanation on a complex real-world situation, and applying scientific processes to unfamiliar problems. At this part of the scale, questions tend to have several scientific or technological elements that need to be linked by students, and their successful synthesis requires several interrelated steps. The construction of evidence-based arguments and communications also requires critical thinking and abstract reasoning. *GREENHOUSE* (Figure 2.33), question 5, is an example of Level 6 and of the competency *explaining phenomena scientifically.* In this question, students must analyse a conclusion to account for other factors that could influence the greenhouse effect. A final example, *GREENHOUSE,* question 4, centres on the competency *using scientific evidence* and asks students to identify a portion of a graph that does not provide evidence supporting a conclusion. Students must locate a portion of two graphs where curves are not both ascending or descending and provide this finding as part of a justification for a conclusion. A full credit response to this question is located at Level 5.

Several of these selected science units contain examples of embedded questions that query students' attitudes about the topics that the unit covers. *GENETICALLY MODIFIED CROPS, ACID RAIN, MARY MONTAGU* and *GRAND CANYON* (Figures 2.22, 2.32, 2.28 and 2.27) all have embedded attitudinal questions. The embedded question (10N) in *GENETICALLY MODIFIED CROPS* asks students to indicate their interest in learning more about various aspects of genetically modified crops. There are two embedded attitudinal questions in *ACID RAIN:* question 10N probes the level of students' interest in the topic of acid rain, while question 10S asks students how much they agree with statements supporting further research in this area. The embedded question in *GRAND CANYON* looks at students' support for scientific inquiry into questions concerning fossils, protection of national parks and rock formations.

Based on the patterns observed when the full question set is reviewed against the proficiency scales, it is possible to characterise the increase in the levels of complexity of competencies measured along the PISA 2006 science scale. This can be done by referring to the ways in which science competencies are associated with questions located at different points ranging from the bottom to the top of the scale. The ascending difficulty of science questions in PISA 2006 is associated with the following characteristics, which require all three competencies but which shift in emphasis as students progress from the identification of issues to the use of evidence to communicate an answer, decision or solution:

- *The degree to which the transfer and application of knowledge is required.* At the lowest levels the application of knowledge is simple and direct. The requirement can often be fulfilled with simple recall of single facts. At higher levels of the scale, individuals are required to identify multiple fundamental concepts and combine categories of knowledge in order to respond correctly.

- *The degree of cognitive demand required to analyse the presented situation and synthesise an appropriate answer.* Related to the discussion of knowledge application, this centres on features such as the depth of scientific understanding required, the range of scientific understandings required and the proximity of the situation to the students' life.

- *The degree of analysis needed to answer the question.* This includes the demands arising from the requirement to discriminate among issues presented in the situation, identify the appropriate knowledge domain *(knowledge of science* and *knowledge about science)*, and use appropriate evidence for claims or conclusions. The analysis may include the extent to which the scientific or technological demands of the situation are clearly apparent or to which students must differentiate among components of the situation to clarify the scientific issues as opposed to other, non-scientific issues.

- *The degree of complexity needed to solve the problem presented.* The complexity may range from a single step where students identify the scientific issue, apply a single fact or concept, and present a conclusion to multi-step problems requiring a search for advanced scientific knowledge, complex decision making, information processing and ability to form an argument.

- *The degree of synthesis needed to answer the question.* The synthesis may range from a single piece of evidence where no real construction of justification or argument is required to situations requiring students to apply multiple sources of evidence and compare competing lines of evidence and different explanations to adequately argue a position.

WHAT STUDENTS CAN DO IN SCIENCE

Student performance in science

PISA summarises student performance on a science scale that provides an overall picture of students' accumulated understanding of science at age 15. The results for the science scale are described below, followed by a more detailed analysis of performance in each of the science competencies (*identifying*

scientific issues, explaining phenomena scientifically and *using scientific evidence*), knowledge domains (*knowledge about science* and *knowledge of science*) and content areas ("Physical systems", "Living systems", and "Earth and space systems").[8]

Results are presented in terms of the percentage of 15-year-olds reaching the six proficiency levels described in Figure 2.8, as well as by an average score on each scale. The distribution of student performance across these proficiency levels is shown in Figure 2.11a.

Figure 2.11a
Percentage of students at each proficiency level on the science scale

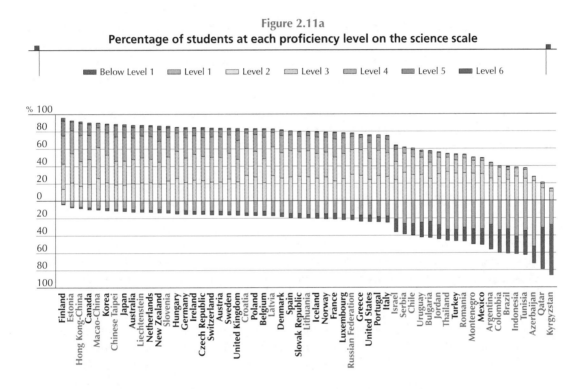

Countries are ranked in descending order of percentage of 15-year-olds at Levels 2, 3, 4, 5 and 6.
Source: OECD PISA 2006 database, Table 2.1a.
StatLink http://dx.doi.org/10.1787/141844475532

Students with a high level of proficiency

The rapidly growing demand for highly skilled workers and growing concerns about ageing populations have translated into a global competition for talent. While basic competencies are generally considered important for the absorption of new technology, high-level competencies are critical for the creation of new technology and innovation. For countries near the technology frontier, this implies that the share of highly educated workers in the labour force is an important determinant of economic growth and social development. There is also mounting evidence that individuals with high-level skills generate relatively large externalities in knowledge creation and utilisation, compared to an "average" individual, which in turn suggests that investing in excellence may benefit all (Minne *et al.*, 2007).[9] This happens, for example, because highly skilled individuals create innovations in various areas (organisation, marketing, design and so forth) that benefit all or that boost technological progress at the frontier. Research has also shown that the effect of the skill level one standard deviation above the mean in the International Adult Literacy Study on economic growth is about six times larger than the effect of the skill level one standard deviation below the mean (Hanushek and Woessmann, 2007).[10]

PISA, therefore, devotes significant attention to the assessment of students at the high end of the skill distribution. On average across OECD countries, 1.3% of 15-year-olds reach the highest level on the PISA science scale, Level 6, but in Finland and New Zealand over 3.9% did so (Table 2.1a). In the United Kingdom, Australia, Japan and Canada, as well as the partner countries/economies Liechtenstein, Slovenia and Hong Kong-China, between 2.1% and 2.9% reached the highest level of science performance and in Germany, the Czech Republic, the Netherlands, the United States[11] and Switzerland as well as the partner countries/economies Chinese Taipei and Estonia between 1.4% and 1.8% reached this level. At age 15, these students can consistently identify, explain and apply scientific knowledge and *knowledge about science* in a variety of complex life situations. They can link different information sources and explanations and use evidence from those sources to justify decisions. They clearly and consistently demonstrate advanced scientific thinking and reasoning, and they demonstrate use of their scientific understanding in support of solutions to unfamiliar scientific and technological situations. Students at this level can use scientific knowledge and develop arguments in support of recommendations and decisions that centre on personal, social, or global situations.

Box 2.2. **Interpreting sample statistics**

Standard errors and confidence intervals. The statistics in this report represent estimates of national performance based on samples of students rather than the values that could be calculated if every student in every country had answered every question. Consequently, it is important to know the degree of uncertainty inherent in the estimates. In PISA 2006, each estimate has an associated degree of uncertainty, which is expressed through a standard error. The use of confidence intervals provides a means of making inferences about the population means and proportions in a manner that reflects the uncertainty associated with sample estimates. Under the usually reasonable assumption of a normal distribution, and unless otherwise noted in this report, there is a 95% chance that the true value lies within the confidence interval.

Judging whether populations differ. The statistics in this report meet standard tests of statistical significance which ensure that, if in fact there is no real difference between two populations, there is no more than a 5% probability that an observed difference between the two samples will erroneously suggest that the populations are different as the result of sampling and measurement error. In the figures and tables showing multiple comparisons of countries' mean scores, multiple comparison significance tests are also employed that limit to 5% the probability that the mean of a given country will erroneously be declared to be different from that of any other country, in cases where there is in fact no difference (Annex A3).

It is noteworthy that the proportion of top-performers cannot be predicted from a country's mean performance. For example, Korea is among the best performing countries on the PISA science test, in terms of students' performance, with an average of 522 score points, while the United States performs below the OECD average, with a score of 489. Nevertheless, the United States has 1.5% and Korea has 1.1% of students at Level 6.

Including Level 5 brings the level of high performers to 9.0% on average across OECD countries. In Finland, 20.9% of the students perform at Levels 5 and 6. The national authorities in Finland attribute the high proportion of top-performers in part to a major development programme for fostering excellence in science education (Luma) that was progressively implemented between 1996 and 2002. Other outcomes attributed to this programme have been rising higher education enrolment in science and technology, increased co-operation between teachers, a greater focus on experimental learning and the establishment of specialised classes or streams in schools which specialise in mathematics and science.

Other countries with large proportions of students in the highest two proficiency levels are New Zealand (17.6%), Japan (15.1%) and Australia (14.6%), as well as the partner economies Hong Kong-China (15.9%) and Chinese Taipei (14.6%). These countries may be best placed to create a pool of talented scientists, provided, of course, their higher education systems offer opportunities for students to develop their skills further and their labour-markets supply attractive science-related jobs. In contrast, countries with few students in the top two levels may face future challenges in doing so.

Box 2.3 **Science performance at age 15 and countries' research intensity**

It is not possible to predict to what extent the performance of today's 15-year-olds in science will influence a country's future performance in research and innovation. However, the figure below portrays the close relationship between a country's proportion of 15-year-olds who scored at Levels 5 and 6 on the PISA science scale and the current number of full-time equivalent researchers per thousand employed. In addition, the correlations between the proportion of 15-year-olds who scored at Levels 5 and 6 and the number of triadic patent families relative to total populations and the gross domestic expenditure on research and development (two other important indicators of the innovative capacity of countries), both exceed 0.5. The corresponding correlations with the PISA mean scores in science are of a similar magnitude. The existence of such correlations does, of course, not imply a causal relationship, as there are many other factors involved.

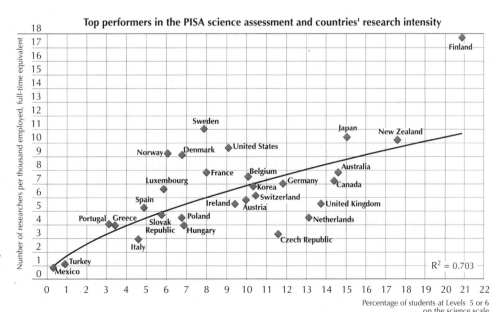

Source: *OECD Main Science and Technology Indicators 2006,* OECD, Paris. Table 2.1a.

Overall, Table 2.1a suggests that the pool of 15-year-olds who are highly proficient in science is distributed very unevenly across countries. Of the 57 countries, nearly one-half (25) have 5% or fewer (based on a round percentage) of their 15-year-olds reaching Level 5 or Level 6, whereas four countries have at least 15% – *i.e.* three times as many – with high science proficiency. Of course, the global pool of scientifically qualified labour also depends on the size of countries. Populous nations like the partner country Russian Federation may still have large numbers of scientists in absolute terms, even if the rather modest numbers of young people proficient at Levels 5 and 6 may in the future contribute to a smaller proportion of individuals choosing scientific careers. However, the variability in percentages in each country with high science proficiency suggests a difference in countries' abilities to staff future knowledge-driven industries with home-grown talent.[12]

Student performance at the lowest levels of proficiency

The number of students at very low proficiency is also an important indicator – not necessarily in relation to scientific personnel but certainly in terms of citizens' ability to participate fully in society and in the labour market. As described earlier, Level 2 has been established as the baseline level, defining the level of achievement on the PISA scale at which students begin to demonstrate the science competencies that will enable them to participate actively in life situations related to science and technology.

Box 2.4 **How seriously do students take the PISA assessment?**

When comparing student performance across countries, the extent to which student performance on international tests might be influenced by the effort that students in different countries invest in the assessment must be considered. Reassuringly, students' self-reports on this subject suggest that the effort they invest in PISA is fairly stable across countries. This finding counters the claim that systematic cultural differences in the effort expended by students invalidate international comparisons.

In PISA 2003, students were asked to imagine an actual situation that was highly important to them personally, so that they would try their very best and put as much effort as they could to do well. They were then asked to report: how they would mark the highest value on the Effort Thermometer shown below; how much effort they put into doing the PISA test compared to the situation they had just imagined; and how much effort they would have invested if their marks from PISA had been counted in their school marks.

The Effort Thermometer shown below provides three 10-point scales for the 41 countries participating in PISA 2003: a High Personal Effort scale, a PISA Effort scale and a School Mark Effort scale. The first scale indicates the maximum effort that students reported investing in a situation that is of high personal importance for them. The second scale shows the rating compared to the High Personal Effort scale for the effort expended in the PISA 2003 assessment. The third scale shows the anticipated expenditure of effort if the assessment were to have high personal relevance for the participant within the school context.

The students generally answered realistically that they would expend more effort if the results in the test were to count towards their school marks. The first bar chart below shows the effort, by country, that students reported putting into PISA 2003. The second indicates by country, the relative effort that the students put into PISA compared with a school test.

...

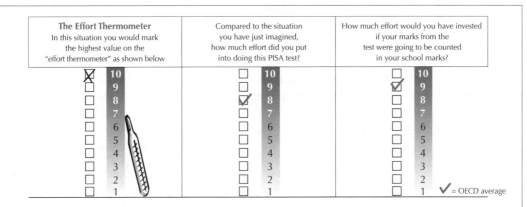

| The Effort Thermometer | Compared to the situation | How much effort would you have invested |
| In this situation you would mark the highest value on the "effort thermometer" as shown below | you have just imagined, how much effort did you put into doing this PISA test? | if your marks from the test were going to be counted in your school marks? |

✔ = OECD average

The analysis established that the reported expenditure of effort by students was fairly stable across countries, which counters the claim that systematic cultural differences in the effort expended by students render international comparisons invalid.

The analysis also showed that effort expenditure was related to student achievement with an effect size similar to variables such as single parent family structure, gender and socio-economic background.

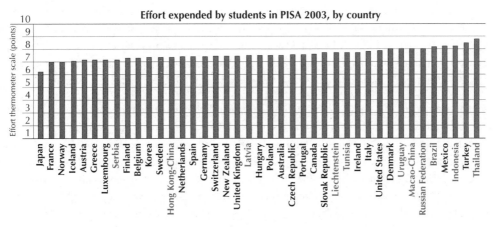

Effort expended by students in PISA 2003, by country

Effort thermometer scale (points)

Japan, France, Norway, Iceland, Austria, Greece, Luxembourg, Serbia, Finland, Belgium, Korea, Sweden, Hong Kong-China, Netherlands, Spain, Germany, Switzerland, New Zealand, United Kingdom, Latvia, Hungary, Poland, Australia, Czech Republic, Portugal, Canada, Slovak Republic, Liechtenstein, Tunisia, Ireland, Italy, United States, Denmark, Uruguay, Macao-China, Russian Federation, Brazil, Mexico, Indonesia, Turkey, Thailand

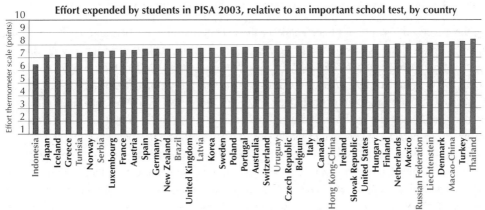

Effort expended by students in PISA 2003, relative to an important school test, by country

Effort thermometer scale (points)

Indonesia, Japan, Iceland, Greece, Tunisia, Norway, Serbia, Luxembourg, France, Austria, Spain, Germany, New Zealand, Brazil, United Kingdom, Latvia, Korea, Sweden, Poland, Portugal, Australia, Switzerland, Uruguay, Czech Republic, Belgium, Italy, Canada, Hong Kong-China, Ireland, Slovak Republic, United States, Hungary, Finland, Netherlands, Mexico, Russian Federation, Liechtenstein, Denmark, Macao-China, Turkey, Thailand

For further details see Butler and Adams, 2007.

53

Across the OECD, on average 19.2% of students are categorised as below Level 2. However, here again there is a substantial variability. In two OECD countries around one-half of the students are not proficient at Level 2: Mexico (50.9%) and Turkey (46.6%). In nine partner countries/economies at least 50% of students do not get to Level 2, and in a further five countries the proportion is between 40% and 49%. In the South and Central American countries that participated in PISA 2006, the figures range from 39.7% for the partner country Chile to 61.0% for the partner country Brazil. In contrast, there are five countries/ economies where around 10% of students or fewer perform below Level 2: Canada (10.0%) and Finland (4.1%) as well as the partner countries/economies Macao-China (10.3%), Hong Kong-China (8.7%) and Estonia (7.7%).

Thus, a level of basic science competency that is held by the overwhelming majority of the population in some countries, and by eight out of ten students on average in OECD countries, is not achieved in many other countries.

Mean performance in science

Figure 2.11b gives a summary of overall performance of different countries on the science scale, in terms of the mean scores (also simply called the science score in this report) achieved by students in each country. Only those differences between countries that are statistically significant should be taken into account (see Box 2.2 for a more detailed description of interpretation of results).[13] Figure 2.11c shows a country's performance relative to other countries by giving an estimated rank order position. It is not possible to give an exact rank order, but for each country there is a range of ranks given within which there is a 95% certainty that the rank will occur. Finland is an exception; its average performance is so far ahead of that of any other country that it can clearly be ranked as number one. Canada, the OECD country with the second highest average score, would range between rank 2 and 3 in the OECD. Japan, the OECD country with the third highest average score would range between rank 2 and 5 in the OECD (Figure 2.11c).

Subsequent chapters of this report examine the relationship between student performance in science and various characteristics of countries, schools and students. When interpreting Figure 2.11b, it is worth noting that the hypothesis that smaller countries tend to perform better is not supported by the data in PISA 2006: there is no relationship between the size of countries and the average performance of 15-year-olds on the PISA science scales. Detailed analysis of the PISA 2003 results showed that there was also no cross-country relationship between the proportion of foreign-born students in countries and the average performance of countries (OECD, 2006b). Last but not least, an analysis undertaken in the context of the PISA 2003 assessment revealed that there were few differences among countries in students' test motivation (Box 2.4).

While the mean score is a useful benchmark for the overall performance of countries, it hides important information on the distribution of performance in countries. Policy makers of countries with similar mean scores may be tempted to make similar policy interventions, whereas in fact the countries may have very different profiles of student performance – one country may have performance clustered around the average, with relatively smaller proportions of students at the extremes while another may have relatively large proportions of students at the lower and upper extremes of the scale. In other cases, there are countries with similar percentages of students in the highest levels of proficiency, but different percentages in the lower levels. For example, Korea is among the best-performing countries in science in PISA 2006, in terms of students' performance, with an average of 522 score points, while the United States performs below the OECD average with a score of 489. Nevertheless, the United States has a similar percentage of students at Levels 5 and 6 (9.1%) as Korea (10.3%). The discrepancy in mean scores between the two countries is partly accounted for by the fact that at the lower levels of proficiency (that is, below Level 2) the United States has 24.4% of students, while Korea has 11.2%.

Mean scores also mask regional differences in results that may require different policy interventions. In Belgium, for example, students in the Flemish Community average 529 score points, a performance that is as high as the levels achieved by students in the Netherlands and Australia, while students in the French Community perform below the OECD average (see the subnational tables in Volume 2).

With these caveats in mind, the following observations can be made

- Students in Finland perform clearly ahead of students in all other countries.

- There is a group of countries which perform below Finland, but which nevertheless still have very high mean scores: Canada, Japan, New Zealand and Australia and the partner countries/economies Hong Kong-China, Chinese Taipei and Estonia. Students in these countries score well above the OECD average – each has a mean score on the scale between 527 and 542 points.

- Of the 30 OECD countries, 20 have scores within 25 points of the OECD average of 500 – this is a closely clustered group of countries, each of which has a mean score very similar to a number of other countries.

- There is a discontinuity in the mean scores below the score for Greece of 473, with the next highest country scoring 454 points and only two OECD countries scoring below 473 points.

Box 2.5 **Interpreting differences in PISA scores: how large a gap?**

What is meant by a difference of, say, 50 points between the scores of two different groups of students? The following comparisons can help to judge the magnitude of score differences.

A difference of 74.7 score points represents one proficiency level on the PISA science scale. This can be considered a comparatively large difference in student performance in substantive terms. For example, with regard to the skills that were described above in the section on the PISA 2006 assessment framework, Level 3 requires students to select facts and knowledge to explain phenomena and apply simple models or inquiry strategies, whereas at Level 2 they are only required to engage in direct reasoning and make literal interpretations.

Another benchmark is that the difference in performance on the science scale between the countries with the highest and lowest mean performance is 241 score points, and the performance gap between the countries with the fifth highest and the fifth lowest mean performance is 143 score points.

Finally, for the 28 OECD countries in which a sizeable number of 15-year-olds in the PISA samples were enrolled in at least two different grades, the difference between students in the two grades implies that one school year corresponds to an average of 38 score points on the PISA science scale (see Table A1.2, Annex A1).[14]

A context for country performance

In as much as it is important to take socio-economic background into account when comparing the performance of any group of students, a comparison of the outcomes of education systems needs to be placed in the context of countries' economic circumstances and the resources that countries can devote to education. This is done in the following analysis by adjusting a country's mean science score for selected social and economic variables at the country level. At the same time such adjustments are always hypothetical and therefore need to be examined with caution. In a global context, the future economic and social prospects of both individuals and countries continue to be dependent on the results they actually achieve, not on the performance that might result if they were to operate under average social and economic conditions.

Figure 2.11b [Part 1/2]
Multiple comparisons of mean performance on the science scale

Column headers (with Mean and S.E.):

Country	Mean	S.E.
Finland	563	(2.0)
Hong Kong-China	542	(2.5)
Canada	534	(2.0)
Chinese Taipei	532	(3.6)
Estonia	531	(2.5)
Japan	531	(3.4)
New Zealand	530	(2.7)
Australia	527	(2.3)
Netherlands	525	(2.7)
Liechtenstein	522	(4.1)
Korea	522	(3.4)
Slovenia	519	(1.1)
Germany	516	(3.8)
United Kingdom	515	(2.3)
Czech Republic	513	(3.5)
Switzerland	512	(3.2)
Macao-China	511	(1.1)
Austria	511	(3.9)
Belgium	510	(2.5)
Ireland	508	(3.2)
Hungary	504	(2.7)
Sweden	503	(2.4)
Poland	498	(2.3)
Denmark	496	(3.1)
France	495	(3.4)
Croatia	493	(2.4)
Iceland	491	(1.6)
Latvia	490	(3.0)
United States	489	(4.2)

Row countries (with Mean and S.E.):

Country	Mean	S.E.
Finland	563	(2.0)
Hong Kong-China	542	(2.5)
Canada	534	(2.0)
Chinese Taipei	532	(3.6)
Estonia	531	(2.5)
Japan	531	(3.4)
New Zealand	530	(2.7)
Australia	527	(2.3)
Netherlands	525	(2.7)
Liechtenstein	522	(4.1)
Korea	522	(3.4)
Slovenia	519	(1.1)
Germany	516	(3.8)
United Kingdom	515	(2.3)
Czech Republic	513	(3.5)
Switzerland	512	(3.2)
Macao-China	511	(1.1)
Austria	511	(3.9)
Belgium	510	(2.5)
Ireland	508	(3.2)
Hungary	504	(2.7)
Sweden	503	(2.4)
Poland	498	(2.3)
Denmark	496	(3.1)
France	495	(3.4)
Croatia	493	(2.4)
Iceland	491	(1.6)
Latvia	490	(3.0)
United States	489	(4.2)
Slovak Republic	488	(2.6)
Spain	488	(2.6)
Lithuania	488	(2.8)
Norway	487	(3.1)
Luxembourg	486	(1.1)
Russian Federation	479	(3.7)
Italy	475	(2.0)
Portugal	474	(3.0)
Greece	473	(3.2)
Israel	454	(3.7)
Chile	438	(4.3)
Serbia	436	(3.0)
Bulgaria	434	(6.1)
Uruguay	428	(2.7)
Turkey	424	(3.8)
Jordan	422	(2.8)
Thailand	421	(2.1)
Romania	418	(4.2)
Montenegro	412	(1.1)
Mexico	410	(2.7)
Indonesia	393	(5.7)
Argentina	391	(6.1)
Brazil	390	(2.8)
Colombia	388	(3.4)
Tunisia	386	(3.0)
Azerbaijan	382	(2.8)
Qatar	349	(0.9)
Kyrgyzstan	322	(2.9)

Legend:

- ▢ Statistically significantly above the OECD average
- ▣ Not statistically significantly different from the OECD average
- ▨ Statistically significantly below the OECD average
- ▲ Mean performance statistically significantly higher than in comparison country
- ○ No statistically significant difference from comparison country
- ▼ Mean performance statistically significantly lower than in comparison country

Source: OECD PISA 2006 database.
StatLink http://dx.doi.org/10.1787/141844475532

Figure 2.11b [Part 2/2]
Multiple comparisons of mean performance on the science scale

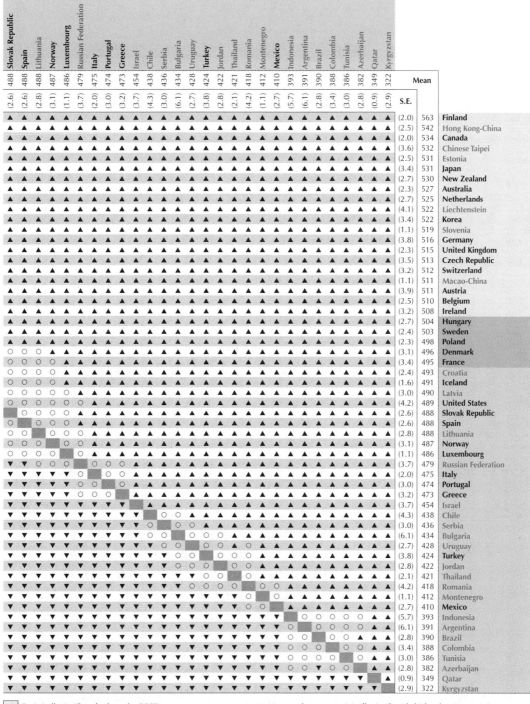

	Statistically significantly above the OECD average	▲ Mean performance statistically significantly higher than in comparison country
	Not statistically significantly different from the OECD average	○ No statistically significant difference from comparison country
	Statistically significantly below the OECD average	▼ Mean performance statistically significantly lower than in comparison country

Source: OECD PISA 2006 database.
StatLink http://dx.doi.org/10.1787/141844475532

Figure 2.11c
Range of rank of countries/economies on the science scale

■ Statistically significantly above the OECD average
■ Not statistically significantly different from the OECD average
■ Statistically significantly below the OECD average

	Science score	S.E.	Science scale Range of rank OECD countries Upper rank	Lower rank	All countries/economies Upper rank	Lower rank
Finland	563	(2.0)	1	1	1	1
Hong Kong-China	542	(2.5)			2	2
Canada	534	(2.0)	2	3	3	6
Chinese Taipei	532	(3.6)			3	8
Estonia	531	(2.5)			3	8
Japan	531	(3.4)	2	5	3	9
New Zealand	530	(2.7)	2	5	3	9
Australia	527	(2.3)	4	7	5	10
Netherlands	525	(2.7)	4	7	6	11
Liechtenstein	522	(4.1)			6	14
Korea	522	(3.4)	5	9	7	13
Slovenia	519	(1.1)			10	13
Germany	516	(3.8)	7	13	10	19
United Kingdom	515	(2.3)	8	12	12	18
Czech Republic	513	(3.5)	8	14	12	20
Switzerland	512	(3.2)	8	14	13	20
Macao-China	511	(1.1)			15	20
Austria	511	(3.9)	8	15	12	21
Belgium	510	(2.5)	9	14	14	20
Ireland	508	(3.2)	10	16	15	22
Hungary	504	(2.7)	13	17	19	23
Sweden	503	(2.4)	14	17	20	23
Poland	498	(2.3)	16	19	22	26
Denmark	496	(3.1)	16	21	22	28
France	495	(3.4)	16	21	22	29
Croatia	493	(2.4)			23	30
Iceland	491	(1.6)	19	23	25	31
Latvia	490	(3.0)			25	34
United States	489	(4.2)	18	25	24	35
Slovak Republic	488	(2.6)	20	25	26	34
Spain	488	(2.6)	20	25	26	34
Lithuania	488	(2.8)			26	34
Norway	487	(3.1)	20	25	27	35
Luxembourg	486	(1.1)	22	25	30	34
Russian Federation	479	(3.7)			33	38
Italy	475	(2.0)	26	28	35	38
Portugal	474	(3.0)	26	28	35	38
Greece	473	(3.2)	26	28	35	38
Israel	454	(3.7)			39	39
Chile	438	(4.3)			40	42
Serbia	436	(3.0)			40	42
Bulgaria	434	(6.1)			40	44
Uruguay	428	(2.7)			42	45
Turkey	424	(3.8)	29	29	43	47
Jordan	422	(2.8)			43	47
Thailand	421	(2.1)			44	47
Romania	418	(4.2)			44	48
Montenegro	412	(1.1)			47	49
Mexico	410	(2.7)	30	30	48	49
Indonesia	393	(5.7)			50	54
Argentina	391	(6.1)			50	55
Brazil	390	(2.8)			50	54
Colombia	388	(3.4)			50	55
Tunisia	386	(3.0)			52	55
Azerbaijan	382	(2.8)			53	55
Qatar	349	(0.9)			56	56
Kyrgyzstan	322	(2.9)			57	57

StatLink ﹍ http://dx.doi.org/10.1787/141844475532

The relative prosperity of some countries allows them to spend more on education, while other countries find themselves constrained by a relatively lower national income. Figure 2.12a displays the relationship between national income as measured by GDP per capita and the average science performance of students in the PISA assessment in each country. The GDP values represent GDP per capita in 2005 at current prices, adjusted for differences in purchasing power between OECD countries (Table 2.6). The figure also shows a trend line that summarises the relationship between GDP per capita and mean student performance in science. It should be borne in mind, however, that the number of countries involved in this comparison is small and that the trend line is therefore strongly affected by the particular characteristics of the countries included in this comparison.

Figure 2.12a
Student performance on the science scale and national income

Relationship between performance in science and GDP per capita, in USD, converted using purchasing power parities (PPPs)

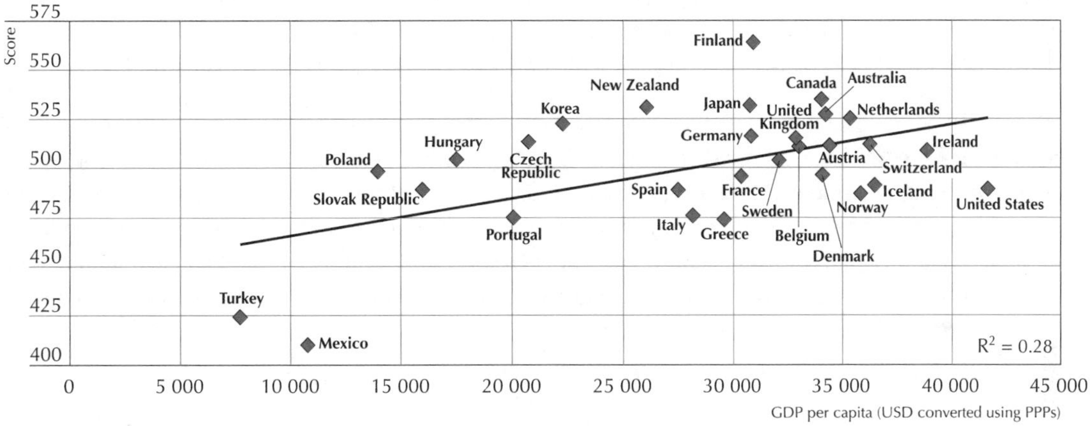

$R^2 = 0.28$

GDP per capita (USD converted using PPPs)

Source: OECD PISA 2006 database, Tables 2.1c and 2.6.
StatLink ⟐ http://dx.doi.org/10.1787/141844475532

The scatter plot suggests that countries with higher national income tend to perform better in science. In fact, the relationship suggests that 28 % of the variation between countries' mean scores can be predicted on the basis of their GDP per capita.[15]

Countries close to the trend line are where the predictor GDP per capita suggests that they would be. Examples include the Slovak Republic, Ireland, Sweden, the United Kingdom, Belgium, Austria and Switzerland. For instance, Ireland outperforms the Slovak Republic in science to an extent that one would predict from the difference in their GDP per capita, as shown in Figure 2.12a. However, the fact that countries deviate from the trend line also suggests that the relationship is not deterministic and linear. Countries above the trend line, such as Finland or New Zealand, have higher mean scores on the PISA science assessment than would be predicted on the basis of their GDP per capita (and on the basis of the specific set of countries used for the estimation of the relationship). Countries below the trend line, such as Italy or the United States, show lower performance than would be predicted from their GDP per capita.[16]

The existence of a correlation does not necessarily mean that there is a causal relationship between the two variables; there are, indeed, likely to be many other factors involved. Figure 2.12a does suggest, however, that countries with higher national income are at a relative advantage. This should be taken into account, in particular, in the interpretation of the performance of countries with comparatively low levels of national income. For some countries, an adjustment for GDP per capita makes a substantial difference to their score (Table 2.6). Examples of countries that see an increase in the score after an adjustment for GDP per capita are Turkey (424 to 463), Mexico (410 to 443), Poland (498 to 525) and the Slovak Republic (488 to 512). Examples of countries that see a decrease in the score after an adjustment are Norway (487 to 472), the United States (489 to 464), Ireland (508 to 489), Switzerland (512 to 497), the Netherlands (525 to 512), Iceland (491 to 475) and Austria (511 to 499).

One can further extend the range of contextual variables to be considered. Given the close interrelationship established in Chapter 4 between student performance and parental levels of educational attainment, an obvious contextual consideration concerns differences in levels of adult educational attainment among the OECD countries. Table 2.6 shows the percentage of the population in the age group 35-to-44 years that have attained upper secondary and tertiary levels of education. This age group roughly corresponds to the age group of parents of the 15-year-olds assessed in PISA. These variables are included in the adjustment in addition to GDP per capita in Table 2.6. Although combining adult attainment with GDP results in a closer relationship with student performance than when GDP is considered alone, the relationship remains far from deterministic and linear as the model underlying the adjustment assumes. A relatively large adjustment of 59 score points is calculated for Turkey, 58 score points for Mexico and 50 score points for Portugal.

While GDP per capita reflects the potential resources available for education in each country, it does not directly measure the financial resources actually invested in education. Figure 2.12b compares countries' actual spending per student, on average, from the age of 6 up to the age of 15, with average student performance in science. Spending per student is approximated by multiplying public and private expenditure on educational institutions per student in 2004 at each level of education by the theoretical duration of education at the respective level, up to the age of 15.[17] The results are expressed in USD using purchasing power parities (OECD, 2007).

Figure 2.12b
Student performance on the science scale and spending per student

Relationship between performance in science and cumulative expenditure on educational institutions per student between the ages of 6 and 15 years, in USD, converted using purchasing power parities (PPPs)

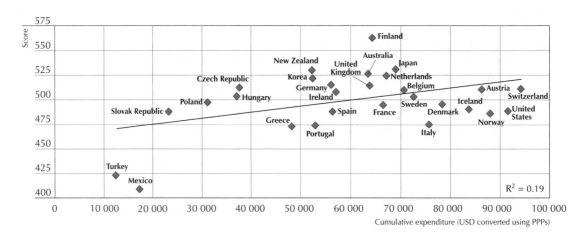

Source: OECD PISA 2006 database, Tables 2.1c and 2.6.
StatLink ⟐☶⟐ http://dx.doi.org/10.1787/141844475532

Figure 2.12b shows a positive relationship between spending per student and mean science performance (see also Table 2.6). As expenditure per student on educational institutions increases, so also does a country's mean performance. However, expenditure per student explains merely 19% of the variation in mean performance between countries.

Deviations from the trend line suggest that moderate spending per student cannot automatically be equated with poor performance by education systems. Spending per student up to the age of 15 years in the Czech Republic and New Zealand are 41% and 57%, respectively, of the spending levels in the United States, but while both the Czech Republic and New Zealand are among the top performers in PISA, the United States performs below the OECD average. Countries that perform significantly higher than would be expected from their spending per student alone include Finland, New Zealand, Australia, Korea and the Czech Republic. In summary, the results suggest that, while spending on educational institutions is a necessary prerequisite for the provision of high-quality education, spending alone is not sufficient to achieve high levels of outcomes.

Gender differences in performance on the science scale

Policy makers have given considerable priority to issues of gender equality, with particular attention being paid to the disadvantages faced by females, even if more recently the education of males is receiving more attention, particularly in the area of *reading literacy*. At age 15, many students are approaching major transitions from education to work, or to further education. Their performance at school, and their motivation and attitudes towards science, can have a significant influence on their further educational and occupational pathways. These, in turn, can have an impact on not only individual career and salary prospects, but also the broader effectiveness with which human capital is developed and utilised in OECD economies and societies.

Across OECD countries, the gender differences in science performance in PISA 2006 tend to be small, both in absolute terms and when compared with the large gender gap in reading performance (see Chapter 6).[18] Only the United Kingdom, Luxembourg, Denmark, the Netherlands, Mexico and Switzerland show a small advantage for males (between 6 and 10 score points) while Turkey and Greece show an advantage for females (between 11 and 12 score points). For the remaining OECD countries there are no statistically significant differences. Among the partner countries, Chile and Brazil show an advantage for males, while Qatar, Jordan, Bulgaria, Thailand, Argentina, Lithuania, Slovenia, Azerbaijan, Latvia and Kyrgyzstan show an advantage for females. For Qatar and Jordan the advantage of females is relatively large, compared with other countries, at 32 and 29 score points, respectively (Table 2.1c).

Thus, overall, gender performance in science is remarkably even, with only a few OECD countries showing significant gender differences. Countries that have concerns over different results by gender in reading and mathematics can look to science as an area where gender equality in performance at age 15 is widespread. However, there are large gender differences in several of the competency and knowledge domain scales, as shown in subsequent parts of this chapter. Moreover, the limited gender differences in science performance have not been reflected in equal choices to study science: on average nearly twice as many males as females in OECD countries are graduating with science degrees (see Table A3.5 in OECD, 2007).

One issue that needs to be taken into account when interpreting the observed gender differences is that males and females, in many countries at least, make different choices in terms of the schools, academic tracks and educational programmes they attend. PISA 2006 compared the observed gender difference in science for all students with estimates of gender differences observed within schools and estimates of gender differences once various programme and school characteristics have been accounted for. In most countries, the gender differences were much larger within schools than they were in the country overall (Table 2.5). In France, for example, males have no overall advantage, but the average gap is 20 score points within schools. Similarly, in Germany and the Slovak Republic, there is no overall advantage of males, but within schools it is 17 score points. Belgium, the Czech Republic and Italy show no performance difference overall but an advantage of males of between 13 and 18 score points within schools. In most countries this reflects the fact that females attend the higher performing, academically oriented tracks and schools at a higher rate than males. From a policy perspective – and for teachers in classrooms – gender differences in science performance, therefore, warrant continued attention. This is the case even if the advantage for males over females within schools and programmes is overshadowed to some extent by the tendency of females to attend higher performing school programmes and tracks.

Last but not least, it is also important to note that gender differences cannot automatically be attributed to features of the education system. The performance advantage of females in all subject areas in Iceland, most notably in rural areas has, for example, been attributed to labour-market incentives that deter males in rural areas from focusing on academic studies by giving them better opportunities to get a well paid job early in life in, for example, the fishing or tourism industries, while academic achievement is frequently seen by females as a lever to social and regional mobility (Ólafsson *et al.,* 2003).

AN OVERVIEW OF STUDENT PERFORMANCE IN DIFFERENT AREAS OF SCIENCE

Student performance on the different science competencies

One of the strengths of PISA 2006 is that it allows examination of students' science competencies and also the science knowledge domains.[19] Understanding the comparative strengths of their students in different science competencies and knowledge domains can inform policy makers and help direct development of strategies (Figure 2.13).

Among countries there are different profiles of students who show stronger skills in *identifying scientific issues, using scientific evidence* or *explaining phenomena scientifically.* It is possible to cluster countries with similar strengths and weaknesses on the science competency scales into four groups, as shown in Figures 2.14a, 2.14b, 2.14c and 2.14d below.[20]

Figures 2.14a, 2.14b, 2.14c and 2.14d show clusters of countries (ranked in order of mean performance on the combined science scale) where, for each country, differences between mean scores on each scale and the mean for science overall are shown.[21] For each scale there are a number of cases that stand out, where the score for a scale is 10 to 20 points higher or lower than the overall science score. These differences are noted with colour coding. Some of the individual cases of differences are also highlighted below. The results show countries in what respects their science education may need to be strengthened. A simplified way of looking at these relative strengths is in terms of a sequence in dealing with science problems: first identifying the problem, then applying knowledge of scientific phenomena, and finally interpreting and using the results. Traditional science teaching may often concentrate on the middle process, *explaining phenomena scientifically*, which requires familiarity with key science knowledge and theories. Yet without being able first to recognise a science problem and then to interpret findings in ways relevant to the real world, students are not fully scientifically literate. A student who has mastered a scientific theory but who is unable to weigh up evidence, for example, will make limited use of science in adult life. In this context, countries with students relatively weak in *identifying scientific issues* or *using scientific evidence* may need to consider the ways in which they acquire wider scientific skills, while those weak in *explaining phenomena scientifically* may need to focus more on mastery of scientific knowledge.

Figure 2.13
Comparison of performance on the different scales in science

Each scale is between 0 to 9.99 score points **higher** than the combined science scale
Each scale is between 10 and 19.99 score points **higher** than the combined science scale
Each scale is between 20 or more score points **higher** than the combined science scale

Each scale is between 0 to 9.99 score points **lower** than the combined science scale
Each scale is between 10 and 19.99 score points **lower** than the combined science scale
Each scale is between 20 or more score points **lower** than the combined science scale

| | | Performance difference between the combined science scale and each scale | | | | | | |
| | | Competencies | | | | Knowledge of science | | |
	Science score	Identifying scientific issues	Explaining phenomena scientifically	Using scientific evidence	Knowledge about science	"Earth and space"	"Living systems"	"Physical systems"
OECD								
Australia	527	8.4	-6.6	4.4	6.6	3.4	-5.1	-11.8
Austria	511	-5.7	5.6	-6.1	-7.3	-8.3	11.3	6.9
Belgium	510	4.7	-7.7	5.6	8.3	-13.9	-7.9	-3.1
Canada	534	-2.6	-3.6	7.1	2.8	5.8	-4.0	-5.5
Czech Republic	513	-12.4	14.6	-12.3	-13.8	13.2	11.9	21.1
Denmark	496	-2.6	5.4	-7.3	-3.2	-9.0	8.9	6.6
Finland	563	-8.4	2.8	4.1	-5.6	-9.0	10.5	-3.6
France	495	3.9	-14.1	15.8	12.2	-5.6	-5.3	-13.0
Germany	516	-5.9	3.4	-0.3	-3.9	-5.4	8.2	0.5
Greece	473	-4.6	3.1	-7.9	-2.5	4.0	1.3	0.8
Hungary	504	-21.3	14.2	-6.9	-11.9	8.6	5.2	29.2
Iceland	491	3.0	-2.7	0.2	1.7	12.1	-9.4	2.6
Ireland	508	7.6	-2.8	-2.4	4.4	-0.2	-2.8	-3.9
Italy	475	-1.2	4.1	-8.4	-3.6	-1.5	12.2	-3.0
Japan	531	-9.3	-4.1	13.0	0.2	-1.1	-5.2	-1.0
Korea	522	-3.1	-10.5	16.3	4.4	10.8	-23.9	7.6
Luxembourg	486	-3.5	-3.1	5.5	1.9	-15.6	12.2	-12.4
Mexico	410	11.7	-3.4	-7.4	3.3	1.9	-7.7	4.6
Netherlands	525	7.7	-3.1	0.7	5.4	-6.8	-15.4	6.2
New Zealand	530	5.8	-8.2	6.4	8.7	-0.8	-2.2	-14.7
Norway	487	2.6	8.7	-14.0	-6.5	10.5	9.6	4.8
Poland	498	-14.7	8.2	-4.1	-7.2	3.5	11.3	-0.7
Portugal	474	12.2	-5.0	-2.1	7.1	5.1	0.7	-12.0
Slovak Republic	488	-13.5	12.6	-10.8	-10.2	14.9	11.4	15.1
Spain	488	0.4	1.9	-3.6	0.4	4.9	9.2	-11.6
Sweden	503	-4.7	6.4	-7.2	-5.2	-5.5	8.4	13.7
Switzerland	512	3.4	-3.7	7.2	2.9	-9.3	0.9	-5.1
Turkey	424	3.7	-0.8	-6.6	1.2	1.3	1.5	-7.7
United Kingdom	515	-1.0	1.9	-1.2	1.8	-10.2	10.6	-6.4
United States	489	3.2	-2.8	-0.4	3.3	15.1	-2.1	-3.7
Partners								
Argentina	391	4.1	-4.8	-5.8	5.9	-7.5	-0.2	-7.8
Azerbaijan	382	-29.6	29.6	-38.1	-27.2	17.9	15.2	50.5
Brazil	390	7.8	-0.1	-12.2	3.3	-15.4	12.6	-5.5
Bulgaria	434	-6.8	10.2	-17.4	-8.5	9.1	11.1	1.6
Chile	438	5.9	-6.1	1.4	4.5	-9.9	-3.8	-5.0
Colombia	388	14.4	-9.0	-4.9	8.4	-17.7	-4.5	-10.0
Croatia	493	0.3	-0.8	-2.9	0.9	4.0	4.5	-0.4
Estonia	531	-15.7	9.2	-0.4	-8.4	9.0	8.4	3.6
Hong Kong-China	542	-14.4	7.0	0.2	-0.6	-17.1	15.4	3.3
Indonesia	393	-0.4	1.1	-7.8	-6.4	8.3	-2.5	-7.4
Israel	454	3.1	-10.5	6.4	12.5	-36.9	4.5	-11.3
Jordan	422	-13.1	15.7	-17.4	-13.5	-1.3	28.1	10.9
Kyrgyzstan	322	-0.7	11.7	-34.0	-13.5	-7.0	7.7	27.3
Latvia	490	-0.9	-3.2	1.1	1.6	4.3	-8.2	5.1
Liechtenstein	522	0.1	-6.0	12.7	4.2	-9.4	1.7	-7.1
Lithuania	488	-11.9	6.5	-1.4	-5.6	-1.4	14.7	2.0
Macao-China	511	-20.8	9.2	0.7	-5.9	-4.9	14.2	6.7
Montenegro	412	-10.7	4.9	-5.2	-4.8	-0.4	18.2	-4.5
Qatar	349	3.1	6.6	-25.5	-6.2	0.3	11.7	8.4
Romania	418	-8.9	7.4	-10.9	-5.6	-11.5	7.8	10.3
Russian Federation	479	-16.6	3.8	1.4	-4.5	2.0	10.5	-0.2
Serbia	436	-5.1	5.2	-10.8	-5.1	4.9	13.9	-0.3
Slovenia	519	-1.8	4.0	-2.8	-8.7	14.7	-2.2	12.1
Chinese Taipei	532	-23.8	12.7	-0.6	-7.0	-3.2	16.9	13.0
Thailand	421	-7.8	-1.1	2.1	0.2	8.9	10.7	-13.7
Tunisia	386	-1.7	-2.2	-3.6	3.8	-33.4	6.2	7.3
Uruguay	428	0.5	-5.2	0.9	3.4	-31.2	4.5	-6.7

Source: OECD PISA database 2006, Tables 2.1c, 2.2c, 2.3c, 2.4c, 2.7, 2.8, 2.9 and 2.10.
StatLink http://dx.doi.org/10.1787/141844475532

One general point of interest in Figures 2.14a-14d is that students in several of the ten countries with the highest science scores overall are particularly strong in *using scientific evidence* and none have this as a relative weakness. The mean score of these ten countries in *using scientific evidence* is 539 points, compared to 533 for science overall. Conversely, the ten weakest countries have either lower or similar mean scores in *using scientific evidence* to their science scores overall, and for the ten countries together the mean is 14 points lower on the *using scientific evidence* scale. This suggests that the ability to interpret and use scientific evidence is more closely related to a high level of science competency within a country. However, note that the relationship does not appear to be continuous, that is, it applies only to the highest and lowest countries but not to all countries above average or to all that are below average in their overall scores.

Figure 2.14a
Countries where students demonstrate relative weakness
in *explaining phenomena scientifically*, but relative strength in other areas

Low level of relative strength (0 to 9.99)	Low level of relative weakness (0 to -9.99)
Medium level of relative strength (10 to 19.99)	Medium level of relative weakness (-10 to -19.99)
High level of relative strength (≥20)	High level of relative weakness (≤-20)

Strength or weakness is relative to the country's score on the combined science scale.
Some of these countries demonstrate relative strength on the *using scientific evidence* scale. This is most pronounced in the cases of France and Korea. The French authorities attribute the relatively stronger performance in France to a curriculum that emphasises scientific reasoning as well as the analysis of data and experiments. This is similar in Korea, where particular emphasis is placed on tables, graphs and experimental results.

	Science score	S.E.	Identifying scientific issues	Explaining phenomena scientifically	Using scientific evidence
New Zealand	530	(2.7)	6	-8	6
Australia	527	(2.3)	8	-7	4
Liechtenstein	522	(4.1)	0	-6	13
Korea	522	(3.4)	-3	-11	16
Switzerland	512	(3.2)	3	-4	7
Belgium	510	(2.5)	5	-8	6
France	495	(3.4)	4	-14	16
Israel	454	(3.7)	3	-10	6

Others in this group demonstrate relative strength in ***identifying scientific issues***

Netherlands	525	(2.7)	8	-3	1
Ireland	508	(3.2)	8	-3	-2
Iceland	491	(1.6)	3	-3	0
United States	489	(4.2)	3	-3	0
Portugal	474	(3.0)	12	-5	-2
Chile	438	(4.3)	6	-6	1
Mexico	410	(2.7)	12	-3	-7
Argentina	391	(6.1)	4	-5	-6
Colombia	388	(3.4)	14	-9	-5

StatLink ᴍᴤᴾ http://dx.doi.org/10.1787/141844475532

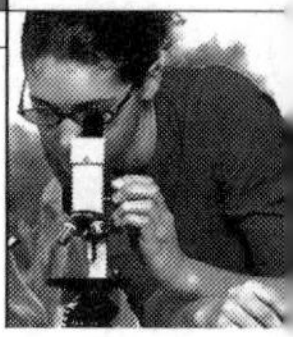

Figure 2.14b
Countries/economies where students demonstrate relative strength in *explaining phenomena scientifically*, but relative weakness in other areas

Low level of relative strength (0 to 9.99)
Medium level of relative strength (10 to 19.99)
High level of relative strength (≥20)

Low level of relative weakness (0 to -9.99)
Medium level of relative weakness (-10 to -19.99)
High level of relative weakness (≤-20)

Some of these countries/economies demonstrate relative weakness in *identifying scientific issues*

	Science score	S.E.	Identifying scientific issues	Explaining phenomena scientifically	Using scientific evidence
Hong Kong-China	542	(2.5)	-14	7	0
Estonia	531	(2.5)	-16	9	0
Macao-China	511	(1.1)	-21	9	1
Poland	498	(2.3)	-15	8	-4
Lithuania	488	(2.8)	-12	7	-1
Russian Federation	479	(3.7)	-17	4	1

Others demonstrate relative weakness both in *using scientific evidence* and in *identifying scientific issues*

	Science score	S.E.	Identifying scientific issues	Explaining phenomena scientifically	Using scientific evidence
Czech Republic	513	(3.5)	-12	15	-12
Hungary	504	(2.7)	-21	14	-7
Slovak Republic	488	(2.6)	-13	13	-11
Jordan	422	(2.8)	-13	16	-17
Azerbaijan	382	(2.8)	-30	30	-38

StatLink http://dx.doi.org/10.1787/141844475532

Figure 2.14c
Countries where students demonstrate relative weakness in *using scientific evidence*

Low level of relative strength (0 to 9.99)
Medium level of relative strength (10 to 19.99)
High level of relative strength (≥20)

Low level of relative weakness (0 to -9.99)
Medium level of relative weakness (-10 to -19.99)
High level of relative weakness (≤-20)

	Science score	S.E.	Identifying scientific issues	Explaining phenomena scientifically	Using scientific evidence
Qatar	349	(0.9)	3	7	-25
Kyrgyzstan	322	(2.9)	-1	12	-34

StatLink http://dx.doi.org/10.1787/141844475532

Figure 2.14d
Countries where students demonstrate relative strength in *using scientific evidence*

Low level of relative strength (0 to 9.99)
Medium level of relative strength (10 to 19.99)
High level of relative strength (≥20)

Low level of relative weakness (0 to -9.99)
Medium level of relative weakness (-10 to -19.99)
High level of relative weakness (≤-20)

This is particularly pronounced in Japan, where the national authorities attribute this relative strength to an emphasis in the curriculum, textbooks and teaching methods on observations and experiments. Japan's relative weakness in the other two competency areas is, in turn, attributed to a lack of science-related activities initiated by students.

	Science score	S.E.	Identifying scientific issues	Explaining phenomena scientifically	Using scientific evidence
Finland	563	(2.0)	-8	3	4
Canada	534	(2.0)	-3	-4	7
Japan	531	(3.4)	-9	-4	13
Luxembourg	486	(1.1)	-3	-3	5
Uruguay	428	(2.7)	1	-5	1
Thailand	421	(2.1)	-8	-1	2

StatLink http://dx.doi.org/10.1787/141844475532

Figure 2.14e [Part 1/3]

Range of rank of countries/economies on the different science scales

	Statistically significantly above the OECD average
	Not statistically significantly different from the OECD average
	Statistically significantly below the OECD average

			Identifying scientific issues scale			
			Range of rank			
			OECD countries		All countries/economies	
	Science score	S.E.	Upper rank	Lower rank	Upper rank	Lower rank
Finland	555	(2.3)	1	1	1	1
New Zealand	536	(2.9)	2	5	2	5
Australia	535	(2.3)	2	5	2	5
Netherlands	533	(3.3)	2	5	2	6
Canada	532	(2.3)	2	5	3	6
Hong Kong-China	528	(3.2)			4	8
Liechtenstein	522	(3.7)			6	12
Japan	522	(4.0)	5	9	6	13
Korea	519	(3.7)	6	11	7	15
Slovenia	517	(1.4)			8	14
Ireland	516	(3.3)	6	12	8	16
Estonia	516	(2.6)			9	16
Belgium	515	(2.7)	7	12	8	16
Switzerland	515	(3.0)	7	12	9	17
United Kingdom	514	(2.3)	7	12	10	17
Germany	510	(3.8)	9	14	12	19
Chinese Taipei	509	(3.7)			13	19
Austria	505	(3.7)	11	15	16	21
Czech Republic	500	(4.2)	12	18	17	24
France	499	(3.5)	13	18	18	24
Sweden	499	(2.6)	13	17	18	23
Iceland	494	(1.7)	16	20	21	26
Croatia	494	(2.6)			20	28
Denmark	493	(3.0)	15	21	20	28
United States	492	(3.8)	15	22	20	30
Macao-China	490	(1.2)			24	29
Norway	489	(3.1)	17	23	22	31
Spain	489	(2.4)	18	23	24	31
Latvia	489	(3.3)			22	32
Portugal	486	(3.1)	19	25	25	33
Poland	483	(2.5)	21	25	29	34
Luxembourg	483	(1.1)	22	25	30	33
Hungary	483	(2.6)	21	25	29	34
Lithuania	476	(2.7)			33	36
Slovak Republic	475	(3.2)	25	28	33	37
Italy	474	(2.2)	26	28	34	37
Greece	469	(3.0)	27	28	36	38
Russian Federation	463	(4.2)			37	39
Israel	457	(3.9)			38	39
Chile	444	(4.1)			40	40
Serbia	431	(3.0)			41	44
Uruguay	429	(3.0)			41	44
Turkey	427	(3.4)	29	30	41	45
Bulgaria	427	(6.3)			41	45
Mexico	421	(2.6)	29	30	43	45
Thailand	413	(2.5)			46	48
Romania	409	(3.6)			46	49
Jordan	409	(2.8)			46	49
Colombia	402	(3.4)			48	52
Montenegro	401	(1.2)			49	52
Brazil	398	(2.8)			49	53
Argentina	395	(5.7)			49	54
Indonesia	393	(5.6)			50	54
Tunisia	384	(3.8)			53	54
Azerbaijan	353	(3.1)			55	56
Qatar	352	(0.8)			55	56
Kyrgyzstan	321	(3.2)			57	57

StatLink ⟐ http://dx.doi.org/10.1787/141844475532

Figure 2.14e [Part 2/3]

Range of rank of countries/economies on the different science scales

Statistically significantly above the OECD average
Not statistically significantly different from the OECD average
Statistically significantly below the OECD average

			Explaining phenomena scientifically scale			
			Range of rank			
			OECD countries		All countries/economies	
	Science score	S.E.	Upper rank	Lower rank	Upper rank	Lower rank
Finland	566	(2.0)	1	1	1	1
Hong Kong-China	549	(2.5)			2	3
Chinese Taipei	545	(3.7)			2	4
Estonia	541	(2.6)			3	4
Canada	531	(2.1)	2	4	5	7
Czech Republic	527	(3.5)	2	6	5	10
Japan	527	(3.1)	2	6	5	10
Slovenia	523	(1.5)			7	12
New Zealand	522	(2.8)	4	10	6	15
Netherlands	522	(2.7)	4	10	7	15
Australia	520	(2.3)	5	10	8	16
Macao-China	520	(1.2)			9	15
Germany	519	(3.7)	4	12	7	18
Hungary	518	(2.6)	6	12	9	18
United Kingdom	517	(2.3)	7	12	11	18
Austria	516	(4.0)	5	13	8	19
Liechtenstein	516	(4.1)			9	20
Korea	512	(3.3)	9	16	15	22
Sweden	510	(2.9)	11	16	16	22
Switzerland	508	(3.3)	12	18	17	24
Poland	506	(2.5)	13	18	19	24
Ireland	505	(3.2)	13	19	19	25
Belgium	503	(2.5)	14	19	20	25
Denmark	501	(3.3)	15	20	21	27
Slovak Republic	501	(2.7)	16	20	21	26
Norway	495	(3.0)	18	21	24	29
Lithuania	494	(3.0)			25	30
Croatia	492	(2.5)			26	30
Spain	490	(2.4)	20	23	27	32
Iceland	488	(1.5)	21	23	28	32
Latvia	486	(2.9)			28	35
United States	486	(4.3)	20	26	27	36
Russian Federation	483	(3.4)			30	37
Luxembourg	483	(1.1)	23	25	32	35
France	481	(3.2)	23	27	32	37
Italy	480	(2.0)	24	27	34	37
Greece	476	(3.0)	25	28	35	38
Portugal	469	(2.9)	28	28	38	38
Bulgaria	444	(5.8)			39	42
Israel	443	(3.6)			39	42
Serbia	441	(3.1)			39	42
Jordan	438	(3.1)			40	43
Chile	432	(4.1)			41	45
Romania	426	(4.0)			43	47
Turkey	423	(4.1)	29	29	43	48
Uruguay	423	(2.9)			44	47
Thailand	420	(2.1)			45	48
Montenegro	417	(1.1)			47	49
Azerbaijan	412	(3.0)			48	50
Mexico	406	(2.7)	30	30	49	50
Indonesia	395	(5.1)			51	53
Brazil	390	(2.7)			51	53
Argentina	386	(6.0)			51	55
Tunisia	383	(2.9)			53	55
Colombia	379	(3.4)			54	55
Qatar	356	(1.0)			56	56
Kyrgyzstan	334	(3.1)			57	57

StatLink ᵫᵫᵫᵫ http://dx.doi.org/10.1787/141844475532

Figure 2.14e [Part 3/3]

Range of rank of countries/economies on the different science scales

Statistically significantly above the OECD average
Not statistically significantly different from the OECD average
Statistically significantly below the OECD average

			Using scientific evidence scale			
			Range of rank			
			OECD countries		All countries/economies	
	Science score	S.E.	Upper rank	Lower rank	Upper rank	Lower rank
Finland	567	(2.3)	1	1	1	1
Japan	544	(4.2)	2	4	2	6
Hong Kong-China	542	(2.7)			2	6
Canada	542	(2.2)	2	4	2	6
Korea	538	(3.7)	2	5	2	8
New Zealand	537	(3.3)	3	6	3	9
Liechtenstein	535	(4.3)			3	10
Chinese Taipei	532	(3.7)			6	11
Australia	531	(2.4)	5	7	7	11
Estonia	531	(2.7)			7	11
Netherlands	526	(3.3)	6	8	9	12
Switzerland	519	(3.4)	7	11	11	16
Slovenia	516	(1.3)			12	16
Belgium	516	(3.0)	8	12	12	18
Germany	515	(4.6)	8	13	12	19
United Kingdom	514	(2.5)	9	13	13	18
Macao-China	512	(1.2)			15	19
France	511	(3.9)	9	14	13	20
Ireland	506	(3.4)	11	15	17	21
Austria	505	(4.7)	11	17	16	23
Czech Republic	501	(4.1)	13	18	19	25
Hungary	497	(3.4)	14	20	20	27
Sweden	496	(2.6)	15	20	21	27
Poland	494	(2.7)	15	21	21	29
Luxembourg	492	(1.1)	17	21	24	29
Iceland	491	(1.7)	18	22	24	30
Latvia	491	(3.4)			23	32
Croatia	490	(3.0)			23	32
Denmark	489	(3.6)	18	23	24	33
United States	489	(5.0)	17	24	22	33
Lithuania	487	(3.1)			26	33
Spain	485	(3.0)	21	24	28	34
Russian Federation	481	(4.2)			30	36
Slovak Republic	478	(3.3)	23	26	32	36
Norway	473	(3.6)	24	27	34	38
Portugal	472	(3.6)	24	27	34	38
Italy	467	(2.3)	26	28	36	39
Greece	465	(4.0)	26	28	36	39
Israel	460	(4.7)			37	39
Chile	440	(5.1)			40	41
Uruguay	429	(3.1)			41	43
Serbia	425	(3.7)			41	44
Thailand	423	(2.6)			41	44
Turkey	417	(4.3)	29	29	42	46
Bulgaria	417	(7.5)			41	48
Romania	407	(6.0)			44	49
Montenegro	407	(1.3)			45	48
Jordan	405	(3.3)			46	49
Mexico	402	(3.1)	30	30	46	49
Indonesia	386	(7.3)			50	54
Argentina	385	(7.0)			50	54
Colombia	383	(3.9)			50	54
Tunisia	382	(3.7)			50	54
Brazil	378	(3.6)			51	54
Azerbaijan	344	(4.0)			55	55
Qatar	324	(1.2)			56	56
Kyrgyzstan	288	(3.8)			57	57

StatLink ᵐᵖ http://dx.doi.org/10.1787/141844475532

In addition to a comparison of mean scores for each of the competencies a country's rank order position in each competency gives an indication of relative strength or weakness of that country in the competency. The range of ranks for each country in each competency is listed in Figure 2.14e above. Similar to the rankings given for the combined science scale in Figure 2.4d, the range of ranks is given with 95% confidence.

Gender differences

As shown before, gender differences on the science scale tend to be modest in most countries. However, on the three competency scales, gender differences are visible, both within individual countries and for two of the scales across the OECD as a whole.

Figure 2.15 and Table 2.2c show that that on the *identifying scientific issues* scale females outperform males on average across OECD countries by 17 score points. In a number of countries the advantage of females is large, for example, in Qatar it is 37 score points, in Bulgaria 34, in Thailand 33, in Jordan 32, and in Greece and Latvia 31 score points.

Figure 2.15
Performance of males and females on the *identifying scientific issues* scale

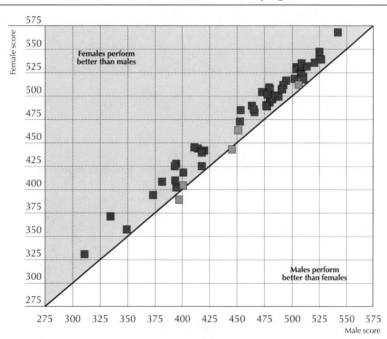

Note: Gender differences that are statistically significant are marked in a darker colour (see Annex A3).
Source: OECD PISA 2006 database, Table 2.2c.
StatLink http://dx.doi.org/10.1787/141844475532

In contrast, Figure 2.16 and Table 2.3c show that on the *explaining phenomena scientifically* scale males outperform females on average across OECD countries by 15 score points. Again, in some cases this difference is large – for example in the partner country Chile it is 34 score points, and among OECD countries, it is 25 score points in Luxembourg, 22 in Hungary and the Slovak Republic, and 21 in the United Kingdom, Denmark, the Czech Republic and Germany. The gender differences on this scale are particularly pronounced at the highest level of proficiency. Across OECD countries the percentage of males in the two highest proficiency levels (Levels 5 and 6) is 11.9% compared to 7.6% for females on the *explaining phenomena scientifically* scale (Table 2.3b).

Figure 2.16

Performance of males and females on the *explaining phenomena scientifically* scale

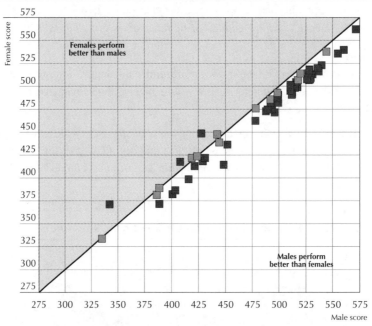

Note: Gender differences that are statistically significant are marked in a darker colour (see Annex A3).
Source: OECD PISA 2006 database, Table 2.3c.
StatLink ⌨ http://dx.doi.org/10.1787/141844475532

Figure 2.17

Performance of males and females on the *using scientific evidence* scale

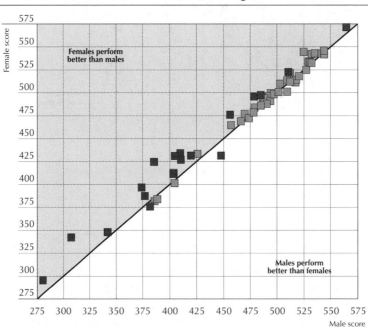

Note: Gender differences that are statistically significant are marked in a darker colour (see Annex A3).
Source: OECD PISA 2006 database, Table 2.4c.
StatLink ⌨ http://dx.doi.org/10.1787/141844475532

In contrast to *identifying scientific issues* and *explaining phenomena scientifically*, Figure 2.17 shows that there are few significant gender differences in the competency *using scientific evidence.*

When interpreting these gender differences in conjunction with the overall performance of countries on the respective scales, the differences imply that males or females sometimes have very different levels of performance in different areas of science. For example, in the Czech Republic, only 7.2% of males reach Level 5 or 6 in *identifying scientific issues,* compared to 17.4% in *explaining phenomena scientifically,* and males' scores on these scales are 492 points and 537 points respectively.[22] Another such contrast is for females in France, 25.2% of whom do not reach Level 2 on the *explaining phenomena scientifically* scale compared to 17.3% on the *identifying scientific issues* scale, with the equivalent figures for reaching Levels 5 or 6 being 4.0% and 9.2%, respectively. Females' mean score in *identifying scientific issues* in France is above the OECD average at 507 points, but their mean performance in *explaining phenomena scientifically* is much lower at 474 points, equivalent to some of the lowest-performing OECD countries.

The striking consistency with which females are stronger in *identifying scientific issues* yet weaker in *explaining phenomena scientifically* may suggest that there is a systematic gender difference in the way students relate to science and to the science curriculum. It appears that males may be better on average at mastering scientific knowledge and females better in distinguishing scientific questions in a given situation. While it should be emphasised that in many countries these differences between the gender groups are small relative to differences within each gender group, overall performance could be raised significantly if the factors behind the gender difference could be identified and tackled.

Student performance in the different knowledge domains

As described before, the PISA 2006 science framework covers two knowledge domains – *knowledge about science* and *knowledge of science.*[23] The second domain can be further divided into the content areas "Physical systems", "Living systems" and "Earth and space systems". A detailed analysis of the strengths and weaknesses of countries in these different categories is particularly valuable for relating PISA 2006 results to national curricula, which are often defined in terms of subject-matter content.

Figure 2.18a shows the differences between the *knowledge about science* domain and the average for the three *knowledge of science* cales[24].

France shows the largest difference in favour of *knowledge about science,* with a 29.2 score point difference between the average score of French students in the *knowledge of science* and the *knowledge about science* domains. Other countries with a performance advantage in the *knowledge about science* domain include Belgium (16.6 score points), New Zealand (14.6 score points), Australia (11.0 score points), the Netherlands (10.7 score points) and Portugal (9.1 score points). Among the partner countries the largest differences in favour of *knowledge about science* were observed in Israel (27.1 score points), Colombia (19.1 score points), Uruguay (14.5 score points), Argentina (11.0 score points), Chile (10.7 score points), Tunisia (10.5 score points) and Liechtenstein (9.1 score points).

There are also countries in which students perform better in the *knowledge of science* domain. Among OECD countries the largest differences are observed in the Czech Republic (29.2 score points), Hungary (26.2 score points) and the Slovak Republic (24.1 score points). These three countries are located in close proximity to each other in Eastern Europe and share similar traditions in science education, in which science is taught with a focus on the accumulation and reproduction of theoretical knowledge in scientific disciplines, with much less emphasis on the nature of scientific work and scientific thinking. For the Czech Republic, the ways in which students learn about the phenomena and their explanations, rather than

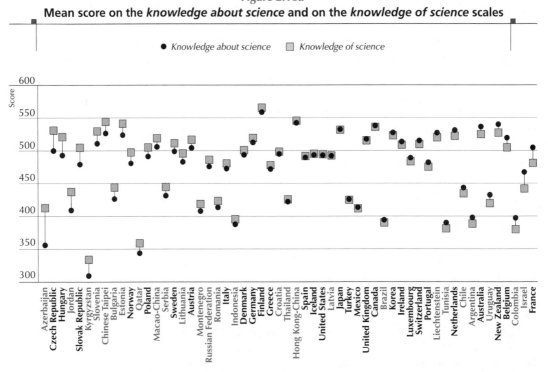

Figure 2.18a
Mean score on the *knowledge about science* and on the *knowledge of science* scales

● *Knowledge about science*   ▢ *Knowledge of science*

Countries are ranked in descending order of the difference between the knowledge of science and the knowledge about science scales.
Source: OECD PISA 2006 database, Tables 2.7, 2.8, 2.9 and 2.10.
StatLink http://dx.doi.org/10.1787/141844475532

discovering scientific phenomena themselves, has been documented through an extensive video study, *Teaching Science in Five Countries: Results from the TIMSS 1999 Video Study* (Roth *et al.*, 2006). Other OECD countries where there is a large difference in favour of *knowledge of science* are Norway (14.8 score points), Poland (11.9 score points) and Sweden (10.8 score points). Some partner countries with relatively better performance in *knowledge of science* are also from the Eastern European region – Slovenia (16.9 score points difference), Bulgaria (15.8 score points), Estonia (15.4 score points), Serbia (11.2 score points) and Lithuania (10.7 score points). In addition to these European countries large differences in favour of *knowledge of science* also occurred in Azerbaijan, Jordan, Kyrgyzstan, Chinese Taipei, Qatar and Macao-China (Figure 2.18a).

Large performance differences between the two knowledge domains do not appear to be related to overall student performance. In some high-performing countries such as Finland and Canada, and in the partner economy Hong Kong-China, there is not a large performance difference between the two knowledge domains, whereas other high performing countries such as New Zealand, Australia and the Netherlands show large differences.

Student performance in the *knowledge of science* domain can be further distinguished in terms of the content areas "Physical systems", "Living systems", "Earth and space systems". This analysis shows performance differences within countries, which provide important insights into curricular patterns in countries. Korea, for example, scores 530 and 533 points on the "Physical systems" and "Earth and space systems" scales, but only 498 points on the "Living systems" scale (Figure 2.19a).

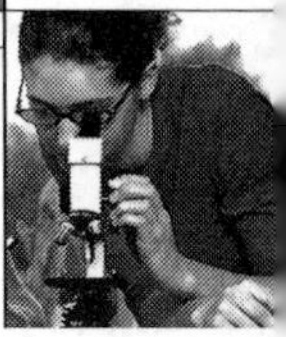

As in the case of the science competencies, it is possible to identify groups of countries with similar strengths and weaknesses on the science content areas.

This section presents for each of the three content areas groups of countries where students are relatively strong or weak compared to the other science content scales. Therefore, each group of countries may include high, average and low performing countries. The emphasis here is not on the ranking across countries of mean performance on each of the three knowledge of science scales, but rather on the relative performance of students on each of these scales within each country. Absolute performance differences on each of the three content areas are presented elsewhere in this chapter. In this section, countries are shown where there is a difference of at least 14 score points on a content area mean score relative to the average of the scores on the other two content areas. This difference is either positive (showing a relative strength) or negative (showing a relative weakness). For countries not included in Figures 2.19a, 2.19b and 2.19c, performance differences across the three content areas of knowledge of science are not so pronounced.

Figure 2.19a shows countries with relative strength and weakness on the "Physical systems" scale. In Hungary, Korea and the Netherlands, and in the partner countries Azerbaijan, Kyrgyzstan and Tunisia the relative strength on "Physical systems" are most pronounced. Countries where students demonstrate relative weakness on the "Physical systems" scale are Portugal and Spain and the partner country Thailand. Generally speaking, the countries here that demonstrate relative weakness in "Physical systems" tend also to be among the countries that have means on the combined science scale less than the OECD average – Portugal (474 score points) and Spain (488 score points) and the partner country Thailand (421 score points).

Figure 2.19a
Countries where students demonstrate relative strength or weakness on the "Physical systems" scale

Students are relatively strong in the "Physical systems" content area

Students are relatively weak in the "Physical systems" content area

		"Physical systems"	"Earth and space systems"	"Living systems"	"Physical systems" mean score compared to the average of the other two content areas
		Mean score	Mean score	Mean score	Score difference
OECD	Hungary	533	512	509	22
	Korea	530	533	498	14
	Netherlands	531	518	509	17
	Portugal	462	479	475	-15
	Spain	477	493	498	-19
Partners	Azerbaijan	433	400	398	34
	Kyrgyzstan	349	315	330	27
	Thailand	407	430	432	-24
	Tunisia	393	352	392	21

StatLink ⬛⬛ http://dx.doi.org/10.1787/141844475532

Figure 2.19b shows countries with relative strength and weakness on the "Earth and space systems" scale. Countries where students demonstrate relative strength on the "Earth and space systems" scale include Korea, the United States and Iceland. Countries that are relatively weak in "Earth and space systems" include France, Austria, Denmark, Sweden and Luxembourg. Although at 463 score points France shows comparatively low performance in this area, its overall mean score is 495, which is not significantly different than the OECD average. This occurs because of a very strong performance by students in Knowledge about science (507 score points). Among partner countries/economies those which demonstrate the largest weaknesses (25 score points or more) in "Earth and space systems" are Tunisia, Israel, Uruguay, Hong Kong-China and Kyrgyzstan. With an overall mean score for science of 542 score points the partner economy Hong Kong-China ranks second after Finland, further underlining its relative weakness in the "Earth and space systems".

Figure 2.19b
Countries/economies where students demonstrate relative strength or weakness on the "Earth and space systems" scale

Students are relatively strong in the "Earth and space systems" content area   Students are relatively weak in the "Earth and space systems" content area

	"Physical systems"	"Earth and space systems"	"Living systems"	"Earth and space systems" mean score compared to the average of the other two content areas
	Mean score	Mean score	Mean score	Score difference
Austria	518	503	522	-17
Denmark	502	487	505	-17
France	482	463	490	-23
Iceland	493	503	481	16
Korea	530	533	498	19
Luxembourg	474	471	499	-16
Sweden	517	498	512	-17
United States	485	504	487	18
Brazil	385	375	403	-19
Hong Kong-China	546	525	558	-27
Israel	443	417	458	-34
Jordan	433	421	450	-21
Kyrgyzstan	349	315	330	-25
Macao-China	518	506	525	-15
Romania	429	407	426	-21
Chinese Taipei	545	529	549	-18
Tunisia	393	352	392	-40
Uruguay	421	397	433	-30

StatLink ᴍᴤ⊓ http://dx.doi.org/10.1787/141844475532

Figure 2.19c shows countries with relative strength and weakness on the remaining content area of *knowledge of science* – "Living systems". Relative strength in this area was demonstrated by students in Luxembourg, the United Kingdom, Finland and France, and in the partner countries/economies Israel, Uruguay, Jordan, Brazil, Hong Kong-China, Montenegro and Tunisia. Students in Finland were especially strong in this area with a mean score of 574. The partner economy Hong Kong-China ranked second with 558 score points. Countries with relative weaknesses in the "Living systems" content area were Korea,

Figure 2.19c
Countries/economies where students demonstrate relative strength or weakness on the "Living systems" scale

☐ Students are relatively strong in the "Living systems" content area   ▨ Students are relatively weak in the "Living systems" content area

	"Physical systems"	"Earth and space systems"	"Living systems"	"Living systems" mean score compared to the average of the other two content areas
	Mean score	Mean score	Mean score	Score difference
Finland	560	554	574	17
France	482	463	490	17
Iceland	493	503	481	-17
Korea	530	533	498	-33
Luxembourg	474	471	499	26
Netherlands	531	518	509	-15
United Kingdom	508	505	525	19
Azerbaijan	433	400	398	-19
Brazil	385	375	403	23
Hong Kong-China	546	525	558	22
Israel	443	417	458	29
Jordan	433	421	450	23
Montenegro	407	411	430	21
Slovenia	531	534	517	-16
Tunisia	393	352	392	19
Uruguay	421	397	433	24

(OECD rows: Finland–United Kingdom; Partners rows: Azerbaijan–Uruguay)

StatLink ⫘ http://dx.doi.org/10.1787/141844475532

Iceland and the Netherlands and the partner countries/economies Azerbaijan and Slovenia. Korea scored well above the OECD average on the other two *knowledge of science* content areas, but with a score (498 score points) not significantly different to the OECD average on the "Living systems" area.

An analysis of the *knowledge of science* content areas by gender reveals also some gender differences (see Figure 2.19d available on line at http://dx.doi.org/10.1787/141844475532).

In all OECD countries except Turkey, males significantly outperform females in the content area "Physical systems", which relates to the structure and properties of matter, changes of matter and energy transformations. In the partner countries, the pattern is similar, with males significantly outperforming females, except in Qatar, Jordan, Azerbaijan, Bulgaria, Argentina, Kyrgyzstan, Thailand and Liechtenstein.

In the *knowledge of science* content area "Physical systems", the OECD country with the largest difference between males and females is Austria with a 45 score point advantage to the males. For Austria, these results are mirrored in other comparative studies, most notably the TIMSS upper secondary assessment (Mullis *et al.,* 1998). Analyses of these data revealed that this gender gap was closely associated with the difference in the cumulative number of physics lessons which males and females attended, essentially because of different programme and study choices (Stadler, 1999). There are four other OECD countries with an advantage for males that is 35 score points or more: the Czech Republic, Luxembourg, Hungary, and the Slovak Republic. Among the partner countries/economies, the largest differences are noted in Chile, with a difference of 40 score points and Hong Kong-China with 34 score points. Other partner countries with differences of 30 or more are Croatia, the Russian Federation (both 30 score points) and Slovenia (31 score points).

These observations support the popular notion that the physical sciences are the domain of males, a finding which is mirrored in a much larger share of males among physics graduates (OECD, 2007).

In the *knowledge of science* content area "Living systems", which refers to cell structure, human biology, the nature of populations and ecosystems, gender patterns are less uniform and there are few significant gender differences. The OECD countries with significant gender differences in this category in favour of males are Mexico, with a difference of 13 score points, Hungary (12 score points), and Denmark, Luxembourg and the Slovak Republic each with a difference of 11 score points. The OECD countries with a significant difference in favour of females are Greece with a difference of 12 score points and Finland, with 10 score points. Among the partner countries, there are seven with differences in favour of males and seven in favour of females. The larger differences in favour of females are in Qatar and Jordan, with 37 and 31 score points, respectively, Bulgaria with a difference of 19 score points, and Thailand and Estonia with 13 and 12 score points, respectively. The larger differences in favour of males are in Chile (27 score points), Chinese Taipei (15 score points), Colombia (13 score points) and Hong Kong-China (12 score points).

In the content area "Earth and space systems", which focuses on the structure and energy of the Earth and its systems, the Earth's history and its place in space, males tend to outperform females, but there are fewer significant differences than observed for Physical Systems. The largest differences in this category are in the Czech Republic (29 score points), Luxembourg (27 score points), Japan, Switzerland and Denmark (26 score points) and the Netherlands (25 score points) and in the partner countries Chile (35 score points), Colombia (26 score points) and Israel and Uruguay (25 score points).

A DETAILED ANALYSIS OF STUDENT PERFORMANCE ON THE SCIENCE COMPETENCY SCALES

The remainder of this chapter provides a detailed description of student performance on the science competency scales.

Student performance in identifying scientific issues

Approximately 22% of the science tasks given to students in PISA 2006 were related to *identifying scientific issues*. Figure 2.20 below shows six sample tasks from this category: one at Level 2, two at Level 3, two at Level 4 and one at Level 6. The knowledge and skills required to attain each level are summarised in the figure.

As described earlier, the main areas of interest in *identifying scientific issues* are recognising issues that are possible to investigate scientifically, identifying keywords to search for scientific information and recognising the key features of a scientific investigation. The scientific knowledge most applicable to the competency *identifying scientific issues* is that associated with an understanding of science processes and of the major content areas of "Physical systems", "Life systems", and "Earth and space systems".

Figure 2.20 [Part 1/2]

Summary descriptions of the six proficiency levels in *identifying scientific issues*

General proficiencies students should have at each level	Tasks a student should be able to do	Examples from released questions

LEVEL 6 1.3% of all students across the OECD area can perform tasks at Level 6 on the *identifying scientific issues* scale.

Students at this level demonstrate an ability to understand and articulate the complex modelling inherent in the design of an investigation.	• Articulate the aspects of a given experimental design that meet the intent of the scientific question being addressed. • Design an investigation to adequately meet the demands of a specific scientific question. • Identify variables that need to be controlled in an investigation and articulate methods to achieve that control.	**ACID RAIN** Question 5 Figure 2.32

LEVEL 5 8.4% of all students across the OECD area can perform tasks at least at Level 5 on the *identifying scientific issues* scale.

Students at this level understand the essential elements of a scientific investigation and thus can determine if scientific methods can be applied in a variety of quite complex, and often abstract contexts. Alternatively, by analysing a given experiment can identify the question being investigated and explain how the methodology relates to that question.	• Identify the variables to be changed and measured in an investigation of a wide variety of contexts. • Understand the need to control all variables extraneous to an investigation but impinging on it. • Ask a scientific question relevant to a given issue.	

LEVEL 4 28.4% of all students across the OECD area can perform tasks at least at Level 4 on the *identifying scientific issues* scale.

Students at this level can identify the change and measured variables in an investigation and at least one variable that is being controlled. They can suggest appropriate ways of controlling that variable. The question being investigated in straightforward investigations can be articulated.	• Distinguish the control against which experimental results are to be compared. • Design investigations in which the elements involve straightforward relationships and lack appreciable abstractness. • Show an awareness of the effects of uncontrolled variables and attempt to take this into account in investigations.	**SUNSCREENS** Questions 2 and 4 Figure 2.23 **CLOTHES** Question 1 Figure 2.26

• • •

77

Figure 2.20 [Part 2/2]

Summary descriptions of the six proficiency levels in *identifying scientific issues*

General proficiencies students should have at each level	Tasks a student should be able to do	Examples from released questions
LEVEL 3 56.7% of all students across the OECD area can perform tasks at least at Level 3 on the *identifying scientific issues* scale.		
Students at this level are able to make judgements about whether an issue is open to scientific measurement and, consequently, to scientific investigation. Given a description of an investigation can identify the change and measured variables.	▪ Identify the quantities able to be scientifically measured in an investigation. ▪ Distinguish between the change and measured variables in simple experiments. ▪ Recognise when comparisons are being made between two tests (but are unable to articulate the purpose of a control).	**ACID RAIN** Question 5 (Partial) Figure 2.32 **SUNSCREENS** Question 3 Figure 2.23
LEVEL 2 81.3% of all students across the OECD area can perform tasks at least at level 2 on the *identifying scientific issues* scale.		
Students at this level can determine if scientific measurement can be applied to a given variable in an investigation. They can recognise the variable being manipulated (changed) by the investigator. Students can appreciate the relationship between a simple model and the phenomenon it is modelling. In researching topics students can select appropriate key words for a search.	▪ Identify a relevant feature being modelled in an investigation. ▪ Show an understanding of what can and cannot be measured by scientific instruments. ▪ Select the most appropriate stated aims for an experiment from a given selection. ▪ Recognise what is being changed (the cause) in an experiment. ▪ Select a best set of Internet search words on a topic from several given sets.	**GENETICALLY MODIFIED CROPS** Question 3 Figure 2.22
LEVEL 1 94.9% of all students across the OECD area can perform tasks at least at Level 1 on the *identifying scientific issues* scale.		
Students at this level can suggest appropriate sources of information on scientific topics. They can identify a quantity that is undergoing variation in an experiment. In specific contexts they can recognise whether that variable can be measured using familiar measuring tools or not.	▪ Select some appropriate sources from a given number of sources of potential information on a scientific topic. ▪ Identify a quantity that is undergoing change, given a specific but simple scenario. ▪ Recognise when a device can be used to measure a variable (within the scope of the student's familiarity with measuring devices).	

StatLink http://dx.doi.org/10.1787/141844475532

Figure 2.21a

Percentage of students at each proficiency level on the *identifying scientific issues* scale

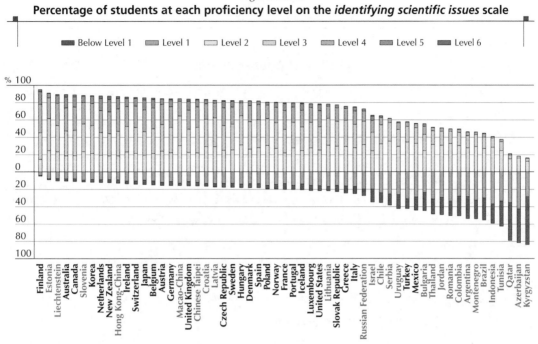

Countries are ranked in descending order of percentage of 15-year-olds at Levels 2, 3, 4, 5 and 6.
Source: OECD PISA 2006 database, Table 2.2a.
StatLink http://dx.doi.org/10.1787/141844475532

It can be seen in Figure 2.21a that across the countries there is a relatively small percentage of students who are capable of carrying out the *identifying scientific issues* tasks at the two highest levels – an average of 8.4% across the OECD countries, slightly less than the percentage for the combined science scale (9.0%). As with the combined science scale, the two countries with the highest percentages of students in these levels are New Zealand and Finland, with 18.5 and 17.2%, respectively. In addition, the Netherlands has 17.0% of students highly proficient at *identifying scientific issues,* compared to 13.1% in science overall, indicating that this area of science is where its strongest students are particularly strong. The partner countries/economies, Hong Kong-China and Liechtenstein have 14.5 and 10.3%, respectively, of students at Levels 5 and 6 of the *identifying scientific issues* scale. The OECD countries with a low percentage of students in these two levels are Mexico and Turkey (0.5%).

As for the combined science scale, Level 2 of the *identifying scientific issues* scale is the level at which students begin to show the skills necessary for future development in *identifying scientific issues.* Across the OECD 18.7% of students are classified as Level 1 or below.

Figure 2.21b (available on line at http://dx.doi.org/10.1787/141844475532) shows the distribution of student performance on the *identifying scientific issues* scale. Figure 2.21c (available on line at http://dx.doi.org/10.1787/141844475532) gives a summary of overall performance of different countries on the *identifying scientific issues* scale, in terms of the mean scores achieved by students in each country. Only those differences between countries that are statistically significant should be taken into account (see Boxes 2.2 and 2.5 for a more detailed description of interpretation of results).

Figure 2.22

GENETICALLY MODIFIED CROPS

GM CORN SHOULD BE BANNED

Wildlife conservation groups are demanding that a new genetically modified (GM) corn be banned.

This GM corn is designed to be unaffected by a powerful new herbicide that kills conventional corn plants. This new herbicide will kill most of the weeds that grow in cornfields.

The conservationists say that because these weeds are feed for small animals, especially insects, the use of the new herbicide with the GM corn will be bad for the environment. Supporters of the use of the GM corn say that a scientific study has shown that this will not happen.

Here are details of the scientific study mentioned in the above article:

- Corn was planted in 200 fields across the country.
- Each field was divided into two. The genetically modified (GM) corn treated with the powerful new herbicide was grown in one half, and the conventional corn treated with a conventional herbicide was grown in the other half.
- The number of insects found in the GM corn, treated with the new herbicide, was about the same as the number of insects in the conventional corn, treated with the conventional herbicide.

GENETICALLY MODIFIED CROPS – *QUESTION 3 (S508Q03)*

Question type: *Multiple choice*
Competency: *Identifying scientific issues*
Knowledge category: *"Scientific enquiry" (knowledge about science)*
Application area: *"Frontiers of science and technology"*
Setting: *Social*
Difficulty: *421*
Percentage of correct answers (OECD countries): *73.6%*

Level 6	707.9
Level 5	633.3
Level 4	558.7
Level 3	484.1
Level 2	409.5
Level 1	334.9
Below Level 1	

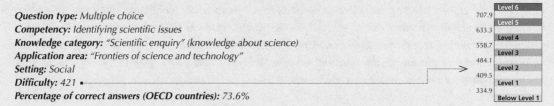

Corn was planted in 200 fields across the country. Why did the scientists use more than one site?

A. So that many farmers could try the new GM corn.

B. To see how much GM corn they could grow.

C. To cover as much land as possible with the GM crop.

D. To include various growth conditions for corn.

Scoring

Full Credit: D. To include various growth conditions for corn.

Comment

Towards the bottom of the scale, typical questions for Level 2 are exemplified by question 3 from the unit GENETICALLY MODIFIED CROPS (Figure 2.22), which is for the competency Identifying scientific issues. Question 3 asks a simple question about varying conditions in a scientific investigation and students are required to demonstrate knowledge about the design of science experiments.

To answer this question correctly in the absence of cues, the student needs to be aware that the effect of the treatment (different herbicides) on the outcome (insect numbers) could depend on environmental factors. Thus, by repeating the test in 200 locations the chance of a specific set of environmental factors giving rise to a spurious outcome can be accounted for. Since the question focuses on the methodology of the investigation it is categorised as "Scientific enquiry". The application area of genetic modification places this at the "Frontiers of science and technology" and given its restriction to one country it can be said to have a social setting.

In the absence of cues this question has the characteristics of Level 4; i.e. the student shows an awareness of the need to account for varying environmental factors and is able to recognise an appropriate way of dealing with that issue. However, the question actually performed at Level 2. This can be accounted for by the cues given in the three distractors. Students likely are able to easily eliminate these as options thus leaving the correct explanation as the answer. The effect is to reduce the difficulty of the question.

GENETICALLY MODIFIED CROPS – *QUESTION 10N (S508Q10N)*

How much interest do you have in the following information?

Tick only one box in each row.

	High Interest	Medium Interest	Low Interest	No Interest
a) Learning about the process by which plants are genetically modified.	$\square_1$	$\square_2$	$\square_3$	$\square_4$
b) Learning why some plants are not affected by herbicides.	$\square_1$	$\square_2$	$\square_3$	$\square_4$
c) Understanding better the difference between cross-breeding and genetic modification of plants.	$\square_1$	$\square_2$	$\square_3$	$\square_4$

Figure 2.23
SUNSCREENS

Mimi and Dean wondered which sunscreen product provides the best protection for their skin. Sunscreen products have a *Sun Protection Factor (SPF)* that shows how well each product absorbs the ultraviolet radiation component of sunlight. A high SPF sunscreen protects skin for longer than a low SPF sunscreen.

Mimi thought of a way to compare some different sunscreen products. She and Dean collected the following:

- two sheets of clear plastic that do not absorb sunlight;
- one sheet of light-sensitive paper;
- mineral oil (M) and a cream containing zinc oxide (ZnO); and
- four different sunscreens that they called S1, S2, S3, and S4.

Mimi and Dean included mineral oil because it lets most of the sunlight through, and zinc oxide because it almost completely blocks sunlight.

Dean placed a drop of each substance inside a circle marked on one sheet of plastic, then put the second plastic sheet over the top. He placed a large book on top of both sheets and pressed down.

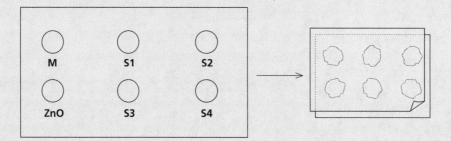

Mimi then put the plastic sheets on top of the sheet of light-sensitive paper. Light-sensitive paper changes from dark grey to white (or very light grey), depending on how long it is exposed to sunlight. Finally, Dean placed the sheets in a sunny place.

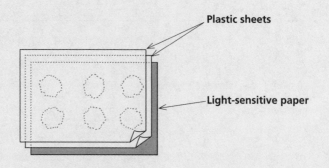

SUNSCREENS – *QUESTION 2 (S447Q02)*

Question type: *Multiple choice*
Competency: *Identifying scientific issues*
Knowledge category: *"Scientific enquiry" (knowledge about science)*
Application area: *"Health"*
Setting: *Personal*
Difficulty: *588* ▪
Percentage of correct answers: *40.5%*

707.9	Level 6
633.3	Level 5
558.7	Level 4
484.1	Level 3
409.5	Level 2
334.9	Level 1
	Below Level 1

Which one of these statements is a scientific description of the role of the mineral oil and the zinc oxide in comparing the effectiveness of the sunscreens?

A. Mineral oil and zinc oxide are both factors being tested.

B. Mineral oil is a factor being tested and zinc oxide is a reference substance.

C. Mineral oil is a reference substance and zinc oxide is a factor being tested.

D. Mineral oil and zinc oxide are both reference substances.

Scoring

Full Credit: D. Mineral oil and zinc oxide are both reference substances.

Comment

This question requires the student to understand the nature of a scientific enquiry in general and to recognise how the effectiveness of the sunscreens is being measured by reference to two substances at the extremes of the measured effect in particular. The application is about protection from UV radiation and the setting has a personal focus.

In addition to being able to recognise the change and measured variables from a description of the experiment, a student gaining full credit can identify the method being used to quantify the measured variable. This locates the question at Level 4.

SUNSCREENS – *QUESTION 3 (S447Q03)*

Question type: *Multiple choice*
Competency: *Identifying scientific issues*
Knowledge category: *"Scientific enquiry" (knowledge about science)*
Application area: *"Health"*
Setting: *Personal*
Difficulty: *499* ▪
Percentage of correct answers (OECD countries): *58.3%*

707.9	Level 6
633.3	Level 5
558.7	Level 4
484.1	Level 3
409.5	Level 2
334.9	Level 1
	Below Level 1

Which one of these questions were Mimi and Dean trying to answer?

A. How does the protection for each sunscreen compare with the others?

B. How do sunscreens protect your skin from ultraviolet radiation?

C. Is there any sunscreen that gives less protection than mineral oil?

D. Is there any sunscreen that gives more protection than zinc oxide?

Scoring

Full credit: A. How does the protection for each sunscreen compare with the others?

Comment

This question requires the student to correctly identify the question that the investigation is trying to answer, i.e. the student needs to recognise variables being measured from the description of the experiment provided. The primary focus of the question is about scientific methodology and is thus classified as "Scientific enquiry". The application is about protection from UV radiation and the setting is personal.

Since the question requires students to identify the change and measured variables it is located at Level 3.

SUNSCREENS – QUESTION 4 (S447Q04)

Question type: Multiple choice
Competency: Identifying scientific issues
Knowledge category: "Scientific enquiry" (knowledge about science)
Application area: "Health"
Setting: Personal
Difficulty: 574
Percentage of correct answers (OECD countries): 43.0%

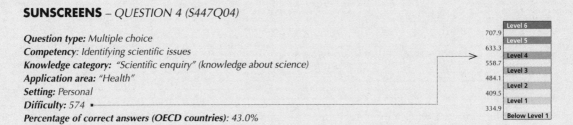

Why was the second sheet of plastic pressed down?

A. To stop the drops from drying out.

B. To spread the drops out as far as possible.

C. To keep the drops inside the marked circles.

D. To make the drops the same thickness.

Scoring

Full Credit: D. To make the drops the same thickness.

Comment

This question involves the technique used to control a variable in a scientific enquiry. The student must recognise that the purpose of the described technique is to assure the sunscreens are the same thickness. Because the methodology of the investigation is the focus of the question it is classified as "scientific enquiry". The application is about protection from UV radiation and the setting is personal.

Correct responses indicate the student is aware that the thickness of the sunscreens would influence the outcome and that this needed to be accounted for in the design of the experiment. Consequently, the question has the characteristics of Level 4.

SUNSCREENS – QUESTION 5 (S447Q05)

Question type: Open-constructed response
Competency: Using scientific evidence
Knowledge category: "Scientific explanations" (knowledge about science)
Application area: "Health"
Setting: Personal
Difficulty: Full Credit 629, Partial Credit 616
Percentage of correct answers (OECD countries): 27.1%

The light-sensitive paper is a dark grey and fades to a lighter grey when it is exposed to some sunlight, and to white when exposed to a lot of sunlight.

Which one of these diagrams shows a pattern that might occur? Explain why you chose it.

Answer: . . . .

Explanation: . . . .

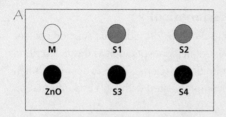

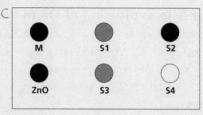

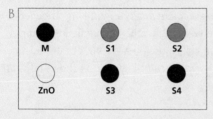

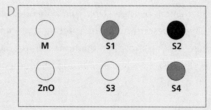

Scoring

Full Credit: A. With explanation that the ZnO spot has stayed dark grey (because it blocks sunlight) and the M spot has gone white (because mineral oil absorbs very little sunlight).

[It is not necessary (though it is sufficient) to include the further explanations that are shown in parentheses.]

A. ZnO has blocked the sunlight as it should and M has let it through.

I chose A because the mineral oil needs to be the lightest shade while the zinc oxide is the darkest.

Partial Credit: A. Gives a correct explanation for either the ZnO spot or the M spot, but not both.

A. Mineral oil provides the lowest resistance against UVL. So with other substances the paper would not be white.

A. Zinc oxide absorbs practically all rays and the diagram shows this.

A because ZnO blocks the light and M absorbs it.

Comment

This question is an example of Level 4 for the competency using scientific evidence. Here, students are given results from an experiment and asked to interpret a pattern of results and explain their conclusion. The question requires the student to demonstrate an understanding of the diagrams shown and then to make a correct selection. Answering correctly requires matching the shades of grey shown in the diagram with the evidence provided in the stimuli of the question and the unit. The student must bring together three pieces of evidence in order to form a conclusion: (1) that mineral oil lets most of the sunlight through while ZnO blocks most of the sunlight; (2) that the light-sensitive paper lightens on exposure to sunlight; and (3) that only one of the diagrams meets both of the criteria. By requiring a conclusion to be drawn that is logically consistent with the available evidence, this question is placed in the category of "Scientific explanations". The application is about protection from UV radiation and the setting is personal.

The student must bring together several pieces of evidence and effectively explain its logical consistency by generating a correct conclusion. This locates the question at Level 4. Separation between full and partial credit lies within Level 4. This can be explained by the similarity in the skills needed to choose the correct diagram. Full-credit responses are identified as having a more complete explanation than those gaining partial credit. The units GREENHOUSE and SUNSCREENS (Figures 2.33 and 2.23) present good examples for Level 3 for the same competency.

Student performance in explaining phenomena scientifically

The competency *explaining phenomena scientifically* is related to the aims of traditional science courses such as physics and biology. In PISA 2006, this centred on basic scientific concepts such as those described in Figure 2.4. What this means for teachers in countries with traditional science courses is a combined emphasis on major concepts fundamental to science disciplines complemented with facts and information associated with basic concepts.

As described earlier, the main areas of interest in *explaining phenomena scientifically* are applying *knowledge of science* in a given situation, describing or interpreting phenomena scientifically and predicting changes, and identifying appropriate descriptions, explanations and predictions. Approximately 46% of the science tasks included in PISA 2006 are related to *explaining phenomena scientifically.* Figure 2.24 shows tasks at proficiency Levels 1, 2, 3, 4, and 6.

Figure 2.24 [Part 1/2]

Summary descriptions of the six proficiency levels in *explaining phenomena scientifically*

General proficiencies students should have at each level	Tasks a student should be able to do	Examples from released questions
LEVEL 6 1.8% of all students across the OECD area can perform tasks at Level 6 on the *explaining phenomena scientifically* scale.		
Students at this level draw on a range of abstract scientific knowledge and concepts and the relationships between these in developing explanations of processes within systems.	• Demonstrate an understanding of a variety of complex, abstract physical, biological or environmental systems. • In explaining processes, articulate the relationships between a number of discrete elements or concepts.	**GREENHOUSE** Question 5 Figure 2.33
LEVEL 5 9.8% of all students across the OECD area can perform tasks at least at Level 5 on the *explaining phenomena scientifically* scale.		
Students at this level draw on knowledge of two or three scientific concepts and identify the relationship between them in developing an explanation of a contextual phenomenon.	• Take a scenario, identify its major component features, whether conceptual or factual, and use the relationships between these features in providing an explanation of a phenomenon. • Synthesise two or three central scientific ideas in a given context in developing an explanation for, or a prediction of, an outcome.	
LEVEL 4 29.4% of all students across the OECD area can perform tasks at least at Level 4 on the *explaining phenomena scientifically* scale.		
Students at this level have an understanding of scientific ideas, including scientific models, with a significant level of abstraction. They can apply a general, scientific concept containing such ideas in the development of an explanation of a phenomenon.	• Understand a number of abstract scientific models and can select an appropriate one from which to draw inferences in explaining a phenomenon in a specific context (*e.g.* the particle model, planetary models, models of biological systems). • Link two or more pieces of specific knowledge, including from an abstract source in an explanation (*e.g.* increased exercise leads to increased metabolism in muscle cells, this in turn requires an increased exchange of gases in the blood supply which is achieved by an increased rate of breathing).	**PHYSICAL EXERCISE** Question 5 Figure 2.29

...

Figure 2.24 [Part 2/2]

Summary descriptions of the six proficiency levels in *explaining phenomena scientifically*

General proficiencies students should have at each level	Tasks a student should be able to do	Examples from released questions
LEVEL 3 56.4% of all students across the OECD area can perform tasks at least at Level 3 on the *explaining phenomena scientifically* scale.		
Students at this level can apply one or more concrete or tangible scientific ideas/concepts in the development of an explanation of a phenomenon. This is enhanced when there are specific cues given or options available from which to choose. When developing an explanation, cause and effect relationships are recognised and simple, explicit scientific models may be drawn upon.	▪ Understand the central feature(s) of a scientific system and, in concrete terms, can predict outcomes from changes in that system (*e.g.* the effect of a weakening of the immune system in a human). ▪ In a simple and clearly defined context, recall several relevant, tangible facts and apply these in developing an explanation of the phenomenon.	**MARY MONTAGU** Question 4 Figure 2.28 **ACID RAIN** Question 2 Figure 2.32 **PHYSICAL EXERCISE** Question 1 Figure 2.29
LEVEL 2 80.4% of all students across the OECD area can perform tasks at least at Level 2 on the *explaining phenomena scientifically* scale.		
Students at this level can recall an appropriate, tangible, scientific fact applicable in a simple and straightforward context and can use it to explain or predict an outcome.	▪ Given a specific outcome in a simple context, indicate, in a number of cases and with appropriate cues the scientific fact or process that has caused that outcome (*e.g.* water expands when it freezes and opens cracks in rocks, land containing marine fossils was once under the sea). ▪ Recall specific scientific facts with general currency in the public domain (*e.g.* vaccination provides protection against viruses that cause disease).	**GRAND CANYON** Question 3 Figure 2.27 **MARY MONTAGU** Questions 2 and 3 Figure 2.28 **GRAND CANYON** Question 5 Figure 2.27
LEVEL 1 94.6% of all students across the OECD area can perform tasks at least at Level 1 on the *explaining phenomena scientifically* scale.		
Students at this level can recognise simple cause and effect relationships given relevant cues. The knowledge drawn upon is a singular scientific fact that is drawn from experience or has widespread popular currency.	▪ Choose a suitable response from among several responses, given the context is a simple one and that recall of a single scientific fact is involved (*e.g.* ammeters are used to measure electric current). ▪ Given sufficient cues, recognise simple cause and effect relationships (*e.g.* Do muscles get an increased flow of blood during exercise? Yes or No).	**PHYSICAL EXERCISE** Question 3 Figure 2.29 **CLOTHES** Question 2 Figure 2.26

StatLink ⬛📄 http://dx.doi.org/10.1787/141844475532

It can be seen in Figure 2.25a, that for the *explaining phenomena scientifically* scale there is a relatively small percentage of students across the countries who are capable of carrying out the tasks at the two highest levels – an average of 9.8% across the OECD countries, slightly more than the percentage for the combined science scale (9.0%). In addition to Finland and New Zealand, and the partner economies, Chinese Taipei and Hong Kong-China, examples of other countries with high percentages of students at these levels are the Czech Republic (15.5%) and the partner countries Estonia and Slovenia with 15.8 and 15.4%, respectively.

These last three countries have considerably more students at high levels of science competency in this scale than in other science competencies, and there is a particularly strong contrast in the case of Estonia, where 15.8% reach Level 5 or 6 on this scale, but only 5.8% on the *identifying scientific issues* scale. Examples of countries with low percentages of students at these two levels are Mexico (0.4%), Turkey (1.5%) and Portugal (2.7%), and the partner countries Indonesia (0.0%), Tunisia (0.1%) and Thailand (0.4%).

Figure 2.25a
Percentage of students at each proficiency level on the
explaining phenomena scientifically **scale**

Below Level 1   Level 1   Level 2   Level 3   Level 4   Level 5   Level 6

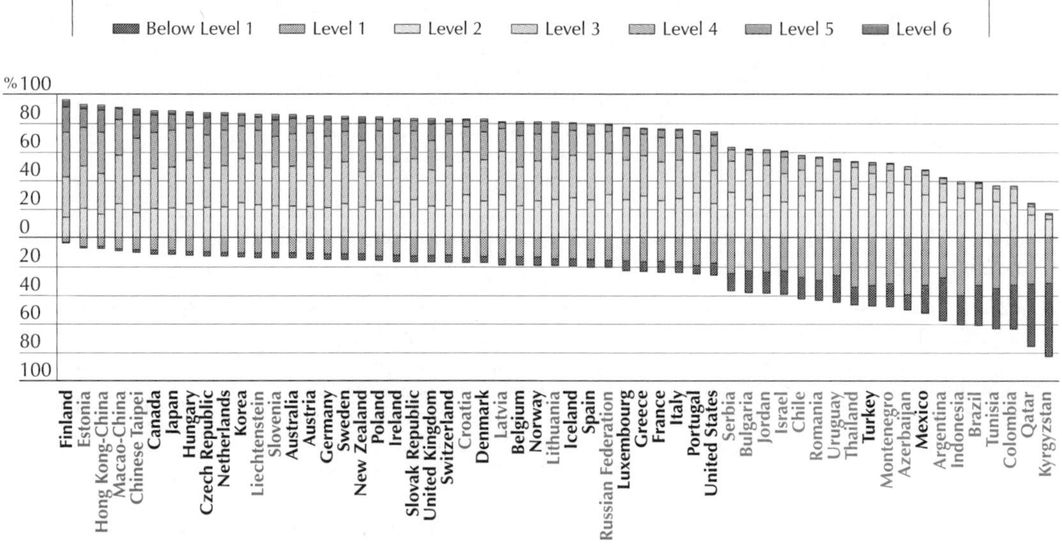

Countries are ranked in descending order of percentage of 15-year-olds at Levels 2, 3, 4, 5 and 6.
Source: OECD PISA 2006 database, Table 2.3a.
StatLink http://dx.doi.org/10.1787/141844475532

As for the combined science scale, Level 2 is the level at which students begin to show the skills necessary for future development in *explaining phenomena scientifically*. Across the OECD countries, 19.6% of students are classified as Level 1 or below. Examples of countries with low percentages in these levels are Finland (4.0%), Canada (11.7%), Japan (11.8%) and Hungary (12.5%), and the partner countries/economies Estonia (7.5%), Hong Kong-China (7.8%), Macao-China (9.5%) and Chinese Taipei (10.4%). Countries with students overrepresented in these lower levels are Mexico (52.8%) and Turkey (47.7%), and the partner countries, Kyrgyzstan (83.1%), Qatar (76.0%), Colombia (63.9%) and Tunisia (63.7%).

Figure 2.25b (available on line at http://dx.doi.org/10.1787/141844475532) shows the distribution of student performance on the *explaining phenomena scientifically* scale. Average country results for *explaining phenomena scientifically* are compared in the multiple comparison chart, Figure 2.25c (available on line at http://dx.doi.org/10.1787/141844475532).

Several of these selected science units contain examples of embedded questions that query students' attitudes. *GENETICALLY MODIFIED CROPS, ACID RAIN,* and *GRAND CANYON* (Figures 2.22, 2.32 and 2.27) all have embedded attitudinal questions (see Chapter 3 for a full discussion of the results of attitudinal questions). The embedded question in *GRAND CANYON* centres on students' support for scientific inquiry into questions concerning fossils, protection of national parks, and rock formations.

Figure 2.26
CLOTHES

Read the text and answer the questions that follow.

CLOTHES TEXT

A team of British scientists is developing "intelligent" clothes that will give disabled children the power of "speech". Children wearing waistcoats made of a unique electrotextile, linked to a speech synthesiser, will be able to make themselves understood simply by tapping on the touch-sensitive material.

The material is made up of normal cloth and an ingenious mesh of carbon-impregnated fibres that can conduct electricity. When pressure is applied to the fabric, the pattern of signals that passes through the conducting fibres is altered and a computer chip can work out where the cloth has been touched. It then can trigger whatever electronic device is attached to it, which could be no bigger than two boxes of matches.

"The smart bit is in how we weave the fabric and how we send signals through it – and we can weave it into existing fabric designs so you cannot see it's in there," says one of the scientists.

Without being damaged, the material can be washed, wrapped around objects or scrunched up. The scientist also claims it can be mass-produced cheaply.

Source: Steve Farrer, "Interactive fabric promises a material gift of the garb", *The Australian*, 10 August 1998.

CLOTHES – *QUESTION 1 (S213Q01)*

Question type: *Complex multiple choice*
Competency: *Identifying scientific issues*
Knowledge category: *"Scientific enquiry" (knowledge about science)*
Application area: *"Frontiers of science and technology"*
Setting: *Social*
Difficulty: *567* •
Percentage of correct answers (OECD countries): *47.9%*

707.9	Level 6
	Level 5
633.3	
	Level 4
558.7	
	Level 3
484.1	
	Level 2
409.5	
	Level 1
334.9	
	Below Level 1

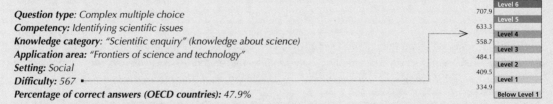

Can these claims made in the article be tested through scientific investigation in the laboratory?

Circle either "Yes" or "No" for each.

The material can be	Can the claim be tested through scientific investigation in the laboratory?
washed without being damaged.	Yes / No
wrapped around objects without being damaged.	Yes / No
scrunched up without being damaged.	Yes / No
mass-produced cheaply.	Yes / No

Scoring

Full Credit: Yes, Yes, Yes, No, in that order.

Comment

The question requires the student to identify the change and measured variables associated with testing a claim about the clothing. It also involves an assessment of whether there are techniques to quantify the measured variable and whether other variables can be controlled. This process then needs to be accurately applied for all four claims. The issue of "intelligent" clothes is in the category "Frontiers of science and technology" and is a community issue addressing a need for disabled children so the setting is social. The scientific skills applied are concerned with the nature of investigation which places the question in the "Scientific enquiry" category.

The need to identify change and measured variables, together with an appreciation of what would be involved in carrying out measurement and controlling variables, locates the question at Level 4.

CLOTHES – *QUESTION 2 (S213Q02)*

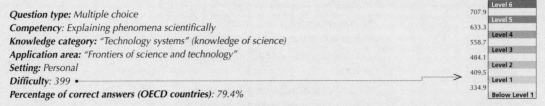

Question type: *Multiple choice*
Competency: *Explaining phenomena scientifically*
Knowledge category: *"Technology systems" (knowledge of science)*
Application area: *"Frontiers of science and technology"*
Setting: *Personal*
Difficulty: *399*
Percentage of correct answers (OECD countries): *79.4%*

	Level 6
707.9	Level 5
633.3	Level 4
558.7	Level 3
484.1	Level 2
409.5	Level 1
334.9	Below Level 1

Which piece of laboratory equipment would be among the equipment you would need to check that the fabric is conducting electricity?

A. Voltmeter
B. Light box
C. Micrometer
D. Sound meter

Scoring

Full Credit: A. Voltmeter.

Comment

In CLOTHES, question 2, the student must simply recall which piece of laboratory equipment would be used to check a fabric's conductivity The question only requires the student to associate electric current with a device used in electric circuits, i.e. the recall of a simple scientific fact. This places the question at Level 1.

Since the focus is a technical device the question lies in the "technology systems" category. PHYSICAL EXERCISE, CLOTHES and GRAND CANYON (Figures 2.29, 2.26 and 2.27) are questions at Level 1 (below the cut-point), at the very bottom of the scale for the competency explaining phenomena scientifically.

Figure 2.27
GRAND CANYON

The Grand Canyon is located in a desert in the USA. It is a very large and deep canyon containing many layers of rock. Sometime in the past, movements in the Earth's crust lifted these layers up. The Grand Canyon is now 1.6 km deep in parts. The Colorado River runs through the bottom of the canyon.

See the picture below of the Grand Canyon taken from its south rim. Several different layers of rock can be seen in the walls of the canyon.

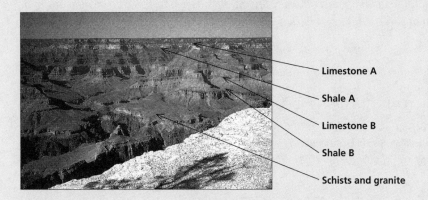

PHYSICAL EXERCISE, CLOTHES and GRAND CANYON (Figures 2.29, 2.26 and 2.27) are questions at Level 1 (below the cut-point), at the very bottom of the scale for the competency Explaining phenomena scientifically.

GRAND CANYON – QUESTION 7 (S426Q07)

Question type: Complex multiple choice
Competency: Identifying scientific issues
Knowledge category: "Scientific enquiry" (knowledge about science)
Application area: "Environment"
Setting: Social
Difficulty: 485
Percentage of correct answers (OECD countries): 61.3%

Level 6	707.9
Level 5	633.3
Level 4	558.7
Level 3	484.1
Level 2	409.5
Level 1	334.9
Below Level 1	

About five million people visit the Grand Canyon national park every year. There is concern about the damage that is being caused to the park by so many visitors.

Can the following questions be answered by scientific investigation? Circle "Yes" or "No" for each question.

Can this question be answered by scientific investigation?	Yes or No?
How much erosion is caused by use of the walking tracks?	Yes / No
Is the park area as beautiful as it was 100 years ago?	Yes / No

Scoring

Full Credit: Both correct: Yes, No in that order.

Comment

This is a complex multiple-choice question, where the students must make a selection of "Yes"or "No"for each of the two options presented. To gain credit a student must correctly answer both of the options presented, in the order "Yes", "No". The student must have some notion of the capacities and limits of scientific investigations, so the question is assessing the competency of identifying scientific issues. The setting of the question is located out side the immediate personal life experiences of the student and the setting is social. The question, at a difficulty level of 485, is just below average difficulty and is placed at the lower part of Level 3. At this level, students can identify clearly described scientific issues in a range of contexts.

GRAND CANYON – *QUESTION 3 (S426Q03)*

Question type: *Multiple choice*
Competency: *Explaining phenomena scientifically*
Knowledge category: *"Earth and space systems" (knowledge of science)*
Application area: *"Environment"*
Setting: *Social*
Difficulty: *451* ■
Percentage of correct answers (OECD countries): *67.6%*

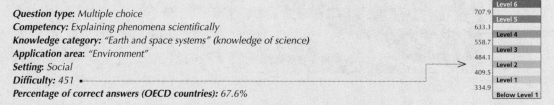

The temperature in the Grand Canyon ranges from below 0 °C to over 40 °C. Although it is a desert area, cracks in the rocks sometimes contain water. How do these temperature changes and the water in rock cracks help to speed up the breakdown of rocks?

A. Freezing water dissolves warm rocks.

B. Water cements rocks together.

C. Ice smoothes the surface of rocks.

D. Freezing water expands in the rock cracks.

Scoring

Full Credit: D. Freezing water expands in the rock cracks.

Comment

This is a multiple-choice question. Choosing the correct explanation for the weathering of rocks involves the student knowing that water freezes when the temperature falls below 0 °C and that water expands when becoming solid ice. The wording of this question does give some cues to the student as to what to eliminate, so its difficulty is lower.

The student needs to recall two tangible scientific facts and apply them in the context of the described conditions in the desert. This locates the question at Level 2.

GRAND CANYON – *QUESTION 5 (S426Q05)*

Question type: Multiple choice
Competency: Explaining phenomena scientifically
Knowledge category: "Earth and space systems" (knowledge of science)
Application area: "Natural resources"
Setting: Social
Difficulty: 411
Percentage of correct answers (OECD countries): 75.8%

707.9	Level 6
633.3	Level 5
558.7	Level 4
484.1	Level 3
409.5	Level 2
334.9	Level 1
	Below Level 1

There are many fossils of marine animals, such as clams, fish and corals, in the Limestone A layer of the Grand Canyon. What happened millions of years ago that explains why such fossils are found there?

A. In ancient times, people brought seafood to the area from the ocean.

B. Oceans were once much rougher and sea life washed inland on giant waves.

C. An ocean covered this area at that time and then receded later.

D. Some sea animals once lived on land before migrating to the sea.

Scoring

Full Credit: C. An ocean covered this area at that time and then receded later.

Comment

The question requires the student to recall the fact that fossils are formed in water and that when the seas recede they may reveal fossils of organisms deposited at an earlier age and then to choose the correct explanation. Credible distractors means the recalled knowledge has to be applied in the context provided. The question is located at Level 2 near the boundary with Level 1.

GRAND CANYON – *QUESTION 10S (S426Q10S)*

How much do you agree with the following statements?
Tick only one box in each row.

	Strongly agree	Agree	Disagree	Strongly disagree
d) The systematic study of fossils is important.	☐₁	☐₂	☐₃	☐₄
e) Action to protect National Parks from damage should be based on scientific evidence.	☐₁	☐₂	☐₃	☐₄
f) Scientific investigation of geological layers is important.	☐₁	☐₂	☐₃	☐₄

Figure 2.28
MARY MONTAGU

Read the following newspaper article and answer the questions that follow.

THE HISTORY OF VACCINATION

Mary Montagu was a beautiful woman. She survived an attack of smallpox in 1715 but she was left covered with scars. While living in Turkey in 1717, she observed a method called inoculation that was commonly used there. This treatment involved scratching a weak type of smallpox virus into the skin of healthy young people who then became sick, but in most cases only with a mild form of the disease.

Mary Montagu was so convinced of the safety of these inoculations that she allowed her son and daughter to be inoculated.

In 1796, Edward Jenner used inoculations of a related disease, cowpox, to produce antibodies against smallpox. Compared with the inoculation of smallpox, this treatment had less side effects and the treated person could not infect others. The treatment became known as vaccination.

MARY MONTAGU – *QUESTION 2 (S477Q02)*

Question type: *Multiple choice*
Competency: *Explaining phenomena scientifically*
Knowledge category: *"Living systems" (knowledge of science)*
Application area: *"Health"*
Setting: *Social*
Difficulty: *436*
Percentage of correct answers (OECD countries): *74.9%*

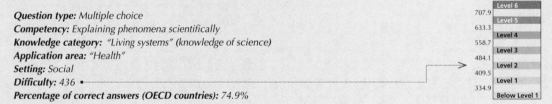

	Level 6
707.9	
	Level 5
633.3	
	Level 4
558.7	
	Level 3
484.1	
	Level 2
409.5	
	Level 1
334.9	
	Below Level 1

What kinds of diseases can people be vaccinated against?

A. Inherited diseases like haemophilia.

B. Diseases that are caused by viruses, like polio.

C. Diseases from the malfunctioning of the body, like diabetes.

D. Any sort of disease that has no cure.

Scoring

Full Credit: B. Diseases that are caused by viruses, like polio.

Comment

To gain credit the student must recall a specific piece of knowledge that vaccination helps prevent diseases, the cause for which is external to normal body components. This fact is then applied in the selection of the correct explanation and the rejection of other explanations. The term "virus" appears in the stimulus text and provides a hint for students. This lowered the difficulty of the question. Recalling an appropriate, tangible scientific fact and its application in a relatively simple context locates the question at Level 2.

MARY MONTAGU – *QUESTION 3 (S477Q03)*

Question type: *Multiple choice*
Competency: *Explaining phenomena scientifically*
Knowledge category: *"Living systems" (knowledge of science)*
Application area: *"Health"*
Setting: *Social*
Difficulty: *431* •
Percentage of correct answers (OECD countries): *75.1%*

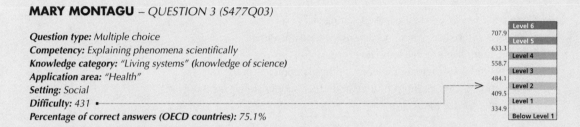

If animals or humans become sick with an infectious bacterial disease and then recover, the type of bacteria that caused the disease does not usually make them sick again.

What is the reason for this?

A. The body has killed all bacteria that may cause the same kind of disease.

B. The body has made antibodies that kill this type of bacteria before they multiply.

C. The red blood cells kill all bacteria that may cause the same kind of disease.

D. The red blood cells capture and get rid of this type of bacteria from the body.

Scoring

Full Credit: B. The body has made antibodies that kill this type of bacteria before they multiply.

Comment

To correctly answer this question the student must recall that the body produces antibodies that attack foreign bacteria, the cause of bacterial disease. Its application involves the further knowledge that these antibodies provide resistance to subsequent infections of the same bacteria. The issue is community control of disease, so the setting is social.

In selecting the appropriate explanation the student is recalling a tangible scientific fact and applying it in a relatively simple context. Consequently, the question is located at Level 2.

MARY MONTAGU – *QUESTION 4 (S477Q04)*

Question type: *Open-constructed response*
Competency: *Explaining phenomena scientifically*
Knowledge category: *"Living systems" (knowledge of science)*
Application area: *"Health"*
Setting: *Social*
Difficulty: *507* •
Percentage of correct answers (OECD countries): *61.7%*

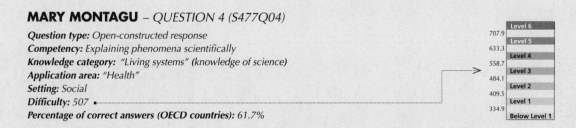

Give one reason why it is recommended that young children and old people, in particular, should be vaccinated against influenza (flu).

....

....

....

Scoring

Full Credit: Responses referring to young and/or old people having weaker immune systems than other people, or similar. For example:

> These people have less resistance to getting sick.
> The young and old can't fight off disease as easily as others.
> They are more likely to catch the flu.
> If they get the flu the effects are worse in these people.
> Because organisms of young children and older people are weaker.
> Old people get sick more easily.

Comment

This question requires the student to identify why young children and old people are more at risk of the effects of influenza than others in the population. Directly, or by inference, the reason is attributed to young children and old people having weaker immune systems. The issue is community control of disease, so the setting is social.

A correct explanation involves applying several pieces of knowledge that are well established in the community. The question stem also provides a cue to the groups having different resistance to disease. This locates the question at Level 3.

MARY MONTAGU – *QUESTION 10S (S477Q10S)*

How much do you agree with the following statements?

Tick only one box in each row.

	Strongly agree	Agree	Disagree	Strongly disagree
a) I am in favour of research to develop vaccines for new strains of influenza.	☐₁	☐₂	☐₃	☐₄
b) The cause of a disease can only be identified by scientific research.	☐₁	☐₂	☐₃	☐₄
c) The effectiveness of unconventional treatments for diseases should be subject to scientific investigation.	☐₁	☐₂	☐₃	☐₄

Figure 2.29
PHYSICAL EXERCISE

Regular but moderate physical exercise is good for our health.

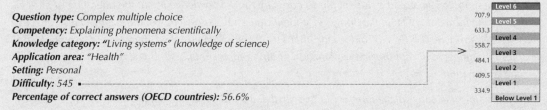

PHYSICAL EXERCISE – *QUESTION 1 (S493Q01)*

Question type: *Complex multiple choice*
Competency: *Explaining phenomena scientifically*
Knowledge category: *"Living systems" (knowledge of science)*
Application area: *"Health"*
Setting: *Personal*
Difficulty: *545*
Percentage of correct answers (OECD countries): *56.6%*

Level 6	707.9
Level 5	633.3
Level 4	558.7
Level 3	484.1
Level 2	409.5
Level 1	334.9
Below Level 1	

What are the advantages of regular physical exercise? Circle "Yes" or "No" for each statement.

Is this an advantage of regular physical exercise?	Yes or No?
Physical exercise helps prevent heart and circulation illnesses.	Yes / No
Physical exercise leads to a healthy diet.	Yes / No
Physical exercise helps to avoid becoming overweight.	Yes / No

Scoring

Full Credit: All three correct: Yes, No, Yes in that order.

Comment

This is a complex multiple-choice question, where the students must make a selection of "Yes"or "No" for each of the three options presented. To gain credit a student must correctly answer all three of the options presented, in the order "Yes", "No", "Yes". The student must have some knowledge of the advantages of physical exercise, so the question is assessing the competency explaining phenomena scientifically. The question is highly relevant to 15-year-olds as it relates to their own personal health. The question, at a difficulty level of 545, is of above-average difficulty and is placed at the upper part of Level 3. At this level, students can select facts and knowledge to explain phenomena and can interpret and use scientific concepts from different disciplines and can apply them directly.

PHYSICAL EXERCISE – *QUESTION 3 (S493Q03)*

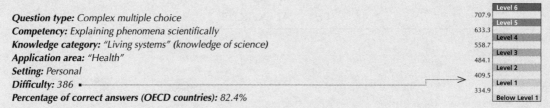

Question type: *Complex multiple choice*
Competency: *Explaining phenomena scientifically*
Knowledge category: *"Living systems" (knowledge of science)*
Application area: *"Health"*
Setting: *Personal*
Difficulty: *386* •
Percentage of correct answers (OECD countries): *82.4%*

Level 6	707.9
Level 5	633.3
Level 4	558.7
Level 3	484.1
Level 2	409.5
Level 1	334.9
Below Level 1	

What happens when muscles are exercised? Circle "Yes" or "No" for each statement.

Does this happen when muscles are exercised?	Yes or No?
Muscles get an increased flow of blood.	Yes / No
Fats are formed in the muscles.	Yes / No

Scoring

Full Credit: Both correct: Yes, No in that order.

Comment

For this question, to gain credit a student has to correctly recall knowledge about the operation of muscles and about the formation of fat in the body, i.e. students must have knowledge of the science fact that active muscles get an increased flow of blood and that fats are not formed when muscles are exercised. This enables the student to accept the first explanation of this complex multiple-choice question and reject the second explanation.

The two simple factual explanations contained in the question are not related to each other. Each is accepted or rejected as an effect of the exercise of muscles and the knowledge has widespread currency. Consequently, the question is located at Level 1. PHYSICAL EXERCISE, CLOTHES and GRAND CANYON (Figures 2.29, 2.26 and 2.27) are at Level 1 (below the cut-point), at the very bottom of the scale for the competency explaining phenomena scientifically.

PHYSICAL EXERCISE – *QUESTION 5 (S493Q05)*

Question type: *Open-constructed response*
Competency: *Explaining phenomena scientifically*
Knowledge category: *"Living systems" (knowledge of science)*
Application area: *"Health"*
Setting: *Personal*
Difficulty: *583* •
Percentage of correct answers (OECD countries): *45.2 %*

Level 6	707.9
Level 5	633.3
Level 4	558.7
Level 3	484.1
Level 2	409.5
Level 1	334.9
Below Level 1	

Why do you have to breathe more heavily when you're doing physical exercise than when your body is resting?

......

......

......

Scoring

Full Credit:

To remove increased levels of carbon dioxide and to supply more oxygen to your body. *[Do not accept "air" instead of "carbon dioxide" or "oxygen".]* For example:

- When you exercise your body needs more oxygen and produces more carbon dioxide. Breathing does this.
- Breathing faster allows more oxygen into the blood and more carbon dioxide to be removed.

To remove *increased* levels of carbon dioxide from your body **or** to supply *more* oxygen to your body, but not both. *[Do not accept "air" instead of "carbon dioxide" or "oxygen".]*

- Because we must get rid of the carbon dioxide that builds up.
- Because the muscles need oxygen. *[The implication is that your body needs **more** oxygen when you are exercising (using your muscles).]*
- Because physical exercise uses up oxygen.
- You breathe more heavily because you are taking more oxygen into your lungs. *[Poorly expressed, but recognises that you are supplied with more oxygen.]*
- Since you are using so much energy your body needs double or triple the amount of air intake. It also needs to remove the carbon dioxide in your body. *[Code 12 for the second sentence – the implication is that more carbon dioxide than usual has to be removed from your body; the first sentence is not contradictory, though by itself it would get Code 01.]*

Comment

For this question the student must explain how breathing more heavily (meaning deeper and more rapidly) is related to an increase in physical activity. Credit is given for an explanation that recognises that exercising muscles requires more oxygen and/or must dispose of more carbon dioxide than when not exercising. Since the student must recall knowledge in order to formulate an explanation the question belongs in the knowledge of science category. Relevant knowledge relates to the physiology of the human body, so the application area is "Health" while the setting is personal.

The student needs to draw on knowledge of body systems in order to relate the gas exchange occurring in the lungs to increased exercise. Consequently, several pieces of specific knowledge are related in order to produce an explanation of the phenomenon. This locates the question at Level 4.

Student performance in using scientific evidence

Approximately 32% of the science tasks presented to students in PISA related to *using scientific evidence*. Sample tasks for this competency are included in units *ACID RAIN* (Figure 2.32), *GREENHOUSE* (Figure 2.33), and *SUNSCREENS* (Figure 2.23). The figures describe sample tasks at Levels 2, 3, 4, and 5. The precise competencies required to perform at different levels of proficiency are described in Figure 2.30.

This competency requires students to synthesise *knowledge of science* and *knowledge about science* as they apply both of these to a life situation or contemporary social problem.

The main features of the competency *using scientific evidence* are: interpreting scientific evidence and making and communicating conclusions; identifying the assumptions, evidence and reasoning behind conclusions; and reflecting on the societal implications of science and technological developments.

The OECD average percentage of students who are capable of carrying out the tasks on the *using scientific evidence* scale at the two highest levels is 11.8% – higher than the 9.0% for the combined science scale. A particularly high percentage of students in Finland (25.0%) are proficient at these levels. Other countries with high percentages at these levels are Japan (22.9%), New Zealand (22.4%), Canada (17.8%), Korea (17.8%) and Australia (17.2%), as well as the partner countries/economies, Liechtenstein (20.7%), Hong Kong-China (17.9%), Chinese Taipei (15.7%), Estonia (13.9%) and Slovenia (12.4%). Of these, Japan and Korea stand out as having around twice the proportion of students rated at Levels 5 and 6 in *using scientific evidence* than they have on either of the other two competency scales.

Box 2.6 **Computer-based assessment of science**

In PISA 2006, countries were given the option of participating in a computer-based assessment of science. This was initially implemented in a field trial by Australia, Austria, Denmark, Iceland, Ireland, Japan, Korea, Norway, Portugal, Scotland and the Slovak Republic, as well as in the partner economy Chinese Taipei, and followed up in greater depth in Denmark, Iceland and Korea. Their mean scores in the computer-based assessment of science were 463, 472 and 504 points, respectively. This compares to the same students' mean scores in the standard PISA science test of 481, 471 and 502 points, respectively (note, however, that these scores are not directly comparable to the normal PISA mean scores as they were analysed separately).

One of the goals of the computer-based assessment of science was to reduce the reading load of the questions, but at the same time retain the science content. It was found that the correlation between the computer-based assessment of science and PISA reading, at 0.73, was lower than the correlation between PISA science and PISA reading (0.83), so by this measure the goal of reducing the reading load was successful.

In each of the three countries there was a significant gender difference in favour of males in the computer-based assessment of science: 45 score points in Denmark, 25 in Iceland and 26 in Korea.

PISA will continue with the development of computer-delivered testing in PISA 2009 with the implementation of an electronic reading assessment.

Figure 2.30 [Part 1/2]

Summary descriptions of the six proficiency levels in *using scientific evidence*

General proficiencies students should have at each level	Tasks a student should be able to do	Examples from released questions
LEVEL 6 2.4% of all students across the OECD area can perform tasks at Level 6 on the *using scientific evidence* scale.		
Students at this level demonstrate an ability to compare and differentiate among competing explanations by examining supporting evidence. They can formulate arguments by synthesising evidence from multiple sources.	• Recognise that alternative hypotheses can be formed from the same set of evidence. • Test competing hypotheses against available evidence. • Construct a logical argument for an hypothesis by using data from a number of sources.	
LEVEL 5 11.8% of all students across the OECD area can perform tasks at Level 5 on the *using scientific evidence* scale.		
Students at this level are able to interpret data from related datasets presented in various formats. They can identify and explain differences and similarities in the datasets and draw conclusions based on the combined evidence presented in those datasets.	• Compare and discuss the characteristics of different datasets graphed on the one set of axes. • Recognise and discuss relationships between datasets (graphical and otherwise) in which the measured variable differs. • Based on an analysis of the sufficiency of the data, make judgements about the validity of conclusions.	**GREENHOUSE** Question 4 Figure 2.33
LEVEL 4 31.6% of all students across the OECD area can perform tasks at Level 4 on the *using scientific evidence* scale.		
Students at this level can interpret a dataset expressed in a number of formats, such as tabular, graphic and diagrammatic, by summarising the data and explaining relevant patterns. They can use the data to draw relevant conclusions. Students can also determine whether the data support assertions about a phenomenon.	• Locate relevant parts of graphs and compare these in response to specific questions. • Understand how to use a control in analysing the results of an investigation and developing a conclusion. • Interpret a table that contains two measured variables and suggest credible relationships between those variables. • Identify the characteristics of a straightforward technical device by reference to diagrammatic representations and general scientific concepts and thus form conclusions about its method of operation.	**SUNSCREENS** Question 5 Figure 2.23 **GREENHOUSE** Question 4 (Partial) Figure 2.33

• • •

101

Figure 2.30 [Part 2/2]

Summary descriptions of the six proficiency levels in *using scientific evidence*

General proficiencies students should have at each level	Tasks a student should be able to do	Examples from released questions
LEVEL 3 56.3% of all students across the OECD area can perform tasks at Level 3 on the *using scientific evidence* scale.		
Students at this level are able to select a piece of relevant information from data in answering a question or in providing support for or against a given conclusion. They can draw a conclusion from an uncomplicated or simple pattern in a dataset. Students can also determine, in simple cases, if enough information is present to support a given conclusion.	• Given a specific question, locate relevant scientific information in a body of text. • Given specific evidence/data, choose between appropriate and inappropriate conclusions. • Apply a simple set of criteria in a given context in order to draw a conclusion or make a prediction about an outcome. • Given a set of functions, determine if they are applicable to a specific machine.	**GREENHOUSE** Question 3 Figure 2.33
LEVEL 2 78.1% of all students across the OECD area can perform tasks at Level 2 on the *using scientific evidence* scale.		
Students at this level are able to recognise the general features of a graph if they are given appropriate cues and can point to an obvious feature in a graph or simple table in support of a given statement. They are able to recognise if a set of given characteristics apply to the function of everyday artifacts in making choices about their use.	• Compare two columns in a simple table of measurements and indicate differences. • State a trend in a set of measurements or simple line or bar graph. • Given a common artifact can determine some characteristics or properties pertaining to the artifact from among a list of properties.	**ACID RAIN** Question 3 Figure 2.32
LEVEL 1 92.1% of all students across the OECD area can perform tasks at Level 1 on the *using scientific evidence* scale.		
In response to a question, students at this level can extract information from a fact sheet or diagram pertinent to a common context. They can extract information from bar graphs where the requirement is simple comparisons of bar heights. In common, experienced contexts students at this level can attribute an effect to a cause.	• In response to a specific question pertaining to a bar graph, make comparisons of the height of bars and give meaning to the difference observed. • Given variation in a natural phenomenon can, in some cases, indicate an appropriate cause (*e.g.* fluctuations in the output of wind turbines may be attributed to changes in wind strength).	

StatLink ⌗⌐ http://dx.doi.org/10.1787/141844475532

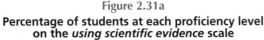

Figure 2.31a
**Percentage of students at each proficiency level
on the *using scientific evidence* scale**

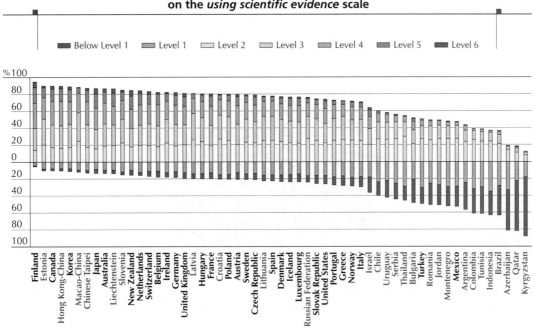

Countries are ranked in descending order of percentage of 15-year-olds at Levels 2, 3, 4, 5 and 6.
Source: OECD PISA 2006 database, Table 2.4a.
StatLink http://dx.doi.org/10.1787/141844475532

As in the other scales, Level 2 of the *using scientific evidence* scale is the level at which students begin to show the skills necessary for future development in *using scientific evidence*. In this scale, 21.9% of students across the OECD countries are classified as Level 1 or below. Countries with large percentages of students at these levels are Mexico (52.8%), Turkey (49.4%) and Italy (29.6%), as well as the partner countries Kyrgyzstan (87.9%), Qatar (81.7%), Azerbaijan (81.2%) and Brazil (63.3%). Some of the countries with lower percentages of students at these levels are Finland (5.4%), Canada (10.2%), Korea (11.1%), Japan (13.3%) and Australia (13.4%), and the partner countries/economies Estonia (10.1%), Hong Kong-China (10.3%), Macao-China (11.8%), Chinese Taipei (13.0%), Liechtenstein (13.6%) and Slovenia (15.1%).

Figure 2.31b (available on line at http://dx.doi.org/10.1787/141844475532) shows the distribution of student performance on the *using scientific evidence* scale. Figure 2.31c (which is also available on line at http://dx.doi.org/10.1787/141844475532) presents the multiple comparison table for the *using scientific evidence* scale. One of the differences observed in this table is the much higher relative standing of Japan and Korea compared to their standing in the other scales. This is largely due to these countries having more students at high levels of proficiency on this scale, as referred to above.

Several of these selected science units contain examples of embedded questions that query students' attitudes. *GENETICALLY MODIFIED CROPS, ACID RAIN,* and *GRAND CANYON* (Figures 2.22, 2.32, and 2.27) all have embedded attitudinal questions (see Chapter 3 for a full discussion of the results of attitudinal questions). Question 10N in *ACID RAIN* probes the level of students' interest in the topic of acid rain and question 10S asks students how much they agree with statements supporting further research.

Figure 2.32
ACID RAIN

Below is a photo of statues called Caryatids that were built on the Acropolis in Athens more than 2500 years ago. The statues are made of a type of rock called marble. Marble is composed of calcium carbonate.

In 1980, the original statues were transferred inside the museum of the Acropolis and were replaced by replicas. The original statues were being eaten away by acid rain.

ACID RAIN – QUESTION 2 (S485Q02)

Question type: Open-constructed response
Competency: Explaining phenomena scientifically
Knowledge category: "Physical systems" (knowledge of science)
Application area: "Hazards"
Setting: Social
Difficulty: 506
Percentage of correct answers (OECD countries): 57.7%

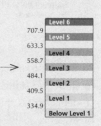

707.9	Level 6
633.3	Level 5
558.7	Level 4
484.1	Level 3
409.5	Level 2
334.9	Level 1
	Below Level 1

Normal rain is slightly acidic because it has absorbed some carbon dioxide from the air. Acid rain is more acidic than normal rain because it has absorbed gases like sulphur oxides and nitrogen oxides as well.

Where do these sulphur oxides and nitrogen oxides in the air come from?

....

....

Scoring

Full Credit:

Any one of car exhausts, factory emissions, burning fossil fuels such as oil and coal, gases from volcanoes or other similar things.

- Burning coal and gas.
- Oxides in the air come from pollution from factories and industries.
- Volcanoes.
- Fumes from power plants. *["Power plants" is taken to include power plants that burn fossil fuels.]*
- They come from the burning of materials that contain sulphur and nitrogen.

Partial Credit:

Responses that include an incorrect as well as a correct source of the pollution. For example:

- Fossil fuel and nuclear power plants. *[Nuclear power plants are not a source of acid rain.]*
- The oxides come from the ozone, atmosphere and meteors coming toward Earth. Also the burning of fossil fuels.

Responses that refer to "pollution" but do not give a source of pollution that is a significant cause of acid rain. For example:

- Pollution.
- The environment in general, the atmosphere we live in – *e.g.* pollution.
- Gasification, pollution, fires, cigarettes. *[It is not clear what is meant by "gasification"; "fires" is not specific enough; cigarette smoke is not a significant cause of acid rain.]*
- Pollution such as from nuclear power plants.

Scoring Comment: *Just mentioning "pollution" is sufficient for Code 1.*

Comment

An example of a question in the middle of the scale is found in ACID RAIN – Question 2 (Figure 2.22). This question requires students to explain the origin of sulphur and nitrogen oxides in the air. Correct responses require students to demonstrate an understanding of the chemicals as originating as car exhaust, factory emission, and burning fossil fuels. Students have to know that sulphur and nitrogen oxides are products of the oxidation of most fossil fuels or arise from volcanic activity.

Students gaining credit display a capacity to recall relevant facts and thus explain that the source of the gases contributing to acid rain was atmospheric pollutants. This locates the question at Level 3. The awareness that oxidation results in the production of these gases places the question in the "Physical systems" content area. Since acid rain is a relatively localised hazard, its setting is social.

Attributing the gases to unspecified pollution is also an acceptable response. Analysis of student responses show little difference in the ability levels of students giving this response compared to those giving the more detailed response. For partial credit and a response considered to be at Level 3, they have simply to state it is a comparison, although if a student states that the acid (vinegar) is necessary for the reaction the response will be considered Level 6. Both responses are linked to the competency identifying scientific issues. ACID RAIN (Figure 2.32) is also related to the competency explaining phenomena scientifically.

The effect of acid rain on marble can be modelled by placing chips of marble in vinegar overnight. Vinegar and acid rain have about the same acidity level. When a marble chip is placed in vinegar, bubbles of gas form. The mass of the dry marble chip can be found before and after the experiment.

ACID RAIN – *QUESTION 3 (S485Q03)*

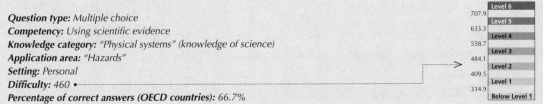

Question type: *Multiple choice*
Competency: *Using scientific evidence*
Knowledge category: *"Physical systems" (knowledge of science)*
Application area: *"Hazards"*
Setting: *Personal*
Difficulty: *460*
Percentage of correct answers (OECD countries): *66.7%*

Level	
707.9	Level 6
633.3	Level 5
558.7	Level 4
484.1	Level 3
409.5	Level 2
334.9	Level 1
	Below Level 1

A marble chip has a mass of 2.0 grams before being immersed in vinegar overnight. The chip is removed and dried the next day. What will the mass of the dried marble chip be?

A. Less than 2.0 grams

B. Exactly 2.0 grams

C. Between 2.0 and 2.4 grams

D. More than 2.4 grams

Scoring

Full Credit: A. Less than 2.0 grams

Comment

For the competency using scientific evidence, question 3 in the unit on ACID RAIN (Figure 2.32) provides a good example for Level 2. The question asks students to use information provided to draw a conclusion about the effects of vinegar on marble, a simple model for the influence of acid rain on marble. Several pieces of information from which a student can draw a conclusion accompany this question. In addition to the descriptive evidence provided, the student also must draw on knowledge that a chemical reaction is the source of the bubbles of gas and that the reaction is drawing, in part, on the chemicals in the marble chip. Consequently, the marble chip will lose mass. Since an awareness of a chemical process is a prerequisite for drawing the correct conclusion this question belongs in the "Physical systems" content area. The application is dealing with the hazard of acid rain, but the experiment relates to the individual and thus the setting is personal.

A student able to correctly respond to this Level 2 question can recognise relevant and obvious cues that outline the logical path to a simple conclusion.

ACID RAIN – QUESTION 5 (S485Q05)

Question type: *Open-constructed response*
Competency: *Identifying scientific issues*
Knowledge category: *"Scientific enquiry" (knowledge about science)*
Application area: *"Hazards"*
Setting: *Personal*
Difficulty: *Full credit 717; Partial credit 513*
Percentage of correct answers (OECD countries): *35.6 %*

707.9	Level 6
633.3	Level 5
558.7	Level 4
484.1	Level 3
409.5	Level 2
334.9	Level 1
	Below Level 1

Students who did this experiment also placed marble chips in pure (distilled) water overnight.

Explain why the students included this step in their experiment.

....

....

Scoring

Full Credit: To show that the acid (vinegar) is necessary for the reaction. For example:

- To make sure that rainwater must be acidic like acid rain to cause this reaction.

- To see whether there are other reasons for the holes in the marble chips.

- Because it shows that the marble chips don't just react with any fluid since water is neutral.

Partial Credit: To compare with the test of vinegar and marble, but it is not made clear that this is being done to show that the acid (vinegar) is necessary for the reaction. For example:

- To compare with the other test tube.

- To see whether the marble chip changes in pure water.

- The students included this step to show what happens when it rains normally on the marble.
- Because distilled water is not acid.
- To act as a control.
- To see the difference between normal water and acidic water (vinegar).

Comment

Students gaining full credit for this question understand that it is necessary to show that the reaction will not occur in water. Vinegar is a necessary reactant. Placing marble chips in distilled water demonstrates an understanding of a control in scientific experiments.

Students who gain partial credit show an awareness that the experiment involves a comparison but do not communicate this in a way that demonstrates they know that the purpose is to show that vinegar is a necessary reactant.

The question requires students to exhibit knowledge about the structure of an experiment and therefore it belongs in the "Scientific enquiry" category. The application is dealing with the hazard of acid rain but the experiment relates to the individual and thus the setting is personal.

A student obtaining credit for the Level 6 component of this question is able to both understand the experimental modelling used and to articulate the method used to control a major variable. A student correctly responding at Level 3 (partial credit) is only able to recognise the comparison that is being made without appreciating the purpose of the comparison.

ACID RAIN – QUESTION 10N (S485Q10N)

How much interest do you have in the following information?

Tick only one box in each row.

	High Interest	Medium Interest	Low Interest	No Interest
d) Knowing which human activities contribute most to acid rain.	□₁	□₂	□₃	□₄
e) Learning about technologies that minimise the emission of gases that cause acid rain.	□₁	□₂	□₃	□₄
f) Understanding the methods used to repair buildings damaged by acid rain.	□₁	□₂	□₃	□₄

ACID RAIN – QUESTION 10S (S485Q10S)

How much do you agree with the following statements?

Tick only one box in each row.

	Strongly agree	Agree	Disagree	Strongly disagree
g) Preservation of ancient ruins should be based on scientific evidence concerning the causes of damage.	□₁	□₂	□₃	□₄
h) Statements about the causes of acid rain should be based on scientific research.	□₁	□₂	□₃	□₄

Figure 2.33
GREENHOUSE

Read the texts and answer the questions that follow.

THE GREENHOUSE EFFECT: FACT OR FICTION?

Living things need energy to survive. The energy that sustains life on the Earth comes from the Sun, which radiates energy into space because it is so hot. A tiny proportion of this energy reaches the Earth.

The Earth's atmosphere acts like a protective blanket over the surface of our planet, preventing the variations in temperature that would exist in an airless world.

Most of the radiated energy coming from the Sun passes through the Earth's atmosphere. The Earth absorbs some of this energy, and some is reflected back from the Earth's surface. Part of this reflected energy is absorbed by the atmosphere.

As a result of this the average temperature above the Earth's surface is higher than it would be if there were no atmosphere. The Earth's atmosphere has the same effect as a greenhouse, hence the term greenhouse effect.

The greenhouse effect is said to have become more pronounced during the twentieth century.

It is a fact that the average temperature of the Earth's atmosphere has increased. In newspapers and periodicals the increased carbon dioxide emission is often stated as the main source of the temperature rise in the twentieth century.

A student named André becomes interested in the possible relationship between the average temperature of the Earth's atmosphere and the carbon dioxide emission on the Earth.

In a library he comes across the following two graphs.

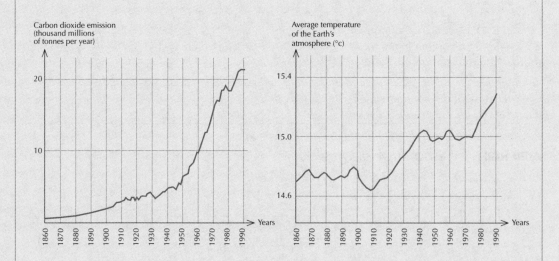

André concludes from these two graphs that it is certain that the increase in the average temperature of the Earth's atmosphere is due to the increase in the carbon dioxide emission.

GREENHOUSE – *QUESTION 3 (S114Q)*

Question type: *Open-constructed response*
Competency: *Using scientific evidence*
Knowledge category: *"Scientific explanations" (knowledge about science)*
Application area: *"Environment"*
Setting: *Global*
Difficulty: *529* •
Percentage of correct answers (OECD countries): *54.0%*

707.9	Level 6
633.3	Level 5
558.7	Level 4
484.1	Level 3
409.5	Level 2
334.9	Level 1
	Below Level 1

What is it about the graphs that supports André's conclusion?

....

....

Scoring

Full Credit:

Refers to the increase of both (average) temperature and carbon dioxide emission. For example:

- As the emissions increased the temperature increased.
- Both graphs are increasing.
- Because in 1910 both the graphs began to increase.
- Temperature is rising as CO_2 is emitted.
- The information lines on the graphs rise together.
- Everything is increasing.
- The more CO_2 emission, the higher the temperature.

Refers (in general terms) to a positive relationship between temperature and carbon dioxide emission. *[Note: This code is intended to capture students' use of terminology such as "positive relationship", "similar shape" or "directly proportional"; although the following sample response is not strictly correct, it shows sufficient understanding to be given credit here.]* For example:

- The amount of CO2 and average temperature of the Earth is directly proportional.
- They have a similar shape indicating a relationship.

Comment

For the competency using scientific evidence, the units GREENHOUSE and SUNSCREENS (Figures 2.33 and 2.23) present good examples for Level 3. In GREENHOUSE, question 3, students must interpret evidence, presented in graphical form, and deduce that the combined graphs support a conclusion that both average temperature and carbon dioxide emission are increasing. The student is required to judge the validity of a conclusion correlating the Earth's atmospheric temperature and the quantity of carbon dioxide emissions by comparing evidence from two graphs having a common time scale. The student must first gain an appreciation for the context by reading a number of descriptive lines of text. Credit is given for recognising that both graphs are rising with time or that there is a positive relationship between the two graphs, thus supporting the stated conclusion. The effects of this environmental issue are global which defines the setting. The skill required by students is to interpret the graphical data supplied so the question belongs in the "Scientific explanations" category.

A student gaining credit for this Level 3 question is able to recognise the simple pattern in two graphical datasets and use this pattern in support of a conclusion.

GREENHOUSE – *QUESTION 4 (S114Q04)*

Question type: Open-constructed response
Competency: Using scientific evidence
Knowledge category: "Scientific explanations" (knowledge about science)
Application area: "Environment"
Setting: Global
Difficulty: Full credit 659; Partial credit 568 •
Percentage of correct answers (OECD countries): 34.5%

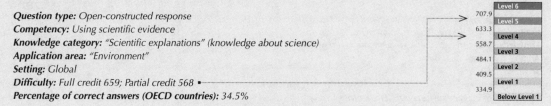

Another student, Jeanne, disagrees with André's conclusion. She compares the two graphs and says that some parts of the graphs do not support his conclusion.

Give an example of a part of the graphs that does not support André's conclusion. Explain your answer.

....
....
....

Scoring

Full Credit:

Refers to one particular part of the graphs in which the curves are not both descending or both climbing and gives the corresponding explanation. For example:

- In 1900–1910 (about) CO_2 was increasing, whilst the temperature was going down.
- In 1980–1983 carbon dioxide went down and the temperature rose.
- The temperature in the 1800s is much the same but the first graph keeps climbing.
- Between 1950 and 1980 the temperature didn't increase but the CO_2 did.
- From 1940 until 1975 the temperature stays about the same but the carbon dioxide emission shows a sharp rise.
- In 1940 the temperature is a lot higher than in 1920 and they have similar carbon dioxide emissions.

Partial Credit:

Mentions a correct period, without any explanation. For example:
- 1930–1933.
- before 1910.

Mentions only one particular year (not a period of time), with an acceptable explanation. For example:
- In 1980 the emissions were down but the temperature still rose.

Gives an example that doesn't support André's conclusion but makes a mistake in mentioning the period. *[Note: There should be evidence of this mistake – e.g. an area clearly illustrating a correct answer is marked on the graph and then a mistake made in transferring this information to the text.]* For example:
- Between 1950 and 1960 the temperature decreased and the carbon dioxide emission increased.

Refers to differences between the two curves, without mentioning a specific period. For example:
- At some places the temperature rises even if the emission decreases.
- Earlier there was little emission but nevertheless high temperature.
- When there is a steady increase in graph 1, there isn't an increase in graph 2, it stays constant. *[Note: It stays constant "overall".]*
- Because at the start the temperature is still high where the carbon dioxide was very low.

Refers to an irregularity in one of the graphs. For example:
- It is about 1910 when the temperature had dropped and went on for a certain period of time.
- In the second graph there is a decrease in temperature of the Earth's atmosphere just before 1910.

Indicates difference in the graphs, but explanation is poor. For example:
- In the 1940s the heat was very high but the carbon dioxide very low. *[Note: The explanation is very poor, but the difference that is indicated is clear.]*

Comment

Another example from GREENHOUSE centres on the competency using scientific evidence and asks students to identify a portion of a graph that does not provide evidence supporting a conclusion. This question requires the student to look for specific differences that vary from positively correlated general trends in these two graphical datasets. Students must locate a portion where curves are not both ascending or descending and provide this finding as part of a justification for a conclusion. As a consequence it involves a greater amount of insight and analytical skill than is required for Q03. Rather than a generalisation about the relation between the graphs, the student is asked to accompany the nominated period of difference with an explanation of that difference in order to gain full credit.

The ability to effectively compare the detail of two datasets and give a critique of a given conclusion locates the full credit question at Level 5 of the scientific literacy scale. If the student understands what the question requires of them and correctly identifies a difference in the two graphs, but is unable to explain this difference, the student gains partial credit for the question and is identified at Level 4 of the scientific literacy scale.

This environmental issue is global which defines the setting. The skill required by students is to interpret data graphically presented so the question belongs in the "Scientific explanations" category.

GREENHOUSE – QUESTION 5 (S114Q)

Question type: Open-constructed response
Competency: Explaining phenomena scientifically
Knowledge category: "Earth and space systems" (knowledge of science)
Application area: "Environment"
Setting: Global
Difficulty: 709 •
Percentage of correct answers (OECD countries): 18.9%

	Level 6
707.9	Level 5
633.3	Level 4
558.7	Level 3
484.1	Level 2
409.5	Level 1
334.9	Below Level 1

André persists in his conclusion that the average temperature rise of the Earth's atmosphere is caused by the increase in the carbon dioxide emission. But Jeanne thinks that his conclusion is premature. She says: "Before accepting this conclusion you must be sure that other factors that could influence the greenhouse effect are constant".
Name one of the factors that Jeanne means.

....

....

Scoring

Full Credit:
Gives a factor referring to the energy/radiation coming from the Sun. For example:
- The sun heating and maybe the earth changing position.
- Energy reflected back from Earth. *[Assuming that by "Earth" the student means "the ground".]*

Gives a factor referring to a natural component or a potential pollutant. For example:

- Water vapour in the air.
- Clouds.
- The things such as volcanic eruptions.
- Atmospheric pollution (gas, fuel).
- The amount of exhaust gas.
- CFC's.
- The number of cars.
- Ozone (as a component of air). *[Note: for references to depletion, use Code 03.]*

Comment

Question 5 of GREENHOUSE (Figure 2.33) is an example of Level 6 and of the competency explaining phenomena scientifically. In this question, students must analyse a conclusion to account for other factors that could influence the greenhouse effect. This question combines aspects of the two competencies identifying scientific issues and explaining phenomena scientifically. The student needs to understand the necessity of controlling factors outside the change and measured variables and to recognise those variables. The student must possess sufficient knowledge of "Earth systems" to be able to identify at least one of the factors that should be controlled. The latter criterion is considered the critical scientific skill involved so this question is categorised as explaining phenomena scientifically. The effects of this environmental issue are global which defines the setting.

As a first step in gaining credit for this question the student must be able to identify the change and measured variables and have sufficient understanding of methods of investigation to recognise the influence of other factors. However, the student also needs to recognise the scenario in context and identify its major components. This involves a number of abstract concepts and their relationships in determining what "other" factors might affect the relationship between the Earth's temperature and the amount of carbon dioxide emissions into the atmosphere. This locates the question near the boundary between Level 5 and 6 in the explaining phenomena scientifically category.

IMPLICATIONS FOR POLICY

Meeting demands for scientific excellence

Meeting a growing demand for science-related qualifications has been a major challenge: A comparison of the ratio between younger and older age cohorts shows that the proportion of individuals with university-level qualifications in the population has, on average across OECD countries, roughly doubled over 30 years while the proportion of science-related graduates has tripled over the same period (OECD, 2007). In particular for countries near the technology frontier, the share of highly educated scientists in the labour force has become an important determinant of economic growth and social development.

While 15-year-olds in OECD countries generally reported a positive disposition towards science – on average across OECD countries 37% reported that they would like to work in a career involving science and 21% reported that they would aspire to a career in advanced science – policymakers need to pay due attention to ensuring that their countries are well prepared to be in the best position to achieve scientific excellence in the future. PISA 2006 shows that, on average across OECD countries, only 9.0% of 15-year-old students perform at the highest two PISA proficiency levels, where students consistently identify, explain and apply scientific knowledge and knowledge about science in a variety of complex life situations, link different information sources and explanations and use evidence from those sources to justify decisions, consistently demonstrate advanced scientific thinking and reasoning, and demonstrate use of their scientific understanding in support of solutions to unfamiliar scientific and technological situations. Moreover, this percentage varies widely across countries. Last but not least, while strong performance in science is associated with students' future-oriented science motivation the results of Chapter 3 suggest that strong science performance alone provides no guarantee for the successful engagement of individuals with science.

Securing strong baseline science competencies

For most of the 20th century, school science curricula, especially in the later stages of secondary education, tended to focus on providing the foundations for the professional training of a small number of scientists and engineers. They mostly presented science in a form that focussed on the knowledge of the science disciplines, while paying less attention to knowledge about science and applications relating to citizens' life and living. However, the influence of scientific and technological advances on today's economies, the central place of information technology in employment, and the increasing presence of science and technology related issues require that all citizens, not just future scientists and engineers, have strong science competencies. The proportion of students at very low proficiency is therefore also an important indicator in terms of citizens' ability to participate fully in society and in the labour market. As described earlier, the science proficiency Level 2 has been established as the baseline level, defining the level of achievement on the PISA science scale at which students begin to demonstrate the science competencies that will enable them to participate actively in life situations related to science and technology. On average across OECD countries, 19.2% of 15-year-old students do not reach this level of proficiency, and in some countries this proportion is more than twice as large. For example, they often confuse key features of an investigation, apply incorrect scientific information, and mix personal beliefs with scientific facts in support of a decision. The level of basic science comptetencies that is held by many students in OECD and participating countries should thus be a serious concern for policymakers in those countries.

More generally, the chapter shows that not just average performance, but also performance patterns, vary widely across countries, requiring different responses from policy makers. For example, Korea is among the best-performing countries in science in PISA 2006, in terms of students' performance, with an average of 522 score points, while the United States performs below the OECD average with a score of 489.

Nevertheless, the United States has a similar percentage of students at Levels 5 and 6 (9.1%) as Korea (10.3%). The discrepancy in mean scores between the two countries is partly accounted for by the fact that at the lower levels of proficiency (that is, below Level 2) the United States has 24.4% of students, while Korea has only 11.2%.

Strengths and weaknesses in different aspects of science

In some countries student performance varies between different areas of science competence and scientific content in important ways. Such variation may be related to differences in curricular emphases, but it can also be an indicator of the effectiveness with which curricula are delivered. While countries make curricular choices in their national context and priorities, examining these choices in the light of the performance of other countries can provide a broader frame of reference for educational policy development. Some countries have a particular need to provide a better grounding of scientific knowledge that allows students to become more proficient at explaining phenomena scientifically. Others may need to think about how students acquire wider science competencies such as interpreting evidence. Similarly, in countries such as France, students show stronger *knowledge about science* than *knowledge of science,* while in the Czech Republic in particular, the reverse is true. This appears to correspond with a different emphasis of the curricula in the two countries, with one focusing on learning scientific reasoning and analysis and the other on mastering scientific information and learning about scientific phenomena. In practice, both of these aspects of scientific knowledge are important. In addition, PISA identifies important differences in the content areas in which students have the strongest *knowledge of science.* The fact that a country like Korea, whose students are among the highest performers among OECD countries in two of the three knowledge areas, performs only at the average level on questions about living systems, is a case in point. A further observation is that there seems to be a pattern in many countries of lower scores in the content area "Earth and space systems" compared to the content areas "Physical systems" and "Living systems". Given that many contemporary situations that citizens encounter have a base in "Earth systems", it seems reasonable to examine curricula to see that students have adequate opportunities to learn concepts and process related to the structure of "Earth systems", energy in "Earth systems", and changes in "Earth systems".

An important objective for future research will be to relate the observed performance patterns to instructional strategies that can be used to help students improve science competencies. Some abilities can be developed in laboratories and demonstrations; for example, using scientific evidence to form an explanation. Other abilities, such as identifying scientific issues may require analysing historical scientific experiments or descriptions of contemporary issues.

Gender differences

Of the three main PISA domains, science is the one where overall gender differences are smallest. In the great majority of countries, there is no significant difference in the average score for males and females. This is good news, showing that science is a subject where gender equality is closer than in mathematics or reading.

However, overall similar average performance in science masks important variation in the relative strengths of males and females on both the three key science competencies and domains of scientific knowledge. For example, across countries females are stronger in *identifying scientific issues,* while males are stronger at *explaining phenomena scientifically.* Conversely, in the scientific content areas, males generally outperform females in "Physical systems", a difference that ranges from 15 score points in Greece, Iceland and Korea to 45 score points in Austria (OECD average 26 score points). While such differences can be attributed to many factors including parental support for science or culture, they may also reveal an emphasis on different educational experiences with science that policymakers can remedy. For example, providing males with increased experience with *identifying scientific issues* (as well as *explaining phenomena scientifically* and *using scientific evidence*) may strengthen these proficiencies. For females, increasing education experiences such as laboratory and investigations in the content area "Physical systems" (*i.e.* physics and chemistry) likewise may compensate for their lower attainment in this content area.

Furthermore, in many countries at least, students make different choices in terms of the schools, tracks and educational programmes they attend. In most countries females attend the higher performing, academically oriented tracks and schools at a higher rate than males. As a result of this, in many countries gender differences in science are substantial within schools or programmes, even if they appear small overall. From a policy perspective – and for teachers in classrooms – gender differences in science performance therefore warrant continued attention. This is the case even if the advantage of males over females within schools and programmes is overshadowed to some extent by the tendency of females to attend higher performing school programmes and tracks.

Last but not least, as shown in Chapter 3, important differences remain also in the ways in which males and females feel about their own academic competencies in science. This too may help to explain why subsequent study of science in higher education remains unbalanced in terms of the disciplines chosen by males and females which, in turn, feed through into future careers.

It needs to be borne in mind that gender differences cannot automatically be attributed to features of the education system. The comparatively large performance advantage of females in all subject areas in Iceland, most notably in rural areas has been attributed to labour-market incentives that distract males in rural areas from focusing on academic studies by giving them better opportunities to get a well paid job early in life in, for example, the fishing or tourism industries, while academic achievement is frequently seen by females as a lever to social and regional mobility.

Do the results matter?

In analysing national results, it must always be borne in mind that variation in student performance within countries is many times larger than the variation between countries. Yet even relatively small differences between countries in the average performance of students, where they are statistically significant, should not be overlooked.

Not all of the variation in the performance of countries in science can be explained by spending on education. Although the analyses reveal a positive association between the two, they also suggest that while spending on educational institutions is a necessary prerequisite for the provision of high-quality education, spending alone is not sufficient to achieve high levels of outcomes. Other factors, including the effectiveness with which resources are invested, play a crucial role.

Does science performance on the PISA assessment matter for the future? It is difficult to assess to what extent performance and success in school is predictive of future success. While there has not been a longitudinal PISA study in science, a follow-up of students in Canada who had participated in the PISA 2000 reading assessment shows that the PISA performance of students at age 15 was a very strong predictor for a successful transition to higher education at age 19 (see Box 6.1 in Chapter 6). What OECD data also show is that individuals who have not completed an upper secondary qualification (still roughly one in five on average across OECD countries, despite significant progress over the last generation) face significantly poorer labour-market prospects. For example, labour force participation rates rise steeply with educational attainment in most OECD countries (OECD, 2007). With very few exceptions, the participation rate for graduates of tertiary education is markedly higher than that for upper secondary graduates which, in turn, is markedly higher than that for individuals without an upper secondary qualification. The gap in male participation rates is particularly wide between upper secondary graduates and those without an upper secondary qualification and the labour force participation rate for women with less than upper secondary attainment is particularly low. Similarly, education and earnings are positively linked, with upper secondary education representing a threshold in many countries beyond which additional education attracts a particularly high premium (OECD, 2007). Last but not least, international comparisons show a pivotal role that education plays in fostering labour productivity, and by implication economic growth – not just as an input linking aggregate output to the stock of productive inputs, but also as a factor strongly associated with the rate of technological progress. The estimated long-run effect on economic output of one additional year of education in the combined OECD area is in the order of between 3 and 6% (OECD, 2006b).

Obviously, learning does not end with compulsory education and modern societies provide various opportunities for individuals to upgrade their knowledge and skills throughout their lives. However, at least when it comes to job-related continuing education and training, on average across OECD countries, about three times as many training hours are invested in employees with a tertiary qualification, as in employees without an upper secondary qualification (OECD, 2007). Thus, initial education combines with other influences to make job-related training beyond school least likely for those who need it most.

This underlines why a solid foundation of knowledge and skills at school is fundamental for the future success of individuals and societies. The results from PISA show that strong educational performance in key subject areas still remains a remote goal for many countries. At the same time, the results also show that some countries succeed in combining strong overall performance with a modest gap between their stronger and weaker performers. Results in these countries pose challenges for other countries, by showing what it is possible to achieve.

Notes

1. When comparing student performance on the PISA tasks that were common between the PISA 2006 and PISA 2003 assessments, but that are not representative of the PISA 2006 assessment, a preliminary analysis suggests that significant performance differences can be observed only for Mexico, Greece and France and for the partner countries Uruguay, Brazil and Tunisia. See Table A7.2 in Annex A7.

2. The model employed to analyse the PISA data was implemented through iterative procedures that simultaneously estimate the probability that a particular person will respond correctly to a given set of test questions, and the probability that a particular question will be answered correctly by a given set of students. Further technical details on the methods used to estimate student ability and question difficulty, and to form the scale, are provided in the *PISA 2006 Technical Report* (OECD, forthcoming).

3. This does not mean that students will always be able to perform questions at or below the difficulty level associated with their own position on the scale, and never be able to do harder questions. Rather, the ratings are based on probability: A student with a given score on the scale is likely to get a question with the same score correct.

4. It should be noted that these are two different ways of categorising the same items: all *knowledge about science* items are *identifying scientific issues* items and all *explaining phenomena scientifically* items are *knowledge of science* items.

5. Technically, the mean score for student performance in science across OECD countries was set at 500 score points and the standard deviation at 100 score points, with the data weighted so that each OECD country contributed equally. Note that this anchoring of the scale was implemented for the combined science scale. The average mean score and standard deviation of the individual science scales can therefore differ from 500 and 100 score points. In the tables in Volume 2, the OECD average standard deviation is less than 100, because it is the arithmetic average of the countries' individual standard deviations – within country deviations are on average smaller than that for the whole pooled OECD sample because they do not include the performance variation across countries for which the standard deviation is 100.

6. Austria, Belgium, Bulgaria, the Czech Republic, Denmark, Estonia, Finland, France, Germany, Greece, Hungary, Ireland, Italy, Latvia, Lithuania, Luxembourg, the Netherlands, Poland, Portugal, Romania, the Slovak Republic, Slovenia, Spain, Sweden and the United Kingdom.

7. For this to be true, students at the bottom of a level have a 0.62 chance of correctly answering the questions at the bottom of that level and a 0.42 chance of answering questions at the top of the level. Students at the top of a level have a 0.62 chance of correctly answering the most difficult questions at that level, and a 0.78 chance of answering the easiest questions.

8. The PISA Science Expert Group chose the four content areas of *knowledge of science* based on current practice and research. A fourth content area, "Technology systems", is not analysed separately because it contains too few questions.

9. At the macro-economic level, skills can lead to positive external effects through research and development activity. Research and development creates new knowledge that is often difficult to appropriate by the producer of the knowledge. This is because new knowledge is at least partially non-excludable and non-rival. Once the new knowledge is produced, other individuals in society can obtain at least a part of it at no cost. The social return to the new knowledge is thus larger than the private return of the producer of the knowledge.

10. Hanushek and Woessmann (2007) have included the shares of individuals that performed one standard deviation above (600 score points) and below (400 score points) on the International Adult Literacy Survey (IALS) scale jointly into a growth regression. The threshold of 400 IALS score points approximated basic literacy and numeracy while the threshold of 600 sought to capture top performance. They found that the effect of the high performance level was about six times larger than the effect of the lower level (and this relationship remained essentially unchanged when various control variables were added).

11. Because of an error in printing the test booklets, in the United States the mean performance in mathematics and science may be mis-estimated by approximately 1 score point. The impact is below one standard error. For details see Annex A3.

12. The proportion of science and engineering occupations in the United States that are filled by tertiary-educated workers born abroad increased from 14 to 22% between 1990 and 2000, and from 24 to 38% when considering solely doctorate-level science and engineering workers (US National Science Board, 2003). In the European Union, 700 000 additional researchers will be

required merely to reach the Lisbon Goals on research in 2010. In acknowledgement of these growing needs for highly-skilled workers, most European economies have started to review their immigration legislation to encourage the settlement of tertiary-educated individuals, and in some cases, to recruit large numbers of international students with a view to granting them residence status upon completion of their studies.

13. The situation is more complex when multiple comparisons are made, as the multiple comparison tables can be used for different types of comparisons. When just two countries are compared at a 95% confidence interval, one can be confident that if there is a significant difference indicated, then this would occur 95% of the time. Although the probability that a particular difference will falsely be declared to be statistically significant is low (5%) in each single comparison, the probability of making such an error increases when several comparisons are made simultaneously. So in a multiple comparison of 20 countries it is possible that a single significant difference may be falsely declared. As the number of countries in PISA increases this likelihood also increases. It is possible to make an adjustment for this which reduces to 5% the maximum probability that differences will be falsely declared as statistically significant at least once among all the comparisons that are made. Such an adjustment, based on the Bonferroni method, was incorporated into the multiple comparison charts in previous PISA reports, in addition to the confidence level for two-way comparisons. The adjusted significance test was used when the interest of readers was to compare a country's performance with that of all other countries. As the number of countries increases, so does the critical value associated with the Bonferroni-adjusted multiple comparisons. In PISA 2000, 31 simultaneous comparisons gave rise to adjusting an $\alpha = 0.05$ significance level to $\alpha = 0.00167$. In PISA 2006, the number of simultaneous comparisons would give rise to an adjusted significance level of $\alpha = 0.000091$. This means that different critical values are applied across cycles. This is especially important to countries when comparing results to other countries with similar results. It is possible that countries with small but significant differences in results in one cycle may be classified as having non-significant differences in the next cycle, despite having much the same results, simply because there are an increased number of participants. For this reason, it was decided not to employ the Bonferroni method for making comparisons in PISA 2006.

14. Column 1 in Table A1.2 estimates the score point difference that is associated with one school year. This difference can be estimated for the 28 OECD countries in which a sizeable number of 15-year-olds in the PISA samples were enrolled in at least two different grades. Since 15-year-olds cannot be assumed to be distributed at random across the grade levels, adjustments had to be made for contextual factors that may relate to the assignment of students to the different grade levels. These adjustments are documented in columns 2 to 7 of the table. While it is possible to estimate the typical performance difference among students in two adjacent grades net of the effects of selection and contextual factors, this difference cannot automatically be equated with the progress that students have made over the last school year but should be interpreted as a lower bound of the progress achieved. This is not only because different students were assessed, but also because the contents of the PISA assessment was not expressly designed to match what students had learned in the preceding school year but was designed more broadly to assess the cumulative outcome of learning in school up to age 15. For example, if the curriculum of the grades in which 15-year-olds are mainly enrolled covers material other than that assessed by PISA (which, in turn, may have been included in earlier school years) then the observed performance difference will underestimate student progress. Accurate measures of student progress can only be obtained through a longitudinal assessment design that focuses on content.

15. For the 29 OECD countries included in this comparison, the correlation between mean student performance in science and GDP per capita is 0.53. The explained variation is obtained as the square of the correlation.

16. Luxembourg was excluded from this comparison, as its spending patterns are an anomaly that relate, in part, to the exceptionally high proportion of foreign nationals and the multi-lingual instructional environment.

17. Cumulative expenditure for a given country is approximated as follows: let n(0), n(1) and n(2) be the typical number of years spent by a student from the age of six up to the age of 15 years in primary, lower secondary and upper secondary education. Let E(0), E(1) and E(2) be the annual expenditure per student in USD converted using purchasing power parities in primary, lower secondary and upper secondary education, respectively. The cumulative expenditure is then calculated by multiplying current annual expenditure E by the typical duration of study n for each level of education i using the following formula:

$$CE = \sum_{i=0}^{2} n(i) * E(i)$$

Estimates for $n(i)$ are based on the International Standard Classification of Education (ISCED) (OECD, 1997).

18. On average across OECD countries, the gender difference is 2 score points in favour of males in science, 38 score points in favour of females in reading (see Table 6.1c) and 11 score points in favour of males in mathematics (see Table 6.2c).

19. This report does not compare student performance in the science competencies with student performance in the different knowledge areas. The reason is that the PISA 2006 competency scales and knowledge domains are *not* two independent sets of scales because: *i)* each item is classified in both ways, so that each item contributes to both scales; *ii)* it follows from the definition of "explaining scientific phenomena" that all items primarily contributing to the assessment of this competency are automatically classified as *knowledge* of *science;* and *iii)* all items classified as *identifying scientific issues* are *knowledge about science* items because of a decision taken during test development to minimise the knowledge of science content in such items so that they were clearly assessing *identifying scientific issues,* not *explaining phenomena scientifically.* These interrelationships between competency and knowledge classification can be observed in Figure 2.10, which shows the two-way classification of the released items. Although *using scientific evidence* items were spread across both *knowledge of science* and *knowledge about science* (roughly in the ratio 1:2), profiles of performance in *identifying scientific issues* and *explaining phenomena scientifically* (including gender differences) will be reflected to a large extent in the corresponding *knowledge about science* and *knowledge of science* profiles.

20. Cluster analysis was used to determine whether countries were similar enough to fall into groups or clusters, with the difference between the mean score on the science competency scales from the overall mean score serving as the criterion variables. The Ward method was employed which uses an analysis of variance approach to evaluate the distances between clusters. This method attempts to minimise the sum of squares of any two hypothetical clusters that can be formed at each step. Cluster analysis was also calculated using the four other main agglomerative methods: the single linkage (nearest neighbour approach); the complete linkage (furthest neighbour); the average linkage; and the Centroid method. Results from the Ward method were most meaningful.

21. The process that takes place to generate the plausible values for each student leads to a standardised average score of 500 across the OECD countries. This average is based on all the items in all scales. When separating out the scales that make up the combined scale their individual mean scores may therefore differ from 500 score points.

22. In the Czech Republic, educators explain this as the result of theoretically oriented instructional material with technical illustrations that are more familiar to males than females.

23. The major focus in PISA 2006 has been on assessing of the competencies that students possess. In addition, a reduced scaling model was applied to generate country means for the different science content areas (except "technology systems" for which there are too few items).

24. The arithmetic average of the three scales was calculated to give this estimate of knowledge of science. The science items were designed to allow full estimates of the results based on competencies rather than content areas. The fourth content area, "technology systems", was not included in the average because there were too few items to generate an estimate. The average, therefore, of the knowledge of science domain can be regarded as an estimate. Significant differences between the two knowledge domains cannot be accurately estimated.

3

A profile of student engagement in science

Introduction 122

Measuring attitudes and engagement in PISA 122
- Notes on the interpretation of the measures 125

Do students support scientific enquiry? 127
- General value of science 127
- Support for scientific enquiry 130
- Personal value of science 133

Do students believe they can succeed in science? 133
- Students' confidence in overcoming difficulties in science 134
- Students' self-concept in science 137

Are students interested in science? 139
- Interest in learning science as a subject 139
- The importance of doing well in science 145
- Motivation to learn science because it is useful 145
- Science-related activities 153

Do students feel responsible towards resources and the environment? 155
- Awareness of environmental issues 155
- Students' level of concern for environmental issues 158
- Optimism regarding environmental issues 158
- Responsibility for sustainable development 161
- Gender differences in responsibility towards resources and the environment 163

Overview of gender differences in science performance and in attitudes towards science 163

Implications for policy 164

INTRODUCTION

Most children come to school ready and willing to learn. International surveys of primary school age children generally reveal high levels of interest and positive attitudes of children to subjects such as science.[1] How can schools foster and strengthen this predisposition and ensure that young adults leave school with the motivation and capacity to continue learning throughout life?

Issues of motivation and attitudes are particularly relevant in science. Science and technology have enabled remarkable achievements over the past 100 years – taking people to the moon and back; eradicating diseases such as small pox; inventing tools such as the computer, on which individuals rely for functions as diverse as calculating the financial return on an investment to controlling the altitude of a plane; and providing communication tools that allow people to remain in contact even when they are separated by thousands of kilometres. However, there remain many scientific challenges, such as technological development, global warming, the depletion of fossil fuel resources, the safe use of nuclear fuels, access to safe water resources, HIV/AIDS, or cancer. Addressing these challenges successfully will require countries to make major investments in scientific infrastructure and to attract qualified individuals into science-related professions, as well as to secure broad public support for scientific endeavour and the capacity of all citizens to use science in relation to their lives. Peoples' attitudes play a significant role in their interest in, attention to, and response to science and technology.

In addition to assessing what scientific and technological knowledge students have acquired and can apply for personal, social and global benefit, PISA 2006 has devoted significant attention to obtaining data on students' attitudes and engagement with science, both as part of the PISA 2006 science assessment and through separate questionnaires. In PISA, attitudes are seen as a key component of an individual's science competency and include an individual's beliefs, motivational orientations and sense of self-efficacy.[2]

MEASURING ATTITUDES AND ENGAGEMENT IN PISA

PISA 2006 gathered data on students' attitudes and engagement with science in four areas: *support for scientific enquiry, self-belief as science learners, interest in science* and *responsibility towards resources and environments* (Figure 3.1). These areas were selected because they provide a summary of students' general appreciation of science, personal beliefs as science learners, specific scientific attitudes and values, and responsibility towards selected science-related issues that have national and international ramifications. Collectively, these measures show levels of engagement of all students – including those who do not aspire to become scientists – even if interest in science is perhaps most relevant for the pursuit of scientific careers.

Support for scientific enquiry is often regarded as an important objective of science education. Appreciation of and support for scientific enquiry implies that students value scientific ways of gathering evidence, reasoning rationally, responding critically and communicating conclusions as they confront life situations related to science. Aspects of this area in PISA 2006 included the use of evidence in making decisions and appreciation for the use of logic and rationality in formulating conclusions. *Self-belief as science learners* is included because students' appraisals of their own abilities in science are an important part of science engagement. Moreover, previous research indicates that science-related self-appraisals tend to be gender-linked and may partially explain gender differences in motivation and achievement in science (Reiss and Park, 2001). *Interest in science* was selected because research has shown that an early interest in science is a predictor for later science learning and/or a career in a science or technology field (OECD, 2006a). PISA 2006 collected data about students' engagement in science-related social issues, their willingness to acquire scientific knowledge and skills, and their consideration of science-related careers. *Responsibility towards resources and environments* is an emerging global concern. Aspects of this in PISA 2006 include students' responsibility for sustainable development and their level of concern about environmental issues.

Figure 3.1
PISA 2006 assessment of attitudes

SUPPORT FOR SCIENTIFIC ENQUIRY

Students who support scientific enquiry:
- Acknowledge the importance of considering different scientific perspectives and arguments.
- Support the use of factual information and rational explanations.
- Express the need for logical and careful processes in drawing conclusions.

Measures include: questions on support for scientific enquiry (integrated into the science assessment); general value of science; personal value of science.

SELF-BELIEF AS SCIENCE LEARNERS

Students with self-belief as science learners believe they can:
- Handle scientific tasks effectively.
- Overcome difficulties to solve scientific problems.
- Demonstrate strong scientific abilities.

Measures include: questions on self-efficacy in science; self-concept in science.

INTEREST IN SCIENCE

Students with interest in science:
- Indicate curiosity in science and science-related issues and endeavours.
- Demonstrate willingness to acquire additional scientific knowledge and skills, using a variety of resources and methods.
- Demonstrate willingness to seek information and have an ongoing interest in science, including consideration of science-related careers.

Measures include: questions on interest in learning science topics (integrated into the science assessment); general interest in science; enjoyment of science; importance of learning science; instrumental motivation to learn science; future-oriented motivation to learn science; expectations for a science-related career at age 30; participation in science-related activities.

RESPONSIBILITY TOWARDS RESOURCES AND ENVIRONMENTS

Students with responsibility towards resources and environments:
- Show a sense of personal responsibility for maintaining a sustainable environment.
- Demonstrate awareness of the environmental consequences of individual actions.
- Demonstrate willingness to take action to maintain natural resources.

Measures include: questions on awareness of environmental issues; level of concern for environmental issues; optimism for the evolution of selected environmental issues; and responsibility for sustainable development.

PISA 2006 gathered data on students' attitudes towards science not only by using a student questionnaire but also by integrating questions about student attitudes towards science in the assessment of student performance. The inclusion of these questions in the science assessment enabled PISA to explore students' attitudes in the context of specific science tasks and thus more concretely than would have been possible when asking general questions about attitudes in a separate questionnaire. Moreover, it enabled PISA to determine whether students' attitudes varied between contexts, and whether the attitudes correlated with students' performance at the level of individual questions or groups of questions.

Students' *support for scientific enquiry* and students' *interest in learning science topics* were directly assessed in the test, using embedded questions that targeted personal, social and global contexts. In the case of students' interest in learning science topics, students were able to report one of the following responses: "high interest", "medium interest", "low interest" or "no interest". Students reporting high interest or medium interest were considered to report an interest in learning science topics. For attitudinal questions measuring students' support for scientific enquiry, students were asked to express their level of agreement using one of the following responses: "strongly agree", "agree", "disagree" or "strongly disagree". Students reporting that they strongly agreed or agreed were considered to support scientific enquiry.

The separate PISA 2006 student questionnaire gathered data on students' attitudes in all four areas, in a non-contextualised manner.

Box 3.1 **An overview of 15-year-olds' attitudes to science**

Students reported appreciating science in general and supporting scientific enquiry.

Among OECD countries, students participating in PISA 2006 reported a general appreciation for science and scientific enquiry:

- 93% agreed that science is important for understanding the natural world.

- 92% agreed that advances in science and technology usually improve people's living conditions.

When asked about scientific enquiry in the context of specific tasks in the PISA 2006 science assessment students expressed high levels of support. However, general support for science needs to be distinguished from the personal value of science:

- 75% agreed that science helps them to understand things around them, but only

- 57% agreed that science is very relevant to them personally.

Students reported confidence as science learners, but this varies according to the task.

In general, among OECD countries, students reported being confident that they could overcome difficulties to solve scientific problems, but this varied significantly for different types of problems.

- 76% reported that they could explain why earthquakes occurred more frequently in some areas than in others.

- 64% reported that they could predict how changes to an environment would affect the survival of certain species.

- 51% reported that they could discuss how new evidence could lead to a change in understanding about the possibility of life on Mars.

More generally, 65% of students reported that they could usually give good answers to test questions on school science topics, but only 47% reported that they found school science topics easy.

Students reported an interest in learning science, but only a minority see themselves using science in the future.

On average across OECD countries, the majority of students participating in PISA 2006 reported that they are motivated to learn science:

- 72% reported that it was important for them to do well in science.

- 67% reported that they enjoyed acquiring new knowledge in science.

- 67% reported that science was useful to them.

When asked about interest in specific science topics examined by the PISA 2006 science assessment, students reported high levels of interest. However, only 56% agreed that science was useful for further studies and only a minority of students saw themselves doing science in the future:

- 21% said they would like to spend their life doing advanced science.

- 37% said they would like to work in a career involving science.

...

124

A minority of students reported engaging regularly in science-related activities. Only:

- 21% regularly watched television programmes about science.
- 20% regularly read science magazines or read science articles in newspapers.
- 13% regularly visited websites on science.
- 8% regularly borrowed books on science.
- 7% regularly listened to radio programmes on science.
- 4% regularly regularly attended a science club.

Students reported a strong sense of responsibility for environmental issues.

The PISA 2006 student questionnaire asked students how they felt about selected environmental issues. On average across OECD countries, less than 5% of students reported that these issues were of no concern to them. However, when asked whether these environmental issues were of direct concern to themselves or other people in their country, the level of concern reported by students varied considerably from country to country. Clearly, some of the environmental issues are of more direct concern in certain countries.

Students' awareness of environmental issues varied considerably according to the issue:

- 73% reported being aware of the consequences of clearing forest for other land use.
- 60% reported being aware of acid rain.
- 35% reported being aware of the use of genetically modified organisms (GMOs).

Students were strongly supportive of policies to promote sustainable development, with over 90% agreeing that industries should be required to prove that they safely dispose of dangerous waste materials; there should be laws to protect the habitats of endangered species and that regular checks should be carried out on the emissions from cars as a condition of their use.

The majority of students reported they believed that selected environmental issues would stay about the same or get worse over the next 20 years; for example, only 21% expressed optimism about energy shortages in the future and only 13% believed that the issues about clearing forests for other land use would improve.

Notes on the interpretation of the measures

Many factors contribute to forming student attitudes about science. Attitudes can be strongly influenced by students' peers in the classroom, the culture of their school, their home and family culture, and more generally their national culture. Furthermore, all of the attitudinal results reported in this chapter are based on students' self-reports. Cultural factors can also influence the way in which responses are given (*e.g.* Heine *et al.*, 1999; van de Vijver and Leung, 1997; Bempechat *et al.*, 2002). Measures on student attitudes therefore need to be constructed and interpreted carefully.

The measures presented in this chapter summarise student responses to a series of related questions. The questions were selected from larger constructs on the basis of theoretical considerations and previous research. Confirmatory factor analysis was conducted to confirm the theoretically expected behaviour of the scales and indices and to validate their comparability across countries (see Annex A10).[3] Each measure provides a set of student "scores" – for example, each student's interest in science is scored on a consistent

125

international scale. However, some care must be taken when comparing the values of these scores among students who come from different cultures, as students in different countries may not always mean the same thing when answering questions about matters like interest in science.

This chapter focuses on those measures for which the analyses confirmed a similar structure across countries and for which the relationship with student performance is also consistent within countries.[4] However, this does not automatically imply that the relationship of the measures with student performance is also consistent across countries. Based on the degree of cross-national consistency in relationships with performance, the measures of student attitudes used in PISA 2006 can be divided into two groups.

For one group of measures – students' self-efficacy, awareness of environmental issues and general value of science – the relationships between the measures and student performance are coherent both within OECD countries and across the pooled OECD sample (with correlations of at least 0.20). For these measures, it is possible to compare reasonably confidently the mean scores across OECD countries – for example, to say that students' sense of self-efficacy in science is stronger in Country A than in Country B.

For a second group of measures – self-concept in science, personal value of science, general interest in science, enjoyment of science, instrumental motivation to learn science, future-oriented motivation to learn science, science-related activities, optimism regarding environmental issues and responsibility for sustainable development – the relationship with student performance is consistent within countries, but differs across countries (in all cases the correlation for the pooled OECD countries is less than 0.20).[5] For these measures, this chapter does not compare mean scores across countries (that is, one cannot necessarily conclude whether students in Country A show more general interest in science than in Country B), but does sometimes highlight results that may be useful to individual countries.

Box 3.2 **Interpreting the PISA indices**

Comparing countries that are above or below the OECD average on each of the attitudinal indices

In describing students in terms of each characteristic (*e.g.* general value of science), indices were constructed on which the average OECD student (*e.g.* the student with an average level of interest) was given an index value of zero and on which about two-thirds of the OECD student population were between the values of -1 and 1 (*i.e.* the index has a standard deviation of 1). Therefore, if countries have negative mean index values this does not necessarily imply that students responded negatively to the underlying questions. Rather in these countries, students responded less positively than students on average across OECD countries. Likewise, in countries with positive mean index values students responded more positively than on average in the OECD area. A good example is on the index of general value of science shown in Figure 3.2. Students in countries that are below the OECD average in Figure 3.2 still reported strong general value of science.

For each attitudinal index there is a corresponding figure showing the percentages of students associated with each question contained within the index and contributing to the mean index value. In all cases the analysis refers only to percentages of students and not to the mean index value.

For both groups of measures it is possible to observe patterns among countries of how a particular characteristic is associated with performance within each country (*i.e.* to conclude whether the extent to which higher-performing students tend to report, for example, more general interest in science is stronger in

Country A than in Country B). The chapter also presents results for both groups of measures on differences among subgroups within countries, analysing how students' gender, as well as their socio-economic and immigrant background are associated with self-reported attitudes to science.

It is also important to bear in mind that in some of the participating countries where comparatively high percentages of students reported that they valued science and were motivated to learn about it, significant proportions of 15-year-olds were not enrolled in formal education. In these countries, these higher percentages may be distorted as they represent only those 15-year-olds who are enrolled in education (see Annex A10). The countries to which this applies include several of the partner countries and throughout the chapter caution should be used in comparing attitudes of students in OECD and these partner countries.

DO STUDENTS SUPPORT SCIENTIFIC ENQUIRY?

One aspect of students' attitudes towards science concerns their general appreciation of science and scientific enquiry, as well as their perceptions of the personal, subjective importance of science. Students' general appreciation of science and scientific enquiry has been shown to be closely related to their epistemological beliefs about science (Fleener, 1996; Hofer and Pintrich, 2002). Therefore, general appreciation of science needs to be considered distinct from personal value of science. Students may not intend to pursue further scientific studies or careers, but may support and value science in general, indicating a belief that scientific advances and knowledge may bring benefits to society. Conversely, a lack of support for scientific enquiry could indicate that students distrust science and may even fear that scientific advances do not support human development.

PISA 2006 produced three measures of students' value of science. Two were constructed from responses to the student questionnaire (the *index of general value of science* and the *index of personal value of science*) and one (*support for scientific enquiry scale*) from answers to questions that were integrated in the science assessment and therefore captured how students value science in relation to specific topics (see the example in Figure 3.3).[6]

General value of science

To what extent do students value the contribution of science and technology for understanding the natural and constructed world and for the improvement of natural, technological and social conditions of life? A strong general value of science would reflect all these things (Carstensen *et al.*, 2003). The majority of students participating in PISA 2006 reported that they valued science (Figure 3.2). On average across OECD countries, students almost universally reported believing that science was important for understanding the natural world and that advances in science and technology usually improve people's living conditions (93 and 92% of students, respectively) and 87% stated a belief that science was valuable to society. This is an important finding. However, a significant proportion of students did not agree that advances in science and technology usually brought social benefits or improved the economy (25 and 20% on average, respectively). This suggests that a significant proportion of students distinguish between science contributing to technical understanding and productivity and a wider conception of it bringing economic and social benefits.

Overall the majority of students in all participating countries reported that they valued science in general. While cross-national analysis seems to indicate that the following comparisons of students' general value of science are valid among OECD countries, comparisons across all participating countries on students' general value of science should be interpreted with caution, since students in different countries may not necessarily interpret questions on these issues in exactly the same way (see Annex A10). In some OECD countries, comparatively fewer students reported valuing science in general. More than 40% of students in Iceland and Denmark did not agree that advances in science and technology usually bring social benefits and similarly for between 32 and 39% of students in France, the United Kingdom, Switzerland, Belgium, New Zealand, Ireland, Sweden, Germany, Austria and Australia and in the partner country Liechtenstein (Figure 3.2). Therefore, although the majority of students in these countries agreed that science contributed to technical understanding and productivity, a significant proportion of students did not agree with the wider conception of it bringing economic and social benefits. However, this does not necessarily mean that students do not value science in these countries. In fact, the vast majority of students in most of the OECD countries did report valuing science in general, but compared to the almost universal level of support expressed in many of the partner countries and economies these percentages are relatively low. Several of the OECD countries that performed above average in the PISA 2006 science assessment are found towards the bottom of Figure 3.2. Conversely, three of the top-performing OECD countries do have students who reported an above-average general value of science: Canada, Finland and Korea.

It is possible to summarise student responses to the questions on the general value of science in an index, on which the average OECD student (*e.g.* the student with average general value of science) was given an index value of zero, and about two-thirds of the OECD student population are between the values of -1 and 1 (*i.e.* the index has a standard deviation of 1). Relating this index to student performance shows that, within every participating country, a strong general value of science is associated with better performance in science – on average an increase of one unit on the index of general value in science is associated with an increase of 28 score points in science. This association is strongest in the United Kingdom, Australia, New Zealand, the Netherlands, Iceland, Finland, Sweden, Ireland and Norway, as well as in the partner country Estonia (an increase of over 30 score points). These performance differences are substantial, given that a difference of 38 score points on the PISA science scale corresponds to the average performance difference between students enrolled in two different grades in the 28 OECD countries in which a sizeable number of 15-year-olds in the PISA samples were enrolled in at least two different grades (see Table A1.2, Annex A1).

Box 3.3 **Comparing differences in attitudes towards science by gender, socio-economic background and immigrant background**

It is useful to compare differences in each attitudinal index between different types of students. This chapter analyses differences between males and females, between students from comparatively favourable and less favourable socio-economic background and between native students and students from an immigrant background. A problem that may occur in such analysis is that the distribution of the index varies across countries. One way to resolve this is to calculate an effect size that accounts for differences in the distributions. An effect size measures the difference between, for example, the general value of science held by male and female students in a given country, relative to the average variation in general value of science scores among male and female students in the country.

An effect size also allows a comparison of differences across measures that differ in their metric. For example, it is possible to compare effect sizes between the PISA 2006 attitudinal indices and the PISA 2006 science assessment scores.

In accordance with common practices, effect sizes of 0.20 are considered small in this volume, effect sizes in the order of 0.50 are considered medium and effect sizes greater than 0.80 are considered large. In the comparisons in this chapter, countries are listed only if the effect sizes are equal to or greater than 0.20, even if smaller differences are still statistically significant.

Figure 3.2
Index of general value of science

A	Science is important for helping us to understand the natural world.
B	Advances in science and technology usually improve people's living conditions.
C	Science is valuable to society.
D	Advances in science and technology usually help to improve the economy.
E	Advances in science and technology usually bring social benefits.

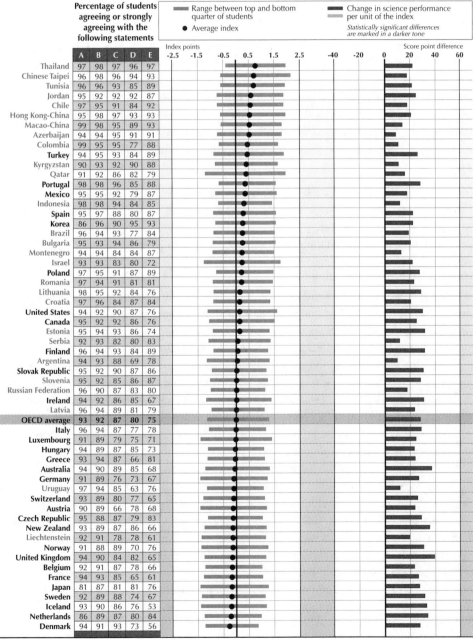

Source: OECD PISA 2006 database, Table 3.5.
StatLink ⟐⟐ http://dx.doi.org/10.1787/141846760512

To what extent is students' general value of science associated with their socio-economic background? To measure the association of socio-economic background with students' general value of science and other measures presented in this chapter effect sizes are calculated showing the difference on the index between students in the top and bottom quarters of the PISA index of economic, social and cultural status (Box 3.3). This analysis only discusses results with an effect size of 0.20 or greater (or -0.20 or less) which are considered to warrant the attention of policy makers. Across all participating countries students' general value of science is positively associated with their socio-economic background (although the effect size is less than 0.20 in the partner countries Serbia, Uruguay and Kyrgyzstan). This relationship is most pronounced in Ireland, the United States, Australia, New Zealand, Sweden, Finland, the United Kingdom, Luxembourg and the Netherlands, and in the partner country Liechtenstein, where the effect sizes are at least 0.50 (Table 3.22).

Among the 33 countries (including 20 OECD countries) where at least 3% of 15-year-olds have an immigrant background, students with an immigrant background in 18 countries reported a general value of science similar to that of their native counterparts. In 10 other countries students with an immigrant background reported a higher general value of science compared to that of their native counterparts, with this being most pronounced in New Zealand, the United Kingdom, Canada and Australia, and in the partner country Qatar. Conversely, in five countries, students with an immigrant background reported a lower general value of science compared to that of their native counter parts; this is most pronounced in the partner countries Estonia and Slovenia (Table 3.23).

Overall, at age 15, males and females report placing equal value on science in general (Table 3.21). Although in the OECD countries slightly higher percentages of males are more likely to have reported a high general value of science, these differences are only significant in a minority of countries (an effect size of at least -0.20 in Iceland, France, the United Kingdom, Denmark and Sweden).

Support for scientific enquiry

When asked in the context of specific tasks in the PISA 2006 science assessment, students tended to report strong levels of support for scientific enquiry. Figure 3.3 shows the percentages of students either agreeing or strongly agreeing with statements supporting scientific enquiry for each of the three released PISA 2006 assessment units *ACID RAIN, GRAND CANYON* and *MARY MONTAGU*. These units are presented in Chapter 2, while the statements used to gauge students' level of support for scientific enquiry are presented in Figure 3.3. Across the science assessment units, students reported, on average, high levels of support for scientific enquiry, with at least 70% of students having agreed with each of the statements. However, there are some interesting variations in level of support for particular scientific enquiries based on the same stimulus. For example, on the unit *MARY MONTAGU* there was almost universal support (94% on average) for research to develop vaccines for new strains of influenza, with at least 95% of students having supported this in 34 of the participating countries. In contrast, the statement that the cause of a disease can only be identified by scientific research did not receive as much support – some 30% of students on average disagreed with this. Students also reported strong support for the remaining statement on the scientific investigation of the effectiveness of unconventional treatments for diseases (87% of students supported this on average). These results indicate that students make a difference between generally supporting scientific evidence and having complete confidence in science as the only way to advance knowledge. Students also reported strong support for the systematic study of fossils and the scientific investigation of geological layers, as well as for the importance of basing statements about the causes of acid rain on scientific research (between 86 and 85% of students on average).

Similar to students' reports on how they valued science in general, results from the scale on support for scientific enquiry show that a stronger support for scientific enquiry is positively associated with science performance in all countries (see Annex A10).

Figure 3.3
Examples of students' support for scientific enquiry

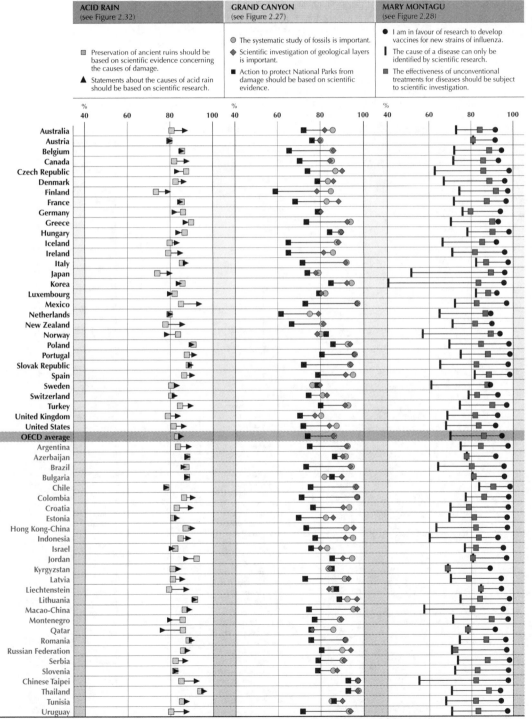

Note: Since cross-country comparisons of the percentages should be made with caution, countries have been ordered alphabetically.
Source: OECD PISA 2006 database.
StatLink ᏘᎦ http://dx.doi.org/10.1787/141846760512

Figure 3.4
Index of personal value of science

A	I find that science helps me to understand things around me.
B	I will use science in many ways when I am an adult.
C	Some concepts in science help me see how I relate to other people.
D	When I leave school there will be many opportunities for me to use science.
E	Science is very relevant to me.

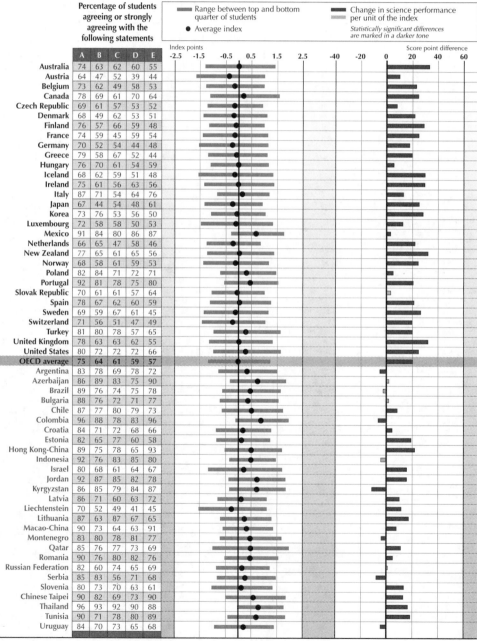

	A	B	C	D	E
Australia	74	63	62	60	55
Austria	64	47	52	39	44
Belgium	73	62	49	58	53
Canada	78	69	61	70	64
Czech Republic	69	61	57	53	52
Denmark	68	49	62	53	51
Finland	76	57	66	59	48
France	74	59	45	59	54
Germany	70	52	54	44	48
Greece	79	58	67	52	44
Hungary	76	70	61	54	59
Iceland	68	62	59	51	48
Ireland	75	61	56	63	56
Italy	87	71	54	64	76
Japan	67	44	54	48	61
Korea	73	76	53	56	50
Luxembourg	72	58	58	50	53
Mexico	91	84	80	86	87
Netherlands	66	65	47	58	46
New Zealand	77	65	61	65	56
Norway	68	58	61	59	53
Poland	82	84	71	72	71
Portugal	92	81	78	75	80
Slovak Republic	70	61	61	57	64
Spain	78	67	62	60	59
Sweden	69	59	67	61	45
Switzerland	71	56	51	47	49
Turkey	81	80	78	57	65
United Kingdom	78	63	63	62	55
United States	80	72	72	72	66
OECD average	**75**	**64**	**61**	**59**	**57**
Argentina	83	78	69	78	72
Azerbaijan	86	89	83	75	90
Brazil	89	76	74	75	78
Bulgaria	88	76	72	71	77
Chile	87	77	80	79	73
Colombia	96	88	78	83	96
Croatia	84	71	72	68	66
Estonia	82	65	77	60	58
Hong Kong-China	89	75	78	65	93
Indonesia	92	76	83	85	80
Israel	80	68	61	64	67
Jordan	92	87	85	82	78
Kyrgyzstan	86	85	79	84	87
Latvia	86	71	60	63	72
Liechtenstein	70	52	49	41	45
Lithuania	87	63	87	67	65
Macao-China	90	73	64	63	91
Montenegro	83	80	78	81	77
Qatar	85	76	77	73	69
Romania	90	76	80	82	76
Russian Federation	82	60	74	65	69
Serbia	85	83	56	71	68
Slovenia	80	73	70	63	61
Chinese Taipei	90	82	69	73	90
Thailand	96	93	92	90	88
Tunisia	90	71	78	80	89
Uruguay	84	70	73	65	68

Legend:
- Range between top and bottom quarter of students
- ● Average index
- Change in science performance per unit of the index
- Statistically significant differences are marked in a darker tone

Note: Since cross-country comparisons of the percentages should be made with caution, countries have been ordered alphabetically.
Source: OECD PISA 2006 database, Table 3.6.
StatLink ⟲ http://dx.doi.org/10.1787/141846760512

The information collected on students' support for scientific enquiry within the science assessment provides further evidence for the conclusions that, in general, students value science.

Personal value of science

While the majority of students reported valuing science in general, to what extent does this translate into science being of personal value? PISA 2006 results show that the personal value of science and science-based reasoning are distinct from general appreciation of science (Figure 3.4). Students may be convinced that science is generally important, but do not necessarily relate this to their own lives and behaviour. This is an important finding for policy makers. On average, 75% of students reported that science helped them to understand things around them. However, fewer students reported that they would use science when they left school or as an adult (59 and 64%, respectively) or reported that concepts in science helped them to see how they relate to other people (61%). Only 57% of students agreed that science was very relevant to them. Comparisons across countries should be made with caution as students may not be answering these questions in the same way in different countries. However, for each country concerned it is still useful to consider the absolute percentages of students who consider science to be very relevant to them: for example, less than 50% of students in Austria, Greece, Sweden, the Netherlands, Finland, Iceland, Germany and Switzerland and in the partner country Liechtenstein reported that science was very relevant to them. In addition, in Austria and the partner country Liechtenstein only around 40% of students agreed that there would be many opportunities for them to use science after they had left school.

In the majority of countries, students from more advantaged socio-economic backgrounds tended to report higher personal value of science (Table 3.22).

Across participating countries, students with an immigrant background reported similar (in 14 countries) or higher (in 16 countries) personal value of science compared to their native counterparts. Countries with the most pronounced differences in personal value of science in favour of students with an immigrant background include the United Kingdom, New Zealand, Denmark, Sweden, Canada, Ireland, Australia and the partner countries Liechtenstein, Latvia and Qatar (Table 3.23). In contrast, students with an immigrant background reported lower personal value of science compared to native students in three countries, with this being most pronounced in the partner country Slovenia.

In 45 of the participating countries, students who reported a higher level of personal value of science performed better in the PISA 2006 science assessment. On average, a one unit increase in the index of personal value of science corresponds to a performance difference of 20 score points in science (Figure 3.4).

DO STUDENTS BELIEVE THEY CAN SUCCEED IN SCIENCE?

Autonomous learning requires both a critical and a realistic judgement of the difficulty of a task as well as the ability to invest enough energy to accomplish it. Learners form views about their own competences and learning characteristics. These views have been shown to have considerable impact on the way they set goals, the learning strategies they use and their performance. Two ways of defining these beliefs are in terms of how much students believe in their own ability to handle tasks effectively and overcome difficulties (self-efficacy) and students' beliefs in their own academic abilities (self-concept).

PISA 2006 includes measures of how much students believe in their own ability to handle tasks effectively and overcome difficulties (the *index of self-efficacy in science*) and students' beliefs in their own academic abilities in science (the *index of self-concept in science*).[7] Both measures of students' self-beliefs are often

133

considered important outcomes of schooling in their own right. Confidence in their abilities in various subjects can feed into students' motivation, learning behaviours and general expectations for their future.

Students' confidence in overcoming difficulties in science

Successful learners are not only confident of their abilities. They also believe that investment in learning can make a difference and help them to overcome difficulties – that is, they have a strong sense of their own efficacy. By contrast, students who lack confidence in their ability to learn what they judge to be important and to overcome difficulties may not find success, not only at school, but also in their adult lives. Self-efficacy goes beyond how good students think they are in subjects such as science. It is more concerned with the kind of confidence that is needed for them to successfully master specific learning tasks, and therefore not simply a reflection of a student's abilities and performance. The relationship between students' self-efficacy and student performance may well be reciprocal; with students with higher academic ability being more confident and higher levels of confidence, in turn, improving students' academic ability.

A strong sense of self-efficacy can affect students' willingness to take on challenging tasks and to make an effort and persist in tackling them: it can thus have a key impact on motivation (Bandura, 1994). PISA 2003 results showed a significant positive association between students' self-efficacy in mathematics and their performance in the mathematics assessment. On average in OECD countries, each unit increase on the index of self-efficacy in mathematics corresponded to a performance difference of 47 score points.

To assess self-efficacy in PISA 2006, students were asked to rate the ease with which they believe they could perform eight listed scientific tasks. For each of the eight scientific tasks, the average percentages of students reporting that they could do it either easily or with a bit of effort vary considerably (Figure 3.5). Cross-national analysis indicates that the following comparisons of students' self-efficacy in science are valid across countries (see Annex A10). Seventy-six per cent of students on average reported that they felt confident explaining why earthquakes occur more frequently in some areas than in others, with the proportion being over 80% of students in Finland, Germany, the Netherlands, the Czech Republic, and Ireland, countries where there is also above-average mean country performance in science. Similarly, 73% of students reported that they could recognise an underlying science question in a newspaper report on a health issue. Students in the Slovak Republic and the Czech Republic, as well as in the partner countries Thailand, Kyrgyzstan, Lithuania and Uruguay, reported comparatively higher levels of confidence in doing this. Between 62 and 64% of students on average reported that they could: interpret the scientific information provided on the labelling of food items; predict how changes to an environment will affect the survival of certain species; and identify the science question associated with the disposal of garbage. Less than 60% of students reported that they could describe the role of antibiotics in the treatment of disease or identify the better of two explanations for the formation of acid rain. Students were least confident with discussing how new evidence could lead to a change of understanding about the possibility of life on Mars, with only 51% on average reporting that they could do so easily or with a bit of effort. In Japan and the partner country Indonesia, only 26% of students reported that they were confident that they could do this.

The majority of countries show no gender differences on the index of self-efficacy in science. In the PISA 2003 mathematics assessment, males reported higher levels of self-efficacy in mathematics (effect sizes of at least 0.20 in 35 of the 40 participating countries), whereas in the PISA 2006 science assessment males reported higher levels of self-efficacy in science only in Japan, the Netherlands, Iceland and Korea and in the partner economy Chinese Taipei (Table 3.21).

Figure 3.5
Index of self-efficacy in science

A   Explain why earthquakes occur more frequently in some areas than in others.
B   Recognise the science question that underlies a newspaper report on a health issue.
C   Interpret the scientific information provided on the labelling of food items.
D   Predict how changes to an environment will affect the survival of certain species.
E   Identify the science question associated with the disposal of garbage.
F   Describe the role of antibiotics in the treatment of disease.
G   Identify the better of two explanations for the formation of acid rain.
H   Discuss how new evidence can lead you to change your understanding about the possibility of life on Mars.

Percentage of students who believe they can perform the following tasks either easily or with a bit of effort

	A	B	C	D	E	F	G	H
Poland	76	76	82	71	62	72	71	59
United States	76	79	71	77	64	63	58	59
Canada	76	78	72	78	64	59	62	57
Jordan	73	74	76	61	75	70	63	50
Portugal	75	75	72	71	76	61	66	57
United Kingdom	75	79	69	77	67	60	61	52
Chinese Taipei	75	74	75	68	75	57	67	52
Czech Republic	81	81	61	67	60	71	57	57
Croatia	73	78	58	65	75	74	71	52
Iceland	79	72	74	72	58	63	55	59
Uruguay	71	81	72	67	64	57	66	58
Norway	78	65	66	66	68	77	76	61
Australia	78	78	68	75	61	59	54	55
Slovak Republic	76	83	77	54	61	63	67	60
Mexico	74	78	62	67	77	57	62	55
Colombia	66	69	69	70	75	60	59	49
Thailand	74	87	73	73	86	61	63	55
Hong Kong-China	70	80	65	69	72	56	75	44
Chile	75	67	71	66	60	56	65	54
Germany	83	78	61	69	62	64	64	44
Serbia	64	75	67	63	71	58	59	51
Netherlands	82	78	60	62	60	66	65	53
Estonia	71	79	71	57	69	59	54	45
Israel	66	80	67	63	65	58	49	54
Finland	83	77	68	56	63	53	48	64
Turkey	73	76	72	65	64	61	57	51
Ireland	81	68	64	63	69	55	64	41
Lithuania	80	81	68	62	68	67	53	52
OECD average	76	73	64	64	62	59	58	51
Russian Federation	68	69	75	51	70	60	49	45
Latvia	77	76	67	62	66	51	52	49
New Zealand	78	73	64	68	58	58	48	50
Montenegro	67	68	68	57	66	63	61	47
Bulgaria	66	71	68	62	72	57	45	46
Argentina	66	73	67	65	62	49	58	52
Brazil	62	76	65	67	76	54	50	42
France	79	65	67	59	52	70	43	54
Hungary	70	72	66	49	74	63	62	35
Sweden	80	67	65	67	58	53	58	54
Spain	73	61	62	59	55	54	61	56
Belgium	67	73	67	64	51	58	57	52
Denmark	78	77	70	59	54	42	49	62
Qatar	66	73	61	62	63	55	53	52
Slovenia	74	74	60	51	60	49	63	49
Macao-China	70	70	59	58	68	49	63	37
Tunisia	53	72	76	59	67	47	41	39
Austria	78	73	53	61	63	55	58	36
Liechtenstein	74	65	51	64	58	58	54	37
Greece	67	67	52	56	61	57	59	42
Luxembourg	78	71	57	65	57	58	49	44
Kyrgyzstan	61	81	68	63	62	53	48	46
Switzerland	77	69	55	62	54	52	45	41
Italy	77	70	63	64	57	46	56	46
Korea	72	68	47	53	65	55	56	39
Romania	57	68	66	52	50	46	51	37
Azerbaijan	52	65	59	53	54	45	39	37
Japan	62	64	44	58	61	33	43	26
Indonesia	43	60	43	40	61	47	28	26

Legend: ▬ Range between top and bottom quarter of students   ● Average index   ▬ Change in science performance per unit of the index   *Statistically significant differences are marked in a darker tone*

Index points: -2.5   -1.5   -0.5   0.5   1.5   2.5

Score point difference: -40   -20   0   20   40   60

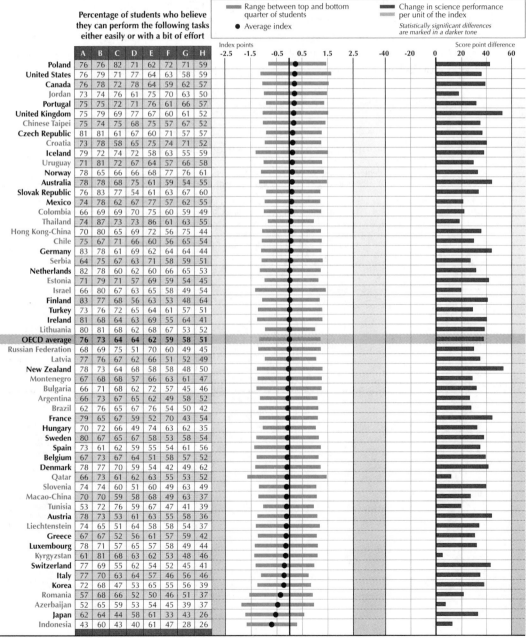

Source: OECD PISA 2006 database, Table 3.3.
StatLink   http://dx.doi.org/10.1787/141846760512

Within each participating country, students' self-efficacy in science shows a positive relationship with science performance. As already mentioned, this relationship may well be reciprocal. In 49 of 57 countries (including all OECD countries) a one unit increase in the index of self-efficacy in science represents a performance difference of at least 20 score points. The relationship between higher self-efficacy and better performance is particularly strong in New Zealand, the United Kingdom, France, Australia, Austria, Germany, Switzerland, Poland, Denmark, Finland and Ireland, as well as in the partner countries Estonia and Croatia, corresponding to a performance difference of at least 40 score points (Figure 3.5). In some countries with above-average performance on the science assessment there are comparatively higher proportions of students reporting self-efficacy in science. These countries include Finland, Canada, Australia, the Netherlands, Germany, the United Kingdom, the Czech Republic and Ireland, as well as the partner countries/economies Hong Kong-China, Estonia and Chinese Taipei (Figure 3.6). However, the opposite is true in other countries performing above average in the PISA science assessment, with notably lower proportions of students reporting self-efficacy in Japan, Korea and Switzerland.

Figure 3.6
Performance in science and self-efficacy in science

Students reporting self-efficacy in science believe they can perform the following tasks either easily or with a bit of effort:

Explain why earthquakes occur more frequently in some areas than in others; recognise the science question that underlies a newspaper report on a health issue; interpret the scientific information provided on the labelling of food items; predict how changes to an environment will affect the survival of certain species; identify the science question associated with the disposal of garbage; describe the role of antibiotics in the treatment of disease; identify the better of two explanations for the formation of acid rain; discuss how new evidence can lead you to change your understanding about the possibility of life on Mars.

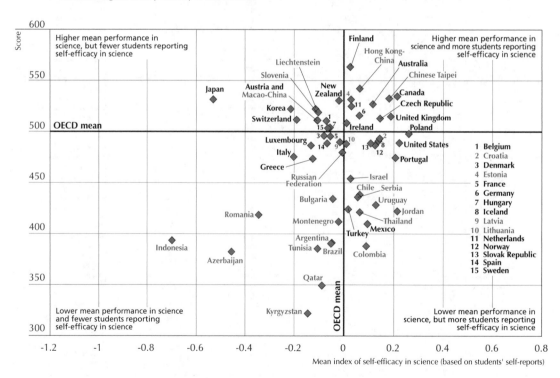

Source: OECD PISA 2006 database, Tables 3.3 and 2.1c.

StatLink ᵃᵢˢᵖ http://dx.doi.org/10.1787/141846760512

Students' self-concept in science

Students' academic self-concept is both an important outcome of education and a trait that correlates strongly with student success. Belief in one's own abilities is highly relevant to successful learning (Marsh, 1986). It can also affect other factors such as well-being and personality development, factors that are especially important for students from less advantaged backgrounds. In contrast to self-efficacy in science, which asks students about their level of confidence in tackling specific scientific tasks, self-concept measures the general level of belief that students have in their academic abilities. To what extent do the 15-year-old students assessed by PISA believe in their own science competencies? On average, 65% of students reported that they could usually give good answers in science tests. Overall, however, a large proportion of students (between 41 and 45% on average) said they were not confident in learning science, reporting that they did not agree that they learned school science topics quickly, or understood concepts or new ideas very well. Furthermore, 47% agreed that school science topics were easy and that learning advanced science would be easy (Figure 3.7).

Box 3.4 **Do students' beliefs about their abilities simply mirror their performance?**

One issue that arises when asking students what they think of their own abilities, especially in terms of whether they can perform scientific tasks, is whether this adds anything of importance to what is known about their abilities from the assessment. In fact, both prior research and the PISA results give strong reasons for assuming that confidence helps to drive learning success, rather than simply reflecting it. In particular:

- Research about the learning process has shown that students need to believe in their own capacities before making necessary investments in learning strategies that will help them to higher performance (Zimmerman, 1999). This finding is also supported by PISA 2000 and PISA 2003: the data suggest that the belief in one's efficacy is a particularly strong predictor of whether a student will control his or her learning.

- Much more of the observed variation in student levels of self-related beliefs occurs within countries, within schools and within classes than would be the case if self-confidence merely mirrored performance. That is to say, in any group of peers, even those with very low levels of science performance, the stronger performers are likely to have relatively high self-confidence, indicating that they base this on the norms they observe around them. This illustrates the importance of the immediate environment in fostering the self-confidence that students need in order to develop as effective learners.

- PISA 2000 showed that students who reported that they were good at verbal tasks did not necessarily also believe that they were good at mathematical tasks, despite the fact that PISA 2000 revealed a high correlation between performance on these two scales. Indeed, in most countries there was, at most, a weak and in some cases negative correlation between verbal and mathematical self-concept (OECD, 2003b). This can again be explained by the assertion that students' ability judgements are made in relation to subjective standards which are in turn based on the contexts they are in. Thus, some students who are confident in reading may be less confident in mathematics partly because it is a relative weak point in relation to their own overall abilities and partly because they are more likely than weak readers to have peers who are good mathematicians.

Figure 3.7
Index of self-concept in science

A	I can usually give good answers to test questions on school science topics.
B	When I am being taught school science, I can understand the concepts very well.
C	I learn school science topics quickly.
D	I can easily understand new ideas in school science.
E	Learning advanced school science topics would be easy for me.
F	School science topics are easy for me.

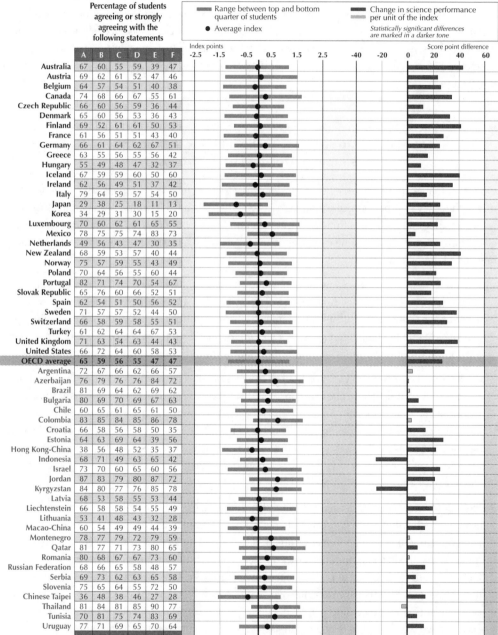

	A	B	C	D	E	F
Australia	67	60	55	59	39	47
Austria	69	62	61	52	47	46
Belgium	64	57	54	51	40	38
Canada	74	68	66	67	55	61
Czech Republic	66	60	56	59	36	44
Denmark	65	60	56	53	36	43
Finland	69	52	61	61	50	53
France	61	56	51	51	43	40
Germany	66	61	64	62	67	51
Greece	63	55	56	55	56	42
Hungary	55	49	48	47	32	37
Iceland	67	59	59	60	50	60
Ireland	62	56	49	51	37	42
Italy	79	64	59	57	54	50
Japan	29	38	25	18	11	13
Korea	34	29	31	30	15	20
Luxembourg	70	60	62	61	65	55
Mexico	78	75	75	74	83	73
Netherlands	49	56	43	47	30	35
New Zealand	68	59	53	57	40	44
Norway	75	57	59	55	43	49
Poland	70	64	56	55	60	44
Portugal	82	71	74	70	54	67
Slovak Republic	65	76	60	66	52	51
Spain	62	54	51	50	56	52
Sweden	71	57	57	52	44	50
Switzerland	66	58	59	58	55	51
Turkey	61	62	64	64	67	53
United Kingdom	71	63	54	63	44	43
United States	66	72	64	60	58	53
OECD average	**65**	**59**	**56**	**55**	**47**	**47**
Argentina	72	67	66	62	66	57
Azerbaijan	76	79	76	76	84	72
Brazil	81	69	64	62	69	62
Bulgaria	80	69	70	69	67	63
Chile	60	65	61	65	61	50
Colombia	83	85	84	85	86	78
Croatia	66	58	56	58	50	35
Estonia	64	63	69	64	39	56
Hong Kong-China	38	56	48	52	35	37
Indonesia	68	71	49	63	65	42
Israel	73	70	60	65	60	56
Jordan	87	83	79	80	87	72
Kyrgyzstan	84	80	77	76	85	78
Latvia	68	53	58	55	53	44
Liechtenstein	66	58	58	54	55	49
Lithuania	53	41	48	43	32	28
Macao-China	60	54	49	49	44	39
Montenegro	78	77	79	72	79	59
Qatar	81	77	71	73	80	65
Romania	80	68	67	67	73	60
Russian Federation	68	66	65	58	48	57
Serbia	69	73	62	63	65	58
Slovenia	75	65	64	55	72	50
Chinese Taipei	36	48	38	46	27	28
Thailand	81	84	81	85	90	77
Tunisia	70	81	75	74	83	69
Uruguay	77	71	69	65	70	64

Note : Since cross-country comparisons of the percentages should be made with caution, countries have been ordered alphabetically.
Source: OECD PISA 2006 database, Table 3.4.
StatLink ⟨ᗝᵴ⟩ http://dx.doi.org/10.1787/141846760512

PISA shows gender differences in students' self-concept in science, but they tend to be small to moderate (Table 3.21). In 22 OECD countries and 8 partner countries/economies, males were more likely than females to agree that, for example, learning school science topics was easy or that they could give good answers to test questions on science topics. On average, gender differences in self-concept in science are slightly less than those observed in mathematics as reported in PISA 2003. In Luxembourg, the Slovak Republic, the Czech Republic, Portugal, Ireland and the partner countries Tunisia, Thailand and Uruguay there are no gender differences in self-concept in science, although there were in self-concept in mathematics in 2003 (effect sizes of 0.20 or above). For several countries the gender differences in favour of males in terms of both self-concept in mathematics in PISA 2003 and self-concept in science in PISA 2006 are consistent (Canada, Denmark, France, Korea, Norway, Spain, Sweden, the United Kingdom and the United States and the partner economy Macao-China). In Iceland, Italy and Japan the gender differences in self-concept are more pronounced for science than they were for mathematics.

In contrast to students who reported high levels of self-efficacy in science, there is not such a uniform or pronounced association between students with strong self-concept in science and higher performance. In 48 of the participating countries (including all of the OECD countries) there is a positive association between students' self-concept in science and student performance in science with the performance difference varying between 6 and 43 score points per unit increase on the index of self-concept in science. The performance difference is at least 20 score points in 28 of the participating countries (Figure 3.7).

It is not surprising that students who perform well in PISA also tend to have high opinions of their abilities. However, as explained in Box 3.4, self-concept is more than simply a mirror of student performance and can have an influence on the learning process. Whether students choose to pursue a particular learning goal is dependent on their appraisal of their abilities and potential in a subject area and on their confidence in being able to achieve this goal even in the face of difficulties.

ARE STUDENTS INTERESTED IN SCIENCE?

Motivation and engagement are often regarded as important driving forces of learning. They can also affect students' quality of life during their adolescence and can influence whether they will successfully pursue further educational or labour market opportunities. In particular, given the importance of science for students' future lives, education systems need to ensure that students have both the interest and the motivation to continue learning in this area beyond school. Interest in and enjoyment of particular subjects, or intrinsic motivation, affects both the degree and continuity of engagement in learning and the depth of understanding reached. This effect has been shown to operate largely independently of students' general motivation to learn. For example, a student who is interested in science and therefore tends to study diligently may or may not show a high level of general learning motivation, and vice versa. Hence, an analysis of the pattern of students' interest in science is important. Such an analysis can reveal strengths and weaknesses in attempts by education systems to promote motivation to learn in various subjects among different sub-groups of students. Furthermore, motivation can be closely linked to students' aspirations for their future careers. For example, future science motivation may be an important indicator of the proportion of students likely to go on to further science studies and/or careers.

Interest in learning science as a subject

Research has shown that an early interest in science is a strong predictor of lifelong science learning and/or a career in a science or technology field (OECD, 2006a). PISA 2006 provided three measures of students' intrinsic motivation to learn science.[8] A high level of intrinsic motivation shows that students are motivated to learn because they are interested in science and enjoy learning about science. Two indices (the *index of general interest in science* and *index of enjoyment of science*) are measured by students' answers to questions in the student questionnaire. These are highly correlated (0.88), even if they are measuring different things. The third measure (*interest in learning science topics* scale) is constructed from responses to questions students answered within the science assessment and relates to levels of interest students expressed in the actual topics used in the assessment.

The PISA 2000 and PISA 2003 assessments revealed differences in students' interest and enjoyment in reading and mathematics. Results in PISA 2000 showed that in general students were interested in reading, although females reported much higher levels of engagement in reading, for example 45% of females reported that reading was one of their favourite hobbies, on average across OECD countries, compared to only 25% of males (OECD, 2001). In contrast, results from PISA 2003 showed that an average of only 38% of students did mathematics because they enjoyed it, although 53% were interested in the things they learned in mathematics (OECD, 2004a). Results from PISA 2006 show that students generally enjoy learning science, with, for example, an average of 63% of students having reported that they were both interested in learning about science and had fun doing so (Figure 3.10).

General interest in science

Interest in a subject can influence the intensity and continuity of student engagement in learning situations. In turn, strong engagement with a subject deepens students' understanding of that subject. The way that science is taught can vary in many ways among classes, among schools and among countries (see Chapter 5). Therefore, in order to measure students' general interest in science subjects PISA 2006 asked students a set of questions on: their level of interest in different subjects, including human biology, astronomy, chemistry, physics, the biology of plants and geology; their general interest in the ways in which scientists design experiments; and their understanding of what is required for scientific explanations. Figure 3.8 shows that the average percentages of students reporting medium or high levels of interest vary significantly among the question set. While the majority of students (68% on average) reported an interest in human biology, students reported less interest in astronomy, chemistry, physics, the biology of plants and the ways in which scientists design experiments (between 46 and 53% on average). Even smaller proportions of students reported interest in what is required for scientific explanations and in geology (36 and 41% on average, respectively).

Similar to the findings for students' value of science, among OECD countries students from higher socio-economic backgrounds tended to report higher general interest in science and this is most pronounced in Ireland, France, Belgium and Switzerland (with an effect size of at least 0.50, see Table 3.22).

Students with an immigrant background reported similar, if not higher, levels of general interest in science than native students in the 20 OECD countries where at least 3% of 15-year-olds have an immigrant background and this is the case in 12 of the 13 partner countries. The largest differences in favour of students with an immigrant background are found in New Zealand, the United Kingdom, Sweden, Australia, Denmark, Spain and Canada, and in the partner country Qatar (Table 3.23). These results mirror those obtained in the context of mathematics as part of the PISA 2003 assessment (OECD, 2005c).

Reported levels of general interest in learning science seem to be similar for males and females across most participating countries (Table 3.21). There are only four partner countries/economies with gender differences on the index of general interest in science: in Thailand it is in favour of females and in Chinese Taipei, Hong Kong-China and Macao-China it is in favour of males.

Figure 3.8
Index of general interest in science

A	Human biology
B	Topics in astronomy
C	Topics in chemistry
D	Topics in physics
E	The biology of plants
F	Ways scientists design experiments
G	Topics in geology
H	What is required for scientific explanations

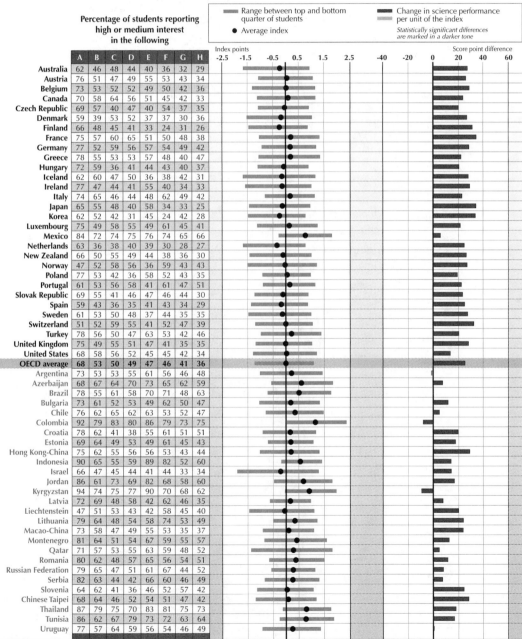

Percentage of students reporting high or medium interest in the following

	A	B	C	D	E	F	G	H
Australia	62	46	48	44	40	36	32	29
Austria	76	51	47	49	55	53	43	34
Belgium	73	53	52	52	49	50	42	36
Canada	70	58	64	56	51	45	42	33
Czech Republic	69	57	40	47	40	54	37	35
Denmark	59	39	53	52	37	37	30	36
Finland	66	48	45	41	33	24	31	26
France	75	57	60	65	51	50	48	38
Germany	77	52	59	56	57	54	49	42
Greece	78	55	53	53	57	48	40	47
Hungary	72	59	36	41	44	43	40	37
Iceland	62	60	47	50	36	38	42	31
Ireland	77	47	44	41	55	40	34	33
Italy	74	65	46	44	48	62	49	42
Japan	65	55	48	40	58	34	33	25
Korea	62	52	42	31	45	24	42	28
Luxembourg	75	49	58	55	49	61	45	41
Mexico	84	72	74	75	76	74	65	66
Netherlands	63	36	38	40	39	30	28	27
New Zealand	66	50	55	49	44	38	36	30
Norway	47	52	58	56	36	59	43	43
Poland	77	53	42	36	58	52	43	35
Portugal	61	53	56	58	41	61	47	51
Slovak Republic	69	55	41	46	47	46	44	30
Spain	59	43	36	35	41	43	34	29
Sweden	61	53	50	48	37	44	35	35
Switzerland	51	52	59	55	41	52	47	39
Turkey	78	56	50	47	63	53	42	46
United Kingdom	75	49	55	51	47	41	35	35
United States	68	58	56	52	45	45	42	34
OECD average	**68**	**53**	**50**	**49**	**47**	**46**	**41**	**36**
Argentina	73	53	53	55	61	56	46	48
Azerbaijan	68	67	64	70	73	65	62	59
Brazil	78	55	61	58	70	71	48	63
Bulgaria	73	61	52	53	49	62	50	47
Chile	76	62	65	62	63	53	52	47
Colombia	92	79	83	80	86	79	73	75
Croatia	78	62	41	38	55	61	51	51
Estonia	69	64	49	53	49	61	45	43
Hong Kong-China	75	62	55	56	56	53	43	44
Indonesia	90	65	55	59	89	82	52	60
Israel	66	47	45	44	41	44	33	34
Jordan	86	61	73	69	82	68	58	60
Kyrgyzstan	94	74	75	77	90	70	68	62
Latvia	72	69	48	58	42	62	46	35
Liechtenstein	47	51	53	43	42	58	45	40
Lithuania	79	64	48	54	58	74	53	49
Macao-China	73	58	47	49	55	53	35	37
Montenegro	81	64	51	54	67	59	55	57
Qatar	71	57	53	55	63	59	48	52
Romania	80	62	48	57	65	56	54	51
Russian Federation	79	65	47	51	61	67	44	52
Serbia	82	63	44	42	66	60	46	49
Slovenia	64	62	41	36	46	52	57	42
Chinese Taipei	68	64	46	52	54	51	47	42
Thailand	87	79	75	70	83	81	75	73
Tunisia	86	62	67	79	73	72	63	64
Uruguay	77	57	64	59	56	54	46	49

Legend:
- Range between top and bottom quarter of students
- ● Average index
- Change in science performance per unit of the index
- *Statistically significant differences are marked in a darker tone*

Note : Since cross-country comparisons of the percentages should be made with caution, countries have been ordered alphabetically.
Source: OECD PISA 2006 database, Table 3.8.
StatLink ᴍᴿ⋑ http://dx.doi.org/10.1787/141846760512

Figure 3.9

Examples of students' interest in learning science topics

Percentage of students reporting high or medium interest in the following:

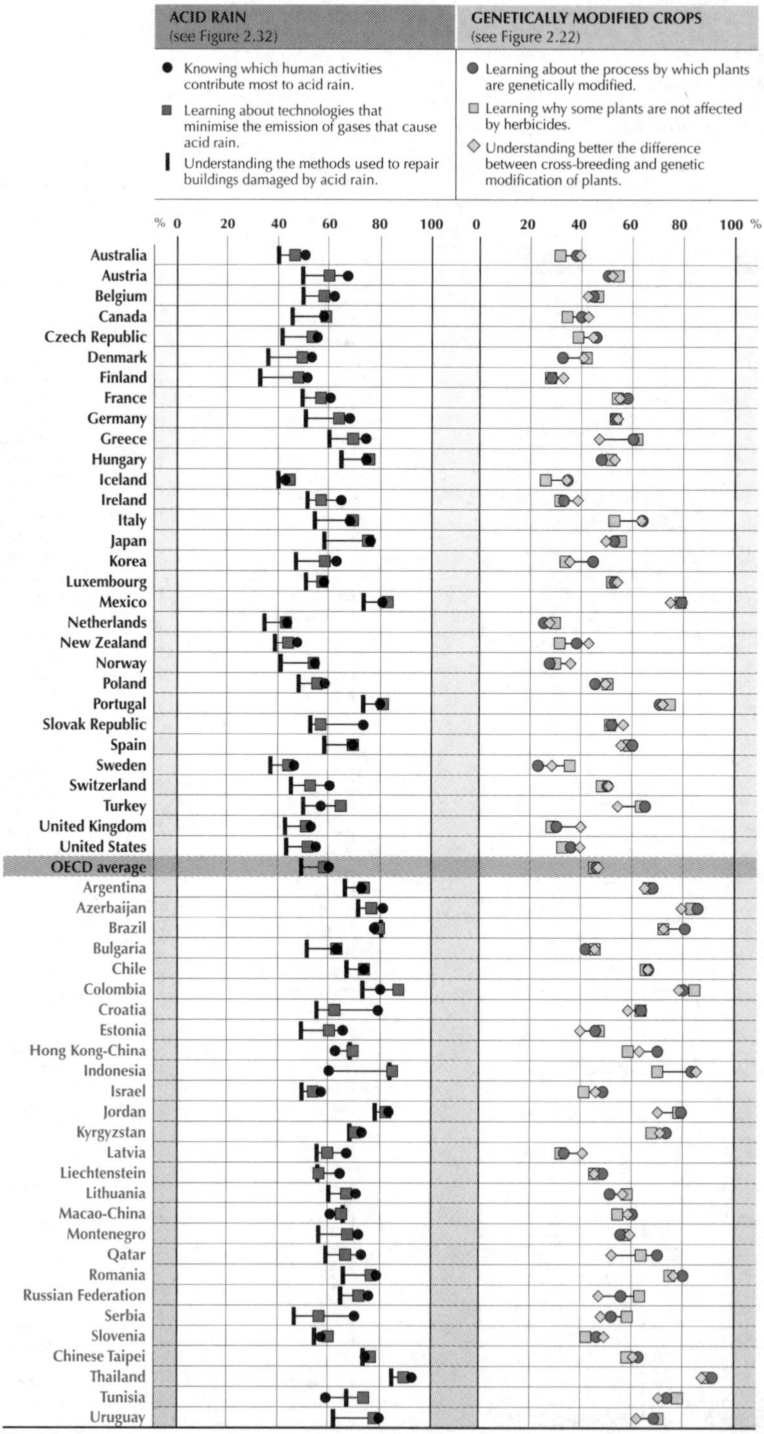

ACID RAIN (see Figure 2.32)	GENETICALLY MODIFIED CROPS (see Figure 2.22)
● Knowing which human activities contribute most to acid rain.	● Learning about the process by which plants are genetically modified.
■ Learning about technologies that minimise the emission of gases that cause acid rain.	▣ Learning why some plants are not affected by herbicides.
▍ Understanding the methods used to repair buildings damaged by acid rain.	◇ Understanding better the difference between cross-breeding and genetic modification of plants.

Note : Since cross-country comparisons of the percentages should be made with caution, countries have been ordered alphabetically.
Source: OECD PISA 2006 database, Table 3.1.
StatLink ⟶ http://dx.doi.org/10.1787/141846760512

In 52 of the participating countries (including all the OECD countries) students with a higher general interest in science performed better in the science assessment. On average across countries there is an associated change of 25 score points for an increase of one unit on the index of general interest in science (Figure 3.8). In 31 of the participating countries higher general interest in science is associated with a performance difference of at least 20 score points. The strongest association between students' general interest in science and their performance is observed in France, Japan, Korea, Switzerland and Finland (35 to 31 score points).

The causal nature of this relationship may well be complex and is difficult to discern. Interest in the subject and performance may be mutually reinforcing and may also be affected by other factors, such as the socio-economic backgrounds of students and their schools. However, whatever the nature of this relationship, a positive disposition towards science remains an important educational goal in its own right.

Interest in learning science topics

PISA 2006 collected more detailed information on students' interest in learning particular science topics included within the science assessment, for example learning about genetically modified crops and acid rain. Using as a stimulus the units presented in Chapter 2 (see Figures 2.22 and 2.32), a set of questions was included to measure students' level of interest in learning and understanding particular aspects of these science topics. Figure 3.9 shows that students expressed different levels of interest between these topics. In general, more students showed an interest in the topic acid rain, with an average of 62% reporting high or medium interest in knowing which human activities contribute most to acid rain, 59% in learning about technologies that minimise the emission of gases that cause acid rain and 49% in understanding the methods used to repair buildings damaged by acid rain. In contrast, 46 to 47% of students on average reported high or medium interest in learning more on the topic of genetically modified crops.

Enjoyment of science

Students who enjoy learning science tend to be emotionally attached to learning and perceive learning science as a meaningful activity (Glaser-Zikuda *et al.*, 2003). In turn, these students are more likely to regulate their learning and to solve problems creatively (Pekrun *et al.*, 2002). A consistent finding from PISA 2006 is that in general students enjoy learning science. On average, when learning science, 67% of students reported enjoying acquiring new knowledge and 63% having fun and being interested in learning. As many as 50% of students reported liking reading about science, although only 43% stated that they were happy doing science problems (Figure 3.10). Comparisons across countries should be made with caution as students may not be answering these questions in the same way in different countries. However, it is still useful to consider the absolute percentages of students who reported that they enjoyed learning science. For example, in the Netherlands, Japan, Poland and Austria, and the partner country Liechtenstein, comparatively few students reported enjoying science and in Poland, the Netherlands and Ireland, less than 50% of the students reported having fun learning about science.

In 37 of the countries, students from more advantaged socio-economic backgrounds tended to report more often that they enjoyed learning science than did students from more disadvantaged socio-economic backgrounds (Table 3.22). This relationship is most pronounced in Iceland, Ireland, Denmark, Australia, Germany and France, and in the partner country Liechtenstein. The reverse is true in Mexico and the partner countries Kyrgyzstan and Serbia, where students from more disadvantaged socio-economic backgrounds reported higher enjoyment of science.

Similar to findings for general interest in science, students with an immigrant background reported similar if not higher enjoyment of science than native students (Table 3.23). The most pronounced differences in favour of students with an immigrant background are found in New Zealand, the United Kingdom, Sweden, the Netherlands, Australia, Spain, Ireland, Canada, Denmark and France, and the partner country Qatar.

Figure 3.10
Index of enjoyment of science

A · I enjoy acquiring new knowledge in science.
B · I generally have fun when I am learning science topics.
C · I am interested in learning about science.
D · I like reading about science.
E · I am happy doing science problems.

Percentage of students agreeing or strongly agreeing with the following statements

- ▬ Range between top and bottom quarter of students
- ● Average index
- ▬ Change in science performance per unit of the index
- Statistically significant differences are marked in a darker tone

	A	B	C	D	E
Australia	67	58	61	43	49
Austria	51	58	44	42	39
Belgium	64	61	68	45	53
Canada	73	73	72	54	49
Czech Republic	70	59	62	47	36
Denmark	55	63	63	48	37
Finland	74	68	68	60	51
France	75	73	77	48	43
Germany	52	63	60	42	38
Greece	71	62	69	59	40
Hungary	71	75	72	61	46
Iceland	66	60	56	53	45
Ireland	68	48	64	45	39
Italy	73	61	73	59	57
Japan	58	51	50	36	29
Korea	70	56	47	45	27
Luxembourg	59	67	55	48	42
Mexico	92	94	85	82	60
Netherlands	56	46	46	41	33
New Zealand	71	62	65	43	55
Norway	69	64	62	48	47
Poland	60	44	44	47	37
Portugal	87	73	84	66	52
Slovak Republic	71	70	57	51	34
Spain	63	59	69	45	27
Sweden	61	62	57	49	34
Switzerland	60	67	55	45	42
Turkey	78	79	79	75	53
United Kingdom	69	55	67	38	53
United States	67	62	65	47	41
OECD average	**67**	**63**	**63**	**50**	**43**
Argentina	72	52	79	58	35
Azerbaijan	86	86	89	83	68
Brazil	86	72	86	67	47
Bulgaria	86	80	88	75	47
Chile	75	77	74	56	46
Colombia	90	89	94	85	71
Croatia	78	63	63	68	39
Estonia	78	63	57	50	40
Hong Kong-China	85	81	77	65	54
Indonesia	96	90	89	90	77
Israel	67	58	57	51	42
Jordan	88	89	84	81	79
Kyrgyzstan	92	91	91	88	76
Latvia	81	72	65	56	26
Liechtenstein	48	58	47	37	38
Lithuania	86	72	73	60	39
Macao-China	86	81	79	72	56
Montenegro	80	60	79	68	53
Qatar	77	76	75	69	57
Romania	86	86	79	80	53
Russian Federation	83	68	60	52	51
Serbia	70	64	76	55	41
Slovenia	58	57	52	52	44
Chinese Taipei	79	65	64	62	43
Thailand	94	91	93	85	75
Tunisia	95	87	91	85	76
Uruguay	74	61	76	61	37

Note : Since cross-country comparisons of the percentages should be made with caution, countries have been ordered alphabetically.
Source: OECD PISA 2006 database, Table 3.9.
StatLink ⬛⬛⬛ http://dx.doi.org/10.1787/141846760512

(This was also the case for general interest in science in all listed countries except France and the Netherlands.) The only countries where native students reported higher levels of enjoyment of science are Germany and the partner countries Serbia and Slovenia but the differences here are not very pronounced (effect sizes of less than 0.20).

In the majority of countries there are no gender differences observed for the index of enjoyment of science (Table 3.21). However, there are small differences in favour of males in Japan, the Netherlands, Korea, the United Kingdom and Norway, and the partner countries/economies Chinese Taipei, Hong Kong-China and Macao-China, and in favour of females in the Czech Republic and Finland, along with the partner countries Uruguay and Lithuania.

PISA 2006 results also suggest that enjoyment of learning science as reported by students is positively associated with student performance in science in 48 of the participating countries (including all of the OECD countries). In 35 of the participating countries one unit on the index of enjoyment of science corresponds to a performance difference of at least 20 score points (Table 3.9). There is a particularly strong relationship between students' enjoyment of science and their performance in the United Kingdom, Australia and New Zealand, where an increase of one unit on the index of enjoyment of science is associated with a change in performance of between 40 and 43 score points. These countries also have an above-average mean performance in PISA 2006 science. In contrast, there is a negative association between enjoyment and performance in the partner countries Kyrgyzstan, Serbia, Colombia and Montenegro, although the effect is below -20 score points in all cases.

The importance of doing well in science

Do students value their academic success in science at school? Is it equally important for them to do well in science as it is for them to do well in mathematics and reading? In PISA 2006, all students still following science courses at school were asked to report how important it was for them to do well in school science, mathematics and reading (see Chapter 5, Figure 5.16 for the proportion of students still following science at school). Students could answer "very important", "important", "of little importance" or "not important at all". Figure 3.11 shows the average percentage of students who reported that doing well in each school subject was important or very important to them. With the exception of only six countries, at least 80% of students following science in each country reported that doing well in reading and mathematics was important to them, and this is at least 90% in 25 countries.

However, compared with reading and mathematics, students still following science courses tend to attribute less importance to doing well in science, with at least 80% of students having reported this in only 22 countries, between 70 and 80% in 19 countries, and between 60 and 70% in 15 countries. In the Czech Republic, only 54% of students reported that doing well in science was important or very important to them.

Motivation to learn science because it is useful

At the age of 15 what proportion of students intend to study science in higher education and maybe eventually work in a scientific career? PISA 2006 provides two measures of students' extrinsic motivation to learn science, that is, of whether students are motivated to learn because they perceive science to be useful to them for either their future studies or careers. Two indices (the *index of instrumental motivation to learn science* and the *index of future-oriented motivation to learn science*) are constructed using information provided by students in answering the student questionnaire.[9]

Figure 3.11
Students' perceptions of the importance of doing well
in science, reading and mathematics

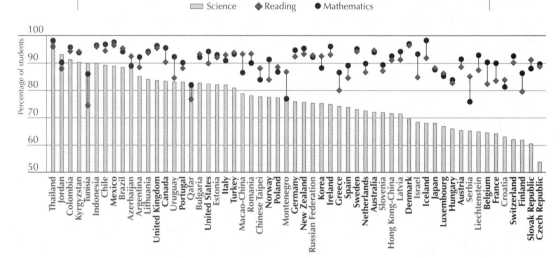

*Average percentage of students still following science courses at school reporting that
doing well in the following subject is important or very important:*

Source: OECD PISA 2006 database, Table 3.7.
StatLink ⌚🖳 http://dx.doi.org/10.1787/141846760512

Instrumental motivation to learn science

Beyond the general interest in science that was reported before, how do 15-year-olds assess the relevance of science to their own life and what role does such external motivation play with regard to their science performance? Given the frequently perceived shortage of students following science in higher education in many countries, it is important that policy makers gain an insight to whether or not this trend is likely to continue. *Instrumental motivation* has been found to be an important predictor for course selection, career choice and performance (Eccles, 1994; Eccles and Wigfield, 1995; Wigfield *et al.,* 1998). In PISA 2006, students' instrumental motivation to learn science was measured by five questions asking students about the importance of learning science for either their future studies or job prospects (see Figure 3.12). These questions referred to students' perceptions of learning school science and therefore not all students responded given that in several countries significant proportions of 15-year-olds no longer study school science (see Chapter 5, Figure 5.16). In general, students perceived science to be useful to them (67% on average across OECD countries) and helpful for their career prospects and future work (between 61 and 63% on average), although a slightly smaller proportion felt that what they learned in science would actually help them get a job or be useful for further studies (56% on average).

In 30 of the countries students from more advantaged socio-economic backgrounds tended to report higher instrumental motivation to learn science compared to students from more disadvantaged socio-economic backgrounds and the effect size is at least 0.20 in 22 countries (Table 3.22). The relationship between socio-economic background and instrumental motivation to learn science is most pronounced in Portugal, Iceland and Finland (an effect size of at least 0.50). In Mexico and three partner countries, students from more disadvantaged socio-economic backgrounds tended to report higher instrumental motivation to learn science, although this relationship is only pronounced in Kyrgyzstan.

Figure 3.12
Index of instrumental motivation to learn science

A I study school science because I know it is useful for me.
B Making an effort in my school science subject(s) is worth it because this will help me in the work I want to do later on.
C Studying my school science subject(s) is worthwhile for me because what I learn will improve my career prospects.
D I will learn many things in my school science subject(s) that will help me get a job.
E What I learn in my school science subject(s) is important for me because I need this for what I want to study later on.

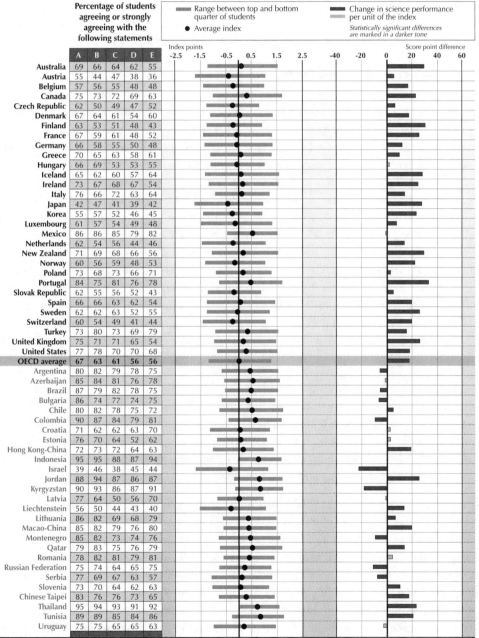

Note : Since cross-country comparisons of the percentages should be made with caution, countries have been ordered alphabetically.
Source: OECD PISA 2006 database, Table 3.10.

StatLink ⬛⬛ http://dx.doi.org/10.1787/141846760512

147

Males and females reported similar levels of instrumental motivation to learn science in the majority of countries. There are only small gender differences on the index of instrumental motivation to learn science in Greece and Austria, and the partner countries/economies Chinese Taipei, Liechtenstein and Hong Kong-China, where males are more motivated than females to learn science. The opposite is true in Ireland and the partner countries Thailand and Jordan (Table 3.21).

Unlike the measures of intrinsic motivation (general interest in science and enjoyment of science) the relationship between the PISA index of instrumental motivation to learn science and science performance is less clear. In 39 of the participating countries (including 28 of the OECD countries) the relationship is positive and a one unit increase in the index of instrumental motivation to learn science corresponds to a performance difference of more than 20 score points in 16 of these countries (Figure 3.12).

Students' future-oriented motivation to learn science

Obviously, the choices that the 15-year-olds assessed in PISA 2006 will make in their future lives cannot be known. However, PISA asked 15-year-olds a series of questions as to their future-oriented motivation to learn science aimed at assessing how many students actually intended to continue their interest in science, either by pursuing further scientific studies or by working in a science-related field. Students were asked what their intentions were with regard to future study or work in science. The motivation behind this was to gain insight into the proportion of students who would use science in their future. On average, according to students' reports on their motivation to use science in the future: 37% would like to work in a career involving science, 31% would like to continue to study science after secondary school, 27% would like to work on science projects as adults and 21% would like to spend life doing advanced science (Figure 3.13). Comparisons across countries should be made with caution as students may not be answering these questions in the same way in different countries. However, for each country concerned it is still useful to consider the absolute percentages of students who reported that they were motivated to use science in the future. Among OECD countries, the percentage of students reporting some form of future-oriented motivation to learn science surpasses 50% only in Mexico and Turkey and in both cases greater percentages of students tended to report more positive attitudes across the measures included in this chapter. The smallest percentages of students reporting future-oriented motivation to learn science are found in Austria, Korea, Japan, the Netherlands, Norway, Switzerland and Sweden and the partner country Liechtenstein.

In 15 of the 20 OECD countries where at least 3% of 15-year-olds have an immigrant background, students with an immigrant background reported higher levels of future-oriented motivation to learn science compared to their native counterparts. The differences in favour of students with an immigrant background are most pronounced in New Zealand, Norway, Sweden, the United Kingdom, Denmark, Ireland, Australia, Canada and Spain, as well as in the partner countries Estonia, Latvia and Qatar (Table 3.23).

OECD data show that the proportion of female students in some of the sciences remains low, while in most countries the majority of students in most other subject areas are now female (OECD, 2007a). For example, on average across OECD countries, only 26% of first university degrees in engineering, manufacturing and construction are awarded to females, for mathematics and computer science it is 29% and for life sciences, physical sciences and agriculture it is 52%. In contrast, for health and welfare or for the humanities and education the proportion of first university-level degrees awarded to females is 72%, and for the social sciences, business, law and services it is 56%. To what extent are those gender differences mirrored in the attitudes of 15-year-olds? According to PISA 2006, similar proportions of male and female 15-year-olds reported that they would like to work in a career involving science, continue to study science after secondary school, work on science projects as adults or spend their life doing advanced science.

Figure 3.13
Index of future-oriented motivation to learn science

A I would like to work in a career involving science.
B I would like to study science after secondary school.
C I would like to work on science projects as an adult.
D I would like to spend my life doing advanced science.

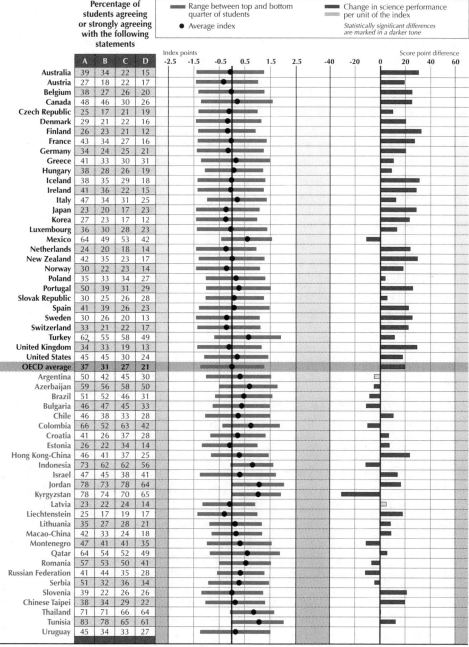

Note : Since cross-country comparisons of the percentages should be made with caution, countries have been ordered alphabetically..
Source: OECD PISA 2006 database, Table 3.11.
StatLink ᵐˢᵖ http://dx.doi.org/10.1787/141846760512

149

However, there are small gender differences in some countries, with more males than females having reported that they were motivated to learn science because they wanted to use it in the future. This is the case in Japan, Greece, Korea, Iceland, the Netherlands, Italy and Germany, as well as in the partner countries/economies Hong Kong-China, Qatar and Macao-China; in the partner economy Chinese Taipei there are pronounced gender differences in favour of males. The Czech Republic is the only participating country where females reported higher levels of future-oriented motivation to learn science (Table 3.21).

How does motivation to pursue science in the future relate to students' performance in the science assessment? Future-oriented motivation to learn science is positively associated with performance in 42 countries and this includes all OECD countries, except Mexico (Figure 3.13). In 20 of the participating countries (including 18 of the OECD countries) a one unit increase in the index of future-oriented motivation to learn science corresponds to a performance difference of more than 20 score points. The strongest relationships between students' motivation to pursue science in the future and performance are in Finland, Iceland and Australia, where an increase of one unit of the index of future-oriented motivation to learn science corresponds to a performance difference of between 30 and 32 score points. There is also a strong positive association with performance in New Zealand, the United Kingdom, Ireland, Japan, France, Portugal, Sweden, Belgium and Canada (between 25 and 29 score points). It is notable that of the 20 countries where the association with performance is strongest (a performance difference of at least 20 score points), 15 perform above the OECD average in the PISA 2006 science assessment. That is, in many high-performing countries future-oriented motivation to learn science is strongly associated with good performance in science.

Do students expect to pursue a scientific career?

In PISA 2006 students also reported their expected career at age 30. From these responses it is possible to identify a group of students who expect to pursue a science-related career. Students' responses were classified using the international standard classification of occupations (ISCO-88[10] [see Annex A10]) and, in accordance with this definition, science-related careers include those that involve a considerable amount of science, but also careers that are beyond the traditional idea of a scientist as someone who works in a laboratory or academic environment. As such, any career that involves tertiary education in a scientific field is considered science-related. Therefore careers like engineer (involving physics), weather forecaster (involving earth science), optician (involving biology and physics) and medical doctor (involving the medical sciences) are all examples of science-related careers.

The percentage of students expecting a science-related career is an indicator of an important educational outcome. In countries where policy makers are concerned about shortages of science professionals in the labour market, analysis of students reporting that they expected science-related careers, in conjunction with other background factors such as the socio-economic background of students and schools, study programmes and gender, could help to identify in which student groups, and to what extent, science orientation may be less pronounced. On average across OECD countries, 25% of students reported that they expected to be in a science-related career at age 30 (Table 3.12). Japan stands out as having only 8% of students expecting a science-related career. This is in stark contrast with the current output of science graduates in Japan, which is around the OECD average (OECD, 2007). In contrast, between 35 and 40% of students report that they expected a science-related career in Portugal, the United States and Canada, and in the partner countries Chile, Jordan and Brazil. This figure is 48% in the partner country Colombia.

In contrast to students' reports on their motivation to use science in the future, PISA 2006 shows small differences between the kinds of jobs males and females expect to have when 30 years old: on average, 27% of females reported that they expected to have a science-related career at age 30, compared to 23.5% of males (Table 3.12). This being said, the nature of the science-related careers that males and females expect may well differ, and PISA does not explore this in greater detail.

Figure 3.14
Students expecting a science-related career and performance in science

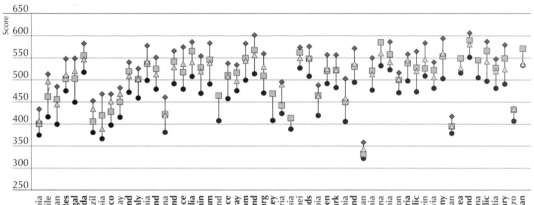

Students who expect a science-related career
- ◆ with at least one parent in a science-related career
- ▣ without a parent in a science-related career

Students who do NOT expect a science-related career
- △ with at least one parent in a science-related career
- ● without a parent in a science-related career

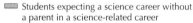 Students expecting a science career without a parent in a science-related career

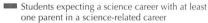 Students expecting a science career with at least one parent in a science-related career

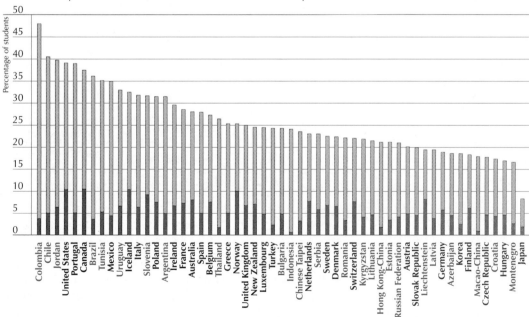

Note: Science performance scores are only shown for groups where there are at least 3% of students.
Source: OECD PISA 2006 database, Table 3.14.

StatLink ⌐🖳🖳 http://dx.doi.org/10.1787/141846760512

To what extent are students' occupational expectations influenced by their parents' occupations? Figure 3.14 shows the percentages of students who expect a science-related career and whether or not those students have parents in a science-related career. This figure shows that, among participating countries, only a minority of students who reported that they expected to be working in a science-related career at age 30 also reported having at least one parent in a science-related career. Similarly, in all but four countries the majority of students with parents in a science-related career reported that they did not expect to pursue a science-related career themselves (Table 3.14). So, students' occupational expectations with regard to occupations in science-related areas seem to be largely uninfluenced by whether or not their parents work in science.

Figure 3.15
Performance in science and proportions of students expecting a science-related career at age 30

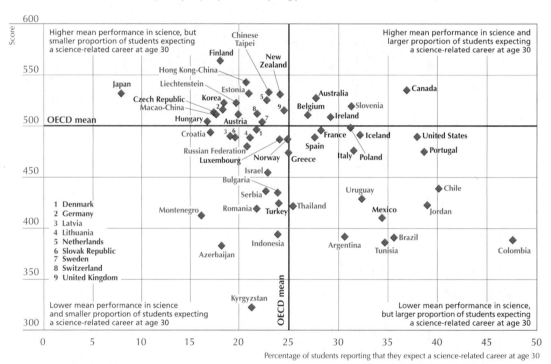

Students expecting a science-related career at age 30 reported one of the following occupations:

Physicists, chemists and related professionals; architects and engineers; physical and engineering science technicians; life science and health professionals (including nursing and midwifery), associate professionals and technicians; safety and quality inspectors; computing professionals.

Source: OECD PISA 2006 database, Tables 3.12 and 2.1c.
StatLink http://dx.doi.org/10.1787/141846760512

Students who reported having a parent in a science-related career did perform better in the PISA 2006 science assessment. This is the case in all countries except Japan. There is a performance difference of at least 60 score points in Turkey, Portugal, France and Luxembourg, as well as in the partner countries Thailand, Chile, Bulgaria and Romania (Table 3.13). Figure 3.14 shows the science performance for four groups of students: those expecting to work in a science-related career at age 30 with at least one parent in a science-related career; those expecting to work in a science-related career at age 30 without a parent in a science-related career; those who do not expect to work in a science-related career at age 30 with at least one parent in a science-related career; and those who do not expect to work in a science-related career at age 30 without a parent in a science-related career. Across countries the best performers among the four groups are students who both expect to work in science themselves and who have at least one parent working in science. Conversely, the lowest performers of the four groups are those students who do not expect to work in science and who do not have a parent working in science. However, in the majority of countries, students who expect to work in a science-related career at age 30 but who do not have a parent working in science perform equally well or better than students who have a parent in a science-related career, but do not expect to work in science themselves.

In the majority of countries with above-average performance in the science assessment less than 25% of students reported that they expected a science-related career at age 30 (Figure 3.15). In Finland, Japan, Korea, Germany and the Czech Republic, and in the partner economy Macao-China, less than 20% of 15-year-olds expected a science-related career at age 30. Conversely, in other countries performing above the OECD average in the science assessment, comparatively high proportions of students reported that they expected a science-related career at age 30. These countries include Canada, Australia, Belgium and Ireland, and the partner country Slovenia.

Science-related activities

Another measure of students' interest in science is the degree to which they pursue science-related activities in their free time.[11] Across countries only a minority of students reported that they engaged regularly in science-related activities (Figure 3.16). On average, students were more likely to report that they regularly watch television programmes on science or read science magazines or articles in newspapers on science (21 and 20%, respectively) than they visit websites on science, borrow books on science and listen to radio programmes on science (13, 8 and 7%, respectively). The vast majority of students (96%) reported that they did do not regularly attend a science club and this was true of almost all students in nine OECD countries. It therefore seems that print and television media have the most influence over students in communicating information about science beyond the classroom. Additionally, in the majority of OECD countries a higher proportion of students reported that they regularly visited websites about science topics than borrowed or bought books about science topics, notably in Norway, Sweden, the United Kingdom, Australia, Switzerland, Germany, the Netherlands, Spain, Denmark, Italy, Canada, the United States and Austria.

Students' socio-economic background is strongly associated with engagement in science-related activities across the majority of countries (Table 3.22). In 38 of the countries the effect size is at least 0.20 and the association is strongest in France, Germany, Korea, Sweden and the United Kingdom, as well as in the partner countries/economies Indonesia and Chinese Taipei (an effect size of at least 0.50). In all these countries, students from less advantaged socio-economic backgrounds are far less likely to report that they engage regularly in activities such as reading science magazines or articles in newspapers on science.

Students with an immigrant background reported that they engaged in science-related activities as often as native students, if not more frequently. Differences in favour of students with an immigrant background are largest in the United Kingdom, Spain, New Zealand, Ireland, Sweden, Australia, Norway, Canada, the United States, the Netherlands and France, and in the partner countries Liechtenstein and Latvia (Table 3.23).

There are small gender differences observed on the index of participation in science-related activities in 13 countries (Table 3.21). In Iceland, Japan, the Netherlands, Norway, Korea, the United States, Sweden, Italy and the United Kingdom, as well as the partner countries/economies Qatar, Chinese Taipei, Hong Kong-China and Macao-China, males are more likely than females to report that they engage in science-related activities, such as reading science magazines or science articles in newspapers.

153

Figure 3.16
Index of science-related activities

- **A** Watch TV programmes about science
- **B** Read science magazines or science articles in newspapers
- **C** Visit web sites about science topics
- **D** Borrow or buy books on science topics
- **E** Listen to radio programmes about advances in science
- **F** Attend a science club

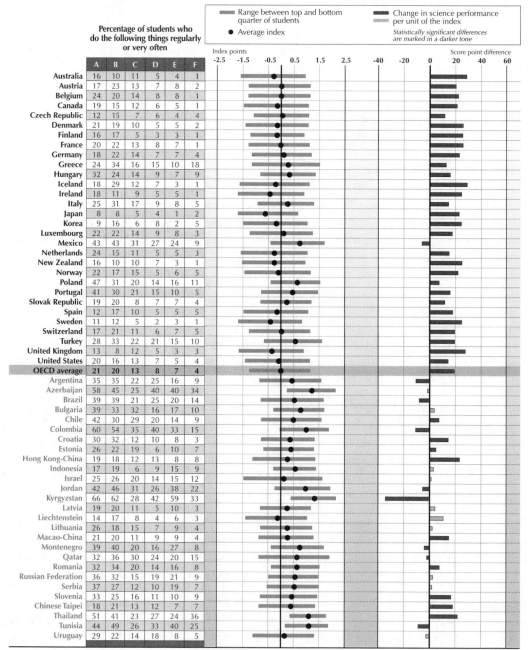

	A	B	C	D	E	F
Australia	16	10	11	5	4	1
Austria	17	23	13	7	8	2
Belgium	24	20	14	8	8	1
Canada	19	15	12	6	5	1
Czech Republic	12	15	7	6	4	4
Denmark	21	19	10	5	5	2
Finland	16	17	5	3	3	1
France	20	22	13	8	7	1
Germany	18	22	14	7	7	4
Greece	24	34	16	15	10	18
Hungary	32	24	14	9	7	9
Iceland	18	29	12	7	3	1
Ireland	18	11	9	5	5	1
Italy	25	31	17	9	8	5
Japan	8	8	5	4	1	2
Korea	9	16	6	8	2	5
Luxembourg	22	22	14	9	8	3
Mexico	43	43	31	27	24	9
Netherlands	24	15	11	5	5	3
New Zealand	16	10	10	7	3	1
Norway	22	17	15	5	6	5
Poland	47	31	20	14	16	11
Portugal	41	30	21	15	10	5
Slovak Republic	19	20	8	7	7	4
Spain	12	17	10	5	5	5
Sweden	11	12	5	2	3	1
Switzerland	17	21	11	6	7	5
Turkey	28	33	22	21	15	10
United Kingdom	13	8	12	5	3	3
United States	20	16	13	7	5	4
OECD average	21	20	13	8	7	4
Argentina	35	35	22	25	16	9
Azerbaijan	58	45	25	40	40	34
Brazil	39	39	21	25	20	14
Bulgaria	39	33	32	16	17	10
Chile	42	30	29	20	14	9
Colombia	60	54	35	40	33	15
Croatia	30	32	12	10	8	3
Estonia	26	22	19	6	10	7
Hong Kong-China	19	18	12	13	8	8
Indonesia	17	19	6	9	15	9
Israel	25	26	20	14	15	12
Jordan	42	46	31	26	38	22
Kyrgyzstan	66	62	28	42	59	33
Latvia	19	20	11	5	10	3
Liechtenstein	14	17	8	4	6	3
Lithuania	26	18	15	7	9	4
Macao-China	21	20	11	9	9	4
Montenegro	39	40	20	16	27	8
Qatar	32	36	30	24	20	15
Romania	32	34	20	14	16	8
Russian Federation	36	32	15	19	21	9
Serbia	37	27	12	10	19	7
Slovenia	33	25	16	11	10	9
Chinese Taipei	18	21	13	12	7	7
Thailand	51	41	23	27	24	36
Tunisia	44	49	26	33	40	25
Uruguay	29	22	14	18	8	5

Note : Since cross-country comparisons of the percentages should be made with caution, countries have been ordered alphabetically.
Source: OECD PISA 2006 database, Table 3.15.
StatLink ⌐⌐⌐ http://dx.doi.org/10.1787/141846760512

In 29 of the OECD countries and in nine of the partner countries there is a positive relationship between engaging in science-related activities and science performance (an increase of one unit on the index of science-related activities corresponds to a performance difference of 19 score points on average) and this is at least 20 score points in 18 of the participating countries (Figure 3.16).

DO STUDENTS FEEL RESPONSIBLE TOWARDS RESOURCES AND THE ENVIRONMENT?

Scientific literacy encompasses the understanding and abilities that empower individuals to make personal decisions and appropriately participate in the formulation of public policies that impact their lives. Examples include public policies involving personal health, natural hazards and the environment. PISA 2006 focused on students' knowledge of environmental issues and their attitudes towards the environment to further understanding of this aspect of students' *scientific literacy*.

Awareness of environmental issues

An individual's attitudes and behaviours with regard to the environment are likely the result of multiple factors including knowledge, awareness, attitudes and social expectations (Bybee, 2005). In PISA 2006 information was collected on students' awareness of a selection of environmental issues.[12] The average level of awareness varies significantly from issue to issue (Figure 3.17). Cross-national analysis suggests that the following comparisons of how aware students are of selected environmental issues can be made across countries. The majority of students (73% on average) reported being aware of the consequences of clearing forest for other land use and this was the case for 80% or more of students in Poland, Turkey, Ireland, Canada, Australia, the Netherlands, Austria and Germany, as well as in the partner countries/economies Hong Kong-China, Chinese Taipei, Macao-China, Latvia, the Russian Federation Estonia, Lithuania and Liechtenstein. Conversely, only between 42 and 50% of students reported being aware of these consequences in Korea, Sweden and Greece. On average, around 60% of students reported being aware of acid rain and the increase of greenhouse gases in the atmosphere, but there are some countries where students reported being less aware of these issues, notably in France, Iceland, Mexico, Switzerland and Turkey, and the partner countries Argentina, Azerbaijan, Chile, Indonesia, Israel, Kyrgyzstan, Qatar, Romania and Tunisia, where there were fewer than 40% of students reporting awareness of one or both of these issues. In contrast, at least 80% of students reported being aware of acid rain in Greece, Ireland and Poland, and in the partner countries/economies Hong Kong-China, Croatia, Chinese Taipei and Slovenia. Nuclear waste is an environmental issue that fewer students reported awareness in general among countries, with an average of 53% of students having reported that they were familiar with this or knew something about it. The highest levels of awareness of nuclear waste were reported in Turkey, the Czech Republic and Austria, as well as in the partner countries Croatia and Slovenia, where at least 65% of students are aware of this. A minority of students reported being aware of the use of genetically modified organisms (GMOs): on average 35% of students reported being aware of GMOs and this is over 50% in Italy and France, as well as in the partner countries Croatia, Thailand, Chinese Taipei and Slovenia (Figure 3.17).

In all countries students from more advantaged socio-economic backgrounds reported higher levels of awareness of environmental issues. Indeed, these differences are pronounced with effect sizes of at least 0.50 in 46 countries (Table 3.22). The relationship with socio-economic background is particularly pronounced in France, Luxembourg, Portugal and Belgium, and the partner economy Chile (effect size of at least 0.80). PISA 2006 results strongly suggest that students from more disadvantaged socio-economic backgrounds are less aware of environmental issues such as acid rain and nuclear waste.

Figure 3.17
Index of students' awareness of environmental issues

A The consequences of clearing forests for other land use
B Acid rain
C The increase of greenhouse gases in the atmosphere
D Nuclear waste
E Use of genetically modified organisms (GMO)

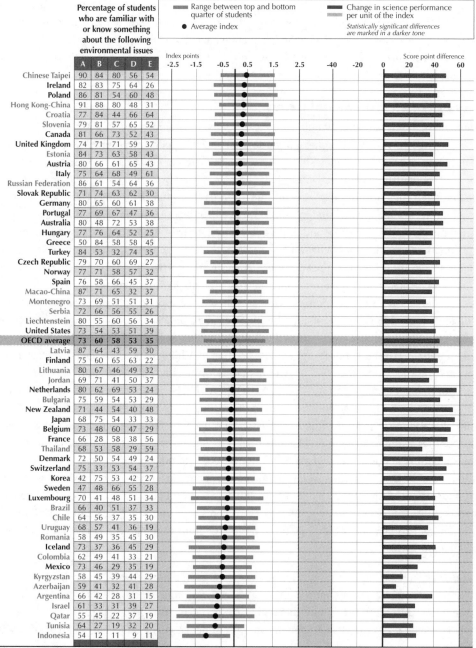

Source: OECD PISA 2006 database, Table 3.16.
StatLink http://dx.doi.org/10.1787/141846760512

The data also suggest that levels of awareness of environmental issues are implicitly linked with students' scientific knowledge. There is a strong association between students' level of environmental awareness and science performance in all participating countries. Among the attitudinal indices presented in this chapter, the index of awareness of environmental issues has the strongest association with science performance. On average an increase of one unit on the index of students' awareness of environmental issues is associated with a performance difference of 44 score points on the PISA science scale and this is at least 20 score points in 54 of the participating countries (including all of the OECD countries). The relationship is particularly strong in the Netherlands, Japan, New Zealand and Belgium, and the partner economy Hong Kong-China. It is worth noting that all these countries performed above average in the PISA 2006 science assessment (Figure 3.18). This suggests not just that students with a strong understanding of science tended to report being aware of environmental threats, but also that relative ignorance in science may cause these issues to go unnoticed by many citizens. It is also true that in the majority of countries with a country mean score in science of less than 450 score points students reported that they were less aware of environmental issues (Figure 3.18).

Figure 3.18
Performance in science and awareness of environmental issues

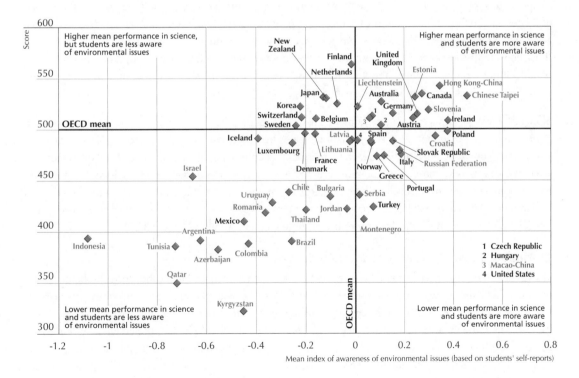

Source: OECD PISA 2006 database, Tables 3.16 and 2.1c.
StatLink ⟦⟧ http://dx.doi.org/10.1787/141846760512

Students' level of concern for environmental issues

How concerned are students about environmental issues? Students were asked to report whether or not a series of selected environmental issues were of serious concern to them and/or other people in their country.[13] The following comparisons across countries reporting how concerned students are about environmental issues should be interpreted with caution, since students in different countries may not answer these questions in exactly the same way. Further, when interpreting the results in Figure 3.19, it is important to remember that students who did not report that a selected environmental issue is of concern in their country may nevertheless have been concerned about this issue in general. In fact, the results show that students are globally concerned about environmental issues: for each of the selected six issues less than 5% of students on average in OECD countries reported that it was not a concern to anyone (see the PISA 2006 database). On average, 92% of students reported that air pollution was a serious concern for them personally or for other people in their country; this is at least 90% of students in 46 of the participating countries. Between 82 and 84% of students on average reported that they believed the extinction of plants and animals, the clearing of forests for other land use and energy shortages were serious environmental concerns, and this is over 90% in Hungary, Japan, Korea, Portugal, Spain and Turkey, as well as in the partner countries/economies Argentina, Brazil, Bulgaria, Chile, Chinese Taipei, Colombia, Croatia, Indonesia, the Russian Federation and Uruguay. Both nuclear waste and water shortages are also of serious concern for students on average (78 and 76% reported this respectively), although water shortages are of serious concern for at least 90% of students in Korea, Mexico, Portugal, Spain, Australia and Turkey, as well as in the partner countries/economies Chile, Colombia, Chinese Taipei, Indonesia, Argentina, Brazil, Jordan, Serbia, Thailand, Uruguay, Bulgaria, Israel, Croatia and the Russian Federation (Figure 3.19).

In stark contrast to students' awareness of environmental issues, students' level of concern for environmental issues is not strongly associated with socio-economic background (effect sizes only surpass 0.20 in France and Greece, and the partner economy Chinese Taipei). In the Czech Republic, students from less favourable socio-economic backgrounds reported greater concern for environmental issues (Table 3.22). PISA 2006 thus shows that students from comparatively more disadvantaged socio-economic backgrounds are often equally, if not more, concerned about environmental issues, even if they are less confident in explaining these issues and they perform lower on related tasks.

Students' level of concern for environmental issues does not have a strong association with science performance. In 35 countries this association is positive (between 3 and 24 score points change in performance on the science scale for each increase of one unit of the index of students' level of concern for environmental issues) and in four countries it is negative (between -4 and -10 score points). The strongest association between increased levels of concern for environmental issues and science performance (a performance difference of at least 20 score points on the PISA science scale) is found in France, Mexico and Greece, as well as in the partner countries Brazil, Argentina and Thailand (Figure 3.19).

Optimism regarding environmental issues

Taking the same set of environmental issues, PISA 2006 asked students whether they thought the problems associated with these issues would improve or get worse over the next 20 years.[14] Similar to the index of levels of concern for environmental issues, comparisons across countries of students' reports on how optimistic they are regarding the evolution of selected environmental issues should be interpreted with caution, since students in different countries may not answer questions on these issues in exactly the same way. Across countries only a minority of students reported that they believed the environmental issues would improve (on average between 13 and 21% of students), with most students being pessimistic about the clearing of forests for other land use (62%) and air pollution (64%) (Figure 3.20; see also the PISA 2006 database).

158

Figure 3.19
Index of students' level of concern for environmental issues

A	Air pollution
B	Extinction of plants and animals
C	Clearing of forests for other land use
D	Energy shortages
E	Nuclear waste
F	Water shortages

Range between top and bottom quarter of students
● Average index

Change in science performance per unit of the index
Statistically significant differences are marked in a darker tone

Percentage of students who believe the following environmental issues to be a serious concern for themselves or other people in their country

	A	B	C	D	E	F
Australia	88	85	87	81	75	92
Austria	95	87	82	78	71	68
Belgium	95	82	76	80	83	68
Canada	93	85	89	80	79	76
Czech Republic	98	84	85	77	85	66
Denmark	86	78	78	75	73	67
Finland	88	74	76	67	74	45
France	95	82	81	80	84	78
Germany	94	87	84	86	85	74
Greece	96	86	84	88	80	87
Hungary	97	94	91	93	84	87
Iceland	84	69	67	62	52	49
Ireland	89	74	75	79	74	67
Italy	97	79	78	86	72	80
Japan	95	92	92	92	88	86
Korea	98	93	93	97	89	97
Luxembourg	92	81	78	78	74	73
Mexico	97	95	94	89	84	96
Netherlands	93	85	75	83	82	66
New Zealand	82	82	81	84	60	80
Norway	83	78	74	64	66	55
Poland	93	83	88	89	72	87
Portugal	97	94	95	94	83	96
Slovak Republic	97	90	83	86	80	83
Spain	97	95	93	94	88	95
Sweden	83	76	74	67	74	52
Switzerland	93	84	80	75	78	66
Turkey	97	94	95	94	92	92
United Kingdom	89	77	74	84	79	76
United States	91	85	87	84	83	81
OECD average	**92**	**84**	**83**	**82**	**78**	**76**
Argentina	97	91	90	91	84	92
Azerbaijan	95	86	84	89	79	88
Brazil	97	93	93	91	87	92
Bulgaria	97	91	92	91	86	91
Chile	98	95	94	96	85	95
Colombia	94	93	94	95	85	95
Croatia	96	93	91	92	87	90
Estonia	96	88	91	86	69	75
Hong Kong-China	95	81	75	86	61	78
Indonesia	95	90	91	93	75	92
Israel	92	86	80	83	73	91
Jordan	94	84	83	90	70	92
Kyrgyzstan	87	82	80	83	75	81
Latvia	94	77	87	82	75	75
Liechtenstein	93	86	79	72	69	60
Lithuania	96	91	91	87	83	80
Macao-China	93	81	81	87	63	88
Montenegro	95	88	86	89	77	89
Qatar	91	77	70	82	69	83
Romania	88	83	84	81	75	82
Russian Federation	95	92	93	91	89	90
Serbia	95	88	89	91	81	92
Slovenia	94	89	86	86	84	86
Chinese Taipei	95	91	92	94	91	94
Thailand	93	88	86	91	73	91
Tunisia	92	75	76	83	56	87
Uruguay	96	91	91	93	75	91

Index points: -2.5 -1.5 -0.5 0.5 1.5 2.5

Score point difference: -40 -20 0 20 40 60

Note : Since cross-country comparisons of the percentages should be made with caution, countries have been ordered alphabetically.
Source: OECD PISA 2006 database, Table 3.17.

StatLink http://dx.doi.org/10.1787/141846760512

159

Figure 3.20

Index of students' optimism regarding environmental issues

A Energy shortages
B Water shortages
C Air pollution
D Nuclear waste
E Extinction of plants and animals
F Clearing of forests for other land use

Percentage of students who believe the problems associated with the environmental issues below will improve over the next 20 years

■ Range between top and bottom quarter of students
● Average index
■ Change in science performance per unit of the index
▨ Statistically significant differences are marked in a darker tone

	A	B	C	D	E	F
Australia	21	18	14	12	12	11
Austria	16	10	10	8	7	5
Belgium	14	13	12	14	10	11
Canada	17	12	13	13	10	10
Czech Republic	33	20	17	14	13	11
Denmark	19	16	13	15	10	10
Finland	14	16	9	8	11	6
France	14	13	11	14	12	12
Germany	16	13	14	13	8	7
Greece	26	21	19	15	14	14
Hungary	13	18	13	13	12	12
Iceland	21	20	13	20	13	11
Ireland	26	27	20	17	16	15
Italy	18	17	14	16	14	12
Japan	22	20	20	17	16	16
Korea	49	23	29	32	22	29
Luxembourg	15	11	13	10	10	8
Mexico	12	16	17	10	20	17
Netherlands	19	23	18	17	13	15
New Zealand	20	14	10	10	12	8
Norway	33	28	30	25	19	15
Poland	18	18	22	23	20	17
Portugal	18	14	18	15	16	15
Slovak Republic	25	19	11	11	12	9
Spain	28	24	17	15	19	15
Sweden	25	25	19	23	14	12
Switzerland	17	13	12	11	10	8
Turkey	23	22	23	16	18	18
United Kingdom	18	22	17	13	13	13
United States	26	22	21	17	18	15
OECD average	**21**	**18**	**16**	**15**	**14**	**13**
Argentina	28	24	22	16	22	18
Azerbaijan	42	43	37	26	32	43
Brazil	23	20	21	18	22	18
Bulgaria	41	43	39	32	30	32
Chile	33	31	22	14	22	19
Colombia	38	30	28	19	28	23
Croatia	21	12	13	12	13	12
Estonia	21	20	12	17	13	11
Hong Kong-China	24	27	23	20	23	18
Indonesia	30	27	24	16	20	16
Israel	33	40	30	21	27	23
Jordan	31	32	36	21	26	25
Kyrgyzstan	44	45	36	31	37	40
Latvia	34	24	15	16	15	10
Liechtenstein	16	8	12	7	7	6
Lithuania	32	26	19	17	17	16
Macao-China	26	27	28	21	26	25
Montenegro	37	41	30	23	30	28
Qatar	41	45	44	30	36	36
Romania	33	35	33	23	22	24
Russian Federation	45	37	26	25	25	20
Serbia	32	31	24	18	23	21
Slovenia	20	12	12	12	11	10
Chinese Taipei	18	19	19	16	21	21
Thailand	36	41	32	25	28	34
Tunisia	29	32	31	20	30	28
Uruguay	18	21	21	12	20	17

Index points: -2.5 -1.5 -0.5 0.5 1.5 2.5

Score point difference: -40 -20 0 20 40 60

Note : Since cross-country comparisons of the percentages should be made with caution, countries have been ordered alphabetically.
Source: OECD PISA 2006 database, Table 3.18.
StatLink ⌖ http://dx.doi.org/10.1787/141846760512

There is a weak to moderate negative association between optimism regarding environmental issues and science performance in all OECD countries (-18 score points on average for a one unit increase on the index and varying between -2 and -36 score points), that is, the more students know about science, the less optimistic they tend to be about environmental issues being successfully addressed. This negative association is at least -20 score points in 25 of the participating countries and is strongest in France and Italy, and in the partner countries Chile, Tunisia and Argentina (between -31 and -36 score points). This suggests that lower performers in the PISA science assessment tend to be more complacent about environmental issues.

In a number of countries students from comparatively more disadvantaged socio-economic backgrounds are more optimistic about how selected environmental issues will evolve over the next 20 years. This is most pronounced in France (-0.52 effect size) and effect sizes are at least -0.20 in 26 countries (Table 3.22).

Responsibility for sustainable development

The PISA 2006 results show that 15-year-old students tend to have strong concern for environmental issues and are somewhat pessimistic about how the associated problems will evolve over time. To what extent do students link societies' actions with these environmental issues and feel responsibility for these issues? To gain a sense of students' responsibility for sustainable development students were asked whether or not they agreed with a selection of seven possible sustainable development policies. Students who responded that they either agreed or strongly agreed were classified as expressing a sense of responsibility for sustainable development.[15] The following comparisons across countries reporting on students' responsibility for sustainable development should be interpreted with caution, since students in different countries may not interpret these questions in exactly the same way. Over 90% of students on average reported supporting policies on the safe disposal of dangerous waste materials, the protection of the habitats of endangered species and making car use contingent upon the regular checks on their emissions, and 82% reported supporting policies to reduce the use of plastic packaging (Figure 3.21). Just under 80% of students expressed support for policies to produce energy from renewable sources, even if this were to increase the cost; indeed, over 90% of students reported supporting this in Portugal and Korea, and in the partner economies Macao-China, Chinese Taipei and Hong Kong-China. Fewer students (69% on average) reported being disturbed by the unnecessary use of electrical appliances and favouring laws to regulate factory emissions even if this would increase the price of products.

A stronger sense of responsibility for sustainable development is associated with higher science performance in all OECD countries (on average an increase of one unit on the index represents a performance difference of 27 score points). That is, students demonstrating higher science competencies in PISA report a stronger sense of responsibility for sustainable development. This association is at least 20 score points in 41 countries and is strongest (at least 30 score points) in the United Kingdom, Greece, France, Ireland, Australia, New Zealand and Iceland (Figure 3.21).

Similar to students' awareness of environmental issues, students from more advantaged socio-economic backgrounds tended to report higher responsibility for sustainable development, although the association is not positive for all countries and is weaker. It is most pronounced in France, the United Kingdom and the partner country Romania (Table 3.22).

PISA 2006 results suggest, therefore, that those students who demonstrate a deeper understanding of science are more aware of environmental issues and have a stronger sense of responsibility for sustainable development. These higher performing students are, however, more pessimistic about how selected environmental issues will evolve over the next 20 years.

Figure 3.21
Index of students' responsibility for sustainable development

A	Industries should be required to prove that they safely dispose of dangerous waste materials.
B	I am in favour of having laws that protect the habitats of endangered species.
C	It is important to carry out regular checks on the emissions from cars as a condition of their use.
D	To reduce waste, the use of plastic packaging should be kept to a minimum.
E	Electricity should be produced from renewable sources as much as possible, even if this increases the cost.
F	It disturbs me when energy is wasted through the unnecessary use of electrical appliances.
G	I am in favour of having laws that regulate factory emissions even if this would increase the price of products.

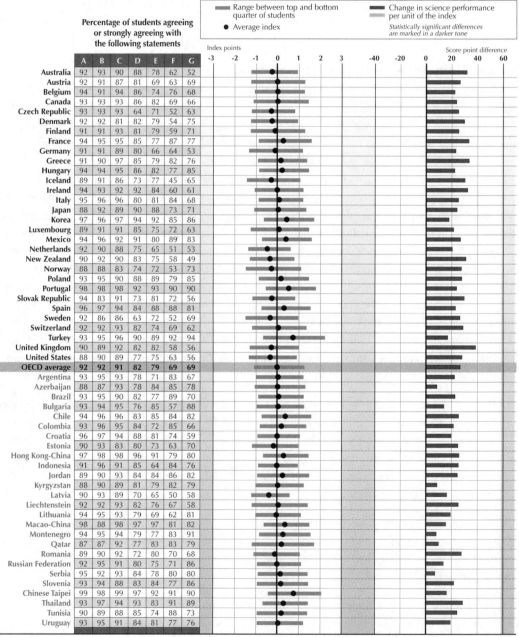

Percentage of students agreeing or strongly agreeing with the following statements

	A	B	C	D	E	F	G
Australia	92	93	90	88	78	62	52
Austria	92	91	87	81	69	63	69
Belgium	94	91	94	86	74	76	68
Canada	93	93	93	86	82	69	66
Czech Republic	93	93	93	64	71	52	63
Denmark	92	92	81	82	79	54	75
Finland	91	91	93	81	79	59	71
France	94	95	95	85	77	87	77
Germany	91	91	89	80	66	64	53
Greece	91	90	97	85	79	82	76
Hungary	94	94	95	86	82	77	85
Iceland	89	91	86	73	77	45	65
Ireland	94	93	92	92	84	60	61
Italy	95	96	96	80	81	84	68
Japan	88	92	89	90	88	73	71
Korea	97	96	97	94	92	85	86
Luxembourg	89	91	91	85	75	72	63
Mexico	94	96	92	91	80	89	83
Netherlands	92	90	88	75	65	51	53
New Zealand	90	92	90	83	75	58	49
Norway	88	88	83	74	72	53	73
Poland	93	95	90	88	89	79	85
Portugal	98	98	98	92	93	90	90
Slovak Republic	94	83	91	73	81	72	56
Spain	96	97	94	84	88	88	81
Sweden	92	86	86	63	72	52	69
Switzerland	92	92	93	82	74	69	62
Turkey	93	95	96	90	89	92	94
United Kingdom	90	89	92	82	82	58	56
United States	88	90	89	77	75	63	56
OECD average	**92**	**92**	**91**	**82**	**79**	**69**	**69**
Argentina	93	95	93	78	71	83	67
Azerbaijan	88	87	93	78	84	85	78
Brazil	93	95	90	82	77	89	70
Bulgaria	93	94	95	76	85	57	88
Chile	94	96	96	83	85	84	82
Colombia	93	96	95	84	72	85	66
Croatia	96	97	94	88	81	74	59
Estonia	90	93	83	80	73	63	70
Hong Kong-China	97	98	98	96	91	79	80
Indonesia	91	96	91	85	64	84	76
Jordan	89	90	93	84	84	86	82
Kyrgyzstan	88	90	89	81	79	82	79
Latvia	90	93	89	70	65	50	58
Liechtenstein	92	92	93	82	76	67	58
Lithuania	94	95	93	79	69	62	81
Macao-China	98	88	98	97	97	81	82
Montenegro	94	95	94	79	77	83	91
Qatar	87	87	92	77	83	83	79
Romania	89	90	92	72	80	70	68
Russian Federation	92	95	91	80	75	71	86
Serbia	95	92	93	84	78	80	80
Slovenia	93	94	88	83	84	77	86
Chinese Taipei	99	98	99	97	92	91	90
Thailand	93	97	94	93	83	91	89
Tunisia	90	89	88	85	74	88	73
Uruguay	93	95	91	84	81	77	76

Range between top and bottom quarter of students
● Average index
Change in science performance per unit of the index
Statistically significant differences are marked in a darker tone

Note : Since cross-country comparisons of the percentages should be made with caution, countries have been ordered alphabetically.
Source: OECD PISA 2006 database, Table 3.19.
StatLink ᵃˢᵖ http://dx.doi.org/10.1787/141846760512

Gender differences in responsibility towards resources and the environment

Males and females reported similar attitudes toward the environment, although there were some gender differences among participating countries (Table 3.21). In general, the results show that males reported being more aware about environmental issues, with significant differences in 12 OECD countries, although females reported being more environmentally aware in the partner countries Jordan, Thailand and Kyrgyzstan. The index of awareness of environmental issues has the strongest relationship with science performance among the attitudinal measures in PISA 2006 and is associated with better performance in all participating countries.

Regarding the outlook on how selected environmental issues will evolve over the next 20 years, males reported being more optimistic than females in 12 OECD countries and in 3 partner countries/economies, but again the gender differences tend to be small. In contrast, females reported stronger levels of concern for environmental issues in 16 OECD countries and in 8 partner countries/economies. Higher values on the index of optimism regarding environmental issues are linked with lower science performance. Males in Finland, Norway, the United Kingdom and Germany reported being both more aware of and more optimistic about environmental issues.

Similarly, there are small gender differences in students' responsibility for sustainable development in nine countries and in all cases females reported high levels of responsibility (Finland, Iceland, Denmark, Norway, Sweden, Canada, Australia and New Zealand and the partner country Thailand).

OVERVIEW OF GENDER DIFFERENCES IN SCIENCE PERFORMANCE AND IN ATTITUDES TOWARDS SCIENCE

The PISA 2006 data suggest that students who demonstrate strong scientific skills and the required competencies to pursue more advanced scientific studies tended not to report aspiring to science careers unless they also valued or enjoyed science. It is therefore important that both males and females have positive values towards science and enjoy it. For a number of participating countries the results suggest that there are no entrenched gender differences in either science performance or attitudes towards science (effect sizes of gender differences are presented in Table 3.21). In Portugal and the partner countries Azerbaijan, Israel and Montenegro there are no significant gender differences at all. In Ireland, Mexico, Poland, the Slovak Republic and Spain, as well as in the partner countries Argentina, Brazil, Colombia, Croatia, Estonia, Indonesia, Romania, the Russian Federation, Serbia, Tunisia and Uruguay, there are moderate gender differences in a maximum of two of the measures, be it performance or attitudinal.

In several countries, however, it is clear that although there are no performance differences between males and females in the science assessment, there are important differences in the attitudes of male and female 15-year-olds. When choosing among an array of subjects what they would like to continue to study in higher education, students are likely to have various motives. Subjects may be useful because they open up career opportunities in areas that interest students or students may just prefer to study subjects that they enjoy learning. In such cases, even moderate differences would be enough to deter students from choosing to pursue the subject further. Gender differences are most prominent in Germany, Iceland, Japan, Korea, the Netherlands and the United Kingdom, and in the partner countries/economies Chinese Taipei, Hong Kong-China and Macao-China where males reported higher values on at least five of the attitudinal measures (although in Iceland, Germany and the Netherlands females reported either higher concern for environmental issues or responsibility for sustainable development). To a lesser extent this is the case also in France, Italy, and the United States. In Austria, Greece, Iceland, Korea and Norway, females have more negative attitudes on at least three of the attitudinal measures, despite the fact that they perform better on the *identifying scientific issues* scale. It is also worthy of note that the majority of these countries perform above average on the science assessment. Conversely, in the partner countries Jordan and Thailand, females both perform better on the science assessment and reported more positive science attitudes (Table 3.21).

163

IMPLICATIONS FOR POLICY

In addition to assessing how students have acquired scientific and technological knowledge and can apply this for personal, social and global benefit, PISA has devoted significant attention to obtaining data on students' attitudes to and engagement with science, both as part of the PISA 2006 assessment and through separate questionnaires. In PISA, attitudes are seen as a key component of an individual's science competency and include an individual's values, motivational orientations and sense of self-efficacy.

In interpreting the results, policy makers should, above all, note that students generally reported very positive attitudes towards science, a finding on which teaching and learning in schools can build. The large majority of 15-year-olds reported that they recognised the important role that science plays in the world and that science was therefore significant in interpreting what goes on around them. Most students expressed a broad interest in science, most considered it relevant at some level to their own lives and the majority thought that they are able generally to master the science problems they are given at school. On the other hand, in certain more specific respects, attitudes towards science are weaker. Only about one-half of students are confident of their ability to interpret certain kinds of scientific evidence and a minority see science as something they will take up in their own future careers. Most students, while concerned about scientific issues such as preserving the environment and in favour of taking measures to tackle such problems, were pessimistic about the prospects that things will improve in these areas, and the more scientific knowledge students have acquired, the more pessimistic they reported being. Significantly fewer believe that science can solve social problems than believe in its ability to bring technological improvements.

Responding to these findings, there are several reasons why governments may wish to develop more positive attitudes to science among young people. One is to enable countries to strengthen their base of science personnel: students who feel positive about science are more likely to be motivated to pursue a scientific career and to develop strong skills in the subject. Being interested in science, enjoying science and having a strong self-concept in science are all positively associated with science performance, albeit moderately. Similarly important is to enable those students who will not end up in science-related careers to engage in science in their lives, in a world where science forms an important part of people's lives and where science competencies help people to achieve their goals. Related to this is the need to ensure that adults as citizens take a responsible attitude towards science in society, supporting scientific endeavour where it can help fulfil social and economic goals, and using science in responding to public issues such as risks to the environment.

The findings summarised above suggest that while students reported positive attitudes to science at a fairly general level, there is much that can be done to encourage them to take a closer interest and to strengthen these attitudes where they are weak. The PISA 2006 results can help point to where these weaknesses exist. Furthermore, they show which attitudes display the most variability between stronger and weaker students, between students of more advantaged and more disadvantaged socio-economic background, between males and females and, for some indicators, across countries. In terms of where the greatest weaknesses in attitudes exist, student self-reports suggest that:

- Students tended to report a stronger belief in the technological potential of science than in its capacity to make social improvements. This suggests both that students exercise critical thinking, but also that in some cases more could be done to demonstrate potential social benefits, with the school curriculum showing the wider potential of scientific advance.

- While students were positive in answering questions about enjoyment of science overall, only 43% on average said that they enjoy doing science problems. The more specific the questions, the lower the interest and enjoyment reported. This suggests that, while students have generally positive feelings about science and recognise its importance, this is not always reflected in their experiences of doing science. This poses a challenge to schools to make science itself more engaging.

- Only a minority of students reported an interest in studying or working in science in the future. This suggests that schools need to more effectively promote scientific careers and create pathways that encourage more students to continue studying the subject.

- Science-related activities outside school attract only a small minority of students on a regular basis. Even regularly watching a science-related television programme, the most commonly cited activity, attracts only one student in five, according to their reports. This suggests that engagement in science could be improved if students could be encouraged to take a broader view of science than just something you do at school.

- Students reported high concern for environmental issues and a strong desire to address them, but reported generally being pessimistic about things improving in this sphere. Despite a general interest in these issues, students know most about certain high profile areas, and for example only about half as many students express awareness of issues related to genetically modified crops as with that of deforestation. Schools have an important task in giving a rounded knowledge of scientific issues beyond those with greatest attention from the media.

The above observations relate to international averages of the attitudes of all students. But in what respects are some students less engaged in science than others, suggesting the need to target interventions on groups with weaker attitudes?

Virtually all of the attitudes discussed in this chapter are, to some degree, associated with student performance in science:

- Typically, more positive attitudes on each of the factors measured are associated with performance differences of around 20 to 30 points more on the PISA science assessment. The greatest difference in this respect was for awareness of environmental issues, with a difference of 44 points, and self-efficacy, with a difference of 38.

- The quarter of students reporting the least awareness of environmental issues were, on average, three times as likely to be among the lowest performing quarter of students in the country. In contrast, there was much less of an association between concern for the environment and performance: this was only significant in about half of countries. This suggests that while there is not much of a problem about students feeling concern for the environment, efforts to raise awareness about specific issues need to focus on weaker students.

- The quarter of students with the lowest sense of self-efficacy in tackling science problems were, on average, over twice as likely to be in the lowest performing quarter of students in the country. PISA cannot show to what extent lack of self-efficacy is a cause or an effect of weakness in *scientific literacy*, but this strong association shows that building students' confidence in their ability to tackle scientific problems is an important part of improving science performance.

Students' socio-economic background also plays an important role in this relationship. The results show that, for example, students from more advantaged backgrounds are significantly more likely to report that they value science in general. Across countries, this effect is relatively small. However, in some countries (Ireland, the United States, Australia, New Zealand, Sweden, Finland, the United Kingdom, Luxembourg and the Netherlands and the partner country Liechtenstein) it is much larger.

To what extent are gender differences in attitudes important? Despite performing equally well as males in most countries, females tend to have a weaker self-concept in science than males. However, this difference remains moderate, ranging from a strong effect in some countries to no difference in others. Perhaps more importantly, in most other respects there is no consistent gender difference across countries in self-reported attitudes towards science. There is also no overall-difference in males' and females' inclination to use science in future studies or jobs. This suggests the basis for an important, positive social change, given the bias towards males in today's scientific personnel. However, there are some countries where attitudinal differences remain significant across a range of measures. In Germany, Iceland, Japan, Korea, the Netherlands and the United Kingdom, and the partner countries/economies Chinese Taipei, Hong Kong-China and Macao-China, males reported higher values on at least five of the attitudinal measures. A smaller range of differences can also be observed in France, Italy and the United States. It is these countries, particularly the first group, who need to continue to ask whether gender differences in science attitudes could be reduced, encouraged by the fact that they have been more or less eliminated in other countries.

Finally, there are certain issues that are particularly important for some countries. PISA shows, for example, that in Japan, Korea and Italy, and in the partner countries Indonesia, Azerbaijan and Romania, self-efficacy is considerably lower than the international average (at least 0.2 standard deviations below the country mean). This suggests that these countries need to build the confidence of their students in their ability to tackle scientific problems. PISA also shows that students in some countries are considerably less aware of environmental issues – this includes a number of partner countries and the OECD countries Mexico, Iceland, Luxembourg, Sweden, Korea, Switzerland and Denmark (at least 0.2 standard deviations below the country mean). These countries could improve coverage of this particular area of *scientific literacy* in the curricula.

Notes

1. See Martin *et. al* (2004).

2. The inclusion of attitudes and the specific areas of attitudes selected for PISA 2006 builds upon Klopfer's structure for the affective domain in science education, and reviews of attitudinal research (OECD, 2006a).

3. For this purpose, a model was estimated separately for each country and collectively for all OECD countries (for details, see Annex A10).

4. The only exception is the measure on students' level of concern for environmental issues, for which the relationship with performance is consistent only in 18 of the 30 OECD countries.

5. These measures showed a consistent relationship with performance in at least 28 of the 30 OECD countries.

6. All three measures have a positive correlation with performance across the pooled OECD countries: the support for scientific enquiry scale correlates 0.25 with student performance, the index of general value of science correlates 0.22 with student performance and the index of personal value correlates 0.12 with student performance. Further, there are positive correlations between each measure and performance within each OECD country. The two indices show moderate reliability (Cronbach's Alpha of 0.75), although the reliability is low in Mexico (0.66), Greece (0.66), Hungary (0.66) and France (0.66).

7. Both measures have high reliability (Cronbach's Alpha of 0.83 for self-efficacy in science and 0.92 for self-concept in science). For the pooled OECD sample both measures are positively correlated with science performance (the correlation between self-efficacy in science and student performance is 0.33 and the correlation between self-concept in science and student performance is 0.15) and there are also positive associations with science performance within each OECD country.

8. Two of the measures are indices based on questions in the student questionnaire and both show high reliability (Cronbach's Alpha of 0.85 for general interest in science and 0.88 for enjoyment of science). These two indices show a weak positive correlation with performance across the pooled OECD sample (the correlation between general interest in science and student performance is 0.13 and the correlation between enjoyment of science and student performance is 0.19) and there are positive correlations with performance within each OECD country. The third measure (the scale of interest in scientific topics) is derived from questions included in the science assessment and has a very weak negative correlation with performance across the pooled OECD sample (-0.06).

9. Both measures show high reliability (Cronbach's Alpha of 0.92). There is a weak positive correlation with performance across the pooled OECD sample for both measures (the correlation between instrumental motivation to learn science and student performance is 0.09 and the correlation between future-oriented science motivation and student performance is 0.08). For the index of instrumental motivation to learn science the within-country correlation with performance is positive in 28 OECD countries and for the index of future-oriented science motivation there is a positive correlation in 29 OECD countries and a negative correlation in Mexico.

10. Note that the classification of ISCO-88 occupations into science-related careers differs from the OECD/Eurostat "Human Resources devoted to science and technology" classification in two main respects. First, it is more specifically related to science. Second, an emphasis is placed on science competencies drawn upon in the course of working in the occupation in question. Thus, for example, while the OECD/Eurostat definition includes mathematics professionals, the PISA definition does not.

11. This measure has a high reliability (Cronbach's Alpha of 0.80) and shows a very weak positive correlation with science performance for the pooled OECD sample (0.04). The within-country correlation with performance is positive in 29 OECD countries and negative in Mexico.

12. This measure has moderate reliability (Cronbach's Alpha of 0.76), but slightly lower reliability in two OECD countries (Greece [0.66] and Hungary [0.69]). There is a positive correlation with science performance (0.43) for the OECD pooled sample and also within each OECD country.

13. The index of level of concern for environmental issues has a high reliability (Cronbach's Alpha of 0.81), although there is lower reliability in Italy (0.69). The measure shows no correlation with science performance for the pooled OECD sample (0.01). The within-country correlation with science performance is positive in only 18 OECD countries and is negative in the Czech Republic and Iceland.

14. The index of optimism regarding environmental issues has moderate reliability (Cronbach's Alpha of 0.79), although this is slightly lower in Austria (0.68) and Germany (0.69). The measure shows weak negative correlation with science performance for the pooled OECD sample (-0.17) and the within-country correlation with science performance is negative in all OECD countries.

15. The index of responsibility for sustainable development has moderate reliability (Cronbach's Alpha of 0.79) and shows a weak positive correlation with science performance for the pooled OECD sample (0.18). The within-country correlation with science performance is positive in all OECD countries.

4

Quality and equity in the performance of students and schools

Introduction 170

Securing consistent standards for schools: a profile of between- and within-school differences in student performance 170

The quality of learning outcomes and equity in the distribution of learning opportunities 173
   ▪ Immigrant status and student performance 174
   ▪ Socio-economic background and student and school performance 181

Socio-economic difference and the role that education policy can play in moderating the impact of socio-economic disadvantage 193

Socio-economic background and the role of parents 196

Implications for policy 198
   ▪ A concentration of low-performing students 199
   ▪ Differing slopes and strengths of socio-economic gradients 200
   ▪ Differing socio-economic profiles 202
   ▪ Differing gradients across schools 203
   ▪ Differing gradients within schools 204

INTRODUCTION

Chapter 2 considered how well students in different countries perform in science at age 15. The analysis revealed considerable variation in the relative standing of countries in terms of their students' capacity to put scientific knowledge and skills to functional use. Differences between countries represent 28% of the variation in student performance in all the countries that took part in the PISA 2006 assessment, and 9% among OECD countries. The remaining performance variation lies between schools and students and it is therefore important to interpret the performance variation among countries jointly with the performance variation between schools and students.[1]

Variation in student performance within countries can have a variety of causes, including: the socio-economic backgrounds of students and schools; the ways in which teaching is organised and delivered in classes; the human and financial resources available to schools; and system-level factors such as curricular differences and organisational policies and practices. Identifying the characteristics of those students, schools and education systems that perform well in a disadvantageous socio-economic context can help policy makers design effective policy levers to overcome inequalities in learning opportunities.

This chapter starts by examining the performance gaps shown in Chapter 2 more closely. It considers, in particular, the extent to which overall variation in student performance relates to differences in the results achieved by different schools. It then looks at the role which the socio-economic contexts of students and schools plays to explain performance differences between students and schools, as an indicator of how equitably learning opportunities are distributed in the different education systems. This is an important consideration over and above average educational performance: the social and financial costs of educational failure are high, because those without the competencies to participate in today's society may be unable to realise thier potential and because they are likely to generate higher costs for healthcare, income support, child welfare and security (OECD, 2007).

The analysis in this chapter builds on analytical work in earlier PISA assessments (OECD, 2001; OECD, 2004; Willms, 2006).

The overall impact of home background on student performance tends to be similar for science, mathematics and reading in PISA 2006. Therefore, to simplify the presentation and avoid repetition, this chapter limits the analysis to student performance in science, the focus area in 2006, and it considers the combined science scale (also referred to as, simply, the science scale) rather than examining the competency and knowledge area scales separately.

SECURING CONSISTENT STANDARDS FOR SCHOOLS: A PROFILE OF BETWEEN- AND WITHIN-SCHOOL DIFFERENCES IN STUDENT PERFORMANCE

Catering for the needs of a diverse student body and narrowing the gaps in student performance represent formidable challenges for all countries. The approaches that countries have chosen to address these demands vary.

Some countries have comprehensive school systems with no, or only limited, institutional differentiation. They seek to provide all students with similar opportunities for learning by requiring each school and teacher to provide for the full range of student abilities, interests and backgrounds. Other countries respond to diversity by grouping students through tracking or streaming, whether between schools or between classes within schools, with the aim of serving students according to their academic potential and/or interests in specific programmes. And in many countries, combinations of the two approaches occur. Even in comprehensive school systems, there may be significant variation in performance levels between schools, due to the socio-economic and

Figure 4.1
Variance in student performance between schools and within schools on the science scale

Expressed as a percentage of the average variance in student performance in OECD countries

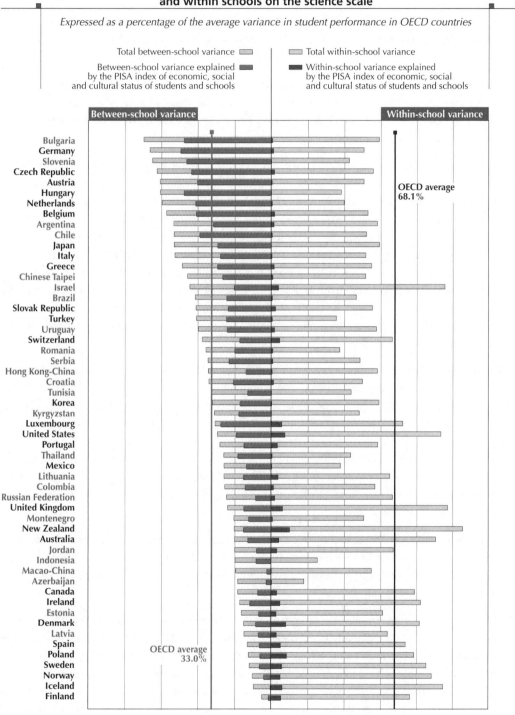

Source: OECD PISA 2006 database, Table 4.1a.
StatLink ⣿⣤ http://dx.doi.org/10.1787/141848881750

cultural characteristics of the communities that are served or due to geographical differences (such as between regions, provinces or states in federal systems, or between rural and urban areas). Finally, there may be differences between individual schools that are more difficult to quantify or describe, part of which could result from differences in the quality or effectiveness of the instruction that those schools deliver. As a result, even in comprehensive systems, the performance levels attained by students may still vary across schools.

How do the policies and historical patterns that shape each country's school system affect and relate to the variation in student performance between and within schools? Do countries with explicit tracking and streaming policies show a higher degree of overall disparity in student performance than countries that have non-selective education systems? Such questions are particularly relevant to countries that observe large variation in overall science performance.

Figure 4.1 shows considerable differences in the extent to which science competencies of 15-year-olds vary within each country (Table 4.1a). The total length of the bars indicates the observed variance in student performance on the PISA science scale. Note that the values in Figure 4.1 are expressed as percentages of the average variance between OECD countries in student performance on the PISA science scale, which is equal to 8 971 units.[2] A value larger than 100 indicates that variance in student performance is greater in the corresponding country than on average among OECD countries. Similarly, a value smaller than 100 indicates below-average variance in student performance. Finland, for example, achieves not only the highest overall performance but has also one of the lowest levels of variation in student performance.[3] By contrast, in New Zealand, the United States, the United Kingdom, Australia and Germany, as well as in the partner countries Israel, Bulgaria and Argentina, the variance in student performance is between 10 and 37.1% larger than the OECD average.[4]

For each country, a distinction is made between the variation attributable to differences in student results attained by students in different schools (between-school variance) and that attributable to the range of student results within schools (within-school variance). The results are also influenced by differences in how schools are defined and organised within countries and by the units that were chosen for sampling purposes.[5] In Figure 4.1, the length of the bars to the left of the central line shows between-school differences and also serves to order countries in the figure. The length of the bars to the right of the central line shows the within-school differences. Therefore, longer segments to the left of the central line indicate greater variation in the mean performance of different schools while longer segments to the right of the central line indicate greater variation among students within schools.

As shown in Figure 4.1, while all countries display considerable within-school variance, in most countries variance in student performance between schools is also considerable. On average across OECD countries, differences in the performance of 15-year-olds between schools account for 33.0% of the OECD average performance variance among students.

In Germany and the partner country Bulgaria, variation in performance between the schools in which 15-year-olds are enrolled is particularly large, about twice as large as the OECD average between-school variance. In the Czech Republic, Austria, Hungary, the Netherlands, Belgium, Japan and Italy, as well as in the partner countries Slovenia, Argentina and Chile, the proportion of between-school variance is still over one-and-a-half times that of the OECD average level (see column 3 in Table 4.1a). Where there is substantial variation in performance between schools and less variation between students within schools, students tend to be grouped in schools in which other students perform at levels similar to their own. This may reflect school choices made by families or residential location, as well as policies on school enrolment or the allocation of students to different curricula in the form of tracking or streaming.

The proportion of between-school variance is only around 14%[6] of the OECD average level in Finland and around 27 and 29% in Iceland and Norway, respectively. Expressed differently, in Finland less than 5% of the overall performance variation of students among OECD countries lies between schools and in Iceland and Norway it is still less than 10%. Other countries in which performance is not very closely related to the schools in which students are enrolled include Ireland, Denmark, Spain, Poland and Sweden, as well as the partner countries Estonia and Latvia (Table 4.1a).

It is noteworthy that Finland and Ireland, and the partner country Estonia, also performed well in PISA 2006, or at least above the OECD average level. Parents in these countries can rely on high and consistent performance standards across schools in the entire education system and may, therefore, be less concerned about choice between schools in order to attain high performance for their children than parents in countries with large performance differences between schools. This also suggests that securing similar student performance among schools is a policy goal that is compatible with the goal of high overall performance standards.

In some countries, student performance or the socio-economic or systemic context of education systems also varies considerably geographically. To capture variation between education systems and regions within countries, some countries have undertaken the PISA surveys at regional levels (*e.g.* Australia, Belgium, Canada, Germany, Italy, Mexico, Spain, Switzerland and the United Kingdom) and, for some of these countries, results at regional levels are presented in Volume 2 of this report. In the case of Spain, differences in student performance between regions tend to be modest. In Belgium, however, student performance in the Flemish Community (at 529 score points) is at a high level (similar to that of students in the Netherlands and Japan) and in the German-speaking Community it is 512, while in the French Community performance is 496 score points. A significant proportion of the performance variation among schools in Belgium, therefore, lies between regions.

While some of the performance variation between schools is attributable to the socio-economic background of students entering the school, some of it is also likely to reflect certain structural features of schools and schooling systems, particularly in systems where students are tracked by ability. Some of the variance in performance between schools may also be attributable to the policies and practices of school administrators and teachers. In other words, there is an added – or subtractive – value associated with attending a particular school. These issues are examined in Chapter 5.

For most countries, these results are similar to those observed in the earlier PISA surveys. However, there are some notable exceptions. For Poland, there was a large decrease in the between-school variance between 2000 and 2003 – from 50.7% of the OECD average total variation in student performance (of which the largest proportion was accounted for by the different school tracks) to 14.9% – and in PISA 2006 Poland has a between-school variance of 12.2% of the average total variation in student performance. Researchers have associated this result with the structural reform of Poland's education system in 1999, which moved towards a more integrated and decentralised education system (see Chapter 5).[7]

Between 2000 and 2006, there were also decreases in the variation among schools in Switzerland (from 45.8 to 37.5%), Belgium (from 65.0 to 57.0%), and in the partner countries Latvia (31.7 to 14.5%) and the Russian Federation (34.4 to 24.1%) – see Tables 4.1a, 4.1b and 4.1c.[8]

THE QUALITY OF LEARNING OUTCOMES AND EQUITY IN THE DISTRIBUTION OF LEARNING OPPORTUNITIES

As much as education has expanded over recent decades, inequalities in educational outcomes as well as in educational and social mobility have persisted in many countries (OECD, 2007). Given that education is a powerful determinant of life chances, equity in education can support equity in life chances. For example, education is a major contributor to the inheritance of economic advantages across generations and to social stratification, but by the same token an accessible policy instrument to increase intergenerational income mobility (OECD, 2006b). Conversely, the long-term social and financial costs of educational inequalities can be high, as those without the competencies to participate socially and economically may not realise their potential and are likely to generate higher costs for health, income support, child welfare and security.

The relative success in provision of appropriate and equitable opportunities for a diverse student body is therefore an important criterion for judging the performance of education systems and PISA devotes significant attention to equity-related issues. To do so, it uses the extent to which socio-economic background relates to student and school performance as a criterion for assessing equity in the distribution of learning opportunities.[9] Where students and schools consistently perform well, irrespective of the socio-economic context, learning opportunities can be considered to be more equitably distributed. In turn, where student and school performance strongly depends on socio-economic background, large inequalities in the distribution of learning opportunities remain and the potential of students remains underutilised.

The results from PISA 2006 show that poor performance in school does not automatically follow from a disadvantaged home background. However, home background remains one of the most powerful factors influencing student performance, explaining an average of 14.4% of the student performance variation in science in the OECD area (Table 4.4a). To assess the impact of socio-economic background on student performance, PISA collected detailed information from students on various aspects relating to the economic, social and cultural status of their families. These included: information on the occupational status of the father and mother (Table 4.8a); the level of education of the father and mother (Table 4.7a); access to educational and cultural resources at home (Table 4.9a) and the country of birth of both the student and his or her father and mother (Table 4.2c). Details on the construction of indices on these measures are given in Annex A1.

Since these various aspects of socio-economic background tend to be highly interrelated, most of the remainder of the report summarises them in a single index, the PISA index of the economic, social and cultural status of students,[10] even though separate data for these are provided in the accompanying data tables indicated above. This index was constructed such that about two-thirds of the OECD student population are between the values of -1 and 1, with an average score of 0 (*i.e.* the mean for the combined student population from participating OECD countries is set to 0 and the standard deviation is set to 1).

However, one attribute of socio-economic background, the immigrant status of students and its relationship to learning outcomes, has received so much attention in the policy discourse that the chapter devotes a separate section to it, which follows next, before the chapter then turns to a more general analysis of the impact of socio-economic background on student and school performance.

Immigrant status and student performance

In most OECD countries, policy makers and the general public are paying increasing attention to issues surrounding international migration. In part, this is a consequence of the growth of immigrant inflows that many OECD countries have experienced over recent decades, whether from globalising economic activities and family reunions in the aftermath of labour migration movements during the 1960s and 1970s, the dissolution of the Eastern Bloc in Europe, or political instability. Between 1990 and 2000 alone, the number of people living outside their country of birth nearly doubled worldwide, to 175 million (OECD, 2006c). Among 15-year-old students, the proportion of students who are foreign born or who have foreign born parents now exceeds 10% in Germany, Belgium, Austria, France, the Netherlands and Sweden as well as the partner countries Croatia, Estonia and Slovenia, and is 15% in the United States, 17% in Jordan, between 21 and 23% in Switzerland, Australia, New Zealand and Canada, and the partner country Israel, 36% in Luxembourg, 37% in Liechtenstein, and over 40% in the partner countries/economies Macao-China, Hong Kong-China and Qatar (Table 4.2c). It should also be borne in mind that these migrant students constitute a very heterogeneous group with a diverse range of skills, backgrounds and motivations.

Considering the anticipated effects of population ageing and ongoing needs for skilled labour, as well as the extent of family reunification, it is likely that migration will remain high on national policy agendas in OECD countries. Although an important subgroup of migrants is highly skilled, many have low skills and are socially disadvantaged (OECD, 2006c). Such disadvantage, along with cultural and ethnic differences, can create many potential divisions and inequities between the host society and newcomers.

The issues go well beyond how migration flows can be channelled and managed, and are increasingly related to how the challenges of integration can be addressed effectively – for both the immigrants themselves and the populations in the countries receiving them. Given the pivotal role of education for success in working life, education and training set the stage for the integration of immigrants into labour markets. They can also contribute to overcoming language barriers and facilitate the transmission of the norms and values that provide a basis for social cohesion.

PISA adds a crucial new perspective to this discussion, by assessing the performance of 15-year-old students with an immigrant background in school. The performance disadvantages of students with an immigrant background that are described here lay out major challenges for education systems. These are unlikely to be resolved on their own, as is illustrated by the fact that, in some countries, the performance disadvantage is as high, or even higher, among second-generation immigrants than among first-generation immigrants. This section compares the performance of a country's students with an immigrant background relative to both the performance of their native peers and the performance of immigrant students in other countries. It also reviews performance differences among first and second-generation immigrants. Following a review of the extent to which such performance differences are attributable to socio-economic and linguistic factors, the section concludes with an analysis of the extent to which immigrant students face inferior or superior schooling conditions in their host countries relative to their native peers.

Among the countries with significant shares of 15-year-olds with an immigrant background,[11] first-generation students – that is, students who were born outside the country of assessment and who also have foreign-born parents – lag, on average, 58 score points behind their native counterparts, a sizeable difference considering that 38 score points are roughly equivalent to the OECD average of a school year's difference (see Box 2.5). Much of this difference remains even after accounting for other socio-economic factors, as shown later in this chapter.

This suggests that schools and societies face major challenges in bringing the human potential that immigrants bring with them fully to fruition. At the same time, Table 4.2c shows a statistically significant performance disadvantage of first-generation immigrant students ranging from 22 score points in Canada and the partner country Croatia to between 77 and 95 score points in Germany, Sweden, Denmark, Austria, Belgium and Switzerland. In contrast, first-generation immigrant students perform at the same level as their native peers in Australia, New Zealand and Ireland as well as in the partner countries/ economies Serbia, Israel, Macao-China and the Russian Federation. Some of these differences can be accounted for by socio-economic factors, as shown later in this section, but substantial cross-country variation remains.

It is noteworthy that across OECD countries there is no positive association between the size of the immigrant student populations and the size of the performance differences between native students and those with an immigrant background.[12] This finding contradicts the frequently made assumption that high levels of immigration will inevitably impair integration.

Without longitudinal data, it is not possible to assess directly to what extent the observed disadvantages of students with an immigrant background are alleviated over successive generations. However, it is possible to compare the performance of second-generation students, who have been born in the country of assessment and therefore have benefited from participation in the same formal education system as their native peers for the same number of years, with that of first-generation students who have started their education in another country. The relatively better performance of second-generation students, as seen in Sweden, Switzerland and Canada, as well as in the partner economies Hong Kong-China and Macao-China, suggests that participation in the education and social system from birth onwards can bring an advantage, although in the cases of Sweden and Switzerland these students still perform below the national average in PISA (Figure 4.2a, Table 4.2c).[13] However, the opposite is observed for New Zealand and the partner countries Israel and Qatar, where second-generation students have lower scores in PISA than their first-generation counterparts. Moreover, comparing the performance of second-generation students with native ones shows strong performance disadvantages in several countries, particularly in Germany, Austria, Denmark, Belgium and the Netherlands, where these students score between 79 and 93 points lower than their native counterparts.

While an analysis of average performance provides a useful summary picture for the situation of students with an immigrant background, a more detailed analysis of the performance distribution is also instructive and shows, in particular, that the science achievement of the highest performers among students with an immigrant background varies much less across countries than the achievement of the lowest performing students with an immigrant background.

In Canada, New Zealand and Australia, and the partner economy Hong Kong-China, 13, 14, 15, and 18%, respectively, of second-generation immigrant students perform at Levels 5 and 6. This is similar to the proportion of top-performers in the native populations of these countries (the OECD average is 6% for second-generation students and 10% for native students). In the United Kingdom, 9% of second-generation immigrants reach the two highest levels on the PISA science scale, compared with 14% in the native population. In the United States the respective proportions are 5 and 10%. In contrast, in Denmark only 1% of second-generation immigrant students were top performers, compared with 7% in the native population (Table 4.2b).

At the bottom end of the scale, 31% of second-generation immigrant students do not reach the baseline Level 2 of science performance. This is the level at which students begin to demonstrate the science competencies that will enable them to participate effectively and productively in life situations related to science and technology. Even in some countries with good science performance overall, there are high proportions of poorly performing immigrants. In Luxembourg, Denmark, the Netherlands, Switzerland, Austria and Germany, for example, the proportion of second-generation students who do not reach Level 2 is at least three times as high as the proportion of native students who do not reach Level 2 (Figure 4.2b, Table 4.2b).

Figure 4.2a
Student performance on the science scale by immigrant status

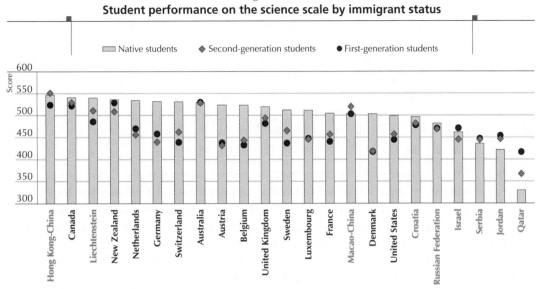

Note: This figure only includes countries with at least 3% of both first-generation and second-generation students.
Countries are ranked in descending order of performance for the native students.
Source: OECD PISA 2006 database, Table 4.2a.
StatLink 🔗 http://dx.doi.org/10.1787/141848881750

Figure 4.2b
Percentage of second-generation versus native students scoring below Level 2 on the science scale

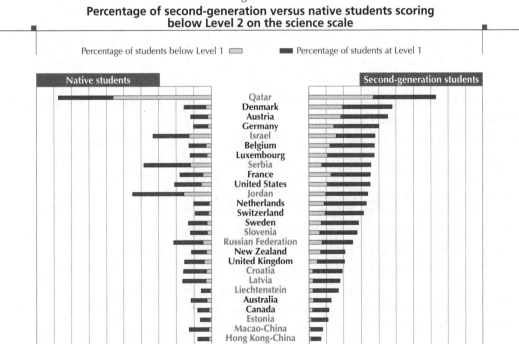

Countries are ranked in descending order of the percentage of second-generation students scoring below Level 2.
Source: OECD PISA 2006 database, Table 4.2b.
StatLink 🔗 http://dx.doi.org/10.1787/141848881750

177

A different country of birth is not the only attribute of immigrant students; in many countries, the association between the language spoken at home and student science performance is as strong as the association between being foreign-born and science performance (Table 4.3a). In Belgium, Austria, Denmark, Luxembourg, Germany, Switzerland and the Netherlands, and the partner countries Liechtenstein and Bulgaria, students who do not speak the language of assessment/instruction, other national dialects or other official languages at home perform between 82 and 102 score points lower on the PISA science scale and they are at least 2.4 times more likely to be in the bottom quarter of science performance (Table 4.3a). In contrast, in Australia and Canada the performance gap is only 19 and 23 score points, respectively, while in the partner countries Israel and Tunisia it is not statistically significant, and in Qatar students with another home language tend to outperform those who speak the language of assessment.

The nature of the educational disadvantage experienced by students who have an ethnic minority background and/or are the children of migrants is substantially influenced by the circumstances from which they come and obviously cannot all be attributed to the education system of the host country. Educational disadvantage in the country of origin can be magnified in the country of adoption even though, in absolute terms, their educational performance might have been raised. These students may be academically disadvantaged either because they are immigrants entering a new education system or because they need to learn a new language in a home environment that may not facilitate this learning.

Furthermore, when interpreting performance gaps between native students and those with a migrant background, it is important to account for differences among countries in terms of such factors as the national origin(s) and socio-economic, educational and linguistic backgrounds of their immigrant populations. The composition of immigrant populations is also shaped by immigration policies and practices and the criteria used to decide who will be admitted into a country vary considerably across countries. While some countries tend to admit relatively large numbers of immigrants each year, often with a low degree of selectivity, other countries have much lower or more selective migrant inflows. In addition, the extent to which the social, educational and occupational status of potential immigrants is taken into account in immigration and naturalisation decisions differs across countries. As a result, immigrant populations tend to have more advantaged backgrounds in some countries than in others. Among the OECD countries:

- Australia, Canada, New Zealand and the United States are countries of immigration, with immigration policies favouring the better qualified (OECD, 2005b).

- In the 1960s and 1970s, European countries such as Austria, Denmark, Germany, Luxembourg, Norway, Sweden and Switzerland recruited temporary immigrant workers, who then settled permanently. Immigration increased again over the last ten years, except in Denmark and Germany. In Austria, Germany and Switzerland, and to a lesser extent in Sweden, immigrants are less likely to have an upper secondary education but more likely to have a tertiary diploma. (OECD, 2005c). This reflects two very different types of migrants – the low-skilled and the highly qualified.

- France, the Netherlands and the United Kingdom draw many immigrants from former colonies, who already know the language of the host country.

- Finland, Greece, Ireland, Italy, Portugal, and Spain, among others, have recently experienced a sharp growth in migration inflows. In Spain, the pace of immigration increased more than tenfold between 1998 and 2004 (OECD, 2006c).

To gauge the extent to which between-country differences in the relative performance of students with a migration background can be attributed to the composition of their immigrant populations, an adjustment for the socio-economic background of students can be made. Table 4.3c examines to what extent the economic, social and cultural status of students with an immigrant background, as well as the language they mainly speak at home, explain their performance disadvantage. In Germany and Denmark, for example, accounting for the socio-economic background of students reduces the performance disadvantage of immigrant students from 85 to 46 score points and from 87 to 49 score points respectively and, across OECD countries, the average reduction is from 54 to 34 score points. However, this reduction tends to be similar across countries and the rank order of countries, in terms of the performance gap between immigrant and native students, remains fairly stable before and after accounting for the socio-economic context.[14] The results suggest that the relative performance levels of students with an immigrant background cannot solely be attributed to the composition of immigrant populations in terms of their educational and socio-economic background. Nor can they be attributed solely to the country of origin: for example, a more detailed analysis of the PISA 2003 survey shows that immigrant students from Turkey performed 31 points better in mathematics in Switzerland than they did in the neighbouring country Germany (OECD, 2005c).

Figure 4.3

Characteristics of schools attended by native students and students with an immigrant background

School characteristics are LESS favourable for students with an immigrant background by:

School characteristics are MORE favourable for students with an immigrant background by:

<<<	at least 0.50 index points	>>>
<<	between 0.20 and 0.49 index points	>>
<	up to 0.19 index points	>

		Percentage of immigrant students[1]	Economic, social and cultural status[1]	Quality of educational resources[1]	Student/teacher ratio[1]	Teacher shortage[1]
OECD	Australia	22				
	Austria	13	<<<		>	
	Belgium	13	<<<		>>	<<
	Canada	21				
	Denmark	8	<<<			
	France	13	<<<	w	w	w
	Germany	14	<<<			<<
	Greece	8	<<	<<		
	Ireland	6				
	Italy	4	<<		>	
	Luxembourg	36	<<<	>		>
	Netherlands	11	<<<			
	New Zealand	21			<<	
	Norway	6	<<<			
	Portugal	6				
	Spain	7	<<		>>	
	Sweden	11	<<		>>	
	Switzerland	22	<<<			
	United Kingdom	9	<<		>>	
	United States	15	<<<		<<	
Partners	Croatia	12	<<			
	Estonia	12				>>
	Hong Kong-China	44	<<<			
	Israel	23	<<			
	Jordan	17	>>	>>	<<	
	Latvia	7		>>		
	Macao-China	74	<<<	>		>
	Montenegro	7	>>		<	<
	Qatar	40	>	>	<<	>
	Russian Federation	9				
	Serbia	9				
	Slovenia	10	<<<	<		

Schools have similar characteristics		9	24	20	24
Schools that immigrant students attend have more favourable characteristics		3	5	6	4
Schools that immigrant students attend have less favourable characteristics		20	2	5	3

1. Scores were standardised within each country sample to make an index which has 0 as the country mean and 1 as the standard deviation within the country.
Source: OECD PISA 2006 database, Table 4.3d.
StatLink ⟐ http://dx.doi.org/10.1787/141848881750

To explore to what extent differences in schooling conditions in the host countries might contribute to the observed outcomes, Figure 4.3 and Table 4.3d examine differences between characteristics of schools attended by immigrant students and native students. The most consistent feature is that immigrant students attend schools with a more disadvantaged socio-economic intake. These differences are particularly pronounced in Denmark, the Netherlands, Luxembourg, Germany, Norway, Austria, the United States, Belgium, France, Switzerland and in the partner countries/economies Slovenia and Hong Kong-China. Only Australia, New Zealand, Portugal, Canada and Ireland and as well as the partner countries the Russian Federation, Serbia, Estonia and Latvia show similar socio-economic contexts in the schools attended by migrant and native students.

Differences in the quality of educational resources, for example instructional materials, computers and science laboratory equipment, between schools attended by immigrant and native students tend to be small (Figure 4.3). However, immigrant students in Greece, Portugal, Denmark and the Netherlands attend schools in which principals report more frequently that the quality of educational resources hinders learning.

In terms of human resources, the schools attended by immigrant and native students tend to be comparable in the majority of countries and where there are differences these are smaller and are often in favour of immigrant students, most notably in Spain, Sweden, the Netherlands, Belgium and the United Kingdom (Figure 4.3), although, in contrast, in Belgium and Germany immigrant students are more likely than their native counterparts to attend schools where teacher shortage is more frequently reported by the school principals (Table 4.3d). Compared to their native peers, immigrant students in the United States, New Zealand and in the partner countries Jordan, Qatar and Montenegro tend to be in schools with higher numbers of students per teacher. In the case of New Zealand and the partner country Jordan immigrant students tend to be in schools with better educational resources and where a lack of qualified teachers is less of a problem compared to their native counterparts.

How well do schools and families encourage and strengthen positive predispositions to learning among students with an immigrant background, thus contributing to laying a foundation for them to leave school with the motivation and capacity to continue learning throughout life? PISA data show that immigrant students report no signs of a lack of engagement in learning science. Students with an immigrant background tend to perform less well on the whole than native students and generally come from less advantaged families. Nevertheless, throughout the OECD area they tend to report higher or comparable levels of future-oriented science motivation, enjoyment of science and personal value of science than do their native peers (Figure 4.4). In fact, only in Germany, and in the partner countries Serbia and Slovenia, do students with an immigrant background report lower levels of science engagement. The consistency of this finding is striking, given the substantial differences between countries in terms of immigration histories, immigrant populations, immigration and integration policies, and the performance of students with an immigration background in PISA. Schools and policy makers could seek to capitalise on the strong engagement of students with an immigrant background, not just in order to strengthen their potential to learn throughout life, but also to help them increase their performance.

Together, the results suggest that some countries appear to be more effective than others in minimising the performance disadvantage for students with a migration background. The most impressive example is the partner economy Hong Kong-China. Here, 25% of students have parents born outside Hong Kong-China and another 19% of students were born outside Hong Kong-China themselves (many of them come from mainland China). And yet, all three student groups – whether native students, first-generation students, or students who speak a language that is different from the language of assessment at home – score well above the OECD average.

180

Figure 4.4

Differences between native students and students with an immigrant background with regard to their personal value of science, enjoyment of science and future-oriented science motivation

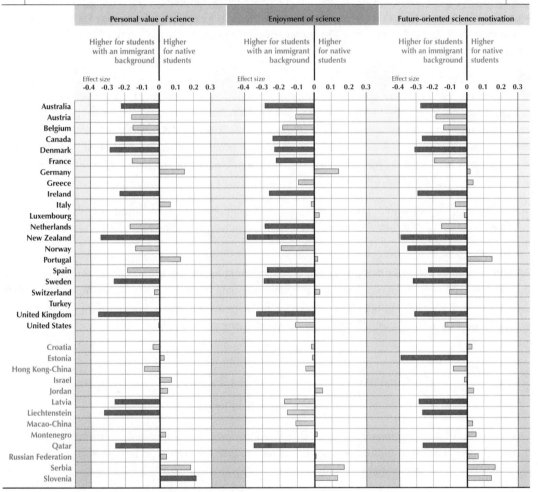

Statistically significant differences and effect sizes with an absolute value greater than 0.2 are marked in a darker tone.
Source: OECD PISA 2006 database, Table 3.23.
StatLink http://dx.doi.org/10.1787/141848881750

Socio-economic background and student and school performance

Achieving an equitable distribution of learning outcomes jointly with high performance standards represents an important challenge for all countries. Analyses at the national level have sometimes been discouraging. For example, using longitudinal methods, researchers who have tracked children's vocabulary development have found that growth trajectories for children from differing socio-economic backgrounds begin to differ early on and that when children enter school the impact of socio-economic background on both cognitive skills and behaviour is already well established (Willms, 2002). Furthermore, during the primary and middle school years, children whose parents have low incomes and low levels of education, or are unemployed or working in low-prestige occupations, are less likely to do well in academic pursuits than children growing up in advantaged socio-economic contexts. They are also less likely to be engaged in curricular and extra-curricular school activities than their more advantaged peers (Datcher, 1982; Finn and Rock, 1997; Johnson *et al.*, 2001; Voelkl, 1995).

The international evidence from PISA is more encouraging in this respect. In all countries, students with more advantaged home backgrounds tend to have higher PISA scores (Table 4.4a). However, a comparison of the relationship between student performance and different aspects of socio-economic background shows that some countries simultaneously demonstrate high average performance together with similar outcomes among students from different socio-economic backgrounds - a finding that was already visible in analyses of the PISA 2003 data (OECD, 2004a). These countries set important benchmarks of what can be achieved in terms of the quality and equity in learning outcomes.

Figure 4.5 depicts the relationship between student performance and the PISA index of economic, social and cultural status that summarises various aspects of socio-economic background, including the occupational status and level of education of the students' father and mother and students' access to educational and cultural resources at home (see Annex A1). The figure describes the relationship for the combined OECD area, with summary statistics on the individual countries shown in Figure 4.6. The figure describes how well students from differing socio-economic backgrounds perform on the PISA science scale.

The relationship between performance and socio-economic background is affected both by how well education systems are performing and the extent of dispersion of the economic, social and cultural factors that make up the index (Box 4.1).

An understanding of this relationship is a useful starting point for analysing the distribution of educational opportunities. From a school policy perspective, understanding the relationship is also important because it indicates how equitably the benefits of schooling are being shared among students from differing socio-economic backgrounds, at least in terms of student performance.

Box 4.1 **How to read Figure 4.5**

Each *dot* on this graph represents 497 15-year-old students drawn randomly from the combined OECD area (this is 10 % of the sampled students). Figure 4.5 plots their performance in science against their economic, social and cultural status.

The vertical axis shows student scores on the science scale, for which the mean is 500. Note that since the standard deviation was set at 100 when the PISA scale was constructed, about two-thirds of the dots fall between 400 and 600. The different shaded areas show the six proficiency levels in science.

The horizontal axis shows values on the PISA index of economic, social and cultural status. This has been constructed to have a mean of 0 and a standard deviation of 1, so that about two-thirds of students are between +1 and –1.

The dark line represents the international socio-economic gradient, which is the best-fitting line showing the association between science performance and socio-economic status across OECD countries.

Since the focus in the figure is not on comparing education systems but on highlighting a relationship throughout the combined OECD area, each student in the combined OECD area contributes equally to this picture – *i.e.* larger countries, with more students in the PISA population, such as Japan, Mexico and the United States, influence the international gradient line more than smaller countries such as Iceland or Luxembourg.

Figure 4.5

**Relationship between student performance in science
and socio-economic background for the OECD area as a whole**

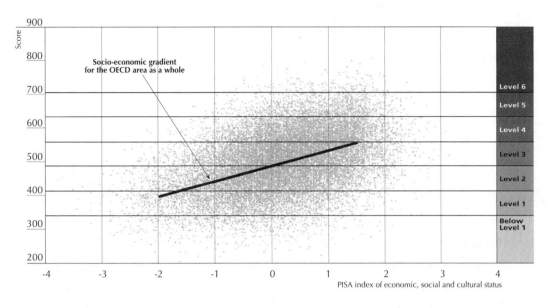

Note: Each dot represents 497 students drawn randomly from the OECD area.
Source: OECD PISA 2006 database.
StatLink 🔗 http://dx.doi.org/10.1787/141848881750

Figure 4.5 points to several findings:

- Students from more advantaged socio-economic backgrounds generally perform better. This finding, already noted above, is shown by the upward slope of the gradient line. Across the OECD countries this advantage averages to 40 score points in science for each increase of one standard deviation in socio-economic background.

- A given difference in socio-economic status is associated with a change in student science performance that is roughly the same throughout the distribution – *i.e.* the marginal benefit of extra socio-economic advantage neither diminishes nor rises by a substantial amount as this advantage grows. This is shown by the fact that the socio-economic gradient is nearly a straight line.

- The relationship between student performance and the PISA index of economic, social and cultural status is not deterministic, in the sense that many disadvantaged students shown on the left of the figure score well above what is predicted by the international gradient line while a sizeable proportion of students from privileged home backgrounds perform below what their home background would predict. For any group of students with similar backgrounds, there is a considerable range of performance.

To what extent is this relationship an inevitable outcome of socio-economic differences, as opposed to an outcome that is amenable to public policy? One approach to answering this question lies in examining to what extent different countries succeed in moderating the relationship between socio-economic background and student performance.

Figure 4.6
How socio-economic background relates to student performance in science

	Mean score	Mean score if the mean ESCS[1] would be equal in all OECD countries	Percentage of explained variance in student performance	Score point difference associated with one unit on the ESCS[1,2] (gradient)	Percentage of students that fall within the lowest 15% of the international distribution on the ESCS[1]
OECD					
Australia	527	519	11.3	43	6.1
Austria	511	502	15.4	46	6.0
Belgium	510	503	19.4	48	8.6
Canada	534	524	8.2	33	4.7
Czech Republic	513	512	15.6	51	7.8
Denmark	496	485	14.1	39	6.5
Finland	563	556	8.3	31	5.6
France	495	502	21.2	54	14.1
Germany	516	505	19.0	46	6.8
Greece	473	479	15.0	37	20.2
Hungary	504	508	21.4	44	15.4
Iceland	491	470	6.7	29	2.4
Ireland	508	510	12.7	39	12.0
Italy	475	478	10.0	31	18.7
Japan	531	533	7.4	39	6.9
Korea	522	522	8.1	32	10.7
Luxembourg	486	483	21.7	41	17.6
Mexico	410	435	16.8	25	52.5
Netherlands	525	515	16.7	44	7.5
New Zealand	530	528	16.4	52	9.0
Norway	487	474	8.3	36	2.3
Poland	498	510	14.5	39	20.8
Portugal	474	492	16.6	28	43.5
Slovak Republic	488	495	19.2	45	13.5
Spain	488	499	13.9	31	29.1
Sweden	503	496	10.6	38	5.6
Switzerland	512	508	15.7	44	11.7
Turkey	424	463	16.5	31	62.7
United Kingdom	515	508	13.9	48	6.6
United States	489	483	17.9	49	11.0
OECD total	491	496	20.2	45	17.9
OECD average	500	500	14.4	40	14.9
Partners					
Argentina	391	416	19.5	38	37.9
Azerbaijan	382	388	4.7	11	33.7
Brazil	390	424	17.1	30	52.9
Bulgaria	434	446	24.1	52	21.1
Chile	438	465	23.3	38	42.3
Colombia	388	411	11.4	23	49.9
Croatia	493	497	12.3	34	13.5
Estonia	531	527	9.3	31	7.3
Hong Kong-China	542	560	6.9	26	37.6
Indonesia	393	425	10.2	21	68.6
Israel	454	448	10.9	43	8.3
Jordan	422	438	11.2	27	34.0
Kyrgyzstan	322	340	8.2	27	35.0
Latvia	490	491	9.7	29	14.7
Lithuania	488	487	15.2	38	14.6
Macao-China	511	523	2.2	13	48.6
Montenegro	412	412	7.5	24	14.4
Romania	418	431	16.6	35	24.1
Russian Federation	479	483	8.1	32	12.6
Serbia	436	440	13.2	33	16.9
Slovenia	519	513	16.7	46	8.7
Chinese Taipei	532	546	12.5	42	20.3
Thailand	421	461	15.9	28	69.4
Tunisia	386	408	9.5	19	56.9
Uruguay	428	446	18.3	34	34.7

Note: Values that are statistically significant are indicated in bold (see Annex A3).
1. ESCS: the PISA index of economic, social and cultural status.
2. Single-level bivariate regression of science performance on the ESCS, the slope is the regression coefficient for the ESCS.
Source: OECD PISA 2006 database, Table 4.4a.
StatLink ⌐🖵🖳 http://dx.doi.org/10.1787/141848881750

In examining Figures 4.5 and 4.6 several aspects of the gradient should be noted, including how strongly socio-economic background predicts performance, how well students with average background perform, how much difference it makes to have stronger or weaker socio-economic background, and how wide are the socio-economic differences in the student population. More specifically, the features of the relationship between socio-economic background and performance can be described in terms of:

- The strength of the relationship between science performance and socio-economic background. This refers to how much individual student performance varies above and below the gradient line. This can be seen for the combined OECD area in Figure 4.5 by the dispersion of dots above and below the line. For individual countries, column 3 of Figure 4.6 (column 3 in Table 4.4a) gives the explained variance, a statistic that summarises the strength of the relationship by indicating the proportion of the observed variation in student performance that can be attributed to the relationship shown by the gradient line. If this number is low, relatively little of the variance in student performance is associated with students' socio-economic background; if it is high, a large part of the performance variation is attributable to socio-economic background. On average across OECD countries, 14.4% of the variation in student performance in science within each country is associated with the PISA index of economic, social and cultural status. This figure is significantly higher than the OECD average in Luxembourg, Hungary, France, Belgium, the Slovak Republic, Germany, the United States, New Zealand and the partner countries Bulgaria, Chile, Argentina and Uruguay.

- The slope of the gradient line is an indication of the extent of inequality in science performance attributable to socio-economic factors (see column 4 in Figure 4.6 and column 4 in Table 4.4a) and is shown by how much student performance changes with a change of one unit on the PISA index of economic, social and cultural status. Steeper gradients indicate a greater impact of economic, social and cultural status on student performance, *i.e.* more inequity. Gentler gradients indicate a lower impact of socio-economic background on student performance, *i.e.* more equity. The OECD countries with the steepest slopes are France, New Zealand, the Czech Republic, the United States, the United Kingdom, Belgium, Germany, Austria and the Slovak Republic; among the partner countries they are Bulgaria, Liechtenstein and Slovenia. In these countries one unit of the PISA index of economic, social and cultural status is associated with a performance difference of between 45 and 54 score points on the science scale. It is important to distinguish the slope from the strength of the relationship as indicated by the variance explained. For example, Germany and the United Kingdom show similar slopes, with one unit of difference on the PISA index of economic, social and cultural status corresponding, on average, to 46 and 48 score points on the science performance scale respectively. However, in the United Kingdom, there are many more exceptions to this general trend; in other words, there are many students from disadvantaged socio-economic backgrounds still achieving well, and many students from advantaged backgrounds with lower performance than predicted, so that the relationship only explains 13.9% of the performance variation. In contrast, in Germany, student performance follows the levels predicted by socio-economic background more closely, with 19.0% of the performance variation explained by socio-economic background. On average across OECD countries, the slope of the gradient is 40 score points.[15] This means that students' scores on the science scale are, on average in OECD countries, 40 score points higher for each extra unit on the PISA index of economic, social and cultural status.

- The level of the gradient lines or the average height – is given in column 1 of Figure 4.6. This shows the average science score reached by those students in each country that have an economic, social and cultural background equal to the average across OECD countries. The level of a gradient for a country can be considered an indication of what would be the overall level of performance of the education system if the economic, social and cultural background of the student population were identical to the

OECD average. Figure 4.7 highlights the difference between the country mean score as predicted from the socio-economic distribution and the actual mean performance score.

- The length of the gradient lines is determined by the range of socio-economic scores for the middle 90% of students (between the 5th and 95th percentiles) in each country (column 5 in Table 4.4a), Columns 5a and 5b in Table 4.4a show the 5th and the 95th percentiles of the PISA index of economic, social and cultural status spanned by the gradient line. The length of the gradient line indicates how widely the student population is dispersed in terms of socio-economic background. Longer projections of the gradient lines, such as in Portugal and Mexico, and the partner country Tunisia, represent a wider dispersion of socio-economic background in the student population within the country in question, whereas shorter projections, such as in Japan or Norway, indicate socio-economically more homogeneous populations.

An analysis of Figure 4.6 points to several findings. First, countries vary in the strength and slope of the relationship between socio-economic background and student performance. The figure not only shows countries with relatively high and low levels of performance on the science scale, but also countries which have greater or lesser degrees of inequality in performance among students from different socio-economic backgrounds. It is worth emphasising the considerable extent of this difference. Consider two students: one from a less advantaged background, say, one standard deviation below the OECD average on the PISA index of economic, social and cultural status and the other from a relatively privileged background, say, one standard deviation above the OECD average on the PISA index of economic, social and cultural status. The predicted performance gap between these two students varies between countries by a factor of over two. Column 4 in Figure 4.6 can be used to calculate this difference. The science score point difference shown in this column is associated with a one standard deviation change in the PISA index of economic, social and cultural status – the two students in this example are separated by two standard deviations. This means that in Portugal this gap is 56 score points, but in France it is 108 score points (in each case double the gradient slope, *i.e.* comparing students two standard deviations apart). The figure also shows clearly that high performance does not have to come at the expense of inequality, as some of the countries with the highest levels of performance have relatively gentle gradients, most notably Finland, Canada, Japan and Korea but also the partner countries/economies Hong Kong-China and Estonia. At the same time, the results show also that overall performance among OECD countries is quite closely related to the slope of the gradient, suggesting that it is more challenging to achieve equity in educational opportunities as overall performance standards rise.

Second, the range of the PISA index of economic, social and cultural status spanned by the gradient lines varies widely between countries. The range is indicated by the length of the line from the 5th percentile value of the index to the 95th percentile – that is the line that spans the values of the middle 90% of the values of the index for each country. For some countries this spread is quite narrow – for example, the range of backgrounds of the middle 90% of the student population spans less than 2.5 index points on the index in Japan, Norway, the Czech Republic and Australia and the partner country the Russian Federation – these countries, therefore have quite a narrow distribution of socio-economic backgrounds to deal with. By contrast, the range is more than 4 index points in Portugal and Mexico and the partner countries Tunisia and Colombia. These figures show that some countries' education systems need to cope with students from a wider range of socio-economic backgrounds than others (see column 5 in Table 4.4a). In countries with large socio-economic disparities in family contexts, even a gentle gradient can lead to large socio-economic disparities.

Third, the gradients for many countries are roughly linear, that is, each increment on the PISA index of economic, social and cultural status is associated with a roughly constant increase in performance on the science scale. One might have expected that the gradients would be steep at low levels of economic, social and cultural status, and then level off at higher status levels, signalling that above a certain level of socio-economic background there would be progressively less advantage in terms of student performance. Indeed, the gradients follow this pattern in some countries, with column 8 in Table 4.4a showing statistically significant negative values on the index of curvilinearity, most notably in Japan and Austria, but also in Italy, Norway, Greece, Germany, Hungary, Canada and Spain, as well as the partner economies Liechtenstein and Macao-China. However, in another group of countries, most notably in Turkey and the United States and the partner country Brazil, and to a lesser extent in the partner countries Israel, Estonia, Thailand, Kyrgyzstan, Tunisia, Chile, Colombia, Indonesia, Azerbaijan, Uruguay and Jordan, they are relatively gentle at low levels of socio-economic status and become steeper at higher levels (with column 8 in Table 4.4a showing statistically significant positive values). In these countries, among the more advanced group of students, home background makes a greater difference to student performance in science. In other words, the greater the socio-economic advantage, the greater the advantage it has in terms of student performance. In the remaining countries, these effects are small and not statistically significant. The finding that in all countries gradients tend to be roughly linear, or only modestly curved across the range of economic, social and cultural status, has an important policy implication. Many socio-economic policies are aimed at increasing resources for the most disadvantaged, either through taxation or by targeting benefits and socio-economic programmes to certain groups. The PISA 2006 results suggest that it is not easy to establish a low economic, social and cultural status baseline, below which performance sharply declines. Moreover, if such status is taken to be a surrogate for the decisions and actions of parents aimed at providing a richer environment for their children – such as taking an interest in their school work – then these findings suggest that there is room for improvement at all levels on the socio-economic continuum. The fact that it is difficult to discern a baseline, however, does not imply that differentiated student support is not warranted.

Figure 4.7

Difference between the unadjusted mean score and the mean score on the science scale if the mean PISA index of economic, social and cultural status were equal in all OECD countries

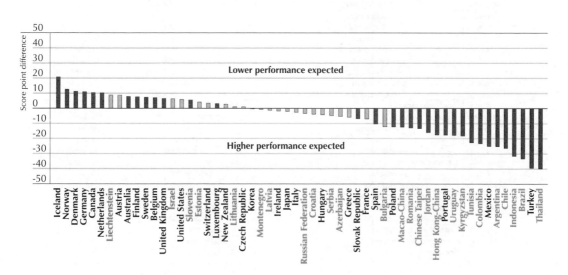

Countries are ranked in descending order of the difference between the unadjusted mean score and the mean score if the mean PISA index of economic, social and cultural status would be equal in all OECD countries.

Note: Statistically significant differences are marked in a darker tone.

Source: OECD PISA 2006 database, Table 4.4a.

StatLink ⟨⟩ http://dx.doi.org/10.1787/141848881750

187

Figure 4.8
Student variability in the distribution of the PISA index of economic, social and cultural status (ESCS)

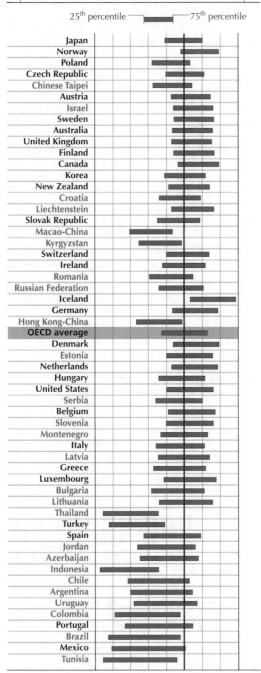

-2.5 -2.0 -1.5 -1.0 -0.5 0 0.5 1.0 1.5
PISA index of economic, social and cultural status

Figure 4.9
School variability in the distribution of the PISA index of economic, social and cultural status (ESCS)

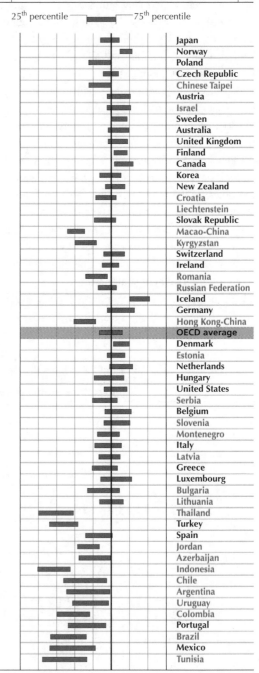

-2.5 -2.0 -1.5 -1.0 -0.5 0 0.5 1.0 1.5
PISA index of economic, social and cultural status

Countries are ranked in ascending order of the interquartile range of the distribution of the student-level ESCS.
Source: OECD PISA 2006 database, Table 4.4b.
StatLink http://dx.doi.org/10.1787/141848881750

Countries are ranked in ascending order of the interquartile range of the distribution of the student-level ESCS.
Source: OECD PISA 2006 database, Table 4.4b.
StatLink http://dx.doi.org/10.1787/141848881750

The variability of many factors described in this report is greater within than between schools. For example, the performance variability in schools is much greater than the variation of schools' average performance. This is true also of students' socioeconomic background. A comparison of the difference between the 25th percentile and the 75th percentile shows that on average across OECD countries this amounts to 1.28 units on the student-level PISA index of economic, social and cultural status, whereas the variability between schools on the same measure averages around half of this figure (0.63 units). This can be seen in Figure 4.9.

Figure 4.10
Performance in science and the impact of socio-economic background

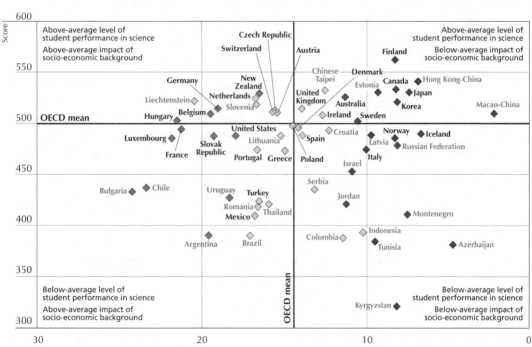

Note: OECD mean used in this figure is the arithmetic average of all OECD countries.
Source: OECD PISA 2006 database, Table 4.4a.
StatLink ⟲ http://dx.doi.org/10.1787/141848881750

Figure 4.10 above summarises the findings by contrasting average performance in science (as shown on the vertical axis) with the strength of the relationship between socio-economic background and science performance, used as explained above as a proxy for equity in the distribution of learning opportunities (as shown on the horizontal axis). Australia, Canada, Finland, Japan and Korea as well as the partner countries/economies Hong Kong-China, Estonia and Macao-China, represented in the upper right quadrant of the figure, are examples of countries that display high levels of student performance in science and, at the same time, a below-average impact of economic, social and cultural status on student performance.

By contrast, the United States, the Slovak Republic and Luxembourg as well as the partner countries Bulgaria, Chile, Argentina and Uruguay, displayed in the lower left quadrant, are examples of countries with below-average student performance in science and an above-average impact of socio-economic background on performance. New Zealand, Germany and Belgium are examples of countries characterised by above-average performance levels but in which performance is comparatively strongly related to socio-economic background. Finally, Iceland, Italy and Norway, as well as the partner countries Azerbaijan, Israel, Jordan, Kyrgyzstan, Latvia, Montenegro, the Russian Federation and Tunisia, are examples of countries in which average performance in science is below the OECD average but not strongly related to student background. Although Mexico and Turkey show below-average performance in science associated with an average impact of socio-economic background, it is important to note that because only around one-half of 15-year-olds in these countries are enrolled in school (the smallest proportion among all participating countries, see Table A3.1) and thus represented in PISA, the impact of socio-economic background on the science performance of 15-year-olds may be underestimated.

Figure 4.10 highlights that countries differ not just in their overall performance, but also in the extent to which they are able to moderate the association between socio-economic background and performance. PISA suggests that maximising overall performance and securing similar levels of performance among students from different socio-economic backgrounds can be achieved simultaneously. The results suggest therefore that quality and equity need not be considered as competing policy objectives.

Across OECD countries, the relationship between socio-economic background and student performance has slightly weakened from PISA 2000 to PISA 2003 and from PISA 2003 to PISA 2006, most notably in reading and to a lesser extent in mathematics and science (Tables 4.4c, d and e). In the Czech Republic and Switzerland, in which this relationship has been particularly strong, the proportion of science performance variation that is explained by socio-economic background fell between PISA 2000 and PISA 2006 by between 5 and 8 percentage points, in Norway by 4.9 percentage points and in Canada by 2.4 percentage points. There was no OECD country in which the relationship between socio-economic background and science performance became stronger between PISA 2000 and PISA 2006. While substantial inequalities remain, it thus seems that some progress towards a more equitable distribution of learning opportunities has been made in OECD countries, particularly in some of those countries where the challenges were most acute. Among the partner countries, the picture is more mixed and where changes have been significant they have all been in the direction of increasing inequalities.[16]

As noted before, when comparing the relationship between socio-economic background and student performance, it is important to take into account marked differences in the distribution of socio-economic characteristics between countries. Figure 4.8 above and Table 4.4a present key characteristics of the distribution of the PISA index of economic, social and cultural status in PISA. Countries with negative mean indices (see column 6 in Table 4.4a), most notably Turkey, Mexico and Portugal and the partner countries/economies Indonesia, Thailand, Tunisia, Brazil, Colombia, Macao-China, Chile, Hong Kong-China, Kyrgyzstan and Argentina are characterised by below-average socio-economic backgrounds and thus face far greater overall challenges in addressing the impact of socio-economic background.

This makes the high performance achieved by students in Hong Kong-China all the more impressive. However, it also places a different perspective on the observed below-average performance of the remaining countries mentioned. In fact, a hypothetical adjustment that assumes an average index of economic, socio-economic and cultural status across OECD countries would result in an increase of science performance in Turkey from 424 to 463 score points, and an increase in Portugal's average performance from 474 to 492 score points, which is on a par with the observed performance level of Iceland.

190

These adjusted scores are shown in Figure 4.7 above. Countries with statistically significant differences above positive 20 score points are (in descending order) Turkey and Mexico and the partner countries Thailand, Brazil, Indonesia, Chile, Argentina, Colombia and Tunisia. In contrast, in countries with above-average socio-economic background this adjustment is negative, suggesting that part of the performance of these countries is attributable to their advantaged socio-economic context, such as Iceland and Norway (accounting for the socio-economic context in these countries would make their performance comparable to the unadjusted performance means of Greece). This also occurs to a lesser extent (in descending order) in Denmark, Germany, Canada, the Netherlands, Austria, Australia, Finland, Sweden, Belgium and the United Kingdom and the partner countries Liechtenstein, Israel and Slovenia, which operate in more favourable socio-economic conditions than the OECD average – adjusting for this advantage would lower their scores. Obviously, such an adjustment is entirely hypothetical – countries operate in a global market place where actual, rather than adjusted, performance is all that counts. Moreover, the adjustment does not take into consideration the complex cultural context of each country. However, in the same way that proper comparisons of the quality of schools focus on the added value that schools provide (accounting for the socio-economic intake of schools when interpreting results), users of cross-country comparisons need to keep in mind the differences among countries in economic, social and educational circumstances.

The challenges that education systems face depend not just on the average socio-economic background of a country. They also depend on the distribution of socio-economic characteristics within countries. Such heterogeneity in socio-economic characteristics can be measured by the standard deviation, within each country, of student values on the PISA index of economic, social and cultural status (see column 7 in Table 4.4a). The greater this socio-economic heterogeneity in the family backgrounds of 15-year-olds, the greater the challenges for teachers, schools and the entire education system. In fact, many of the countries with below-average socio-economic backgrounds, most notably Mexico and Portugal, and the partner countries Tunisia, Brazil, Colombia, Uruguay and Chile also face the difficulty of significant heterogeneity in the socio-economic backgrounds of 15-year-olds.

Some countries with similar average levels of socio-economic background differ widely in the socio-economic heterogeneity of their populations. For example, both Italy and Japan have a level in the PISA index of economic, social and cultural status that is near the OECD average. However, while Japan has the most homogeneous distribution of socio-economic characteristics among OECD countries, Italy has a comparatively wide variation. In countries in which the student population is very heterogeneous, similar socio-economic gradients will have a much larger impact on the performance gap than in countries that have socio-economically more homogeneous student populations. For example, Finland and Spain have socio-economic gradients with similar slopes: *i.e.* in both countries a given socio-economic difference is associated with a similar difference in performance. Since the distribution of socio-economic characteristics is much more heterogeneous in Spain than in Finland, the performance gap among students in the top and bottom quarters of the PISA index of economic, social and cultural background is much larger in Spain than in Finland (Table 4.4a).

Countries with a low average level of socio-economic background and a wide distribution of socio-economic characteristics face particular challenges in meeting the needs of disadvantaged students, even more so if the distribution of socio-economic background characteristics is skewed towards disadvantage, as indicated by a positive index of skewness in Table 4.4a (see column 9). For example, in Turkey and Mexico, as well as in the partner countries Thailand, Indonesia, Tunisia and Brazil, more than one-half of all students come from a socio-economic background below that experienced by the least advantaged 15% of students in OECD countries (see column 10 in Table 4.4a). By contrast, in Norway, Iceland and Canada, less than 5% of students have a socio-economic background below that of the least advantaged 15% of all OECD students.

191

Figure 4.11

Within-school and between-school socio-economic effect[1]

	Effect of the PISA index of economic, social and cultural status (ESCS)			
	Overall effect of ESCS[2]	Within-school effect of ESCS[3]	Between-school effect of ESCS[4]	Index of inclusion[5]
	Student-level score point difference associated with one unit of the ESCS	Student-level score point difference associated with one unit of the student-level ESCS	School-level score point difference associated with one unit of the school mean ESCS	Proportion of ESCS variance within schools
Australia	43	29	56	0.77
Austria	46	10	110	0.71
Belgium	48	17	102	0.73
Canada	33	23	44	0.81
Czech Republic	51	19	120	0.73
Denmark	39	32	41	0.87
Finland	31	30	10	0.91
France	w	w	w	w
Germany	46	14	114	0.75
Greece	37	16	66	0.66
Hungary	44	7	85	0.54
Iceland	29	29	-5	0.85
Ireland	39	28	48	0.79
Italy	31	7	87	0.76
Japan	39	5	133	0.76
Korea	32	9	80	0.74
Luxembourg	41	24	69	0.77
Mexico	25	6	37	0.60
Netherlands	44	11	123	0.78
New Zealand	52	41	55	0.82
Norway	36	31	29	0.88
Poland	39	35	21	0.76
Portugal	28	17	32	0.69
Slovak Republic	45	21	56	0.63
Spain	31	24	21	0.76
Sweden	38	32	34	0.87
Switzerland	44	26	70	0.82
Turkey	31	9	65	0.69
United Kingdom	48	32	71	0.83
United States	49	34	51	0.74
OECD total	45			
OECD average	40	21	64	0.76
Argentina	38	13	57	0.61
Azerbaijan	11	7	15	0.63
Brazil	30	8	48	0.61
Bulgaria	52	13	68	0.49
Chile	38	11	54	0.47
Colombia	23	11	31	0.60
Croatia	34	14	83	0.78
Estonia	31	22	42	0.81
Hong Kong-China	26	9	64	0.76
Indonesia	21	1	42	0.67
Israel	43	26	69	0.76
Jordan	27	18	28	0.75
Kyrgyzstan	27	6	75	0.74
Latvia	29	21	35	0.80
Liechtenstein	49	c	c	c
Lithuania	38	24	47	0.73
Macao-China	13	7	15	0.67
Montenegro	24	11	65	0.80
Qatar	m	m	m	m
Romania	35	12	60	0.66
Russian Federation	32	20	39	0.76
Serbia	33	12	75	0.74
Slovenia	46	7	121	0.74
Chinese Taipei	42	14	107	0.77
Thailand	28	8	42	0.50
Tunisia	19	4	36	0.64
Uruguay	34	14	45	0.62

OECD (rows Australia–United States), *Partners* (rows Argentina–Uruguay)

1. In some countries, sub-units within schools were sampled instead of schools as administrative units and this may affect the estimation of school-level effects.
2. Single-level bivariate regression of science performance on the ESCS, the slope is the regression coefficient for the ESCS.
3. Two-level regression of science performance on student ESCS and school mean ESCS: within-school slope for ESCS and variance explained by the model at the student level.
4. Two-level regression of science performance on student ESCS and school mean ESCS: between-school slope for ESCS and variance explained by the model at the school level.
5. The index of inclusion is derived from the intra-class correlation for ESCS as 1- the intra class correlation coefficient.
Source: OECD PISA 2006 database, Table 4.4b.
StatLink ᵺᵺᵺ http://dx.doi.org/10.1787/141848881750

SOCIO-ECONOMIC DIFFERENCE AND THE ROLE THAT EDUCATION POLICY CAN PLAY IN MODERATING THE IMPACT OF SOCIO-ECONOMIC DISADVANTAGE

Many of the factors of socio-economic disadvantage are not directly amenable to education policy, at least not in the short term. For example, the educational attainment of parents can only gradually improve, and average family wealth depends on the long-term economic development of a country as well as the development of a culture which promotes individual savings. The importance of socio-economic disadvantage, and the realisation that aspects of such disadvantage only change over extended periods of time, give rise to a vital question for policy makers: to what extent can schools and school policies moderate the impact of socio-economic disadvantage on student performance? The overall relationship between socio-economic background and student performance provides an important indicator of the capacity of education systems to provide equitable learning opportunities. However, from a policy perspective, the relationship between socio-economic background and school performance is even more important as it indicates how equity is interrelated with systemic aspects of education.

Figure 4.1 reveals large differences among countries in the extent to which student performance varies among schools. How is within-school and between-school variation attributable to socio-economic background? Making such an analysis helps illuminate which policies might aid in simultaneously increasing overall student performance and moderating the impact of socio-economic background (*i.e.* to raise and flatten a country's socio-economic gradient line). The following examines the impact of socio-economic difference on student performance, as measured by the socio-economic gradient. To this end, the gradient for a country can be broken down into two parts: a within-school gradient and a between-school gradient. The within-school gradient describes how students' socio-economic background is related to their performance within a common school environment. The between-school gradient describes how schools' average level of performance is related to the average economic, social and cultural status of their student intake.[17]

Figures 4.14a-f at the end of this chapter, show the average performance and the socio-economic composition of the student intake, for each school in the PISA sample. As elsewhere in this chapter, socio-economic composition is measured by the mean PISA index of economic, social and cultural status in the school. Each dot in Figures 4.14a-f represents one school, with the size of the dot proportionate to the number of 15-year-olds enrolled in the school. This shows first that in some countries students are highly segregated along socio-economic lines, whether because of residential segregation, economic factors or selection within the school system. The figures also show the overall gradient between socio-economic background and student performance (black line in Figures 4.14a-f). Finally, the figures display the between-school gradient (thick dashed black line in Figures 4.14a-f) and the average within-school gradient (blue line in Figures 4.14a-f). Schools above the between-school gradient line (thick dashed black line) perform better than would be predicted by their socio-economic intake. Schools below the between-school gradient line perform lower than expected.

Figure 4.12 compares the slopes of within-school and between-school gradients across countries. The slopes represent, respectively, the gap in predicted scores of two students within a school separated by a fixed amount of socio-economic background, and the gap in predicted scores of two students with identical socio-economic backgrounds attending different schools where the average background of their fellow-students is separated by the same fixed amount. The slopes were estimated with a multilevel model that included the PISA index of economic, social and cultural status at the student and school levels. The lengths of the bars in Figure 4.12 indicate the differences in scores on the PISA science scale that are associated with a difference of one-half of an international standard deviation on the PISA index of economic, social and cultural status for the individual student (grey bar) and for the average of the student's school (blue bar). One-half a student-level standard deviation was chosen as the benchmark for measuring performance gaps because this value describes realistic differences between schools in terms of their socio-economic composition: on average across OECD countries, the difference between the 75th and 25th quartiles of the distribution of the school mean PISA index of economic, social and cultural status is 0.63 of a student-level standard deviation. This value ranges from 0.45 standard deviations or less in Norway, Finland, the Czech Republic, Denmark and Sweden, to 0.90 or more standard deviations in Mexico and Portugal, and the partner countries Tunisia, Argentina, Chile, Uruguay, Brazil, Thailand and Colombia (see column 11 in Table 4.4b).

Figure 4.12
Effects of students' and schools' socio-economic background on student performance in science

Differences in performance on the science scale associated with one-half of a student-level standard deviation on the PISA index of economic, social and cultural status

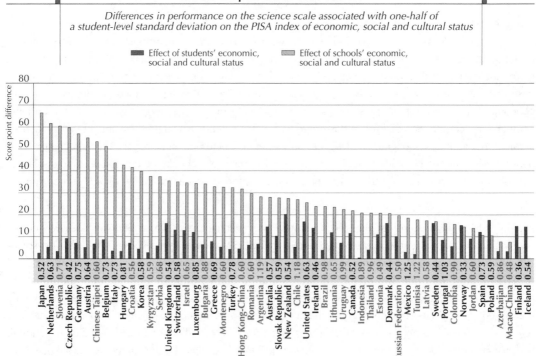

Note: Data on blue background are values of the interquartile range of the school-level average PISA index of economic, social and cultural status.
Source: OECD PISA 2006 database, Table 4.4b.
StatLink ⟨⟨⟨ http://dx.doi.org/10.1787/141848881750

In almost all countries, and for all students, the relatively long blue bars in Figure 4.12 indicate the clear advantage in attending a school whose students are, on average, from more advantaged socio-economic backgrounds. Regardless of their own socio-economic background, students attending schools in which the average socio-economic background is high tend to perform better than when they are enrolled in a school with a below-average socio-economic intake. In the majority of OECD countries the effect of the average economic, social and cultural status of students in a school – in terms of performance variation across students – far outweighs the effects of the individual student's socio-economic background.

All of this is perhaps not surprising, but the magnitude of the differences is striking. In Japan, Netherlands, the Czech Republic, Germany, Austria, Belgium, Italy, Hungary and Korea, and the partner countries/economies Slovenia, Chinese Taipei and Croatia, the effect on student performance of a school's average economic, social and cultural status is very substantial. In these countries, one-half of a unit on the PISA index of economic, social and cultural status at the school level is equivalent to between 40 and 67 score points (one-half of the value shown in column 7 in Table 4.4b). Consider the case of two hypothetical students in any of these countries, living in families with average socio-economic background, as measured by the PISA index of economic, social and cultural status. One student attends a school in a socio-economically advantaged area, in which the mean PISA index of economic, social and cultural status of the school's intake is one-quarter of a (student-level) standard deviation above the OECD average. Most of this student's peers will therefore come from families that are more affluent than his or her own. The other student attends a school in a more disadvantaged area: the school's mean economic, social and cultural background is one-quarter of a standard deviation below the OECD average, so that the student comes from a more affluent family than his or her peers. The result indicates that the first student would be likely to have a much higher science performance than the second student, by between 40 and 67 score points depending on the country in this list.

Socio-economic differences at student levels are much less predictive of performance than the schools' socio-economic context. Consider the case of two students in the same country living in families whose different economic, social and cultural status give them scores on the index that are one-quarter of a student-level standard deviation above, and one-quarter below, the mean. If these students attend the same school, with an average socio-economic profile, they would have a much smaller gap in their predicted performance – a mere 3 score points in Japan, Mexico and Hungary and 4 score points in Italy, Turkey and Korea and the partner country/economy Macao-China and Azerbaijan (one-half of the value shown in column 2 in Table 4.4b).

It needs to be borne in mind that differences in the averages of schools' socio-economic backgrounds are naturally smaller than comparable differences between individual students, given that every school's intake is mixed in terms of socio-economic variables. To aid in the interpretation, the typical range of the average socio-economic status of schools has been added to Figure 4.12.

Not all of the contextual effect is attributable to peer group effects, but socio-economic advantage of students and their families often also goes along with a better learning environment and access to better educational resources at school. Also, the manner in which students are allocated to schools within a district or region, or to classes and programmes within schools, can have implications for the contextual effect, in terms of the teaching and learning conditions in schools that are associated with educational outcomes. A number of studies (e.g. Baker et al., 2002) have found that schools with a higher average socio-economic status among their student intake are likely to have: fewer disciplinary problems, better teacher-student relations, higher teacher morale, and a general school climate that is oriented towards higher performance. Such schools also often have a faster-paced curriculum. Talented and motivated teachers are more likely to be attracted to schools with higher socio-economic status and less likely to transfer to another school or to leave the profession. Some of the contextual effect associated with high socio-economic status may also stem from peer interactions that occur as talented students work with each other. The potential influence of such school factors is examined further in Chapter 5.

Some of the contextual effect might also be due to factors for which PISA does not account. For example, the parents of a student attending a more socio-economically advantaged school may, on average, be more engaged in the student's learning at home. This may be so even though their socio-economic background is comparable to that of the parents of a student attending a less-privileged school. Also relevant to the previously mentioned example of the two hypothetical students of similar ability, who attend schools with different average socio-economic intakes, is the fact that because no data on the students' earlier achievement are available from PISA, it is not possible to infer ability and motivation. Therefore, it is also not possible to determine whether and to what extent the school background directly or indirectly determines students' performance (for example, indirectly through a process of student selection or self-selection).

Two different messages emerge about the ways to increase both quality and equity. On the one hand, socio-economic segregation may bring benefits for the advantaged that will enhance the performance of the elite and, perhaps as a consequence, overall average performance. On the other hand, segregation of schools is likely to decrease equity. However, there is strong evidence that this dilemma can be resolved, as shown by those countries that have achieved both high quality and high equity. Just how other countries might match this is the key question. Moving all students to schools with higher socio-economic status is a logical impossibility and the results shown in Figure 4.12 should not lead to the conclusion that transferring a group of students from a school with a low socio-economic intake to a school with a high socio-economic intake would automatically result in the gains suggested by Figure 4.12. That is, the estimated contextual effects shown in Figure 4.12 are descriptive of the distribution of school performance, and should not necessarily be interpreted in a causal sense.

In any attempt to develop education policy in the light of the above findings, there needs to be some understanding of the nature of the formal and informal selection mechanisms that contribute to between-school socio-economic segregation and the effect of this segregation on students' performance. In some countries, socio-economic segregation may be firmly entrenched through residential segregation in major cities, or by a large urban/rural socio-economic divide. In other countries, structural features of the education system tend to stream or track students from different socio-economic contexts into programmes with different curricula and teaching practices. The policy options are either to reduce socio-economic segregation or to mitigate its effects (see Chapter 5).

SOCIO-ECONOMIC BACKGROUND AND THE ROLE OF PARENTS

As part of the PISA 2006 assessment, 16 countries complemented the perspectives of students and school principals with data collected from parents.[18] These data provide important insights too as regarding the role which parents can play in raising student performance and moderating the impact of socio-economic background.

Parents' responses show, for example, a close relationship between their child's involvement in science-related activities at age 10 and their science performance at age 15.

Students whose parents reported that their child had, at the age of 10, read books on scientific discoveries "very often" or "regularly", performed 39 score points higher in PISA 2006 (on average across the 16 countries that administered the parent questionnaire) than did students whose parents reported that their children had done this "never" or "only sometimes". This performance advantage is roughly equivalent to the average performance difference associated with one school year (see Box 2.5). The performance advantage was largest in New Zealand, Luxembourg and Iceland, where it corresponded to between 53 and 60 score points on the science scale (Table 4.14).

Parents in the bottom quarter of the socio-economic distribution were less likely to report that their child had read books on scientific discoveries often or very often. In fact, in the top quarter of the socio-economic distribution the percentage was, at 18% on average across the 16 countries, almost twice as large as for the bottom quarter (10%). It is noteworthy, however, that in most countries the performance advantage of students in the bottom quarter of the socio-economic distribution who had read books on scientific discoveries very often or often at age 10, according to their parents, remained significant. In Denmark, for example, the performance advantage is 64 score points even in the socio-economically most disadvantaged quarter and in Iceland, Luxembourg and Germany it is still 35 score points or larger (for data see *www.pisa.oecd.org*). This suggests that educational activities in childhood can make up for a sizeable part of socio-economic disadvantage.

Similar effects for socio-economically disadvantaged families, though slightly less pronounced, are observed for children who very often or regularly watched TV programmes about science at age 10 or who watched, read or listened to science fiction. The relationships are mixed for the frequency with which 10-year-olds have visited websites about science topics or attended a science club, according to the reports of parents, but the percentages of students with these activities were generally small.

Parents' views of their child's school with regard to, for example, high performance aspirations, the disciplinary climate or the competence and dedication of the teachers, were also important predictors for student performance. Students of parents who strongly agreed or agreed that achievement standards are high in their child's school scored, on average across the 16 countries, 21 points higher than students with parents who disagreed or strongly disagreed with that statement (Table 4.12). In Korea and Germany, as well as in the partner countries/economies Croatia and Hong Kong-China, the advantage was between 30 and 48 score points. Some of this performance difference is accounted for by socio-economic factors, but, in most countries, the performance advantage of students whose parents reported high standards of achievement remained large both in the top and bottom quarters of the socio-economic distribution (for data see *www.pisa.oecd.org*).

Figure 4.13

Socio-economic background and the role of parents

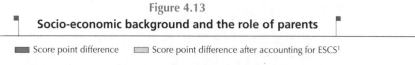

Score point difference between students whose parents answered "strongly agree or agree" and those whose parents answered "strongly disagree or disagree" on the following statements:

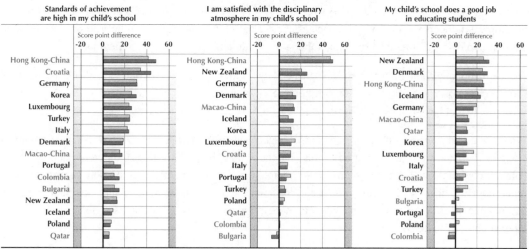

1. ESCS: the PISA index of economic, social and cultural status.
Source: OECD PISA 2006 database, Table 4.12.
StatLink 🔗 http://dx.doi.org/10.1787/141848881750

A somewhat smaller, but still sizeable, performance advantage (12 score points on average across the 16 countries), was observed for students whose parents reported being satisfied with the disciplinary atmosphere in their child's schools. This advantage was as high as 21 score points in Germany and 25 score points in New Zealand, and 49 score points in the partner economy Hong Kong-China (Table 4.12). However, while the percentage of parents reporting to be satisfied with the disciplinary atmosphere in their child's school was, on average, around 80% both among the top and bottom quarters of the socio-economic distribution, the performance advantage associated with this was about three times larger (at 18 score points) for the top socio-economic group than for the bottom socio-economic group.

The picture was similar for parents who reported that their child's school did a good job in educating students. An average performance advantage of 6 score points was observed for students of parents who strongly agreed or agreed that most of their child's school teachers seemed competent and dedicated. This is developed further in Chapter 5 (Table 5.7).

Students whose parents said they "strongly agree" or "agree" that their child's school provided regular and useful information on their child's progress scored, on average across the 16 countries, 9 points lower than those whose parents did not (Table 5.7). It is noteworthy that this perception is strongly related to the socio-economic background of families, with parents agreeing strongly or agreeing with this statement typically representing more disadvantaged socio-economic backgrounds. One interpretation is that parents from socio-economically more advantaged families have higher expectations with regard to obtaining feedback from schools.

IMPLICATIONS FOR POLICY

Home background influences educational success and experiences at school often appear to reinforce its effects. Although PISA shows that poor performance in school does not automatically follow from a disadvantaged socio-economic background, socio-economic background does appear to be a powerful influence on performance.

This represents a significant challenge for public policy striving to provide learning opportunities for all students irrespective of their socio-economic backgrounds. National research evidence from various countries has often been discouraging. Often simply because of limited between-school variation, schools have appeared to make little difference. And most importantly, either because privileged families are better able to reinforce and enhance the effect of schools, or because schools are better able to nurture and develop young people from privileged backgrounds, it has often appeared that schools reproduce existing patterns of privilege, rather than bringing about a more equitable distribution of outcomes.

The internationally comparative perspective that emerges from PISA is more encouraging. While all countries show a clear positive relationship between home background and educational outcomes, some countries demonstrate that high average quality and equity in educational outcomes can go together.

What are useful strategies in moving towards this goal, given the respective contexts in which countries operate? The characteristics described in this chapter display themselves in very different patterns across different countries. Strategies for improvement therefore need to be tailored accordingly. It is not easy to think about how all these characteristics interact. As a starting point, it helps to recap the different dimensions described in this chapter and to look at certain more or less average countries on each dimension to which other countries can be compared.

Figures 4.14a-f summarise the three levels at which the relationship between student background has been considered. One is the overall relationship within a country – what could be predicted about the performance of any student in the country if their socio-economic background was known. A second is the relationship within a given school – what could be predicted about a student's performance within a given school. The third is the relationship when comparing schools – what could be predicted about a school's average performance if the background of its intake was known.

On each of these dimensions, several factors are important. The two central aspects of the relationship are how much performance difference is associated with a given socio-economic difference within and between schools (slope) and how strong the predictions mentioned above are likely to be (explained variance). Also relevant is the amount of socio-economic variability within a country and the overall performance differences within a country.

These patterns can help inform the way in which policies are targeted (Willms, 2006). Options (which may be relevant in combination) include:

- Targeting low performance, regardless of students' background, either by targeting low-performing schools or low-performing students within schools, depending on the extent to which low performance is concentrated by school. Examples include early prevention programmes that target children who are deemed to be at risk of school failure when they enter early childhood programmes or school. Other systems provide late prevention or recovery programmes for children who fail to progress at a normal rate during the first few years of elementary school. Some performance-targeted programmes aim to provide a modified curriculum for students with high academic performance, such as programmes for gifted students.

- Targeting disadvantaged children through a specialised curriculum, additional instructional resources or economic assistance for these students. This is indicated by a relatively strong socio-economic gradient accounting for a substantial proportion of performance variation. Again, this can be either at a school or an individual level, depending on the strength of the inter-school socio-economic gradient, and also the extent to which schools are segregated by socio-economic background.

- More universal policies that rely mainly on raising standards for all students. In countries with weaker gradients and less variation in student performance, these will play a greater role. Such policies can relate to altering the content and pace of the curriculum, improving instructional techniques, introducing full-day schooling, altering the school-entry age, or increasing the time spent on language classes.

The following examples illustrate a range of different patterns observed in the PISA 2006 science data that point to different kinds of policy interventions.

A concentration of low-performing students

In some countries, the key issue to address is a relatively high number of students with low proficiency in science and other competencies. Chapter 2 shows that in some countries, most students are relatively weak in science. In others, there are relatively large numbers with low proficiency even though substantial numbers also demonstrate high proficiency. In Mexico and Turkey, as well as the partner countries Kyrgyzstan, Qatar, Azerbaijan, Tunisia, Indonesia, Brazil, Colombia, Argentina, Montenegro, Romania, Thailand, Jordan, Bulgaria and Uruguay, the absolute number of poorly performing students is high, with more than 40% of 15-year-old students performing at Level 1 or below.

In another group, the proportion of poor performers is moderate in absolute terms compared to other countries but high in relative terms within the country. For example, the United States has 9.1% of students performing at Levels 5 or 6, roughly the OECD average, but almost one-quarter (24.4%) on Level 1 or below in science. New Zealand, one of the best performing countries on average, still has 13.7% of students performing at Level 1 or below. Other countries with a comparatively large gap between better and poorer performing students include France, Germany, Japan and the United Kingdom. It is this second group where a focus on low performance is most clearly indicated, since in countries where very large numbers perform poorly, help for low performers does not constitute a particularly targeted policy.

Differing slopes and strengths of socio-economic gradients

A question that often confronts school administrators is whether efforts to improve student performance should be targeted mainly at those with low performance or those with a disadvantaged socio-economic background. The overall slope of the socio-economic gradient, together with the proportion of performance variation that is explained by socio-economic background, are useful indicators for assessing this question. As noted before, there is an important distinction between the slope of the socio-economic gradient referring to the size of the performance gap associated with a given amount of socio-economic difference and its strength which is associated with how closely students conform to the predictions of the gradient line. Figure 4.14a shows some contrasting patterns on these two measures.

Figure 4.14a
Relationship between school performance and schools' socio-economic background in Denmark, Portugal, Korea and the United Kingdom

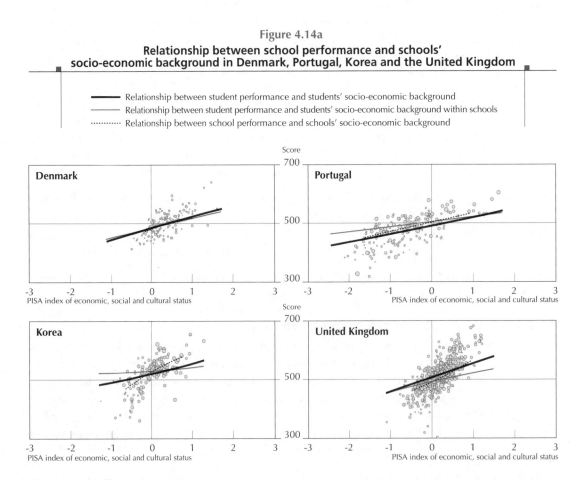

Note: Each symbol represents one school in the PISA sample, with the size of the symbols proportional to the number of 15-year-olds enrolled.
Source: OECD PISA 2006 database.
StatLink 🔗 http://dx.doi.org/10.1787/141848881750

In countries with relatively shallow gradients, *i.e.* where predicted student performance tends to be similar across socio-economic groups, policies that specifically target students from disadvantaged backgrounds would not by themselves address the needs of many of the country's low-performing students.

While Portugal and Korea have gradients of similar steepness, less steep than the OECD average, their gradients differ greatly in terms of their strength. In Korea's case (8.1%), the relationship is only one-half as strong as in Portugal (16.6%), which accounts for more performance variation than the average (Table 4.4a).

On the other hand, comparing the United Kingdom (a country with a steeper than average gradient) with Portugal provides a different picture. The United Kingdom's gradient has only an average strength (13.9%). Thus, whereas students in Portugal pay on average a lower penalty than those in the United Kingdom for a disadvantaged background, Portugal may find it more feasible to reduce this gap by targeting disadvantaged students. Countries where the relationship is relatively stronger will find that socio-economically targeted policies will be more likely to reach the students who most need help, indicating a greater need to combine them with performance targeted policies.

Portugal (with a 28 score point gradient), Iceland (29), Turkey (31), Finland (31), Italy (31), Spain (31), Korea (32) and Canada (33), are characterised by gradients that are flatter than the OECD average level of 40 score points for a one standard deviation change in socio-economic background (Table 4.4a). In these countries, a relatively smaller proportion of low-performing students come from disadvantaged backgrounds and also school performance is largely unrelated to a school's socio-economic intake. Thus, by themselves, policies that specifically target students from disadvantaged backgrounds would not address the needs of many of the country's low-performing students. Moreover, if the goal is to ensure that most students achieve some minimum level of performance, socio-economically targeted policies in these countries would be providing services to a sizeable proportion of students who have high performance levels.

By contrast, in countries where the impact of socio-economic background on student performance is strong, socio-economically targeted policies would direct more of the resources towards students who are likely to require these services. As an illustration, compare Norway and the Slovak Republic (Figure 4.14c and 4.14e respectively). By focusing on actions indicated by the left area of the chart, socio-economically targeted policies would exclude many schools and students in Norway with comparatively low performance but from advantaged backgrounds shown in the bottom right area of the graph. By contrast, performance-targeted policies would reach most of the lower-performing students and schools. In the Slovak Republic, where the relationship between socio-economic background and student performance is much stronger, socio-economically targeted interventions are likely to have a much stronger impact, as a much larger proportion of students and schools are located in the lower-left quadrant of the figure.

However, the case for socio-economically targeted policies can still be over-stated for countries with steep socio-economic gradients. In countries with steep socio-economic gradients, but where the variation explained by socio-economic background is only moderate, there tends to be a sizeable group of poorly performing students with a more advantaged socio-economic background. Consider, for example, the Czech Republic which has an above-average gradient of 51, but moderate variation explained (15.6%). As the vertical cut-off point in Figure 4.14e shifts to the left – *i.e.* as the picture focuses on more disadvantaged socio-economic background – the proportion of schools and students with low levels of performance which is not covered by these policies increases. Thus, in such situations socio-economically targeted policies are likely to miss a large proportion of students who have relatively poor performance.

Different socio-economic profiles

The degree of socio-economic differences within a country is important contextual information when interpreting the socio-economic gradient. For example, Canada and Spain have similar socio-economic gradients, but the range of scores on the PISA index of economic, social and cultural status between the 5th and 95th percentile of students is 35% larger in Spain than in Canada (Table 4.4a). This helps explain why in Canada, socio-economic background accounts for less than average variation in performance, whereas in Spain the performance gap between the bottom and top quarters of the socio-economic distributions is much larger than in Canada. Countries thus need to take account of the socio-economic profile of their student populations when thinking about how to target policies. The situation is similar when comparing Mexico and Spain, although in addition, Mexico has a highly skewed distribution of family background, with a high concentration of socio-economically disadvantaged students, which suggests the need for compensatory policies to help the most disadvantaged students, despite the fact that the slope of the gradient is modest. In Sweden on the other hand, a relatively equal society means that differences between students of different backgrounds have a relatively small effect, and policies targeting socio-economic reform are unlikely to be the dominant means of raising performance.

Figure 4.14b

Relationship between school performance and schools' socio-economic background in Sweden and Mexico

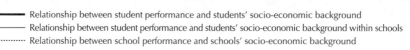

——— Relationship between student performance and students' socio-economic background
——— Relationship between student performance and students' socio-economic background within schools
·········· Relationship between school performance and schools' socio-economic background

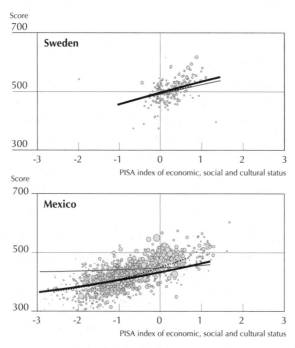

Note: Each symbol represents one school in the PISA sample, with the size of the symbols proportional to the number of 15-year-olds enrolled.
Source: OECD PISA 2006 database.
StatLink ⌨📊 http://dx.doi.org/10.1787/141848881750

Differing gradients across schools

The relationship between a school's socio-economic intake and student performance can vary in several ways. One feature is the extent to which a student who goes to a school with a socio-economically more advantaged intake can be predicted to perform better in science. A second is how close students come to this prediction – the strength of the relationship. However, a third feature that is very important in contrasting different countries is the extent to which schools differ in their socio-economic intake. It would not matter much if students' opportunities were strongly affected by a socio-economic difference in intake in a country where most schools' intake was similar.

This point can be illustrated by comparing four countries – the United States (with a between-school gradient around the OECD average), Germany, (with a comparatively steep between-school gradient), and Spain and Norway (with comparatively shallow between-school gradients). In Germany, about three-quarters of the difference in student performance across schools is accounted for by socio-economic factors (Table 4.1a). Spain on the other hand has one of the shallowest slopes of performance between schools with different intakes, but still close to 50% of between-school variance associated with socio-economic background. A significant factor is that the degree of separation of students into different schools is considerable, and the range of socio-economic differences between the upper and lower quartile of schools ranked by intake is the same as that of Germany (Table 4.4b). In contrast, this difference in intake is less than one-half as large in Norway.

Figure 4.14c
Relationship between school performance and schools' socio-economic background in United States, Germany, Spain and Norway

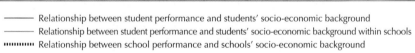

——— Relationship between student performance and students' socio-economic background
——— Relationship between student performance and students' socio-economic background within schools
·········· Relationship between school performance and schools' socio-economic background

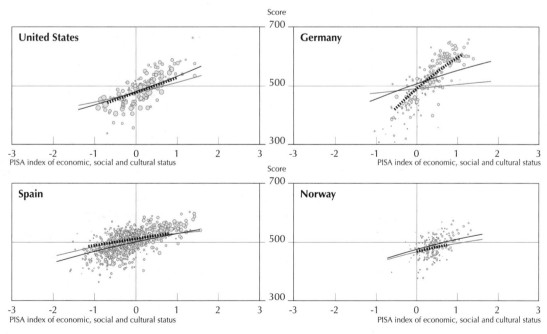

Note: Each symbol represents one school in the PISA sample, with the size of the symbols proportional to the number of 15-year-olds enrolled.
Source: OECD PISA 2006 database.
StatLink ᘛᕰᕰ᎐ http://dx.doi.org/10.1787/141848881750

This helps explain why despite having a steeper gradient than Spain, Norway has considerably less of its between-school difference in performance associated with socio-eonomic difference – at 38%, one of the lowest in the survey. Note also that in Norway and Spain, the overall amount of between-school difference in performance is low. Looking at these factors together, it is particularly countries where school performance varies considerably and where a high level of variation is accounted for by between-school socio-economic factors that need to consider whether socio-eonomic segregation by school is harming equity or overall performance.

Differing gradients within schools

To some extent, school systems that separate students into different schools by ability can expect to have narrower differences in student performance within each school, both overall and relative to socio-economic background. This is broadly the pattern observed in practice. However, differences between countries here tend to be smaller than in the comparisons of effects between schools. Thus even Finland and New Zealand, which in other respects represent one of the least and one of the most unequal countries respectively in terms of PISA results, are not very dissimilar on this measure. And in no country do within-school socio-eonomic differences in performance account for more than 11% of all performance variation. A general conclusion is that while there may be some instances where socio-economic differences in performance within schools need to be addressed, in no country can such measures succeed on their own in creating more even student performance.

Figure 4.14d
**Relationship between school performance and schools'
socio-economic background in Belgium, Switzerland, New Zealand and Finland**

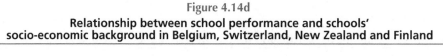

——— Relationship between student performance and students' socio-economic background
━━━ Relationship between student performance and students' socio-economic background within schools
·········· Relationship between school performance and schools' socio-economic background

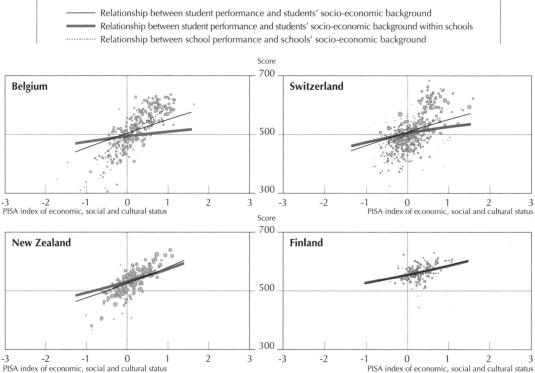

Note: Each symbol represents one school in the PISA sample, with the size of the symbols proportional to the number of 15-year-olds enrolled.
Source: OECD PISA 2006 database.
StatLink ⏎ http://dx.doi.org/10.1787/141848881750

These results tend to focus the attention of policy makers on the schooling system, particularly on features of the secondary education system. This is natural, as PISA is an assessment of students at age 15. Indeed, the analyses pertaining to school effectiveness presented in this report are based on data describing school offerings at the late primary or secondary levels. However, PISA is not an assessment of what young people learned during their previous year at school, or even during their secondary school years. It is an indication of the learning development that has occurred since birth. A country's results in PISA depend on the quality of care and stimulation provided to children during infancy and the pre-school years, as well as on the opportunities children have to learn both in school and at home during the elementary and secondary school years.

Improving quality and equity therefore require a long-term view and a broad perspective. For some countries, this may mean taking measures to safeguard the healthy development of young children or to improve early childhood education. For others, it may mean socio-economic reforms that enable families to provide better care for their children. And in many, it may mean efforts to increase socio-economic inclusion and improve school offerings.

Figure 4.14e [Part 1/5]

**Relationship between school performance and schools' socio-economic background:
school mean score 300-700**

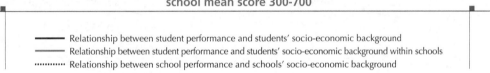

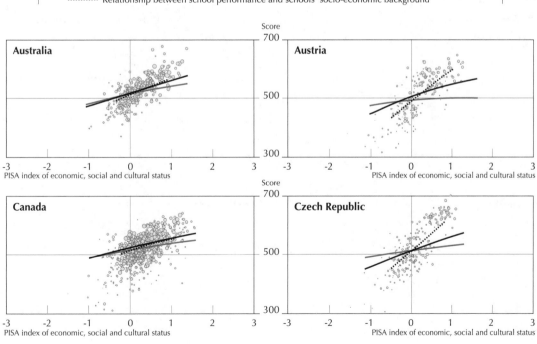

Note: Each symbol represents one school in the PISA sample, with the size of the symbols proportional to the number of 15-year-olds enrolled.
Source: OECD PISA 2006 database.
StatLink http://dx.doi.org/10.1787/141848881750

Figure 4.14e [Part 2/5]
Relationship between school performance and schools' socio-economic background:
school mean score 300-700

—— Relationship between student performance and students' socio-economic background
—— Relationship between student performance and students' socio-economic background within schools
·········· Relationship between school performance and schools' socio-economic background

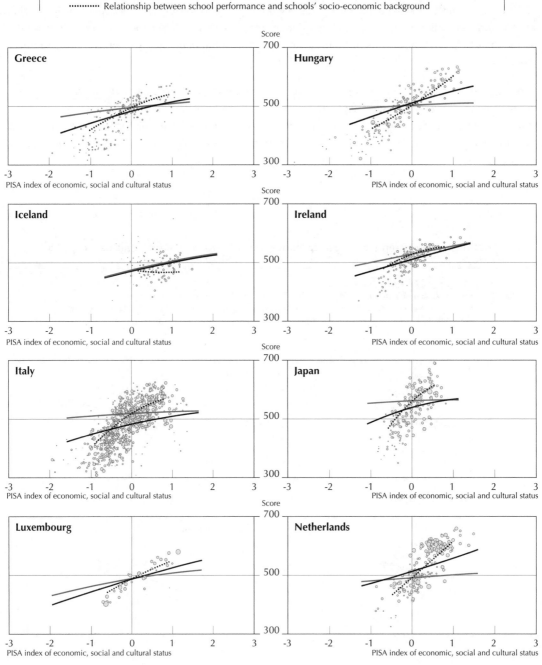

Note: Each symbol represents one school in the PISA sample, with the size of the symbols proportional to the number of 15-year-olds enrolled.
Source: OECD PISA 2006 database.
StatLink ᗛᔕᓬ http://dx.doi.org/10.1787/141848881750

Figure 4.14e [Part 3/5]

Relationship between school performance and schools' socio-economic background:
school mean score 300-700

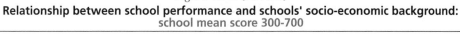

——— Relationship between student performance and students' socio-economic background
——— Relationship between student performance and students' socio-economic background within schools
·········· Relationship between school performance and schools' socio-economic background

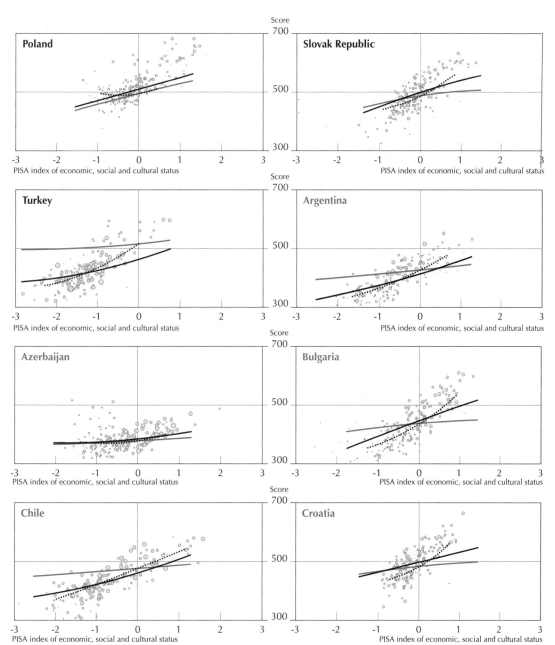

Note: Each symbol represents one school in the PISA sample, with the size of the symbols proportional to the number of 15-year-olds enrolled.
Source: OECD PISA 2006 database.
StatLink 🔢 http://dx.doi.org/10.1787/141848881750

207

Figure 4.14e [Part 4/5]
Relationship between school performance and schools' socio-economic background:
school mean score 300-700

——— Relationship between student performance and students' socio-economic background
——— Relationship between student performance and students' socio-economic background within schools
············ Relationship between school performance and schools' socio-economic background

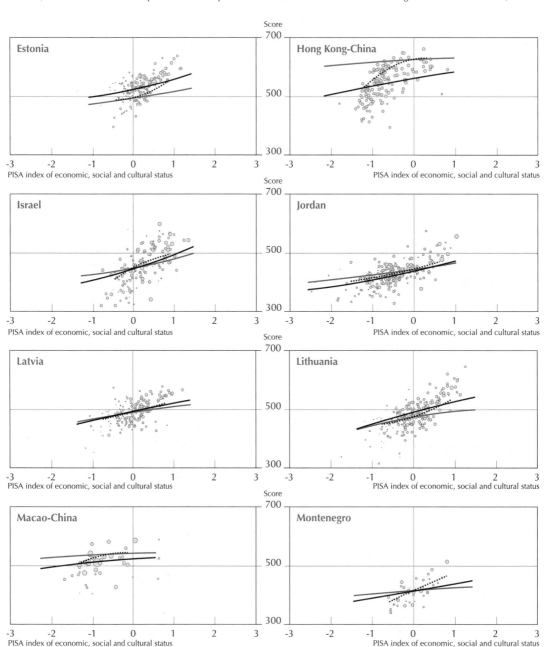

Note: Each symbol represents one school in the PISA sample, with the size of the symbols proportional to the number of 15-year-olds enrolled.
Source: OECD PISA 2006 database.
StatLink ᴍᴤ☐ http://dx.doi.org/10.1787/141848881750

Figure 4.14e [Part 5/5]
Relationship between school performance and schools' socio-economic background:
school mean score 300-700

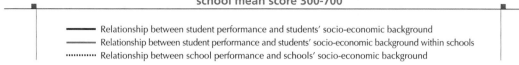

——— Relationship between student performance and students' socio-economic background
——— Relationship between student performance and students' socio-economic background within schools
·············· Relationship between school performance and schools' socio-economic background

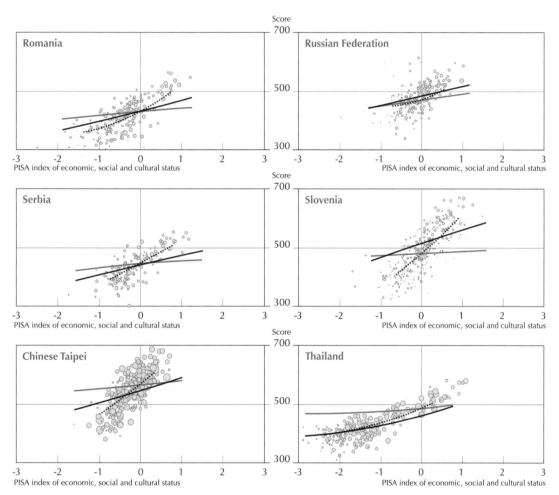

Note: Each symbol represents one school in the PISA sample, with the size of the symbols proportional to the number of 15-year-olds enrolled.
Source: OECD PISA 2006 database.
StatLink ⫿⫾⫿ http://dx.doi.org/10.1787/141848881750

Figure 4.14f
Relationship between school performance and schools' socio-economic background:
school mean score 200-600 and 100-500

——— Relationship between student performance and students' socio-economic background
——— Relationship between student performance and students' socio-economic background within schools
·········· Relationship between school performance and schools' socio-economic background

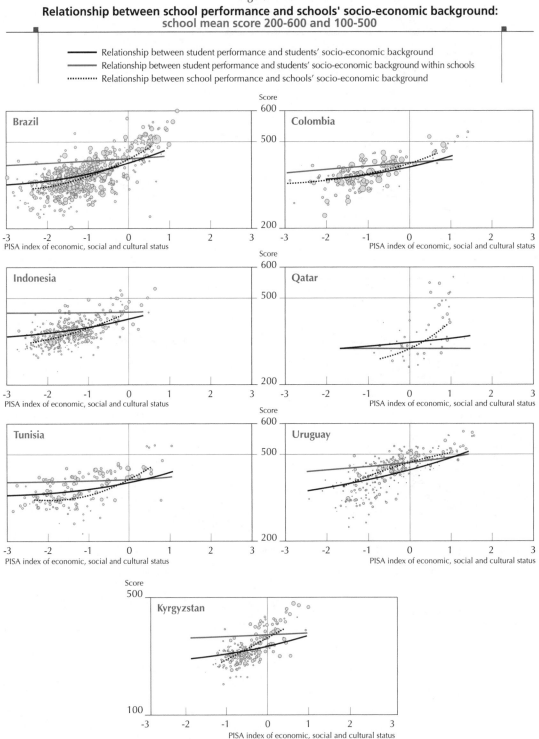

Note: Each symbol represents one school in the PISA sample, with the size of the symbols proportional to the number of 15-year-olds enrolled.
Source: OECD PISA 2006 database.
StatLink ⬛⬛ http://dx.doi.org/10.1787/141848881750

Notes

1. The partitioning of the total variance in the science scale was estimated with a three-level model including the student-, school-, and system-level. Scores on the combined science scale were used as the outcome variable.

2. Variation is expressed by statistical variance. This is obtained by squaring the standard deviation referred to in Chapter 2. The statistical variance rather than the standard deviation is used for this comparison to allow for the decomposition of the components of variation in student performance. For reasons explained in the *PISA 2006 Technical Report* (OECD, forthcoming), and most importantly because the data in this table only account for students with valid data on their socio-economic background, the variance differs slightly from the square of the standard deviation shown in Chapter 2. The *PISA 2006 Technical Report* also explains why, for some countries, the sum of the between-school and within-school variance components differs slightly from the total variance. The average is calculated over the OECD countries.

3. Turkey and Mexico show also comparatively low variation in student performance but in these countries, as well as in many of the partner countries, enrolment rates among 15-year-olds are comparatively low (see Annex A3) which suggests that the variability in performance among 15-year-olds in the population may be significantly underestimated.

4. The OECD average level is calculated simply as the arithmetic mean of the respective country values. This average differs from the square of the OECD average standard deviation shown in Chapter 2, since the latter includes the performance variation among countries whereas the former simply averages the within-country performance variation across countries.

5. For example, in some countries the schools in the PISA sample were defined as administrative units (even if they spanned several geographically separate institutions, as in Italy); in others they were defined as those parts of larger educational institutions that serve 15-year-olds; in others they were defined as physical school buildings; and in yet others they were defined from a management perspective (*e.g.* entities having a principal). The *PISA 2006 Technical Report* provides an overview of how schools were defined. Note also that, because of the manner in which students were sampled, the within-school variance includes performance variation between classes as well as between students.

6. This figure is obtained by dividing the percentage of between-school variance of the country by the OECD average between-school variance.

7. Before 1999, the school system provided three tracks following eight years of primary education, an academic secondary track, an academic track with a practical orientation, and a vocational track oriented towards direct entry into the labour market. The system introduced in 1999 provided six years of primary education followed by three years of subject-oriented general lower secondary education, followed by a tracked system of upper secondary education.

8. Although science performance cannot be compared between PISA 2000, PISA 2003 and PISA 2006, the proportion of variation between schools can be reasonably compared.

9. This is measured by the proportion of the variance in student performance that is explained by the PISA index of economic, social and cultural status (see Annex A1for the definition of this index).

10. The **PISA index of economic, social and cultural status** was created to capture a range of aspects of a student's family and home background in addition to occupational status. It was derived from the following variables: the **international socio-economic index of occupational status** of the father or mother whichever is higher; the level of education of the father or mother whichever is higher converted into years of schooling (for the conversion of levels of education into years of schooling see Table A1.1); and the **index of home possessions** obtained by asking students whether they had at their home: a desk to study at, a room of their own, a quiet place to study, a educational software, a link to the Internet, their own calculator, classic literature, books of poetry, works of art (*e.g.* paintings), books to help with their school work, a dictionary, a dishwasher, a DVD player or VCR, three other country-specific items, as well as the number of cellular phones, televisions, computers, cars and books at home. The rationale for the choice of these variables was that socio-economic status is usually seen as being determined by occupational status, education and wealth. As no direct measure on parental income was available from PISA (except for those countries which undertook the PISA Parent Questionnaire), access to relevant household items was used as a proxy. The student scores on the index are factor scores derived from a Principal Component Analysis which are standardised to have an OECD mean of zero and a standard deviation of one. For more details see Annex A1. See Tables 4.7a, 4.7b, 4.7c, 4.8b, and 4.9b for data on the individual components of the PISA index of economic, social and cultural status and Table 4.4a for values relating to the index.

11. For the purpose of this analysis these are those countries in which 15-year-old students with an immigrant background represent at least 3% of the 15-year-old student population.

12. For OECD countries there is no association (the cross-county correlation is equal to -.02, p = 0.921) and for all countries the association is slightly negative (the cross-county correlation is equal to -.35 and p = 0.045). That is, when all countries are considered the performance gap tends to be smaller in countries with higher proportions of immigrants.

13. Cross-country differences in the average performance of first and second-generation immigrant students can be influenced by differences in the composition of the immigrant population between successive generations, for example, the 15-year-olds in the first generation might have come from a different set of countries, or in different proportions, than the parents of 15-year-olds of second-generation immigrants. However, analyses of the PISA 2003 survey have shown that even students from the same countries of origin show considerable differences in their performance across the different host countries (OECD, 2005b).

14. The rank order correlation is 0.95.

15. The percentage of variance explained on average across OECD countries and the average slope across countries are different from the OECD average and the total shown in Table 4.9 since the latter also reflect the between-country differences.

16. See Note 8.

17. The decomposition is a function of the between-school slope, the average within-school slope, and η^2, which is the proportion of variation in socio-economic background that is between schools. The statistic η^2 can be considered a measure of segregation by socio-economic background (Willms and Paterson, 1995), which theoretically can range from zero for a completely desegregated system in which the distribution of socio-economic background is the same in every school, to one for a system in which students within schools have the same level of socio-economic background, but the schools vary in their average socio-economic background. One can also think of the term, $1 - \eta^2$, as an index of socio-economic inclusion, which would range from zero for a segregated schooling system to one for a fully desegregated schooling system. The overall gradient is related to the within- and between-school gradients through the segregation and inclusion indices: $\beta_t = \eta^2 * \beta_b + (1 - \eta^2) * \beta_w$, where β_t is the overall gradient, β_b is the between-school gradient, and β_w is the average within-school gradient.

18. These countries were Denmark, Germany, Iceland, Italy, Korea, Luxembourg, New Zealand, Poland, Portugal and Turkey, as well as the partner countries/economies Bulgaria, Colombia, Croatia, Hong Kong-China, Macao-China and Qatar. In examining the results from the PISA parent questionnaire, it should be noted that in some countries non-response was considerable. Countries with considerable missing data in the parent questionnaire are listed in the following together with the proportion of missing data in brackets: Portugal (11%), Italy (14%), Germany (20%), Luxembourg (24%), New Zealand (32%), Iceland (36%) and Qatar (40%).

5

School and system characteristics and student performance in science

Introduction 214

Admittance, selection and grouping policies 216
- School admittance policies 216
- Institutional differentiation and grade repetition 220
- Ability grouping within schools 223
- The relationship between school admittance, selection and ability grouping and
  student performance in science 225

Public and private stakeholders in the management and financing of schools 229
- The relationship between public and private stakeholders in the management and financing
  of schools and student performance in science 229

The role of parents: school choice and parental influence on schools 232
- The relationship between school choice and parental influence on schools
  and student performance in science 236

Accountability arrangements 237
- Nature and use of accountability systems 240
- Feedback on student performance to parents and the public 240
- The existence of standards-based external examinations 242
- The relationship between accountability policies and student performance in science 243

Approaches to school management and the involvement of stakeholders in decision making 245
- Involvement of school staff in decision making at school 245
- Involvement of stakeholders in decision making 249
- The relationship between school autonomy and student performance in science 252

School resources 254
- Human resources reported by school principals 254
- Material resources reported by school principals 256
- Learning time and educational resources reported by students and school principals 258
- The relationship between school resources and student performance in science 262

The joint impact of school and system resources, practices, and policies on student performance 264

**The joint impact of school and system resources, practices, and policies on the relationship
between socio-economic background and student performance in science** 272

Implications for policy 275

INTRODUCTION

Chapter 4 showed the considerable impact that socio-economic background can have on student performance and, by implication, on the distribution of educational opportunities. At the same time, many factors of socio-economic disadvantage are not directly amenable to education policy, at least not in the short term. For example, the educational attainment of parents can only gradually improve and average family wealth depends on the long-term economic and social development of a country. The importance of socio-economic disadvantage, and the realisation that aspects of such disadvantage only change over extended periods of time, give rise to vital questions for policy makers: what can schools and school policies do to raise overall student performance? And similarly, what can they do to moderate the impact that socio-economic background has on student performance, thus promoting a more equitable distribution of learning opportunities?

Studies such as PISA can address these questions only up to a point. This is both because many important contextual factors cannot be captured by international comparative surveys of this kind and because such surveys do not examine processes over time and thus do not allow cause and effect to be firmly established (Box 5.1). However, it is possible to describe both the learning environment of schools and education systems and the results achieved, using multilevel analysis.[1]

PISA 2000, PISA 2003 and PISA 2006 examined school factors selected on the basis of three strands of research:

- Studies on effective teaching and instruction, which tend to focus on classroom management and teaching strategies, such as students' opportunity to learn, time on task, monitoring performance at classroom levels, approaches to teaching, and differentiation practices.

- Studies on school effectiveness, which focus on organisational and managerial characteristics of schools, such as school and classroom climate, performance orientation, school autonomy and educational leadership, evaluation strategies and practices, parental involvement and staff development.

- Studies on resource inputs, which focus, for example, on school size, student/teaching staff ratios, the quality of schools' physical infrastructures and of their educational resources, teacher experience, training and compensation, and how these translate into educational outcomes.

The questions that the various PISA surveys asked students, school principals and parents were drawn up from these three areas, concentrating on those aspects that had received support in earlier empirical research. No data were collected from teachers, mainly because teaching is a cumulative process and because in most countries 15-year-old students are taught by multiple teachers. It has not yet been possible to establish a methodology to link students and teachers in surveys like PISA in ways such that meaningful inferences can be made as to the influence of teacher characteristics and behaviour on learning outcomes. Therefore, inferences on teaching and learning are only made indirectly from the perspective of students and school principals.

This chapter focuses on the following six groups of school and system-level factors:

- Admitting, grouping and selecting
- School management and funding
- Parental pressure and choice
- Accountability policies
- School autonomy
- School resources (human, material and educational)

Box 5.1 **Interpreting the data from schools and their relationship to student performance**

The PISA 2006 indices are based on students' and school principals' reports of the learning environment and organisation of schools and of the social and economic contexts in which learning takes place. Several of the PISA 2006 indices summarise the responses of students or school principals to a series of related questions. The questions were selected from larger constructs on the basis of theoretical considerations and previous research. Structural equation modelling was used to confirm the theoretically expected dimensions of the indices and to validate their comparability across countries. For this purpose, a model was estimated separately for each country, as well as collectively for all OECD countries. For detailed information on the construction of the PISA 2006 indices and the models, see Annexes A1 and A8.

Several limitations of the information collected from principals should be taken into account in the interpretation of the data:

- On average, only 300 principals were surveyed in each OECD country and in seven countries fewer than 170 principals were surveyed.

- Although principals are able to provide information about their schools, generalising from a single source of information for each school (and then matching that information with students' reports) is not straightforward. Most importantly, students' performance usually relates to the work of many teachers in various subject areas.

- The learning environment in which 15-year-olds find themselves and which PISA examines may only be partially indicative of the learning environment that shaped their educational experiences earlier in their schooling career, particularly in education systems where students progress through different types of educational institutions at the lower secondary and upper secondary levels. To the extent that the current learning environment of 15-year-olds differs from that of their earlier school years, the contextual data collected by PISA is an imperfect proxy for the cumulative learning environments of students, and their effect on learning outcomes is therefore likely to be underestimated.

- The definition of the school in which students are taught is not straightforward in some countries, because 15-year-olds may be in different school types that vary in the level of education provided or the programme destination.[2] Because of the manner in which students were sampled, the within-school variation includes variation between classes as well as variation between students.

- The study of school resources requires precision that might not be easily captured in surveys, especially surveys with time restrictions that affect what can be requested of respondents. For example, a principal may not have accurate data on such matters as class sizes in specific subjects, nor the time or resources to gather such data. Moreover, it is important to associate specific resources with specific students rather than school averages to ascertain how a change in one type of resource might impact student performance. The combination of these restrictions limits the ability of PISA to provide direct statistical estimates of the effects of school resources on educational outcomes. Caution is therefore required in interpreting the school resource indicators bearing in mind that there are potential measurement problems and omitted variables. However, despite these caveats, the information from the school questionnaire can be instructive as it provides important insights into the ways in which national and sub-national authorities implement their educational objectives.

• • •

215

In using results from non-experimental data on school performance such as the PISA database, it is also important to bear in mind the distinction between school effects and the effects of schooling, particularly when interpreting the modest association between factors such as school resources, policies, and institutional characteristics and student performance. The effect of schooling is the influence on performance of not being schooled versus being schooled, which, as a set of well-controlled studies has shown, can have significant impact not only on knowledge but also on fundamental cognitive skills (*e.g.* Blair *et al.*, 2005; Ceci, 1991; Downing and Martinez, 2002). School effects are education researchers' shorthand way of referring to the effect on academic performance of attending one school or another, usually schools that differ in resources or policies or institutional characteristics. Where schools and school systems do not vary in fundamental ways, the school effect can be modest. Nevertheless, modest school effects should not be confused with a lack of an effect by schooling.

Where data based on reports from school principals or parents are presented in this report, it has been weighted so that it reflects the number of 15-year-olds enrolled in each school.

Under each of these headings, the chapter examines the relevant features of school policies, practices and institutional characteristics, as well as their relationship with student performance before and after accounting for demographic and socio-economic background factors. The chapter also examines the relationship between the factors and the impact which socio-economic background has on student performance in order to gauge how these factors contribute to equity in the distribution of educational opportunities.

The analyses in this chapter were undertaken separately with science, reading and mathematics as learning outcomes. Since the results did not vary in fundamental ways across the different subject areas, the results are discussed only for science performance.

ADMITTANCE, SELECTION AND GROUPING POLICIES

As noted in Chapter 4, catering to an increasingly diverse student body such that all students benefit from effective instruction represents formidable challenges for education systems. The approaches that countries have taken to address this challenge vary: some have non-selective school systems that seek to provide all students with similar opportunities for learning by requiring that each school caters to the full range of student performance. Other countries respond to diversity explicitly by forming groups of students through selection either between schools or between classes within schools, with the aim of serving students according to their academic potential and/or interests in specific programmes. PISA 2006 collected information on school admittance policies, the degree of institutional stratification in education systems and the approaches to within-school differentiation that schools pursue.

School admittance policies

Admission and placement policies establish frameworks for the selection of students for academic programmes and for streaming students according to career goals and educational needs. In countries with large performance differences between programmes and schools or where socio-economic segregation is firmly entrenched through residential segregation, admission and grouping policies have high stakes for parents and students. Effective schools may be more successful in attracting motivated students and in retaining good teachers; conversely, a "brain drain" of students and staff risks causing the deterioration of other schools. Moreover, once admitted to school, students become members of a community of peers and adults and, as shown in Chapter 4, the socio-economic context of the school in which students are enrolled tends to be much more strongly related to student learning outcomes than students' individual socio-economic background.

To assess the academic selectivity of education systems, school principals were asked to what extent they considered the following when admitting students to their schools: students' residence; students' academic records (including placement tests); recommendations from feeder schools; parents' endorsement of the instructional or religious philosophy of the school; students' needs or desires for a specific programme; and the past or present attendance of other family members at the school.

Among these criteria, students' residence in a particular area tended to be the most frequently reported one. On average, across OECD countries, 47% of 15-year-old students are enrolled in schools whose school principals reported that students' residence was a prerequisite or a high priority for school admittance. However, this ranges from less than 10% in Belgium, Hungary and Mexico, and the partner countries/economies Croatia, Macao-China, Hong Kong-China, Slovenia, Chile, Serbia and Argentina, to over 80% in Iceland, Poland, the United States and Switzerland, and the partner country Tunisia (Figure 5.1).

Students' academic records followed as the next most frequently reported criterion, at 27% on average across OECD countries. These records may involve a formal test, an informal assessment of attainment or a formal qualification. Such academic selection can have positive features. It may help both stronger and weaker performers by adapting learning environments to the needs of each group, permitting each group to learn at its own pace, providing a reward in the form of entrance to a desired institution or a track that encourages attainment. On the other hand, it could also be argued that academic selection hinders the learning of those who are not selected because: high quality and high status programmes and institutions are naturally in high demand and when academic selection is used to choose entrants, those with initially weaker attainment can end up with lower quality education; weaker performers are not able to benefit from the expectations and aspirations of stronger performers and thus improve their own performance; sorting based on attainment can stigmatise those who do not meet the attainment standard, labelling them as poor performers and reducing their prospects in future education or in the labour market; and prior attainment levels, particularly at young ages, are a weak guide to future potential (Brunello *et al.,* 2006). Since many initial differences in performance are attributable to socio-economic background, the differential impact of socio-economic background on life chances could also be increased. In Japan, the Netherlands, Austria, Hungary, Korea and Switzerland, and in the partner countries/economies Serbia, Croatia, Bulgaria, Hong Kong-China, Montenegro, Macao-China, Indonesia, Romania, Qatar and Chinese Taipei, more than one-half of 15-year-olds are enrolled in schools whose principals reported that consideration of students' academic records was a prerequisite or at least of high priority when deciding on school admittance. In contrast, in Iceland, Sweden, Ireland, Spain, Denmark, Finland, Greece, Portugal, Italy, the United States, Australia, New Zealand and the United Kingdom, and the partner countries Argentina, Brazil and Uruguay, this is the case for less than 10% of students (Figure 5.1).

Students' need or desire for a specific programme follows next, with an OECD average of 19%, and attendance of other family members at the school (past or present) follows with an OECD average of 17%. Recommendations from feeder schools are at an OECD average of 13%, but there is considerable variation in this criterion across schools. Less than 1% of 15-year-olds students in Sweden and Norway are enrolled in schools in which recommendations from feeder schools are a prerequisite or of high priority for admittance and in 34 countries this is less than 10%, while it is 90% in the Netherlands and 40% in Switzerland, as well as 59% in the partner economy Macao-China. The parents' endorsement of the instructional or religious philosophy of the school is a prerequisite or high priority in the admission of 12% of students on average, across OECD countries (Figure 5.1).

217

Figure 5.1 [Part 1/2]
School admittance policies

Percentage of students in schools where the principal reported the following as a "prerequisite" or a "high priority"
for admittance at their school

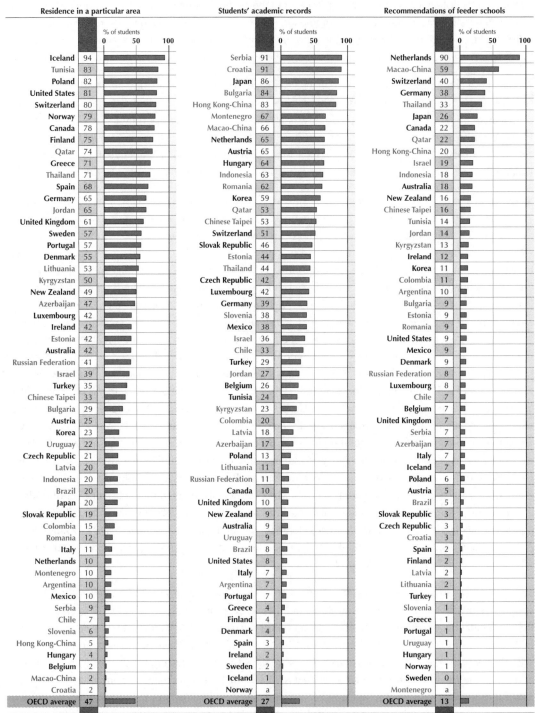

Residence in a particular area		Students' academic records		Recommendations of feeder schools	
Iceland	94	Serbia	91	Netherlands	90
Tunisia	83	Croatia	91	Macao-China	59
Poland	82	Japan	86	Switzerland	40
United States	81	Bulgaria	84	Germany	38
Switzerland	80	Hong Kong-China	83	Thailand	33
Norway	79	Montenegro	67	Japan	26
Canada	78	Macao-China	66	Canada	22
Finland	75	Netherlands	65	Qatar	22
Qatar	74	Austria	65	Hong Kong-China	20
Greece	71	Hungary	64	Israel	19
Thailand	71	Indonesia	63	Indonesia	18
Spain	68	Romania	62	Australia	18
Germany	65	Korea	59	New Zealand	16
Jordan	65	Qatar	53	Chinese Taipei	16
United Kingdom	61	Chinese Taipei	53	Tunisia	14
Sweden	57	Switzerland	51	Jordan	14
Portugal	57	Slovak Republic	46	Kyrgyzstan	13
Denmark	55	Estonia	44	Ireland	12
Lithuania	53	Thailand	44	Korea	11
Kyrgyzstan	50	Czech Republic	42	Colombia	11
New Zealand	49	Luxembourg	42	Argentina	10
Azerbaijan	47	Germany	39	Bulgaria	9
Luxembourg	42	Slovenia	38	Estonia	9
Ireland	42	Mexico	38	Romania	9
Estonia	42	Israel	36	United States	9
Australia	42	Chile	33	Mexico	9
Russian Federation	41	Turkey	29	Denmark	9
Israel	39	Jordan	27	Russian Federation	8
Turkey	35	Belgium	26	Luxembourg	8
Chinese Taipei	33	Tunisia	24	Chile	7
Bulgaria	29	Kyrgyzstan	23	Belgium	7
Austria	25	Colombia	20	United Kingdom	7
Korea	23	Latvia	18	Serbia	7
Uruguay	22	Azerbaijan	17	Azerbaijan	7
Czech Republic	21	Poland	13	Italy	7
Latvia	20	Lithuania	11	Iceland	7
Indonesia	20	Russian Federation	11	Poland	6
Brazil	20	Canada	10	Austria	5
Japan	20	United Kingdom	10	Brazil	5
Slovak Republic	19	New Zealand	9	Slovak Republic	3
Colombia	15	Australia	9	Czech Republic	3
Romania	12	Uruguay	9	Croatia	3
Italy	11	Brazil	8	Spain	2
Netherlands	10	United States	8	Finland	2
Montenegro	10	Italy	7	Latvia	2
Argentina	10	Argentina	7	Lithuania	2
Mexico	10	Portugal	7	Turkey	1
Serbia	9	Greece	4	Slovenia	1
Chile	7	Finland	4	Greece	1
Slovenia	6	Denmark	4	Portugal	1
Hong Kong-China	5	Spain	3	Uruguay	1
Hungary	4	Ireland	2	Hungary	1
Belgium	2	Sweden	2	Norway	1
Macao-China	2	Iceland	1	Sweden	0
Croatia	2	Norway	a	Montenegro	a
OECD average	**47**	**OECD average**	**27**	**OECD average**	**13**

Source: OECD PISA 2006 database, Table 5.1.
StatLink http://dx.doi.org/10.1787/141887160188

Figure 5.1 [Part 2/2]
School admittance policies

Percentage of students in schools where the principal reported the following as a "prerequisite" or a "high priority" for admittance at their school

Parents' endorsement of the instructional or religious philosophy of the school — % of students (0, 50, 100)

Country	%
Bulgaria	48
Thailand	48
Belgium	40
Qatar	35
Indonesia	35
Israel	33
Australia	27
Ireland	27
Hungary	23
Denmark	20
Netherlands	19
New Zealand	19
Colombia	19
Azerbaijan	17
Russian Federation	17
Argentina	16
Chinese Taipei	16
Canada	15
Spain	14
Hong Kong-China	13
Chile	12
United Kingdom	12
Jordan	12
Romania	12
Macao-China	12
Czech Republic	11
Brazil	11
Germany	11
Austria	10
Italy	10
Portugal	10
Latvia	10
Finland	10
Iceland	10
Estonia	9
Japan	9
Serbia	8
Kyrgyzstan	7
Slovak Republic	7
Luxembourg	7
Uruguay	6
Mexico	6
Poland	6
United States	5
Slovenia	5
Lithuania	4
Greece	4
Montenegro	4
Korea	4
Tunisia	3
Sweden	3
Norway	2
Switzerland	2
Turkey	1
Croatia	1
OECD average	**12**

Students' needs or desires for a special programme — % of students (0, 50, 100)

Country	%
Bulgaria	75
Serbia	71
Slovenia	64
Romania	48
Latvia	46
Thailand	44
Austria	44
Portugal	41
Canada	37
Italy	33
Hungary	30
Japan	29
Tunisia	27
Israel	26
Australia	25
Indonesia	25
Chinese Taipei	22
United States	22
Germany	22
Switzerland	21
Argentina	20
Colombia	20
Netherlands	20
New Zealand	19
Russian Federation	19
Iceland	19
Slovak Republic	18
Qatar	17
Finland	17
Denmark	17
Jordan	16
Kyrgyzstan	15
Korea	15
Ireland	14
Greece	14
Belgium	13
Spain	13
Chile	12
Mexico	12
Luxembourg	11
Macao-China	11
Uruguay	11
Czech Republic	10
Sweden	10
United Kingdom	10
Estonia	9
Montenegro	9
Croatia	8
Lithuania	8
Hong Kong-China	7
Brazil	6
Turkey	5
Azerbaijan	5
Poland	5
Norway	3
OECD average	**19**

Attendance of other family members at the school — % of students (0, 50, 100)

Country	%
Bulgaria	51
Spain	48
Australia	42
Luxembourg	41
Ireland	37
Qatar	34
United Kingdom	33
Portugal	31
New Zealand	31
Argentina	27
Canada	26
Macao-China	25
Greece	24
Denmark	24
Thailand	19
Germany	17
Hong Kong-China	17
Chile	16
Lithuania	15
Jordan	13
Russian Federation	13
Finland	13
Austria	13
Tunisia	12
Israel	12
Sweden	12
Italy	11
Latvia	11
Kyrgyzstan	11
Mexico	11
Serbia	10
Belgium	10
Iceland	10
Estonia	10
United States	10
Chinese Taipei	9
Indonesia	8
Romania	7
Uruguay	7
Azerbaijan	6
Brazil	6
Slovenia	6
Japan	6
Colombia	5
Poland	5
Norway	5
Netherlands	4
Czech Republic	4
Hungary	4
Turkey	3
Slovak Republic	3
Montenegro	2
Switzerland	2
Croatia	1
Korea	1
OECD average	**17**

Source: OECD PISA 2006 database, Table 5.1.
StatLink ⧉ http://dx.doi.org/10.1787/141887160188

Institutional differentiation and grade repetition

Many education systems contain mechanisms for dividing students into separate types of education, with different curricula, different qualifications at the end of the programme and different expectations for the transition to further education or work, representing different tracks. Commonly, more academic tracks offer readier access to university-level education, and vocational tracks provide training for particular jobs or trades in the labour market (although these may also provide options for continued education).

One device to differentiate among students is the use of different institutions or programmes that seek to separate students, in accordance with their performance or other characteristics. Where students are stratified based on their performance, this is often done on the assumption that their talents will develop best in a learning environment in which they can stimulate each other equally well, and that an intellectually homogeneous student body will be conducive to the efficiency of teaching.

The measures shown in Table 5.2 range from essentially undivided secondary education until the age of 15 years to systems with four or more school types or distinct educational programmes (the Czech Republic, the Slovak Republic, Austria, Belgium, Germany, Ireland, Luxembourg, the Netherlands, and Switzerland, and the partner countries Montenegro and Qatar).

Figure 5.2
Interrelationships between institutional factors
Measured by the cross-country correlation of the relevant variables

▨ OECD countries
▨ All participating countries

1 Number of school types or distinct educational programmes available to 15-year-olds
2 Proportion of 15-year-olds enrolled in programmes that give access to vocational studies at the next programme level or direct access to the labour market
3 First age of selection in the education system
4 Proportion of repeaters in participating schools (lower secondary education)
5 Proportion of repeaters in participating schools (upper secondary education)
6 Mean performance on the science scale
7 Variance of student performance on the science scale
8 Total variance expressed as a percentage of the average variance in student performance across OECD countries
9 Variance between schools expressed as a percentage of the average variance in student performance across OECD countries
10 Strength of the relationship between student performance and the PISA index of economic, social and cultural status
11 Existence of standards-based external examinations

	1 Corr. coef.[1]	1 P-value[1]	2 Corr. coef.[1]	2 P-value[1]	3 Corr. coef.[1]	3 P-value[1]	4 Corr. coef.[1]	4 P-value[1]	5 Corr. coef.[1]	5 P-value[1]	6 Corr. coef.[1]	6 P-value[1]	7 Corr. coef.[1]	7 P-value[1]	8 Corr. coef.[1]	8 P-value[1]	9 Corr. coef.[1]	9 P-value[1]	10 Corr. coef.[1]	10 P-value[1]	11 Corr. coef.[1]	11 P-value[1]
1			**0.56**	**(0.00)**	**-0.86**	**(0.00)**	0.05	(0.81)	0.24	(0.21)	-0.15	(0.45)	-0.05	(0.81)	-0.07	(0.70)	**0.72**	**(0.00)**	**0.52**	**(0.00)**	0.10	(0.62)
2	**0.31**	**(0.02)**			**-0.50**	**(0.01)**	-0.05	(0.80)	0.12	(0.56)	0.17	(0.40)	0.03	(0.89)	0.01	(0.97)	**0.59**	**(0.00)**	0.17	(0.39)	0.15	(0.45)
3	**-0.66**	**(0.00)**	-0.24	(0.08)			0.01	(0.97)	-0.14	(0.47)	0.23	(0.23)	0.12	(0.52)	0.14	(0.45)	**-0.75**	**(0.00)**	**-0.53**	**(0.00)**	-0.03	(0.86)
4	-0.12	(0.40)	-0.15	(0.29)	-0.05	(0.73)			**0.93**	**(0.00)**	-0.20	(0.28)	-0.14	(0.47)	-0.14	(0.45)	-0.03	(0.86)	0.29	(0.12)	**-0.41**	**(0.03)**
5	0.04	(0.76)	-0.05	(0.73)	-0.13	(0.33)	**0.91**	**(0.00)**			-0.22	(0.24)	-0.15	(0.42)	-0.17	(0.38)	0.13	(0.51)	0.33	(0.08)	-0.31	(0.10)
6	0.12	(0.37)	0.05	(0.73)	-0.06	(0.68)	**-0.30**	**(0.03)**	-0.22	(0.10)			**0.47**	**(0.01)**	**0.46**	**(0.01)**	-0.03	(0.88)	-0.30	(0.10)	0.29	(0.12)
7	0.08	(0.55)	-0.04	(0.79)	-0.14	(0.30)	-0.09	(0.52)	0.00	(0.99)	**0.48**	**(0.00)**			**1.00**	**(0.00)**	0.24	(0.20)	0.11	(0.55)	-0.03	(0.88)
8	0.06	(0.67)	-0.04	(0.77)	-0.13	(0.35)	-0.10	(0.48)	-0.02	(0.91)	**0.46**	**(0.00)**	**0.99**	**(0.00)**			0.21	(0.27)	0.11	(0.56)	-0.03	(0.89)
9	**0.54**	**(0.00)**	**0.29**	**(0.04)**	**-0.65**	**(0.00)**	0.02	(0.88)	0.18	(0.17)	-0.02	(0.91)	**0.39**	**(0.00)**	**0.39**	**(0.00)**			**0.50**	**(0.00)**	-0.01	(0.96)
10	0.24	(0.08)	0.05	(0.71)	**-0.48**	**(0.00)**	0.10	(0.44)	0.22	(0.10)	0.07	(0.61)	**0.43**	**(0.00)**	**0.42**	**(0.00)**	**0.51**	**(0.00)**			-0.09	(0.64)
11	0.14	(0.31)	-0.07	(0.62)	0.08	(0.54)	**-0.48**	**(0.00)**	**-0.42**	**(0.00)**	0.26	(0.05)	0.06	(0.63)	0.07	(0.61)	-0.04	(0.78)	-0.16	(0.25)		

Note: The proportion of explained variance is obtained by squaring the correlations shown in this figure.
1. Values that are statistically significant at the 5% level ($p<0.05$) are indicated in bold.
Source: OECD PISA 2006 database, Table 5.2.
StatLink ▨▨ http://dx.doi.org/10.1787/141887160188

Simple cross-country comparisons across OECD countries show that, while the number of school types or distinct educational programmes available to 15-year-olds is not related to average country performance in science (see column 6 and row 1 in Figure 5.2), it accounts for 52% of the share of the OECD average variation that lies between schools (see column 9 and row 1 in Figure 5.2).[3] The picture is similar when the partner countries and economies are included, although the relationship is slightly weaker then (29% see column 1 and row 9 in Figure 5.2).

Even more important, the number of school types or distinct educational programmes accounts for 27% of the cross-country variation among OECD countries in the strength of the relationship between socio-economic background and student performance (see column 10 and row 1 in Figure 5.2). In other words, in countries with a larger number of distinct programme types, socio-economic background tends to have a significantly larger impact on student performance, suggesting that stratification tends to be associated with socio-economic segregation. One aspect of such differentiation is the separate provision of academic and vocational programmes. Vocational programmes differ from academic ones not only with regard to their subject-matter content, but also in that they generally prepare students for specific types of occupations and, in some cases, for direct entry into the labour market. The proportion of students enrolled in vocational educational programmes varies from 1% or less in one-third of the OECD countries and one-half of the partner countires/economies to over one-half of students in the Netherlands (55%), and in the partner countries Serbia (76%), Montenegro (68%) and Slovenia (52%) (Table 5.2).

An important dimension of tracking and streaming is the age at which decisions between different school types are generally made and therefore at which students and their parents are faced with choices. Such decisions occur very early in Austria and Germany, at the age of 10 years. By contrast, in countries such as New Zealand, Spain and the United States no formal differentiation takes place between schools until the completion of secondary education (Table 5.2). While there is no relationship between the age of selection and country mean performance, the share of the variation in student performance that lies between schools tends to be much higher in countries with early selection policies. In fact, the age of selection accounts for more than half of the between-school differences across OECD countries (see column 9 and row 3 in Figure 5.2) and it accounts for 42% of the between-school differences across all participating countries (see column 3 and row 9 in Figure 5.2). While this in itself is not surprising because variation in school performance could be considered an intended outcome of educational tracking, the findings also show that education systems with lower ages of selection tend to show much larger socio-economic disparities, with the age of selection explaining 28% of the country average of the strength of the relationship between the PISA index of economic, social and cultural status and student performance in OECD countries (see column 10 and row 3 in Figure 5.2). The reason why the age at which differentiation begins is closely associated with socio-economic selectivity may be explained by the fact that students are more dependent upon their parents and their parental resources when they are younger. In systems with a high degree of institutional differentiation, parents from higher socio-economic backgrounds are in a better position to promote their children's chances than in a system in which such decisions are taken at a later age, and students themselves play a bigger role.

Grade repetition can also be considered as a form of differentiation in that it seeks to adapt curriculum content to student performance. In most countries, the requirement to repeat a year typically follows a formal or informal assessment of the student by the teachers towards the end of the school year, which suggests that the student has not adequately understood the material taught or reached the expected level of competence although sometimes repetition reflects failure in only some subjects. School principals were asked what percentage of students in their school repeated a grade at the levels of lower and upper secondary education

(ISCED 2 and 3, respectively), in the previous year of schooling. Across OECD countries, principals reported an average retention rate of 3 and 4% respectively. However, the proportions vary widely across countries: both in lower and upper secondary education, retention rates of 10% or more were reported in Portugal and Spain, as well as in the partner countries Tunisia, Uruguay, Argentina and Brazil. In the partner economy Macao-China, this was reported for lower secondary education, and in Luxembourg, for upper secondary education (Table 5.2). The results from PISA 2003 (*www.pisa.oecd.org*) show that, across countries, the performance of students who have repeated a school year remains lower than the national average. A number of other studies have also compared outcomes for those students who repeated years with others who were promoted despite poor results and found that grade repetition had little benefit and often led to the stigmatisation of the students concerned. It should be noted that the full economic costs of grade repetition, including the additional year of tuition plus the opportunity costs of one year of a student's time, which will mainly affect the student in the form of lower life-time earnings, typically after a delay, tend on average to be in the order of USD 20 000 per student per year repeated (OECD, 2005d).

An explanation for these results is not straightforward. There is no intrinsic reason why institutional differentiation should necessarily lead to the greater variation in student performance, or the greater socio-economic selectivity that the data show. If teaching homogeneous groups of students is more efficient than teaching heterogeneous groups, this should increase the overall level of student performance rather than the dispersion of scores. However, in homogeneous environments, while high-performing students may profit from the wider opportunities to learn from one another, and stimulate each other's performance, low performers may not be able to access effective models and support.

It may also be that in institutionally differentiated systems it is easier to move students not meeting certain performance standards to other schools, tracks or streams with lower performance expectations, rather than investing the effort to raise their performance. Finally, it could be that a learning environment that has a greater variety of student abilities and backgrounds may stimulate teachers to use approaches that involve a higher degree of individual attention for students.

The question, of course, remains whether institutional differentiation might still contribute to raising overall performance levels. This question cannot be answered conclusively with a cross-sectional survey such as PISA. The five OECD countries that show both above-average science performance and below-average impact of socio-economic background on student performance – namely Australia, Canada, Finland, Japan and Korea – do not track students early. The OECD countries with more stratified education systems tend to perform less well, but this tendency is small and not statistically significant.

While educational structures are deeply embedded in the historical and cultural context of countries, they are not static. Indeed, across OECD countries there has been a significant trend from highly stratified towards more integrated educational structures since the 1960s (Field *et al.,* 2007). The Nordic countries were among the first to make the change more than a generation ago, while Spain introduced such a reform as recently as the early 1990s by adding two more years of comprehensive schooling. The most recent example is Poland, which delayed the separation of students into different institutional tracks by one year, and since the reform of the schooling structure in Poland[4] was implemented between the PISA 2000 and PISA 2003 assessments, it warrants further discussion in this context. As shown in Chapter 4, for Poland there was a large decrease in the between-school variance between PISA 2000 and PISA 2003 for science, from 50.7% of the OECD average variation in student performance, of which the largest proportion was accounted for by the different school tracks, to 14.9%. Poland is now among the countries with the lowest between-school variance (12.2% in PISA 2006; see Tables 4.1a, 4.1b and 4.1c) – a result that researchers have associated with the fact that the 15-year-old students assessed by PISA were no longer separated into different school tracks.

An important question remains, of course, as to whether the more integrated structure of the education system in Poland merely led to a redistribution of the performance variance among schools or whether it induced genuine improvement in learning outcomes. A more detailed analysis of changes in the performance on the PISA measures in Poland sheds light on this. First of all, as described in Chapter 6, Poland showed the second largest increase in average reading performance among OECD countries, an increase of 17 score points between PISA 2000 and PISA 2003 and a further increase of 11 score points between PISA 2003 and PISA 2006. In the initial period, most of that increase occurred at the lower end of the performance distribution: in the PISA 2000 assessment, 23.3% of the students had scored at Level 1 or below. In the vocationally oriented track (comprising 23% of the student population) this proportion amounted to almost three quarters. It appears that students in this track benefited most from the more integrated school system, as the proportion of poor performers in the student population, those who scored at Level 1 or below, dropped from 23.3% to 16.8% in PISA 2003 and to 16.1% in PISA 2006. The question arises, of course, as to whether the more integrated school system was disadvantageous for the better performers. The results from PISA lend no support to this hypothesis, however. On the contrary, the proportion of students at the highest two performance levels increased from 25% in PISA 2000 to 29% in PISA 2003 and to 35% in PISA 2006. The results were very similar for mathematics.

Ability grouping within schools

Apart from institutional differentiation, students can be also grouped within the schools they attend. The rationale behind this practice is much the same as for institutional differentiation, namely to be able to meet the students' needs better by creating a more homogeneous learning environment.

PISA asked school principals to report whether students were grouped by ability into different classes or within their class, and were asked whether these groupings were carried through for all subjects, for some subjects (without specifying which), or not at all.[5] From these questions, three different forms of ability grouping within schools can be identified. On average across OECD countries, 14% of 15-year-olds are in schools reporting there is ability grouping for all subjects within schools (between and/or within classes); 54% are in schools reporting there is ability grouping for some subjects but not for all subjects within schools; and 33% are in schools reporting there is no ability grouping takes place (Figure 5.3 and Table 5.3).

Across countries, the proportions of 15-year-olds in these three forms of ability grouping within schools vary considerably. Over 85% of 15-year-olds were in schools where school principals did not report any form of ability grouping in Greece, and between 52% and 67% in Poland, Italy, Austria, Belgium, Norway, Germany and Turkey, and in the partner countries/economies Serbia, Croatia, Chinese Taipei, Slovenia, Macao-China and Uruguay.

However, in the United Kingdom, Ireland, New Zealand, Australia and Canada, as well as in the partner countries Israel, Azerbaijan and Thailand, over 90% of 15-year-olds are in schools where school principals reported ability grouping for all or some subjects, and in all of these countries, the age of first selection in the education system is 15 or above (Tables 5.2 and 5.3).

In the Netherlands, Luxembourg, and Switzerland and the partner countries Tunisia, Indonesia, Montenegro, Qatar, Thailand, Brazil, Colombia and the Russian Federation over 40% of 15-year-olds are in schools where school principals reported the grouping of students within schools based on their ability for all subjects. On the other hand, this is 5% or below in Greece, Finland, Hungary, Norway, Poland, Austria and Australia, and the partner country Slovenia (Figure 5.3).

223

Figure 5.3

Ability grouping within schools and student performance in science

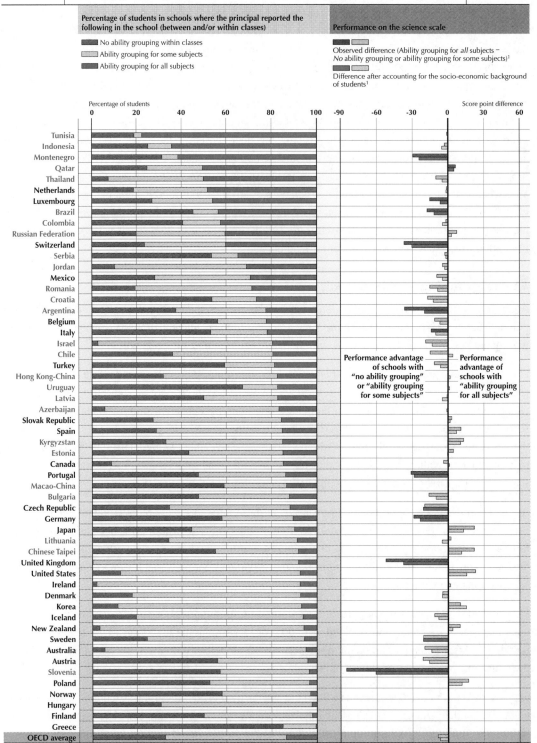

1. Statistically significant differences are marked in a darker tone.
Source: OECD PISA 2006 database, Table 5.3.
StatLink http://dx.doi.org/10.1787/141887160188

How does ability grouping within schools for all subjects, compared to no ability grouping or ability grouping only for some subjects, relate to student performance? In six OECD countries and four partner countries the science performance in schools that reported ability grouping for all subjects is lower; only in the partner country Qatar is it slightly higher than in schools without ability grouping or ability grouping only for some subjects (Figure 5.3).[6]

After accounting for the students' home backgrounds, students in schools that practise no ability grouping or ability grouping only for some subjects outperform those with ability grouping for all subjects in the United Kingdom, Switzerland, Portugal, Germany, the Czech Republic, Sweden and Luxembourg, as well as in the partner countries Slovenia, Montenegro, Argentina and Brazil, with the differences ranging between 7 and 61 score points.

The relationship between school admittance, selection and ability grouping and student performance in science

When assessing the extent to which the above factors relate to student and school performance, the individual effects of the factors on learning outcomes cannot simply be added, since they are interrelated. In the following, the effect of each factor is considered in turn, but in a model that takes the other factors into account. This section also shows the effect of these factors in Australia, Canada, Finland, Japan and Korea, the five OECD countries that show both above-average performance in science and a below-average impact of socio-economic background on performance. At the end of the chapter, a more elaborated version of the model is presented that also incorporates other school and system-level factors.

Across Australia, Canada, Finland, Japan and Korea (see the top-right quadrant in Figure 4.10), on average, 8% of 15-year-olds are enrolled in schools which reported practising ability grouping for all subjects within schools (OECD average 14%). This varies from 2% in Finland to 15% in Canada. In four out of these five countries, the first selection in education systems is at the age of 15 or later (OECD average 13.6). The number of school types or distinct educational programmes available to 15-year-ods is 1.6 on average: ranging from one programme in three countries to two in Japan and three in Korea (OECD average 2.5). On the other hand, considerable variation can be observed with regard to the academic selectivity of school admittance across these five countries. On average across these five countries, 26% of 15-year-olds are in schools with high academic selectivity, defined as schools reporting that academic records or feeder school recommendations were a prerequisite for school admittance (OECD average 19%), while 33% are in schools with low academic selectivity, defined as schools reporting that neither academic records nor feeder school recommendations were considered for school admittance (OECD average 42%). While the figures for high and low academic selectivity are 72% and 1% in Japan, they are 3% and 79% in Finland (Table 5.22).

As shown in Chapter 4, socio-economic factors play a role both at the level of individual students and through the aggregate context they provide for learning in schools. To examine this, the following analysis takes into account both the individual socio-economic background of students, as measured by the PISA index of economic, social and cultural status, and the socio-economic intake of the school, as measured by the school average of the same index. To examine the net relationship between admittance, selection and grouping policies and science performance, adjustments were made for demographic and socio-economic factors.[7] Such an adjustment allows a comparison of schools that are operating in similar socio-economic contexts. The net effects resulting from such an adjustment may, however, provide an incomplete picture of the true effect of admittance, selection and grouping policies because some of the performance differences are jointly attributable to admittance arrangements and socio-economic factors. For example, selection could reinforce socio-economic factors such that students from more

225

disadvantaged socio-economic backgrounds tend to be redirected to schools with lower performance expectations. Conversely, the interpretation of the school factors without an adjustment for the contextual factors (referred to as gross models in this chapter) ignores differences in the composition of schools and the country context. Gross and net effects are therefore both relevant. Parents and other stakeholders, for example, may be most interested in the overall performance results of schools, including any effects that are conferred by the socio-economic intake of schools, whereas those interested in the quality and effectiveness of schools and education systems may be primarily interested in the net effects.

The factors considered in both the net and gross models are the ones described in the preceding sections: school admittance based on academic record and recommendation of feeder schools, ability-grouping within school for all subjects, the age of first selection, and the number of distinct study programmes offered to 15-year-old students in a country (Box 5.2).[8]

Not surprisingly, schools reporting higher degrees of academic selectivity, where a student's academic record and/or recommendations from feeder schools are a prerequisite for admittance to the school, tend to perform better. Across the participating countries, the advantage amounts to 30.4 score points on the PISA science scale, equivalent to almost a school year; however, this is reduced to 18.1 score points after accounting for demographic and socio-economic factors (see the first table in Box 5.2). While these results suggest that individual schools benefit from more restrictive admission policies, this does not answer the question of how academic selectivity plays out for the education system as a whole. Do education systems in which schools have a higher degree of academic selectivity perform better or worse overall, all other things being equal? A separate model examined whether having a greater proportion of selective schools had an impact on the overall performance of the education system, beyond the individual school effect. The results show that there is no statistically significant compositional effect, that is, while selective schools tend to perform better, school systems with a greater proportion of selective schools do not perform better, other factors being equal.[9]

While an examination of the extent to which school or system-level variables relate to the overall performance of students is important, it is equally important to examine how those factors relate to equity-related issues. PISA assesses equity in the education system by the strength of the relationship between student performance and the socio-economic background of students and schools, measured through the PISA index of economic, social and cultural status (Table 5.20a).[10] The greater the dependence of educational performance on socio-economic factors, the less efficiently the human potential of the students is utilised and the greater the inequalities in educational opportunities. This part of the analysis therefore seeks to assess whether particular school and system-level factors are associated with the impact of socio-economic background on student performance. This is assessed by measuring the increase or decrease in the impact which one unit of the PISA index of economic, social and cultural status has, on average, on student performance in science. The results of this analysis suggest that whether individual students are in academically more selective schools or not does not appear to affect the impact which their socio-economic background has on their performance (see the second table in Box 5.2).

A similar analysis can be undertaken for school practices relating to ability grouping. Students in schools where principals reported that students in their school were grouped by ability for all subjects within the school, tend to perform lower in science, an effect which amounts to 10.2 score points in the gross model and 4.5 points in the net model (see the first table in Box 5.2). At the same time, whether students are in schools that practise or do not practise within-school ability grouping for all subjects appears to have no association with the impact that socio-economic background has on student performance (see the second table in Box 5.2).

Box 5.2 **Multilevel models: Admitting, grouping and selecting**

Admitting, grouping and selecting and student performance

	Gross		Net	
	Change in score	p-value	Change in score	p-value
School with ability grouping for all subjects within school (1=ability grouping between and/or within classes for all subjects; 0=no ability grouping or ability grouping for some subjects within school)	-10.2	(0.000)	-4.5	(0.002)
School with high academic selectivity of school admittance (1= academic record and/or recommendation of feeders schools are of prerequisite for student admittance; 0=others)	30.4	(0.000)	18.1	(0.000)
School with low academic selectivity of school admittance (1= neither academic record nor recommendation of feeders schools is considered for student admittance; 0=others)	-14.5	(0.000)	-1.6	(0.264)
System with early selection (each additional year between the first age of selection and the age of 15)	-4.2	(0.331)	-0.4	(0.927)
System-level number of school types or distinct educational programmes available to 15-year-olds	6.9	(0.357)	3.3	(0.607)

Admitting, grouping and selecting and the impact of socio-economic background

	Increase in score points in science corresponding to one unit increase of the student's PISA index of economic, social and cultural status		Increase in score points in science corresponding to one unit increase of the school average of the PISA index of economic, social and cultural status	
	Change in relationship	p-value	Change in relationship	p-value
School with ability grouping for all subjects within school (1=ability grouping between and/or within classes for all subjects; 0=no ability grouping or ability grouping for some subjects within school)	0.6	(0.311)		
School with high academic selectivity of school admittance (1= academic record and/or recommendation of feeders schools are of prerequisite for student admittance; 0=others)	-1.2	(0.139)		
School with low academic selectivity of school admittance (1= neither academic record nor recommendation of feeders schools is considered for student admittance; 0=others)	1.1	(0.084)		
System with early selection (each additional year between the first age of selection and the age of 15)	-1.3	(0.056)	6.6	(0.009)
System-level number of school types or distinct educational programmes available to 15-year-olds	-1.3	(0.294)	6.2	(0.049)

Notes: The analysis is based on 55 participating countries. The p-value (probability value) is the likelihood that a given multilevel analysis regression coefficient has been obtained by chance alone, and its real value is equal to zero. Thus, the smaller the p-value, the more likely that a given system or school-level variable is related to science performance. Data in shaded cells are statistically significant. Statistical significance was tested at the 0.5% level (p<0.005) for the school-level factors and at the 10% level (p<0.1) for the system-level factors as there are more than 14 000 cases at the school-level and only 55 cases at the system level in the analysis (in order to balance the Type I and Type II errors). A Type I error means that a conclusion can be drawn from the multilevel analysis results that a given institutional variable is related to science performance, when this is not the case; a Type II error means that a conclusion can be drawn from the multilevel analysis results that a given institutional variable is not related to science performance, when this is the case. In the net model, the following demographic and socio-economic background factors are accounted for: at the student level, the PISA index of economic, social and cultural status of student, gender, students' and parents' country of birth and the language spoken at home; at the school level, the socio-economic intake of the school, the school location and the school size; and at the country level, the national average economic, social and cultural status.

More detailed results for the first table are presented in Table 5.19a and for the second table in Table 5.20a. The model is described in Annex A8.

227

Figure 5.4
**Impact of the socio-economic background of students and schools
on student performance in science, by tracking systems**

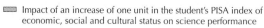
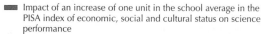

□ Impact of an increase of one unit in the student's PISA index of
economic, social and cultural status on science performance

■ Impact of an increase of one unit in the school average in the
PISA index of economic, social and cultural status on science
performance

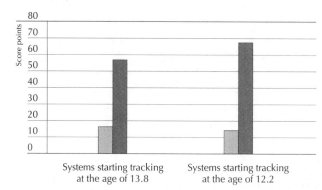

Note: Across the 55 countries, the average years spent between the first age of selection in the education system and the age of 15 is 1.2 and the standard deviation is 1.6. "System starting tracking at the age of 13.8" is a system starting tracking at the average stage (subtracting 1.2 years from the age of 15). "System starting tracking at the age of 12.2" is a system starting tracking at an early stage (one standard deviation earlier than the average therefore subtracting 1.6 years from the age of 13.8).
Source: OECD PISA 2006 database, Table 5.19a.
StatLink ▱▱ http://dx.doi.org/10.1787/141887160188

Whether, and at what age, students are placed in different institutional tracks or not is not related to student performance (see the first table in Box 5.2). However, institutional tracking is closely related to the impact which socio-economic background has on student performance (see the second table in Box 5.2): The earlier students are stratified into separate institutions or programmes, the stronger is the impact which the school's average socio-economic background has on performance. In fact, for each additional year that students are stratified into different institutions before the age of 15 – when they were tested by PISA – the impact which one unit of the school's average PISA index of economic, social and cultural status has on student performance increases by 6.6 score points. Similarly, with each additional educational programme into which 15-year-olds can be tracked, the impact which the school's average socio-economic composition has on student performance increases by 6.2 score points. On the other hand, the results suggest that the socio-economic segregation that is associated with tracking does create a more homogenous environment within schools, which is reflected in a slight decrease of the impact of students' background on performance within schools. However, this decrease is much smaller than the increase associated with the school's socio-economic impact. Thus, on balance, early selection into different institutional tracks appears to reinforce socio-economic inequalities in learning opportunities. This explains why the overall impact of socio-economic background on student performance is so much higher in highly stratified and early selective school systems. Figure 5.4 presents a comparison between education systems starting tracking at the age of 13.8 years (see the bars on the left in Figure 5.4) and education systems starting tracking 1.6 years earlier, which is equivalent to one standard deviation across the 55 countries in the model (see the bars on the right in Figure 5.4). The length of the bars in light grey represents the impact of one unit increase in the PISA index of economic, social and cultural status of students on performance in science and the length of the bars in dark grey represents the impact of one unit increase in the school average of the PISA index of economic, social and cultural status on performance in science.

PUBLIC AND PRIVATE STAKEHOLDERS IN THE MANAGEMENT AND FINANCING OF SCHOOLS

School education is mainly a public enterprise. Nevertheless, with an increasing variety of educational opportunities, programmes and providers, governments are forging new partnerships to mobilise resources for education and to design new policies that allow the different stakeholders to participate more fully and to share costs and benefits more equitably.

On average across OECD countries, 4% of 15-year-olds are enrolled in schools that reported being privately managed and predominantly privately financed (referred to as government-independent private schools) (Figure 5.5). In accordance with OECD standards, these are schools in which principals reported management by non-governmental organisations such as churches, trade unions or business enterprises and/or have governing boards consisting mostly of members not selected by a public agency. At least 50% of their funds come from private sources, such as fees paid by parents, donations, sponsorships or parental fund-raising, and other non-public sources.

There are only a few countries in which such a model of private education is common. Only in Japan, Korea, Mexico and Spain, and in the partner countries/economies Chinese Taipei, Macao-China, Indonesia, Jordan, Uruguay, Colombia and Thailand, is the proportion of students enrolled in independent private schools greater than 10%. By contrast, in more than one-half of the participating countries, independent private schools do not exist or 3% or less of 15-year-olds are enrolled in such schools (Figure 5.5).

Private education is not only a way of mobilising resources from a wider range of funding sources; it is sometimes also regarded as a way of making education more cost-effective. Publicly financed schools are not necessarily also publicly managed. Instead, governments can transfer funds to public and private educational institutions according to various allocation mechanisms (OECD, 2007). By making the funding for educational institutions dependent on parents' choosing to enrol their children, governments sometimes seek to introduce incentives for institutions to organise programmes and teaching in ways that better meet diverse student requirements and interests, thus reducing the costs of failure and mismatches. Direct public funding of institutions based on student enrolments or student credit-hours is one model for this. Giving money to students and their families (through, for example, scholarships or vouchers) to spend in public or private educational institutions of their choice is another method.

Schools that are privately managed but predominantly financed through the public purse (defined here as government-dependent private schools) are a much more common model of private schooling in OECD countries than are privately financed schools. On average across the OECD countries with comparable data, 11% of 15-year-olds are enrolled in government-dependent private schools. In Ireland and the Netherlands, as well as in the partner economies Macao-China and Hong Kong-China, the range lies between 55 and 91% (Figure 5.5).[11]

The relationship between public and private stakeholders in the management and financing of schools and student performance in science

Across Australia, Canada, Finland, Japan and Korea, the five OECD countries with both above-average performance in science and below-average impact of socio-economic background on performance (see the top-right quadrant in Figure 4.10), on average, 22% of 15-year-olds are in schools that reported being managed privately and 75% of total funding comes from public sources (OECD average 17% and 85 % respectively). However, there is considerable variation in this among these five countries: in Finland, 3% of 15-year-olds are in schools that are managed privately and all of the funding comes from public sources, while in Korea 46% of 15-year-olds are in schools managed privately and only 47% of funding comes from public sources (Table 5.22).

229

Figure 5.5
Public and private schools

◻ Observed performance difference

▨ Performance difference after accounting for the socio-economic background of students

▮ Performance difference after accounting for the socio-economic background of students and schools

	Percentage of students enrolled in public schools	Percentage of students enrolled in private schools		Performance difference between public and private schools (government-dependent and government-independent schools)
		Government-dependent	Government-independent	
Macao-China	4	69	28	
Hong Kong-China	7	91	2	
Netherlands	33	67	0	
Ireland	42	55	3	
Chile	47	45	8	
Korea	54	32	15	
Indonesia	61	13	26	
Chinese Taipei	65	0	35	
Spain	65	25	10	
Argentina	67	25	8	
Japan	70	1	29	
Israel	73	20	6	
Denmark	76	23	1	
Jordan	81	1	18	
Colombia	83	5	12	
Thailand	83	6	10	
Hungary	84	13	3	
Uruguay	85	0	15	
Luxembourg	86	14	0	
Mexico	90	0	10	
Austria	91	8	1	
Portugal	91	7	2	
Qatar	91	0	9	
Sweden	92	8	0	
Slovak Republic	92	7	0	
Brazil	92	0	8	
United States	93	1	7	
Canada	93	4	3	
United Kingdom	94	0	6	
Germany	94	6	0	
Greece	95	0	5	
Switzerland	95	1	4	
New Zealand	96	0	4	
Czech Republic	96	4	0	
Italy	96	1	2	
OECD average	**86**	**10**	**4**	

Performance advantage of **private** schools — Performance advantage of **public** schools

Score point difference: -120 -100 -80 -60 -40 -20 0 20 40 60 80

Source: OECD PISA 2006 database, Table 5.4.
StatLink ⟐ http://dx.doi.org/10.1787/141887160188

How do these institutional arrangements relate to school performance? This question is difficult to answer, not only because student characteristics sometimes differ between public and private schools, but also because in some countries private schools are unevenly spread across different school types, such as general and vocational programmes, which may, in turn, be related to performance. On average across the countries with a significant share of private enrolment, students in private schools outperform students in public schools in 21 countries, while public schools outperform private ones in four countries.[12] The performance advantage of private schools is 25 score points, on average across OECD countries.

It amounts to between 17 and 63 score points in Denmark, Portugal, Sweden, Ireland, Hungary, Spain, Canada, Mexico, and the United States, and the partner countries/economies Colombia, Chile, Macao-China and Jordan, to between 76 and 96 score points in Greece, New Zealand and the United Kingdom, as well as in the partner countries Argentina, Uruguay and Qatar, and to 107 score points in the partner country Brazil (Figure 5.5).

In the interpretation of these figures, it is important to recognise that there are many factors that affect school choice. Insufficient family wealth can, for example, be an important impediment to students wanting to attend independent private schools with a high level of tuition fees. Even government-dependent private schools that charge no tuition fees can cater for a different clientele or apply more restrictive transfer or selection practices.

One way to examine this is to adjust for differences in the socio-economic background of students and schools. The results for this are also shown in Figure 5.5. If the family background of students is accounted for, an average advantage remains for private schools although it diminishes to 8 score points. The net advantage of private schools is between 16 and 48 score points in Spain, Sweden, Mexico, Ireland, Canada, the United States, Greece and New Zealand, and in the partner countries/economies Colombia, Chile, Uruguay, Macao-China, Jordan and Argentina. It is between 51 and 90 score points in the United Kingdom, as well as in the partner countries Brazil and Qatar.

The picture changes further when in addition to students' family background the socio-economic background of schools' intakes is also taken into account. The impact of this contextual effect, which was discussed in detail in Chapter 4, on school performance is strong and, once it is accounted for, public schools have an advantage of 12 score points over private schools, on average across OECD countries. Once the impact of students' and schools' socio-economic background is accounted for, Canada is the only OECD country where private schools outperform public schools in a way that is statistically significant, although that is more commonly the case in the partner countries/economies Qatar, Brazil, Jordan and Macao-China.[13] Conversely, in Switzerland, Japan, the Czech Republic, Greece, Italy, Mexico and Luxembourg, as well as in the partner countries/economies Chinese Taipei, Uruguay and Thailand, public schools outperform private schools once the socio-economic context of students and schools is accounted for.

That said, while the performance of private schools does not tend to be superior once socio-economic factors have been accounted for, in many countries they may still pose an attractive alternative for parents looking to maximise the benefits for their children, including those benefits that are conferred to students through the socio-economic level of schools' intake.

In addition to the country-specific results shown in Figure 5.5, multilevel models were also employed to estimate the gross and net relationships between public or private school management and school performance (see the first table in Box 5.3). The results suggest that, without adjusting for demographic and socio-economic factors, private management of schools is associated with better performance,[14] as is the share of private investment in school financing. However, neither effect is visible once demographic and socio-economic factors have been accounted for. This suggests that private schools may realise their advantage not only from the socio-economic advantage that students bring with them, but even more so because their combined socio-economic intake allows them to create a learning environment that is more conducive to learning.[15] Analysis was also undertaken to assess whether public or private management and funding affects the relationship between socio-economic background and performance and no impact was found, that is the data do not lend support to the hypothesis that a greater proportion of private schools is associated with larger socio-economic disparities in schooling outcomes (see the second table in Box 5.3).

231

Box 5.3 **Multilevel models: School management and funding – public or private**

School management and funding and student performance

	Gross		Net	
	Change in score	p-value	Change in score	p-value
School being privately managed (1=private; 0=public)	20.0	(0.002)	-2.6	(0.353)
School with high proportion of school funding from government sources (each additional 10% of funding from government sources)	-3.2	(0.000)	0.3	(0.436)

School management and funding and the impact of socio-economic background

	Increase in score points in science corresponding to one unit increase of the student's PISA index of economic, social and cultural status	
	Change in relationship	p-value
School being privately managed (1=private; 0=public)	-0.7	(0.382)
School with high proportion of school funding from government sources (each additional 10% of funding from government sources)	0.2	(0.174)

Note: See Box 5.2 for general notes.

More detailed results in the first table are presented in Table 5.19b and those in the second table are in Table 5.20b. The model is described in Annex A8.

THE ROLE OF PARENTS: SCHOOL CHOICE AND PARENTAL INFLUENCE ON SCHOOLS

Apart from the direct influence that parent groups have gained in some countries with respect to being an integral body in decision making at school (see section "Approaches to school management and the involvement of stakeholders in decision making" below), parents may also exert indirect influence on schools, most obviously when they can choose the school for their child. In recent years, some countries have increased the extent of choice, particularly in secondary education. This is partly because the demand for choice from parents appears to be increasing and partly because a market, or quasi-market, in schooling is thought to push individual schools to improve quality and contain costs (*e.g.* Hoxby, 2002).

To provide an assessment of the role of choice, school principals were asked to indicate whether there are other schools in the local area with which they compete for students. For 60% of students, on average across OECD countries, parents have, in the above sense, a choice of two or more other schools for their children (Figure 5.6). School choice is particularly prevalent in Australia, the Slovak Republic, the United Kingdom, New Zealand and Japan, as well as in the partner countries/economies Indonesia, Hong Kong-China, Chinese-Taipei, Macao-China and Latvia, where more than 80% of 15-year-olds are enrolled in schools where school principals reported a choice of at least two alternatives to their own school.

On the other hand, in Iceland, Norway, and Switzerland, and in the partner countries Qatar and Uruguay, the parents of at least one-half of the students have effectively no choice, according to school principals. However, caution is required when interpreting these results, as the existence of other schools in the local area does not automatically imply that all parents have access to these, particularly if they are privately managed. In some countries, this also depends on whether 15-year-old students are enrolled at the primary or secondary level of education.

Figure 5.6
School choice

Percentage of students in schools where the principal reported the following number of schools competing for the students in the same area

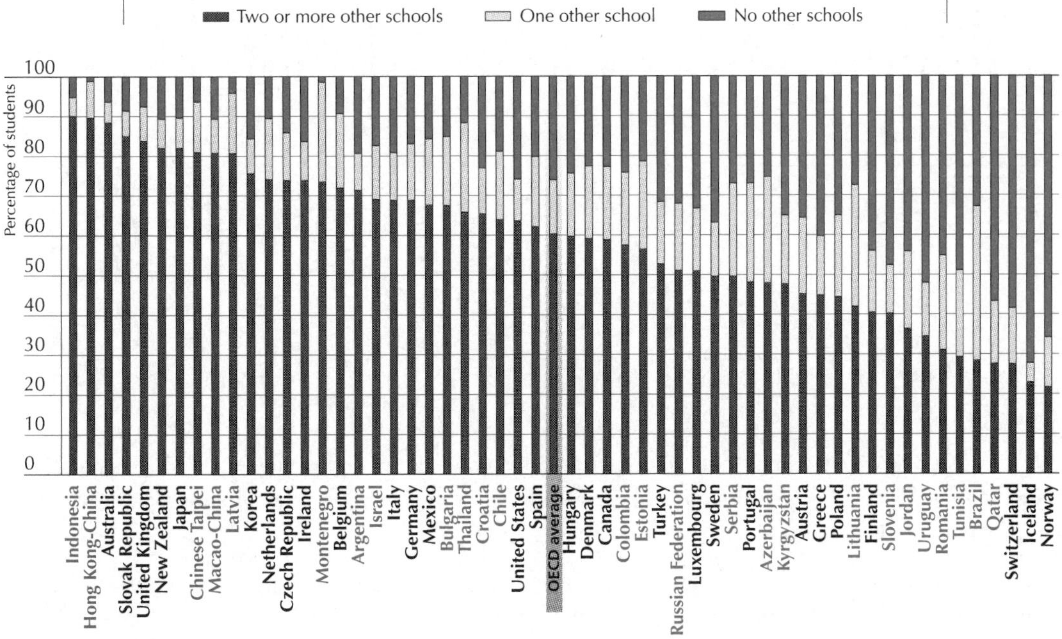

■ Two or more other schools   ☐ One other school   ■ No other schools

Source: OECD PISA 2006 database, Table 5.5.
StatLink ⬛⬛ http://dx.doi.org/10.1787/141887160188

To what extent do school principals experience parental pressure on the school to achieve high academic standards among students? On average, across OECD countries, 21% of students are enrolled in schools where school principals reported constant pressure from many parents who expected the school to set very high academic standards and to have the students achieve them, while 47% of students are enrolled in schools in which a minority of parents exert pressure to achieve higher academic standards among students (Figure 5.7). According to the reports from school principals, parental expectations for high academic standards are particularly high in New Zealand, Sweden and Ireland where more than 40% of students are enrolled in schools that reported constant pressure from many parents. On the other hand, parental pressure on schools is largely absent for 32% of students on average across OECD countries. In Finland – the best performing country – this is the case for 79% of students.

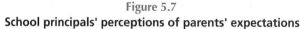

Figure 5.7
School principals' perceptions of parents' expectations

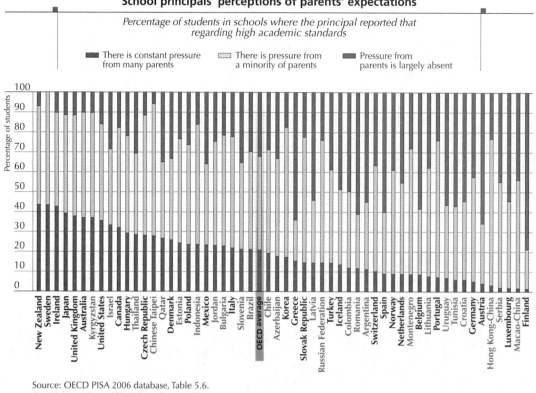

Source: OECD PISA 2006 database, Table 5.6.
StatLink http://dx.doi.org/10.1787/141887160188

As part of the PISA 2006 assessment, 16 countries complemented the perspectives of students and school principals with data collected from parents (Figure 5.8).[16] These data provide an additional perspective on the demands and expectations placed upon schools.

- On average across the 16 countries, 86% of the 15-year-olds' parents strongly agreed or agreed that their child's school did a good job in educating students, and in each of the 16 individual countries this figure is over 76%. Students whose parents agreed or strongly agreed that the school did a good job in educating students performed 11 score points higher than those students whose parents disagreed or strongly disagreed. In New Zealand, Denmark and Iceland, as well as the partner economy Hong Kong-China, this performance advantage exceeds 24 score points.

- On average, 76% of the parents strongly agreed or agreed that standards of achievement were high in their child's school, a figure which ranges from around 54% in the partner economy Hong Kong-China to more than 85% in Poland, New Zealand and the partner countries Bulgaria and Colombia. Again, students whose parents considered that their school had high standards tended to perform better, on average across the 16 countries by 21 score points. In Germany and Korea, and the partner countries/economies Hong Kong-China and Croatia, the performance advantage is between 30 and 48 score points.

- On average, 81% of the parents reported being satisfied with the disciplinary atmosphere in their child's school, and particularly so in Luxembourg and New Zealand, and in the partner countries/economies Hong Kong-China, Macao-China, Colombia and Croatia. On average, parental satisfaction with the disciplinary atmosphere in their children's school is associated with a performance advantage of 12 score points.

Figure 5.8
Parents' perceptions of school quality

Percentage of students whose parents "agree or strongly agree" and difference in science performance between students whose parents "agree or strongly agree" and those who "disagree or strongly disagree" with the following statements regarding the school their children attend[1]

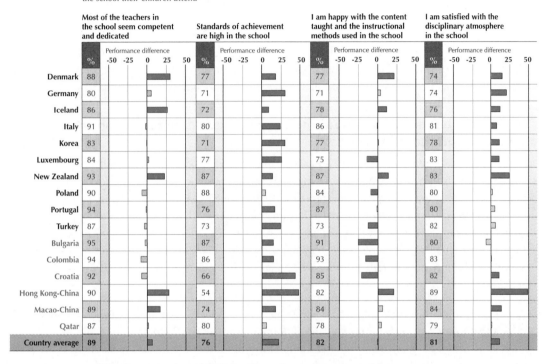

	Most of the teachers in the school seem competent and dedicated %	Standards of achievement are high in the school %	I am happy with the content taught and the instructional methods used in the school %	I am satisfied with the disciplinary atmosphere in the school %
Denmark	88	77	77	74
Germany	80	71	71	74
Iceland	86	72	78	76
Italy	91	80	86	81
Korea	83	71	77	78
Luxembourg	84	77	75	83
New Zealand	93	87	87	83
Poland	90	88	84	80
Portugal	94	76	87	80
Turkey	87	73	73	82
Bulgaria	95	87	91	80
Colombia	94	86	93	83
Croatia	92	66	85	82
Hong Kong-China	90	54	82	89
Macao-China	89	74	84	84
Qatar	87	80	78	79
Country average	89	76	82	81

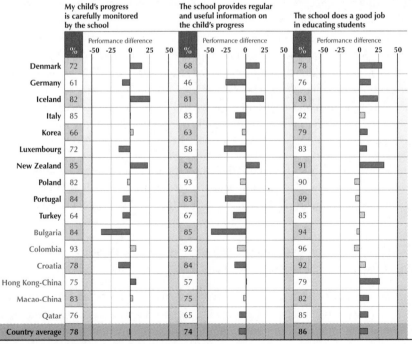

	My child's progress is carefully monitored by the school %	The school provides regular and useful information on the child's progress %	The school does a good job in educating students %
Denmark	72	68	78
Germany	61	46	76
Iceland	82	81	83
Italy	85	83	92
Korea	66	63	79
Luxembourg	72	58	83
New Zealand	85	82	91
Poland	82	93	90
Portugal	84	83	89
Turkey	64	67	85
Bulgaria	84	85	94
Colombia	93	92	96
Croatia	78	84	92
Hong Kong-China	75	57	79
Macao-China	83	75	82
Qatar	76	65	85
Country average	78	74	86

1. Statistically significant differences are marked in a darker tone.
Source: OECD PISA 2006 database, Table 5.7.
StatLink ⟨⟩ http://dx.doi.org/10.1787/141887160188

235

- On average, 89% of the parents agreed or strongly agreed that their child's teachers seemed competent and dedicated, and this ranges from around 80% in Germany, Korea and Luxembourg to more than 90% in Portugal, New Zealand, Italy and Poland, as well as the partner countries Bulgaria, Colombia and Croatia. The relationship of this measure with student performance is inconsistent across countries, but is positive on average (6 score points).

- On average, 74% of the parents agreed or strongly agreed that the school provided regular and useful information on their child's progress, but this ranges from less than 50% in Germany to over 90% in Poland and the partner country Colombia. The relationship of this measure with student performance is inconsistent across countries, but is negative on average (9 score points).

The relationship between school choice and parental influence on schools and student performance in science

Across Australia, Canada, Finland, Japan and Korea, the five OECD countries with both an above-average student performance in science and a below-average impact of socio-economic background on student performance (see the top-right quadrant in Figure 4.10), 80% of 15-year-olds are in schools which reported competing with one or more other schools in the area for students (OECD average 74%). This varies from 56% in Finland to 94% in Australia. Similarly, on average, 73% of 15-year-olds are in schools whose principals reported that the schools were receiving constant pressure from many parents or pressure from a minority of parents, but this ranges from only 21% in Finland to 90% in Australia (OECD average 68%) (Table 5.22).

Two multilevel models were employed to assess the (gross and net) association between school choice and perceived parental pressure on student performance in science (see the first table in Box 5.4). The results suggest that students in schools competing with other schools for the students in the same area tend to perform better, but this effect is no longer visible when demographic and socio-economic factors are accounted for. However, students in systems with a greater proportion of schools competing with other schools tend to perform better even after accounting for demographic and socio-economic factors. These results suggest that whether students are in competitive schools or not does not matter for their performance when socio-economic factors are accounted for, but it does matter whether school systems offer higher proportions of competitive schools. Students in education systems with 85% of schools competing with other schools tend to perform 6.7 score points higher in science than students in education systems where 75% of schools are competitive, regardless of whether the particular schools that students attend are competitive or not.[17]

Similarly, students in schools whose principals perceived themselves to be under pressure from parents to maintain high academic standards tended to perform better than students in schools without pressure, but there is no statistically significant association when demographic and socio-economic factors are accounted for.

None of the factors related to parents' pressure and choice were found to have a statistically significant association with educational equity (see the second table in Box 5.4).

It is difficult to interpret relationships between such factors as school choice, schools' admittance policies and school performance, because more selective schools may perform better simply because they do not accept poorly performing students and not necessarily because they provide better services. The last section will examine the joint impact of all the factors discussed so far on student performance in science.

Box 5.4 **Multilevel models: Parental pressure and choice**

Parental pressure and choice and student performance

	Gross		Net	
	Change in score	p-value	Change in score	p-value
School with high level of competition (1=one or more other schools compete for students; 0=no other schools compete for students)	17.9	(0.000)	1.9	(0.245)
School with high levels of perceived parental pressure (1=there is pressure from parents; 0=pressure from parent is largely absent)	11.2	(0.000)	2.0	(0.228)
System with high proportion of competitive schools (each additional 10% of competitive schools)	3.1	(0.525)	6.7	(0.076)

Parental pressure and choice and the impact of socio-economic background

	Increase in score points in science corresponding to one unit increase of the student's PISA index of the economic, social and cultural status		Increase in score points in science corresponding to one unit increase of the school average of the PISA index of the economic, social and cultural status	
	Change in relationship	p-value	Change in relationship	p-value
School with high level of competition (1=one or more other schools compete for students; 0=no other schools compete for students)	1.0	(0.083)		
School with high levels of perceived parental pressure (1=there is pressure from parents; 0=pressure from parent is largely absent)	1.0	(0.058)		
System with high proportion of competitive schools (each additional 10% of competitive schools)	-0.8	(0.291)	3.5	(0.211)

Note: See Box 5.2 for general notes.
More detailed results in the first table are presented in Table 5.19c and those in the second table are in Table 5.20c. The model is described in Annex A8.

ACCOUNTABILITY ARRANGEMENTS

The shift in public and governmental concern, away from mere control over the resources and content of education toward a focus on outcomes has, in many countries, driven the establishment of standards for the quality of the work of educational institutions. The approaches to standard-setting that countries pursue range from the definition of broad educational goals up to the formulation of concise performance expectations in well-defined subject areas.

The establishment of performance standards has, in turn, driven the establishment of accountability systems. Over the last decade, assessments of student performance have become common in many OECD countries – and often the results are widely reported and used in public debate, as well as by those concerned with school improvement. However, the rationale for assessments and the nature of the instruments used vary greatly within and across countries. Methods employed in OECD countries include different forms of external assessment, external evaluation or inspection, and schools' own quality assurance and self-evaluation efforts.

Given the importance that accountability systems now play in the policy and public debate and given the diverse accountability arrangements across OECD countries (OECD, 2007), the PISA 2006 assessment collected data on the nature of accountability systems and the ways in which the resulting information was used and made available to various stakeholders and the public at large.

Figure 5.9 [Part 1/2]
Use of achievement data for accountability purposes

Percentage of students in schools where the principal reported that achievement data were

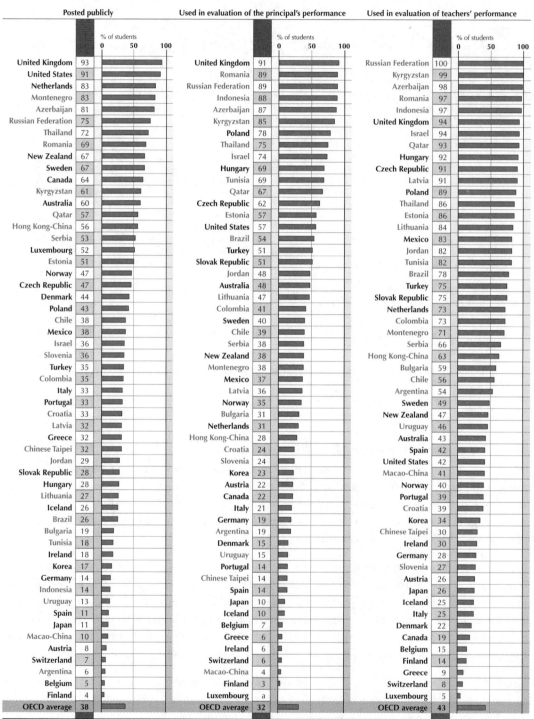

Posted publicly		Used in evaluation of the principal's performance		Used in evaluation of teachers' performance	
United Kingdom	93	United Kingdom	91	Russian Federation	100
United States	91	Romania	89	Kyrgyzstan	99
Netherlands	83	Russian Federation	89	Azerbaijan	98
Montenegro	83	Indonesia	88	Romania	97
Azerbaijan	81	Azerbaijan	87	Indonesia	97
Russian Federation	75	Kyrgyzstan	85	United Kingdom	94
Thailand	72	Poland	78	Israel	94
Romania	69	Thailand	75	Qatar	93
New Zealand	67	Israel	74	Hungary	92
Sweden	67	Hungary	69	Czech Republic	91
Canada	64	Tunisia	69	Latvia	91
Kyrgyzstan	61	Qatar	67	Poland	89
Australia	60	Czech Republic	62	Thailand	86
Qatar	57	Estonia	57	Estonia	86
Hong Kong-China	56	United States	57	Lithuania	84
Serbia	53	Brazil	54	Mexico	83
Luxembourg	52	Turkey	51	Jordan	82
Estonia	51	Slovak Republic	51	Tunisia	82
Norway	47	Jordan	48	Brazil	78
Czech Republic	47	Australia	48	Turkey	75
Denmark	44	Lithuania	47	Slovak Republic	75
Poland	43	Colombia	41	Netherlands	73
Chile	38	Sweden	40	Colombia	73
Mexico	38	Chile	39	Montenegro	71
Israel	36	Serbia	38	Serbia	66
Slovenia	36	New Zealand	38	Hong Kong-China	63
Turkey	35	Montenegro	38	Bulgaria	59
Colombia	35	Mexico	37	Chile	56
Italy	33	Latvia	36	Argentina	54
Portugal	33	Norway	35	Sweden	49
Croatia	33	Bulgaria	31	New Zealand	47
Latvia	32	Netherlands	31	Uruguay	46
Greece	32	Hong Kong-China	28	Australia	43
Chinese Taipei	32	Croatia	24	Spain	42
Jordan	29	Slovenia	24	United States	42
Slovak Republic	28	Korea	23	Macao-China	41
Hungary	28	Austria	22	Norway	40
Lithuania	27	Canada	22	Portugal	39
Iceland	26	Italy	21	Croatia	39
Brazil	26	Germany	19	Korea	34
Bulgaria	19	Argentina	19	Chinese Taipei	30
Tunisia	18	Denmark	15	Ireland	30
Ireland	18	Uruguay	15	Germany	28
Korea	17	Portugal	14	Slovenia	27
Germany	14	Chinese Taipei	14	Austria	26
Indonesia	14	Spain	14	Japan	26
Uruguay	13	Japan	10	Iceland	25
Spain	11	Iceland	10	Italy	25
Japan	11	Belgium	7	Denmark	22
Macao-China	10	Greece	6	Canada	19
Austria	8	Ireland	6	Belgium	15
Switzerland	7	Switzerland	6	Finland	14
Argentina	6	Macao-China	4	Greece	9
Belgium	5	Finland	3	Switzerland	8
Finland	4	Luxembourg	a	Luxembourg	5
OECD average	**38**	**OECD average**	**32**	**OECD average**	**43**

Source: OECD PISA 2006 database, Table 5.8.
StatLink ⌐⌐⌐ http://dx.doi.org/10.1787/141887160188

Figure 5.9 [Part 2/2]

Use of achievement data for accountability purposes

Percentage of students in schools where the principal reported that achievement data were

Used in decisions about instructional resource allocation to the school		Tracked over time by an administrative authority	
Chile	87	Russian Federation	100
Indonesia	86	Kyrgyzstan	98
United States	79	United States	97
Romania	77	United Kingdom	92
Thailand	76	New Zealand	92
Kyrgyzstan	75	Mexico	91
Israel	72	Canada	91
Brazil	71	Montenegro	90
New Zealand	69	Estonia	88
Azerbaijan	69	Brazil	88
Russian Federation	66	Australia	88
Colombia	66	Netherlands	86
Tunisia	64	Qatar	84
United Kingdom	63	Sweden	83
Australia	58	Croatia	83
Portugal	57	Iceland	82
Canada	57	Thailand	82
Italy	54	Tunisia	82
Jordan	53	Turkey	81
Hong Kong-China	51	Jordan	81
Ireland	47	Luxembourg	80
Sweden	46	Colombia	80
Spain	43	Chile	79
Qatar	42	Poland	78
Turkey	33	Slovak Republic	76
Latvia	33	Lithuania	74
Denmark	31	Bulgaria	71
Argentina	31	Israel	71
Macao-China	31	Romania	70
Korea	30	Slovenia	70
Lithuania	27	Portugal	69
Germany	26	Azerbaijan	69
Switzerland	25	Uruguay	66
Belgium	23	Serbia	66
Montenegro	21	Spain	64
Austria	19	Indonesia	63
Chinese Taipei	19	Hong Kong-China	62
Estonia	19	Austria	60
Mexico	18	Belgium	56
Slovak Republic	15	Czech Republic	56
Bulgaria	15	Germany	55
Netherlands	14	Finland	54
Serbia	14	Norway	53
Uruguay	14	Korea	52
Poland	12	Latvia	52
Norway	11	Macao-China	50
Croatia	11	Argentina	50
Czech Republic	9	Greece	49
Hungary	9	Ireland	48
Finland	7	Hungary	40
Luxembourg	7	Switzerland	36
Japan	6	Denmark	34
Iceland	3	Chinese Taipei	32
Greece	1	Italy	22
Slovenia	a	Japan	16
OECD average	30	OECD average	65

Source: OECD PISA 2006 database, Table 5.8.
StatLink ⟨图⟩ http://dx.doi.org/10.1787/141887160188

239

Nature and use of accountability systems

There is considerable debate as to how school-performance data can best be developed and harnessed to raise educational aspirations, establish transparency over the performance of educational objectives and content, and provide a useful reference framework for teachers to understand and foster student learning while avoiding the risks of narrowing the curriculum and teaching to the test. PISA asked school principals to indicate whether achievement data were tracked over time by an administrative authority, whether such data were used in the evaluation of the teachers' or principal's performance, and whether such data were used in decisions about instructional resource allocation to and within the school.

On average across OECD countries, 65% of 15-year-olds are enrolled in schools that reported that achievement data were tracked over time by an administrative authority. However, this ranges from over 90% in the United States, the United Kingdom, New Zealand, Mexico and Canada, and in the partner countries the Russian Federation and Kyrgyzstan, to over 80% in Australia, the Netherlands, Sweden, Iceland, Turkey and Luxembourg, and the partner countries Montenegro, Estonia, Brazil, Qatar, Croatia, Thailand, Tunisia, Jordan and Colombia, to less than 36% in Switzerland, Denmark, Italy and Japan, and in the partner economy Chinese Taipei (Figure 5.9).

On average across OECD countries, 43% of 15-year-olds were enrolled in schools which reported using achievement data in the evaluation of teacher performance. In the United Kingdom, Hungary and the Czech Republic, as well as the partner countries the Russian Federation, Kyrgyzstan, Azerbaijan, Romania, Indonesia, Israel, Qatar and Latvia, this is more than 90%. In Poland and Mexico, as well as the partner countries Thailand, Estonia, Lithuania, Jordan and Tunisia, it is still more than 80%. However, in Luxembourg, Switzerland and Greece this was reported by less than 10% of the schools and in Finland, Belgium and Canada in less than 20% of the schools. In most countries, achievement data are used more frequently to evaluate the performance of teachers than of principals, sometimes considerably so (Figure 5.9).

The use of achievement data for decisions on instructional resource allocations tends to be less common. On average across OECD countries, 30% of 15-year-olds are enrolled in schools that reported such practices, but this varies from over 85% in the partner countries Chile and Indonesia to less than 10% in Greece, Iceland, Japan, Luxembourg, Finland, Hungary and the Czech Republic.

Feedback on student performance to parents and the public

There remain diverging views on how results from evaluation and assessment can and should be used. Some see them primarily as tools to reveal best practices and identify shared problems in order to encourage teachers and schools to improve and develop more supportive and productive learning environments. Others extend their purpose to support contestability of public services or market-mechanisms in the allocation of resources, *e.g.* by making comparative results of schools publicly available to facilitate parental choice or by having funds following students. A widely debated question relates to the extent and ways in which information on student performance should be made available to parents and the public at large. PISA examined both to what extent information on student performance is made available to parents, as well as to what extent information on school performance is made available to the public at large.

On average across OECD countries, the majority of students (54%) are enrolled in schools, where school principals reported giving feedback to parents on their child's performance relative to the performance of other students at the school. In the Slovak Republic and the partner countries Indonesia, Azerbaijan, Romania, Serbia, Jordan, Kyrgyzstan and the Russian Federation, this holds for more than 90% of students, while in Sweden, Finland and Italy this is only between 12 and 19% (Figure 5.10).

Figure 5.10
School accountability to parents

Percentage of students in schools where the principal reported that the school provided information to parents on student performance relative to

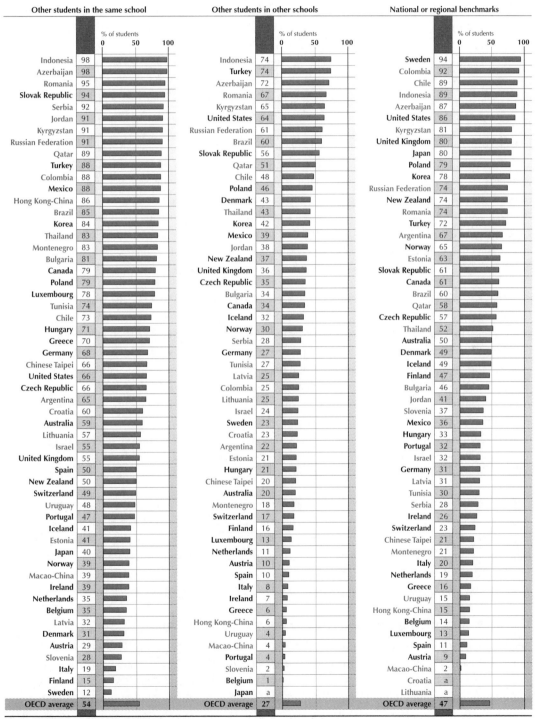

Other students in the same school		Other students in other schools		National or regional benchmarks	
Indonesia	98	Indonesia	74	Sweden	94
Azerbaijan	98	Turkey	74	Colombia	92
Romania	95	Azerbaijan	72	Chile	89
Slovak Republic	94	Romania	67	Indonesia	89
Serbia	92	Kyrgyzstan	65	Azerbaijan	87
Jordan	91	United States	64	United States	86
Kyrgyzstan	91	Russian Federation	61	Kyrgyzstan	81
Russian Federation	91	Brazil	60	United Kingdom	80
Qatar	89	Slovak Republic	56	Japan	80
Turkey	88	Qatar	51	Poland	79
Colombia	88	Chile	48	Korea	78
Mexico	88	Poland	46	Russian Federation	74
Hong Kong-China	86	Denmark	43	New Zealand	74
Brazil	85	Thailand	43	Romania	74
Korea	84	Korea	42	Turkey	72
Thailand	83	Mexico	39	Argentina	67
Montenegro	83	Jordan	38	Norway	65
Bulgaria	81	New Zealand	37	Estonia	63
Canada	79	United Kingdom	36	Slovak Republic	61
Poland	79	Czech Republic	35	Canada	61
Luxembourg	78	Bulgaria	34	Brazil	60
Tunisia	74	Canada	34	Qatar	58
Chile	73	Iceland	32	Czech Republic	57
Hungary	71	Norway	30	Thailand	52
Greece	70	Serbia	28	Australia	50
Germany	68	Germany	27	Denmark	49
Chinese Taipei	66	Tunisia	27	Iceland	49
United States	66	Latvia	25	Finland	47
Czech Republic	66	Colombia	25	Bulgaria	46
Argentina	65	Lithuania	25	Jordan	41
Croatia	60	Israel	24	Slovenia	37
Australia	59	Sweden	23	Mexico	36
Lithuania	57	Croatia	23	Hungary	33
Israel	55	Argentina	22	Portugal	32
United Kingdom	55	Estonia	21	Israel	32
Spain	50	Hungary	21	Germany	31
New Zealand	50	Chinese Taipei	20	Latvia	31
Switzerland	49	Australia	20	Tunisia	30
Uruguay	48	Montenegro	18	Serbia	28
Portugal	47	Switzerland	17	Ireland	26
Iceland	41	Finland	16	Switzerland	23
Estonia	41	Luxembourg	13	Chinese Taipei	21
Japan	40	Netherlands	11	Montenegro	21
Norway	39	Austria	10	Italy	20
Macao-China	39	Spain	10	Netherlands	19
Ireland	39	Italy	8	Greece	16
Netherlands	35	Ireland	7	Uruguay	15
Belgium	35	Greece	6	Hong Kong-China	15
Latvia	32	Hong Kong-China	6	Belgium	14
Denmark	31	Uruguay	4	Luxembourg	13
Austria	29	Macao-China	4	Spain	11
Slovenia	28	Portugal	4	Austria	9
Italy	19	Slovenia	2	Macao-China	2
Finland	15	Belgium	1	Croatia	a
Sweden	12	Japan	a	Lithuania	a
OECD average	54	OECD average	27	OECD average	47

Source: OECD PISA 2006 database, Table 5.9.
StatLink ⫘ http://dx.doi.org/10.1787/141887160188

In many OECD countries, the reporting of student performance information to parents is more commonly done relative to national benchmarks than relative to other students in the school. For example, in Sweden only 12% of 15-year-olds are enrolled in schools that reported performance data to parents relative to those of other students in the school, while 94% of 15-year-olds are enrolled in schools reporting data relative to national or regional standards or benchmarks. The pattern is similar in Japan, Finland, Norway, the United Kingdom, New Zealand, the United States as well as the partner country Estonia. Overall, in Sweden, the United States, the United Kingdom and Japan, as well as the partner countries Colombia, Chile, Indonesia, Azerbaijan and Kyrgyzstan, more than 80% of 15-year-olds are enrolled in schools that report student performance data to parents relative to national or regional standards or benchmarks, while this is below 20% in Austria, Spain, Luxembourg, Belgium, Greece, the Netherlands and Italy, as well as the partner countries/economies Macao-China, Hong Kong-China and Uruguay (Figure 5.10).

It is far less common for parents to receive information on student performance in their school relative to students in other schools. Across OECD countries, an average of 27% of students are enrolled in schools that reported providing information to parents on the academic performance of the students as a group relative to students in the same grade in other schools. Use of this practice varies, ranging from less than 10% in Belgium, Portugal, Greece, Ireland, Italy and Spain, as well as the partner countries/economies Slovenia, Macao-China, Uruguay and Hong Kong-China, to over 60% in Turkey and the United States, as well as in the partner countries Indonesia, Azerbaijan, Romania, Kyrgyzstan and the Russian Federation (Figure 5.10).

Providing assessment information to parents is one thing, but a more widely debated question in many countries is to what extent and how results from accountability systems should be made publicly available. Some contend that there should be an effort towards making public all evidence from the evaluation of public policy (with appropriate analyses) in order to provide evidence to taxpayers and the users of schools on whether the schools are delivering the expected results, to provide a basis for intervening across the systems where results in priority areas are unsatisfactory, to enhance trust in government, or to improve the quality of policy debate. Others consider that the publication of school performance data will be counterproductive as it is subject to erroneous interpretation, particularly when no adjustment for socio-economic background is made. Also debated are what types of reporting have proven most effective, in terms of raising performance and engaging teachers and schools in school improvement and to what extent the information schools and parents receive goes beyond the performance of their own school. PISA asked school principals to report whether achievement data from their school are posted publicly.

In the United Kingdom and the United States, school principals of more than 90% of 15-year-olds enrolled in school reported that school achievement data were posted publicly; in the Netherlands, as well as the partner countries Montenegro and Azerbaijan, this is still the case for more than 80%. In contrast, in Finland, Belgium, Switzerland and Austria, as well as in the partner country Argentina, this is the case for less than 10% of the students and in Japan, Spain, Germany, Korea and Ireland, and in the partner countries/economies Macao-China, Uruguay, Indonesia, Tunisia and Bulgaria it holds for less than 20% (Figure 5.9).

The existence of standards-based external examinations

Another aspect relating to accountability systems concerns the existence of external examinations. PISA collected data on the existence of standards-based external examinations, *i.e.* examinations that are keyed to a specific school subject and assess a major portion of what students studying this subject are expected to know or be able to do (Bishop 1998, 2001).[18] These define performance relative to an external standard, not relative to other students in the classroom or school. Perhaps more importantly, such examinations usually have real consequences for the students' progression or certification in the education system.

While in some countries, the standards-based external examination during or at the end of secondary education is the same for all students, in other countries, *e.g.* the United Kingdom, students have a choice between different examination levels for a given subject.

Table 5.2 provides an overview of the existence of such examinations for science in the participating countries. In federal countries, figures with decimals represent the proportion of the reporting sub-national entities that have such examinations in science. [19]

The relationship between accountability policies and student performance in science

Across Australia, Canada, Finland, Japan and Korea, the five OECD countries that show both an above-average student performance in science and a below-average impact of socio-economic background on performance (see the top-right quadrant in Figure 4.10), on average 56% of 15-year-olds attend schools that reported informing parents of children's performance relative to other students in school (this varies from 15% in Finland to 79% in Canada, and the OECD average is 54%), 63% are in schools that reported informing parents of children's performance relative to national benchmarks (this varies from 47% in Finland to 80% in Japan, and the OECD average is 47%), and 22% are in schools that reported informing parents of children's performance relative to other schools (this varies from 0% in Japan to 42% in Korea and the OECD average is 26%). On average across these five countries, 31% of 15-year-olds attend schools that reported posting achievement data publicly (this varies from 4% in Finland to 64% in Canada and the OECD average is 38%), 21% are in schools that reported using achievement data for evaluating principals (this varies from 3% in Finland to 48% in Australia and the OECD average is 31%), 27% are in schools that reported using achievement data for evaluating teachers (this varies from 14% in Finland to 43% in Australia and the OECD average is 43%), 32% are in schools that reported using achievement data for allocating resources to schools (this varies from 6% in Japan to 58% in Australia and the OECD average is 30%), and 60% are in schools that reported achievement data tracked over time (this varies from 16% in Japan to 91% in Canada and the OECD average is 65%). In all five countries, standards-based external examinations exist (Table 5.22).

How do accountability policies and practices relate to the performance of countries? This is difficult to answer, most notably because these policies and practices are often closely interrelated with other school policies and practices (see also the last section in this chapter). The models in Box 5.5 focus on the impact on student performance of regular use of school-level statistics on student performance, of feedback provided to parents and the public and of standards-based external examinations in the country.

As in preceding sections of the chapter, such factors are considered in this model both before and after accounting for the socio-economic context of students, schools and countries, which is achieved by examining the relationship between accountability systems and educational performance before and after an adjustment for demographic and socio-economic factors. The results suggest that, on average across countries and taking into account all other aspects of accountability systems examined in this model, students in countries with a standards-based external examination performed 36.1 score points higher on the PISA science scale, roughly equivalent to a school-year's progress (see the first table in Box 5.5). This association is still positive, yet no longer statistically significant,[20] once demographic and socio-economic background factors are taken into account. Students in schools posting their results publicly performed 14.7 score points better than students in schools that did not, and this association remained positive even after the demographic and socio-economic background of students and schools is accounted for. For the other aspects of accountability policies as measured by PISA, the relationships with performance are weaker and not statistically significant. None of the accountability policies have a statistically significant association with the impact that socio-economic background has on student performance.

Box 5.5 **Multilevel models: Accountability policies**

Accountability policies and student performance

	Gross		Net	
	Change in score	p-value	Change in score	p-value
School informing parents of children's performance relative to other students in the school (1=yes; 0=no)	4.7	(0.140)	2.8	(0.139)
School informing parents of children's performance relative to national benchmarks (1=yes; 0=no)	4.2	(0.100)	1.8	(0.228)
School informing parents of students' performance relative to other schools (1=yes; 0=no)	-5.0	(0.013)	-1.4	(0.352)
School posting achievement data publicly (1=yes; 0=no)	14.7	(0.000)	6.6	(0.000)
School using achievement data for evaluating principals (1=yes; 0=no)	-2.3	(0.354)	0.0	(0.993)
School using achievement data for evaluating teachers (1=yes; 0=no)	4.3	(0.076)	-0.5	(0.711)
School using achievement data for allocating resources to schools (1=yes; 0=no)	-4.8	(0.034)	-4.3	(0.007)
School with achievement data tracked over time (1=yes; 0=no)	-2.4	(0.327)	-1.2	(0.443)
System with standards-based external examinations (ratio of existence)	36.1	(0.028)	17.0	(0.226)

Accountability policies and the impact of socio-economic background

	Increase in score points in science corresponding to one unit increase of the student's PISA index of economic, social and cultural status		Increase in score points in science corresponding to one unit increase of the school average of the PISA index of economic, social and cultural status	
	Change in relationship	p-value	Change in relationship	p-value
School informing parents of children's performance relative to other students in the school (1=yes; 0=no)	-0.5	(0.327)		
School informing parents of children's performance relative to national benchmarks (1=yes; 0=no)	1.1	(0.058)		
School informing parents of students' performance relative to other schools (1=yes; 0=no)	-0.4	(0.557)		
School posting achievement data publicly (1=yes; 0=no)	1.3	(0.012)		
School using achievement data for evaluating principals (1=yes; 0=no)	0.2	(0.789)		
School using achievement data for evaluating teachers (1=yes; 0=no)	0.4	(0.566)		
School using achievement data for allocating resources to schools (1=yes; 0=no)	-0.3	(0.599)		
School with achievement data tracked over time (1=yes; 0=no)	-0.4	(0.514)		
System with standards-based external examinations (ratio of existence)	2.8	(0.290)	12.7	(0.120)

Note: See Box 5.2 for general notes.

More detailed results for the first table are presented in Table 5.19d and those for the second table are in Table 5.20d. The model is described in Annex A8.

APPROACHES TO SCHOOL MANAGEMENT AND THE INVOLVEMENT OF STAKEHOLDERS IN DECISION MAKING

Involvement of school staff in decision making at school

Increased autonomy over a wide range of institutional operations has been a main aim of restructuring and school reform since the early 1980s, the objective being to raise performance levels through devolving responsibility to the frontline and encouraging responsiveness to local needs. This has involved enhancing the decision-making responsibility and accountability of principals and, in some cases, the management responsibilities of teachers or department heads. Nonetheless, while school autonomy may stimulate responsiveness to local requirements, it is sometimes seen as creating mechanisms for choice favouring groups in society that are already advantaged.

In order to gauge the extent to which school staff have a say in decisions relating to school policy and management, PISA 2006 asked principals to report whether the teachers, the principal, the school's governing board, the regional or local education authorities or the national education authority had considerable responsibility for: appointing and dismissing teachers, establishing teachers' starting salaries and increases, formulating school budgets and allocating them within the school, establishing student disciplinary policies and assessment policies, approving students for admittance to school, choosing which textbooks to use, determining which courses were offered and their content. Figure 5.11 shows the percentage of students enrolled in schools whose principals reported that only schools had considerable responsibility, both schools and regional and/or national educational authorities had considerable responsibilities, or only regional and/or national educational authorities had considerable responsibilities for various aspects of school management.

Caution is required in interpreting the proportion of schools having considerable responsibility presented in Figure 5.11. First, because the arrangements for the distribution of decision making vary so widely across countries, the questions to school principals had to be kept quite general. The responses may therefore depend on how school principals interpreted the questions in their respective contexts. For example, when school principals were asked who has considerable responsibility for formulating the school budget, some school principals might have related this question to the regular budget of the school, while others may not have had any involvement in the regular budget and may therefore have related the question to supplementary budgets, *i.e.* contributions from parents or the community. In addition, school principals could identify multiple stakeholders who had a considerable responsibility. Since the degree of responsibility that each stakeholder had was not identified, the responses were given equal weight, irrespective of the actual influence the stakeholders had on the different aspects of decision making.

Unlike private sector enterprises, Figure 5.11 shows that schools in most countries have little say in the establishment of teachers' starting salaries. Except for the United States, the Netherlands, the Czech Republic, Sweden, the United Kingdom, Hungary, and the Slovak Republic, as well as partner countries/economies Macao-China, Chile and Indonesia, less than one-third of 15-year-olds are enrolled in schools whose principals reported that only schools had considerable responsibility for the establishment of teachers' starting salaries (OECD average 22%). The scope to reward teachers financially, once they have been hired, is likewise limited. Only in the United States and the United Kingdom, as well as in the partner countries/economies Macao-China and Thailand, are more than two-thirds of the students enrolled in schools whose principals reported that only schools had considerable responsibility for determining teachers' salary increases (OECD average 21%).

Figure 5.11 [Part 1/2]
Involvement of schools in decision making

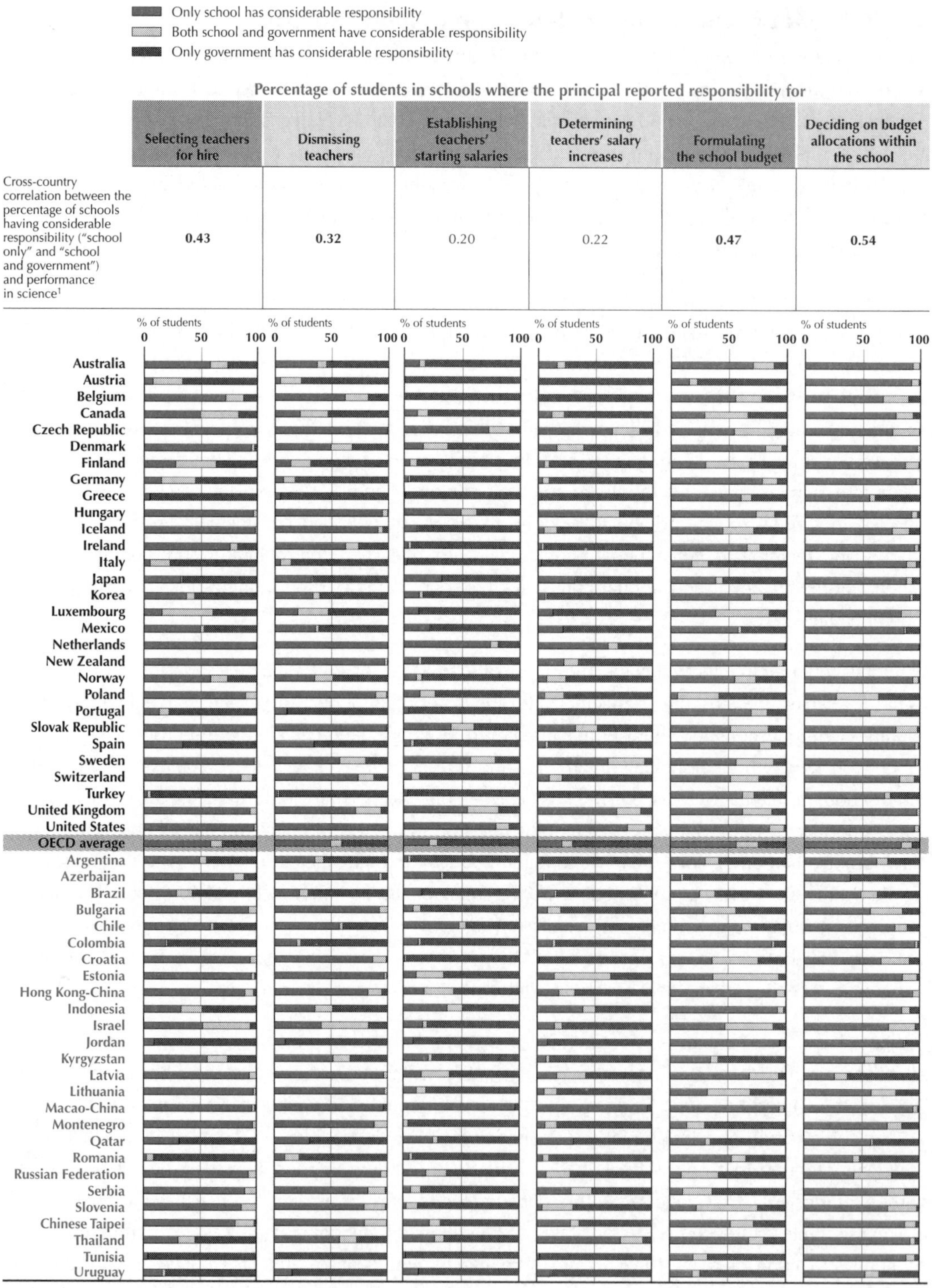

■■■ Only school has considerable responsibility
▧▧▧ Both school and government have considerable responsibility
■■■ Only government has considerable responsibility

	Percentage of students in schools where the principal reported responsibility for					
	Selecting teachers for hire	Dismissing teachers	Establishing teachers' starting salaries	Determining teachers' salary increases	Formulating the school budget	Deciding on budget allocations within the school
Cross-country correlation between the percentage of schools having considerable responsibility ("school only" and "school and government") and performance in science[1]	**0.43**	**0.32**	0.20	0.22	**0.47**	**0.54**

1. Values that are statistically significant at the 5% level (p<0.05) are indicated in bold.
Source: OECD PISA 2006 database, Table 5.10.
StatLink ⟲ http://dx.doi.org/10.1787/141887160188

Figure 5.11 [Part 2/2]

Involvement of schools in decision making

■ Only school has considerable responsibility
▨ Both school and government have considerable responsibility
■ Only government has considerable responsibly

Percentage of students in schools where the principal reported responsibility for

	Establishing student disciplinary policies	Establishing student assessment policies	Approving students for admission to the school	Choosing which textbooks are used	Determining course content	Deciding which courses are offered
Cross-country correlation between the percentage of schools having considerable responsibility ("school only" and "school and government") and performance in science[1]	0.41	0.43	0.27	0.51	0.52	0.58

Australia
Austria
Belgium
Canada
Czech Republic
Denmark
Finland
Germany
Greece
Hungary
Iceland
Ireland
Italy
Japan
Korea
Luxembourg
Mexico
Netherlands
New Zealand
Norway
Poland
Portugal
Slovak Republic
Spain
Sweden
Switzerland
Turkey
United Kingdom
United States
OECD average
Argentina
Azerbaijan
Brazil
Bulgaria
Chile
Colombia
Croatia
Estonia
Hong Kong-China
Indonesia
Israel
Jordan
Kyrgyzstan
Latvia
Lithuania
Macao-China
Montenegro
Qatar
Romania
Russian Federation
Serbia
Slovenia
Chinese Taipei
Thailand
Tunisia
Uruguay

1. Values that are statistically significant at the 5% level (p<0.05) are indicated in bold.
Source: OECD PISA 2006 database, Table 5.10.
StatLink http://dx.doi.org/10.1787/141887160188

There is greater flexibility for schools with regard to the appointment and dismissal of teachers. On average across OECD countries, 59% of 15-year-olds are enrolled in schools whose principals reported that only schools had considerable responsibility for the appointment of teachers, and the figure is 50% for the dismissal of teachers. However, there is great variability across countries in this. In the Slovak Republic, New Zealand, the Netherlands, the Czech Republic, Iceland, Sweden, the United States and Hungary, as well as in the partner countries/economies Lithuania, Montenegro, Macao-China and Estonia, more than 95% of 15-year-olds are enrolled in schools reporting that only schools have considerable responsibility for the appointment of teachers. In Portugal, Germany and Luxembourg, as well as in the partner countries Uruguay and Colombia, this is less than 20%, while in Turkey, Greece, Italy and Austria, and the partner countries Romania, Tunisia and Jordan, it is less than 10%.

The roles that schools play in the formulation of their budgets vary significantly too. While in Poland and the partner country Azerbaijan 10% or less of students are enrolled in schools that reported that only the school has considerable responsibility for formulating their school budget, it is more than 90% in the Netherlands and New Zealand and in the partner countries/economies Jordan, Macao-China, Indonesia and Hong Kong-China (OECD average 57%). With the exception of Poland and the partner countries Brazil, the Russian Federation, Romania, Azerbaijan and Latvia, the majority of 15-year-olds are in schools that reported that only the schools had considerable responsibility for decisions concerning how money is spent. In many countries, this holds for virtually all enrolled students (OECD average 84%).

Another area where the involvement of schools varies considerably across countries concerns the setting of course content and course offerings.[21] In Japan, Poland and Korea, as well as in the partner countries/economies Macao-China and Thailand, over 90% of 15-year-olds are enrolled in schools reporting that only schools have considerable responsibility for the determination of course content. This is 10% or less in Greece, Luxembourg and Turkey and in the partner countries Tunisia, Serbia, Montenegro, Uruguay, Croatia, Jordan and Bulgaria (OECD average 43%). Concerning decisions in offering courses, in Japan and New Zealand, as well as in the partner countries/economies Thailand and Hong Kong-China, over 90% of 15-year-olds are in schools whose principals reported that only schools had considerable responsibility for this. This figure is less than 10% in Luxembourg and Greece and the partner countries Tunisia, Serbia and Croatia (OECD average 51%). Both schools and regional and/or national educational authorities tend to have considerable responsibility for the determination of course content and course offerings (OECD average 27%), compared to other aspects of school management.

The picture shows less variability when it comes to disciplinary policies, the choice of textbooks and admission policies, where schools in most countries tended to report having considerable responsibility. On average, across OECD countries, 82, 80 and 74% of students, respectively, are enrolled in schools reporting that only schools have considerable responsibility in these areas (Figure 5.11).

Also assessment policies are an area where the majority of students are in schools whose principals reported that only schools had considerable responsibility (OECD average: 63%). However, in Luxembourg and Greece and the partner countries Bulgaria, Croatia, Slovenia and Uruguay, this is true for less than one-fifth of the students. Moreover, in most OECD countries, the majority of 15-year-olds are enrolled in schools whose principals reported that national authorities had a direct influence on decision making in student assessment. In Greece and Luxembourg, as well as in the partner country Tunisia, this figure is 70% or more.

While in Greece and Turkey, as well as in the partner countries Tunisia, Jordan and Uruguay, school involvement[22] tended to be low across the various areas of decision making, in others, such as the Netherlands, the United States, the Czech Republic, the United Kingdom, Sweden, Hungary and New Zealand, and the partner countries/economies Macao-China, Estonia and Hong Kong-China, it tended to be high.

There are some countries where the involvement of schools varies considerably across the different areas of decision making. For example, in Turkey only 6 and 11% of 15-year-olds are enrolled in schools that reported having considerable responsibility for the appointment of teachers, and for determining course content, respectively, whereas 84% reported considerable responsibility for approving student admittance and 72% for formulating the school budget. Conversely, in Austria only 23% of 15-year-olds are in schools whose principals reported considerable responsibility for formulating the school budget, whereas the percentages are high for decisions on course offerings (81%), course content (79%) and approving admittance (92%).

The association between the different aspects of school autonomy and student performance within a given country is often weak, in many cases simply because decision-making responsibilities are established at national levels so that there is little variation on these measures within countries. However, when looking at the relationships across countries, the data suggest that in those countries in which principals reported, on average, higher degrees of autonomy in most of the above aspects of decision making, the average performance in science tends to be higher, as indicated by the cross-country correlations shown in the top of Figure 5.11. For example, the percentage of schools that reported having considerable responsibility for decisions on course content accounts for 27% of the cross-country performance differences in science performance. For decisions on budget allocations within the school it is 29%, for decisions on the choice of textbooks it is 26%, and for decisions on formulating the school budget it is 22%. For the remaining aspects of decision making the cross-country relationship is weaker but it remains statistically significant except for the aspects concerning teacher starting salaries and salary increases. Obviously, these cross-country relationships can also be affected by many other factors.

Involvement of stakeholders in decision making

Important differences among countries also emerge in the ways in which stakeholders outside and inside the school are involved in decision making. Across the four decision-making areas of staffing, budgeting, instructional content and assessment practices, and among seven stakeholder groups that were considered, school principals most frequently reported that regional or national education authorities exerted a direct influence on decision making, followed by school governing boards, teacher groups, external examination boards and then by employers in the enterprise sector, parent groups and student groups (Tables 5.12a-d).[23] However, across OECD countries the frequency with which school principals reported the direct influence on decision making of a certain stakeholder varies across the four areas of decision making. The involvement of schools' governing boards is predominantly related to budgeting (62%), and to a lesser extent to staffing (34%), assessment practices (29%) and instructional content (22%). Naturally, external examination boards have most of their influence on assessment practices (40%), and to a lesser extent on instructional content (22%). Teacher groups tend to have significant influence over assessment practices (59%) and instructional content (56%) and to a lesser extent on staffing (29%) and budgeting (24%). The direct influence of parent and student groups on the different areas of decision making seems generally very limited.

Figure 5.12 shows that decision-making patterns clearly vary considerably across countries. For example, while the direct influence of regional or national education authorities tends to be most frequently cited in all four areas of decision making, there are exceptions: in Sweden, Iceland, Norway, the Slovak Republic and Hungary, and in the partner countries Estonia, Bulgaria, Montenegro and the Russian Federation, for example, only between 7 and 20% of 15-year-olds are enrolled in schools whose school principals reported that regional or national authorities exerted a direct influence on decisions relating to staffing (OECD average 54%) (Table 5.12a). Similarly, in Iceland, Sweden, Turkey and Greece, and the

partner countries Colombia and Jordan, the corresponding percentage of decisions relating to budgeting is only between 5 and 20% (OECD average 50%) (Table 5.12b); in Denmark, Poland and Korea, the percentage for decisions relating to instructional content is only 12, 29 and 31%, respectively (OECD average 66%) (Table 5.12c); and in Italy and Japan, and the partner country Azerbaijan, the percentage for decisions relating to assessment practices is only 17, 23 and 21% respectively (OECD average 59%) (Table 5.12d).

Figure 5.12
Direct influence of stakeholders on decision making at school

Percentage of students enrolled in schools where the principals reported that the respective stakeholders exert a direct influence on decision making at school

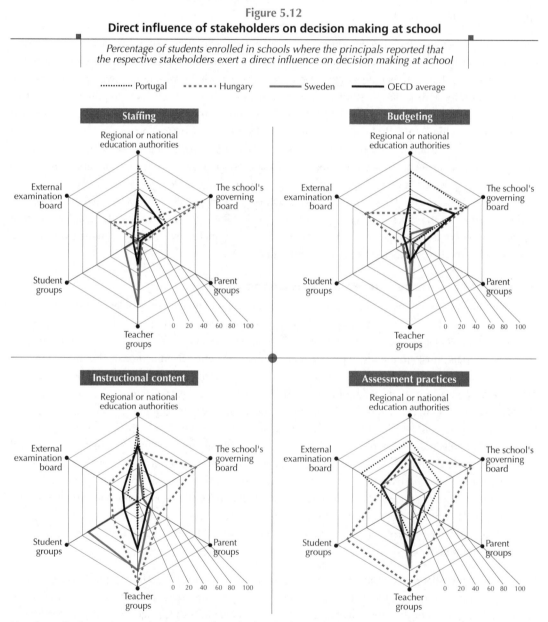

Note: Portugal is shown as an example of a country where school principals tended to report that regional or national education authorities exert a direct influence on all four areas of decision making; Hungary is an example of a country where school principals tended to report that the school's governing board exerts a direct influence on all four areas of decision making; and Sweden is an example of a country where school principals tended to report that teacher groups exert a direct influence on all four areas of decision making.

Source: OECD PISA 2006 database, Tables 5.12a, 5.12b, 5.12c and 5.12d.

StatLink ⫘⫘⫘ http://dx.doi.org/10.1787/141887160188

Also with regard to the involvement of teacher groups, such as staff associations, curriculum committees and trade unions, there tends to be considerable variation across countries. For example, while in Hungary, Poland, Japan, Finland, the Czech Republic, the United States, Sweden, the Netherlands, Italy and Germany, as well as in the partner countries/economies Estonia, Colombia, Indonesia, Thailand, Slovenia, Latvia, Lithuania, Hong Kong-China, the Russian Federation and Croatia, more than 70% of 15-year-olds are enrolled in schools whose principals reported a direct influence of teacher groups on decisions relating to instructional content, this is 10% or less in Iceland and the partner countries Tunisia and Israel (OECD average 56%). In the areas of assessment practices, staffing and budgeting, the OECD averages are 59, 29 and 24%, respectively (Tables 5.12a - d).

In New Zealand, the United States, the United Kingdom, Italy, Belgium, Greece, Luxembourg, Korea and Spain, as well as in the partner countries/economies Hong Kong-China and Croatia, more than 80% of 15-year-olds are enrolled in schools whose principals reported that the school's governing board exerted a direct influence on decisions regarding budget (OECD average 62%). However, in Denmark and Poland, and the partner countries/economies Azerbaijan and Chinese Taipei, this is the case for less than 5%. On average across OECD countries, 34% of students are in schools that reported the school governing board having a direct influence on staffing, but this figure varies widely across countries. In New Zealand, the Netherlands and Ireland, as well as the partner countries/economies Chile, Macao-China and Liechtenstein, between one half and three quarters of the students are in schools where school principals reported that the governing board exerted a direct influence on decision making on staff matters; in the United Kingdom, the United States, Switzerland and Belgium, and the partner countries/economies Chinese Taipei, Serbia and Hong Kong-China, the proportion is more than 80%, and it is up to 91% in Hungary. At the other extreme, the school governing board influences staffing decisions for less than 10% of 15-year-olds enrolled at schools in Greece, Italy, Turkey, Denmark, Austria, Norway, Korea and Germany, as well as in the partner countries Tunisia, Colombia, Bulgaria and Jordan, and for less than 1% in Poland. In the areas of instructional content and assessment practices, the school governing board's role is comparatively more limited with the proportions being 22 and 29%, respectively, on average, across OECD countries (Tables 5.12a - d).

The role of external examination boards is naturally strongest in relation to assessment practices, but in some countries, schools also frequently reported that examination boards have a direct influence on matters relating to instructional content. However, countries differ widely in this area. In New Zealand, the United Kingdom, Ireland, Australia and the Netherlands, as well as the partner countries/economies Hong Kong-China and Thailand, more than three-quarters of 15-year-olds are enrolled in schools whose principals reported that external examination boards exerted a direct influence on decisions relating to assessment practices. In Austria, Greece, Spain, Sweden, Japan and Germany, and the partner country Israel, such examination boards either do not exist or do not have a significant role (OECD average 40%). In the areas of instructional content, budgeting and staffing, the respective OECD averages are 22%, 10% and 7% (Tables 5.12a - d).

In order to identify institutional connections that may exist between schooling and the labour market, principals were also asked to what extent business and industry have a direct influence on the students' curriculum. On average across OECD countries, 11% of 15-year-olds are in schools in which business and industry exert considerable influence on the curriculum, for 53%, the influence is considered to be minor or indirect, and for 36%, business and industry have no influence on the curriculum. While these figures also vary considerably across countries there are 50% or more students enrolled in schools in Austria and the partner country Indonesia who reported that business and industry influence the curriculum considerably (Figure 5.13).

251

Figure 5.13

Influence of business and industry on the school curriculum

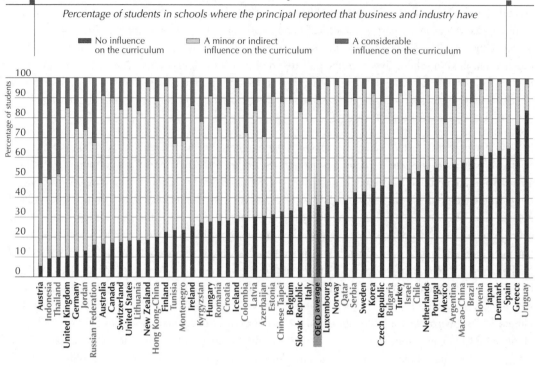

Source: OECD PISA 2006 database, Table 5.11.
StatLink ᐧ᠍᠍ᠯᠯ http://dx.doi.org/10.1787/141887160188

The relationship between school autonomy and student performance in science

To analyse the association between different aspects of school autonomy and student outcomes in science, three indices of school autonomy have been developed by using principal component analysis: school autonomy in staffing, school autonomy in budgeting and school autonomy in educational content.[24] So, are there any common features in Australia, Canada, Finland, Japan and Korea, the five OECD countries that show both above-average student performance in science and a below-average impact of socio-economic background on student performance (see the top-right quadrant in Figure 4.10). First, schools in all five countries are characterised by a relatively low degree of autonomy in staffing (OECD average -0.02). In contrast, all five countries (except for Canada) are characterised by a high degree of autonomy in educational content, compared to the average of 55 countries (OECD average 0.15). The picture varies concerning autonomy in budgeting: schools in Australia and Korea have, on average, a high degree of autonomy, while schools in Canada and Japan have a low degree of autonomy in budgeting matters, compared to the average of 55 countries (OECD average 0.19) (Table 5.22).

The associations between the different aspects of school autonomy and student performance have been examined in a multilevel model. After accounting for demographic and socio-economic background factors, school level autonomy indices in staffing, educational content, and budgeting do not show a statistically significant association with student performance (see the first table in Box 5.6). However, a system-level composition effect appears with regard to school autonomy in educational content as well as budgeting. Students in educational systems giving more autonomy to schools to choose textbooks, to determine course content, and to decide which courses to offer, tend to perform better regardless of whether the schools which individual students attend have higher degrees of autonomy or not (an increase of one unit on the index corresponds to an increase of 20.3 score points in science). Similarly, students in educational systems that give more autonomy to schools to formulate the school budget and to decide on budget allocations within the school tend to perform better regardless of whether the schools that individual students attend have higher degrees of autonomy or not (an increase of one unit on the index corresponds to an increase of 22.5 score points in science). School autonomy variables do not appear to have an impact on the relationship between socio-economic background and science performance, that is, greater school autonomy is not associated with a more inequitable distribution of learning opportunities (see the second table in Box 5.6).

Box 5.6 **Multilevel models: School autonomy**

School autonomy and student performance

	Gross		Net	
	Change in score	p-value	Change in score	p-value
School autonomy index in staffing (effect of one standard deviation of the index)	9.5	(0.000)	-3.4	(0.005)
School autonomy index in educational content (effect of one standard deviation of the index)	0.9	(0.573)	-0.8	(0.368)
School autonomy index in budgeting (effect of one standard deviation of the index)	1.1	(0.457)	1.5	(0.045)
System average of school autonomy index in staffing (effect of one standard deviation of the index)	0.7	(0.936)	1.5	(0.829)
System average of school autonomy index in educational content (effect of one standard deviation of the index)	22.1	(0.019)	20.3	(0.004)
System average of school autonomy index in budgeting (effect of one standard deviation of the index)	27.2	(0.056)	22.5	(0.048)

School autonomy and the impact of socio-economic background

	Increase in score points in science corresponding to one unit increase of the student's PISA index of the economic, social and cultural status		Increase in score points in science corresponding to one unit increase of the school average of the PISA index of the economic, social and cultural status	
	Change in relationship	p-value	Change in relationship	p-value
School autonomy index in staffing (effect of one standard deviation of the index)	0.0	(0.943)		
School autonomy index in educational content (effect of one standard deviation of the index)	0.4	(0.394)		
School autonomy index in budgeting (effect of one standard deviation of the index)	0.1	(0.675)		
System average of school autonomy index in staffing (effect of one standard deviation of the index)	1.8	(0.311)	2.8	(0.683)
System average of school autonomy index in educational content (effect of one standard deviation of the index)	1.3	(0.495)	-1.3	(0.806)
System average of school autonomy index in budgeting (effect of one standard deviation of the index)	1.0	(0.765)	6.6	(0.436)

Note: See Box 5.2 for general notes.

More detailed results for the first table are presented in Table 5.19e and those for the second table are in Table 5.20e. The model is described in Annex A8.

SCHOOL RESOURCES

Effective schools require the right combination of trained and talented personnel, adequate educational resources and facilities and motivated students ready to learn. In the public debate, resources such as class and school sizes, the quality of the school's materials, perceived staff shortages, and teacher quality are frequently associated with performance. This section describes important school resources including human, material and educational resources and then examines their relationship with student performance and with the impact that socio-economic background has on student performance. When examining school resource factors within the framework of PISA, it is important to keep in mind the challenges that were outlined in Box 5.1.

Human resources reported by school principals

In order to gauge the extent to which schools were able to employ an adequate supply of science teachers, school principals were asked if their school had any science teacher vacancies in the academic year in which PISA 2006 was conducted, and, if yes, whether the vacancies had been filled. The results show that, on average, across OECD countries, 3% of students are in schools which reported that one or more science teaching positions remained vacant, 59% are enrolled in schools which reported that all vacant science teaching positions had been filled either with newly appointed staff or by reassigning existing staff, and 38% are in schools with no vacancies in science teaching positions. However, the proportion of 15-year-olds in schools with vacant science teacher positions ranged from less than 1% in Portugal, Greece, Poland, Italy, Spain, Ireland, the Slovak Republic, Sweden and Switzerland as well as the partner countries Bulgaria, Hong Kong-China, Tunisia, Lithuania and Romania, to between 5 and 10% in Turkey, the United Kingdom, as well as the partner countries/economies Colombia, Jordan, Slovenia, Israel, Chinese Taipei and Brazil, and to over 10% in Germany and Luxembourg and in the partner countries Indonesia, Kyrgyzstan and Azerbaijan (Figure 5.14).

In addition, PISA 2006 sought school principals' views on the extent to which instruction was hindered by a lack of qualified teachers in key subject areas. Not surprisingly, the principals of schools where all the science teaching positions were filled were less likely to report that the lack of qualified science teachers hindered the school's capacity to provide instruction compared to the school principals of schools where there were vacancies in science teaching positions. For example, on average across OECD countries 65% of principals in schools where there were vacancies reported that instruction was hindered by a lack of qualified science teachers, but only 16% of principals in schools where there were no vacancies reported the same. However, in some countries school principals considered that instruction was hindered by a lack of science teachers even in schools where there were no vacancies. For example, in Turkey, Mexico and Germany, as well as in Kyrgyzstan, Azerbaijan, Jordan, Chile and the Russian Federation, 30% or more of those schools with all science teaching positions filled reported that instruction was hindered by the lack of qualified science teachers to a greater or lesser extent. Some of the differences in the level of vacancies across countries may be due to differences in required qualifications for being a science teacher (Figure 5.14).

In examining human resources, it is important to assess not only average levels of human resources, but also how these are distributed within countries. PISA established an index of teacher shortage by using responses from school principals to questions about the extent to which the shortage or inadequacy of teachers in science, languages, mathematics and other subjects hindered the school's capacity to provide instruction. The index has a mean value of zero and a standard deviation of one across OECD countries. Positive values indicate that school principals more frequently reported that the lack of qualified teachers hinders instruction than is the case on average across OECD countries, while negative values suggest the reverse. In Finland, the Czech Republic, Austria and Sweden, as well as in the partner countries Bulgaria and Croatia, school principals' perceptions about the impact of teacher shortage vary relatively little across schools, while in Turkey and Belgium, as well as in the partner countries/economies Kyrgyzstan, Qatar, Jordan, the Russian Federation, Macao-China, Colombia, Brazil and Azerbaijan, there is considerable between-school variation (Figure 5.14).

Figure 5.14

School principals' reports on vacant science teaching positions and their perceptions of the supply of qualified science teachers

	Percentage of students in schools where the principal reported				Index of teacher shortage
	No vacant science teaching positions to be filled	All vacant science teaching positions filled	No vacant science teaching positions or all vacant science teaching positions filled of which a lack of qualified science teachers hinders instruction to some extent or a lot	One or more vacant science teaching positions not filled	▬ Range between top and bottom quarter of students[1] ● Average index
Indonesia	6	60		34	
Kyrgyzstan	3	72		25	
Luxembourg	38	43		19	
Azerbaijan	55	32		13	
Germany	40	48		12	
Brazil	9	81		10	
Chinese Taipei	19	71		10	
United Kingdom	19	73		9	
Turkey	63	30		7	
Israel	23	69		7	
Slovenia	23	70		7	
Jordan	9	85		6	
Colombia	56	39		5	
Australia	22	75		4	
Finland	59	37		4	
Serbia	41	56		3	
Austria	56	41		3	
Hungary	57	40		3	
Russian Federation	7	90		3	
Japan	11	86		3	
Netherlands	34	63		3	
United States	27	71		3	
Uruguay	45	52		3	
Chile	35	62		3	
Qatar	20	78		3	
Mexico	49	49		2	
Czech Republic	54	44		2	
Thailand	41	57		2	
Estonia	55	43		2	
Denmark	37	61		2	
Montenegro	48	50		2	
Croatia	27	71		2	
Macao-China	14	84		2	
Canada	18	80		2	
Argentina	37	61		2	
Iceland	31	67		2	
New Zealand	19	79		2	
Korea	80	19		1	
Latvia	34	65		1	
Belgium	25	74		1	
Switzerland	42	57		1	
Sweden	27	72		1	
Romania	41	58		1	
Slovak Republic	3	97		1	
Lithuania	54	45		1	
Ireland	55	44		1	
Spain	36	64		0	
Italy	33	66		0	
Poland	73	27		0	
Greece	31	69		0	
Portugal	25	75		0	
Bulgaria	69	31		0	
Hong Kong-China	50	50		0	
Tunisia	69	31		0	
OECD average	38	59		3	

1. Range between top and bottom quarter of students is not presented for the countries where more than 50% of students have the same value on the index.
Source: OECD PISA 2006 database, Table 5.13 and 5.14.
StatLink ⌐╦╗ http://dx.doi.org/10.1787/141887160188

As another indicator of the quality of human resources in schools, the average number of students per teacher was computed, based on the school principals' reports on the number of male and female students and the number of full-time and part-time teachers in their schools. The total number of students was divided by the total number of full-time equivalent teachers. There are 10 or less 15-year-old students per full-time equivalent teacher in Portugal, Greece, Belgium, Italy, Luxembourg, as well as in the partner country Azerbaijan, while there are over 20 students per full-time equivalent teacher in Mexico, as well as in the partner countries/economies Chile, Colombia, Thailand and Macao-China, and over 30 students in the partner country Brazil (Table 5.14).

Material resources reported by school principals

Ensuring the availability of an adequate physical infrastructure and supply of educational resources does not guarantee good learning outcomes, but the absence of such resources could negatively affect learning. School principals were asked to report on the extent to which the school's capacity to provide instruction was hindered by the shortage or inadequacy of several types of resources, including: science laboratory equipment, instruction materials such as textbooks, computers for instruction, Internet connectivity, computer software for instruction, library materials and audio-visual resources (see Figure 5.15). On average across OECD countries, only a minority of 15-year-olds are in schools where school principals reported that a shortage or inadequacy of these educational resources hindered the school's capacity to provide instruction to a greater or lesser extent. There was particularly little concern about the shortage or inadequacy of Internet connectivity or instructional materials: 20 and 25% of students, respectively, were enrolled in schools where school principals reported that instruction was hindered by a shortage of these resources. In contrast, school principals expressed more concern about the supply of laboratory equipment, particularly in the Slovak Republic, Turkey, Mexico, Iceland, Poland, Norway and Hungary, as well as in many of the partner countries, where the majority of 15-year-olds were enrolled in schools where school principals reported that a shortage or inadequacy of laboratory equipment hindered learning.

A composite index of educational resources summarises principals' responses to the seven questions on the adequacy or shortage of educational resources. The index was inverted so that positive values on the index reflect a below-average concern among school principals that the shortage or inadequacy of educational resources hinders the capacity to provide instruction. This index shows that few principals in Switzerland, Japan and Australia, as well as the partner economy Chinese Taipei perceived inadequacy of educational resources as hindering their schools' capacity to provide instruction, while in the partner countries Kyrgyzstan, Indonesia, Azerbaijan, Montenegro, the Russian Federation, and Colombia, many school principals expressed such concern (Figure 5.15). However, when interpreting these figures, it should be borne in mind that school principals did not provide an objective measure of the condition of educational resources, but rather their perceptions of whether a shortage or inadequacy of educational resources hindered the capacity to provide instruction in their schools. Caution is therefore required in comparing responses across schools and countries. Still, principals' perceptions can shape their behaviour in important ways and should therefore be considered.

The variation in school principals' assessments regarding these educational resources, expressed as the difference between the bottom and top quarters of the index, was particularly low in Norway and the Slovak Republic, as well as in the partner countries Lithuania, Estonia, Bulgaria, Latvia, Serbia, and Tunisia, while in Mexico and Australia, as well as in the partner countries/economies Uruguay, Chinese Taipei, Indonesia, Argentina, Brazil, Qatar and Israel, school principals' perceptions differed most considerably across schools (Figure 5.15).

Figure 5.15

Material resources – index of the quality of schools' educational resources

A — Shortage or inadequacy of audio-visual resources
B — Shortage or inadequacy of library materials
C — Shortage or inadequacy of computer software for instruction
D — Lack or inadequacy of Internet connectivity
E — Shortage or inadequacy of computers for instruction
F — Shortage or inadequacy of instructional materials (*e.g.* textbooks)
G — Shortage or inadequacy of science laboratory equipment

Percentage of students in schools whose principals reported that the capacity to provide instruction was hindered by the following

	A	B	C	D	E	F	G
Australia	17	16	26	17	34	14	23
Austria	23	21	20	11	24	22	40
Belgium	36	38	32	24	42	22	38
Canada	30	27	32	19	38	25	36
Czech Republic	41	34	31	15	39	30	40
Denmark	37	19	31	15	39	34	34
Finland	46	40	40	19	37	25	42
Germany	31	32	30	19	27	20	39
Greece	46	54	56	13	24	10	35
Hungary	24	25	24	12	15	32	52
Iceland	19	17	0	8	24	37	58
Ireland	52	57	54	30	55	15	49
Italy	31	24	34	13	21	16	45
Japan	34	24	29	16	19	0	25
Korea	54	52	36	17	32	15	49
Luxembourg	30	38	0	0	42	0	0
Mexico	65	54	62	60	59	43	67
Netherlands	21	12	33	23	39	12	34
New Zealand	26	12	25	0	42	16	18
Norway	42	47	65	24	46	39	56
Poland	39	38	48	7	33	35	56
Portugal	50	37	70	33	52	26	48
Slovak Republic	59	66	53	23	39	66	75
Spain	42	36	51	23	43	13	40
Sweden	36	30	41	14	46	26	28
Switzerland	15	17	16	11	16	14	30
Turkey	71	63	56	36	61	61	72
United Kingdom	24	24	26	19	37	21	28
United States	20	20	24	15	33	17	33
OECD average	37	34	38	20	37	25	42
Argentina	51	33	56	56	51	33	55
Azerbaijan	86	66	88	85	81	58	84
Brazil	57	58	73	61	76	45	77
Bulgaria	66	56	51	29	48	40	77
Chile	47	53	55	24	50	44	72
Colombia	64	69	77	69	70	72	71
Croatia	62	44	66	28	46	50	76
Estonia	53	39	47	10	44	37	66
Hong Kong-China	23	22	30	6	23	15	11
Indonesia	79	76	68	83	59	59	75
Israel	39	33	27	15	37	25	40
Jordan	61	47	66	70	67	39	51
Kyrgyzstan	93	90	94	95	90	95	93
Latvia	49	39	42	20	49	45	78
Lithuania	49	29	53	18	51	28	67
Macao-China	29	33	27	16	21	19	17
Montenegro	76	69	71	65	79	70	87
Qatar	58	35	38	40	43	21	38
Romania	64	40	67	38	59	63	76
Russian Federation	84	77	83	64	80	64	87
Serbia	61	52	57	50	58	50	67
Slovenia	21	12	24	7	21	21	26
Chinese Taipei	23	24	22	13	17	14	26
Thailand	58	54	53	40	45	40	59
Tunisia	65	70	62	52	78	26	43
Uruguay	52	46	58	57	60	50	42

Range between top and bottom quarter of students
● Average index[1]
Change in science performance per unit of the index

Index points: -3.5 -2.5 -1.5 -0.5 0.5 1.5 2.5
Score point difference: -50 -30 -10 10 30

1. Higher mean value indicates that school principals perceived that the quality of schools' educational resources hindered instruction to a lesser extent.
Source: OECD PISA 2006 database, Table 5.15.
StatLink ⟐ http://dx.doi.org/10.1787/141887160188

257

School principals also reported the number of computers available for instruction in their schools, which, divided by the total number of students in the school, provides an indicator of the availability of computers for instruction per student. The number of computers available for instruction per student varies widely across countries. Five or less students share one computer for instruction in the United Kingdom, Australia, Luxembourg, Austria, the United States and Norway, while 25 or more students share one computer for instruction in the partner countries Azerbaijan, Kyrgyzstan, Tunisia, Brazil, Montenegro, Indonesia and the Russian Federation (Table 5.15).

Learning time and educational resources reported by students and school principals

Students reported on whether or not they were learning science in 2006 and, if so, how these courses were delivered. For example, students may have been following compulsory or optional courses in general science, biology, physics or chemistry in any number of combinations or even no longer learning science at school. An aged-based sample, such as in PISA, implies that students can be drawn from a number of different grades and in some countries science may be a compulsory subject up to a certain number of years in school, but not after. In 43 out of 56 countries where data are available, at least 80% of 15-year-old students are still following some form of science education at school, whether a compulsory course, optional course or combination of both (Figure 5.16 and Table 5.16). In 24 of the participating countries at least 90% of students are enrolled in a science class at age 15. At least 95% of 15-year-old students reported following science courses in Finland, the Slovak Republic, Iceland and France, and in the partner countries Latvia, Slovenia and Montenegro, and all students reported following science courses in Norway and Poland and the partner country Russian Federation.

There are many ways in which 15-year-olds are exposed to science at school. Important differences between countries or between regions within countries relate to the organisation of science content. In some countries, students take a general science course, sometimes called "integrated science", where they study a variety of concepts drawn from the physical, biological or earth sciences. Another type of curriculum will have separate courses in biology, physics, chemistry and earth sciences, with students taking all or some of these during a school year. In still other systems, coursework is grouped thematically and science as a separate course is not offered, with students drawing on their science knowledge and skills to answer specific problems within a theme at the same time that they draw on their skills in other disciplines, such as geography or writing. It is also possible that students might experience a combination of all of these approaches.

PISA has examined different arrangements for science instruction. Norway is the only country where all students at age 15 follow a compulsory general science course. Compulsory general science courses are also attended by between 70 and 90% of students in 13 of the participating countries and this is the case for at least 80% of the students in Korea, Japan, Finland, Iceland and Canada and in the partner countries Thailand and Indonesia. In contrast, there are no general science courses (whether compulsory or optional) offered to students at age 15 in Austria, France, Greece, Hungary, Luxembourg, Poland and the Slovak Republic, or in the partner countries Azerbaijan, Bulgaria, Croatia, Lithuania and Serbia. All students in Poland are enrolled in compulsory biology, chemistry and physics classes, while in all other 11 countries students are enrolled for the most part in compulsory biology, chemistry or physics classes. Similarly, the majority of students in the partner country the Russian Federation follow compulsory science courses in biology, chemistry and physics at age 15 and only 3% follow compulsory general science courses. Finland stands out as a country where the majority of students follow both compulsory general science courses and compulsory specific courses in biology, chemistry and physics (Figure 5.16 and Table 5.16).

Figure 5.16
Percentage of students following science courses at age 15

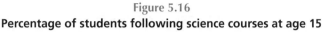

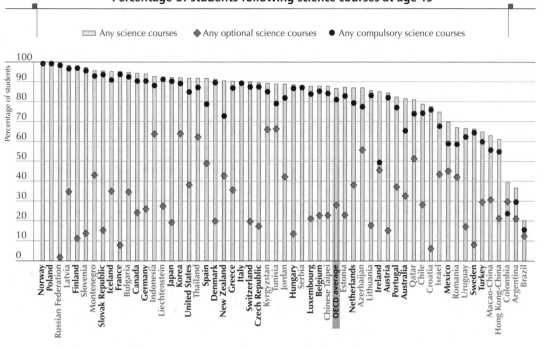

Source: OECD PISA 2006 database, Table 5.16.
StatLink http://dx.doi.org/10.1787/141887160188

Through exposure to science at school and out of school, students have the opportunity to explore and absorb some of the facts, principles and skills associated with science. It is therefore to be expected that the amount of time spent learning science would be associated with the level of student performance in science. In PISA 2006, students were asked to estimate the amount of time, in hours, that they spent on science in regular lessons, in out-of school lessons, and doing study or homework by themselves. The same question was asked of the students regarding reading and mathematics.

On average across OECD countries, 28.7% of students reported that they had four hours or more of regular science lessons at school. This percentage rises to 64.8% in New Zealand, 61.9% in the United Kingdom, 56.8% in Canada, and 49.1% in the United States. Among the partner countries/economies, the percentage is between 40% and 46% in Macao-China, the Russian Federation, Colombia and Hong Kong-China. In Norway, only 6.9% of students reported that they studied science at school for four hours or more per week (Figure 5.17 and Table 5.17).

There are a number of countries where the majority of students reported that they took two hours or less of science at school each week. This is the case in the Slovak Republic, the Netherlands and Luxembourg and also in the partner countries Kyrgyzstan, Romania, Chile and Argentina.

Activities external to the classroom can enhance students' learning in science, as they can provide a motivation for students and help to place science in a real-life context. In PISA 2006 school principals were asked about their schools' provision for such activities. The activities include going on excursions, participating in science competitions and science fairs, engaging in extracurricular science projects, and belonging to a science-related club. A single index was developed from principals' responses to these five individual questions.

Figure 5.17
Students' time spent on learning

Percentage of students who spend four hours or more per week in regular lessons

□ Science　◆ Reading　▲ Mathematics

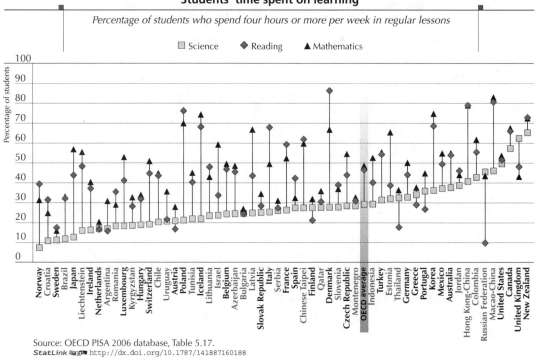

Source: OECD PISA 2006 database, Table 5.17.
StatLink http://dx.doi.org/10.1787/141887160188

The most common activity to promote the learning of science is taking students on excursions. Across OECD countries, 89% of students attend schools where the principals reported this activity. This figure is over 97% in the Slovak Republic, Poland and Hungary and in the partner countries Romania, Lithuania, the Russian Federation, Latvia, Qatar and Slovenia. Among OECD countries, Japan reported the least use of excursions, with 30% of the students attending schools where the principals reported this activity (Figure 5.18 and Table 5.18).

Across the OECD, 54% of students were in schools where principals reported that participation in science competitions was encouraged. Science competitions are very common in Poland, where all of the students attended schools where principals reported this activity, and the figure is still over 95% in Australia and in the partner countries Kyrgyzstan and the Russian Federation. Science competitions are not as popular in Japan, where just 6% of students were in schools where principals reported participation in them. The figure is also low in Denmark (10%) and Norway (16%).

Science clubs are less prevalent across OECD countries (on average, 38% of students were in schools where principals reported to provide these), the corresponding figure for science fairs is 39% and for extracurricular science projects, 45%.

The prevalence of these activities can be summarised in an index. The countries with an index value of more than one-half of a standard deviation below the OECD average, *i.e.* the countries in which schools provide such activities to a lesser extent, are Japan (-1.16), Denmark (-0.83), Iceland (-0.71), Finland (-0.60) and the Netherlands (-0.51). Those countries with the values of over one-half of a standard deviation above the OECD average are the Slovak Republic (0.70), Portugal (0.66), Hungary (0.62), Poland (0.58), Korea (0.54) and New Zealand (0.51) and the partner countries/economies Thailand (1.34), the Russian Federation (1.19), Lithuania (1.19), Slovenia (1.15), Hong Kong-China (0.92), Estonia (0.90), Jordan (0.87), Colombia (0.82), Romania (0.77), Chinese Taipei (0.76), Kyrgyzstan (0.76) and Qatar (0.59).

Figure 5.18

Index of school activities to promote the learning of science

A	Excursions and field trips
B	Science competitions
C	Extracurricular science projects
D	Science fairs
E	Science clubs

Percentage of students in schools whose principals reported that the school promoted engagement with science using the following activities

■ Range between top and bottom quarter of students[1]
● Average index

	A	B	C	D	E
Thailand	96	93	89	97	84
Russian Federation	99	98	80	83	84
Lithuania	99	91	76	98	80
Slovenia	97	80	79	85	92
Hong Kong-China	90	91	83	52	91
Estonia	97	88	88	81	50
Jordan	90	75	84	80	67
Colombia	87	62	75	71	93
Romania	100	92	55	62	71
Chinese Taipei	89	72	71	73	76
Kyrgyzstan	94	98	36	75	79
Slovak Republic	99	81	44	70	78
Portugal	94	62	86	62	64
Hungary	97	84	38	69	72
Qatar	97	78	71	66	41
Poland	99	100	51	27	78
Korea	80	86	44	49	87
New Zealand	94	91	57	72	32
United States	92	58	65	50	73
Czech Republic	97	78	50	61	47
Macao-China	69	91	96	34	46
Canada	95	64	64	55	48
United Kingdom	87	72	60	35	73
Australia	97	98	70	31	31
Tunisia	78	49	51	56	83
Montenegro	83	81	57	31	68
Serbia	65	84	43	41	83
Azerbaijan	91	79	29	42	68
Brazil	84	39	86	82	5
Israel	87	62	65	32	53
Spain	95	37	36	57	69
Latvia	99	91	86	6	14
Croatia	90	75	58	49	21
Luxembourg	93	41	56	69	33
Ireland	93	54	53	64	21
Argentina	80	51	65	72	16
Bulgaria	86	78	52	20	a
Italy	96	34	75	16	39
OECD average	**89**	**54**	**45**	**39**	**38**
Uruguay	83	32	60	57	33
Mexico	75	72	54	39	21
Indonesia	74	63	45	25	60
Germany	95	43	34	29	47
Turkey	78	54	48	29	39
Belgium	91	52	48	35	5
Switzerland	95	22	29	47	35
Chile	74	36	47	44	39
Austria	91	35	30	27	27
Greece	87	67	23	9	11
Sweden	81	56	29	24	7
Norway	94	16	42	36	1
Netherlands	89	35	40	21	8
Finland	94	37	23	9	9
Iceland	95	25	23	7	5
Denmark	87	10	18	25	3
Japan	30	6	19	11	49

Index points: -2.5, -1.5, -0.5, 0.5, 1.5, 2.5

1. Range between top and bottom quarter of students is not presented for the countries where more than 50% of students have the same value on the index.
Source: OECD PISA 2006 database, Table 5.18.
StatLink ⓜ🖇 http://dx.doi.org/10.1787/141887160188

The relationship between school resources and student performance in science

Across Australia, Canada, Finland, Japan and Korea, the five OECD countries that show above-average student performance in science and a below-average impact of socio-economic background on student performance (see the top-right quadrant in Figure 4.10), there is considerable variation in school resources. On average across the five countries, for example, there are 14.1 students per teacher, but this varies from 11.3 in Finland to 16.7 in Canada (OECD average 13.4). Across the five countries, five students share one computer for instruction, which varies from 4 students in Australia to 7 students in Finland (OECD average 7). The extent of school principals' perception of a lack of qualified teachers hindering instruction is below the OECD average in Japan, Korea and Finland, but higher than the OECD average in Australia and Canada. School principals tend to perceive school educational resources as adequate in Japan and Australia, but this is not the case in Finland and Korea. Across the five countries, the average students' learning time for regular lessons in school per week is 11.5 hours, varying from 9.7 hours in Finland to 12.9 hours in Canada (OECD average 10.6); the average students' learning time for out-of school lessons is 2.3 hours, varying from 1.1 hours in Finland to 4.8 hours in Korea (OECD average 2.4); and the average students' learning time for self-study or homework is 4.3 hours per week, varying from 3.1 hours in Japan to 5.3 hours in Canada (OECD average 4.9). School principals in Korea, Canada and Australia tended to more frequently report that schools provided activities to promote students' learning of science than the OECD average, while this was less frequently the case in Japan and Finland (Table 5.22).

This remainder of this section examines the relationship between school principals' views on human, material and educational resources and science performance. Since the various aspects of school resources are interrelated, it is not possible to estimate the total impact of the school resources on student performance by simply adding up the factors examined in the previous section. Only a joint examination of the various factors makes it possible to estimate their collective impact on student and school performance.

As in previous sections of this chapter, the relationships between school resources and student performance are analysed before and after taking demographic and socio-economic factors into account. Examining the impact of school-resource factors after an adjustment for the demographic and socio-economic factors allow a comparison of schools that are operating in similar contexts. Conversely, the interpretation of the school factors without an adjustment for the contextual factors ignores differences in the composition of schools and the country context. That said, the unadjusted gross effects may give a more realistic picture of the choices that parents face if they wish to select a school for their children. Parents and other stakeholders, for example, are naturally most interested in the overall performance results of schools, including any effects that are conferred by the socio-economic intake of schools, whereas the added value that schools provide may only be a secondary consideration for them.

The following model incorporates both aspects providing both gross effects (prior to an adjustment for socio-economic factors) and net effects (after an adjustment for demographic and socio-economic factors). For methodological reasons, composite indices have been used rather than single-item statements wherever these could be constructed. The following factors are included in the model: the index of teacher shortage, the student-teacher ratio, the index of the school's educational resources and the ratio of computers used for instructional purposes to the number of students at school, the learning time in school (over all subjects), and the time spent on homework assignments, the time spent in taking out-of-school lessons, as well as the presence of school activities promoting science and the science courses taken by the school's students in the current or previous school year.

As shown in the first table in Box 5.7, the school average students' learning time in science, mathematics and language during regular lessons in school, the school average students' learning time for self-study or homework, the school average level of providing learning opportunity in science, and the index of school

Box 5.7 **Multilevel models: School resources**

School resources and student performance	Gross		Net	
	Change in score	p-value	Change in score	p-value
Human resource indicators				
School average number of students per teacher (one additional student per teacher)	0.33	(0.121)	-0.16	(0.304)
School-level index of teacher shortage (effect of one standard deviation of the index)	-4.14	(0.000)	-1.55	(0.073)
Material resource indicators				
School average number of computers for instruction per student (one additional computer per student)	-12.5	(0.359)	2.5	(0.817)
School-level index of quality of school educational resources (effect of one standard deviation of the index)	5.14	(0.000)	0.17	(0.798)
Educational resource indicators				
School average students' learning time for regular lessons in school (one additional hour per week)	14.3	(0.000)	8.7	(0.000)
School average students' learning time for out-of-school lessons (one additional hour per week)	-12.9	(0.000)	-9.0	(0.000)
School average students' learning time for self-study or homework (one additional hour per week)	3.8	(0.004)	3.1	(0.001)
School providing opportunity of learning science (each additional 10% of students taking any science course)	1.7	(0.080)	1.4	(0.016)
School average index of school activities to promote students' learning of science (effect of one standard deviation of the index)	7.07	(0.000)	2.89	(0.000)

School resources and the impact of socio-economic background	Increase in score points in science corresponding to one unit increase of the student's PISA index of economic, social and cultural status	
	Change in relationship	p-value
Human resource indicators		
School average number of students per teacher (one additional student per teacher)	0.00	(0.909)
School-level index of teacher shortage (effect of one standard deviation of the index)	-0.04	(0.865)
Material resource indicators		
School average number of computers for instruction per student (one additional computer per student)	-6.6	(0.004)
School-level index of quality of school educational resources (effect of one standard deviation of the index)	0.35	(0.141)
Educational resource indicators		
School average students' learning time for regular lessons in school (one additional hour per week)	0.6	(0.003)
School average students' learning time for out-of-school lessons (one additional hour per week)	-0.8	(0.020)
School average students' learning time for self-study or homework (one additional hour per week)	-0.1	(0.850)
School providing opportunity of learning science (each additional 10% of students taking any science course)	0.1	(0.438)
School average index of school activities to promote students' learning of science (effect of one standard deviation of the index)	0.49	(0.117)

Note: See Box 5.2 for general notes.

More detailed results for the first table are presented in Table 5.19f and those for the second table are in Table 5.20f. The model is described in Annex A8.

activities to promote students' learning of science are all positively associated with science performance both before and after accounting for contextual factors.[25] After accounting for background factors and all other factors in the model, students in schools with one additional hour of regular lessons per week tend to perform 8.7 score points higher; students in schools with one additional hour of self-study and homework perform 3.1 score points higher; and students in schools with one unit more in the index of school activities to promote students' learning of science tend to perform 2.9 score points higher.

In the gross models, the index of teacher shortage is negatively related to science performance, *i.e.* students in schools that reported a higher incidence of teacher shortage tended to perform worse, while the index of the quality of the school's educational resources is positively related to science performance. However, the effect of both factors disappears when accounting for contextual factors in the net model.

There is a statistically significant association between average learning time in school and the impact which socio-economic background has on student performance (see the second table in Box 5.7). One unit increase in students' PISA index of economic, social and cultural status is equivalent to an advantage of 16.1 score points in science performance in schools with the average in-class learning time (10 hours), but this association increases to 16.7 score points in schools with 11 hours in-class learning time per week (Table 5.20f). The results also suggest that the higher the number of computers for instruction per student, the lower the impact which individual socio-economic background has on science performance. In schools with longer average learning time there could be a large gap in the students' learning time among students within schools and students with more advantaged socio-economic backgrounds might study for longer hours in schools than their schoolmates with less advantaged socio-economic background; this would be reflected in the greater impact of socio-economic background on student performance in schools with longer average learning time. Also, students in schools with a greater number of computers per students schools might have opportunities to access educational resources in their school that enhance their learning regardless of their socio-economic backgrounds; this would be reflected in the lesser impact of socio-economic background on student performance in schools with a greater number of computers per student. However, the nature and causality in such relationships are not established.

THE JOINT IMPACT OF SCHOOL AND SYSTEM RESOURCES, PRACTICES, AND POLICIES ON STUDENT PERFORMANCE

The preceding sections examined various aspects of school systems. These aspects can also be interrelated. For example, it is possible that schools that are well resourced also tend to be the ones that use the most effective teaching practices. A next step in the analysis is therefore to look at these factors jointly. This analysis provides valuable insights in two ways. First, it shows the overall amount of variation in student performance that is associated with the school and system-level factors considered in this chapter. Second, it allows for discernment of the extent to which the individual policies and practices have unique effects – an association with performance that is not explained only by their association with other factors that tend to go together with strong performance, including socio-economic background. As before, it needs to be taken into account that some of these factors have been measured more extensively than others and that many other factors that potentially have an influence on learning outcomes have not been measured by PISA. For example, much of the current research on school effectiveness concludes that teacher quality is a powerful predictor of learning outcomes (Wright, Horn and Sanders, 1997; Wayne and Youngs, 2001; and Loeb, 2003) but it has not been possible to establish measures on this in PISA. Readers should also keep in mind the methodological caveats described in Box 5.1.

The model examined below is based on student data from 55 participating countries, with each country given equal weight. Because the number of systems was small compared to the number of factors measured by PISA, the model was constructed in two steps. First, the relationship between science performance and six groups of school factors was examined, group-by-group, simultaneously at student, school and system-levels. The six factors were those discussed in preceding sections of this chapter: policies of admitting, grouping and selecting students, the role of public and private stakeholders in school management and funding, parental pressure and choice, accountability policies, school autonomy, and school resources. Afterwards, the individual factors from the different groups that had a statistically significant relationship with science performance[26] (see the first table in Boxes 5.2 to 5.7) in these analyses were jointly examined in a combined multilevel model (Table 5.19g). The relationship between these factors and science performance was estimated both before and after accounting for socio-economic variables at student, school and system-levels. As in the preceding sections, the former are referred to as gross effects while the latter are referred to as net effects (Box 5.8).[27]

Box 5.8 Combined multilevel model for student performance

	Gross		Net	
	Change in score	p-value	Change in score	p-value
Admitting, grouping and selecting				
School with ability grouping for all subjects within school (1=ability grouping between and/or within classes for all subjects; 0=no ability grouping or ability grouping for some subjects within school)	-7.6	(0.000)	-4.5	(0.000)
School with high academic selectivity of school admittance (1=academic records and/or feeder school recommendations are a prerequisite for student admittance; 0=others)	18.5	(0.000)	14.4	(0.000)
School with low academic selectivity of school admittance (1=neither academic records nor feeder school recommendations are considered for student admittance; 0=others)	-7.0	(0.002)	-1.3	(0.378)
School management and funding				
School with high proportion of school funding from government sources (each additional 10% funding from government sources)	-2.1	(0.000)		
Parental pressure and choice				
School with high level of competition (1=one or more other schools compete for students; 0=no other schools compete for students)	6.0	(0.002)		
System with high proportion of competitive schools (each additional 10% of competitive schools)	-4.6	(0.178)		
Accountability policies				
School posting achievement data publicly (1=yes; 0=no)	5.3	(0.000)	3.5	(0.001)
School autonomy				
School autonomy index in budgeting (effect of one standard deviation of the index)	1.4	(0.155)	0.9	(0.188)
System average of school autonomy index in budgeting (effect of one standard deviation of the index)	28.6	(0.023)	25.7	(0.008)
School resources				
School-level index of teacher shortage (effect of one standard deviation of the index)	-3.5	(0.000)		
School-level index of quality of school educational resources (effect of one standard deviation of the index)	3.9	(0.000)		
School average students' learning time for regular lessons in school (one additional hour per week)	14.0	(0.000)	8.8	(0.000)
School average students' learning time for out-of-school lessons (one additional hour per week)	-11.7	(0.000)	-8.6	(0.000)
School average students' learning time for self-study or homework (one additional hour per week)	3.8	(0.002)	3.1	(0.000)
School average index of school activities to promote students' learning of science (effect of one standard deviation of the index)	6.7	(0.000)	2.9	(0.000)

Note: See Box 5.2 for general notes.
More detailed results are presented in Table 5.19g. The detailed model is described in Annex A8.

The net combined model, which includes demographic and socio-economic background factors, as well as the school and system-level factors in the net model shown in Box 5.8, explains 40% of the total performance variance (Figure 5.19a). Of the 40% of explained variance, 19% lies between countries/economies (equivalent to almost three-quarters of total variance between countries), 18% lies between schools within countries/economies (equivalent to over two-thirds of the total variance between schools) and 2% lies between students within schools (equivalent to one-twentieth of the total variance between students).

Figure 5.19a
Variance and explained variance in science performance at student, school, and system levels

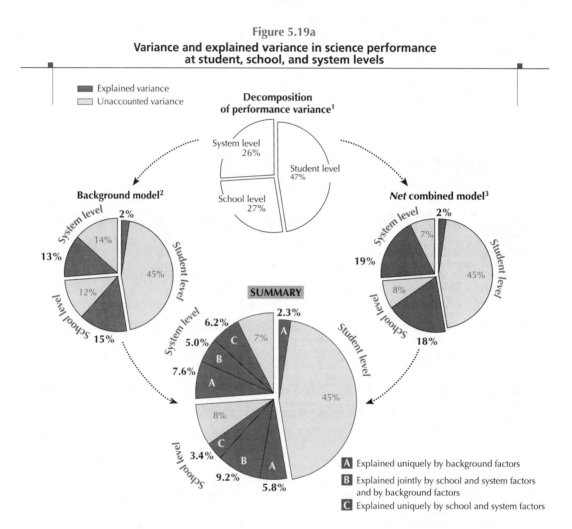

1. This model shows how much of the overall performance variation lies between students, schools, and countries/economies (see Model 0a in Table 5.19g.)
2. This model includes only the demographic and socio-economic background factors such as the PISA index of of economic, social and cultural status (ESCS) of students, the squared term of the ESCS, the gender, immigrant status, language spoken at home, the school location, the school size, the squared term of school size and the school average ESCS, and system average ESCS (see Model 0b in Table 5.19g).
3. This model includes school and system level factors such as ability grouping for all subjects within the school, high and low academic selectivity for school admittance, school accountability (posting achievement data publicly), school autonomy in budgeting (and percentage of schools with autonomy in budgeting in a country), school average students' learning time for regular lessons in school, for out-of-school lessons, and for self-study or homework, and school activities to promote students' learning of science, in addtion to the demographic and socio-economic background factors included in the background model (see Model 2N in Table 5.19g).
Source: OECD PISA 2006 database, Table 5.19g.
StatLink ⏴⏵ http://dx.doi.org/10.1787/141887160188

It is also possible to examine how much of the performance variation between schools factors in the net model shown in Box 5.8 explain in each country. The performance variation uniquely explained by the selected set of school factors, the performance variation uniquely explained by the demographic and socio-economic factors, the performance variation jointly explained by the school factors and the demographic and socio-economic factors, and the unexplained performance variation between schools is shown in Figure 5.19b. The overall length of the bar in the figure represents the performance variation between schools expressed as a percentage of the average performance variation between schools across OECD countries. The percentages in the second column reflect the percentage of the performance variation between schools that is explained by the model relative to the total performance variation between schools in each country. On average across OECD countries, 81% of the between-school variation in performance within countries is explained by the model[28] and this exceeds 90% in Luxembourg, New Zealand and Germany,but is less than 60% or less in Canada, Norway and Finland, and the partner country Indonesia and 31% in the partner country Azerbaijan. In most countries, more than half of the performance variation between schools is jointly explained by the school factors and the demographic and socio-economic factors (Figure 5.19b).

Beyond showing what proportion of the performance variation the school factors explain, the models also estimate the size of their effect on school performance. The first five school factors and the one system factor listed below have effects on science performance both before and after accounting for the socio-economic context. In contrast, the last four school factors listed below have effects on science learning before accounting for the socio-economic contextual factors, but the effects are no longer statistically significant after accounting for the socio-economic context (Box 5.8):

School factors that are associated with performance even after accounting for demographic and socio-economic background

- School principals' reports regarding the practice of ability grouping for all subjects within schools (students in schools practicing ability grouping for all subjects within schools score 4.5 points lower than students in school practicing no ability grouping or ability grouping only for some subjects, all other things being equal).

- School principals' reports regarding high academic selectivity of school admittance (students in schools in which academic records or feeder school recommendations were a prerequisite for school admittance score 14.4 points higher than students in schools applying a moderate selective admittance policy, all other things being equal).

- School principals' reports regarding whether the school's achievement data are posted publicly (students in schools posting achievement data publicly score 3.5 points higher compared with students in schools not posting achievement data publicly, all other things being equal).

- School principals' reports regarding the school average time students invest in learning for science, mathematics and language at school (students in schools with one additional average hour per week score 8.8 points higher, all other things being equal), out-of school lessons (students in schools with one additional average hour per week score 8.6 points lower, all other things being equal), and self-study (students in schools with one additional average hour per week score 3.1 points higher, all other things being equal).

- School principals' reports regarding school activities to promote students' learning of science (one additional unit of this index is equivalent to an advantage of 2.9 score points in student performance, all other things being equal).

System factor that is associated with performance even after accounting for demographic and socio-economic background

- Education systems where schools have a higher degree of autonomy in budgeting (students in education systems with one additional standard deviation on the index of autonomy in budgeting score 25.7 points higher, all other things being equal).

267

Figure 5.19b
School-level variance and explained variance in science performance, by country

▦ Unaccounted between-school variance
▦ Between-school variance uniquely accounted for by demographic and socio-economic factors
▦ Between-school variance uniquely accounted for by school factors
▦ Between-school variance jointly accounted for by demographic and socio-economic factors and school factors

	Between-school variance as a percentage of the total variance within each country	Explained between-school variance as a percentage of the total between-school variance within each country	Between-school variance in student performance in science as a percentage of the average between-school variance across OECD countries
Germany	57	91	
Bulgaria	54	83	
Slovenia	60	86	
Hungary	61	88	
Czech Republic	53	82	
Austria	55	85	
Netherlands	60	86	
Belgium	52	87	
Chile	50	90	
Argentina	48	80	
Italy	50	78	
Japan	47	73	
Greece	47	81	
Chinese Taipei	47	75	
Turkey	53	82	
Luxembourg	30	99	
Switzerland	36	80	
Slovak Republic	42	73	
Israel	31	67	
Brazil	47	69	
Uruguay	40	71	
Croatia	40	82	
OECD average	33	81	
Serbia	41	78	
Romania	49	75	
Korea	35	83	
Hong Kong-China	37	76	
Tunisia	42	78	
United States	24	85	
Portugal	32	83	
Kyrgyzstan	39	72	
Thailand	37	83	
New Zealand	17	93	
Lithuania	28	77	
United Kingdom	20	79	
Colombia	30	72	
Montenegro	28	85	
Mexico	40	67	
Russian Federation	27	61	
Australia	18	72	
Macao-China	26	76	
Ireland	17	84	
Jordan	23	65	
Estonia	21	75	
Indonesia	43	59	
Canada	19	57	
Denmark	16	69	
Latvia	19	66	
Sweden	12	75	
Spain	15	66	
Poland	14	67	
Iceland	9	69	
Norway	11	59	
Azerbaijan	50	31	
Finland	6	60	

Source: OECD PISA 2006 database, Table 5.21a.
StatLink ⟐ http://dx.doi.org/10.1787/141887160188

School factors that are associated with performance only before taking demographic and socio-economic background into account

- School principals' reports regarding the level of funding from government (students in schools with an additional 10% of public funding score 2 points lower, all other things being equal).

- School principals' reports regarding whether there is one or more other schools in the area that compete for the students (students in schools competing with other schools score 6.0 points higher compared to students in schools not competing with other schools for students, all other things being equal).

- School principals' perceptions of the lack of qualified teachers hindering instruction (students in schools with one additional unit of this index score 3.5 points lower, all other things being equal);

- School principals' positive evaluations of the quality of educational materials at their school (students in schools with one additional unit of this index score 3.9 points better, all other things being equal);

The school and system-level factors with statistically significant effects in both the gross and net models (Box 5.8 and Model 2G and Model 2N in Table 5.19g) present an interesting story about the association of school and system characteristics with science performance. Even after accounting for a host of salient student, school, and country background factors, some specific factors remain important predictors of student performance. These factors provide some clues to policy amenable practices that schools and countries are undertaking that could enhance performance beyond the standard set of educational resources.

The above analysis shows that, in terms of school resources, the schools that enhance their students' science performance are ones that manage resources in such a way as to increase in-school learning time, encourage students' self-study, and provide extra learning activities that promote science including science clubs, science fairs, science competitions, extracurricular science projects, and excursions and field trips. Although separately these additional resources are only modestly associated with enhanced student performance, taken together they point to a substantial impact (Box 5.8 and Table 5.19g).

The school factors in the net combined model were also examined country by country with a two-level model consisting of student and school levels. The net effects on science performance of school factors as well as the demographic and socio-economic background of students and schools are presented in Table 5.21b and Figure 5.20. The results show that the net effects of additional learning time in science, mathematics and language during regular school lessons are significantly positive in all countries except in Iceland and Sweden. The net effect varies from 2 to 17 score points, and one additional in-school learning hour per week is associated with an increase of over 10 score points in science performance in Greece, Turkey, Portugal, Hungary and the Czech Republic and in the partner countries/economies Tunisia, Argentina, Romania, Israel, the Russian Federation, Macao-China, Hong Kong-China, Montenegro, Chile, Latvia and Brazil. The net effect of additional learning time for self-study or homework is statistically significantly positive in 21 OECD countries and 11 partner countries/economies. The net effect is between 10 and 12 score points in Switzerland, Sweden, Japan, the United States and the partner economy Hong Kong-China, and between 15 to 20 score points in Belgium, Korea and the Netherlands and in the partner economy Chinese Taipei. The net effect is slightly negative but statistically significant in Greece, Austria and Turkey and in the partner country Tunisia. Schools with activities that promote students' learning in science tend to perform better, even after accounting for the demographic and socio-economic background of students and schools. The net effect associated with a one unit increase in this index is statistically significantly positive in 15 OECD countries and 12 partner countries/economies with the variation of the effect between 2 to 12 score points in science. The net effect is over 7 score points in science in Poland, Switzerland and Germany and in the partner countries/economies Macao-China, Bulgaria and Azerbaijan. The net effect is negative in the following three countries: Iceland (-6.5), Luxembourg (-6.3) and Finland (-4.5) (Figure 5.20 and Table 5.21b).

269

Figure 5.20 [Part 1/2]

Net association of school factors with student performance in science

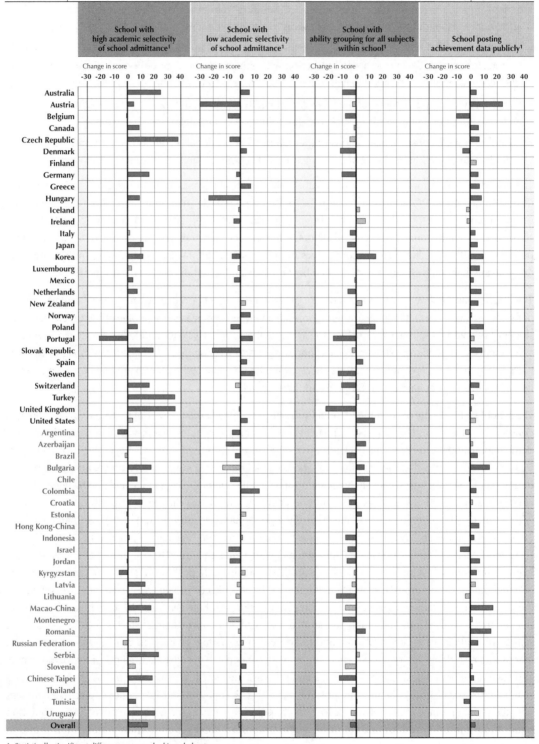

1. Statistically significant differences are marked in a darker tone.
Source: OECD PISA 2006 database, Table 5.19g and Table 5.21b.
StatLink http://dx.doi.org/10.1787/141887160188

Figure 5.20 [Part 2/2]

Net association of school factors with student performance in science

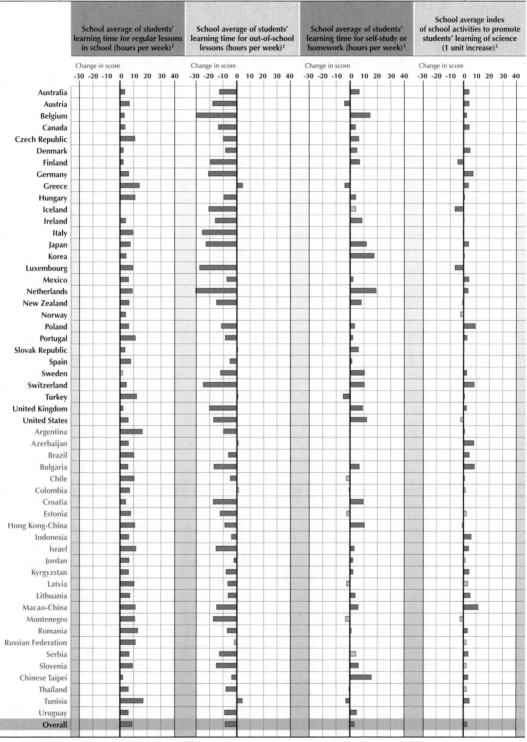

1. Statistically significant differences are marked in a darker tone.
Source: OECD PISA 2006 database, Table 5.19g and Table 5.21b.
StatLink http://dx.doi.org/10.1787/141887160188

The results of the model illustrated in Box 5.8 also shed light on other education policy issues. For example, when the 55 countries are examined jointly, schools that publicly communicate students' performance have a gross performance advantage of 5.3 score points and of 3.5 score points after accounting for socio-economic factors (Box 5.8 and Table 5.19g). This association can be observed in 17 OECD countries and 12 partner countries and economies: the net effect of schools is greatest in Austria at 23.9 score points, but is also between 8 to 17 score points in the Netherlands, Hungary, the Slovak Republic, Korea and Poland and in the partner countries/economies Thailand, Bulgaria, Romania and Macao-China (Figure 5.20 and Table 5.21b).

Students in schools that do not use ability grouping or use ability grouping only for some subjects but not for all subjects within the school score 7.6 points higher than students in other schools and the net effect is 4.5 score points when jointly examining the 55 countries (Box 5.8 and Table 5.19g). The net effect of practicing ability grouping for all subjects is negative in 11 OECD countries and 10 partner countries and economies, varying from -4 to -22 score points. The net effect is between -11 and -22 score points in Switzerland, Denmark, Sweden and Portugal and the Unitde Kingdom, and in the partner economy Chinese Taipei and the partner country Lithuania. However, in nine countries, there is a positive net effect, which ranges between 4 and 10 score points in Spain and in the partner countries Estonia, Bulgaria, Romania, Azerbaijan and Chile, and amounts to over 11 score points in Korea (14.5), Poland (14.1) and the United States (13.6) (Figure 5.20 and Table 5.21b).

Students in schools in which academic records or feeder school recommendations were a prerequisite for school admittance score 18.5 score points higher than students in other schools. This effect barely decreases when socio-economic contextual factors are accounted for. It is, however, important to note that if in one country highly selective schools are performing better than non-selective schools, it does not follow that if more schools became selective, overall results would improve.[29]

Students in systems with more schools having autonomy in formulating the school budget and deciding on budget allocations within school tend to perform better in science, even after accounting for the background factors (Box 5.8 and Table 5.19g).

In the gross combined model, students in schools with adequate science teachers and educational materials perform better than students in other schools. However, these effects are not statistically significant when socio-economic context factors are accounted for. This suggests that some school material resources and the background factors are strongly interrelated; for example in some countries students with more advantaged socio-economic backgrounds attend schools with better qualified science teachers and educational materials. Similarly, the performance difference between students in publicly and privately funded schools as well as the performance advantage for students in schools with competing other schools in the same area for students disappear after accounting for demographic and socio-economic background factors.

THE JOINT IMPACT OF SCHOOL AND SYSTEM RESOURCES, PRACTICES, AND POLICIES ON THE RELATIONSHIP BETWEEN SOCIO-ECONOMIC BACKGROUND AND STUDENT PERFORMANCE IN SCIENCE

As shown in Chapter 4, the extent to which the performance of students and schools depends on socio-economic factors varies considerably across schools and education systems. In some schools or educational systems, students' academic performances are strongly related to socio-economic background, while in others, learning outcomes depend much less on socio-economic background conditions.

This section examines the joint influence of the various school policies and practices that have been discussed in this chapter on the strength of the association between students' socio-economic background on science performance, with the objective to identify school and system-level factors that potentially enhance equity in the distribution of learning opportunities.

Because the number of school factors measured by PISA far exceeds the number of participating education systems, a two-step modelling process was applied. First, indicators from each of the six groups of factors considered in this chapter (policies of admitting, grouping and selecting students, the role of public and private stakeholders in the governance and financing of schools, parental school choice and performance pressure on schools, accountability arrangements, school autonomy, and school resources) are examined separately as to their impact on the relationship between students' socio-economic background and performance (see the second tables in Box 5.2 to 5.7 and Tables 5.20a-f). Afterwards, the individual factors from the different groups that had a statistically significant impact on the relationship between socio-economic background and student performance in these analyses are examined jointly (see Box 5.9 and Table 5.20g).[30]

Box 5.9 **Combined multilevel model for the impact of socio-economic background**

	Increase in score points in science corresponding to one unit increase of the student's PISA index of economic, social and cultural status		Increase in score points in science corresponding to one unit increase of the school average of the PISA index of economic, social and cultural status	
	Change in relationship	p-value	Change in relationship	p-value
System with early selection (each additional year between the first age of selection and the age of 15)	-1.9	(0.004)	8.9	(0.000)
School average students' learning time for regular lessons in school (one additional hour per week)	0.7	(0.000)		

Note: See Box 5.2 for general notes.
More detailed results are presented in Table 5.20g. The model is described in Annex A8.

There are two factors among those tested in the model that are closely related to equity in the distribution of learning opportunities even after accounting for other school and system-level factors. These are consistent with the results from the models examining institutional characteristics separately. These are the school average of student learning time for science, mathematics and language at school, and the age at which students are placed into distinct school types (Box 5.7 and Box 5.2). One additional hour per week of student learning time at school is equivalent to an increase in the within-school relationship between the students' socio-economic background and science performance by 0.7 score points for a one-unit increase in the student's PISA index of economic, social and cultural status. In education systems where students are placed into different types of schools or distinct educational programmes at an early stage in their educational career, the impact of student socio-economic background on performance within a school is slightly weakened, but the impact of socio-economic composition of the school that students attend on student performance is considerably strengthened beyond the impact of the students' own socio-economic background on science performance. For instance, each additional year spent in separate school types is associated with a decrease in the within-school relationship between the students' socio-economic background and science performance by 1.9 score points for a one-unit increase in the PISA index of economic, social and cultural status. On the other hand, when educational tracking is brought forward

by one year, the impact of schools' socio-economic composition on student performance increases by 8.9 for a one-unit increase in the school average PISA index of economic, social and cultural status, beyond the impact of the individual students' socio-economic background. These results suggest that educational tracking tends to reinforce socio-economic segregation between schools.

Comparing students across countries according to the time they spend learning in class, it can been seen that no matter where students come from in terms of their socio-economic background, those in schools with longer average in-class learning time tend to perform better than students in schools with average in-class learning time (Figure 5.21). Therefore, even though the effect of socio-economic background on performance is stronger in schools with longer in-class learning, this does not suggest that learning time should be reduced for these students, as students from all socio-economic contexts benefit from being in schools with longer in-class learning.

Figure 5.21
**Relationship between student's economic, social and cultural status
and student performance in science, by learning time at school**

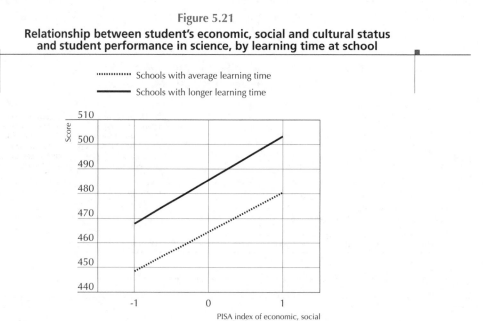

Note: Across the 55 countries, the average regular lesson hours per week is 10.2 and the standard deviation is 2.4. "Schools with average learning time" corresponds to schools with 10.2 hours regular lessons per week. "Schools with longer learning time" corresponds to schools with 12.6 hours regular lessons per week (one standard deviation longer than the average).
Source: OECD PISA 2006 database, Table 5.20g.
StatLink http://dx.doi.org/10.1787/141887160188

The same can be done by examining the impact of early tracking (Figure 5.22). The left panel in Figure 5.22 presents the relationships between the individual student's socio-economic background (on the horizontal axis) and student performance (on the vertical axis) for schools with a disadvantaged socio-economic intake; the middle panel represents schools with a socio-economic intake that is similar to the OECD average, and the right panel represents schools with an advantaged socio-economic intake.

On the surface, it seems that the relationship between the individual socio-economic background of students and performance is weaker in the institutionally stratified systems, as mirrored in the relatively flatter socio-economic gradients within schools. However, in the socio-economically disadvantaged schools, students tend to perform equally poorly in systems that are stratified at early stages in their education, whatever

Figure 5.22
Relationship between student economic, social and cultural status and student performance in science, by tracking system

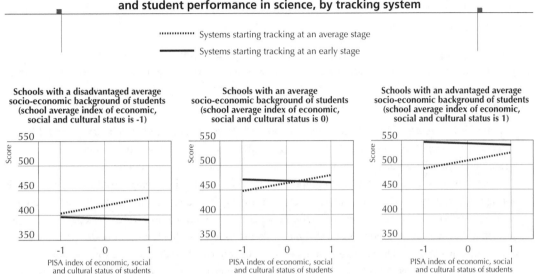

Note: Across the 55 countries, the average years spent between the first age of selection in the education system and the age of 15 is 1.2 and the standard deviation is 1.6. "Systems starting tracking at an average stage" corresponds to systems starting tracking at the age of 13.8 (subtracting 1.2 years from the age of 15). "Systems starting tracking at an early stage" corresponds to systems starting tracking at the age of 12.2 (one standard deviation earlier than the average).

Source: OECD PISA 2006 database, Table 5.20g.

StatLink ᵃᵐᵖ http://dx.doi.org/10.1787/141887160188

their individual socio-economic background (solid line in the left panel), while all students, whatever their individual socio-economic background, tend to show equally high performance in the socio-economically advantaged schools (solid line in the right panel). This gap between schools in the systems with early tracking is much larger than the gap in more comprehensive systems even though there is no difference in the overall level of performance between systems starting tracking early and comprehensive systems. Systems starting tracking early thus tend to be associated with larger socio-economic inequalities, while not showing to gains in average performance.

IMPLICATIONS FOR POLICY

This chapter has identified a range of school characteristics that have a bearing on learning outcomes, on differences in these outcomes across schools and on the extent to which differences are associated with the uneven distribution of students across schools according to their socio-economic background.

Such findings cannot provide precise policy prescriptions based on direct measurement of the effects of various policy measures on achievement. This is partly because of the methodological caveats listed in Box 5.1, and partly because a large-scale survey like PISA cannot look at the details of policy and practice within schools at a micro level.

Conversely, the findings can start to answer some types of questions that national surveys cannot address. These include questions about the overall effects of school system differences, questions about which of a broad range of school factors seem to have a consistent, measurable association with performance and questions about the extent to which these associations interact with socio-economic background.

PISA can thus help inform broad strategies in the pursuit of quality and equity within school systems, by showing which factors seem to be most closely connected with performance and to what extent socio-economic differences in results are linked to socio-economic differences in access to resources and to schools with positive features.

A number of groups of school characteristics show a relationship with performance. When each group is looked at separately, the effect tends to be modest, yet where it is statistically significant across thousands of schools in dozens of countries, it is worth examining further. At this level, the main sections of this chapter identify:

- *Differences in patterns of results according to how students are admitted to schools, grouped across schools and grouped within schools.* Most importantly, in school systems where students are divided into different school groups at relatively early ages, the socio-economic differences in results by age 15 are relatively large through school compositional effects, while the average level of performance is not higher compared to comprehensive education systems. This suggests that countries practising early tracking need to pay particular attention to the students grouped into schools with a disadvantaged socio-economic background and the extent to which this may increase differences in performance without leading to gains in overall level of performance. A smaller effect is the slightly lower overall performance of schools that group students by ability for all subjects internally, suggesting that such a policy might potentially hinder learning of certain students more than it enhances learning of others.

- *Higher performance in privately funded schools and in schools that compete for students, but no statistically significant effect in either case once the combined effect of individual student socio-economic background and the average socio-economic background of all students in the school are taken into account.* There is no statistically significant difference in the impact of student's socio-economic difference on performance between public and private schools, nor between schools competing with other schools and schools not competing. That said, while the performance of private schools does not tend to be superior once demographic and socio-economic factors have been accounted for, in many countries they may still pose an attractive alternative for parents looking to maximise the benefits for their children, including those benefits that are conferred on students through the socio-economic level of schools' intake.

- *Higher performance in schools that keep track of student performance at a public level.* The public posting of results by schools continues to have an effect on performance even after all other school and demographic and socio-economic factors that were measured have been accounted for. The strength of these effects across so many countries suggests that the impetus provided by external monitoring of standards, rather than relying principally on schools and individual teachers to uphold them, can make a real difference to results. PISA itself has encouraged countries not to take internally assessed education standards for granted, and is now indicating a strong effect within countries of the discipline provided by subjecting schools to external assessment with publicly visible results.

- *Higher performance in countries giving more autonomy to schools to formulate the school budget and to decide on budget allocations within the school even after accounting for other school and system level factors as well as demographic and socio-economic factors.* Similarly, students in educational systems that give more autonomy to schools in educational matters such as text books and courses offered, tend to perform better, but this effect is not significant after accounting for some other school and system level factors. These results suggest that greater autonomy has a general impact within school systems, perhaps deriving from the greater independence of school managers in systems that authorise choice of responses to local conditions.

- *A modest relationship between certain aspects of school resources and student outcomes.* However, much of this relationship disappears when one accounts for the socio-economic status of students, suggesting that the resources themselves may not be causing the better results since in many cases schools with better material and human resources also have students from relatively favourable socio-economic backgrounds. Of the resource factors that remain statistically significant net of socio-economic status, the most noticeable is learning time in class. Students who spend more time in class tend to do somewhat better. Schools providing activities enhancing students' science learning perform better.

A larger question is whether specific policy interventions responding to these effects are likely to be overshadowed by the high number of other influences on student performance, whether in terms of the multiple aspects of the school learning environment and organisation not covered by any given policy or in terms of contextual influences including the socio-economic background of the students attending each school. The later section of the above analysis addresses this issue by looking at the combined influence of selected school factors each of which appears to have an impact beyond its association with students' socio-economic background and with other school factors. These factors are:

- Student learning time, most importantly in school classes, but also out of school classes and private study
- Activities to promote science learning in schools
- Public posting of achievement data
- Ability grouping for all subjects within schools (which appears to have a small negative effect)
- The degree to which a school selects its students
- The system providing schools with more autonomy in budgeting

An overall measure of the combined effect of these six factors suggests that about one-quarter of variation in students' science performance can be associated with the ways in which these factors vary across countries and across schools, once the variation explained by demographic and socio-economic differences has been taken into account. However, most of this effect is not attributable to the school factors acting wholly independently of demographic and socio-economic factors, but rather a combined effect of the two. For example, schools that have longer learning hours also tend to enrol more socio-economically advantaged students, and while the higher predicted performance of such students can only partially account for the superior performance of such schools, the effects of longer hours and higher intake appear to reinforce each other. At a policy level, this suggests that the potential for improving results through such school factors needs to be considered in combination with the extent to which schools with favourable characteristics are being accessed mainly by more advantaged students. The challenge is to find ways of spreading such characteristics to a wider section of the student population.

In this context, a crucial question for school systems is whether there are policies that can systematically improve equity without threatening quality. In terms of the distribution of finite resources, this is not straightforward, since it is difficult to calculate whether lowering resources for socio-economically advantaged students and schools might harm students' performance more than improving resources for socio-economically disadvantaged students and schools would improve results. Even if this were not to lower the average score, it is possible that it would reduce the number of high-performing students, which in itself is undesirable. However, what is noticeable about the strongest effects measured in this chapter is that they are not the ones most closely associated with finite material resources, such as the distribution of good teachers. Rather, such effects are related to how schools and the school system are run – for example, the amount of time that students spend in class and the extent to which schools are accountable for their results. Delivering such advantages to one student is not obviously at the expense of another.

277

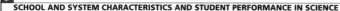
A more complex issue relates to the effects of selection and differentiation. It is clearly not possible for every school to raise its students' performance by becoming more selective about its intake. However, one clear-cut finding from PISA is that differentiation at an early age damages equity without any discernible benefit for quality. That is to say, in systems that separate children early in secondary school, their results by the age of 15 differ more than average according to socio-economic background, with no systematic benefit in terms of the average performance. A number of countries with early differentiation of students by institution have already delayed or reduced the degree of separation in recent years. This evidence suggests that others should consider doing so.

Notes

1. In the countries with multiple school systems, the results presented in this chapter relate to the overall picture, not necessarily to the features of individual school systems.

2. For instance, in some countries some of the schools in the PISA sample were defined as administrative units even if they spanned several geographically separate institutions, as in Italy; in some they were defined as those parts of larger educational institutions that serve 15-year-olds; in others they were defined as physical school buildings; and in yet others they were defined from a management perspective (*e.g.* entities having a principal). The *PISA 2006 Technical Report* (OECD, forthcoming) provides an overview of how schools were defined.

3. The proportion of explained variation is obtained by squaring the correlation shown in Figure 5.2.

4. Before 1999, the school system provided three tracks following eight years of primary education, an academic secondary track, an academic track with a practical orientation, and a vocational track oriented towards direct entry into the labour market. The system introduced in 1999 provided six years of primary education followed by three years of subject-oriented general lower secondary education, followed by a tracked system of upper secondary education.

5. The term "grouping" often refers to an instructional strategy that can be used effectively in any class, irrespective of the existence of tracking or streaming. Students can be grouped according to interests, capabilities on particular tasks, group or collective projects, and so on. However, in the context of PISA, "ability grouping" refers to tracking or streaming, which means students being assigned to classes with different levels of academic challenge or content according to their perceived or measured abilities. School principals were asked to report on whether students were grouped by ability into different classes as well if students were grouped by ability within their classes. Therefore, the ability grouping analysed in this section does not include grouping on the basis of different curricula.

6. These opposite effects of ability grouping may be partly due to different forms of grouping. For example, high performing students are grouped in some schools or countries, while low-performing students are grouped in others.

7. At the student level, the following variables were taken into account: the parental occupation and education, as well as students' access to home educational and cultural resources, as expressed in the PISA index of economic, social and cultural status, gender, the country of birth of the student and his or her parents, as well as the language spoken at home. At the school level, the socio-economic intake of the school, as measured by the school-level aggregate of the economic, social and cultural status of the 15-year-olds attending this school, the school location and the school size were taken into account. At the country level, the national occupational profile and the country average of students' family and home background as measured by the country average PISA index of economic, social and cultural status were taken into account. Separate models were also estimated with GDP per capita instead of the country average PISA index of economic, social and cultural status in order examine the robustness of the index. Both models led to very similar results.

8. France and Qatar were not included in this analysis. France did not provide data from school principals. Qatar had a large number of missing observations in the factors used to construct the index of economic, social and cultural status.

9. Results of the model including the proportion of highly selective schools in the country show that this variable does not have a statistically significant association with student performance (the change in score is 2.6 and the p-value is 0.918).

10. The gradient between the PISA index of economic, social and cultural status and student performance in science is used as a measure of equity. All of the models for the impact of socio-economic background in this chapter also control for other background factors such as students' gender, migration status, and language spoken at home as well as school location, school size, school average socio-economic background and the country wealth indicator.

11. In accordance with OECD standards, public schools are defined as educational instructional institutions that are accounted for and managed directly by a public education authority or agency; or controlled and managed either by a government agency directly or by a governing body (council, committee, etc.), most of whose members were either appointed by a public authority or elected by public franchise. Private schools are defined as educational instructional institutions that are accounted for and managed by a non-governmental organisation (*e.g.* a church, a trade union or a business enterprise) or if their governing board consisted mostly of members not selected by a public agency.

12. For the comparisons in this section, government-dependent and government-independent private schools were combined as otherwise the number of schools would have been too small to allow for reliable comparisons. Moreover, only countries with at least 3% of students enrolled in private schools were included in these comparisons.

13. It is important to note that over 96% of 15-year-olds are in private schools in Macao-China.

14. The score point difference between public and private schools in Table 5.4 is the result of a comparison of these two different school types within each country, while the effect of private management in this multilevel model is the effect after controlling for the funding source (public/private). This explains why the average of the score point difference between public and private schools in Table 5.4 is larger than the effect of public management found in the multilevel model.

15. An examination at the level of the education system shows that countries with a higher proportion of privately managed schools tend to perform slightly better, even after controlling for demographic and socio-economic factors. In other words, students in education systems with a higher proportion of privately managed schools tend to perform better, regardless of whether the schools that they attend are privately managed or not.

16. These countries were Denmark, Germany, Iceland, Italy, Korea, Luxembourg, New Zealand, Poland, Portugal and Turkey, and the partner countries/economies Bulgaria, Colombia, Croatia, Hong Kong-China, Macao-China and Qatar. In examining the results from the PISA parent questionnaire, it should be noted that in some countries non-response was considerable. Countries with considerable missing data in the parent questionnaire are listed in the following together with the proportion of missing data in brackets: Portugal (11%), Italy (14%), Germany (20%), Luxembourg (24%), New Zealand (32%), Iceland (36%) and Qatar (40%).

17. Across the 55 countries, on average, students are in education systems where 75% of schools are competitive.

18. Standards-based external examinations are defined according to John Bishop's definition of "curriculum-based external examination system" (CBEES). CBEES has the following characteristics: it produces signals of student accomplishments that have real consequences for the student and it defines achievement relative to an external standard, not relative to other students in the classroom or the school. To enable fair comparisons of achievement across schools and across students at different schools, it is organised by discipline and keyed to the content of specific course sequences, which focuses the responsibility for preparing the student for particular exams on one or a small group of teachers; it signals multiple levels of achievement in the subject and not only a pass-fail signal, and it covers almost all secondary school students (Bishop 1998, 2001).

19. Data were collected through the OECD's Programme on Indicators of Education Systems (INES). In partner countries/economies, the National Project Managers for PISA were asked to complete a questionnaire. For the partner countries, decimals given represent the proportion of academic and vocation programmes, when a standards-based external examination exits only in some programmes.

20. It is statistically significant at the 12% level.

21. It is important to note that schools' decisions in determining course content and course offerings could be affected by the existence of external standards-based examinations, even if schools have a considerable responsibility in this area.

22. This covers responses to both the category "only school has a considerable responsibility" and the category "both school and government have a considerable responsibility" in the corresponding question to school principals.

23. The relative influence of the seven stakeholder groups was determined by averaging the percentage of 15-year-olds whose school principals reported that the stakeholder group in question has a direct influence across the four decision-making areas of staffing, budgeting, instructional content and assessment practices.

24. The index of school autonomy in staffing consists of the following components: school's relative responsibility in selecting teachers for hire (0.811), dismissing teachers (0.833), establishing teachers' starting salaries (0.797), and determining teachers' salary increases (0.791). The index of school autonomy in budgeting consists of the following components: school relative responsibility in formulating the school budget (0.827) and deciding on budget allocations within the school (0.827). The index of school autonomy in educational content consists of three components: school's relative responsibility in choosing which textbooks are used (0.794), determining course content (0.837), and deciding which course are offered (0.824). The figures in brackets are the respective factor loadings. The school's relative responsibility is computed by assigning the value 1 when only schools ("principals or teachers" and/or "school governing board") have a considerable responsibility and governments

("regional or local education authority" and/or "national education authority") have no responsibility; assigning the value 0 when both schools and governments have considerable responsibilities; and assigning the value -1 when only governments have considerable responsibilities.

25. The variable "learning time at out-of-school lessons" is not included in the discussion here even though it is included in the model. The reason for this is that this factor cannot be regarded as a school resource, and it was included in the model as a control variable in order to interpret the in-school and homework learning time in a comprehensive framework of total learning time. In the model, out-of-school lessons, such as tutoring and other shadow education, have a negative association with performance. This may be because students with poor performance in science seek remediation through learning outside of school resources (Baker *et al.*, 2001).

26. The criteria for inclusion of factors was a p-value below 10% for system-level factors, and a p-value below 0.5% for school level factors, in order to balance the Type I and Type II statistical errors at the two levels, taking into account the fact that data from around 14,000 schools enter the analysis at school level, whereas 55 observations are processed at the system-level.

27. Since the gross models and the net models were built up independently, the final gross combined model and the final net combined model include different sets of school and system-level factors.

28. This figure is different from the explained variance in Model 2N (69%) as the former is based on the two-level model consisting of the student and school levels, while the latter is based on the three-level model including the system level in addition to the student and school levels.

29. See note 9.

30. See note 26.

6

A profile of student performance in reading and mathematics from PISA 2000 to PISA 2006

Introduction 284

What students can do in reading 284
- A profile of PISA reading questions 286

Student performance in reading 293
- The mean performances of countries/economies in reading 295
- How student performance in reading has changed 301
- Gender differences in reading 303

What students can do in mathematics 304
- A profile of PISA mathematics questions 304

Student performance in mathematics 312
- The mean performances of countries/economies in mathematics 315
- How student performance in mathematics has changed 319
- Gender differences in mathematics 320

Implications for policy 321
- Reading 321
- Mathematics 322
- Gender differences 323

INTRODUCTION

PISA shows countries where their education systems stand relative to others, in terms of the performance of 15-year-old students. Equally important, PISA monitors changes in educational outcomes over time and tracks changes in factors related to student and school performance, including the attitudes and expectations of students, the learning environment at school, and factors relating to school policies and practices.

This chapter makes comparisons over time where they are possible based on full assessments of subject domains.[1] PISA 2006 provides the second assessment of reading since PISA 2000, when the first full assessment of reading took place, and the first assessment of mathematics since PISA 2003, when the first full assessment of mathematics took place. This chapter provides an overview of student performance in reading and mathematics, and how this has changed since PISA 2000 and PISA 2003.

While the results do provide a basis for comparison across surveys, some limitations must be noted when interpreting change over time:

- First, since data are only available for three points in time for reading and two points for mathematics, it is not yet possible to assess to what extent the observed differences are indicative of longer-term trends.

- Second, while the overall approach to measurement used by PISA is consistent across cycles, small refinements continue to be made, so it would not be prudent to read too much into small changes in results. Furthermore, errors from sampling, as well as measurement errors, are inevitably introduced when assessments are linked through a limited number of common assessment tasks over time. To account for this, the confidence band for comparisons over time has been widened correspondingly and only changes that are indicated as statistically significant in this chapter should be considered.[2]

- Third, some countries cannot be included in comparisons between PISA 2000 and PISA 2003 and PISA 2006 for methodological reasons. Among OECD countries, the Slovak Republic and Turkey joined PISA only since the PISA 2003 survey. The PISA 2000 sample for the Netherlands did not meet the PISA response rate standards and mean scores for the Netherlands were therefore not reported for PISA 2000. In Luxembourg, the assessment conditions were changed in substantial ways between the PISA 2000 and PISA 2003 survey and results are therefore only comparable between PISA 2003 and PISA 2006.[3] The PISA 2000 and PISA 2003 samples for the United Kingdom did not meet the PISA response rate standards and so data from the United Kingdom are not comparable with other countries.[4] In addition, for the United States, no reading results are available for PISA 2006,[5] and for Austria, there have been modifications to the weighting of their PISA 2000 data.[6]

With those provisos in mind, there are a number of informative comparisons that can be made over time in reading and mathematics.

WHAT STUDENTS CAN DO IN READING

Reading literacy focuses on the ability of students to use written information in situations which they encounter in their life. In PISA, *reading literacy* is defined as understanding, using and reflecting on written texts, in order to achieve one's goals, to develop one's knowledge and potential and to participate in society (OECD, 2006a). This definition goes beyond the traditional notion of decoding information and literal interpretation of what is written towards more applied tasks. The concept of *reading literacy* in PISA is defined by three dimensions: the format of the reading material, the type of reading task or reading aspects, and the situation or the use for which the text was constructed.

The first dimension, the text format, classifies the reading material or texts into *continuous* and *non-continuous texts*. *Continuous texts* are typically composed of sentences that are, in turn, organised into paragraphs. These may fit under larger structures such as sections, chapters and books. *Non-continuous texts* are organised differently from *continuous texts;* they require a different reading approach and can be classified according to their format.

The second dimension is defined by the three reading aspects. Some tasks required students to *retrieve information* – that is, to locate single or multiple pieces of information in a text. Other tasks required students to *interpret texts* – that is, to construct meaning and draw inferences from written information. The third type of task required students to *reflect on and evaluate texts* – that is, to relate written information to their prior knowledge, ideas and experiences.

The third dimension, the situation or context, reflects the categorisation of texts based on the author's intended use, the relationship with other persons implicitly or explicitly associated with the text, and the general content. The situations included in PISA and selected to maximise the diversity of content included in the *reading literacy* assessment were *reading for private use* (personal), *reading for public use, reading for work* (occupational) and *reading for education.*

A full description of the conceptual framework underlying the PISA assessment of *reading literacy* is provided in *Assessing Scientific, Reading and Mathematical Literacy: A Framework for PISA 2006* (OECD, 2006a).

Since reading was the focus of the PISA 2000 survey, the framework and instruments for measuring *reading literacy* were fully developed at that stage, and an OECD mean score of 500 points was established for PISA 2000 as the benchmark against which reading performance has since been measured. In PISA 2003 and PISA 2006, when the focus shifted to mathematics and then science, the area of reading was given smaller amounts of assessment time than in PISA 2000 with 60 instead of 210 minutes devoted to reading, allowing an update on overall performance rather than the kind of in-depth analysis of knowledge and skills shown in the PISA 2000 report.[7] In PISA 2000, student performance in reading was reported separately for each of the three aspects described above. In PISA 2003 and PISA 2006, however, smaller amounts of testing time for reading only allow reading to be reported on a single combined scale.

As in PISA 2000 and PISA 2003, reading scores in PISA 2006 are reported according to five levels of proficiency, corresponding to tasks of varying difficulty (see Chapter 2 for a more detailed description of the development of proficiency levels in PISA). The establishment of proficiency levels in reading makes it possible not only to rank students' performance but also to describe what students can do. Each successive reading level is associated with tasks of ascending difficulty. The tasks at each level of *reading literacy* were judged by panels of experts to share certain features and requirements and to differ consistently from tasks at either higher or lower levels. The assumed difficulty of tasks was then validated empirically on the basis of student performance in participating countries. An analysis of the range of tasks provides some indication of an ordered set of knowledge-construction skills and strategies. For example, the easiest of these tasks, *retrieval,* requires students to locate explicitly stated information according to a single criterion where there is little, if any, competing information in the text, or to identify the main theme of a familiar text, or to make a simple connection between a piece of the text and everyday life. In general, the information is prominent in the text and the text itself is less dense and less complex in structure. In contrast, harder retrieval tasks require students to locate and sequence multiple pieces of deeply embedded information, sometimes in accordance with multiple criteria. Often there is competing information in the text that shares some features with the information required for the answer. Similarly, with tasks requiring *interpretation* or *reflection and evaluation,* those at the lower end differ from those at the higher end in terms of the processes needed to answer them correctly, the degree to which the reading strategies required for a correct answer are signalled in the question or the instructions, the level of complexity and familiarity of the text and the quantity of competing or distracting information present in the text.

Students at a particular level not only demonstrate the knowledge and skills associated with that level but also the proficiencies required at lower levels. For example, all students proficient at Level 3 are also proficient at Levels 1 and 2. All students at a given level are expected to answer at least half of the items at that level correctly. Students scoring below 335 score points, *i.e.* those who do not reach Level 1, are not able to routinely show the most basic reading skills that PISA seeks to measure. While such performance should not be interpreted to mean that those students have no literacy skills at all, performance below Level 1 does signal serious deficiencies in students' ability to use *reading literacy* as a tool for the acquisition of knowledge and skills in other areas.

Figure 6.1 presents an overall profile of proficiency on the *reading literacy* scale, with the length of the various shadings on the bars showing the percentage of students proficient at each level.

Figure 6.1
Percentage of students at each proficiency level on the reading scale

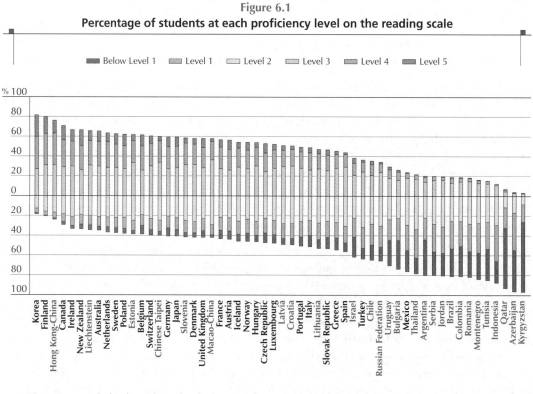

Countries are ranked in descending order of percentage of 15-year-olds at Levels 3, 4 and 5.
Source: OECD PISA 2006 database, Table 6.1a.
StatLink http://dx.doi.org/10.1787/142046885031

A profile of PISA reading questions

A selection of sample questions has been included to provide a better understanding of the type of questions that are encountered in a PISA test.

Each question presented in this section includes the actual text as seen by the students and is categorised according to the PISA 2006 reading framework, which considers each question's situation, text format, aspect, proficiency level and score point difficulty.

Figure 6.2
A map of selected items in reading

Level	READING
5	(631) LABOUR – Question 16
4	(581) GRAFFITI – Question 14
3	(485) LABOUR – Question 16
2	(478) LAKE CHAD – Question 11
1	(356) RUNNERS – Question 1
Below 1	

>625.6
552.9
480.2
407.5
334.8

The *LABOUR* unit, shown below, has questions at both Level 3 and Level 5. Tasks in the *LABOUR* unit are classified as non-continuous in terms of text format. The unit is based on a tree diagram showing the structure and distribution of a national labour force. The diagram is published in an economics textbook for upper secondary school students, so that the text is classified as educational in terms of situation. Although originating from one country, the terms and definitions used are those established by the OECD and the stimulus can therefore be regarded as international.

The *LABOUR* unit represents the kind of reading text that adults are likely to encounter and need to be able to interpret in order to participate fully in the economic and political life of a modern society. It comprises five questions representing all three aspects and spanning Levels 2 to 5. One of the questions is reproduced here – it is a question that has two different score points and students can obtain one or the two depending on the quality of their response.

Typically, the requirement to use conditional information – that is, information found outside the main body of a text – significantly increases the difficulty of a task. This is clearly demonstrated by the two categories of this task, since the difference between full-credit and partial-credit answers is, substantively, the application or non-application of conditional information to correctly identified numerical information in the body of the text. The difference in difficulty of these two categories of response is more than two proficiency levels.

The stimulus for the unit *GRAFFITI* consists of two letters posted on the Internet. The tasks simulate typical literacy activities, since as readers we often synthesise, and compare and contrast ideas from two or more different sources.

Because they are published on the Internet, the *GRAFFITI* letters are classified as public in terms of situation. They are classified as argumentation within the broader classification of continuous texts, as they set forth propositions and attempt to persuade the reader to a point of view.

The subject matter of *GRAFFITI* was expected to be interesting for 15-year-olds: the implied debate between the writers as to whether graffiti makers are artists or vandals would represent a real issue in the minds of the test-takers.

The four questions from the *GRAFFITI* unit used to measure reading proficiency in PISA 2000 range in difficulty from Level 2 to Level 4 and address the aspects of interpreting texts and reflection and evaluation. The question presented here is at Level 4.

The relative difficulty of the task, and of other similar PISA reading tasks, suggests that many 15-year-olds are not practised in drawing on formal knowledge about structure and style to make critical evaluations of texts.

Figure 6.3
LABOUR

The tree diagram below shows the structure of a country's labour force or "working-age population". The total population of the country in 1995 was about 3.4 million.

The labour force structure, year ended 31 March 1995 (000s)[1]

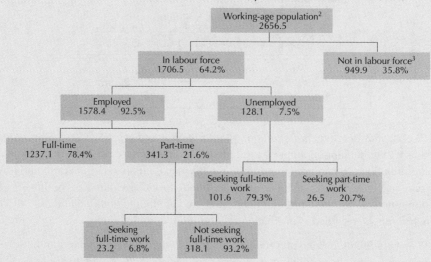

1. Numbers of people are given in thousands (000s).
2. The working-age population is defined as people between the ages of 15 and 65.
3. People "Not in labour force" are those not actively seeking work and/or not available for work.
Source: D. Miller, *Form 6 Economics*, ESA Publications, Box 9453, Newmarker, Auckland, NZ, p. 64.

LABOUR – QUESTION 16

Situation: *Reading for education*
Text format: *Non-continuous*
Aspect: *Retrieving information*
Difficulty: *485 – Percentage of correct answers (OECD countries): 64.9%* •
          631 – Percentage of correct answers (OECD countries): 27.9% •

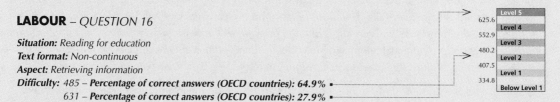

How many people of working age were not in the labour force? (Write the **number** of people, not the percentage.)

Comment

The question presented here yields responses at two levels of difficulty, with the partial-credit response category falling within Level 3 with a score of 485 and the full-credit category within Level 5 with a score of 631.

For full credit (Level 5) students are required to locate and combine a piece of numerical information in the main body of the text (the tree diagram) with information in a footnote – that is, outside the main body of the text. In addition, students have to apply this footnoted information in determining the correct number of people fitting into this category. Both of these features contribute to the difficulty of this task, which is one of the most difficult retrieving information tasks in the PISA reading assessment.

For partial credit (Level 3) this task merely requires students to locate the number given in the appropriate category of the tree diagram. They are not required to use the conditional information provided in the footnote to receive partial credit. Even without this important information the task is still moderately difficult.

Figure 6.4
GRAFFITI

The two letters below come from the Internet and are about graffiti. Graffiti is illegal painting and writing on walls and elsewhere. Refer to the letters to answer the questions below.

I'm simmering with anger as the school wall is cleaned and repainted for the fourth time to get rid of graffiti. Creativity is admirable but people should find ways to express themselves that do not inflict extra costs upon society.

Why do you spoil the reputation of young people by painting graffiti where it's forbidden? Professional artists do not hang their paintings in the streets, do they? Instead they seek funding and gain fame through legal exhibitions.

In my opinion buildings, fences and park benches are works of art in themselves. It's really pathetic to spoil this architecture with graffiti and what's more, the method destroys the ozone layer. Really, I can't understand why these criminal artists bother as their "artistic works" are just removed from sight over and over again.

Helga

There is no accounting for taste. Society is full of communication and advertising. Company logos, shop names. Large intrusive posters on the streets. Are they acceptable? Yes, mostly. Is graffiti acceptable? Some people say yes, some no.

Who pays the price for graffiti? Who is ultimately paying the price for advertisements? Correct. The consumer.

Have the people who put up billboards asked your permission? No. Should graffiti painters do so then? Isn't it all just a question of communication – your own name, the names of gangs and large works of art in the street?

Think about the striped and chequered clothes that appeared in the stores a few years ago. And ski wear. The patterns and colours were stolen directly from the flowery concrete walls. It's quite amusing that these patterns and colours are accepted and admired but that graffiti in the same style is considered dreadful.

Times are hard for art.

Sophia

Source: Mari Hankala.

GRAFFITI – *QUESTION 5*

Situation: *Reading for public use*
Text format: *Continuous*
Aspect: *Reflecting on and evaluating the content of a text*
Difficulty: 581
Percentage of correct answers (OECD countries): 45.2%

625.6	Level 5
552.9	Level 4
480.2	Level 3
407.5	Level 2
334.8	Level 1
	Below Level 1

We can talk about **what** a letter says (its content).

We can talk about **the way** a letter is written (its style).

Regardless of which letter you agree with, in your opinion, which do you think is the better letter?

Explain your answer by referring to **the way** one or both letters are written.

Comment

The most difficult task associated with the GRAFFITI texts falls within Level 4 with a score of 581. It requires students to use formal knowledge to evaluate the writer's craft by comparing the two letters. In the three-aspect categorisation, this task is classified as reflection and evaluation regarding the form of a text, since to answer it, readers need to draw on their own understanding of what constitutes good writing.

Full credit may be given for many types of answers, including those dealing with one or both writers' tone or argumentative strategies, or with the structure of the piece. Students are expected to explain their opinion with reference to the style or form of one or both letters. Reference to criteria such as style of writing, structure of argument, cogency of argument, tone, register used and strategies for persuading the reader are given full credit, but terms such as "better arguments" need to be substantiated.

Figure 6.5
LAKE CHAD

Diagram A shows changing levels of Lake Chad, in Saharan North Africa. Lake Chad disappeared completely in about 20000 BC, during the last Ice Age. In about 11000 BC it reappeared. Today, its level is about the same as it was in AD 1000.

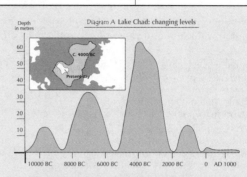

Diagram A Lake Chad: changing levels

Diagram B shows Saharan rock art (ancient drawings or paintings found on the walls of caves) and changing patterns of wildlife.

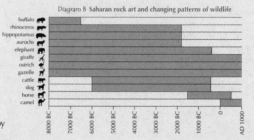

Diagram B Saharan rock art and changing patterns of wildlife

Source: Copyright Bartholomew Ltd 1988. Extracted from *The Times Atlas of Archaeology* and reproduced by permission of Harper Collins Publishers.

LAKE CHAD – QUESTION 11

Situation: *Reading for public use*
Text format: *Non-continuous*
Aspect: *Retrieving information*
Difficulty: *478* •
Percentage of correct answers (OECD countries): 65.1%

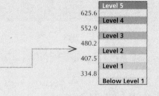

What is the depth of Lake Chad today?
A. About two metres.
B. About fifteen metres.
C. About fifty metres.
D. It has disappeared completely.
E. The information is not provided.

Scoring

Full Credit: A. About two metres.

Comment

The task shown here is a Level 2 retrieving information task with a score of 478 that requires students to locate and combine pieces of information from a line graph and the introduction.

The word "today" in the question can be directly matched in the relevant sentence of the introduction, which refers to the depth of the lake "today" being the same as it was in AD 1000. The reader needs to combine this information with information from Diagram A by locating AD 1000 on the graph and then by reading off the depth of the lake at this date. Competing information is present in the form of multiple dates in Diagram A, and the repetition of "AD 1000" in Diagram B. Nevertheless, the task is relatively easy because key information is supplied explicitly in the prose introduction. Most students who did not select the correct alternative A, "About two metres", selected E, "The information is not provided." This is probably because they looked only at Diagram A, rather than combining the relevant part of Diagram A with information from the introduction.

Figure 6.6
RUNNERS

Feel good in your runners

For 14 years the Sports Medicine Centre of Lyon (France) has been studying the injuries of young sports players and sports professionals. The study has established that the best course is prevention… and good shoes.

Knocks, falls, wear and tear...

Eighteen per cent of sports players aged 8 to 12 already have heel injuries. The cartilage of a footballer's ankle does not respond well to shocks, and 25% of professionals have discovered for themselves that it is an especially weak point. The cartilage of the delicate knee joint can also be irreparably damaged and if care is not taken right from childhood (10–12 years of age), this can cause premature osteoarthritis. The hip does not escape damage either and, particularly when tired, players run the risk of fractures as a result of falls or collisions.

According to the study, footballers who have been playing for more than ten years have bony outgrowths either on the tibia or on the heel.

Source: Revue ID (16) 1-15 June 1997.

This is what is known as "footballer's foot", a deformity caused by shoes with soles and ankle parts that are too flexible.

Protect, support, stabilise, absorb

If a shoe is too rigid, it restricts movement. If it is too flexible, it increases the risk of injuries and sprains. A good sports shoe should meet four criteria:

Firstly, it must *provide exterior protection*: resisting knocks from the ball or another player, coping with unevenness in the ground, and keeping the foot warm and dry even when it is freezing cold and raining.

It must *support the foot*, and in particular the ankle joint, to avoid sprains, swelling and other

problems, which may even affect the knee.

It must also provide players with good *stability* so that they do not slip on a wet ground or skid on a surface that is too dry.

Finally, it must *absorb shocks*, especially those suffered by volleyball and basketball players who are constantly jumping.

Dry feet

To avoid minor but painful conditions such as blisters or even splits or athlete's foot (fungal infections), the shoe must allow evaporation of perspiration and must prevent outside dampness from getting in. The ideal material for this is leather, which can be water-proofed to prevent the shoe from getting soaked the first time it rains.

RUNNERS – QUESTION 1

Situation: *Reading for education*
Text format: *Continuous*
Aspect: *Developing an interpretation*
Difficulty: 356 •
Percentage of correct answers (OECD countries): 84.6%

	Level 5
625.6	Level 4
552.9	Level 3
480.2	Level 2
407.5	Level 1
334.8	Below Level 1

What does the author intend to show in this text?

A. That the quality of many sports shoes has greatly improved.

B. That it is best not to play football if you are under 12 years of age.

C. That young people are suffering more and more injuries due to their poor physical condition.

D. That it is very important for young sports players to wear good sports shoes.

Scoring

Full Credit: A. That the quality of many sports shoes has greatly improved.

Comment

This task is classified as developing an interpretation rather than retrieving information. There are at least two features that make this task easy. First, the required information is located in the introduction, which is a short section of text. Secondly, there is a good deal of redundancy, the main idea in the introduction being repeated several times throughout the text. Reading tasks tend to be relatively easy when the information they require the reader to use is either near the beginning of the text or repeated. This task meets both of these criteria.

The question is intended to discover whether students can form a broad understanding. Only small percentages of students did not select the correct answer, and they were spread over the three alternative answers A, B and C. The smallest percentage and least able selected alternative B, "That it is best not to play football if you are under 12 years of age." These students may have been trying to match words from the question with the text, and linked "12" in alternative B with two references to 12-year-olds near the beginning of the article.

291

In the *LAKE CHAD* unit, the stimulus is classified as non-continuous on the text format dimension. The unit presents two graphs from an archaeological atlas. Diagram A is a line graph and Diagram B is a horizontal histogram. A third *non-continuous text* type is represented in this unit by a small map of the lake embedded in Diagram A. Two very short passages of prose are also part of the stimulus. By juxtaposing these pieces of information the author invites the reader to infer a connection between the changing water levels of Lake Chad over time, and the periods in which certain species of wildlife inhabited its surroundings.

This is a type of text that might typically be encountered by students in an educational setting. Nevertheless, because the atlas is published for the general reader the text is classified as public in the situation dimension. The full set of five questions in the unit covers all three aspects. The questions range in difficulty from Level 1 to Level 4. The question presented here is at Level 2 where tasks based on *non-continuous texts,* like *LAKE CHAD*, may require combining information from different displays, whereas Level 1 non-continuous tasks typically focus on discrete pieces of information, usually within a single display.

RUNNERS contains a piece of expository prose from a magazine produced for adolescent students. It is classed as belonging to the *reading for education* situation. One of the reasons for its selection as part of the PISA reading instrument is its subject, which was considered of interest for 15-year-olds. The article includes a cartoon-like illustration and is broken up by subheadings. Within the *continuous text* format category, it is an example of expository writing in that it provides an outline of a mental construct, laying out a set of criteria for judging the quality of running shoes in terms of their fitness for young athletes.

Question 1 from *RUNNERS* falls within Level 1 with a score of 356. It requires the reader to recognise the article's main idea in a text about a familiar topic.

Figure 6.7 [Part 1/2]
Summary descriptions for the five proficiency levels in reading

Level	Lower score limit	What students can typically do
5		Locate and possibly sequence or combine multiple pieces of deeply embedded information, some of which may be outside the main body of the text. Infer which information in the text is relevant to the task. Deal with highly plausible and/or extensive competing information. Either construe the meaning of nuanced language or demonstrate a full and detailed understanding of a text. Critically evaluate or hypothesise, drawing on specialised knowledge. Deal with concepts that are contrary to expectations and draw on a deep understanding of long or complex texts. In *continuous texts* students can analyse texts whose discourse structure is not obvious or clearly marked, in order to discern the relationship of specific parts of the text to its implicit theme or intention. In *non-continuous texts*, students can identify patterns among many pieces of information presented in a display which may be long and detailed, sometimes by referring to information external to the display. The reader may need to realise independently that a full understanding of the section of text requires reference to a separate part of the same document, such as a footnote.
	625.6	
4		Locate and possibly sequence or combine multiple pieces of embedded information, each of which may need to meet multiple criteria, in a text with familiar context or form. Infer which information in the text is relevant to the task. Use a high level of text-based inference to understand and apply categories in an unfamiliar context, and to construe the meaning of a section of text by taking into account the text as a whole. Deal with ambiguities, ideas that are contrary to expectation and ideas that are negatively worded. Use formal or public knowledge to hypothesise about or critically evaluate a text. Show accurate understanding of long or complex texts. In *continuous texts* students can follow linguistic or thematic links over several paragraphs, often in the absence of clear discourse markers, in order to locate, interpret or evaluate embedded information or to infer psychological or metaphysical meaning. In *non-continuous texts* students can scan a long, detailed text in order to find relevant information, often with little or no assistance from organisers such as labels or special formatting, to locate several pieces of information to be compared or combined.
	552.9	...

Figure 6.7 [Part 2/2]

Summary descriptions for the five proficiency levels in reading

3	Locate, and in some cases recognise, the relationship between pieces of information, each of which may need to meet multiple criteria. Deal with prominent competing information. Integrate several parts of a text in order to identify a main idea, understand a relationship or construe the meaning of a word or phrase. Compare, contrast or categorise taking many criteria into account. Deal with competing information. Make connections or comparisons, give explanations, or evaluate a feature of text. Demonstrate a detailed understanding of the text in relation to familiar, everyday knowledge, or draw on less common knowledge. In *continuous texts* students can use conventions of text organisation, where present, and follow implicit or explicit logical links such as cause and effect relationships across sentences or paragraphs in order to locate, interpret or evaluate information. In *non-continuous texts* students can consider one display in the light of a second, separate documents or displays, possibly in a different format, or combine several pieces of spatial, verbal and numeric information in a graph or map to draw conclusions about the information represented.
480.2	
2	Locate one or more pieces of information, each of which may be required to meet multiple criteria. Deal with competing information. Identify the main idea in a text, understand relationships, form or apply simple categories, or construe meaning within a limited part of the text when the information is not prominent and low-level inferences are required. Make a comparison or connections between the text and outside knowledge, or explain a feature of the text by drawing on personal experience and attitudes. In *continuous texts* students can follow logical and linguistic connections within a paragraph in order to locate or interpret information; or synthesise information across texts or parts of a text in order to infer the author's purpose. In *non-continuous texts* students demonstrate a grasp of the underlying structure of a visual display such as a simple tree diagram or table, or combine two pieces of information from a graph or table.
407.5	
1	Locate one or more independent pieces of explicitly stated information, typically meeting a single criterion, with little or no competing information in the text. Recognise the main theme or author's purpose in a text about a familiar topic, when the required information in the text is prominent. Make a simple connection between information in the text and common, everyday knowledge. In *continuous texts* students can use redundancy, paragraph headings or common print conventions to form an impression of the main idea of the text, or to locate information stated explicitly within a short section of text. In *non-continuous texts* students can focus on discrete pieces of information, usually within a single display such as a simple map, a line graph or a bar graph that presents only a small amount of information in a straightforward way, and in which most of the verbal text is limited to a small number of words or phrases.
334.8	

STUDENT PERFORMANCE IN READING

The proficiency levels used in reading in the PISA 2006 assessment are the same as those established for reading when it was the major area of assessment in 2000. The process used to produce proficiency levels in reading is similar to that described in detail for science in Chapter 2. In reading there are five levels of proficiency.

Proficiency at Level 5 (scores higher than 625.6 points)

Students proficient at Level 5 on the *reading literacy* scale are capable of completing sophisticated reading tasks, such as locating and using information that is difficult to find in unfamiliar texts; showing detailed understanding of such texts and inferring which information in the text is relevant to the task; and being able to evaluate critically and build hypotheses, draw on specialised knowledge, and accommodate concepts that may be contrary to expectations.

The proportion of students in participating countries performing at the highest PISA proficiency level in reading is of interest as today's proportion of students performing at these levels may influence the contribution which each country will contribute towards future global knowledge.

In the OECD area, an average of 8.6% of the students are at Level 5. In Korea, 21.7% of the students are at this level, as are more than 15% of the students in Finland and New Zealand. In Canada 14.5% of students are at this level and more than 11% are in Ireland, Poland and Belgium and the partner economy Hong Kong-China. In contrast, less than 1% of the students in Mexico reach Level 5 and in the partner countries/economies Indonesia, Kyrgyzstan, Azerbaijan, Tunisia, Jordan, Thailand Serbia, Romania, and Montenegro it is less than one-half of a percent (Figure 6.1 and Table 6.1a).

It is of course possible for countries with quite similar percentages of students in Level 5 to have different mean scores. This is due to the countries having different percentages of students in the lower proficiency levels. An example is provided by Finland and New Zealand. These two countries have similar percentages of students in Level 5 with 16.7 and 15.9% respectively, but averages which are significantly different. This can be partly explained by the fact that Finland has only 4.8% of students in Level 1 or below, whereas New Zealand has 14.5% of students in these levels. Finland has a mean score of 547 and New Zealand has a mean score of 521.

Proficiency at Level 4 (scores higher than 552.9 but lower than or equal to 625.6 points)

Students proficient at Level 4 on the *reading literacy* scale are capable of difficult reading tasks, such as locating embedded information, dealing with ambiguities and critically evaluating a text. In the OECD area, an average 29.3% of students are proficient at Level 4 or above (that is, at Levels 4 and 5) (Figure 6.1 and Table 6.1a). Over one-half of the students in Korea and at least 40% of those in Finland, Canada, New Zealand and the partner economy Hong Kong-China attain at least Level 4. With the exception of Mexico, Turkey, Spain and Greece, at least 20% of students in each OECD country reach at least Level 4.

Proficiency at Level 3 (scores higher than 480.2 but lower than or equal to 552.9 points)

Students proficient at Level 3 on the *reading literacy* scale are capable of reading tasks of moderate complexity, such as locating multiple pieces of information, making links between different parts of a text and relating it to familiar everyday knowledge. In the OECD area, an average 57.1% of students are proficient at least at Level 3 (that is, at Levels 3, 4 and 5) on the *reading literacy* scale (Figure 6.1 and Table 6.1a). In 6 of the 30 OECD countries (Korea, Finland, Canada, Ireland, New Zealand and Australia), and in two partner countries/economies (Hong Kong-China and Liechtenstein), over 65% of 15-year-old students are proficient at least at Level 3. This level is the individual proficiency level at which most students are placed, with 27.8% of students on average in the OECD area.

Proficiency at Level 2 (scores higher than 407.5 but lower than or equal to 480.2 points)

Students proficient at Level 2 are capable of basic reading tasks, such as locating straightforward information, making low-level inferences of various types, working out what a well-defined part of a text means and using some outside knowledge to understand it. Across the OECD, an average of 79.9% of students is proficient at Level 2 or above on the *reading literacy* scale. In every OECD country except Mexico, Turkey, the Slovak Republic and Greece at least 73% of students are at Level 2 or above (Figure 6.1 and Table 6.1a). In Finland 95.2% of the students are at Level 2 and above. Other countries with more than 85% of students at Level 2 and above are (in ascending order) New Zealand, Australia, Ireland, Canada, Korea and the partner countries/economies Liechtenstein, Estonia, Macao-China and Hong Kong-China.

Proficiency at Level 1 (scores higher than 334.8 but lower than or equal to 407.5 points) or below

Reading literacy, as defined in PISA, focuses on the knowledge and skills required to apply reading for learning rather than on the technical skills acquired in learning to read. Since comparatively few young adults in OECD countries have not acquired technical reading skills, PISA does not seek to measure such things as the extent to which 15-year-old students are fluent readers or how well they spell or recognise words. In line with most contemporary views about *reading literacy*, PISA focuses on measuring the extent to which individuals are able to construct, expand and reflect on the meaning of what they have read in a wide range of texts common both within and beyond school. The simplest reading tasks that can still be associated with this notion of *reading literacy* are those at Level 1. Students proficient at this level are capable of completing only the simplest reading tasks developed for PISA, such as locating a single piece of information, identifying the main theme of a text or making a simple connection with everyday knowledge.

Students performing below 334.8 score points – that is, below Level 1 – are not likely to demonstrate success on the most basic type of reading that PISA seeks to measure. This does not mean that they have no literacy skills. Nonetheless, their pattern of answers in the assessment is such that they would be expected to solve fewer than one-half of the tasks in a test made up of items drawn solely from Level 1. Such students have serious difficulties in using *reading literacy* as an effective tool to advance and extend their knowledge and skills in other areas. Students with *reading literacy* skills below Level 1 may therefore be at risk not only of difficulties in their initial transition from education to work, but also of failure to benefit from further education and learning opportunities throughout life.

Across the OECD, an average of 12.7% of students perform at Level 1, and 7.4% perform below Level 1, but there are wide differences between countries. In Finland and Korea, less than 6% of students perform at or below Level 1. In all other OECD countries, the percentage of students performing at or below Level 1 ranges from 11.0% (Canada) to 47.0% (Mexico) (Figure 6.1 and Table 6.1a).

The OECD countries with at least 25% of students at or below Level 1 are (in descending order): Mexico, Turkey, the Slovak Republic, Greece, Italy and Spain. For partner countries, those with more than 50% of students at or below Level 1 are Kyrgyzstan, Qatar, Azerbaijan, Tunisia, Indonesia, Argentina, Montenegro, Colombia, Brazil, Romania, Serbia and Bulgaria.

Education systems with large proportions of students performing below, or even at, Level 1 should be concerned that significant numbers of their students may not be acquiring the necessary literacy knowledge and skills to benefit sufficiently from their educational opportunities. This situation is even more troublesome in light of the extensive evidence suggesting that it is difficult in later life to compensate for learning gaps in initial education. OECD data suggest indeed that job-related continuing education and training often reinforce the skill differences with which individuals leave initial education (OECD, 2007). Adult literacy skills and participation in continuing education and training are strongly related, even after controlling for other characteristics affecting participation in training. Literacy skills and continuing education and training appear to be mutually reinforcing, with the result that training is least commonly pursued by those adults who need it most.

The mean performances of countries/economies in reading

The discussion above has focused on comparisons of the distributions of student performance between countries. One way to summarise student performance and to compare the relative standing of countries in reading is by way of countries' mean scores on the PISA assessment. Countries with high average performance will have a considerable economic and social advantage.

In PISA 2006, the OECD average score for reading is 492 score points. This score is slightly lower than the average score of 500 for the PISA 2000 assessment, which is partially explained by the fact that Turkey and the Slovak Republic, which both perform below the OECD average, joined PISA in 2003. However, among the countries that provided comparable data for both PISA 2000 and PISA 2006, the average performance in PISA 2006 remains broadly similar to that in PISA 2000.

Figure 6.8a [Part 1/2]

Multiple comparisons of mean performance on the reading scale

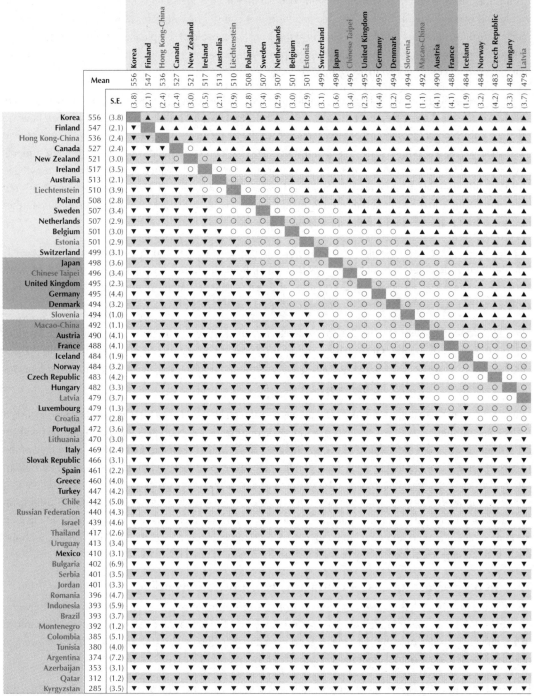

Statistically significantly above the OECD average

Not statistically significantly different from the OECD average

Statistically significantly below the OECD average

▲ Mean performance statistically significantly higher than in comparison country

○ No statistically significant difference from comparison country

▼ Mean performance statistically significantly lower than in comparison country

Source: OECD PISA 2006 database.
StatLink ᐧᐧᐧ http://dx.doi.org/10.1787/142046885031

Figure 6.8a [Part 2/2]

Multiple comparisons of mean performance on the reading scale

Luxembourg (479)	Croatia (477)	Portugal (472)	Lithuania (470)	Italy (469)	Slovak Republic (466)	Spain (461)	Greece (460)	Turkey (447)	Chile (442)	Russian Federation (440)	Israel (439)	Thailand (417)	Uruguay (413)	Mexico (410)	Bulgaria (402)	Serbia (401)	Jordan (401)	Romania (396)	Indonesia (393)	Brazil (393)	Montenegro (392)	Colombia (385)	Tunisia (380)	Argentina (374)	Azerbaijan (353)	Qatar (312)	Kyrgyzstan (285)	Mean	S.E.	Country
▲	▲	▲	▲	▲	▲	▲	▲	▲	▲	▲	▲	▲	▲	▲	▲	▲	▲	▲	▲	▲	▲	▲	▲	▲	▲	▲	▲	556	(3.8)	Korea
▲	▲	▲	▲	▲	▲	▲	▲	▲	▲	▲	▲	▲	▲	▲	▲	▲	▲	▲	▲	▲	▲	▲	▲	▲	▲	▲	▲	547	(2.1)	Finland
▲	▲	▲	▲	▲	▲	▲	▲	▲	▲	▲	▲	▲	▲	▲	▲	▲	▲	▲	▲	▲	▲	▲	▲	▲	▲	▲	▲	536	(2.4)	Hong Kong-China
▲	▲	▲	▲	▲	▲	▲	▲	▲	▲	▲	▲	▲	▲	▲	▲	▲	▲	▲	▲	▲	▲	▲	▲	▲	▲	▲	▲	527	(2.4)	Canada
▲	▲	▲	▲	▲	▲	▲	▲	▲	▲	▲	▲	▲	▲	▲	▲	▲	▲	▲	▲	▲	▲	▲	▲	▲	▲	▲	▲	521	(3.0)	New Zealand
▲	▲	▲	▲	▲	▲	▲	▲	▲	▲	▲	▲	▲	▲	▲	▲	▲	▲	▲	▲	▲	▲	▲	▲	▲	▲	▲	▲	517	(3.5)	Ireland
▲	▲	▲	▲	▲	▲	▲	▲	▲	▲	▲	▲	▲	▲	▲	▲	▲	▲	▲	▲	▲	▲	▲	▲	▲	▲	▲	▲	513	(2.1)	Australia
▲	▲	▲	▲	▲	▲	▲	▲	▲	▲	▲	▲	▲	▲	▲	▲	▲	▲	▲	▲	▲	▲	▲	▲	▲	▲	▲	▲	510	(3.9)	Liechtenstein
▲	▲	▲	▲	▲	▲	▲	▲	▲	▲	▲	▲	▲	▲	▲	▲	▲	▲	▲	▲	▲	▲	▲	▲	▲	▲	▲	▲	508	(2.8)	Poland
▲	▲	▲	▲	▲	▲	▲	▲	▲	▲	▲	▲	▲	▲	▲	▲	▲	▲	▲	▲	▲	▲	▲	▲	▲	▲	▲	▲	507	(3.4)	Sweden
▲	▲	▲	▲	▲	▲	▲	▲	▲	▲	▲	▲	▲	▲	▲	▲	▲	▲	▲	▲	▲	▲	▲	▲	▲	▲	▲	▲	507	(2.9)	Netherlands
▲	▲	▲	▲	▲	▲	▲	▲	▲	▲	▲	▲	▲	▲	▲	▲	▲	▲	▲	▲	▲	▲	▲	▲	▲	▲	▲	▲	501	(3.0)	Belgium
▲	▲	▲	▲	▲	▲	▲	▲	▲	▲	▲	▲	▲	▲	▲	▲	▲	▲	▲	▲	▲	▲	▲	▲	▲	▲	▲	▲	501	(2.9)	Estonia
▲	▲	▲	▲	▲	▲	▲	▲	▲	▲	▲	▲	▲	▲	▲	▲	▲	▲	▲	▲	▲	▲	▲	▲	▲	▲	▲	▲	499	(3.1)	Switzerland
▲	▲	▲	▲	▲	▲	▲	▲	▲	▲	▲	▲	▲	▲	▲	▲	▲	▲	▲	▲	▲	▲	▲	▲	▲	▲	▲	▲	498	(3.6)	Japan
▲	▲	▲	▲	▲	▲	▲	▲	▲	▲	▲	▲	▲	▲	▲	▲	▲	▲	▲	▲	▲	▲	▲	▲	▲	▲	▲	▲	496	(3.4)	Chinese Taipei
▲	▲	▲	▲	▲	▲	▲	▲	▲	▲	▲	▲	▲	▲	▲	▲	▲	▲	▲	▲	▲	▲	▲	▲	▲	▲	▲	▲	495	(2.3)	United Kingdom
▲	▲	▲	▲	▲	▲	▲	▲	▲	▲	▲	▲	▲	▲	▲	▲	▲	▲	▲	▲	▲	▲	▲	▲	▲	▲	▲	▲	495	(4.4)	Germany
▲	▲	▲	▲	▲	▲	▲	▲	▲	▲	▲	▲	▲	▲	▲	▲	▲	▲	▲	▲	▲	▲	▲	▲	▲	▲	▲	▲	494	(3.2)	Denmark
▲	▲	▲	▲	▲	▲	▲	▲	▲	▲	▲	▲	▲	▲	▲	▲	▲	▲	▲	▲	▲	▲	▲	▲	▲	▲	▲	▲	494	(1.0)	Slovenia
▲	▲	▲	▲	▲	▲	▲	▲	▲	▲	▲	▲	▲	▲	▲	▲	▲	▲	▲	▲	▲	▲	▲	▲	▲	▲	▲	▲	492	(1.1)	Macao-China
▲	▲	▲	▲	▲	▲	▲	▲	▲	▲	▲	▲	▲	▲	▲	▲	▲	▲	▲	▲	▲	▲	▲	▲	▲	▲	▲	▲	490	(4.1)	Austria
▲	▲	▲	▲	▲	▲	▲	▲	▲	▲	▲	▲	▲	▲	▲	▲	▲	▲	▲	▲	▲	▲	▲	▲	▲	▲	▲	▲	488	(4.1)	France
▲	▲	▲	▲	▲	▲	▲	▲	▲	▲	▲	▲	▲	▲	▲	▲	▲	▲	▲	▲	▲	▲	▲	▲	▲	▲	▲	▲	484	(1.9)	Iceland
○	○	▲	▲	▲	▲	▲	▲	▲	▲	▲	▲	▲	▲	▲	▲	▲	▲	▲	▲	▲	▲	▲	▲	▲	▲	▲	▲	484	(3.2)	Norway
○	○	▲	▲	▲	▲	▲	▲	▲	▲	▲	▲	▲	▲	▲	▲	▲	▲	▲	▲	▲	▲	▲	▲	▲	▲	▲	▲	483	(4.2)	Czech Republic
○	○	▲	▲	▲	▲	▲	▲	▲	▲	▲	▲	▲	▲	▲	▲	▲	▲	▲	▲	▲	▲	▲	▲	▲	▲	▲	▲	482	(3.3)	Hungary
○	○	○	○	▲	▲	▲	▲	▲	▲	▲	▲	▲	▲	▲	▲	▲	▲	▲	▲	▲	▲	▲	▲	▲	▲	▲	▲	479	(3.7)	Latvia
■	○	○	▲	▲	▲	▲	▲	▲	▲	▲	▲	▲	▲	▲	▲	▲	▲	▲	▲	▲	▲	▲	▲	▲	▲	▲	▲	479	(1.3)	Luxembourg
○	■	○	○	▲	▲	▲	▲	▲	▲	▲	▲	▲	▲	▲	▲	▲	▲	▲	▲	▲	▲	▲	▲	▲	▲	▲	▲	477	(2.8)	Croatia
○	○	■	○	○	○	▲	▲	▲	▲	▲	▲	▲	▲	▲	▲	▲	▲	▲	▲	▲	▲	▲	▲	▲	▲	▲	▲	472	(3.6)	Portugal
▼	○	○	■	○	○	▲	▲	▲	▲	▲	▲	▲	▲	▲	▲	▲	▲	▲	▲	▲	▲	▲	▲	▲	▲	▲	▲	470	(3.0)	Lithuania
▼	▼	○	○	■	○	▲	○	▲	▲	▲	▲	▲	▲	▲	▲	▲	▲	▲	▲	▲	▲	▲	▲	▲	▲	▲	▲	469	(2.4)	Italy
▼	▼	○	○	○	■	○	○	▲	▲	▲	▲	▲	▲	▲	▲	▲	▲	▲	▲	▲	▲	▲	▲	▲	▲	▲	▲	466	(3.1)	Slovak Republic
▼	▼	▼	▼	▼	○	■	○	▲	▲	▲	▲	▲	▲	▲	▲	▲	▲	▲	▲	▲	▲	▲	▲	▲	▲	▲	▲	461	(2.2)	Spain
▼	▼	▼	▼	○	○	○	■	▲	▲	▲	▲	▲	▲	▲	▲	▲	▲	▲	▲	▲	▲	▲	▲	▲	▲	▲	▲	460	(4.0)	Greece
▼	▼	▼	▼	▼	▼	▼	▼	■	○	○	○	▲	▲	▲	▲	▲	▲	▲	▲	▲	▲	▲	▲	▲	▲	▲	▲	447	(4.2)	Turkey
▼	▼	▼	▼	▼	▼	▼	▼	○	■	○	○	▲	▲	▲	▲	▲	▲	▲	▲	▲	▲	▲	▲	▲	▲	▲	▲	442	(5.0)	Chile
▼	▼	▼	▼	▼	▼	▼	▼	○	○	■	○	▲	▲	▲	▲	▲	▲	▲	▲	▲	▲	▲	▲	▲	▲	▲	▲	440	(4.3)	Russian Federation
▼	▼	▼	▼	▼	▼	▼	▼	○	○	○	■	▲	▲	▲	▲	▲	▲	▲	▲	▲	▲	▲	▲	▲	▲	▲	▲	439	(4.6)	Israel
▼	▼	▼	▼	▼	▼	▼	▼	▼	▼	▼	▼	■	○	○	▲	▲	▲	▲	▲	▲	▲	▲	▲	▲	▲	▲	▲	417	(2.6)	Thailand
▼	▼	▼	▼	▼	▼	▼	▼	▼	▼	▼	▼	○	■	○	○	▲	▲	▲	▲	▲	▲	▲	▲	▲	▲	▲	▲	413	(3.4)	Uruguay
▼	▼	▼	▼	▼	▼	▼	▼	▼	▼	▼	▼	○	○	■	○	○	▲	▲	▲	▲	▲	▲	▲	▲	▲	▲	▲	410	(3.1)	Mexico
▼	▼	▼	▼	▼	▼	▼	▼	▼	▼	▼	▼	▼	○	○	■	○	○	○	○	○	○	▲	▲	▲	▲	▲	▲	402	(6.9)	Bulgaria
▼	▼	▼	▼	▼	▼	▼	▼	▼	▼	▼	▼	▼	▼	○	○	■	○	○	○	○	▲	▲	▲	▲	▲	▲	▲	401	(3.5)	Serbia
▼	▼	▼	▼	▼	▼	▼	▼	▼	▼	▼	▼	▼	▼	▼	○	○	■	○	○	○	▲	▲	▲	▲	▲	▲	▲	401	(3.3)	Jordan
▼	▼	▼	▼	▼	▼	▼	▼	▼	▼	▼	▼	▼	▼	▼	○	○	○	■	○	○	○	○	▲	▲	▲	▲	▲	396	(4.7)	Romania
▼	▼	▼	▼	▼	▼	▼	▼	▼	▼	▼	▼	▼	▼	▼	○	○	○	○	■	○	○	○	○	▲	▲	▲	▲	393	(5.9)	Indonesia
▼	▼	▼	▼	▼	▼	▼	▼	▼	▼	▼	▼	▼	▼	▼	○	○	○	○	○	■	○	○	▲	▲	▲	▲	▲	393	(3.7)	Brazil
▼	▼	▼	▼	▼	▼	▼	▼	▼	▼	▼	▼	▼	▼	▼	○	▼	▼	○	○	○	■	○	▲	▲	▲	▲	▲	392	(1.2)	Montenegro
▼	▼	▼	▼	▼	▼	▼	▼	▼	▼	▼	▼	▼	▼	▼	▼	▼	▼	○	○	○	○	■	○	○	▲	▲	▲	385	(5.1)	Colombia
▼	▼	▼	▼	▼	▼	▼	▼	▼	▼	▼	▼	▼	▼	▼	▼	▼	▼	▼	○	▼	▼	○	■	○	▲	▲	▲	380	(4.0)	Tunisia
▼	▼	▼	▼	▼	▼	▼	▼	▼	▼	▼	▼	▼	▼	▼	▼	▼	▼	▼	▼	▼	▼	○	○	■	▲	▲	▲	374	(7.2)	Argentina
▼	▼	▼	▼	▼	▼	▼	▼	▼	▼	▼	▼	▼	▼	▼	▼	▼	▼	▼	▼	▼	▼	▼	▼	▼	■	▲	▲	353	(3.1)	Azerbaijan
▼	▼	▼	▼	▼	▼	▼	▼	▼	▼	▼	▼	▼	▼	▼	▼	▼	▼	▼	▼	▼	▼	▼	▼	▼	▼	■	▲	312	(1.2)	Qatar
▼	▼	▼	▼	▼	▼	▼	▼	▼	▼	▼	▼	▼	▼	▼	▼	▼	▼	▼	▼	▼	▼	▼	▼	▼	▼	▼	■	285	(3.5)	Kyrgyzstan

Legend:

- ☐ Statistically significantly above the OECD average
- ▨ Not statistically significantly different from the OECD average
- ▨ Statistically significantly below the OECD average

- ▲ Mean performance statistically significantly higher than in comparison country
- ○ No statistically significant difference from comparison country
- ▼ Mean performance statistically significantly lower than in comparison country

Source: OECD PISA 2006 database.
StatLink ⟹ http://dx.doi.org/10.1787/142046885031

Figure 6.8b
Range of rank of countries/economies on the reading scale

Statistically significantly above the OECD average
Not statistically significantly different from the OECD average
Statistically significantly below the OECD average

	Mean score	S.E.	Reading scale			
			Range of rank			
			OECD countries		All countries/economies	
			Upper rank	Lower rank	Upper rank	Lower rank
Korea	556	(3.8)	1	1	1	1
Finland	547	(2.1)	2	2	2	2
Hong Kong-China	536	(2.4)			3	3
Canada	527	(2.4)	3	4	4	5
New Zealand	521	(3.0)	3	5	4	6
Ireland	517	(3.5)	4	6	5	8
Australia	513	(2.1)	5	7	6	9
Liechtenstein	510	(3.9)			6	11
Poland	508	(2.8)	6	10	7	12
Sweden	507	(3.4)	6	10	7	13
Netherlands	507	(2.9)	6	10	8	13
Belgium	501	(3.0)	8	13	10	17
Estonia	501	(2.9)			10	17
Switzerland	499	(3.1)	9	14	11	19
Japan	498	(3.6)	9	16	11	21
Chinese Taipei	496	(3.4)			12	22
United Kingdom	495	(2.3)	11	16	14	22
Germany	495	(4.4)	10	17	12	23
Denmark	494	(3.2)	11	17	14	23
Slovenia	494	(1.0)			16	21
Macao-China	492	(1.1)			18	22
Austria	490	(4.1)	12	20	15	26
France	488	(4.1)	14	21	18	28
Iceland	484	(1.9)	17	21	23	28
Norway	484	(3.2)	16	22	22	29
Czech Republic	483	(4.2)	16	22	22	30
Hungary	482	(3.3)	17	22	23	30
Latvia	479	(3.7)			24	31
Luxembourg	479	(1.3)	20	22	26	30
Croatia	477	(2.8)			26	31
Portugal	472	(3.6)	22	25	29	34
Lithuania	470	(3.0)			30	34
Italy	469	(2.4)	23	25	31	34
Slovak Republic	466	(3.1)	23	26	31	35
Spain	461	(2.2)	25	27	34	36
Greece	460	(4.0)	25	27	34	36
Turkey	447	(4.2)	28	28	37	39
Chile	442	(5.0)			37	40
Russian Federation	440	(4.3)			37	40
Israel	439	(4.6)			38	40
Thailand	417	(2.6)			41	42
Uruguay	413	(3.4)			41	44
Mexico	410	(3.1)	29	29	41	44
Bulgaria	402	(6.9)			42	50
Serbia	401	(3.5)			44	48
Jordan	401	(3.3)			44	48
Romania	396	(4.7)			44	50
Indonesia	393	(5.9)			44	51
Brazil	393	(3.7)			46	51
Montenegro	392	(1.2)			47	50
Colombia	385	(5.1)			48	53
Tunisia	380	(4.0)			51	53
Argentina	374	(7.2)			51	53
Azerbaijan	353	(3.1)			54	54
Qatar	312	(1.2)			55	55
Kyrgyzstan	285	(3.5)			56	56

Source: OECD PISA 2006 database.
StatLink ⎯⎯⎯ http://dx.doi.org/10.1787/142046885031

The following section looks at the mean reading scores of countries participating in PISA 2006. When interpreting mean performance, only those differences between countries which are statistically significant should be taken into account. Figure 6.8a shows those pairs of countries where the difference in their mean scores is sufficient to say with confidence that the higher performance by sampled students in one country holds for the entire population of enrolled 15-year-olds. Read across the row for a country to compare its performance with the countries listed along the top of the figure. The coding indicates whether the average performance of the country in the row is lower than that of the comparison country, not statistically different from or higher than it.

Because the figures are derived from samples, it is also not possible to determine a precise rank of the performance of a country among the participating countries. It is, however, possible to determine a range of ranks between which the country's rank lies with 95% likelihood.[8] This range of ranks is shown in the Figure 6.8b.

In Korea, performance on the *reading literacy* scale is above that of any other OECD country, even higher than in Finland, which was the top-performer in reading in PISA 2000 and PISA 2003. Korea's country mean, 556 score points, is nearly one proficiency level above the OECD average of 492 score points in PISA 2006. Other OECD countries with mean performances statistically significantly above the OECD average include Finland (547 score points), Canada (527 score points), New Zealand (521 score points), Ireland (517 score points), Australia (513 score points), Poland (508 score points), Sweden (507 score points), the Netherlands (507 score points), Belgium (501 score points) and Switzerland (499 score points), as well as the partner countries/economies Hong Kong-China (536 score points), Liechtenstein (510 score points), Estonia (501 score points) and Slovenia (494 score points). Seven OECD countries perform around the OECD average: Austria, Denmark, France, Germany, Japan, and the United Kingdom, as well as the partner economies Chinese Taipei and Macao-China.[9] Among OECD countries, differences are quite large – 146 score points separate the mean scores of the highest and lowest performing OECD countries, and when the partner countries/economies are included along with the OECD countries, the range expands to 271 score points.

Although there are large differences in the mean performance between countries, the variation in performance between students within each country is much larger. One of the major challenges faced by education systems is to encourage high performance while at the same time minimising poor performance. The question of poor performance is particularly relevant to *reading literacy* because levels of *reading literacy* have a significant impact on the welfare of individuals, the state of society and the economic standing of countries in the international arena (OECD, 2003). Inequality in this context can be examined through the performance distribution as seen by the gap in performance between the 5th and the 95th percentiles (Table 6.1c). Among OECD countries, Finland and Korea show the narrowest distributions in the OECD with this difference equivalent to 265 and 289 score points, respectively, while at the same time these two countries show the strongest overall performance. In the OECD area, the Czech Republic, Belgium, Germany, Austria, Italy, the Slovak Republic and New Zealand show the largest gaps between the 5th and 95th percentiles, which is almost one standard deviation more than in Finland and Korea. With the exception of Belgium and New Zealand, none of these countries perform better than the OECD average.

Box 6.1 **How well does PISA performance at age 15 predict future educational success?**

Three studies suggest that PISA performance in reading is closely related to subsequent outcomes such as completion of high school and participation in post-secondary education.

The Canadian Youth in Transition Survey (YITS) is a longitudinal survey which investigates patterns of and influences on major educational, training and work transitions in young people's lives (Knighton and Bussiere, 2006). In 2000, 29 330 15-year-old students in Canada participated in PISA. Four years later, the educational outcomes of the same students, then aged 19, were assessed and the association of these outcomes with PISA reading performance at age 15 was examined. The analysis showed that youths' performance on the PISA reading test at the age of 15 was highly predictive of high school completion and students' successful transition into post-secondary education by the age of 19. As shown in the figure below around one-quarter (28%) of youth in the lowest reading proficiency levels (Level 1 and below) had pursued some form of post-secondary education. The participation rates increased to 45% for those at Level 2, 65% for those at Level 3, 76% for those at Level 4 and 88% for those at Level 5. Youths' reading proficiency levels continue to have a very strong effect on post-secondary participation even after accounting for other factors known to be related to post-secondary participation, such as gender, parental education, mother tongue, family income or place of residence. Further analysis shows that students who had achieved Level 2 in reading at age 15 were more than twice as likely to participate in post-secondary education at age 19, even after controlling for socio-economic factors, and that those who had completed Level 5 were almost 17 times as likely to participate in post-secondary education.

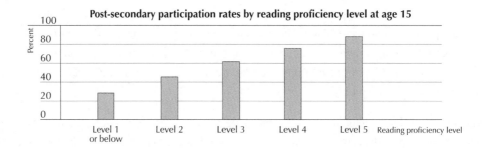

Post-secondary participation rates by reading proficiency level at age 15

A study undertaken in Denmark led to very similar results, in that the percentage of youth who had completed post-compulsory, general or vocational upper secondary education (ungdomsuddannelse) by age 19 was closely related to their PISA reading performance at age 15.

Australia used the PISA 2003 cohort as the basis for further study and looked at performance in mathematics as a guide to future educational success. The first follow-up took place in 2006 (Hillman and Thomson, 2006)[10] and shows similar figures to those of the Canadian study, with an increasing probability of completing Year 12 for each proficiency level achieved in mathematics at age 15.

For more information, visit: *http://www.pisa.gc.ca/yits.shtml* (YITS); *http://www.sfi.dk/sw19649.asp* (the Danish study) and *www.acer.edu.au* (the Australian study).

How student performance in reading has changed

After a first glimpse of change over time from PISA 2000 to PISA 2003, PISA 2006 offers information about performance trends in reading since PISA 2000, when the first full assessment of reading took place. It therefore allows policy makers to monitor improvements in learning outcomes both in absolute terms and relative to improvement in other countries.

Across OECD countries, performance in PISA reading has remained broadly similar between PISA 2000 and PISA 2006. This, in itself, is noteworthy because most countries have significantly increased their investment in education in recent years. As shown in Table 2.6, between 1995 and 2004 expenditure per primary and secondary student increased by 39% in real terms, on average across OECD countries. In the short period between 2000, when the first PISA assessment was undertaken, and 2004, the average increase amounted to 22% and in 6 OECD countries to between 30 and 61%.

At the same time, the data also show that some countries have achieved significant improvements in learning outcomes, and some of these with moderate increases in costs.

Two OECD countries (Korea and Poland) and five partner countries/economies (Chile, Liechtenstein, Indonesia, Latvia and Hong Kong-China) have seen rises in reading performance since PISA 2000.

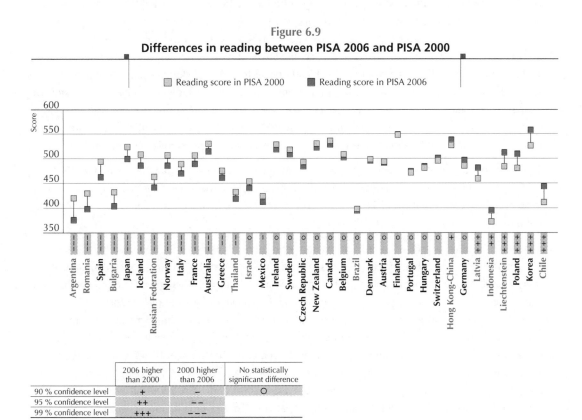

Figure 6.9
Differences in reading between PISA 2006 and PISA 2000

	2006 higher than 2000	2000 higher than 2006	No statistically significant difference
90 % confidence level	+	–	O
95 % confidence level	++	– –	
99 % confidence level	+++	– – –	

Countries are ranked in ascending order of score difference between PISA 2006 and PISA 2000.
Source: OECD PISA 2006 database, Table 6.3a.
StatLink http://dx.doi.org/10.1787/142046885031

- Korea increased its reading performance between PISA 2000 and PISA 2006 from an already high level by 31 score points, thus reaching the highest reading performance among all participating countries – even surpassing Finland, the performance of which remained stable at a high level (Table 6.3a). Korea achieved this increase mainly by significantly raising performance standards among the better performing students, while the performance at the lower end of the distribution remained essentially unchanged (Table 6.3c). Indeed, at the 95th percentile, the point above which the 5% best performing students score, reading performance rose by 59 score points, to 688 score points, at the 90th percentile still by 55 score points and at the 75th percentile by 44 score points. In contrast, there was no significant change at the 5th and 10th percentiles for Korea. The Korean authorities attribute the improvement in reading performance to a new curriculum under which essay tests gained much greater emphasis. Furthermore, universities have also introduced and expanded use of essay test scores in admission screenings with opportunities for students to formulate and present their own thoughts and opinions. This has provided additional incentives for better-performing high-school students to enhance their reading and reasoning skills in order to gain access to the university of their choice.

- Hong Kong-China has been another country that has seen a significant increase, by 11 score points since PISA 2000, from an already high level of reading performance, reaching 536 score points in PISA 2006. Here the change was mainly driven by improvements among the lowest performing students, with the 5th percentile rising by 21 score points, and to a lesser degree in the other percentiles.

- Poland increased its reading performance by 17 score points between PISA 2000 and PISA 2003 and another 11 score points between PISA 2003 and PISA 2006 and now performs, at 508 score points, for the first time clearly above the OECD average. Between these two assessments, Poland raised its average performance mainly through increases at the lower end of the performance distribution (*i.e.* 5th, 10th and 25th percentiles). As a result, in PISA 2003 fewer than 5% of students fell below performance standards that had not been reached by the bottom 10% of Polish students in PISA 2000. Extensive analyses at the national level (see also Chapter 5) have associated this improvement with the reform of the schooling systems in 1999, which now provides more integrated educational structures. Since PISA 2003, performance in Poland has risen more evenly across the performance spectrum.

- The other countries that have seen significant performance increases in reading between PISA 2000 and PISA 2006 – Chile (33 score points between PISA 2000 and PISA 2006), Liechtenstein (28 score points), Indonesia (22 score points) and Latvia (21 score points) – all, with the exception of Liechtenstein, perform significantly below the OECD average.

A number of countries saw a decline in their reading performance between PISA 2000 and PISA 2006: nine OECD countries (in descending order) – Spain, Japan, Iceland, Norway, Italy, France, Australia, Greece and Mexico, as well as five partner countries, Argentina, Romania, Bulgaria, Russian Federation and Thailand. In France, Japan and Mexico, as well as the partner country Thailand, for example, performance declined slightly at the higher end of the student performance distribution, but declined markedly at the lower end. It is noteworthy that, among the countries with above-average performance levels only Australia has seen a statistically significant decline in their students' reading performance, by 15 score points, which is attributable to a decline at the higher end of the performance spectrum. The other countries with a significant decline in reading performance between PISA 2000 and PISA 2006, all perform around or below the OECD average level. Of this latter group, Japan and Iceland had previously performed above the OECD average. For the Czech Republic, the better performers have seen improvements, while performance declined at the lower end of the performance distribution. In Switzerland, performance standards rose at the lower end of the distribution.

Gender differences in reading

In the first two PISA surveys, significant differences in favour of females were observed in all OECD countries, a pattern that is mirrored in the PISA 2006 assessment. Analyses of earlier PISA assessments explain the gender gap as being due to the greater engagement of females with most forms of reading, the fact that they read a greater diversity of material and that they have an increased propensity to use both school and community libraries (OECD, 2002).

The OECD countries with the largest gender difference in PISA 2006 are Greece (57 score points), Finland (51 score points), Iceland (48 score points), Norway (46 score points), the Czech Republic (46 score points), Austria (45 score points), Turkey (44 score points), Germany (42 score points), the Slovak Republic (42 score points), Italy (41 score points), Belgium, Hungary, Poland and Sweden (all 40 score points). The partner countries with large differences are Qatar (66 score points), Bulgaria (58 score points), Jordan (55 score points), Argentina, Slovenia, and Thailand each with 54 score points difference (Figure 6.10 and Table 6.1c).

The OECD countries with the smallest gender differences are the Netherlands (24 score points), the United Kingdom (29 score points), Denmark (30 score points), Japan and Switzerland (both 31 score points) and Luxembourg (32 score points). Among the partner countries/economies, Chile, Indonesia and Colombia show the lowest gender difference and in Azerbaijan (20 score points), Chinese Taipei (21 score points) and Macao-China (26 score points) it is still comparatively small.

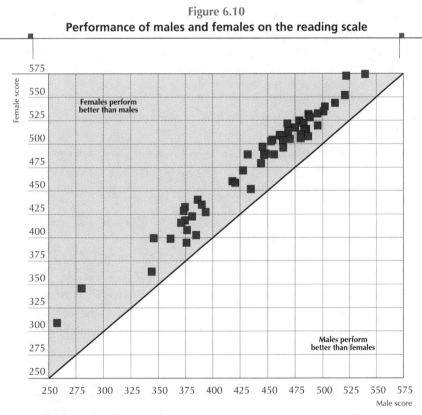

Figure 6.10
Performance of males and females on the reading scale

Note: Gender differences that are statistically significant are marked in a darker colour (see Annex A3).
Source: OECD PISA 2006 database, Table 6.1c.
StatLink http://dx.doi.org/10.1787/142046885031

It is noteworthy that on average across OECD countries, females are 38 score points ahead of their male counterparts, which mirrors the significant performance advantages observed for females in both PISA 2000 and PISA 2003. In Korea males increased their performance by 20 score points but females at twice that rate (41 score points).

PISA 2009 will return the focus of PISA to reading. This will provide countries with information about the changes that may have occurred in the nine years between the PISA surveys in which reading is the major domain of assessment.

WHAT STUDENTS CAN DO IN MATHEMATICS

PISA uses a concept of *mathematical literacy* that is concerned with the capacity of students to analyse, reason and communicate effectively as they pose, solve and interpret mathematical problems in a variety of situations involving quantitative, spatial, probabilistic or other mathematical concepts. The publication, *Assessing Scientific, Reading and Mathematical Literacy: A Framework for PISA 2006* (OECD, 2006a), through which OECD countries established the guiding principles for comparing mathematics performance across countries in PISA, defines *mathematical literacy* as "…an individual's capacity to identify and understand the role that mathematics plays in the world, to make well-founded judgements and to use and engage with mathematics in ways that meet the needs of that individual's life as a constructive, concerned and reflective citizen" (OECD, 2006a).

Students' mathematics knowledge and skills were assessed according to three dimensions relating to: the mathematical content to which different problems and questions relate; the processes that need to be activated in order to connect observed phenomena with mathematics and then to solve the respective problems; and the situations and contexts that are used as sources of stimulus materials and in which problems are posed.

Mathematics was the focus of the PISA 2003 survey and the PISA 2003 mean for OECD countries was set at 500. This mean score is the benchmark against which mathematics performance in PISA 2006 is compared in this report and will be the benchmark for such comparisons in the future. However, it must be noted that in PISA 2006 the area of mathematics was given a smaller amount of assessment time than in PISA 2003, when mathematics was a major domain, with 120 instead of 210 minutes devoted to mathematics, allowing an update on overall performance rather than the kind of in-depth analysis of knowledge and skills shown in the PISA 2003 report (OECD, 2004a).

A profile of PISA mathematics questions

A selection of sample questions has been included to allow the reader a better understanding of the type of questions that are encountered in a PISA mathematics test. The sample questions described in the following section were released following the implementation of the PISA 2003 survey. Similar to reading, there were no further mathematics questions released after PISA 2006. A map of these selected questions is shown in Figure 6.11. The selected questions have been ordered according to their difficulty, with the most difficult of these scores at the top, and the least difficult at the bottom.

Towards the top of the scale, the items that are displayed typically involve a number of different elements, and require high levels of interpretation. Situations are typically unfamiliar, hence requiring some degree of thoughtful reflection and creativity. Questions usually demand some form of argument, often in the form of an explanation. Typical activities involved include: interpreting complex and unfamiliar data; imposing a mathematical construction on a complex real-world situation; and using mathematical modelling processes.

Figure 6.11
A map of selected items in mathematics

Level	MATHEMATICS
6	(687) CARPENTER – Question 1
5	(620) TEST SCORES – Question 16
4	(586) EXCHANGE RATE – Question 11
3	(525) GROWING UP – Question 7
2	(421) STAIRCASE – Question 2
1	(406) EXCHANGE RATE – Question 9
Below 1	

>669.3

607.0

544.7

482.4

420.1

357.8

At this part of the scale, items tend to have several elements that need to be linked by students, and their successful negotiation typically requires a strategic approach to several interrelated steps. For example, Question 1 from *CARPENTER* presents students with four diagrams and they have to ascertain which of these (there could be more than one) would be suitable for a garden bed given a certain length of timber for the perimeter. The question requires geometrical understanding and application.

Around the middle of the scale, items require substantial interpretation, frequently of situations that are relatively unfamiliar or unpractised. They often demand the use of different representations of the situation, including more formal mathematical representations, and the thoughtful linking of those different representations in order to promote understanding and facilitate analysis. They often involve a chain of reasoning or a sequence of calculation steps, and can require students to express reasoning through a simple explanation. Typical activities include: interpreting a set of related graphs; interpreting text, relating this to information in a table or graph, extracting the relevant information and performing some calculations; using scale conversions to calculate distances on a map; and using spatial reasoning and geometric knowledge to perform distance, speed and time calculations. For example, *GROWING UP* presents students with a graph of the average height of young males and young females from the ages of 10 to 20 years. Question 7 from *GROWING UP* asks students to identify the period in their life when females are on average taller than males of the same age. Students have to interpret the graph to understand exactly what is being displayed. They also have to relate the graphs for males and females to each other and determine how the specified period is shown then accurately read the relevant values from the horizontal scale.

Near the bottom of the scale, items set in simple and relatively familiar contexts require only the most limited interpretation of the situation, as well as direct application of well-known mathematical knowledge in familiar situations. Typical activities are reading a value directly from a graph or table, performing a very simple and straightforward arithmetic calculation, ordering a small set of numbers correctly, counting familiar objects, using a simple currency exchange rate, identifying and listing simple combinatorial outcomes. For example, Question 9 from *EXCHANGE RATE* presents students with a simple rate for exchanging Singapore dollars (SGD) into South African rand (ZAR), namely 1 SGD = 4.2 ZAR. The question requires students to apply the rate to convert 3000 SGD into ZAR. The rate is presented in the form of a familiar equation, and the mathematical step required is direct and reasonably obvious.

Figure 6.12
CARPENTER

A carpenter has 32 metres of timber and wants to make a border around a garden bed. He is considering the following designs for the garden bed.

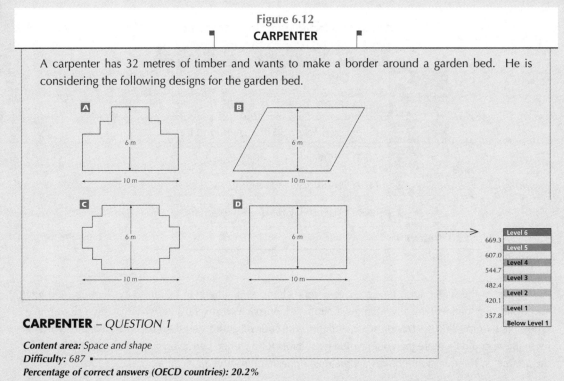

CARPENTER – *QUESTION 1*

Content area: *Space and shape*
Difficulty: *687* •
**Percentage of correct answers (OECD countries): 20.2%*

Circle either "Yes" or "No" for each design to indicate whether the garden bed can be made with 32 metres of timber.

Garden bed design	Using this design, can the garden bed be made with 32 metres of timber?
Design A	Yes / No
Design B	Yes / No
Design C	Yes / No
Design D	Yes / No

Scoring

Full Credit: Yes, No, Yes, Yes in that order.

Comment

This complex multiple-choice item is situated in an educational context, since it is the kind of quasi-realistic problem that would typically be seen in a mathematics class, rather than being a genuine problem likely to be met in an occupational setting. While not regarded as typical, a small number of such problems have been included in PISA. However, the competencies needed for this problem are certainly relevant and part of mathematical literacy. This item illustrates Level 6 with a difficulty of 687 score points. The item belongs to the space and shape content area. The students need the competence to recognise that for the purpose of solving the question the two-dimensional shapes A, C and D have the same perimeter, therefore they need to decode the visual information and see similarities and differences. The students need to see whether or not a certain border-shape can be made with 32 metres of timber. In three cases this is rather evident because of the rectangular shapes. But the fourth is a parallelogram, requiring more than 32 metres. This use of geometrical insight and argumentation skills and some technical geometrical knowledge locates this item at Level 6.

Figure 6.13
TEST SCORE

The diagram shows the results on a science test for two groups, labelled as Group A and Group B. The mean score for Group A is 62.0 and the mean for Group B is 64.5. Students pass this test when their score is 50 or above.

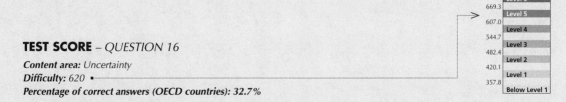

Scores on a science test

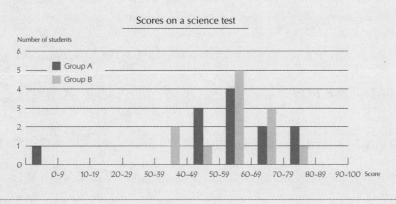

TEST SCORE – *QUESTION 16*

Content area: *Uncertainty*
Difficulty: *620* •────────────────
**Percentage of correct answers (OECD countries): 32.7%*

669.3	Level 6
607.0	Level 5
544.7	Level 4
482.4	Level 3
420.1	Level 2
357.8	Level 1
	Below Level 1

Looking at the diagram, the teacher claims that Group B did better than Group A in this test.

The students in Group A don't agree with their teacher. They try to convince the teacher that Group B may not necessarily have done better.

Give one mathematical argument, using the graph that the students in Group A could use.

Comment

This open-constructed response item is situated in an educational context. It has a difficulty of 620 score points. The educational context of this item is one that all students are familiar with: comparing test scores. In this case a science test has been administered to two groups of students: A and B. The results are given to the students in two different ways: in words with some data embedded and by means of two graphs in one grid. The problem is to find arguments that support the statement that Group A actually did better than Group B, given the counter-argument of one teacher that Group B did better – on the grounds of the higher mean for Group B. The item falls into the content area of uncertainty. Knowledge of this area of mathematics is essential, as data and graphical representations play a major role in the media and in other aspects of our daily experience. The students have a choice of at least three arguments here. The first one is that more students in Group A pass the test; a second one is the distorting effect of the outlier in the results of Group A; and finally Group A has more students that scored 80 or over. Students who are successful have applied statistical knowledge in a problem situation that is somewhat structured and where the mathematical representation is partially apparent. They also need reasoning and insight to interpret and analyse the given information, and they must communicate their reasons and arguments. Therefore the item clearly illustrates Level 5.

Figure 6.14
EXCHANGE RATE – *QUESTION 11*

Mei-Ling from Singapore was preparing to go to South Africa for 3 months as an exchange student. She needed to change some Singapore dollars (SGD) into South African rand (ZAR).

EXCHANGE RATE – *QUESTION 11*

Content area: Quantity
Difficulty: 586 ■————————————————————————
Percentage of correct answers (OECD countries): 40.5%

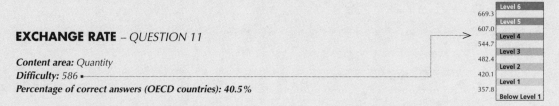

During these 3 months the exchange rate had changed from 4.2 to 4.0 ZAR per SGD.

Was it in Mei-Ling's favour that the exchange rate now was 4.0 ZAR instead of 4.2 ZAR, when she changed her South African rand back to Singapore dollars? Give an explanation to support your answer.

Scoring

Full Credit: Yes, with adequate explanation.

Comment

This open-constructed response item is situated in a public context and has a difficulty of 586 score points. As far as the mathematics content is concerned students need to apply procedural knowledge involving number operations: multiplication and division, which along with the quantitative context, places the item in the quantity area. The competencies needed to solve the problem are not trivial: students need to reflect on the concept of exchange rate and its consequences in this particular situation. The mathematisation required is of a rather high level although all the required information is explicitly presented: not only is the identification of the relevant mathematics somewhat complex, but also the reduction to a problem within the mathematical world places significant demands on the student. The competency needed to solve this problem can be described as using flexible reasoning and reflection. Explaining the results requires some communication skills as well. The combination of familiar context, complex situation, non-routine problem, the need for reasoning, insight and communication places the item in Level 4.

Figure 6.15
GROWING UP

In 1998 the average height of both young males and young females in the Netherlands is represented in this graph.

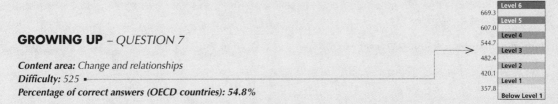

GROWING UP – *QUESTION 7*

Content area: Change and relationships
Difficulty: 525 ■
Percentage of correct answers (OECD countries): 54.8%

669.3	Level 6
607.0	Level 5
544.7	Level 4
482.4	Level 3
420.1	Level 2
357.8	Level 1
	Below Level 1

According to this graph, on average, during which period in their life are females taller than males of the same age?

Scoring

Full Credit: Responses giving the correct interval (from 11 to 13 years) or stating that girls are taller than boys when they are 11 and 12 years old.

Comment

This item, with its focus on age and height means that it lies in the change and relationships content area - it has a difficulty of 420 (Level 1). The students are asked to compare characteristics of two datasets, interpret these datasets and draw conclusions. The competencies needed to successfully solve the problem involve the interpretation and decoding of reasonably familiar and standard representations of well known mathematical objects. Students need thinking and reasoning competencies to answer the question: "Where do the graphs have common points?" and argumentation and communication competencies to explain the role these points play in finding the desired answer. Students who score partial credit are able to show that their reasoning and/or insight was well directed, but they fail in coming up with a full, comprehensive answer. They properly identify ages like 11 and/or 12 and/or 13 as being part of an answer but fail to identify the continuum from 11 to 13 years. The item provides a good illustration of the boundary between Level 1 and Level 2. The full credit response to this item illustrates Level 3, as it has a difficulty of 525 score points. Students who score full credit are not only able to show that their reasoning and/or insight is well directed, but they also come up with a full, comprehensive answer. Students who solve the problem successfully are adept at using graphical representations, making conclusions and communicating their findings.

309

Figure 6.16
STAIRCASE

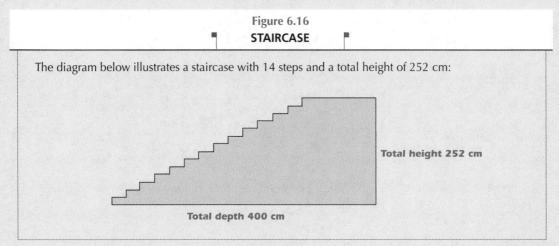

The diagram below illustrates a staircase with 14 steps and a total height of 252 cm:

Total height 252 cm

Total depth 400 cm

STAIRCASE – *QUESTION 2*

Content area: *Space and shape*
Difficulty: *421* ■
Percentage of correct answers (OECD countries): 78.3%

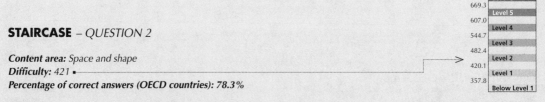

What is the height of each of the 14 steps?

Height: ....cm.

Scoring

Full Credit: 18

Comment

This short open-constructed response item is situated in a daily life context for carpenters and therefore is classified as having an occupational context. It has a difficulty of 421 score points. One does not need to be a carpenter to understand the relevant information; it is clear that an informed citizen should be able to interpret and solve a problem like this that uses two different representation modes: language, including numbers, and a graphical representation. But the illustration serves a simple and non-essential function: students know what stairs look like. This item is noteworthy because it has redundant information (the depth is 400 cm) that is sometimes considered by students as confusing, but such redundancy is common in real-world problem solving. The context of the stairs places the item in the space and shape content area, but the actual procedure to carry out is a simple division. All the required information, and even more than required, is presented in a recognisable situation, the students can extract the relevant information from a single source, and, in essence the item makes use of a single representational mode. Combined with the application of a basic algorithm makes this item fit, although barely, at Level 2.

Figure 6.17
EXCHANGE RATE – *QUESTION 9*

Mei-Ling from Singapore was preparing to go to South Africa for 3 months as an exchange student. She needed to change some Singapore dollars (SGD) into South African rand (ZAR).

EXCHANGE RATE – *QUESTION 9*

Content area: Quantity
Difficulty: 406
Percentage of correct answers (OECD countries): 79.9%

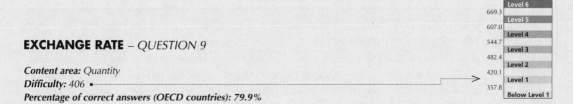

Mei-Ling found out that the exchange rate between Singapore dollars and South African rand was:
1 SGD = 4.2 ZAR

Mei-Ling changed 3000 Singapore dollars into South African rand at this exchange rate.

How much money in South African rand did Mei-Ling get?

Scoring

Full Credit: 12 600 ZAR (unit not required).

Comment

This short constructed-response item is situated in a public context. It has a difficulty of 406 score points. Experience in using exchange rates may not be common to all students, but the concept can be seen as belonging to skills and knowledge for citizenship. The mathematics content is restricted to one of the four basic operations: multiplication. This places the item in the quantity area, and more specifically: operations with numbers. As far as the competencies are concerned, a very limited form of mathematisation is needed: understanding a simple text, and linking the given information to the required calculation. All the required information is explicitly presented. Thus the competency needed to solve this problem can be described as performance of a routine procedure and/or application of a standard algorithm. The combination of a familiar context, a clearly defined question and a routine procedure places the item in Level 1.

311

STUDENT PERFORMANCE IN MATHEMATICS

The proficiency levels used in mathematics in PISA 2006 are the same as those established for mathematics when it was the major area of assessment in PISA 2003. The process used to produce proficiency levels in mathematics is similar to that described in detail for science in Chapter 2. In mathematics there are six levels of proficiency.

Figure 6.18
Summary descriptions of the six proficiency levels in mathematics

Level	Lower score limit	What students can typically do
6	669.3	At Level 6 students can conceptualise, generalise, and utilise information based on their investigations and modelling of complex problem situations. They can link different information sources and representations and flexibly translate among them. Students at this level are capable of advanced mathematical thinking and reasoning. These students can apply this insight and understandings along with a mastery of symbolic and formal mathematical operations and relationships to develop new approaches and strategies for attacking novel situations. Students at this level can formulate and precisely communicate their actions and reflections regarding their findings, interpretations, arguments, and the appropriateness of these to the original situations.
5	607.0	At Level 5 students can develop and work with models for complex situations, identifying constraints and specifying assumptions. They can select, compare, and evaluate appropriate problem solving strategies for dealing with complex problems related to these models. Students at this level can work strategically using broad, well-developed thinking and reasoning skills, appropriate linked representations, symbolic and formal characterisations, and insight pertaining to these situations. They can reflect on their actions and formulate and communicate their interpretations and reasoning.
4	544.7	At Level 4 students can work effectively with explicit models for complex concrete situations that may involve constraints or call for making assumptions. They can select and integrate different representations, including symbolic ones, linking them directly to aspects of real-world situations. Students at this level can utilise well-developed skills and reason flexibly, with some insight, in these contexts. They can construct and communicate explanations and arguments based on their interpretations, arguments, and actions.
3	482.4	At Level 3 students can execute clearly described procedures, including those that require sequential decisions. They can select and apply simple problem solving strategies. Students at this level can interpret and use representations based on different information sources and reason directly from them. They can develop short communications reporting their interpretations, results and reasoning.
2	420.1	At Level 2 students can interpret and recognise situations in contexts that require no more than direct inference. They can extract relevant information from a single source and make use of a single representational mode. Students at this level can employ basic algorithms, formulae, procedures, or conventions. They are capable of direct reasoning and making literal interpretations of the results.
1	357.8	At Level 1 students can answer questions involving familiar contexts where all relevant information is present and the questions are clearly defined. They are able to identify information and to carry out routine procedures according to direct instructions in explicit situations. They can perform actions that are obvious and follow immediately from the given stimuli.

Proficiency at Level 6 (scores higher than 669.3 points)

Students proficient at Level 6 on the mathematics scale are capable of advanced mathematical thinking and reasoning. These students can apply insight and understandings, along with a mastery of symbolic and formal mathematical operations and relationships, to develop new approaches and strategies for attacking novel situations. Students at this level can formulate and precisely communicate their actions and *reflections* regarding their findings, interpretations, arguments, and the appropriateness of these to the original situations.

In the OECD area, an average of 3.3% of students are at Level 6. In Korea, 9.1% of the students are at this level, and 6% or more in the Czech Republic, Finland, Belgium and Switzerland. The partner economies, Chinese Taipei and Hong Kong-China have 11.8 and 9.0% of students at this level, respectively. In contrast, 0.1% of the students in Mexico reach Level 6 and in the partner countries Colombia, Tunisia, Indonesia, Kyrgyzstan and Jordan, this is even lower.

It can be seen from Tables 6.2a and 6.2c that the average score of two countries with similar levels of students at Level 6 can be influenced by the percentage of students at Level 1. For example, Estonia and France have similar percentages of students at Level 6 with 2.6% each, but averages which are significantly different – Estonia's average score (515) is significantly higher than that of France (496).This can be partially explained by the fact that Estonia has a relatively small percentage of students at Level 1 (2.7%), whereas France has 8.4% of students at this level.

Proficiency at Level 5 (scores higher than 607.0 but lower than or equal to 669.3 points)

Students proficient at Level 5 on the mathematics scale can develop and work with models for complex situations, identifying constraints and specifying assumptions. They can select, compare, and evaluate appropriate problem solving strategies for dealing with complex problems related to these models. Students at this level can work strategically using broad, well-developed thinking and reasoning skills, appropriate linked representations, symbolic and formal characterisations, and insight pertaining to these situations.

In the OECD area, an average of 13.4% of students are proficient at Levels 5 or 6 (Figure 6.19 and Table 6.2a). With 27.1%, Korea is the OECD country with the highest percentage of students in these two levels. Finland, Switzerland, Belgium and the Netherlands all have more than 20% of students at these levels and the partner economies Chinese Taipei and Hong Kong-China have 31.9 and 27.7%, respectively. With the exception of Mexico and Turkey, at least 5% of students in each OECD country reaches Level 5.

Proficiency at Level 4 (scores higher than 544.7 but lower than or equal to 607.0 points)

Students proficient at Level 4 on the mathematics scale can work effectively with explicit models for complex concrete situations that may involve constraints or call for making assumptions. They can select and integrate different representations, including symbolic, linking them directly to aspects of real-world situations. Students at this level can utilise well-developed skills and reason flexibly, with some insight, in these contexts. In the OECD area, an average of 32.5% of students are proficient at Level 4 or above (that is, at Levels 4, 5 and 6) (Figure 6.19 and Table 6.2a). In Korea, Finland and the partner economies Chinese Taipei and Hong Kong-China, the majority of students perform at this level. In Switzerland, the Netherlands, Belgium, Canada, Japan and New Zealand, as well as the partner countries/economies Liechtenstein and Macao-China, over 40% do so. However, in Mexico, Turkey, Greece, Italy, Portugal, the United States and Spain, as well as the majority of the partner countries/economies, less than one-quarter of students attain Level 4.

313

Proficiency at Level 3 (scores higher than 482.4 but lower than or equal to 544.7 points)

Students proficient at Level 3 on the mathematics scale can execute clearly described procedures, including those that require sequential decisions. They can select and apply simple problem solving strategies. Students at this level can interpret and use representations based on different information sources. They can develop short communications reporting their interpretations, results and reasoning. In the combined OECD area, an average of 56.8% of students are proficient at least at Level 3 (that is, at Levels 3, 4, 5 and 6) on the mathematics scale (Figure 6.19 and Table 6.2a). In 6 of the 30 OECD countries (Finland, Korea, Canada, the Netherlands, Switzerland and Japan), and in the partner countries/economies Hong Kong-China, Chinese Taipei, Macao-China and Liechtenstein, over 67% of 15-year-old students are proficient at least at Level 3.

Figure 6.19
Percentage of students at each proficiency level on the mathematics scale

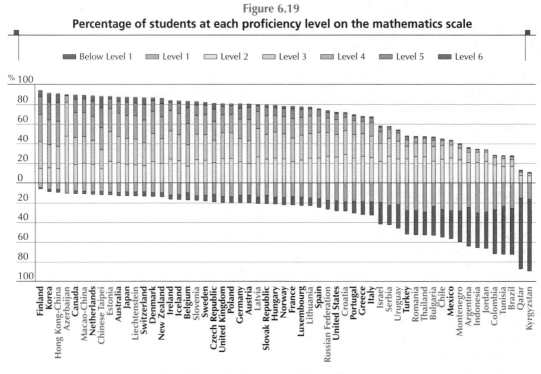

Countries are ranked in descending order of percentage of 15-year-olds at Levels 2, 3, 4, 5 and 6.
Source: OECD PISA 2006 database, Table 6.2a.
StatLink http://dx.doi.org/10.1787/142046885031

Proficiency at Level 2 (scores higher than 420.1 but lower than or equal to 482.4 points)

Students proficient at Level 2 can interpret and recognise situations in contexts that require no more than direct inference. They can extract relevant information from a single source and make use of a single representational mode. Students at this level can employ basic algorithms, formulae, procedures or conventions. They are capable of direct reasoning and making literal interpretations of the results. This level represents a baseline level of mathematics proficiency on the PISA scale at which students begin to demonstrate the kind of literacy skills that enable them to actively use mathematics, which are considered fundamental for future development and use of mathematics. In the OECD area, an average of 78.7% of students are proficient at Level 2 or above. In Finland and Korea and the partner economy Hong Kong-China, more than 90% of students perform at or above this threshold. In every OECD country except Portugal, Greece, Italy, Turkey and Mexico at least 70% of students are at Level 2 or above (Figure 6.19 and Table 6.2a).

Proficiency at Level 1 (scores higher than 357.8 but lower than or equal to 420.1 points) or below

Students proficient at Level 1 can answer questions involving familiar contexts where all relevant information is present and the questions are clearly defined. They are able to identify information and to carry out routine procedures according to direct instructions in explicit situations. They can perform actions that are obvious and follow immediately from the given stimuli.

Students performing below 357.8 score points – that is, below Level 1 – usually do not demonstrate success on the most basic type of mathematics that PISA seeks to measure. Their pattern of answers in the assessment is such that they would be expected to solve fewer than half of the tasks in a test made up of items drawn solely from Level 1. Such students will have serious difficulties in using mathematics as an effective tool to benefit from further education and learning opportunities throughout life.

In the OECD area, an average of 13.6% of students perform at Level 1, and 7.7% perform below Level 1, but there are wide differences between countries. In Finland and Korea, and the partner economy Hong Kong-China, less than 10% of students perform at or below Level 1. In all other OECD countries, the percentage of students performing at or below Level 1 ranges from 10.8% in Canada to 56.5% in Mexico (Figure 6.19 and Table 6.2a).

The mean performances of countries/economies in mathematics

As in the case of reading, the performance of countries can be summarised by a mean score. As explained above, because mathematics was the focus of the PISA 2003 survey, the PISA 2003 mean for OECD countries was set at 500 and establishes the benchmark against which mathematics performance in PISA 2006 is compared. For PISA 2006, the OECD average score in mathematics appears, at 498 score points, slightly lower than the score of 500 in PISA 2003, but this difference is not statistically significant.

When interpreting mean performance, only those differences between countries which are statistically significant should be taken into account. Figure 6.20a shows those pairs of countries where the difference in their mean scores is sufficient to say with confidence that the higher performance by sampled students in one country holds for the entire population of enrolled 15-year-olds. Read across the row for a country to compare its performance with the countries listed along the top of the figure. The colour-coding indicates whether the average performance of the country in the row is lower than that of the comparison country, not statistically different from or higher than it.

Four countries/economies outperformed all other countries in PISA 2006: the OECD countries Finland and Korea and the partner economies Chinese Taipei and Hong Kong-China. Each of these four had a mean score more than 16 score points above that of any other OECD country. These countries' mean scores of 548, 547, 549 and 547 respectively are also more than half of a proficiency level above the OECD average of 498 score points in PISA 2006. Other countries with mean performances statistically significantly above the OECD average include the Netherlands, Switzerland, Canada, Japan, New Zealand, Belgium, Australia, Denmark, the Czech Republic, Iceland and Austria, as well as the partner countries/economies Liechtenstein, Macao-China, Estonia and Slovenia. Countries that performed around the OECD average were Germany, Sweden, Ireland, France, the United Kingdom and Poland.

Because the figures are derived from samples, it is not possible to determine a precise rank of the performance of a country among the participating countries. It is, however, possible to determine a range of ranks between which the country's rank lies with 95% likelihood (Figure 6.20b).

Figure 6.20a [Part 1/2]
Multiple comparisons of mean performance on the mathematics scale

	Mean	S.E.
Chinese Taipei	549	(4.1)
Finland	548	(2.3)
Hong Kong-China	547	(2.7)
Korea	547	(3.8)
Netherlands	531	(2.6)
Switzerland	530	(3.2)
Canada	527	(2.0)
Macao-China	525	(1.3)
Liechtenstein	525	(4.2)
Japan	523	(3.3)
New Zealand	522	(2.4)
Belgium	520	(3.0)
Australia	520	(2.2)
Estonia	515	(2.7)
Denmark	513	(2.6)
Czech Republic	510	(3.6)
Iceland	506	(1.8)
Austria	505	(3.7)
Slovenia	504	(1.0)
Germany	504	(3.9)
Sweden	502	(2.4)
Ireland	501	(2.8)
France	496	(3.2)
United Kingdom	495	(2.1)
Poland	495	(2.4)
Slovak Republic	492	(2.8)
Hungary	491	(2.9)
Luxembourg	490	(1.1)
Norway	490	(2.6)
Lithuania	486	(2.9)
Latvia	486	(3.0)
Spain	480	(2.3)
Azerbaijan	476	(2.3)
Russian Federation	476	(3.9)
United States	474	(4.0)
Croatia	467	(2.4)
Portugal	466	(3.1)
Italy	462	(2.3)
Greece	459	(3.0)
Israel	442	(4.3)
Serbia	435	(3.5)
Uruguay	427	(2.6)
Turkey	424	(4.9)
Thailand	417	(2.3)
Romania	415	(4.2)
Bulgaria	413	(6.1)
Chile	411	(4.6)
Mexico	406	(2.9)
Montenegro	399	(1.4)
Indonesia	391	(5.6)
Jordan	384	(3.3)
Argentina	381	(6.2)
Colombia	370	(3.8)
Brazil	370	(2.9)
Tunisia	365	(4.0)
Qatar	318	(1.0)
Kyrgyzstan	311	(3.4)

Comparison countries (column headers, with mean and S.E.): Chinese Taipei 549 (4.1), Finland 548 (2.3), Hong Kong-China 547 (2.7), Korea 547 (3.8), Netherlands 531 (2.6), Switzerland 530 (3.2), Canada 527 (2.0), Macao-China 525 (1.3), Liechtenstein 525 (4.2), Japan 523 (3.3), New Zealand 522 (2.4), Belgium 520 (3.0), Australia 520 (2.2), Estonia 515 (2.7), Denmark 513 (2.6), Czech Republic 510 (3.6), Iceland 506 (1.8), Austria 505 (3.7), Slovenia 504 (1.0), Germany 504 (3.9), Sweden 502 (2.4), Ireland 501 (2.8), France 496 (3.2), United Kingdom 495 (2.1), Poland 495 (2.4), Slovak Republic 492 (2.8), Hungary 491 (2.9), Luxembourg 490 (1.1), Norway 490 (2.6)

Legend:
- ☐ Statistically significantly above the OECD average
- ■ Not statistically significantly different from the OECD average
- ▨ Statistically significantly below the OECD average
- ▲ Mean performance statistically significantly higher than in comparison country
- ○ No statistically significant difference from comparison country
- ▼ Mean performance statistically significantly lower than in comparison country

Source: OECD PISA 2006 database.
StatLink ⌨ http://dx.doi.org/10.1787/142046885031

Figure 6.20a [Part 2/2]
Multiple comparisons of mean performance on the mathematics scale

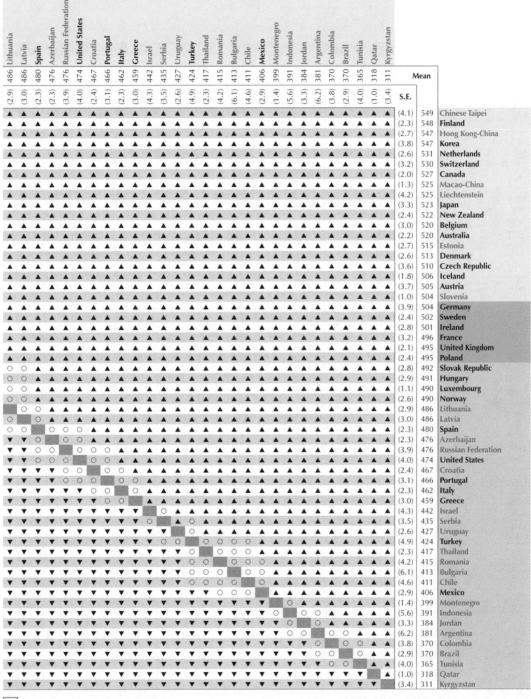

Statistically significantly above the OECD average — ▲ Mean performance statistically significantly higher than in comparison country

Not statistically significantly different from the OECD average — ○ No statistically significant difference from comparison country

Statistically significantly below the OECD average — ▼ Mean performance statistically significantly lower than in comparison country

Source: OECD PISA 2006 database.
StatLink ᴹᶠᴾ http://dx.doi.org/10.1787/142046885031

Figure 6.20b
Range of rank of countries/economies on the mathematics scale

Statistically significantly above the OECD average
Not statistically significantly different from the OECD average
Statistically significantly below the OECD average

			Mathematics scale			
			Range of rank			
			OECD countries		**All countries/economies**	
	Mean score	**S.E.**	**Upper rank**	**Lower rank**	**Upper rank**	**Lower rank**
Chinese Taipei	549	(4.1)			1	4
Finland	548	(2.3)	1	2	1	4
Hong Kong-China	547	(2.7)			1	4
Korea	547	(3.8)	1	2	1	4
Netherlands	531	(2.6)	3	5	5	8
Switzerland	530	(3.2)	3	6	5	9
Canada	527	(2.0)	3	6	5	10
Macao-China	525	(1.3)			7	11
Liechtenstein	525	(4.2)			5	13
Japan	523	(3.3)	4	9	6	13
New Zealand	522	(2.4)	5	9	8	13
Belgium	520	(3.0)	6	10	8	14
Australia	520	(2.2)	6	9	10	14
Estonia	515	(2.7)			12	16
Denmark	513	(2.6)	9	11	13	16
Czech Republic	510	(3.6)	10	14	14	20
Iceland	506	(1.8)	11	15	16	21
Austria	505	(3.7)	10	16	15	22
Slovenia	504	(1.0)			17	21
Germany	504	(3.9)	11	17	16	23
Sweden	502	(2.4)	12	17	17	23
Ireland	501	(2.8)	12	17	17	23
France	496	(3.2)	15	22	21	28
United Kingdom	495	(2.1)	16	21	22	27
Poland	495	(2.4)	16	21	22	27
Slovak Republic	492	(2.8)	17	23	23	30
Hungary	491	(2.9)	18	23	24	31
Luxembourg	490	(1.1)	20	23	26	30
Norway	490	(2.6)	19	23	25	31
Lithuania	486	(2.9)			27	32
Latvia	486	(3.0)			27	32
Spain	480	(2.3)	24	25	31	34
Azerbaijan	476	(2.3)			32	35
Russian Federation	476	(3.9)			32	36
United States	474	(4.0)	24	26	32	36
Croatia	467	(2.4)			35	38
Portugal	466	(3.1)	25	27	35	38
Italy	462	(2.3)	26	28	37	39
Greece	459	(3.0)	27	28	38	39
Israel	442	(4.3)			40	41
Serbia	435	(3.5)			40	41
Uruguay	427	(2.6)			42	43
Turkey	424	(4.9)	29	29	41	45
Thailand	417	(2.3)			43	46
Romania	415	(4.2)			43	47
Bulgaria	413	(6.1)			43	48
Chile	411	(4.6)			44	48
Mexico	406	(2.9)	30	30	46	48
Montenegro	399	(1.4)			49	50
Indonesia	391	(5.6)			49	52
Jordan	384	(3.3)			50	52
Argentina	381	(6.2)			50	53
Colombia	370	(3.8)			52	55
Brazil	370	(2.9)			53	55
Tunisia	365	(4.0)			53	55
Qatar	318	(1.0)			56	56
Kyrgyzstan	311	(3.4)			57	57

Source: OECD PISA 2006 database.
StatLink ⟨⟩ http://dx.doi.org/10.1787/142046885031

The performance difference between high and low-performing students is shown in Table 6.2c. Among OECD countries, Finland and Ireland show the narrowest distributions between the 5th and 95th percentile in the OECD with this difference equivalent to 266 and 268 score points respectively. From the partner countries/economies, some of the lower performing countries such as Azerbaijan, Indonesia and Thailand have a narrow distribution ranging from 153 to 269 score points, while, at the same time, Estonia, one of the higher performing partner countries has a score difference across this range of 264 score points. On the other hand, Austria, Switzerland, Germany, the Czech Republic and Belgium have quite large differences in the performances of their students between the 5th and 95th percentiles. In Belgium this reflects partly the performance differences between the different communities.

How student performance in mathematics has changed

As noted before, it is only possible to compare the results of PISA 2006 mathematics with those of PISA 2003. Because only two data points are involved any inferences should be made with caution. Across OECD countries as a whole, mathematics performance has remained unchanged between PISA 2003 and PISA 2006, the difference of 2 score points for the OECD average not being statistically significant (Table 6.3b).

Figure 6.21
Differences in mathematics between PISA 2006 and PISA 2003

☐ Mathematics score in PISA 2003   ■ Mathematics score in PISA 2006

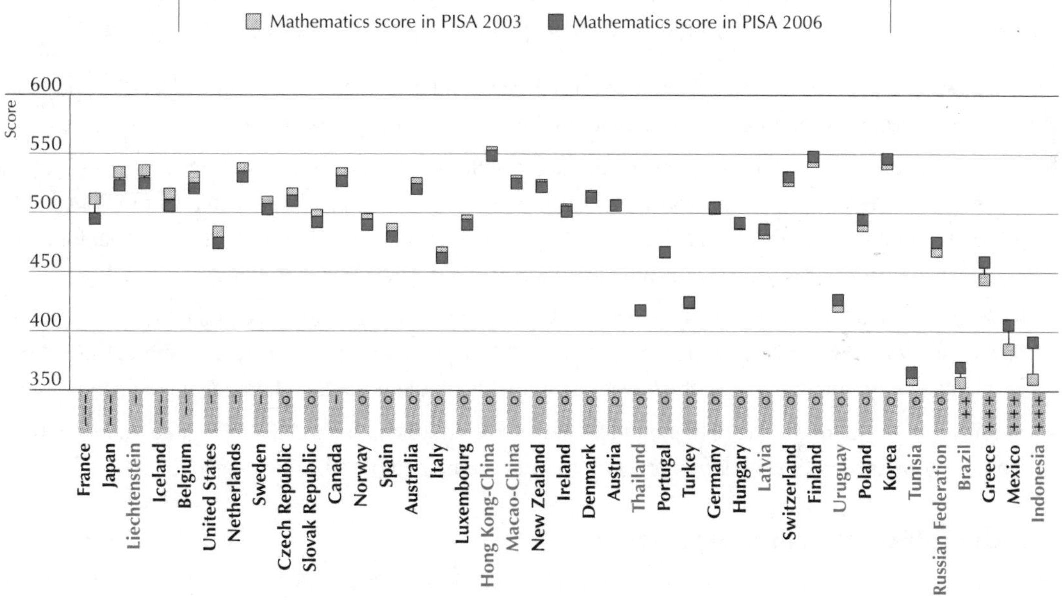

	2006 higher than 2003	2003 higher than 2006	No statistically significant difference
90 % confidence level	+	–	O
95 % confidence level	++	– –	
99 % confidence level	+++	– – –	

Countries are ranked in ascending order of score difference between PISA 2006 and PISA 2003.
Source: OECD PISA 2006 database, Table 6.3b.
StatLink ⟐ http://dx.doi.org/10.1787/142046885031

319

For most countries, performance in mathematics remained broadly unchanged between PISA 2003 and PISA 2006. However, for a few countries there are notable performance differences.

Two OECD countries, Mexico and Greece, and two partner countries, Indonesia and Brazil, show higher performance in PISA 2006 than in PISA 2003.

- In Mexico mathematics performance was 20 score points higher in PISA 2006 than in PISA 2003 but at 406 score points it is still well below the OECD average. In reading, Mexican females performed significantly higher in PISA 2006 than in PISA 2003 while the performance of males remained unchanged; in mathematics both males and females saw similar performance increases between the two surveys.

- In Greece, mathematics performance was 14 score points higher in PISA 2006 than in PISA 2003. Most of the increase was driven by changes in the lower and middle range of the performance distribution. It is also noteworthy that the performance difference is mainly due to the significantly higher performance of females in PISA 2006. In contrast, in reading there was no significant performance difference between PISA 2003 and PISA 2006.

- In Indonesia, mathematics performance was 31 score points higher in PISA 2006 than in PISA 2003, which was, as in the case of reading, largely driven by the higher performance of males in PISA 2006.

- In Brazil, mathematics performance was 13 score points higher in PISA 2006 than in PISA 2003, which was mainly driven by performance improvements at the lower end of the distribution.

Mathematics performance in PISA 2006 was significantly lower in France (15 score points), essentially because of an increase in students at the lower end of the performance distribution. Among the partner countries in Liechtenstein performance in PISA 2006 was 11 score points lower than in PISA 2003 (Table 6.3b).

Some countries in which overall performance has remained relatively stable between PISA 2003 and PISA 2006 have nevertheless seen significant changes in the distribution of performance.

- In Australia, Denmark and Turkey, performance at the bottom at the mathematics performance distribution was higher in PISA 2006 than in PISA 2003, *i.e.* the lowest performing students did better in PISA 2006, while performance decreased at the higher end of the performance distribution. This meant that for these countries there was no overall significant difference between PISA 2006 and PISA 2003.

- In Belgium, Canada, Iceland, Japan, the Netherlands and Sweden performance at the higher end of the distribution was lower in PISA 2006 than in PISA 2003, the better performing students did worse in PISA 2006, while performance among the lower end of the distribution remained broadly unchanged.

- In Tunisia, performance at the higher end of the distribution was higher in PISA 2006 than in PISA 2003, while performance at the lower end of the distribution remained broadly unchanged.

Gender differences in mathematics

The performance advantage of males remained unchanged between PISA 2003 and PISA 2006, at 11 score points.

The largest gender differences are observed in Austria and Japan with 23 and 20 score point advantages for males respectively and a difference of 28 and 22 score points in the partner countries Chile and Colombia respectively. The other countries with mathematics scores significantly higher for males are Germany, the United Kingdom, Italy, Luxembourg, Portugal, Australia, the Slovak Republic, Canada, Switzerland, the Netherlands and Finland, and the partner country Brazil. The only country where females significantly outperformed males in mathematics is Qatar (Table 6.2c).

Figure 6.22
Performance of males and females on the mathematics scale

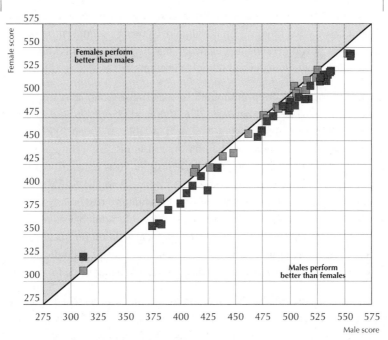

Note: Gender differences that are statistically significant are marked in a darker colour (see Annex A3).
Source: OECD PISA 2006 database, Table 6.2c.
StatLink ⌐⌐⌐ http://dx.doi.org/10.1787/142046885031

IMPLICATIONS FOR POLICY

Reading

The results for PISA 2006 show wide differences between countries in the knowledge and skills of 15-year-olds in reading. Differences between countries represent, however, only a fraction of overall variation in student performance. Catering for such a diverse client base and narrowing the gaps in student performance represents formidable challenges for all countries: An average of 8.6% of 15-year-olds reach the highest reading level in PISA, demonstrating the ability to complete sophisticated reading tasks, to show detailed understanding of texts and the relevance of their components, and to evaluate information critically and build hypotheses drawing on specialised knowledge. At the other end of the scale, an average of 7.4% of students do not reach proficiency Level 1. They fail to demonstrate routinely the most basic knowledge and skills that PISA seeks to measure. These students may still be able to read in a technical sense, but they show serious difficulties in applying reading as a tool to advance and extend their knowledge and skills in other areas. Although the proportion of these students is below 2% in two OECD countries and one partner country, it exceeds 20% in Mexico and in 15 partner countries/economies (Table 6.1a). The existence of even a small but significant minority of students who, near the end of compulsory schooling, lack the foundation of literacy skills needed for further learning, must be of concern to policy makers seeking to make lifelong learning a reality for all. This is particularly important in the face of mounting evidence that continuing education and training beyond school tend to reinforce rather than to mitigate skill differences resulting from unequal success in initial education (OECD, 2007).

In the OECD countries, the proportion of low performers at or below Level 1 is, on average, 20%. Parents, educators, and policy makers in systems with large proportions of students performing at or below Level 1 need to recognise that significant numbers of students are not benefiting sufficiently from available educational opportunities and are not acquiring the necessary knowledge and skills to do so effectively in their further school careers and beyond. The longitudinal studies undertaken by Australia, Canada and Denmark (Box 6.1 above) provide compelling evidence that performance at Level 1 in PISA at age 15 is highly predictive of failure to advance beyond school education.

When looking at performance changes over time, the results suggest that, across the OECD area, reading performance has generally remained flat between PISA 2000 and PISA 2006. This needs to be seen in the context of significant rises in expenditure levels. As shown in Table 2.6, been 1995 and 2004 expenditure per primary and secondary student increased by 39% in real terms, on average across OECD countries. In the short period between 2000, when the first PISA assessment was undertaken and 2004, the average increase amounted to 22% and in 6 OECD countries to between 30 and 61%. The increase in expenditure can be understood when looking at the determinants of expenditure, particularly the place and mode of educational provision (OECD, 2007). The labour intensiveness of traditional education accounts for the predominance of teachers' salaries in overall costs and pay scales based on qualifications and automatic increases make these costs rise over time. However, the data also suggest that education generally has not re-invented itself yet in ways that other professions have to provide better value for money.

At the same time, the results from PISA also show that some countries have achieved significant improvements in learning outcomes. Korea and Poland illustrate the level of progress that is possible. They achieved progress in very different ways and with different starting points, with low proficiency a much greater issue in Poland than in Korea at the time of the first PISA survey.

Korea increased its reading performance between PISA 2000 and PISA 2006 from an already high level by 31 score points, equivalent to roughly a school year, thus reaching the highest reading performance among all participating countries and surpassing Finland. In PISA 2000, Korea had fewer weak readers than any other country – only 5.7% at Level 1 or below (see Table 2.1a, OECD, 2001). But it also had very few readers with very strong performance, with only 5.7% at Level 5 compared to 9.5% on average and over 18% in Finland and New Zealand. As can be seen in Table 6.3c, from 2000 to 2006 Korea improved its average mainly by significantly raising performance standards among the better performing students, while the performance at the lower end of the distribution remained essentially unchanged.

In Poland, the picture was very different in PISA 2000, with nearly one in four students (23.3%) at Level 1 or below (see Table 2.1a, OECD, 2001). As can be seen in Table 6.3c, from 2000 to 2003 Poland raised its average performance mainly through increases at the lower end of the performance distribution (*i.e.* the 5th, 10th and 25th percentiles). Extensive analysis at the national level has associated this improvement with the reform of the schooling systems in 1999, which now provides more integrated educational structures. Since PISA 2003, performance in Poland has risen more evenly across the performance spectrum.

These exceptional cases demonstrate how, within a relatively short period of six years, significant progress can be achieved.

Mathematics

With the growing role of science, mathematics and technology in modern life, the objectives of personal fulfilment, employment and full participation in society increasingly require that all adults, not just those aspiring to a scientific career, should be mathematically, scientifically and technologically literate. The performance of a country's best students in mathematics and related subjects may have implications for the role that that country will play in tomorrow's advanced technology sector, and for its overall international competitiveness. Conversely, deficiencies among lower-performing students in mathematics can have negative consequences for individuals' labour-market and earnings prospects and for their capacity to participate fully in society.

Not surprisingly, policy makers and educators alike attach great importance to mathematics education. Addressing the increasing demand for mathematical skills requires excellence throughout education systems, and it is therefore essential to monitor how well countries provide young adults with fundamental skills in this area.

The wide disparities in student performance in mathematics within most countries, evident from the analysis in this chapter, suggest that excellence throughout education systems still remains a remote goal and that countries need to serve a wide range of student abilities, including those who perform exceptionally well and also those most in need. At the same time, some of the best-performing countries have achieved their results while displaying a modest gap between their stronger and weaker performers.

To what extent is the observed variation in student performance on the PISA 2006 mathematics assessment a reflection of the innate distribution of students' abilities and thus a challenge for education systems that cannot be influenced directly by education policy? The analysis in this chapter has shown not only that the magnitude of within-country disparities in mathematics performance varies widely between countries, but also that wide disparities in performance are not a necessary condition for a country to attain a high level of overall mathematics performance. Although more general contextual factors need to be considered when such disparities are compared between countries, public policy may therefore have the potential to make an important contribution to providing equal opportunities and equitable learning outcomes for all students. Showing that countries differ not just in their mean performance, but also in the extent to which they are able to close the gap between the students with the lowest and the highest levels of performance and to reduce some of the barriers to equitable distribution of learning outcomes is an important finding which has direct relevance for policy makers.

Although changes can so far only be traced over a relatively short, three-year period, significant changes have been noted of which Mexico within the OECD and the partner country Indonesia have shown the most marked improvement. In both of these countries, the great majority of students were at Level 1 or below in PISA 2003, but both have made a start in reducing this proportion: from 66.0% to 56.5% in Mexico and from 78.1% to 65.8% in Indonesia (see Table 2.5a, OECD 2004).

Gender differences

Policy makers have given considerable priority to issues of gender equality, with particular attention being paid to the disadvantages faced by females. The results of PISA point to successful efforts in many countries but also to a growing problem for males, particularly in reading and at the lower tail of the performance distribution. Indeed, in reading the gender gap remains wide, with a 38 score point advantage for females. In mathematics, females remain at a disadvantage in many countries, on average, but the advantage of males, in those countries where this persists, is mainly due to high levels of performance of a comparatively small number of males. Analysis of these differences in PISA 2000 and PISA 2003, respectively, revealed lower engagement of males in reading, and higher anxiety of females in mathematics. Data on these measures were not collected in PISA 2006 as the student questionnaire was devoted to science-related issues – the PISA 2009 assessment will provide an update of student engagement in reading.

Beyond what is shown in this chapter, analyses in PISA 2003 suggested that the different career and occupational choices made later by males and females correspond strikingly with the pattern of gender difference in PISA mathematics performance, and even more so with gender differences in attitudes and approaches to mathematics at age 15 (OECD, 2004a). One issue that needs to be taken into account when interpreting the observed gender differences is that males and females, in many countries at least, make different choices in terms of the schools, tracks and educational programmes they attend. PISA 2003 compared the observed gender difference for all students with estimates of gender differences observed within schools and estimates of gender differences once various programme and school characteristics have been accounted for. In most countries, the gender differences were much larger within schools than they were overall. In Belgium, Germany and Hungary, for example, males had an overall advantage of 8, 9 and 8 score points, respectively, on the mathematics scale (see Table 2.5c, PISA 2003), but the average gap increased to 26, 31 and 26 points within schools (see Table 2.5d, PISA 2003). In these countries, that was a reflection of the fact that females attend the higher performing, academically oriented tracks and schools at a higher rate than males. If the programme and school characteristics measured by PISA were taken into account,[11] then the estimated gender differences increased even further in many countries. From a policy perspective – and for teachers in classrooms – gender differences in mathematics performance thus warrant continued attention. This is the case even if the advantage of males over females within schools and programmes is overshadowed to some extent by the tendency of females to attend higher performing school programmes and tracks.

This conclusion is reinforced by a comparison made in PISA 2003, when PISA also measured student performance in problem solving, reported in *Problem Solving For Tomorrow's World: First Measures of Cross-curricular Competencies from PISA 2003* (OECD, 2004c). This suggested that males and females perform roughly equally in analytical reasoning skills, which also form one component of mathematics tasks. The gender difference in mathematics appeared to correspond to the contexts in which tasks are embedded at school, rather than to the underlying mathematical reasoning skills.

At the same time, some countries do appear to provide a learning environment that benefits both genders equally, either as a direct result of educational efforts or because of a more favourable societal context or both. The wide variation in gender gaps among countries suggests that the current differences are not inevitable outcomes of differences between young males and females and that effective policies and practices can overcome what were long taken to be inevitable outcomes of differences between males and females in interests, learning styles and, even, in underlying capacities.

Notes

1. Note that in PISA 2003, more limited assessments of change in mathematics and science were also made, comparing mathematics as a minor domain in PISA 2000 with a subset of the questions asked when it was a major domain in PISA 2003 and comparing science as a minor domain in those two years. Now that all domains have been fully developed, however, comparisons will only be made from the point where each was first used as a major domain.

2. Normally, when making comparisons between two concurrent means, the significance is indicated by calculating the ratio of the difference of the means to the standard error of the difference of the means – if the absolute value of this ratio is greater than 1.96 then a true difference is indicated with 95% confidence. When comparing two means taken at different times, as in the different PISA surveys, an extra error term, known as the linking error is introduced and the resulting statement of significant difference is more conservative. The linking errors used in PISA 2006 are slightly larger than the linking errors used in PISA 2003. For full details see the *PISA 2006 Technical Report* (OECD, forthcoming).

3. For Luxembourg changes were implemented in the assessment conditions between PISA 2000 and PISA 2003 with regard to organisational and linguistic aspects in order to improve compliance with OECD standards and to better reflect the national characteristics of the school system. In PISA 2000, students in Luxembourg had been given one assessment booklet, with the languages of testing chosen by each student one week prior to the assessment. In practice, however, familiarity with the language of assessment became an important barrier for a significant proportion of students in Luxembourg in PISA 2000. In PISA 2003 and PISA 2006, therefore, students were each given two assessment booklets – one in each of the two languages of instruction – and could choose their preferred language immediately prior to the assessment. This provided for assessment conditions that are more comparable with those in countries that have only one language of instruction and resulted in a fairer assessment of the performance of students in mathematics, science, reading and problem solving. As a result of this change in procedures, the assessment conditions and hence the assessment results for Luxembourg cannot be compared between PISA 2000 and PISA 2003. Assessment conditions between PISA 2003 and PISA 2006 have not been changed and therefore results can be compared.

4. In PISA 2000, the initial response rate for the United Kingdom fell 3.7% short of the minimum requirement. At that time, the United Kingdom provided evidence to the PISA Consortium that permitted an assessment of the expected performance of the non-participating schools and on the basis of which the PISA Consortium concluded that the response-bias was likely negligible and the results were therefore nevertheless included in the international report. In PISA 2003, the United Kingdom's response rate was such that required sampling standards were not met and further investigation by the PISA Consortium did not confirm that the resulting response bias was negligible. Therefore, these data were not deemed internationally comparable and were not included in most types of comparisons. For PISA 2006, the more stringent standards are being applied and PISA 2000 and PISA 2003 data for the United Kingdom are therefore not included in the comparisons of this chapter.

5. In the United States because of an error in printing the test booklets, some of the reading items had incorrect instructions and the mean performance in reading cannot be accurately estimated. The impact of the error on estimates of student performance is likely to exceed one standard error of sampling. For details see Annex A3. This was not the case for science and mathematics items.

6. As noted in the *PISA 2000 Technical Report* (OECD, 2002), the Austrian sample for the PISA 2000 assessment did not adequately cover students enrolled in combined school and work-based vocational programmes as required by the technical standards for PISA. The published PISA 2000 estimates for Austria were therefore biased (OECD, 2001). This non-conformity was corrected in the PISA 2003 assessment. To allow reliable comparisons, adjustments and modified student weights were developed which make the PISA 2000 estimates comparable to those obtained in PISA 2003 (OECD Working Paper No. 5 "PISA 2000: Sample Weight Problems in Austria" available at *http://www.oecd.org/edu/working papers,* presents further details on this issue).

7. To ensure comparability in calculating trends, the 28 reading items used in PISA 2006 are a subset of the 141 items used in PISA 2000. The same items were used in PISA 2003 and PISA 2006. The items were selected taking the relative balance of aspects of the framework into account so that, for example, the proportion of items falling into each task classification is similar.

8. The relative probability of a country assuming each rank-order position on each scale is determined from the country mean scores, their standard errors and the covariance between the performance scales of two assessment areas.

9. Comparisons of a particular country's average score with the OECD average are based on a recomputed OECD average that excludes the data from the country in question. This is done to avoid dependency between the two averages.

10. Hillman, K. and S. Thomson (2006), *Pathways from PISA: LSAY and the 2003 PISA sample two years on,* ACER, Melbourne.

11. For more details on types of programme and school characteristics, see Annex A1.

325

References

Autor, D., Levy, F. and **R. J. Murnane,** "The Skill Content of Recent Technical Change", *Quarterly Journal of Economics* 118, M.I.T. Press, Cambridge, pp. 1279-1334.

Baker, D., B. Goesling and **G. Letendre** (2002), "Socio-economic Status, School Quality and National Economic Development: A Cross-national Analysis of the 'Heyneman-Loxley Effect' on Mathematics and Science Achievement", *Comparative Education Review* 46.3, University of Chicago Press, Chicago, pp. 291-312.

Bandura, A. (1994), *Self-Efficacy: The Exercise of Control,* Freeman, New York.

Baumert, J. and **O. Köller** (1998), "Interest Research in Secondary Level I: An Overview" in L. Hoffmann *et al.* (eds.), *Interest and Learning,* Institute for Science Education at the University of Kiel, Kiel.

Bempechat, J., N.V. Jimenez and **B.A. Boulay** (2002), "Cultural-Cognitive Issues in Academic Achievement: New Directions for Cross-National Research", in A.C. Porter and A. Gamoran (eds.), *Methodological Advances in Cross-national Surveys of Educational Achievement,* National Academic Press, Washington, D.C.

Bishop, J. (1998), "Do Curriculum-based External Exit Exam Systems Enhance Student Achievement?", CPRE Research Report Series RR-40, Consortium for Policy Research in Education, University of Pennsylvania, Philadelphia.

Bishop, J. (2001), "How External Exit Exams Spur Achievement", in F. Mane and M. Bishop (eds.) *Educational Leadership,* Association for Supervision and Curriculum Development, Baltimore.

Blair, C., D. Gamson, S. Thorne and **D. Baker** (2005), "Rising Mean IQ: Cognitive Demand of Mathematics Education for Young Children, Population Exposure to Formal Schooling, and the Neurobiology of the Prefrontal Cortex", *Intelligence* 33, Elsevier, pp. 93-106.

Brunello, G. and **D. Checchi** (2006) "Does School Tracking Affect Equality of Opportunity? New International Evidence", IZA Discussion Papers 2348, Institute for the Study of Labor (IZA), Bonn.

Butler, J. and **R. Adams** (2007) "The Impact of Differential Investment of Student Effort on the Outcomes of International Studies", *Journal of Applied Measurement* 8.3, JAM Press, Maple Grove, pp. 279-304.

Bybee, R. (1997), *Achieving Scientific Literacy: From Purposes to Practices,* Heinemann, Portsmouth.

Bybee, R. (2005), "Scientific Literacy and the Environment," essay prepared for the OECD PISA Science Forum, Poland, August 2005.

Carstensen, C., J. Rost and **M. Prenzel** (2003), "Proposal for Assessing the Affective Domain", document prepared for the PISA Science Expert Group Meeting, Las Vegas, 7-8 October 2003.

Ceci, S. (1991), "How Much Does Schooling Influence General Intelligence and Its Cognitive Components? A Reassessment of the Evidence", *Developmental Psychology* 27.5, American Psychological Association, Washington, D.C., pp. 703–722.

Cohen, J. and **P. Cohen.** (1985), *Applied Multiple Regression and Correlation Analysis for the Behavioural Sciences* (2nd ed.), Erlbaum, Hillsdale.

Datcher, L. (1982), "Effects of Community and Family Background on Achievement", *Review of Economics and Statistics* 64.1, M.I.T Press, Cambridge, pp. 32-41.

Downey, D., P. von Hippel and **B. Broh** (2004), "Are Schools the Great Equalizer? Cognitive Inequality During the Summer Months and School Year", *American Sociological Review* 69, American Sociological Association, Washington, D.C., pp. 613-635.

Eccles, J. S. (1994), "Understanding Women's Educational and Occupational Choice: Applying the Eccles et al. Model of Achievement-related Choices", Psychology of Women Quarterly 18, Blackwell Publishing, Oxford, pp. 585-609.

Eccles, J.S. and **A. Wigfield** (1995), "In the Mind of the Achiever: The Structure of Adolescents' Academic Achievement-related Beliefs and Self-perceptions", *Personality and Social Psychology Bulletin* 21, Sage, London, pp. 215-225.

Fensham, P.J. (2000), "Time to Change Drivers for Scientific Literacy", *Canadian Journal of Science, Mathematics, and Technology Education* 2, University of Toronto Press, Toronto, pp. 9-24.

Field, S., M. Kuczera and **B. Pont** (2007), *No More Failures: Ten Steps to Equity in Education,* OECD, Paris.

Finn, J. and **D.A. Rock** (1997), "Academic Success Among Students at Risk for School Failure", *Journal of Applied Psychology* 82.2, American Psychological Association, Washington, D.C., pp. 221-234.

Ganzeboom, H.B.G., P.M. De Graaf and **D.J. Treiman** (1992), "A Standard International Socio-economic Index of Occupational Status", *Social Science Research* 21.1, Elsevier Ltd., pp. 1-56.

Glaser-Zikuda, M., P. Mayring and **C. von Rhoeneck** (2003), "An Investigation of the Influence of Emotional Factors on Learning Physics Interaction", *International Journal of Science Education* 25.4, Routledge, Taylor & Francis Group, London, pp. 489-507.

Hanushek, E.A. and **L. Wößmann** (2007), *Education Quality and Economic Growth,* World Bank, Washington, DC.

Harris, K-L and **K. Farrell** (2007), "The Science Shortfall: An Analysis of the Shortage of Suitably Qualified Science Teachers in Australian Schools and the Policy Implications for Universities", *Journal of Higher Education Policy and Management* 29.2, Routledge, Victoria, pp. 159-171.

Hart, B. and **T.R. Risely** (1995), *Meaningful Differences in the Everyday Experience of Young American Children,* Brookes, Baltimore.

Hillman, K. and **S. Thomson** (2006f), *Pathways from PISA: LSAY and the 2003 PISA Sample Two Years On,* ACER, Melbourne.

Heine, S.J., Lehman, D.R., Markus, H.R. and **Kitayama, S.** (1999), "Is There a Universal Need for Positive Self-regard?", *Psychological Review* 106.4, American Psychological Association, Washington, D.C. , pp. 766-794.

Hoxby, C. M. (2002), "How School Choice Affects the Achievement of Public School Students," in Paul Hill (ed.), *Choice with Equity,* Hoover Press, Stanford.

Jones, M.P. (1996), "Indicator and Stratification Methods for Missing Explanatory Variables in Multiple Linear Regression", *Journal of the American Statistical Association* 91, American Statistical Association, Alexandria, pp. 222-230.

Johnson, M. K., R. Crosnoe and **G.H. Elder** (2001), "Students' Attachment and Academic Engagement: The Role of Race and Ethnicity", *Sociology of Education* 74, American Sociological Association, Washington, D.C., pp.318-340.

Knighton, T. and **P. Bussiere** (2006), "Educational Outcomes at Age 19 Associated with Reading Ability at Age 15" (research paper), Statistics Canada, Ottawa.

Law, N. (2002), "Scientific Literacy: Charting the Terrains of a Multifaceted Enterprise", *Canadian Journal of Science, Mathematics, and Technology Education* 2, Ontario Institute for Studies in Education, University of Toronto, Toronto, pp. 151–176.

Levy, F. and **R.J. Murnane** (2006), "How Computerized Work and Globalization Shape Human Skill Demands", working paper, available at: http://web.mit.edu/flevy/www/computers_offshoring_and_skills.pdf.

Loeb, Susanna (2001) "Teacher Quality: Its Enhancement and Potential for Improving Pupil Achievement," in D. Monk *et al.* (eds.), *Improving Educational Productivity,* Information Age Publishing Inc., Greenwich.

Marsh, H.W. (1986), "Verbal and Math Self-concepts: An Internal/External Frame of Reference Model", *American Educational Research Journal* 23.1, American Educational Research Association , Washington, D.C., pp. 129-149.

Martin, M.O., Mullis, I.V.S., Gonzalez, E.J. and **S.J. Chrostowski** (2004), *Findings From IEA's Trends in International Mathematics and Science Study at the Fourth and Eighth Grades,*TIMSS & PIRLS International Study Center, Boston College, Chestnut Hill.

Martinez, M. (2000), *Education as the Cultivation of Intelligence,* Erlbaum, Hillsdale.

Mayer, V.J. and **Y. Kumano** (2002), "The Philosophy of Science and Global Science Lliteracy", in V.J. Mayer (ed.), *Global Science Literacy,* Kluwer Academic Publishers, Dordrecht.

Mullis, I.V.S., M.O. Martin, A.E. Beaton, E.J. Gonzalez, D.J. Kelly and **T.A. Smith** (1998), *Mathematics and Science Achievement in the Final Year of Secondary School: IEA's Third International Mathematics and Science Study,* Center for the Study of Testing, Evaluation, and Educational Policy, Boston College, Chestnut Hill.

Pekrun, R., T. Götz, W. Titz and **R.P. Perry** (2002), "Academic Emotions in Students' Self-regulated Learning and Achievement: A Program of Quantitative and Qualitative Research", *Educational Psychologist* 37, Routledge, Taylor & Francis Group, London pp. 91-106.

OECD (1999), *Measuring Student Knowledge and Skills – A New Framework for Student Assessment,* OECD, Paris.

OECD (2001), *Knowledge and Skills for Life – First Results from PISA 2000,* OECD, Paris.

OECD (2002), *PISA 2000 Technical Report,* OECD, Paris.

OECD (2003), *The PISA 2003 Assessment Framework – Reading, Mathematical and Scientific Literacy,* OECD, Paris.

OECD (2004a), *Learning for Tomorrow's World – First Results from PISA 2003,* OECD, Paris.

OECD (2004b), *PISA 2003 Data Analysis Manual,* OECD, Paris.

OECD (2004c), *Problem Solving for Tomorrow's World – First Measures of Cross-curricular Competencies from PISA 2003,* OECD, Paris.

OECD (2005a), *PISA 2003 Technical Report,* OECD, Paris.

OECD (2005b), *Trends in International Migration: SOPEMI – 2004 Edition,* OECD, Paris.

OECD (2005c), *Where Immigrant Students Succeed – A Comparative Review of Performance and Engagement in PISA 2003,* OECD, Paris.

OECD (2005d), *Education at a Glance – OECD Indicators 2005,* OECD, Paris.

OECD (2006a), *Assessing Scientific, Reading and Mathematical Literacy: A Framework for PISA 2006,* OECD, Paris.

OECD (2006b), *Education at a Glance – OECD Indicators 2006,* OECD, Paris

OECD (2006c), *International Migration Outlook 2006,* OECD, Paris.

OECD (2007), *Education at a Glance – OECD Indicators 2007,* OECD, Paris.

OECD (forthcoming), *PISA 2006 Technical Report,* OECD, Paris.

Ólafsson, R.F., Halldórsson, A.M. and **Júlíus K. Björnsson** (2003) "Gender and the Urban-rural Differences in Mathematics and Reading: An Overview of PISA 2003 Results in Iceland", *Northern Lights on PISA: Unity and Diversity in the Nordic Countries in PISA 2000,* Svein Lie, Pirjo Linnakylä and Astrid Roe (eds.), Department of Teacher Education and School Development, University of Oslo, Oslo.

Osborne, J., S. Simon and **S. Collins** (2003), "Attitudes Towards Science: A Review of the Literature and Its Implications", *International Journal of Science Education* 25:9, Routledge, pp. 1049-1079.

Raudenbush, S.W. and **A.S. Bryk** (2002), *Hierarchical Linear Models: Applications and Data Analysis Methods,* Sage, London.

Roth, K. J., S. L. Druker, H.E. Garnier, M. Lemmens, C. Chen, T. Kawanaka, D. Rasmussen, S. Trubacova, D. Warvi, Y. Okamoto, P. Gonzales, J. Stigler and **R. Gallimore** (2006), *Teaching Science in Five Countries: Results From the TIMSS 1999 Video Study,* NCES, Washington, D.C.

Snijders, T. and **R. Bosker** (1999) *Multilevel Analysis: An Introduction to Basic and Advanced Multilevel Modelling,* Sage, London.

Stadler, H. (1999), "Fachdidaktische Analyse der österreichischen SchülerInnenergebnisse bei TIMSS Pop 3 – Betrachtung der Ergebnisse in geschlechtsspezifischer Hinsicht" [Analysis of the results of TIMSS Pop 3 with a focus on gender issues], *Zweiter Zwischenbericht zum Projekt IMST – Innovations in Mathematics and Science Teaching, Teil I (im Auftrag des BMUK),* University of Klagenfurt, Klagenfurt.

Van de Vijver, F. and **K. Leung** (1997), "Methods and Data Analysis of Comparative Research", in J. W. Berry, Y., H. Poortinga and J. Pandey (eds.), *Handbook of Cross-Cultural Psychology, Vol. 1 Theory and Method,* Allyn and Bacon, Needham Heights, M.A.

Voelkl, K.E. (1995), "School Warmth, Student Participation, and Achievement", *Journal of Experimental Education* 63.2, HELDREF Publications, Washington, D.C., pp. 127-138.

Warm, T.A. (1985), "Weighted Maximum Likelihood Estimation of Ability in Item Response Theory with Tests of Finite Length", *Technical Report CGI-TR-85-08,* U.S. Coast Guard Institute, Oklahoma City.

Wayne, A.J. and **P. Youngs** (2003) "Teacher Characteristics and Student Achievement Gains: A Review", *Review of Educational Research* 73.1, American Educational Research Association, pp. 89-122.

Wigfield, A., J.S. Eccles and **D. Rodriguez** (1998), "The Development of Children's Motivation in School Context", *Review of Research in Education* 23, 73-118, American Educational Research Association, Washington, D.C.

Willms, J.D. (2002), *Vulnerable Children: Findings from Canada's National Longitudinal Survey of Children and Youth,* University of Alberta Press, Edmonton.

Willms, J.D. (2004), "Student Performance and Socio-economic Background", unpublished research, University of New Brunswick.

Willms, J.D. (2006), *Learning Divides: Ten Policy Questions About the Performance and Equity of Schools and Schooling Systems,* UNESCO Institute for Statistics, Montreal.

Willms, J.D. and **L. Paterson** (1995), "A Multilevel Model for Community Segregation", *Journal of Mathematical Sociology* 20.1, Routledge, Taylor & Francis Group, London, pp. 23-40.

Wright, S.P., Horn, S.P. and **W.L. Sanders** (1997), "Teacher and Classroom Context Effects on Student Achievement: Implications for Teacher Evaluation", *Journal of Personnel Evaluation in Education* 11, Springer Netherlands, pp. 57-67.

Annex A

TECHNICAL BACKGROUND

All tables in Annex A are available on line
at http://dx.doi.org/10.1787/142050165315

Annex A1: Construction of indices and other derived measures from the student, school and parent context questionnaires

Annex A2: The PISA target population, the PISA samples and the definition of schools

Annex A3: Standard errors, significance tests and subgroup comparisons

Annex A4: Quality assurance

Annex A5: Development of the PISA assessment instruments

Annex A6: Reliability of the coding of responses to open-ended items

Annex A7: Comparison of results from the PISA 2000, PISA 2003 and PISA 2006 assessments

Annex A8: Technical notes on multilevel regression analysis

Annex A9: SPSS syntax to prepare data files for multilevel regression analysis

Annex A10: Technical notes on measures of students' attitudes to science

ANNEX A1

CONSTRUCTION OF INDICES AND OTHER DERIVED MEASURES FROM THE STUDENT, SCHOOL AND PARENT CONTEXT QUESTIONNAIRES

This section explains the indices derived from the student, school and parent context questionnaires in PISA 2006.

Several of PISA's measures reflect indices that summarise responses from students or school representatives (typically principals) to a series of related questions. The questions were selected from larger constructs on the basis of theoretical considerations and previous research. Structural equation modelling was used to confirm the theoretically expected behaviour of the indices and to validate their comparability across countries. For this purpose, a model was estimated separately for each country and collectively for all OECD countries.

For a detailed description of other PISA indices and details on the methods see the *PISA 2000 Technical Report* (OECD, 2002), the *PISA 2003 Technical Report* (OECD, 2005a) and the *PISA 2006 Technical Report* (OECD, forthcoming).

Unless otherwise indicated, where an index involves multiple questions and student responses, the index was scaled using a weighted maximum likelihood estimate (WLE) (Warm, 1985), using a one-parameter item response model, (a partial credit model was used in the case of items with more than two categories). The scaling was done in three stages:

- The item parameters were estimated from equal-sized sub-samples of students from each OECD country.
- The estimates were computed for all students and all schools by anchoring the item parameters obtained in the preceding step.
- The indices were then standardised so that the mean of the index value for the OECD student population was zero and the standard deviation was one (countries being given equal weight in the standardisation process).

Sequential codes were assigned to the different response categories of the questions in the sequence in which the response categories appeared in the student, school or parent questionnaires. Where indicated in this section, these codes were inverted for the purpose of constructing indices or scales.

It is important to note that negative values for an index do not necessarily imply that students responded negatively to the underlying questions. A negative value merely indicates that the respondents answered less positively than all respondents did on average across OECD countries. Likewise, a positive value on an index indicates that the respondents answered more favourably, or more positively, than respondents did, on average, in OECD countries.

Terms enclosed in brackets < > in the following descriptions were replaced in the national versions of the student, school and parent questionnaires by the appropriate national equivalent. For example, the term <qualification at ISCED level 5A> was translated in the United States into "Bachelor's degree, post-graduate certificate program, Master's degree program or first professional degree program". Similarly the term <classes in the language of assessment> in Luxembourg was translated into "German classes" or "French classes" depending on whether students received the German or French version of the assessment instruments.

Student-level variables

Student background

Parental occupations and students' expected occupation

Students were asked to report their mothers' and fathers' occupations. Students were also asked to report on their expected occupation at age 30. The open-ended responses for occupations were then coded in accordance with the International Standard Classification of Occupations (ISCO 1988).

The **PISA international socio-economic index of occupational status** was derived from students' responses on parental occupation. The index captured the attributes of occupations that convert parents' education into income. The index was derived by the optimal scaling of occupation groups to maximise the indirect effect of education on income through occupation and to minimise the direct effect of education on income, net of occupation (both effects being net of age).

For more information on the methodology, see Ganzeboom *et al.* (1992). The ***highest international socio-economic index of occupational status*** corresponds to the highest ***international socio-economic index of occupational status*** of either the father or the mother.

The variables on students' expected occupation and their fathers' and mothers' occupations were also transformed into four socio-economic categories: *i)* white-collar high-skilled: legislators, senior officials and managers, professionals, technicians and associate professionals; *ii)* white-collar low-skilled: service workers, shop and market sales workers and clerks; *iii)* blue-collar high-skilled: skilled agricultural and fishery workers and craft and related trades workers; and *iv)* blue-collar low-skilled: plant and machine operators and assemblers and elementary occupations.

Economic, social and cultural status

The ***PISA index of economic, social and cultural status*** was created to capture wider aspects of a student's family and home background in addition to occupational status. It was derived from the following variables: the ***highest international socio-economic index of occupational status*** (HISCEI) of the father or mother; the ***index of highest educational level of parents*** (HISCED) converted into years of schooling (for the conversion of levels of education into years of schooling see Table A1.1); and the ***index of home possessions*** obtained by asking students whether they had at their home: a desk to study at, a room of their own, a quiet place to study, a computer they can use for school, an educational software, a link to the Internet, their own calculator, classic literature, books of poetry, works of art (*e.g.* paintings), books to help with their school work, a dictionary, a dishwasher, a DVD player or VCR, the number of cellular phones, televisions, computers, cars and books at home, and three other country-specific items. The rationale for the choice of these variables was that socio-economic status is usually seen as being determined by occupational status, education and wealth. As no direct measure on parental income was available from PISA (except for those countries which undertook the Parent Questionnaire), access to relevant household items was used as a proxy. The student scores on the index are factor scores derived from a Principal Component Analysis which are standardised to have an OECD mean of zero and a standard deviation of one.

Principal Component Analysis was also performed for each participating country to determine to what extent the components of the index operate in similar ways across countries. The analysis revealed that patterns of factor loadings were very similar across countries, with all three components contributing to a similar extent to the index. For the occupational component, the average factor loading was 0.81, ranging from 0.72 to 0.87 across countries. For the educational component, the average factor loading was 0.80, ranging from 0.73 to 0.86 across countries. For the wealth component, the average factor loading was 0.73, ranging from 0.55 to 0.83 across countries. The reliability of the index ranged from 0.52 to 0.80. These results support the cross-national validity of the ***PISA index of economic, social and cultural status.***

The ***PISA index of economic, social and cultural status*** used in the PISA 2000 analysis was derived from five indices: the ***index of highest occupational status of parents*** (HISEI), the ***index of highest educational level of parents*** (in number of years of education according to ISCED classification), the ***index of family wealth,*** the ***index of cultural possessions*** and the ***index of home educational resources.*** Also, for the question on parental levels of education no distinction had been made in PISA 2000 between university-level (ISCED 5A) and non-university tertiary education (ISCED 5B).

The ***PISA index of economic, social and cultural status*** for PISA 2003 was derived from three variables related to family background: the ***index of highest educational level of parents*** (in number of years of education according to ISCED classification), the ***index of highest occupational status of parents*** (HISEI), and the ***index of home possessions.*** However, in PISA 2003, the number of cellular phones, computers, cars and televisions were not included in the index, and the number of books at home was dichotomised.

The components comprising the ***PISA index of economic, social and cultural status*** for 2006 also include home possessions, the ***index of highest occupational status of parents*** (HISEI) and the ***index of highest educational level of parents*** (HISCED) converted into years of schooling, but for PISA 2006 there were additional items and national item parameters were used. The scale construction was done through Item Response Theory (IRT) scaling with item parameters estimated first for common items separately for each country. The sum of the common items' parameters was constrained to zero for each country. Next, these item parameters were anchored and the remaining items were added, and each country was scaled separately.

333

This being said, the correlation between the PISA 2003 and PISA 2006 indices is very high (R of 0.96). This shows that different methods of computation of the indices did not have a major impact on the results. For more information on this index see the *PISA 2006 Technical Report* (OECD, forthcoming).

Educational level of parents

Parental education is a family background variable that is often used in the analysis of educational outcomes. Indices were constructed using information on the ***educational level of the father,*** the ***educational level of the mother,*** and the highest level of education between the two parents, referred to as the ***index of highest educational level of parents*** (HISCED). Students were asked to identify the highest level of education of their mother and father on the basis of national qualifications, which were then coded in accordance with the International Standard Classification of Education (ISCED 1997, see OECD, 1999) in order to obtain internationally comparable categories of educational attainment. The resulting categories were: (0) for no completion of <ISCED Level 1>; (1) for the completion of <ISCED Level 1> (primary education); (2) for completion of <ISCED Level 2> (lower secondary education); (3) for the completion of <ISCED Level 3B or 3C> (vocational/pre-vocational upper secondary education, aimed in most countries at providing direct entry into the labour market); (4) for completion of <ISCED Level 3A> (upper secondary education, aimed in most countries at gaining entry into tertiary-type A [university level] education) and/or <ISCED Level 4> (non-tertiary post-secondary); (5) for qualifications in <ISCED 5B> (vocational tertiary); and (6) for completion of <ISCED Level 5A, 6> (tertiary-type A and advanced research programmes).

As noted above, the highest level of educational attainment of the parents was also converted into years of schooling using the conversion coefficients shown in Table A1.1. Students who reported that their parents had not completed <ISCED Level 1> were assigned a value of 3 years because for most parents it would be unlikely that they had no school education at all.

Immigrant background

The ***index of immigrant background*** was derived from students' responses to questions about whether or not they, their mother and their father were born in the country of assessment or in another country. The response categories were then grouped into three categories: *i)* "native" students (those students born in the country of assessment or who had at least one parent born in that country); *ii)* "second-generation" students (those born in the country of assessment but whose parents were born in another country); and *iii)* "first-generation" students (those born outside the country of assessment and whose parents were also born in another country). For some comparisons, first-generation and second-generation students were grouped together as "students with an immigrant background".

Language used at home

Students were asked which language they speak at home most of the time. The ***index of language spoken at home*** distinguishes between students who *i)* use the language of assessment most of the time at home, *ii)* use another national language most of the time at home and *iii)* use another language most of the time at home.

In most countries, the languages were individually identified and were coded internationally to allow for further research and analysis in this area.

Availability of household possessions indicating family wealth

This index was derived from three sets of items: *i)* whether students had a room of their own, a link to the Internet, a dishwasher and a DVD or VCR player; *ii)* how many of the following items they had at their home: cellular phones, televisions, computers and cars; and *iii)* three country-specific items thought to indicate wealth defined by each country. The scale construction was done through IRT scaling with positive values indicating higher levels of family wealth. National item parameters were estimated for each country and the sum of the common international items' parameters was constrained to zero.

Home educational resources

The ***index of home educational resources*** was derived from students' reports on the availability of the following items in their home: *i)* a desk to study at; *ii)* a quiet place to study; *iii)* a computer they can use for school work; *iv)* educational software; *v)* their own calculator; *vi)* books to help with their school work; and *vii)* a dictionary. Scale construction was done using IRT scaling and positive values indicate higher levels of home educational resources. National item parameters were estimated for each country.

[Part 1/2]
Table A1.1 Levels of parental education converted into years of schooling

	Did not go to school	Completed ISCED Level 1 (primary education)	Completed ISCED Level 2 (lower secondary education)	Completed ISCED Levels 3B or 3C (upper secondary education providing direct access to the labour market or to ISCED 5B programmes)
OECD				
Australia	0.0	6.0	10.0	11.0
Austria	0.0	4.0	9.0	12.0
Belgium	0.0	6.0	9.0	12.0
Canada	0.0	6.0	9.0	12.0
Czech Republic	0.0	5.0	9.0	11.0
Denmark	0.0	6.0	9.0	12.0
England, Wales and Northern Ireland	0.0	6.0	9.0	12.0
Finland	0.0	6.0	9.0	12.0
France	0.0	5.0	9.0	12.0
Germany	0.0	4.0	10.0	13.0
Greece	0.0	6.0	9.0	11.5
Hungary	0.0	4.0	8.0	10.5
Iceland	0.0	7.0	10.0	13.0
Ireland	0.0	6.0	9.0	12.0
Italy	0.0	5.0	8.0	12.0
Japan	0.0	6.0	9.0	12.0
Korea	0.0	6.0	9.0	12.0
Luxembourg	0.0	6.0	9.0	12.0
Mexico	0.0	6.0	9.0	12.0
Netherlands	0.0	6.0	10.0	
New Zealand	0.0	5.5	10.0	11.0
Norway	0.0	6.0	9.0	12.0
Poland	0.0		8.0	11.0
Portugal	0.0	6.0	9.0	12.0
Scotland	0.0	7.0	11.0	13.0
Slovak Republic	0.0	4.5	8.5	12.0
Spain	0.0	5.0	8.0	10.0
Sweden	0.0	6.0	9.0	11.5
Switzerland	0.0	6.0	9.0	12.5
Turkey	0.0	5.0	8.0	11.0
United States	0.0	6.0	9.0	
Partners				
Argentina	0.0	6.0	10.0	12.0
Azerbeidjan	0.0	4.0	9.0	11.0
Brazil	0.0	4.0	8.0	11.0
Bulgaria	0.0	4.0	8.0	12.0
Chile	0.0	6.0	8.0	12.0
Colombia	0.0	5.0	9.0	11.0
Croatia	0.0	4.0	8.0	11.0
Estonia	0.0	4.0	9.0	12.0
Hong Kong-China	0.0	6.0	9.0	11.0
Indonesia	0.0	6.0	9.0	12.0
Israel	0.0	6.0	9.0	12.0
Jordan	0.0	6.0	10.0	12.0
Kyrgyzstan	0.0	4.0	8.0	11.0
Latvia	0.0	3.0	8.0	11.0
Liechtenstein	0.0	5.0	9.0	11.0
Lithuania	0.0	3.0	8.0	11.0
Macao-China	0.0	6.0	9.0	11.0
Montenegro	0.0	4.0	8.0	11.0
Qatar	0.0	6.0	9.0	12.0
Romania	0.0	4.0	8.0	11.5
Russian Federation	0.0	4.0	9.0	11.5
Serbia	0.0	4.0	8.0	11.0
Slovenia	0.0	4.0	8.0	11.0
Chinese Taipei	0.0	6.0	9.0	12.0
Thailand	0.0	6.0	9.0	12.0
Tunisia	0.0	6.0	9.0	12.0
Uruguay	0.0	6.0	9.0	12.0

StatLink ⌨ http://dx.doi.org/10.1787/142050165315

[Part 2/2]

Table A1.1 Levels of parental education converted into years of schooling

		Completed ISCED Level 3A (upper secondary education providing access to ISCED 5A and 5B programmes) and/or ISCED Level 4 (non-tertiary post-secondary)	Completed ISCED Level 5A (university level tertiary education) or ISCED Level 6 (advanced research programmes)	Completed ISCED Level 5B (non-university tertiary education)
OECD	Australia	12.0	15.0	14.0
	Austria	12.5	17.0	15.0
	Belgium	12.0	17.0	14.5
	Canada	12.0	17.0	15.0
	Czech Republic	13.0	16.0	16.0
	Denmark	12.0	17.0	15.0
	England, Wales and Northern Ireland	13.0	16.0	15.0
	Finland	12.0	16.5	14.5
	France	12.0	15.0	14.0
	Germany	13.0	18.0	15.0
	Greece	12.0	17.0	15.0
	Hungary	12.0	16.5	13.5
	Iceland	14.0	18.0	16.0
	Ireland	12.0	16.0	14.0
	Italy	13.0	17.0	16.0
	Japan	12.0	16.0	14.0
	Korea	12.0	16.0	14.0
	Luxembourg	13.0	17.0	16.0
	Mexico	12.0	16.0	14.0
	Netherlands	12.0	16.0	
	New Zealand	12.0	15.0	14.0
	Norway	12.0	16.0	14.0
	Poland	12.0	16.0	15.0
	Portugal	12.0	17.0	15.0
	Scotland	13.0	16.0	16.0
	Slovak Republic	12.0	17.5	13.5
	Spain	12.0	16.5	13.0
	Sweden	12.0	15.5	14.0
	Switzerland	12.5	17.5	14.5
	Turkey	11.0	15.0	13.0
	United States	12.0	16.0	14.0
Partners	Argentina	12.0	17.0	14.5
	Azerbeidjan	11.0	17.0	14.0
	Brazil	11.0	16.0	14.5
	Bulgaria	12.0	17.5	15.0
	Chile	12.0	17.0	16.0
	Colombia	11.0	15.5	14.0
	Croatia	12.0	17.0	15.0
	Estonia	12.0	16.0	15.0
	Hong Kong-China	13.0	16.0	14.0
	Indonesia	12.0	15.0	14.0
	Israel	12.0	15.0	15.0
	Jordan	12.0	16.0	14.5
	Kyrgyzstan	10.0	15.0	13.0
	Latvia	11.0	16.0	16.0
	Liechtenstein	13.0	17.0	14.0
	Lithuania	11.0	16.0	15.0
	Macao-China	12.0	16.0	15.0
	Montenegro	12.0	16.0	15.0
	Qatar	12.0	16.0	15.0
	Romania	12.5	16.0	14.0
	Russian Federation	12.0	15.0	
	Serbia	12.0	17.0	14.5
	Slovenia	12.0	16.0	15.0
	Chinese Taipei	12.0	16.0	14.0
	Thailand	12.0	16.0	14.0
	Tunisia	13.0	17.0	16.0
	Uruguay	12.0	17.0	15.0

StatLink 🔗 http://dx.doi.org/10.1787/142050165315

Cultural possessions at home

The *index of cultural possessions at home* was derived from students' reports on the availability of the following items in their home: classic literature (examples were given), books of poetry and works of art (examples were given). Scale construction was performed through IRT scaling and positive values indicate higher levels of cultural possessions. National item parameters were estimated for each country.

Learning and instruction

Grade

Data on the grade in which students are enrolled were obtained both from the Student Questionnaire and from the Student Tracking Forms. The relationship between the grade and student performance was estimated through a multilevel model accounting for the following background variables: *i)* the **PISA index of economic, social and cultural status**; *ii)* the **PISA index of economic, social and cultural status** squared; *iii)* the school mean of the **PISA index of economic, social and cultural status**; *iv)* an indicator as to whether students were foreign born (first-generation students); *v)* the percentage of first-generation students in the school; and *vi)* students' gender.

Table A1.2 presents the results of the multilevel model. Column 1 in Table A1.2 estimates the score point difference that is associated with one grade level (or school year). This difference can be estimated for the 28 OECD countries in which a sizeable number of 15-year-olds in the PISA samples were enrolled in at least two different grades. Since 15-year-olds cannot be assumed to be distributed at random across the grade levels, adjustments had to be made for the above-mentioned contextual factors that may relate to the assignment of students to the different grade levels. These adjustments are documented in columns 2 to 7 of the table. While it is possible to estimate the typical performance difference among students in two adjacent grades net of the effects of selection and contextual factors, this difference cannot automatically be equated with the progress that students have made over the last school year but should be interpreted as a lower boundary of the progress achieved. This is not only because different students were assessed but also because the content of the PISA assessment was not expressly designed to match what students had learned in the preceding school year but more broadly to assess the cumulative outcome of learning in school up to age 15. For example, if the curriculum of the grades in which 15-year-olds are enrolled mainly includes material other than that assessed by PISA (which, in turn, may have been included in earlier school years) then the observed performance difference will underestimate student progress.

In order to adjust for between-country variation the *index of relative grade* indicates whether students are at the modal grade in a country (value of 0), or whether they are below or above the modal grade (-x grades, +x grades).

Motivational factors

General interest in science

The *index of general interest in science* was derived from students' level of interest in learning the following topics: *i)* topics in physics; *ii)* topics in chemistry; *iii)* the biology of plants; *iv)* human biology; *v)* topics in astronomy; *vi)* topics in geology; *vii)* ways scientists design experiments; and *viii)* what is required for scientific explanations. A four-point scale with the response categories "high interest", "medium interest", "low interest" and "no interest" was used. All items were inverted for IRT scaling and positive values on this new index for PISA 2006 indicate higher levels of interest in science.

Enjoyment of science

The *index of enjoyment of science* was derived from students' level of agreement with the following statements: *i)* I generally have fun when I am learning <broad science> topics; *ii)* I like reading about <broad science>; *iii)* I am happy doing <broad science> problems; *iv)* I enjoy acquiring new knowledge in <broad science>; and *v)* I am interested in learning about <broad science>. A four-point scale with the response categories "strongly agree", "agree", "disagree" and "strongly disagree" was used. All items were inverted for IRT scaling and positive values on this new index for PISA 2006 indicate higher levels of enjoyment of science.

[Part 1/1]

Table A1.2 A multilevel model to estimate grade effects in science performance, after accounting for selected background variables

	Grade		PISA index of economic, social and cultural status		PISA index of economic, social and cultural status squared		School mean PISA index of economic, social and cultural status		First-generation students		Percentage of first-generation students in the school		Gender – student is a female		Intercept	
	Coef.	S.E.	Coef.	S.E.	Coef.	S.E.	Coef.	S.E.	Coef.	S.E.	Coef.	S.E.	Coef.	S.E.	Coef.	S.E.
OECD																
Australia	36.6	(2.04)	27.9	(1.51)	-2.3	(1.17)	58.1	(2.12)	-8.5	(2.45)	0.0	(0.04)	-1.5	(1.89)	512.0	(1.54)
Austria	30.3	(2.00)	6.0	(1.76)	-3.4	(1.04)	103.9	(2.56)	-48.4	(3.99)	0.1	(0.07)	-14.8	(2.81)	519.8	(2.26)
Belgium	46.2	(1.56)	12.9	(1.12)	-0.9	(0.65)	78.5	(1.85)	-21.1	(3.48)	-0.1	(0.04)	-16.9	(1.65)	527.3	(1.30)
Canada	47.1	(2.01)	21.2	(1.57)	-2.2	(1.14)	38.6	(2.15)	-15.4	(2.90)	-0.1	(0.03)	-9.2	(1.85)	529.0	(1.45)
Czech Republic	36.6	(3.40)	16.4	(1.56)	-1.7	(1.38)	116.3	(2.85)	-25.8	(9.25)	-0.6	(0.29)	-17.1	(2.83)	545.3	(2.57)
Denmark	44.0	(2.84)	26.2	(1.88)	1.7	(1.23)	26.7	(4.27)	-47.2	(6.24)	-0.2	(0.12)	-12.5	(2.68)	493.3	(2.38)
Finland	32.8	(4.04)	25.9	(1.65)	2.9	(1.43)	14.5	(3.86)	-66.3	(11.46)	-0.8	(0.24)	0.8	(2.82)	557.3	(2.19)
France	50.2	(3.76)	15.1	(1.85)	1.5	(1.28)	69.4	(3.16)	-24.7	(4.39)	0.0	(0.07)	-18.0	(2.02)	537.2	(2.07)
Germany	36.2	(1.83)	7.4	(1.58)	0.6	(0.99)	97.7	(2.08)	-32.4	(3.30)	-0.4	(0.06)	-18.6	(2.28)	498.8	(1.97)
Greece	21.9	(3.03)	14.6	(1.55)	-2.3	(1.20)	56.1	(2.03)	-0.7	(5.63)	-0.1	(0.11)	-3.8	(3.06)	486.4	(2.23)
Hungary	20.2	(1.98)	4.1	(1.35)	-0.4	(0.94)	79.3	(3.03)	-3.9	(7.83)	-1.0	(0.49)	-26.8	(2.36)	523.3	(1.46)
Iceland	c	c	30.3	(2.91)	-1.7	(1.63)	-8.8	(5.92)	-55.5	(14.29)	-0.1	(0.46)	6.3	(3.06)	479.8	(4.71)
Ireland	19.7	(1.64)	28.2	(1.88)	-0.8	(1.29)	45.8	(2.91)	-7.9	(7.71)	-0.5	(0.20)	-2.6	(3.23)	504.9	(2.84)
Italy	35.7	(2.01)	4.3	(1.04)	-1.2	(0.61)	78.5	(1.63)	-30.5	(5.54)	0.3	(0.08)	-14.5	(2.00)	504.0	(1.29)
Japan	0.0	(0.00)	5.6	(2.13)	-3.4	(2.28)	131.2	(2.33)	-32.4	(24.75)	-1.6	(0.71)	-3.3	(2.55)	536.6	(1.86)
Korea	44.0	(7.91)	8.8	(1.88)	2.3	(1.30)	82.0	(2.63)	35.3	(26.74)	17.4	(1.97)	0.3	(3.43)	520.9	(2.01)
Luxembourg	38.6	(1.64)	14.1	(1.54)	-1.8	(0.81)	60.3	(2.60)	-33.6	(3.57)	0.1	(0.07)	-12.1	(2.30)	487.5	(2.75)
Mexico	9.8	(1.80)	7.1	(1.15)	0.7	(0.49)	31.3	(0.96)	-37.2	(7.79)	-1.7	(0.14)	-13.4	(1.77)	464.8	(1.06)
Netherlands	30.4	(1.80)	5.9	(1.26)	0.4	(0.98)	121.0	(1.66)	-27.4	(5.35)	0.3	(0.05)	-17.2	(2.19)	517.2	(1.91)
New Zealand	43.4	(5.03)	39.2	(1.92)	3.5	(1.62)	58.0	(3.85)	-13.7	(4.29)	-0.2	(0.08)	-3.4	(3.99)	531.3	(2.91)
Norway	59.8	(14.97)	30.0	(2.25)	-2.8	(1.56)	26.4	(5.67)	-33.6	(7.74)	-0.2	(0.15)	3.2	(3.33)	470.6	(3.01)
Poland	76.2	(6.29)	32.2	(1.57)	0.6	(1.07)	18.0	(3.34)	-9.8	(47.14)	-4.3	(1.21)	-5.0	(2.31)	520.5	(1.92)
Portugal	50.8	(1.27)	11.2	(1.27)	1.5	(0.55)	14.8	(1.80)	-14.8	(4.93)	-0.4	(0.08)	-15.6	(2.22)	539.2	(2.06)
Slovak Republic	28.9	(5.12)	19.3	(1.78)	-2.9	(1.18)	47.1	(4.38)	-30.2	(15.86)	-0.7	(0.58)	-14.7	(2.72)	522.5	(2.73)
Spain	69.1	(1.54)	11.8	(1.17)	-2.4	(0.77)	14.1	(1.41)	-28.2	(5.40)	-0.1	(0.07)	-16.9	(1.83)	546.7	(1.44)
Sweden	56.5	(5.73)	28.6	(2.65)	-0.6	(1.40)	28.4	(6.37)	-43.6	(5.24)	-0.1	(0.10)	-1.4	(2.68)	499.0	(2.35)
Switzerland	42.6	(2.28)	17.6	(1.28)	-1.1	(0.97)	49.7	(1.99)	-47.4	(2.95)	-0.7	(0.04)	-17.1	(2.12)	538.6	(1.44)
Turkey	-1.7	(3.43)	13.7	(2.58)	2.3	(0.96)	64.4	(1.72)	-2.6	(8.16)	0.5	(0.20)	2.1	(2.60)	516.1	(2.08)
United Kingdom	34.1	(5.62)	32.2	(2.07)	-2.4	(1.49)	68.7	(2.67)	-8.5	(5.14)	-0.1	(0.06)	-9.6	(2.42)	505.6	(1.80)
United States	31.7	(2.73)	30.3	(1.90)	3.2	(1.15)	43.7	(2.82)	-20.1	(4.92)	0.0	(0.07)	-6.7	(2.58)	483.4	(2.01)
Partners																
Argentina	38.3	(2.71)	12.4	(2.07)	0.1	(1.16)	44.0	(2.49)	2.3	(9.47)	0.0	(0.21)	-1.1	(3.98)	445.9	(2.32)
Azerbaijan	5.8	(1.17)	6.2	(1.08)	0.6	(0.61)	16.7	(1.12)	-9.2	(5.59)	0.1	(0.05)	6.9	(1.57)	387.9	(1.21)
Brazil	32.8	(1.23)	9.2	(1.77)	1.2	(0.68)	34.8	(1.46)	-7.7	(6.17)	-1.2	(0.14)	-14.9	(2.18)	453.1	(1.61)
Bulgaria	17.3	(3.22)	12.3	(1.69)	-0.9	(1.10)	61.9	(4.14)	-15.8	(26.14)	-4.7	(0.75)	-3.1	(3.06)	453.4	(2.17)
Chile	34.3	(2.74)	10.7	(1.54)	0.8	(0.65)	43.9	(1.78)	-48.3	(14.58)	1.1	(0.52)	-18.2	(2.61)	490.8	(1.90)
Colombia	27.2	(1.77)	9.3	(2.53)	1.2	(0.95)	22.7	(2.47)	-9.1	(25.95)	-7.5	(0.82)	-18.2	(3.44)	443.5	(2.55)
Croatia	22.1	(2.52)	12.0	(1.47)	-2.6	(1.15)	85.4	(2.33)	-9.1	(3.08)	0.0	(0.09)	-14.4	(2.62)	508.6	(2.20)
Estonia	40.9	(2.85)	16.8	(1.58)	2.8	(1.80)	34.6	(2.90)	-4.6	(4.24)	-1.0	(0.06)	-4.5	(2.48)	550.2	(2.28)
Hong Kong-China	35.2	(1.83)	4.7	(2.42)	0.7	(1.03)	76.0	(3.28)	17.6	(3.00)	0.6	(0.07)	-22.1	(2.37)	595.2	(2.48)
Indonesia	14.6	(1.53)	3.0	(2.02)	0.7	(0.62)	34.4	(1.37)	-27.5	(15.99)	-0.6	(0.19)	-8.8	(1.46)	437.6	(2.06)
Israel	30.9	(6.01)	26.0	(2.35)	3.1	(1.53)	64.9	(3.54)	-0.2	(4.48)	0.5	(0.07)	-2.1	(4.34)	429.6	(3.20)
Jordan	61.7	(5.19)	22.5	(1.78)	3.3	(0.75)	18.7	(1.77)	6.5	(3.40)	0.3	(0.06)	19.0	(4.17)	433.4	(2.84)
Kyrgyzstan	20.9	(2.13)	6.1	(1.80)	0.8	(0.85)	64.9	(2.60)	3.2	(6.96)	2.6	(0.25)	3.7	(2.35)	356.5	(2.11)
Latvia	49.0	(3.82)	16.1	(2.13)	-0.4	(1.96)	34.0	(3.24)	-1.4	(4.76)	-0.6	(0.08)	-1.7	(2.61)	505.8	(2.55)
Liechtenstein	41.5	(7.61)	17.8	(4.98)	-6.5	(3.37)	102.8	(15.95)	-16.8	(7.38)	-0.4	(0.31)	-13.3	(6.31)	527.0	(12.38)
Lithuania	37.1	(2.99)	21.9	(1.48)	-2.9	(1.32)	44.8	(2.76)	10.1	(11.54)	-1.3	(0.16)	0.1	(2.50)	494.7	(2.03)
Macao-China	39.5	(1.33)	3.8	(2.18)	-0.7	(1.01)	3.4	(6.31)	15.1	(2.56)	0.2	(0.27)	-24.1	(2.70)	539.7	(16.36)
Montenegro	19.3	(3.56)	9.1	(1.47)	-1.4	(1.40)	62.3	(5.29)	14.9	(4.78)	-0.4	(0.27)	-9.2	(2.40)	416.1	(2.89)
Qatar	24.7	(1.81)	1.4	(1.20)	0.3	(0.80)	23.6	(2.84)	32.6	(2.44)	1.0	(0.06)	14.4	(5.46)	302.6	(4.15)
Romania	26.6	(6.64)	11.3	(2.82)	-0.6	(1.23)	55.5	(2.76)	4.1	(34.39)	17.4	(1.18)	-12.6	(2.60)	448.9	(2.03)
Russian Federation	39.1	(0.93)	18.3	(0.32)	-0.4	(0.22)	57.1	(0.58)	-24.5	(2.33)	0.2	(0.09)	-9.3	(0.47)	514.0	(0.41)
Serbia	17.2	(7.90)	10.3	(1.26)	-2.1	(1.05)	73.7	(2.66)	-3.7	(3.17)	0.4	(0.09)	-13.4	(2.15)	452.3	(1.95)
Slovenia	24.5	(5.25)	1.8	(1.44)	1.3	(1.18)	121.7	(2.87)	-32.3	(3.98)	-0.2	(0.09)	-20.5	(2.51)	504.5	(1.91)
Chinese Taipei	4.7	(2.93)	14.0	(1.39)	1.3	(1.38)	105.6	(1.87)	-43.6	(12.15)	-2.5	(0.29)	-8.9	(2.19)	578.0	(1.74)
Thailand	26.2	(2.19)	14.4	(2.37)	3.0	(0.86)	34.7	(1.67)	-44.7	(19.34)	-0.5	(0.29)	5.5	(2.12)	487.7	(1.67)
Tunisia	36.5	(1.47)	5.7	(1.58)	1.3	(0.53)	15.3	(1.74)	-16.2	(9.00)	-1.6	(0.55)	-11.1	(2.43)	443.7	(2.07)
Uruguay	34.4	(2.62)	14.9	(1.49)	2.5	(0.69)	26.7	(2.33)	-0.7	(18.15)	0.8	(0.57)	-11.5	(2.79)	471.8	(2.13)

StatLink ᵐˢᵖ http://dx.doi.org/10.1787/142050165315

Instrumental motivation in science

The **index of instrumental motivation to learn science** was derived from students' level of agreement with the following statements: *i)* making an effort in my <school science> subject(s) is worth it because this will help me in the work I want to do later on; *ii)* what I learn in my <school science> subject(s) is important for me because I need this for what I want to study later on; *iii)* I study <school science> because I know it is useful for me; *iv)* studying my <school science> subject(s) is worthwhile for me because what I learn will improve my career prospects; and *v)* I will learn many things in my <school science> subject(s) that will help me get a job. A four-point scale with the response categories "strongly agree", "agree", "disagree" and "strongly disagree" was used. All items were inverted for IRT scaling and positive values on this new index for PISA 2006 indicate higher levels of instrumental motivation to learn science.

Future-oriented motivation to learn science

The **index of future-oriented motivation to learn science** was derived from students' level of agreement with the following statements: *i)* I would like to work in a career involving <broad science>; *ii)* I would like to study <broad science> after <secondary school>; *iii)* I would like to spend my life doing advanced <broad science>; and *iv)* I would like to work on <broad science> projects as an adult. A four-point scale with the response categories "strongly agree", "agree", "disagree" and "strongly disagree" was used. All items were inverted so that positive values on this new index for PISA 2006 indicate higher levels of motivation to use science in the future.

Science self-beliefs

Self-efficacy in science

The **index of self-efficacy in science** was derived from students' beliefs in their ability to perform the following tasks on their own: *i)* recognise the science question that underlies a newspaper report on a health issue; *ii)* explain why earthquakes occur more frequently in some areas than in others; *iii)* describe the role of antibiotics in the treatment of disease; *iv)* identify the science question associated with the disposal of garbage; *v)* predict how changes to an environment will affect the survival of certain species; *vi)* interpret the scientific information provided on the labelling of food items; *vii)* discuss how new evidence can lead you to change your understanding about the possibility of life on Mars; and *viii)* identify the better of two explanations for the formation of acid rain. A four-point scale with the response categories "I could do this easily", "I could do this with a bit of effort", "I would struggle to do this on my own" and "I couldn't do this" was used. All items were inverted for IRT scaling and positive values on this new index for PISA 2006 indicate higher levels of self-efficacy in science.

Self-concept in science

The **index of self-concept in science** was derived from students' level of agreement with the following statements: *i)* learning advanced <school science> topics would be easy for me; *ii)* I can usually give good answers to <test questions> on <school science> topics; *iii)* I learn <school science> topics quickly; *iv)* <school science> topics are easy for me; *v)* when I am being taught <school science>, I can understand the concepts very well; and *vi)* I can easily understand new ideas in <school science>. A four-point scale with the response categories "strongly agree", "agree", "disagree" and "strongly disagree" was used. The items were inverted for scaling and positive values on this new index for PISA 2006 indicate a positive self-concept in science.

Value beliefs regarding science

General value of science

The **index of general value of science** was derived from students' level of agreement with the following statements: *i)* advances in <broad science and technology> usually improve people's living conditions; *ii)* <broad science> is important for helping us to understand the natural world; *iii)* advances in <broad science and technology> usually help improve the economy; *iv)* <broad science> is valuable to society; and *v)* advances in <broad science and technology> usually bring social benefits. A four-point scale with the response categories "strongly agree", "agree", "disagree" and "strongly disagree" was used. The items were inverted for scaling and positive values on this new index for PISA 2006 indicate positive student perceptions of the general value of science.

339

Personal value of science

The **index of personal value of science** was derived from students' level of agreement with the following statements: *i)* some concepts in <broad science> help me see how I relate to other people; *ii)* I will use <broad science> in many ways when I am an adult; *iii)* <broad science> is very relevant to me; *iv)* I find that <broad science> helps me to understand the things around me; *v)* when I leave school there will be many opportunities for me to use <broad science>; and *vi)* some concepts in <broad science> help me see how I relate to other people. A four-point scale with the response categories "strongly agree", "agree", "disagree" and "strongly disagree" was used. The items were inverted for scaling and positive values on this new index for PISA 2006 indicate positive student perceptions of the personal value of science.

Science activities

The **index of students' science-related activities** was derived from the frequency with which students did the following things: *i)* watch TV programmes about <broad science>; *ii)* borrow or buy books on <broad science> topics; *iii)* visit web sites about <broad science> topics; *iv)* listen to radio programmes about advances in <broad science>; *v)* read <broad science> magazines or science articles in newspapers; and *vi)* attend a <science club>. A four-point scale with the response categories "very often", "regularly", "sometimes" and "never or hardly ever" was used. The items were inverted for scaling and positive values on this new index for PISA 2006 indicate higher frequencies of students' science activities.

Scientific literacy and the environment

Awareness of environmental issues

The **index of students' awareness of environmental issues** was derived from students' beliefs regarding their own level of information on the following environmental issues: *i)* the increase of greenhouse gases in the atmosphere; *ii)* the use of genetically modified organisms (<GMO>); *iii)* acid rain; *iv)* nuclear waste; and *v)* the consequences of clearing forests for other land use. A four-point scale with the response categories "I have never heard of this", "I have heard of this but I would not be able to explain what it is really about", "I know something about this and could explain the general issue" and "I am familiar with this and I would be able to explain this well" was used. The items were inverted for scaling and positive values on this new index for PISA 2006 indicate higher levels of students' awareness of environmental issues.

Level of concern for environmental issues

The **index of students' level of concern for environmental issues** was derived from students' level of concern about the following environmental issues: *i)* air pollution; *ii)* energy shortages; *iii)* extinction of plants and animals; *iv)* clearing of forests for other land use; *v)* water shortages; and *vi)* nuclear waste. A four-point scale with the response categories "this is a serious concern for me personally as well as others", "this is a serious concern for other people in my country but not me personally", "this is a serious concern for people in other countries" and "this is not a serious concern to anyone" was used. The items were inverted for scaling and positive values on this new index for PISA 2006 indicate higher levels of students' concerns about environmental issues.

Optimism regarding environmental issues

The **index of students' optimism regarding environmental issues** was derived from students' optimism concerning the development over the next 20 years of the problems associated with the following environmental issues: *i)* air pollution; *ii)* energy shortages; *iii)* extinction of plants and animals; *iv)* clearing of forests for other land use; *v)* water shortages; and *vi)* nuclear waste. A three-point scale with the response categories "improve", "stay about the same" and "get worse" was used. The items were inverted for scaling and positive values on this new index for PISA 2006 indicate higher levels of students' optimism about environmental issues.

Responsibility for sustainable development

The **index of students' responsibility for sustainable development** was derived from students' level of agreement with the following statements: *i)* it is important to carry out regular checks on the emissions from cars as a condition of their use; *ii)* it disturbs me when energy is wasted through the unnecessary use of electrical appliances; *iii)* I am in favour of having laws that regulate factory emissions even if this would increase the price of products; *iv)* to reduce waste, the use of plastic packaging should be kept to a minimum; *v)* industries should be required to prove that they safely dispose of dangerous waste materials; *vi)* I am in favour of having laws that protect the habitats of endangered species; and *vii)* electricity should be produced from renewable sources as much as possible, even if this increases the cost. A four-point scale with the response categories "strongly agree", "agree", "disagree" and "strongly disagree" was used. The items were inverted for scaling and positive values on this new index for PISA 2006 indicate higher levels of students' responsibility for sustainable development.

Science-related careers

School preparation for science-related careers

The *index of school preparation for science-related careers* was derived from students' level of agreement with the following statements: *i)* the subjects available at my school provide students with the basic skills and knowledge for a <science-related career>; *ii)* the <school science> subjects at my school provide students with the basic skills and knowledge for many different careers; *iii)* the subjects I study provide me with the basic skills and knowledge for a <science-related career>; and *iv)* my teachers equip me with the basic skills and knowledge I need for a <science-related career>. A four-point scale with the response categories "strongly agree", "agree", "disagree" and "strongly disagree" was used. All items were inverted and positive values on this new index for PISA 2006 indicate higher levels of agreement with usefulness of schooling for this purpose.

Student information on science-related careers

The *index of student information on science-related careers* was derived from students' beliefs about their level of information about the following topics: *i)* <science-related careers> that are available in the job market; *ii)* where to find information about <science-related careers>; *iii)* the steps students need to take if they want a <science-related career>; and *iv)* employers or companies that hire people to work in <science-related careers>. A four-point scale with the response categories "very well informed", "fairly informed", "not well informed" and "not informed at all" was used. All items were inverted and positive values on this new index for PISA 2006 indicate higher levels of information about science-related careers.

Science teaching and learning

Interaction in science teaching and learning

The *index of interaction in science teaching and learning* was derived from students' responses about the frequency with which the following activities occur when learning <school science> topics at school: *i)* students are given opportunities to explain their ideas; *ii)* the lessons involve students' opinions about the topics; *iii)* there is a class debate or discussion; and *iv)* the students have discussions about the topics. A four-point scale with the response categories "in all lessons", "in most lessons", "in some lessons" and "never or hardly ever" was used. All items were inverted and positive values on this new index for PISA 2006 indicate higher frequencies of interactive science teaching.

Hands-on activities in science teaching and learning

The *index of hands-on activities in science teaching and learning* was derived from students' responses about the frequency with which the following activities occur when learning <school science> topics at school: *i)* students spend time in the laboratory doing practical experiments; *ii)* students are required to design how a <school science> question could be investigated in the laboratory; *iii)* students are asked to draw conclusions from an experiment they have conducted; and *iv)* students do experiments by following the instructions of the teacher. A four-point scale with the response categories "in all lessons", "in most lessons", "in some lessons" and "never or hardly ever" was used. All items were inverted and positive values on this new index for PISA 2006 indicate higher frequencies of this type of science teaching.

Student investigations in science teaching and learning

The *index of student investigations in science teaching and learning* was derived from students' responses about the frequency with which the following activities occur when learning <school science> topics at school: *i)* students are allowed to design their own experiments; *ii)* students are given the chance to choose their own investigations; and *iii)* students are asked to do an investigation to test out their own ideas. A four-point scale with the response categories "in all lessons", "in most lessons", "in some lessons" and "never or hardly ever" was used. All items were inverted and positive values on this new index for PISA 2006 indicate higher frequencies of this type of science teaching.

Focus on model or applications in science teaching and learning

The **index of focus on model or applications in science teaching and learning** was derived from students' responses about the frequency with which the following activities occur when learning <school science> topics at school: *i)* the teacher explains how a <school science> idea can be applied to a number of different phenomena (*e.g.* the movement of objects, substances with similar properties); *ii)* the teacher uses science to help students understand the world outside school; *iii)* the teacher clearly explains the relevance of <broad science> concepts to our lives; and *iv)* the teacher uses examples of technological application to show how <school science> is relevant to society. A four-point scale with the response categories "in all lessons", "in most lessons", "in some lessons" and "never or hardly ever" was used. All items were inverted and positive values on this new index for PISA 2006 indicate higher frequencies of this type of science teaching.

Information and Communication Technology (ICT) familiarity

ICT Internet/entertainment use

The **index of ICT Internet/entertainment use** was derived from students' responses about the frequency with which they use computers for the following reasons: *i)* browse the Internet for information about people, things, or ideas; *ii)* play games; *iii)* use the Internet to collaborate with a group or team; *iv)* download software from the Internet (including games); and *v)* download music from the Internet and *vi)* for communication (*e.g.* e-mail or "chat rooms"). A five-point scale with the response categories "almost every day", "once or twice a week", "a few times a month", "once a month or less" and "never" was used. All items were inverted and positive values on this index indicate high frequencies of ICT use.

ICT program/software use

The **index of ICT program/software use** was derived from students' responses about the frequency with which they use computers for the following reasons: *i)* write documents (*e.g.* with <Word® or WordPerfect®>); *ii)* use spreadsheets (*e.g.* <Lotus 1 2 3® or Microsoft Excel®>); *iii)* drawing, painting or using graphics programs; *iv)* use educational software such as mathematics programs; and *v)* writing computer programs. A five-point scale with the response categories "almost every day", "once or twice a week", "a few times a month", "once a month or less" and "never" was used. All items were inverted and positive values on this index indicate high frequencies of ICT use.

Self-confidence in ICT Internet tasks

The **index of self-confidence in ICT Internet tasks** was derived from students' beliefs about their ability to perform the following tasks on a computer: *i)* chat online; *ii)* search the Internet for information; *iii)* download files or programs from the Internet; *iv)* attach a file to an e-mail message; *v)* download music from the Internet; and *vi)* write and send e-mails. A four-point scale with the response categories "I can do this very well by myself", "I can do this with help from someone", "I know what this means but I cannot do it" and "I don't know what this means" was used. All items were inverted for IRT scaling and positive scores on this index indicate high self-confidence.

Self-confidence in ICT high-level tasks

The index of self-confidence in ICT high-level tasks was derived from students' beliefs about their ability to perform the following tasks on a computer: *i)* use software to find and get rid of computer viruses; *ii)* edit digital photographs or other graphic images; *iii)* create a database (*e.g.* using <Microsoft Access®>); *iv)* use a word processor (*e.g.* to write an essay for school); *v)* use a spreadsheet to plot a graph; *vi)* create a presentation (*e.g.* using <Microsoft PowerPoint®>); *vii)* create a multi-media presentation (with sound, pictures, video); and *viii)* construct a web page. A four-point scale with the response categories "I can do this very well by myself", "I can do this with help from someone", "I know what this means but I cannot do it" and "I don't know what this means" was used. All items were inverted for IRT scaling and positive values on this index indicate high self-confidence.

School-level variables

School characteristics

School size

The **index of school size** contains the total enrolment at school based on the enrolment data provided by the school principal, summing the number of males and females at a school.

Proportion of females enrolled at school

The **index of proportion of females enrolled at school** provides the proportion of females at the school based on the enrolment data provided by the school principal, dividing the number of females by the total of males and females at a school.

School type

Schools are classified as either public or private according to whether a private entity or a public agency has the ultimate power to make decisions concerning its affairs. The **index of school type** has three categories: *i)* public schools controlled and managed by a public education authority or agency; *ii)* "government-dependent" private schools which principals reported to be managed by non-governmental organisations such as churches, trade unions or business enterprises and/or having governing boards consisting mostly of members not selected by a government agency and which receive 50% or more of their core funding from government agencies; and *iii)* "government-independent" private schools which principals reported to be controlled by a non-government organisation or with a governing board not selected by a government agency which receive less than 50% of their core funding from government agencies.

Admittance policies and instructional context

Academic selectivity

School principals were asked about admittance policies at their school. The **index of academic selectivity** was constructed from principals' responses to how much consideration was given to the following factors when students were admitted to the school, based on a scale from the response categories "not considered", "considered", "high priority" or "pre-requisite": *i)* residence in a particular area; *ii)* students' academic record (including placement tests); *iii)* recommendation of feeder schools; *iv)* parents' endorsement of the instructional or religious philosophy of the school; *v)* student need or desire for a special programme; and *vi)* attendance of other family members at the school (past or present). A school was considered to have selective admittance policies if students' academic records or a recommendation from a feeder school was a high priority or a pre-requisite for admittance. It was considered a school with non-selective admittance if both factors were not considered for admittance.

Ability grouping

School principals were asked about ability grouping policies at their school. Principals were asked to indicate whether students are grouped by ability *i)* into different classes or *ii)* within their classes and whether this is the case for all subjects, for some subjects or not at all. The **index of ability grouping** was derived from assigning schools to one of three categories: *i)* schools with no ability grouping for any subjects, *ii)* schools with one of these forms of ability grouping for some subjects and *iii)* schools with one of these forms of ability grouping for all subjects.

School management

School principals were asked to report whether the principal or teachers, the < school governing board>, the < regional or local education authority > or < the national education authority > had a considerable responsibility for: *i)* selecting teachers for hire; *ii)* firing teachers; *iii)* establishing teachers' starting salaries; *iv)* determining teachers' salary increases; *v)* formulating school budgets; *vi)* deciding on budget allocations within the school; *vii)* establishing student disciplinary policies; *viii)* establishing student assessment policies; *ix)* approving students for admittance to school; *x)* choosing which textbooks to use; *xi)* determining course content; and *xii)* deciding which courses are offered. The **index of resource autonomy** was derived from the number of decisions related to school resources that are a school's responsibility (criteria *i* to *vi* above). The **index of curricular autonomy** was derived from the number of decisions that relate to curriculum that are a school's responsibility (criteria *viii, x, xi* and *xii* above).

School resources

School's educational resources

The *index of the school's educational resources* was derived from seven items measuring the school principals' perceptions of potential factors hindering instruction at school: *i)* shortage or inadequacy of science laboratory equipment; *ii)* shortage or inadequacy of instructional materials (*e.g.* textbooks); *iii)* shortage or inadequacy of computers for instruction; *iv)* lack or inadequacy of Internet connectivity; *v)* shortage or inadequacy of computer software for instruction; *vi)* shortage or inadequacy of library materials; and *vii)* shortage or inadequacy of audio-visual resources. A four-point scale with the response categories "not at all", "very little", "to some extent", and "a lot" was used. All items were inverted for scaling and positive values indicate positive evaluations of this aspect. This index was constructed using IRT scaling.

Teacher shortage

The *index on teacher shortage* was derived from items measuring the school principals' perceptions of potential factors hindering instruction at school. These factors are a lack of: *i)* qualified science teachers; *ii)* qualified mathematics teachers; *iii)* qualified <test language> teachers; and *iv)* qualified teachers of other subjects. For PISA 2006 these items were administered together with other items on the school's infrastructure. A four-point scale with the response categories "not at all", "very little", "to some extent" and "a lot" was used. The items were not inverted for scaling and positive values indicate school principals' reports of higher teacher shortage at a school. This index was constructed using IRT scaling.

School activities

School activities to promote the learning of science

The *index of school activities to promote the learning of science* was derived from school principals' responses indicating whether their school is involved in any of the following activities to promote engagement with science among students in <national modal grade for 15-year-olds>: *i)* science clubs; *ii)* science fairs; *iii)* science competitions; *iv)* extracurricular science projects (including research); and *v)* excursions and field trips. Positive values indicate higher levels of school activities in this area.

School activities for learning of environmental topics

The *index of school activities for learning of environmental topics* was derived from school principals' responses indicating whether their school organises any of the following activities to provide opportunities to students in <national modal grade for 15-year-olds> to learn about environmental topics: *i)* <outdoor education>; *ii)* trips to museums; *iii)* trips to science and/or technology centres; *iv)* extracurricular environmental projects (including research); and *v)* lectures and/or seminars (*e.g.* guest speakers). Positive values indicate higher levels of school activities in this area.

Parent variables

The following indices are based on the optional parent questionnaire, a new feature in PISA 2006 that was administered in 10 OECD and 6 partner countries/economies.[1]

Students' past science activities

The *index of students' past science activities* was derived from responses by parents of 15-year-old students regarding the frequency with which their child did the following things at age 10: *i)* watched TV programmes about science; *ii)* read books on scientific discoveries; *iii)* watched, read or listened to science fiction; *iv)* visited web sites about science topics; and *v)* attended a science club. A four-point scale with the response categories "very often", "regularly", "sometimes" and "never" was used. The items were inverted for scaling and positive values on this index indicate higher frequencies of students' past science activities.

. . . .

1. Countries participating in the optional parent questionnaire included Denmark, Germany, Iceland, Italy, Korea, Luxembourg, New Zealand, Poland, Portugal and Turkey as well as the partner countries/economies Bulgaria, Colombia, Croatia, Hong Kong-China, Macao-China and Qatar.

Parents' perception of school quality

The ***index of parents' perception of school quality*** was derived from the level of agreement by parents of 15-year-old students with the following statements: *i)* most of my child's school teachers seem competent and dedicated; *ii)* standards of achievement are high in my child's school; *iii)* I am happy with the content taught and the instructional methods used in my child's school; *iv)* I am satisfied with the disciplinary atmosphere in my child's school; *v)* my child's progress is carefully monitored by the school; *vi)* my child's school provides regular and useful information on my child's progress; and *vii)* my child's school does a good job in educating students. A four-point scale with the response categories "strongly agree", "agree", "disagree" and "strongly disagree" was used. The items were inverted for scaling and positive values on this index indicate positive evaluations of the school's quality.

Parents' views on the importance of science learning

The ***index of parents' views on the importance of science learning*** was derived from the level of agreement by parents of 15-year-old students with the following statements: *i)* it is important to have good scientific knowledge and skills in order to get any good job in today's world; *ii)* employers generally appreciate strong scientific knowledge and skills among their employees; *iii)* most jobs today require some scientific knowledge and skills; and *iv)* it is an advantage in the job market to have good scientific knowledge and skills. A four-point scale with the response categories "strongly agree", "agree", "disagree" and "strongly disagree" was used. The items were inverted for scaling and positive values on this index indicate beliefs of the greater importance of science learning.

Parents' reports on science career motivation

The ***index of parents' reports on science career motivation*** was derived from the responses by parents of 15-year-old students stating whether: *i)* the child shows an interest to work in a <science-related career>; *ii)* they expect their child will go into a <science-related career>; *iii)* their child has shown interest in studying science after completing <secondary school>; and *iv)* they expect their child will study science after completing <secondary school>. The items were inverted for scaling and positive values on this index indicate higher levels of science career motivation.

Parents' general value of science

The ***index of parents' general value of science*** was derived from the level of agreement by parents of 15-year-old students with the following statements: *i)* advances in <broad science and technology> usually improve people's living conditions; *ii)* <broad science> is important for helping us to understand the natural world; *iii)* advances in <broad science and technology> usually help improve the economy; *iv)* <broad science> is valuable to society; and *v)* advances in <broad science and technology> usually bring social benefits. A four-point scale with the response categories "strongly agree", "agree", "disagree" and "strongly disagree" was used. The items were inverted for scaling and positive values indicate positive perceptions of the general value of science.

Parents' personal value of science

The ***index of parents' personal value of science*** was derived from the level of agreement by parents of 15-year-old students with the following statements: *i)* some concepts in <broad science> help me to see how I relate to other people; *ii)* there are many opportunities for me to use <broad science> in my everyday life; *iii)* <broad science> is very relevant to me; and *iv)* I find that <broad science> helps me to understand the things around me. A four-point scale with the response categories "strongly agree", "agree", "disagree" and "strongly disagree" was used. Items were inverted for scaling and positive values indicate positive perceptions of the personal value of science.

Parents' level of concern for environmental issues

The ***index of parents' level of concern for environmental issues*** was derived from the level of concern by parents of 15-year-old students regarding the following environmental issues: *i)* air pollution; *ii)* energy shortages; *iii)* extinction of plants and animals; *iv)* clearing of forests for other land use; *v)* water shortages; and *vi)* nuclear waste. A four-point scale with the response categories "this is a serious concern for me personally as well as others", "this is a serious concern for other people in my country but not me personally", "this is a serious concern for people in other countries" and "this is not a serious concern to anyone" was used. The items were inverted for scaling and positive values on this index indicate higher levels of concerns about environmental issues.

Parents' optimism regarding environmental issues

The *index of parents' optimism regarding environmental issues* was derived from the optimism shown by parents of 15-year-old students concerning the development over the next 20 years of the problems associated with the following environmental issues: *i)* air pollution; *ii)* energy shortages; *iii)* extinction of plants and animals; *iv)* clearing of forests for other land use; *v)* water shortages; and *vi)* nuclear waste. A three-point scale with the response categories "improve", "stay about the same" and "get worse" was used. All items were inverted for scaling and positive values indicate higher levels of parents' optimism about environmental issues.

ANNEX A2

THE PISA TARGET POPULATION, THE PISA SAMPLES AND THE DEFINITION OF SCHOOLS

The definition of the PISA target population

PISA 2006 provides an assessment of the cumulative yield of education and learning at a point at which most young adults are still enrolled in initial education.

A major challenge for an international survey is to operationalise such a concept in ways that guarantee the international comparability of national target populations.

Differences between countries in the nature and extent of pre-primary education and care, the age of entry to formal schooling and the institutional structure of educational systems do not allow the definition of internationally comparable grade levels of schooling. Consequently, international comparisons of educational performance typically define their populations with reference to a target age group. Some previous international assessments have defined their target population on the basis of the grade level that provides maximum coverage of a particular age cohort. A disadvantage of this approach is that slight variations in the age distribution of students across grade levels often lead to the selection of different target grades in different countries, or between education systems within countries, raising serious questions about the comparability of results across, and at times within, countries. In addition, because not all students of the desired age are usually represented in grade-based samples, there may be a more serious potential bias in the results if the unrepresented students are typically enrolled in the next higher grade in some countries and the next lower grade in others. This would exclude students with potentially higher levels of performance in the former countries and students with potentially lower levels of performance in the latter.

In order to address this problem, PISA uses an age-based definition for its target population, *i.e.* a definition that is not tied to the institutional structures of national education systems: PISA assesses students who were aged between 15 years and 3 (complete) months and 16 years and 2 (complete) months at the beginning of the assessment period and who were enrolled in an educational institution, regardless of the grade levels or type of institution in which they were enrolled, and regardless of whether they were in full-time or part-time education (15-year-olds enrolled in Grade 6 or lower were excluded from PISA 2006, but, among the countries participating in PISA 2006, such students only exist in significant numbers in a very small number of countries). Educational institutions are generally referred to as schools in this publication, although some educational institutions (in particular some types of vocational education establishments) may not be termed schools in certain countries. As expected from this definition, the average age of students across OECD countries was 15 years and 9 months. The range in country means was 3 months and 2 days (0.26 years) from the minimum country mean of 15 years and 8 months to the maximum country mean of 15 years and 11 months.

As a result of this population definition, PISA makes statements about the knowledge and skills of a group of individuals who were born within a comparable reference period, but who may have undergone different educational experiences both within and outside schools. In PISA, these knowledge and skills are referred to as the yield of education at an age that is common across countries. Depending on countries' policies on school entry and promotion, these students may be distributed over a narrower or a wider range of grades. Furthermore, in some countries, students in PISA's target population are split between different education systems, tracks or streams.

If a country's scale scores in reading, scientific or mathematical literacy are significantly higher than those in another country, it cannot automatically be inferred that the schools or particular parts of the education system in the first country are more effective than those in the second. However, one can legitimately conclude that the cumulative impact of learning experiences in the first country, starting in early childhood and up to the age of 15 and embracing experiences both in school and at home, have resulted in higher outcomes in the literacy domains that PISA measures.

The PISA target population did not include residents attending schools in a foreign country. It does, however, include foreign nationals attending schools in the country of assessment.

To accommodate countries that desired grade-based results for the purpose of national analyses, PISA 2006 provided an international option to supplement age-based sampling with grade-based sampling.

Population coverage

All countries attempted to maximise the coverage of 15-year-olds enrolled in education in their national samples, including students enrolled in special educational institutions. As a result, PISA 2006 reached standards of population coverage that are unprecedented in international surveys of this kind.

The sampling standards used in PISA permitted countries to exclude up to a total of 5% of the relevant population either by excluding schools or by excluding students within schools. All but two countries, Canada (6.35%) and Denmark (6.07%), achieved this standard and in 32 countries the overall exclusion rate was less than 2%. When language exclusions were accounted for (*i.e.* removed from the overall exclusion rate), Denmark no longer had exclusion rates greater than 5%. For details, see *www.pisa.oecd.org*.

Exclusions within the above limits include:

- **At the school level:** *i)* schools which were geographically inaccessible or where the administration of the PISA assessment was not considered feasible; and *ii)* schools that provided teaching only for students in the categories defined under "within-school exclusions", such as schools for the blind. The percentage of 15-year-olds enrolled in such schools had to be less than 2.5% of the nationally desired target population (0.5% maximum for *i)* and 2% maximum for *ii)*). The magnitude, nature and justification of school-level exclusions are documented in the *PISA 2006 Technical Report* (OECD, forthcoming).

- **At the student level:** *i)* students with an intellectual disability; *ii)* students with a functional disability; and *iii)* students with limited assessment language proficiency. Students could not be excluded solely because of low proficiency or normal discipline problems. The percentage of 15-year-olds excluded within schools had to be less than 2.5% of the nationally desired target population.

Table A2.1 describes the target population of the countries participating in PISA 2006. Further information on the target population and the implementation of PISA sampling standards can be found in the *PISA 2006 Technical Report* (OECD, forthcoming).

- **Column 1** shows the **total number of 15-year-olds** according to the most recent available information, which in most countries meant the year 2005 as the year before the assessment.

- **Column 2** shows the number of 15-year-olds enrolled in schools in grades 7 or above (as defined above), which is referred to as the **eligible population.**

- **Column 3** shows the **national desired target population**. Countries were allowed to exclude up to 0.5% of students *a priori* from the eligible population, essentially for practical reasons. The following *a priori* exclusions exceed this limit but were agreed with the PISA Consortium: Azerbaijan excluded 5.7% of its population in occupied regions; Canada excluded 1.1% of its population from Territories and Aboriginal reserves; France excluded 3.98% of its students in its *territoires d'outre-mer* and other institutions; Indonesia excluded 4.4% of its students from four provinces because of security reasons; and Kyrgyzstan excluded 3.0% of its population in remote, inaccessible schools.

- **Column 4** shows the number of students enrolled in schools that were excluded from the national desired target population either from the sampling frame or later in the field during data collection.

- **Column 5** shows the size of the national desired target population after subtracting the students enrolled in excluded schools. This is obtained by subtracting column 4 from column 3.

- **Column 6** shows the percentage of students enrolled in excluded schools. This is obtained by dividing column 4 by column 3 and multiplying by 100.

- **Column 7** shows the **number of students participating in PISA 2006.** Note that this number does not account for 15-year-olds assessed as part of additional national options.

- **Column 8** shows the **weighted number of participating students**, *i.e.* the number of students in the nationally defined target population that the PISA sample represents.

[Part 1/2]

Table A2.1 PISA target populations and samples

		Population and sample information				
		Total population of 15-year-olds	Total enrolled population of 15-year-olds at grade 7 or above	Total in national desired target population	Total school-level exclusions	Total in national desired target population after all school-level exclusions and before within-school exclusions	School-level exclusion rate (%)
		(1)	(2)	(3)	(4)	(5)	(6)
OECD	Australia	270 115	256 754	255 554	1 371	254 183	0.54
	Austria	97 337	92 149	92 149	401	91 748	0.43
	Belgium	124 943	124 557	124 216	2 957	121 259	2.38
	Canada	426 967	428 876	424 238	5 141	419 097	1.21
	Czech Republic	127 748	124 764	124 764	1 124	123 640	0.90
	Denmark	66 989	65 984	65 984	1 871	64 113	2.84
	Finland	66 232	66 232	66 232	1 257	64 975	1.90
	France	809 375	809 375	777 194	19 397	757 797	2.50
	Germany	951 535	1 062 920	1 062 920	6 009	1 056 911	0.57
	Greece	107 505	110 663	110 663	640	110 023	0.58
	Hungary	124 444	120 061	120 061	3 230	116 831	2.69
	Iceland	4 820	4 777	4 777	16	4 761	0.33
	Ireland	58 667	57 648	57 510	50	57 460	0.09
	Italy	578 131	639 971	639 971	16	639 955	0.00
	Japan	1 246 207	1 222 171	1 222 171	16 604	1 205 567	1.36
	Korea	660 812	627 868	627 868	3 461	624 407	0.55
	Luxembourg	4 595	4 595	4 595	0	4 595	0.00
	Mexico	2 200 916	1 383 364	1 383 364	0	1 383 364	0.00
	Netherlands	197 046	193 769	193 769	57	193 712	0.03
	New Zealand	63 800	59 341	59 341	451	58 890	0.76
	Norway	61 708	61 449	61 373	412	60 961	0.67
	Poland	549 000	546 000	546 000	10 400	535 600	1.90
	Portugal	115 426	100 816	100 816	0	100 816	0.00
	Slovak Republic	79 989	78 427	78 427	1 355	77 072	1.73
	Spain	439 415	436 885	436 885	3 930	432 955	0.90
	Sweden	129 734	127 036	127 036	2 330	124 706	1.83
	Switzerland	87 766	86 108	86 108	2 130	83 978	2.47
	Turkey	1 423 514	800 968	782 875	970	781 905	0.12
	United Kingdom	779 076	767 248	767 248	12 879	754 369	1.68
	United States	4 192 939	4 192 939	4 192 939	19 710	4 173 229	0.47
Partners	Argentina	662 686	579 222	579 222	2 393	576 829	0.41
	Azerbaijan	139 119	139 119	131 235	780	130 455	0.59
	Brazil	3 390 471	2 374 044	2 357 355	0	2 357 355	0.00
	Bulgaria	89 751	88 071	88 071	1 733	86 338	1.97
	Chile	299 426	255 459	255 393	2 284	253 109	0.89
	Colombia	897 477	543 630	543 630	2 814	540 816	0.52
	Croatia	54 500	51 318	51 318	548	50 770	1.07
	Estonia	19 871	19 623	19 623	569	19 054	2.90
	Hong Kong-China	77 398	75 542	75 542	678	74 864	0.90
	Indonesia	4 238 600	3 119 393	2 983 254	9 388	2 973 866	0.31
	Israel	122 626	109 370	109 370	1 770	107 600	1.62
	Jordan	138 026	126 708	126 708	0	126 708	0.00
	Kyrgyzstan	128 810	94 922	92 109	1 617	90 492	1.76
	Latvia	34 277	33 659	33 534	932	32 602	2.78
	Liechtenstein	422	362	362	0	362	0.00
	Lithuania	53 931	51 808	51 761	613	51 148	1.18
	Macao-China	8 835	6 648	6 648	6	6 642	0.09
	Montenegro	9 190	8 973	8 973	155	8 818	1.72
	Qatar	8 053	7 865	7 865	0	7 865	0.00
	Romania	341 181	241 890	240 661	2 943	237 718	1.22
	Russian Federation	2 243 924	2 077 231	2 077 231	43 425	2 033 806	2.09
	Serbia	88 584	80 692	80 692	1 811	78 881	2.24
	Slovenia	23 431	23 018	23 018	228	22 790	0.99
	Chinese Taipei	334 391	318 691	318 691	2 972	315 719	0.93
	Thailand	895 924	727 860	727 860	7 234	720 626	0.99
	Tunisia	153 331	153 331	153 331	0	153 331	0.00
	Uruguay	52 119	40 815	40 815	97	40 718	0.24

Note: For a full explanation of the details in this table please refer to the *PISA 2006 Technical Report* (OECD, forthcoming).
StatLink ᴹˢᴾ http://dx.doi.org/10.1787/142050165315

[Part 2/2]
Table A2.1 PISA target populations and samples

		Population and sample information					Coverage indices		
		Number of participating students	Weighted number of participating students	Number of excluded students	Weighted number of excluded students	Within-school exclusion rate (%)	Overall exclusion rate (%)	Coverage Index 1: Coverage of national desired population	Coverage Index 2: Coverage of national enrolled population	Coverage Index 3: Coverage of 15-year-old population
		(7)	(8)	(9)	(10)	(11)	(12)	(13)	(14)	(15)
OECD	Australia	14 170	234 940	234	2 935	1.23	1.76	0.98	0.98	0.87
	Austria	4 927	89 925	94	1 586	1.73	2.16	0.98	0.98	0.92
	Belgium	8 857	123 161	28	401	0.32	2.70	0.97	0.97	0.99
	Canada	22 646	370 879	1 681	20 339	5.20	6.35	0.94	0.93	0.87
	Czech Republic	5 932	128 827	8	203	0.16	1.06	0.99	0.99	1.01
	Denmark	4 532	57 013	170	1 960	3.32	6.07	0.94	0.94	0.85
	Finland	4 714	61 387	135	1 650	2.62	4.47	0.96	0.96	0.93
	France	4 716	739 428	28	3 876	0.52	3.00	0.97	0.93	0.91
	Germany	4 891	903 512	37	6 017	0.66	1.22	0.99	0.99	0.95
	Greece	4 873	96 412	65	1 397	1.43	2.00	0.98	0.98	0.90
	Hungary	4 490	106 010	31	1 103	1.03	3.69	0.96	0.96	0.85
	Iceland	3 789	4 624	95	96	2.04	2.37	0.98	0.98	0.96
	Ireland	4 585	55 114	93	59 792	1.67	1.76	0.98	0.98	0.94
	Italy	21 773	520 055	363	8 984	1.70	1.70	0.98	0.98	0.90
	Japan	5 952	1 113 701	0	0	0.00	1.36	0.99	0.99	0.89
	Korea	5 176	576 669	4	625	0.11	0.66	0.99	0.99	0.87
	Luxembourg	4 567	4 733	193	9 493	3.92	3.92	0.96	0.96	1.03
	Mexico	30 971	1 190 420	49	1 221 440	0.27	0.27	1.00	1.00	0.54
	Netherlands	4 871	189 576	7	227	0.12	0.15	1.00	1.00	0.96
	New Zealand	4 823	53 398	222	58 443	3.84	4.58	0.95	0.95	0.84
	Norway	4 692	59 884	156	1 764	2.86	3.51	0.96	0.96	0.97
	Poland	5 547	515 993	18	1 685	0.33	2.22	0.98	0.98	0.94
	Portugal	5 109	90 079	112	95 300	2.05	2.05	0.98	0.98	0.78
	Slovak Republic	4 731	76 201	11	193	0.25	1.98	0.98	0.98	0.95
	Spain	19 604	381 686	557	401 848	2.65	3.52	0.96	0.96	0.87
	Sweden	4 443	126 393	122	3 471	2.67	4.46	0.96	0.96	0.97
	Switzerland	12 193	89 651	186	842	0.93	3.38	0.97	0.97	1.02
	Turkey	4 942	665 477	1	130	0.02	0.14	1.00	0.98	0.47
	United Kingdom	13 152	732 004	229	12 033	1.62	3.27	0.97	0.97	0.94
	United States	5 611	3 578 040	254	142 517	3.83	4.28	0.96	0.96	0.85
Partners	Argentina	4 339	523 048	4	636	0.12	0.53	0.99	0.99	0.79
	Azerbaijan	5 184	122 208	0	0	0.00	0.59	0.99	0.94	0.88
	Brazil	9 295	1 875 461	19	6 438	0.34	0.34	1.00	0.99	0.55
	Bulgaria	4 498	74 326	0	0	0.00	1.97	0.98	0.98	0.83
	Chile	5 235	233 526	28	1 259	0.54	1.43	0.99	0.99	0.78
	Colombia	4 478	537 262	2	541 743	0.03	0.55	0.99	0.99	0.60
	Croatia	5 213	46 523	38	382	0.81	1.87	0.98	0.98	0.85
	Estonia	4 865	18 662	50	23 580	1.10	3.97	0.96	0.96	0.94
	Hong Kong-China	4 645	75 145	1	21	0.03	0.93	0.99	0.99	0.97
	Indonesia	10 647	2 248 313	0	0	0.00	0.31	1.00	0.95	0.53
	Israel	4 584	93 347	72	1 339	1.41	3.01	0.97	0.97	0.76
	Jordan	6 509	90 267	73	1 042	1.14	1.14	0.99	0.99	0.65
	Kyrgyzstan	5 904	80 674	42	521	0.64	2.39	0.98	0.95	0.63
	Latvia	4 719	29 232	26	33 980	0.44	3.21	0.97	0.96	0.85
	Liechtenstein	339	353	3	3	0.84	0.84	0.99	0.99	0.84
	Lithuania	4 744	50 329	28	264	0.52	1.70	0.98	0.98	0.93
	Macao-China	4 760	6 417	0	0	0.00	0.09	1.00	1.00	0.73
	Montenegro	4 455	7 734	0	0	0.00	1.72	0.98	0.98	0.84
	Qatar	6 265	7 271	3	3	0.04	0.04	1.00	1.00	0.90
	Romania	5 118	223 887	0	0	0.00	1.22	0.99	0.98	0.66
	Russian Federation	5 799	1 810 856	60	20 576	1.12	3.19	0.97	0.97	0.81
	Serbia	4 798	73 907	6	78 713	0.12	2.36	0.98	0.98	0.83
	Slovenia	6 595	20 595	45	27 236	0.48	1.46	0.99	0.99	0.88
	Chinese Taipei	8 815	293 513	21	922	0.31	1.24	0.99	0.99	0.88
	Thailand	6 192	644 125	5	353	0.05	1.05	0.99	0.99	0.72
	Tunisia	4 640	138 491	2	52	0.04	0.04	1.00	1.00	0.90
	Uruguay	4 839	36 011	5	39	0.11	0.34	1.00	1.00	0.69

Note: For a full explanation of the details in this table please refer to the *PISA 2006 Technical Report* (OECD, forthcoming).
StatLink ᴍᴤ█ http://dx.doi.org/10.1787/142050165315

- Each country attempted to maximise the coverage of PISA's target population within the sampled schools. In the case of each sampled school, all eligible students, namely those 15 years of age, regardless of grade, were first listed. Sampled students who were to be excluded had still to be included in the sampling documentation, and a list drawn up stating the reason for their exclusion. ***Column 9*** indicates the **total number of excluded students**, which is further described and classified into specific categories in Table A2.2. ***Column 10*** indicates the **weighted number of excluded students,** *i.e.* the overall number of students in the nationally defined target population represented by the number of students excluded from the sample, which is also described and classified by exclusion categories in Table A2.2. Excluded students were excluded based on four categories: *i)* students with an intellectual disability – student has a mental or emotional disability and is cognitively delayed such that he/she cannot perform in the PISA testing situation; *ii)* students with a functional disability – student has a moderate to severe permanent physical disability such that he/she cannot perform in the PISA testing situation; *iii)* students with a limited assessment language proficiency – student is unable to read or speak any of the languages of the assessment in the country and would be unable to overcome the language barrier in the testing situation (typically a student who has received less than one year of instruction in the languages of the assessment may be excluded); and *iv) other* – a category defined by the national centres and approved by the international centre.

- ***Column 11*** shows the **percentage of students excluded within schools**. This is calculated as the weighted number of excluded students (column 10), divided by the weighted number of excluded and participating students (column 8 plus column 10) then multiplied by 100.

- ***Column 12*** shows the **overall exclusion rate** which represents the weighted percentage of the national desired target population excluded from PISA either through school-level exclusions or through the exclusion of students within schools. It is calculated as the school-level exclusion rate (column 6 divided by 100) plus within-school exclusion rate (column 11 divided by 100) multiplied by 1 minus the school-level exclusion rate (column 6 divided by 100). This result is then multiplied by 100. Two countries, Canada and Denmark, had exclusion rates higher than 5% (see also *www.pisa.oecd.org* for further information on these exclusions). When language exclusions were accounted for (*i.e.* removed from the overall exclusion rate), Denmark no longer had an exclusion rate greater than 5%.

- ***Column 13*** presents an index of the **extent to which the national desired target population is covered by the PISA sample**. Canada and Denmark were the only countries where the coverage is below 95%.

- ***Column 14*** presents an index of the **extent to which 15-year-olds enrolled in schools are covered by the PISA sample**. The index measures the overall proportion of the national enrolled population that is covered by the non-excluded portion of the student sample. The index takes into account both school-level and student-level exclusions. Values close to 100 indicate that the PISA sample represents the entire education system as defined for PISA 2006. The index is the weighted number of participating students (column 8) divided by the weighted number of participating and excluded students (column 8 plus column 10), times the nationally defined target population (column 5) divided by the eligible population (column 2) (times 100). The only countries where the coverage is below 95% are Canada, Denmark and France as well as the partner country Azerbaijan.

- ***Column 15*** presents an index of the **coverage of the 15-year-old population**. This index is the weighted number of participating students (column 8) divided by the total population of 15-year-old students (column 1).

This high level of coverage contributes to the comparability of the assessment results. For example, even assuming that the excluded students would have systematically scored worse than those who participated, and that this relationship is moderately strong, an exclusion rate in the order of 5% would likely lead to an overestimation of national mean scores of less than 5 score points (on a scale with an international mean of 500 score points and a standard deviation of 100 score points). This assessment is based on the following calculations: If the correlation between the propensity of exclusions and student performance is 0.3, resulting mean scores would likely be overestimated by 1 score point if the exclusion rate is 1%, by 3 score points if the exclusion rate is 5%, and by 6 score points if the exclusion rate is 10%. If the correlation between the propensity of exclusions and student performance is 0.5, resulting mean scores would be overestimated by 1 score point if the exclusion rate is 1%, by 5 score points if the exclusion rate is 5%, and by 10 score points if the exclusion rate is 10%. For this calculation, a model was employed that assumes a bivariate normal distribution for the propensity to participate and performance. For details see the *PISA 2000 Technical Report* (OECD, 2001).

[Part 1/2]
Table A2.2 **Exclusions**

		Student exclusions (Unweighted)				
		Number of excluded students with disability (Code 1)	Number of excluded students with disability (Code 2)	Number of excluded students because of language (Code 3)	Number of excluded students for other reasons (Code 4)	Total number of excluded students
		(1)	(2)	(3)	(4)	(5)
OECD	Australia	25	167	42	0	234
	Austria	1	29	64	0	94
	Belgium	2	13	13	0	28
	Canada	125	1 372	184	0	1 681
	Czech Republic	0	2	6	0	8
	Denmark	11	60	58	41	170
	Finland	5	105	25	0	135
	France	3	9	16	0	28
	Germany	3	19	15	0	37
	Greece	1	9	3	52	65
	Hungary	2	11	1	17	31
	Iceland	6	65	24	0	95
	Ireland	8	40	15	30	93
	Italy	24	270	69	0	363
	Japan	0	0	0	0	0
	Korea	0	4	0	0	4
	Luxembourg	1	24	168	0	193
	Mexico	40	6	3	0	49
	Netherlands	6	1	0	0	7
	New Zealand	25	111	82	4	222
	Norway	8	103	45	0	156
	Poland	5	7	0	6	18
	Portugal	10	90	12	0	112
	Slovak Republic	2	8	1	0	11
	Spain	40	359	158	0	557
	Sweden	8	88	26	0	122
	Switzerland	9	62	115	0	186
	Turkey	0	0	1	0	1
	United Kingdom	29	151	49	0	229
	United States	24	192	38	0	254
Partners	Argentina	3	1	0	0	4
	Azerbaijan	0	0	0	0	0
	Brazil	13	6	0	0	19
	Bulgaria	0	0	0	0	0
	Chile	16	8	4	0	28
	Colombia	1	1	0	0	2
	Croatia	6	32	0	0	38
	Estonia	6	44	0	0	50
	Hong Kong-China	0	0	1	0	1
	Indonesia	0	0	0	0	0
	Israel	22	18	32	0	72
	Jordan	38	9	26	0	73
	Kyrgyzstan	33	4	5	0	42
	Latvia	20	5	1	0	26
	Liechtenstein	0	3	0	0	3
	Lithuania	4	19	0	5	28
	Macao-China	0	0	0	0	0
	Montenegro	0	0	0	0	0
	Qatar	2	0	1	0	3
	Romania	0	0	0	0	0
	Russian Federation	6	52	2	0	60
	Serbia	1	2	3	0	6
	Slovenia	5	25	15	0	45
	Chinese Taipei	1	20	0	0	21
	Thailand	0	4	1	0	5
	Tunisia	2	0	0	0	2
	Uruguay	3	1	1	0	5

Exclusion codes:

Code 1: Functional disability – student has a moderate to severe permanent physical disability.

Code 2: Intellectual disability – student has a mental or emotional disability and has either been tested as cognitively delayed or is considered in the professional opinion of qualified staff to be cognitively delayed.

Code 3: Limited assessment language proficiency – student is not a native speaker of any of the languages of the assessment in the country and has been resident in the country for less than one year.

Code 4: Other defined by the national centres and approved by the international centre.

Note: For a full explanation of other details in this table please refer to the *PISA 2006 Technical Report* (OECD, forthcoming).
StatLink ⟨⟩ http://dx.doi.org/10.1787/142050165315

[Part 2/2]
Table A2.2 Exclusions

		Student exclusion (Weighted)				
		Weighted number of excluded students with disability (Code 1)	Weighted number of excluded students with disability (Code 2)	Number of excluded students because of language (Code 3)	Weighted number of excluded students for other reasons (Code 4)	Total weighted number of excluded students
		(6)	(7)	(8)	(9)	(10)
OECD	Australia	355	2 056	524	0	2 935
	Austria	11	576	999	0	1 586
	Belgium	38	190	173	0	401
	Canada	2 061	14 565	3 714	0	20 339
	Czech Republic	0	47	155	0	203
	Denmark	119	710	670	462	1 960
	Finland	64	1 287	299	0	1 650
	France	421	1 277	2 179	0	3 876
	Germany	418	3 000	2 599	0	6 017
	Greece	37	255	55	1 050	1 397
	Hungary	64	469	12	559	1 103
	Iceland	6	66	24	0	96
	Ireland	80	401	153	304	937
	Italy	563	6 713	1 707	0	8 984
	Japan	0	0	0	0	0
	Korea	0	625	0	0	625
	Luxembourg	1	24	168	0	193
	Mexico	2 005	659	553	0	3 217
	Netherlands	191	36	0	0	227
	New Zealand	243	1 068	792	32	2 135
	Norway	96	1 159	509	0	1 764
	Poland	468	656	0	561	1 685
	Portugal	215	1 467	208	0	1 890
	Slovak Republic	30	149	14	0	193
	Spain	441	6 354	3 591	0	10 386
	Sweden	354	2 406	711	0	3 471
	Switzerland	42	229	571	0	842
	Turkey	0	0	130	0	130
	United Kingdom	1 482	7 698	2 853	0	12 033
	United States	14 376	109 160	18 981	0	142 517
Partners	Argentina	594	41	0	0	636
	Azerbaijan	0	0	0	0	0
	Brazil	5 344	1 094	0	0	6 438
	Bulgaria	0	0	0	0	0
	Chile	734	395	130	0	1 259
	Colombia	107	78	0	0	186
	Croatia	49	332	0	0	382
	Estonia	41	167	0	0	208
	Hong Kong-China	0	0	21	0	21
	Indonesia	0	0	0	0	0
	Israel	408	327	603	0	1 339
	Jordan	481	118	443	0	1 042
	Kyrgyzstan	417	45	59	0	521
	Latvia	94	30	6	0	130
	Liechtenstein	0	3	0	0	3
	Lithuania	27	200	0	37	264
	Macao-China	0	0	0	0	0
	Montenegro	0	0	0	0	0
	Qatar	2	0	1	0	3
	Romania	0	0	0	0	0
	Russian Federation	1 724	18 393	459	0	20 576
	Serbia	14	31	41	0	86
	Slovenia	6	50	42	0	98
	Chinese Taipei	50	872	0	0	922
	Thailand	0	232	121	0	353
	Tunisia	52	0	0	0	52
	Uruguay	28	6	5	0	39

Exclusion codes:

Code 1: Functional disability – student has a moderate to severe permanent physical disability.

Code 2: Intellectual disability – student has a mental or emotional disability and has either been tested as cognitively delayed or is considered in the professional opinion of qualified staff to be cognitively delayed.

Code 3: Limited assessment language proficiency – student is not a native speaker of any of the languages of the assessment in the country and has been resident in the country for less than one year.

Code 4: Other defined by the national centres and approved by the international centre.

Note: For a full explanation of other details in this table please refer to the *PISA 2006 Technical Report* (OECD, forthcoming).
StatLink ᔥᔥ http://dx.doi.org/10.1787/142050165315

Sampling procedures and response rates

The accuracy of any survey results depends on the quality of the information on which national samples are based as well as on the sampling procedures. Quality standards, procedures, instruments and verification mechanisms were developed for PISA that ensured that national samples yielded comparable data and that the results could be compared with confidence.

Most PISA samples were designed as two-stage stratified samples (where countries applied different sampling designs, these are documented in the *PISA 2006 Technical Report* [OECD, forthcoming]). The first stage consisted of sampling individual schools in which 15-year-old students could be enrolled. Schools were sampled systematically with probabilities proportional to size, the measure of size being a function of the estimated number of eligible (15-year-old) students enrolled. A minimum of 150 schools were selected in each country (where this number existed), although the requirements for national analyses often required a somewhat larger sample. As the schools were sampled, replacement schools were simultaneously identified, in case a sampled school chose not to participate in PISA 2006.

In the case of Iceland, Liechtenstein, Luxembourg and Qatar, all schools and all eligible students within schools were included in the sample. However, since not all students in the PISA samples were assessed in all assessment areas, these national samples represent a complete census only in respect of the assessment of *scientific literacy* as the major assessment area.

Experts from the PISA Consortium performed the sample selection process for each participating country and monitored it closely in those countries where they selected their own samples.

The second stage of the selection process sampled students within sampled schools. Once schools were selected, a list of each sampled school's 15-year-old students was prepared. From this list, 35 students were then selected with equal probability (all 15-year-old students were selected if fewer than 35 were enrolled).

Data quality standards in PISA required minimum participation rates for schools as well as for students. These standards were established to minimise the potential for response biases. In the case of countries meeting these standards, it was likely that any bias resulting from non-response would be negligible, *i.e.* typically smaller than the sampling error.

A minimum response rate of 85% was required for the schools initially selected. Where the initial response rate of schools was between 65 and 85%, however, an acceptable school response rate could still be achieved through the use of replacement schools. This procedure brought with it a risk of increased response bias. Participating countries were, therefore, encouraged to persuade as many of the schools in the original sample as possible to participate. Schools with a student participation rate between 25 and 50% were not regarded as participating schools, but data from these schools were included in the database and contributed to the various estimations. Data from schools with a student participation rate of less than 25% were excluded from the database.

PISA 2006 also required a minimum participation rate of 80% of students within participating schools. This minimum participation rate had to be met at the national level, not necessarily by each participating school. Follow-up sessions were required in schools in which too few students had participated in the original assessment sessions. Student participation rates were calculated over all original schools, and also over all schools whether original sample or replacement schools, and from the participation of students in both the original assessment and any follow-up sessions. A student who participated in the original or follow-up cognitive sessions was regarded as a participant. Those who attended only the questionnaire session were included in the international database and contributed to the statistics presented in this publication if he or she provided at least a description of his or her father's or mother's occupation.

Table A2.3 shows the response rates for students and schools, before and after replacement.

- *Column 1* shows the **weighted participation rate of schools before replacement**. This is obtained by dividing column 2 by column 3.

- *Column 2* shows the **weighted number of responding schools before school replacement** (weighted by student enrolment).

[Part 1/3]
Table A2.3 Response rates

		Initial sample – before school replacement				
		Weighted school participation rate before replacement (%)	Weighted number of responding schools (weighted also by enrolment)	Weighted number of schools sampled (responding and non-responding) (weighted also by enrolment)	Number of responding schools (unweighted)	Number of responding and non-responding schools (unweighted)
		(1)	(2)	(3)	(4)	(5)
OECD	Australia	98.40	247 212	251 222	349	356
	Austria	98.77	91 471	92 606	197	203
	Belgium	81.54	100 785	123 597	236	288
	Canada	83.20	348 248	418 565	850	941
	Czech Republic	72.87	91 281	125 259	198	264
	Denmark	87.24	49 865	57 156	189	218
	Finland	100.00	65 086	65 086	155	155
	France	96.68	732 366	757 512	179	187
	Germany	98.15	932 815	950 350	223	227
	Greece	92.51	96 973	104 827	176	192
	Hungary	94.70	108 354	114 425	180	189
	Iceland	98.35	4 819	4 900	135	151
	Ireland	100.00	57 245	57 245	164	164
	Italy	90.53	564 533	623 570	753	874
	Japan	87.27	1 032 152	1 182 688	171	196
	Korea	99.24	572 256	576 637	153	155
	Luxembourg	100.00	4 955	4 955	31	31
	Mexico	95.46	1 281 867	1 342 898	1 115	1 184
	Netherlands	75.70	151 039	199 533	146	194
	New Zealand	91.69	54 182	59 090	162	179
	Norway	90.47	54 613	60 369	193	213
	Poland	95.41	507 651	532 061	209	222
	Portugal	94.87	94 835	99 961	165	174
	Slovak Republic	92.42	70 860	76 671	170	190
	Spain	98.26	416 539	423 904	682	686
	Sweden	99.59	126 611	127 133	197	199
	Switzerland	95.44	77 940	81 660	496	512
	Turkey	97.16	773 777	796 371	155	160
	United Kingdom	76.05	569 438	748 796	439	587
	United States	68.95	2 689 741	3 901 131	145	209
Partners	Argentina	95.08	547 775	576 125	168	179
	Azerbaijan	94.86	123 718	130 423	163	172
	Brazil	98.01	2 300 530	2 347 346	606	629
	Bulgaria	98.76	82 248	83 281	178	180
	Chile	83.08	207 183	249 370	161	196
	Colombia	93.53	500 567	535 166	154	167
	Croatia	98.59	48 081	48 768	159	163
	Estonia	98.98	19 071	19 267	167	169
	Hong Kong-China	68.57	52 768	76 956	106	156
	Indonesia	99.72	2 249 728	2 256 019	349	352
	Israel	89.89	95 231	105 941	139	167
	Jordan	100.00	99 088	99 088	210	210
	Kyrgyzstan	99.58	89 863	90 240	200	201
	Latvia	97.57	31 740	32 532	171	175
	Liechtenstein	100.00	362	362	12	12
	Lithuania	96.85	48 989	50 584	190	197
	Macao-China	100.00	6 608	6 608	43	43
	Montenegro	94.64	7 363	7 780	49	51
	Qatar	98.02	7 260	7 407	128	137
	Romania	100.00	231 533	231 533	174	174
	Russian Federation	100.00	1 848 221	1 848 221	209	209
	Serbia	98.67	76 534	77 568	160	163
	Slovenia	97.42	21 983	22 565	355	365
	Chinese Taipei	98.03	420 165	428 630	235	240
	Thailand	97.70	705 353	721 963	208	212
	Tunisia	100.00	153 009	153 009	152	152
	Uruguay	96.30	38 378	39 854	270	280

StatLink ⟨⟩ http://dx.doi.org/10.1787/142050165315

[Part 2/3]
Table A2.3 Response rates

		Final sample – after school replacement				
		Weighted school participation rate after replacement (%)	Weighted number of responding schools (weighted also by enrolment)	Weighted number of schools sampled (responding and non-responding) (weighted also by enrolment)	Number of responding schools (unweighted)	Number of responding and non-responding schools (unweighted)
		(6)	(7)	(8)	(9)	(10)
OECD	Australia	98.85	248 321	251 222	350	356
	Austria	98.77	91 471	92 606	197	203
	Belgium	93.59	115 646	123 563	269	288
	Canada	86.23	360 867	418 514	861	941
	Czech Republic	93.87	117 526	125 202	244	264
	Denmark	96.47	55 068	57 085	209	218
	Finland	100.00	65 086	65 086	155	155
	France	96.68	732 366	757 512	179	187
	Germany	99.05	941 356	950 350	225	227
	Greece	99.35	104 124	104 810	189	192
	Hungary	100.00	114 266	114 266	189	189
	Iceland	98.35	4 819	4 900	135	151
	Ireland	100.00	57 245	57 245	164	164
	Italy	97.47	607 860	623 619	796	874
	Japan	92.38	1 092 616	1 182 688	181	196
	Korea	99.89	575 984	576 637	154	155
	Luxembourg	100.00	4 955	4 955	31	31
	Mexico	96.20	1 291 872	1 342 898	1 128	1 184
	Netherlands	94.25	187 953	199 423	183	194
	New Zealand	96.06	56 762	59 090	170	179
	Norway	95.40	57 582	60 359	203	213
	Poland	99.99	532 150	532 197	221	222
	Portugal	98.73	98 593	99 863	172	174
	Slovak Republic	99.93	76 865	76 920	188	190
	Spain	100.00	424 621	424 621	686	686
	Sweden	99.59	126 611	127 133	197	199
	Switzerland	99.09	81 345	82 095	509	512
	Turkey	100.00	794 826	794 826	160	160
	United Kingdom	88.15	660 503	749 270	494	587
	United States	79.09	3 085 548	3 901 521	166	209
Partners	Argentina	96.19	554 186	576 125	171	179
	Azerbaijan	99.37	129 952	130 775	171	172
	Brazil	99.24	2 329 154	2 346 988	617	629
	Bulgaria	99.35	82 548	83 092	179	180
	Chile	87.89	219 082	249 283	173	196
	Colombia	99.22	530 585	534 764	165	167
	Croatia	99.80	48 727	48 823	161	163
	Estonia	100.00	19 261	19 261	169	169
	Hong Kong-China	93.76	72 564	77 392	146	156
	Indonesia	100.00	2 256 019	2 256 019	352	352
	Israel	93.45	99 541	106 520	149	167
	Jordan	100.00	99 088	99 088	210	210
	Kyrgyzstan	100.00	90 240	90 240	201	201
	Latvia	100.00	32 532	32 532	175	175
	Liechtenstein	100.00	362	362	12	12
	Lithuania	100.00	50 584	50 584	197	197
	Macao-China	100.00	6 608	6 608	43	43
	Montenegro	94.64	7 363	7 780	49	51
	Qatar	98.02	7 260	7 407	128	137
	Romania	100.00	231 533	231 533	174	174
	Russian Federation	100.00	1 848 221	1 848 221	209	209
	Serbia	99.96	77 539	77 568	162	163
	Slovenia	97.71	22 049	22 565	356	365
	Chinese Taipei	98.10	420 394	428 529	236	240
	Thailand	100.00	721 552	721 552	212	212
	Tunisia	100.00	153 009	153 009	152	152
	Uruguay	96.30	38 378	39 854	270	280

StatLink http://dx.doi.org/10.1787/142050165315

[Part 3/3]
Table A2.3 Response rates

		Final sample – students within schools after school replacement			
		Weighted student participation rate after replacement (%)	Number of students assessed (weighted)	Number of students sampled (assessed and absent) (weighted)	Number of students assessed (unweighted)	Number of students sampled (assessed and absent) (unweighted)
		(11)	(12)	(13)	(14)	(15)
OECD	Australia	86.30	200 410	232 221	14 071	16 590
	Austria	90.81	80 765	88 942	4 925	5 542
	Belgium	92.98	107 247	115 343	8 857	9 492
	Canada	81.43	258 789	317 822	22 201	26 329
	Czech Republic	90.62	110 435	121 869	5 927	6 560
	Denmark	89.51	49 249	55 018	4 510	5 035
	Finland	92.78	56 954	61 387	4 714	5 082
	France	89.78	641 681	714 695	4 684	5 218
	Germany	92.26	825 350	894 612	4 884	5 294
	Greece	95.24	91 494	96 070	4 871	5 116
	Hungary	93.12	98 716	106 010	4 490	4 823
	Iceland	83.32	3 781	4 538	3 781	4 538
	Ireland	83.75	46 160	55 114	4 585	5 469
	Italy	92.30	467 291	506 270	21 753	23 465
	Japan	99.55	1 028 039	1 032 727	5 952	5 971
	Korea	99.04	570 786	576 314	5 176	5 229
	Luxembourg	96.49	4 567	4 733	4 567	4 733
	Mexico	96.40	1 101 670	1 142 760	30 885	32 119
	Netherlands	90.15	161 900	179 592	4 848	5 375
	New Zealand	87.03	44 638	51 291	4 823	5 535
	Norway	87.81	50 232	57 205	4 692	5 345
	Poland	91.70	473 144	515 945	5 547	6 074
	Portugal	86.74	77 053	88 828	5 092	5 862
	Slovak Republic	93.19	70 837	76 011	4 729	5 095
	Spain	88.48	337 710	381 686	19 604	21 328
	Sweden	91.37	115 210	126 095	4 443	4 851
	Switzerland	94.94	84 366	88 861	12 191	12 778
	Turkey	97.59	649 451	665 477	4 942	5 057
	United Kingdom	87.65	565 955	645 688	13 050	15 182
	United States	91.00	2 589 680	2 845 841	5 611	6 179
Partners	Argentina	89.31	447 966	501 589	4 297	4 854
	Azerbaijan	98.02	119 024	121 433	5 184	5 284
	Brazil	90.83	1 692 354	1 863 114	9 246	10 408
	Bulgaria	94.47	69 821	73 907	4 498	4 768
	Chile	93.72	192 205	205 089	5 233	5 585
	Colombia	93.89	500 459	533 020	4 478	4 787
	Croatia	95.63	44 400	46 431	5 213	5 455
	Estonia	94.89	17 708	18 662	4 865	5 119
	Hong Kong-China	91.51	64 124	70 071	4 645	5 073
	Indonesia	97.81	2 199 184	2 248 313	10 647	10 918
	Israel	90.57	79 246	87 498	4 584	5 058
	Jordan	96.26	86 890	90 267	6 509	6 791
	Kyrgyzstan	97.08	78 319	80 674	5 904	6 074
	Latvia	96.66	28 255	29 232	4 719	4 885
	Liechtenstein	96.03	339	353	339	353
	Lithuania	93.76	47 189	50 329	4 744	5 061
	Macao-China	97.57	6 261	6 417	4 760	4 882
	Montenegro	93.23	6 821	7 317	4 367	4 681
	Qatar	87.34	6 224	7 126	6 224	7 126
	Romania	99.83	223 503	223 887	5 118	5 129
	Russian Federation	96.02	1 738 842	1 810 856	5 799	6 036
	Serbia	93.91	69 375	73 877	4 798	5 112
	Slovenia	91.50	18 489	20 206	6 576	7 194
	Chinese Taipei	97.75	283 168	289 675	8 815	8 988
	Thailand	98.74	636 028	644 125	6 192	6 266
	Tunisia	94.53	130 922	138 491	4 640	4 905
	Uruguay	88.24	30 693	34 784	4 779	5 380

StatLink ⛓ http://dx.doi.org/10.1787/142050165315

- *Column 3* shows the **weighted number of sampled schools before school replacement** (including both responding and non responding schools) (weighted by student enrolment).

- *Column 4* shows the **unweighted number of responding schools before school replacement**.

- *Column 5* shows the **unweighted number of responding and non responding schools before school replacement**.

- *Column 6* shows the **weighted participation rate of schools after replacement**. This is obtained by dividing column 7 by column 8.

- *Column 7* shows the **weighted number of responding schools after school replacement** (weighted by student enrolment).

- *Column 8* shows the **weighted number of schools sampled after school replacement** (including both responding and non-responding schools) (weighted by student enrolment).

- *Column 9* shows the **unweighted number of responding schools after school replacement**.

- *Column 10* shows the **unweighted number of responding and non responding schools after school replacement**.

- *Column 11* shows the **weighted student participation rate after replacement**. This is obtained by dividing column 12 by column 13.

- *Column 12* shows the **weighted number of students assessed.**

- *Column 13* shows the **weighted number of students sampled** (including both students that were assessed and students who were absent on the day of the assessment).

- *Column 14* shows the **unweighted number of students assessed.** Note that any students in schools with student response rates less than 50% were not included in these rates (both weighted and unweighted).

- *Column 15* shows the **unweighted number of students sampled** (including both students that were assessed and students who were absent on the day of the assessment). Note that any students in schools where fewer than half of the eligible students were assessed, were not included in these rates (neither weighted nor unweighted).

Definition of schools

In some countries, sub-units within schools were sampled instead of schools and this may affect the estimation of the between-school variance components. In Austria, the Czech Republic, Hungary, Italy and Japan, and the partner countries Romania and Slovenia, schools with more than one study programme were split into the units delivering these programmes. In the Netherlands, for schools with both lower and upper secondary programmes, schools were split into units delivering each programme level. In the partner country Uruguay, schools where instruction is delivered in shifts were split into the corresponding units. In the Flemish Community of Belgium, in case of multi-campus schools, implantations (campuses) were sampled whereas in the French part, in case of multi-campus schools the larger administrative units were sampled. In Australia, for schools with more than one campus, the individual campuses were listed for sampling. In Argentina, schools that had more than one campus had the locations listed for sampling. In the Slovak Republic, in the case of schools with both Slovak and Hungarian offered as the language of instruction, schools were split into units delivering each language of instruction. In Spain, the schools in the Basque region with multi-linguistic models were split into linguistic models for sampling.

ANNEX A3

STANDARD ERRORS, SIGNIFICANCE TESTS AND SUBGROUP COMPARISONS

The statistics in this report represent estimates of national performance based on samples of students rather than values that could be calculated if every student in every country had answered every question. Consequently, it is important to have measures of the degree of uncertainty of the estimates. In PISA, each estimate has an associated degree of uncertainty, which is expressed through a standard error. The use of confidence intervals provides a way to make inferences about the population means and proportions in a manner that reflects the uncertainty associated with the sample estimates. From an observed sample statistic it can, under the assumption of a normal distribution, be inferred that the corresponding population result would lie within the confidence interval in 95 out of 100 replications of the measurement on different samples drawn from the same population.

In many cases, readers are primarily interested in whether a given value in a particular country is different from a second value in the same or another country, *e.g.* whether females in a country perform better than males in the same country. In the tables and charts used in this report, differences are labelled as statistically significant when a difference of that size, smaller or larger, would be observed less than 5% of the time, if there was actually no difference in corresponding population values. Similarly, the risk of reporting a correlation as significant if there is, in fact, no correlation between two measures, is contained at 5%.

Throughout the report, significance tests were undertaken to assess the statistical significance of the comparisons made.

Differences in performance between PISA 2000, PISA 2003 and PISA 2006

Differences in average performance between PISA 2000, PISA 2003 and PISA 2006 were tested for statistical significance. Figures marked in bold indicate that performance between PISA 2000, PISA 2003 and PISA 2006 is statistically significantly different at the 95% confidence level. Figures marked in bold and italic indicate that performance between PISA 2000, PISA 2003 and PISA 2006 is statistically significantly different at the 90% confidence level. See Annex A7 for notes on the interpretation of differences between the PISA 2000, PISA 2003 and PISA 2006 assessments.

Gender differences

Gender differences in student performance or other indices were tested for statistical significance. Positive differences indicate higher scores for males while negative differences indicate higher scores for females. Generally, differences marked in bold in the data tables in Volume 2 of this report are statistically significant at the 95% confidence level.

Performance differences between top and bottom quartiles

Differences in average performance between the top quarter and the bottom quarter on the PISA indices were tested for statistical significance. Figures marked in bold indicate that performance between the top and bottom quarter of students on the respective index is statistically significantly different at the 95% confidence level.

Change in the performance per unit of the index

For many tables, the difference in student performance per unit of the index shown was calculated. Figures in bold indicate that the differences are statistically significantly different from zero at the 95% confidence level.

Relative risk or increased likelihood

The relative risk is a measure of association between an antecedent factor and an outcome factor. The relative risk is simply the ratio of two risks, *i.e.* the risk of observing the outcome when the antecedent is present and the risk of observing the outcome when the antecedent is not present. Figure A3.1 presents the notation that is used in the following.

Figure A3.1
Labels used in a two-way table

p_{11}	p_{12}	$p_{1.}$
p_{21}	p_{22}	$p_{2.}$
$p_{.1}$	$p_{.2}$	$p_{..}$

$p_{..}$ is equal to $\frac{n_{..}}{n_{..}}$, with $n_{..}$ the total number of students and $p_{..}$ is therefore equal to 1, $P_{i.}$, $P_{.j}$ respectively represent the marginal probabilities for each row and for each column. The marginal probabilities are equal to the marginal frequencies divided by the total number of students. Finally, the P_{ij} represent the probabilities for each cell and are equal to the number of observations in a particular cell divided by the total number of observations.

In PISA, the rows represent the antecedent factor with the first row for "having the antecedent" and the second row for "not having the antecedent" and the columns represent the outcome with, the first column for "having the outcome" and the second column for "not having the outcome". The relative risk is then equal to:

$$RR = \frac{(p_{11} / p_{1.})}{(p_{21} / p_{2.})}$$

Figures in bold in the data tables presented in Volume 2 of this report indicate that the relative risk is statistically significantly different from 1 at the 95% confidence level.

Differences in percentages between PISA 2000, PISA 2003 and PISA 2006

Where percentages are compared between the PISA 2000, PISA 2003 and PISA 2006 samples, differences were tested for statistical significance. Figures in bold in the data tables presented in Volume 2 of this report indicate statistically significantly different percentages at the 95% confidence level. When comparing data between PISA 2003 and PISA 2000, it should be borne in mind that in PISA 2000 school principals were asked to report with regard to the situation of 15-year-olds in their school whereas in PISA 2003 school principals were asked to reflect the situation in the entire school in their responses. Similarly, in PISA 2000 students were asked to reflect the situation in their language classes whereas in PISA 2003 they were asked to reflect the situation in their mathematics classes. In PISA 2006 students and principals were asked questions similar to those in PISA 2003, except that the focus was on science instead of mathematics.

Difference in the science performance between public and private schools

Differences in the performance between public and private schools were tested for statistical significance. For this purpose, government-dependent and government-independent private schools were jointly considered. Positive differences represent higher scores for public schools while negative differences represent higher scores for private schools. Figures in bold in the data tables presented in Volume 2 of this report indicate statistically significant different scores at the 95% confidence level.

Difference in the science performance between native students and students with an immigrant background

Differences in the performance between native and non-native students were tested for statistical significance. For this purpose, first-generation and second-generation students were jointly considered. Positive differences represent higher scores for native students, while negative differences represent higher scores for first-generation and second-generation students. Figures in bold in the data tables presented in Volume 2 of this report indicate statistically significantly different scores at the 95% confidence level.

Effect sizes

Sometimes it is useful to compare differences in an index between groups, such as males and females, across countries. A problem that may occur in such instances is that the distribution of the index varies across countries. One way to resolve this is to calculate an effect size that accounts for differences in the distributions. An effect size measures the difference between, say, the self-efficacy in science of male and female students in a given country, relative to the average variation in self-efficacy in science scores among male and female students in the country.

An effect size also allows a comparison of differences across measures that differ in their metric. For example, it is possible to compare effect sizes between the PISA indices and the PISA test scores, as when, for example, gender differences in performance in science are compared with the gender differences in several of the indices.

In accordance with common practices, effect sizes less than 0.20 are considered small in this volume, effect sizes in the order of 0.50 are considered medium, and effect sizes greater than 0.80 are considered large. Many comparisons in this report consider differences only if the effect sizes are equal to or greater than 0.20, even if smaller differences are still statistically significant; figures in bold in the data tables presented in volume 2 of this report indicate values equal to or greater than 0.20. Values smaller than 0.20 but that due to rounding are shown as 0.20 in tables and figures have not been highlighted. Light shading represents the absolute value of effect size is equal or more than 0.2 and less than 0.5; medium shading represents the absolute value of effect size is equal or more than 0.5 and less than 0.8; and dark shading represents the absolute value of effect size is equal or more than 0.8.

The effect size between two subgroups is calculated as:

$$\frac{m_1 - m_2}{\sqrt{\dfrac{\sigma_1^2 + \sigma_2^2}{2}}}$$

m_1 and m_2 respectively represent the mean values for the subgroups 1 and 2. σ_1^2 and σ_2^2 respectively represent the values of variance for the subgroups 1 and 2. The effect size between the two subgroups 1 and 2 is calculated as dividing the mean difference between the two subgroups ($m_1 - m_2$), by the square root of the sum of the subgroup's variance ($\sigma_1^2 + \sigma_2^2$) divided by 2.

Skewness of a distribution

The skewness for the distribution of socio-economic background was calculated. Negative values for the skewness indicate a longer tail of students from disadvantaged socio-economic background while positive values indicate a longer tail of students from advantaged socio-economic backgrounds.

Results from the United States

In the United States an error in printing the test booklets, in which the pagination was changed and instructions for some reading items directed students to the wrong page, may have affected student performance. The potential impact of the printing error on student performance was estimated by examining the relative performance of students in the United States on the item set that was common between PISA 2006 and PISA 2003, after controlling for performance on the items that were not likely to be affected by the printing error.

The predicted effect of the printing error on student mean performance on the mathematics and science tests was one score point. Mathematics and science performance data for the United States, therefore, have been retained.

The predicted effect of the printing error and the wrong directions on student mean performance on the reading test was up to 6 score points, and thus exceeds one standard error of sampling. Reading performance data for the United States are therefore excluded from this publication and the PISA database.

ANNEX A4
QUALITY ASSURANCE

Quality assurance procedures were implemented in all parts of PISA 2006, as was also done in all previous PISA surveys.

The consistent quality and linguistic equivalence of the PISA 2006 assessment instruments were facilitated by providing countries with equivalent source versions of the assessment instruments in English and French and requiring countries (other than those assessing students in English and French) to prepare and consolidate two independent translations using both source versions. Precise translation and adaptation guidelines were supplied, also including instructions for the selection and training of the translators. For each country, the translation and format of the assessment instruments (including test materials, marking guides, questionnaires and manuals) were verified by expert translators appointed by the PISA Consortium (whose mother tongue was the language of instruction in the country concerned and who were knowledgeable about education systems) before they were used in the PISA 2006 Field Trial and Main Study. For further information on the PISA translation procedures see the *PISA 2006 Technical Report* (OECD, forthcoming).

The survey was implemented through standardised procedures. The PISA Consortium provided comprehensive manuals that explained the implementation of the survey, including precise instructions for the work of School Co-ordinators and scripts for Test Administrators for use during the assessment sessions. Proposed adaptations to survey procedures, or proposed modifications to the assessment session script, were submitted to the PISA Consortium for approval prior to verification. The PISA Consortium then verified the national translation and adaptation of these manuals.

To establish the credibility of PISA as valid and as unbiased and to encourage uniformity in the administration of the assessment sessions, Test Administrators in participating countries were selected using the following criteria: it was required that the Test Administrator not be the reading, mathematics or science instructor of any students in the sessions he or she would administer for PISA; it was recommended that the Test Administrator not be a member of the staff of any school where he or she would administer for PISA; and it was considered preferable that the Test Administrator not be a member of the staff of any school in the PISA sample. Participating countries organised an in-person training session for Test Administrators.

Participating countries were required to ensure that: Test Administrators worked with the School Co-ordinator to prepare the assessment session, including updating student tracking forms and identifying excluded students; no extra time was given for the cognitive items (while it was permissible to give extra time for the student questionnaire); no instrument was administered before the two one-hour parts of the cognitive session; Test Administrators recorded the student participation status on the student tracking forms and filled in a Session Report Form; no cognitive instrument was permitted to be photocopied; no cognitive instrument could be viewed by school staff before the assessment session; and that Test Administrators returned the material to the national centre immediately after the assessment sessions.

National Project Managers were encouraged to organise a follow-up session when more than 15% of the PISA sample was not able to attend the original assessment session.

National Quality Monitors from the PISA Consortium visited all national centres to review data-collection procedures. Finally, School Quality Monitors from the PISA Consortium visited a sample of 15 schools during the assessment. For further information on the field operations see the *PISA 2006 Technical Report* (OECD, forthcoming).

Marking procedures were designed to ensure consistent and accurate application of the marking guides outlined in the PISA Operations manuals. National Project Managers were required to submit proposed modifications to these procedures to the Consortium for approval. Reliability studies to analyse the consistency of marking were implemented, these are discussed in more detail below.

Software specially designed for PISA facilitated data entry, detected common errors during data entry, and facilitated the process of data cleaning. Training sessions familiarised National Project Managers with these procedures.

For a description of the quality assurance procedures applied in PISA and the results see the *PISA 2006 Technical Report* (OECD, forthcoming).

ANNEX A5

DEVELOPMENT OF THE PISA ASSESSMENT INSTRUMENTS

The development of the PISA 2006 assessment instruments was an interactive process between the PISA Consortium, various international expert groups working under the auspices of the OECD, the PISA Governing Board and national experts. A panel of international experts led, in close consultation with participating countries, the identification of the range of skills and competencies in the respective assessment domains that were considered to be crucial for an individual's capacity to fully participate in and contribute to a successful modern society. A description of the assessment domains – the assessment framework – was then used by participating countries, and other test development professionals, as they contributed assessment materials. The development of this assessment framework involved the following steps:

- Development of a working definition for the assessment area and description of the assumptions that underlay that definition;

- Evaluation of how to organise the set of tasks constructed in order to report to policy-makers and researchers on performance in each assessment area among 15-year-old students in participating countries;

- Identification of a set of key characteristics to be taken into account when assessment tasks were constructed for international use;

- Operationalisation of the set of key characteristics to be used in test construction, with definitions based on existing literature and the experience of other large-scale assessments;

- Validation of the variables, and assessment of the contribution which each made to the understanding of task difficulty in participating countries; and

- Preparation of an interpretative scheme for the results.

The frameworks were agreed at both scientific and policy levels and subsequently provided the basis for the development of the assessment instruments. The frameworks are described in *Assessing Scientific, Reading and Mathematical Literacy: A Framework for PISA 2006* (OECD 2006a). They provided a common language and a vehicle for participating countries to develop a consensus as to the measurement goals of PISA.

Assessment items were then developed to reflect the intentions of the frameworks and were piloted in a Field Trial in all participating countries before a final set of items was selected for the PISA 2006 Main Study. Tables A5.1, A5.2 and A5.3 show the distribution of PISA 2006 assessment items according to the various dimensions of the PISA frameworks.

Due attention was paid to reflecting the national, cultural and linguistic variety among OECD countries. As part of this effort the PISA Consortium used professional test item development teams in several different countries. In addition to the items that were developed by the international experts working with the PISA Consortium, assessment material was contributed by participating countries. The Consortium's multi-national team of test developers deemed a substantial amount of this submitted material as appropriate given the requirements laid out by the PISA assessment frameworks. As a result, the item pool included assessment items from Australia, Austria, Belgium, Canada, the Czech Republic, Finland, France, Germany, Greece, Italy, Korea, the Netherlands, New Zealand, Norway, Sweden and Switzerland.

Each item included in the assessment pool was rated by each country: *i)* for potential cultural, gender or other bias; *ii)* for relevance to 15-year-olds in school and non-school contexts; and *iii)* for familiarity and level of interest. A first consultation of countries on the item pool was undertaken as part of the process of developing the Field Trial assessment instruments. A second consultation was undertaken after the Field Trial to assist in the final selection of items for the Main Study.

Following the Field Trial, in which all items were tested in all participating countries, test developers and expert groups considered a variety of aspects in selecting the items for the Main Study: *i)* the results from the Field Trial, *ii)* the outcome of the item review from countries, and *iii)* queries received during the Field Trial marking process. The test developers and expert groups selected a final set of items in October 2005 which, following a period of negotiation, was adopted by participating countries at both scientific and policy levels.

[Part 1/1]

Table A5.1   Distribution of items by the dimensions of the PISA framework for the assessment of science

Context	Number of items	Number of multiple-choice items	Number of complex multiple-choice items	Number of closed-constructed response items	Number of open-constructed response items	Number of short response items
Distribution of science items by content area						
Knowledge of science "Physical systems"	17	8	3	2	4	0
Knowledge of science "Living systems"	25	9	7	1	8	0
Knowledge of science "Earth and space"	12	5	2	1	4	0
Knowledge of science "Technology systems"	8	2	3	0	3	0
Knowledge about science "Scientific enquiry"	25	9	10	0	6	0
Knowledge about science "Scientific explanations"	21	5	4	1	11	0
Total	**108**	**38**	**29**	**5**	**36**	**0**
Distribution of science items by science competencies						
Identifying scientific issues	24	9	10	0	5	0
Explaining phenomena scientifically	53	22	11	4	16	0
Using scientific evidence	31	7	8	1	15	0
Total	**108**	**38**	**29**	**5**	**36**	**0**
Distribution of science items by situation or context						
Personal	29	13	6	4	6	0
Social	59	21	16	0	22	0
Global	20	4	7	1	8	0
Total	**108**	**38**	**29**	**5**	**36**	**0**

StatLink ᴍˢᴾ http://dx.doi.org/10.1787/142050165315

[Part 1/1]

Table A5.2   Distribution of items by the dimensions of the PISA framework for the assessment of *reading literacy*

Context	Number of items	Number of multiple-choice items	Number of complex multiple-choice items	Number of closed-constructed response items	Number of open-constructed response items	Number of short response items
Distribution of reading items by format						
Continuous texts	18	8	1	0	9	0
Non-continuous texts	10	1	0	4	1	4
Total	**28**	**9**	**1**	**4**	**10**	**4**
Distribution of reading items by type of reading task						
Retrieve information	8	1	1	3	0	3
Interpret texts	13	8	0	1	3	1
Reflect on and evaluate texts	7	0	0	0	7	0
Total	**28**	**9**	**1**	**4**	**10**	**4**
Distribution of reading items by the situation or the use for which the text was constructed						
Reading for private use (personal)	6	2	0	1	3	0
Reading for public use	7	1	0	2	3	1
Reading for work (occupational)	7	1	1	1	2	2
Reading for education	8	5	0	0	2	1
Total	**28**	**9**	**1**	**4**	**10**	**4**

StatLink ᴍˢᴾ http://dx.doi.org/10.1787/142050165315

The Main Study included 37 science units with 108 test items and 32 embedded attitude questions. 13 of these units originated from material submitted by participating countries. 23 of the units came from one of the Consortium teams, and one originated as TIMSS material. The Main Study instruments also included 31 mathematics units (48 items) and eight reading units (28 items).

[Part 1/1]

Table A5.3 Distribution of items by the dimensions of the PISA framework for the assessment of mathematics

Context	Number of items	Number of multiple-choice items	Number of complex multiple-choice items	Number of closed-constructed response items	Number of open-constructed response items	Number of short response items
Distribution of mathematics items by topic						
Change and relationships	13	1	2	2	7	1
Quantity	13	3	2	2	0	6
Space and shape	11	3	2	2	3	1
Uncertainty	11	5	3	0	1	2
Total	48	12	9	6	11	10
Distribution of mathematics items by competency cluster						
Reproduction	11	5	0	2	2	2
Connections	24	3	7	2	4	8
Reflection	13	4	2	2	5	0
Total	48	12	9	6	11	10
Distribution of mathematics items by situation or context						
Personal	9	3	2	1	1	2
Public	18	7	2	3	3	3
Occupational	1	0	0	0	0	1
Educational	7	1	3	2	1	0
Scientific	12	1	2	0	5	4
Intra-mathematical	1	0	0	0	1	0
Total	48	12	9	6	11	10

StatLink ⟨⟩ http://dx.doi.org/10.1787/142050165315

Five item types were used in the PISA assessment instruments:

- *Open-constructed response items:* These items required students to construct a longer response, allowing for the possibility of a broad range of divergent, individual responses and differing viewpoints. These items usually asked students to relate information or ideas in the stimulus text to their own experience or opinions, with the acceptability depending less on the position taken by the student than on the ability to use what they had read when justifying or explaining that position. Partial credit was often permitted for partially correct or less sophisticated answers, and all of these items were marked by hand.

- *Closed-constructed response items:* These items required students to construct their own responses, there being a limited range of acceptable answers. Most of these items were scored dichotomously with a few items included in the marking process.

- *Short-response items:* These items required students to provide a brief answer, as in the closed-constructed response items, but here there was a wider range of possible answers. These items were marked by hand, thus allowing for dichotomous, as well as partial, credit.

- *Complex multiple-choice items:* These items required students to make a series of choices, usually binary. Students indicated their answer by circling a word or short phrase (for example "yes" or "no") for each point. These items were scored dichotomously for each choice, yielding the possibility of full or partial credit for the whole item.

- *Multiple-choice items:* These items required students to circle a letter to indicate one choice among four or five alternatives, each of which might be a number, a word, a phrase or a sentence. They were scored dichotomously.

PISA 2006 was designed to yield group-level information in a broad range of content. The PISA assessment of science included material allowing for a total of 210 minutes of assessment time. The mathematics assessment included 120 minutes of assessment time while the reading assessment included 60 minutes of assessment time. Each student, however, sat assessments lasting a total of 120 minutes.

In order to cover the intended broad range of content while meeting the limit of 120 minutes of individual assessment time, the assessment in each assessment area was divided into clusters, organised into thirteen booklets. There were seven 30-minute science clusters, four 30-minute clusters for mathematics and two 30-minute clusters for reading. This means that in PISA 2006, every student answered some science items as part of the assessment.

This assessment design was balanced so that each item cluster appeared four times, once in each of four possible locations in a booklet. Further, each cluster appeared once with each other cluster. The final design, therefore, ensured that a representative sample responded to each cluster of items.

For further information on the development of the PISA assessment instruments and the PISA assessment design, see the *PISA 2006 Technical Report* (OECD, forthcoming).

ANNEX A6

RELIABILITY OF THE CODING OF RESPONSES TO OPEN-ENDED ITEMS

The process of coding responses to open-ended items was an important step in ensuring the quality and comparability of PISA results.

Detailed guidelines contributed to a response coding process that was accurate and consistent across countries. The coding guidelines consisted of coding manuals, training materials for recruiting coders, and workshop materials used for the training of national coders. Before national training, the PISA Consortium organised training sessions to present the material and train the coding co-ordinators from the participating countries. The latter were then responsible for training their national coders.

For each assessment item, the relevant coding manual described the aim of the question and how to code students' responses to each item. This description included the credit labels – full credit, partial credit or no credit – attached to the possible categories of responses. PISA 2006 also included a system of double-digit coding for some mathematics and science items in which the first digit represented the score and the second digit represented different strategies or approaches that students used to solve the problem. The second digit generated national profiles of student strategies and misconceptions. By way of illustration, the coding manuals also included real examples of students' responses (drawn from the Field Trial) accompanied by a rationale for their classification.

In each country, a sub-sample of assessment booklets was coded independently by four coders and examined by the PISA Consortium. In order to examine the consistency of this coding process in more detail within each country and to estimate the magnitude of the variance components associated with the use of coders, the PISA Consortium conducted an inter-coder reliability study on the sub-sample of assessment booklets. Homogeneity analysis was applied to the national sets of multiple coding and compared with the results of the Field Trial. For details see the *PISA 2006 Technical Report* (OECD, forthcoming).

At the between-country level, an International Coding Review (ICR) was implemented to check on the consistency of application of response coding standards across all participating countries. The objective of this study was to estimate potential bias (either leniency or harshness) in the coding standards applied in each national centre, and to express this potential bias in "PISA units". The ICR was implemented in two stages described here.

The first stage involved selection of a random sample of work from each adjudicated PISA entity (covering each of the three domains, and selecting a representative proportion of each language involved) that had already been subject to the multiple coder study, and coding of that work a fifth time by an independent trained multilingual reviewer. The code assigned by this independent reviewer was referred to as the "verifier code". A statistical analysis of the consistency between the score from the verifier code and the reported score was then carried out in order to identify cases where the verifier codes differed significantly from the codes underlying the reported scores.

The statistic used to assess coding consistency in each country was the average difference across items in a an assessment area between the verifier score and the reported score. When that difference was statistically significant (based on the standard errors for the country mean calculated from PISA 2003 data, or on a fixed criterion for new countries), all of those items were identified as being potentially discrepant, and requiring further review.

For any country where there appeared to be a serious potential problem, a second stage was warranted in order to confirm that any observed discrepancy between national codes and verifier codes indicated a problem with the national coding, and not with the standards applied by the verifier. The second stage involved international adjudication by senior Consortium staff of a random sample of about 20 student responses from each set (data from an adjudicated entity for a particular assessment area) that had been flagged as a result of the analysis in Stage 1. Where necessary, student responses were back-translated into English, and the responses together with the four national codes and the verifier code for these selected cases were reviewed by the international adjudicator in each assessment area. The adjudicator assigned a code to each response, and the corresponding score was compared to the verifier scores, and to the national scores.

Based on the results of the analysis of these data, it is expected that it will be possible to estimate a potential bias, in PISA units, of the coding in each adjudicated entity. The results of the International Coding Review will be reported in the *PISA 2006 Technical Report* (OECD, forthcoming).

ANNEX A7

COMPARISON OF RESULTS FROM THE PISA 2000, PISA 2003 AND PISA 2006 ASSESSMENTS.

The reading reporting scales used for PISA 2006, PISA 2003 and PISA 2000 are directly comparable. The mathematics reporting scale used for PISA 2006 is directly comparable to the scale used for PISA 2003. The science reporting scale used in PISA 2006 provides a base for comparison of results in the future. In the year where a given assessment area is the focus, the mean performance score is set at 500 for OECD countries – that is, reading was the focus of the PISA 2000 survey, so the PISA 2000 mean score for OECD countries was set at 500. The same was done for mathematics in PISA 2003 and for science in PISA 2006.

The PISA 2000, PISA 2003 and PISA 2006 assessments of reading, mathematics and science are linked assessments. That is, the sets of items used to assess each of mathematics, reading and science in PISA 2000, PISA 2003 and PISA 2006 include a subset of common items. Between PISA 2000 and PISA 2003 there were 20 items that were used in both assessments for mathematics, in reading there were 28 items used in both assessments and for science 25 items were used in both assessments. These common items are referred to as link items. PISA 2006 included 8 reading items that were also used in PISA 2000 and PISA 2003. All PISA 2006 mathematics items were also used in PISA 2003.

To establish common reporting metrics for PISA, the difficulty of the link items, measured on different occasions, is compared. Using procedures that are detailed in the *PISA 2006 Technical Report* (OECD, forthcoming), the comparison of the item difficulties on the different occasions was used to determine a score transformation that allows the reporting of the data on a common scale. The change in the difficulty of each of the individual link items is used in determining the transformation.

As each item provides slightly different information about the link transformation it follows that the chosen sample of link items will influence the estimated transformation. This means that if an alternative set of link items had been chosen the resulting transformation would be slightly different. The consequence is an uncertainty in the transformation due to the sampling of the link items, just as there is an uncertainty in values such as country means due to the use of a sample of students.

[Part 1/1]

Table A7.1 **Linking errors**

PISA survey cycles	Assessment domain	Linking error
2006-2003	Mathematics	1.38
2006-2003	Reading	4.47
2006-2000	Reading	4.98
2003-2000	Reading	5.31
2003-2000	Science	3.11

StatLink ⟨⟩ http://dx.doi.org/10.1787/142050165315

The uncertainty that results from the link-item sampling is referred to as linking error and this error must be taken into account when making certain comparisons between PISA 2000, PISA 2003 and PISA 2006 results. Just as with the error that is introduced through the process of sampling students, the exact magnitude of this linking error can only be estimated. As with sampling errors, the likely range of magnitude for the errors is represented as a standard error. The linking errors are listed in Table A7.1. In computing the statistical significance of the difference in scores between different PISA cycles, the calculation of the standard error of the difference includes the linking error in addition to the standard errors of the two individual scores. For example to calculate the standard error on the difference between scores obtained for a country in 2000 and 2003 the following formula is applied when $\sigma^2_{(\hat{\mu}_{2000})}$ and $\sigma^2_{(\hat{\mu}_{2003})}$ represent the standard errors for the results of PISA 2000 and PISA 2003, respectively, and $\sigma^2_{(linking\ error)}$ represents the linking error between PISA 2000 and PISA 2003:

$$SE = \sqrt{\sigma^2_{(\hat{\mu}_{2000})} + \sigma^2_{(\hat{\mu}_{2003})} + \sigma^2_{(linking\ error)}}$$

[Part 1/1]

Table A7.2 Comparison of science link items in the three PISA surveys

	PISA 2000		PISA 2006		PISA 2006		PISA 2006		PISA 2003		Difference between PISA 2006 and PISA 2003 science scores based on link items present in both assessments
	All science items on the PISA 2000 scale		All science items on the PISA 2006 scale		All science items on the PISA 2000 scale		Link items on the PISA 2000 scale		Link items on the PISA 2000 scale		
	Mean	S.E.	Mean	S.E.	Mean	S.E.	Mean	S.E.	Mean	S.E.	
	(1)		(2)		(3)		(4)		(5)		(6)
OECD											
Australia	528	3.5	527	2.3	521	2.2	530	3.1	529	2.2	0.7
Austria	505	2.6	511	3.9	505	3.8	498	5.1	496	3.5	1.8
Belgium	496	4.3	510	2.5	505	2.4	511	3.0	514	2.5	-3.0
Canada	529	1.6	534	2.0	528	2.0	532	2.5	527	2.0	4.9
Czech Republic	511	2.4	513	3.5	507	3.4	512	5.0	519	3.9	-6.9
Denmark	481	2.8	496	3.1	491	3.0	490	4.0	482	3.4	8.4
Finland	538	2.5	563	2.0	556	2.0	565	2.5	556	2.4	8.8
France	500	3.2	495	3.4	490	3.3	499	4.2	515	3.2	**-16.2**
Germany	487	2.4	516	3.8	510	3.7	518	4.4	514	4.0	3.2
Greece	461	4.9	473	3.2	469	3.1	480	4.0	459	3.9	**20.5**
Hungary	496	4.2	504	2.7	499	2.6	492	3.4	495	2.9	-2.8
Iceland	496	2.2	491	1.6	486	1.6	483	2.1	490	2.0	-7.2
Ireland	513	3.2	508	3.2	503	3.1	509	3.8	518	3.1	-8.7
Italy	478	3.1	475	2.0	471	2.0	465	2.5	468	3.1	-3.5
Japan	550	5.5	531	3.4	525	3.3	548	4.1	547	4.4	0.2
Korea	552	2.7	522	3.4	516	3.3	544	4.2	554	3.8	-10.4
Luxembourg	443	2.3	486	1.1	481	1.0	476	1.4	476	1.8	-0.6
Mexico	422	3.2	410	2.7	407	2.6	391	3.0	368	3.8	**22.7**
Netherlands	529	4.0	525	2.7	519	2.7	526	3.7	532	3.5	-6.1
New Zealand	528	2.4	530	2.7	524	2.6	521	3.1	522	2.7	-0.6
Norway	500	2.8	487	3.1	482	3.0	480	3.5	476	3.3	4.3
Poland	483	5.1	498	2.3	493	2.3	495	3.4	486	3.2	9.0
Portugal	459	4.0	474	3.0	470	2.9	454	3.9	455	3.9	-1.0
Slovak Republic	m	m	488	2.6	484	2.5	469	3.8	475	3.5	-5.8
Spain	491	3.0	488	2.6	484	2.5	484	3.0	474	2.7	10.2
Sweden	512	2.5	503	2.4	498	2.3	501	3.1	508	3.1	-7.0
Switzerland	496	4.4	512	3.2	506	3.1	513	3.6	513	3.9	0.3
Turkey	m	m	424	3.8	421	3.7	400	5.2	403	6.3	-2.4
United Kingdom	532	2.7	515	2.3	509	2.2	521	3.0	527	3.1	-5.7
United States	499	7.3	489	4.2	484	4.1	473	4.7	487	3.2	-13.5
Partners											
Argentina	396	8.6	391	6.1	389	5.9	377	6.3	m	m	m
Azerbaijan	m	m	382	2.8	380	2.7	379	3.8	m	m	m
Brazil	375	3.3	390	2.8	388	2.7	376	3.5	357	4.5	**19.0**
Bulgaria	m	m	434	6.1	431	6.0	434	7.5	m	m	m
Chile	415	3.4	438	4.3	435	4.2	420	5.2	m	m	m
Colombia	m	m	388	3.4	386	3.3	387	4.4	m	m	m
Croatia	m	m	493	2.4	488	2.4	486	3.4	m	m	m
Estonia	m	m	531	2.5	525	2.5	538	3.1	m	m	m
Hong Kong-China	541	3.0	542	2.5	536	2.4	563	3.0	561	4.4	1.4
Indonesia	393	3.9	393	5.7	391	5.6	391	7.5	373	2.9	17.7
Israel	434	9.0	454	3.7	450	3.6	454	4.8	m	m	m
Jordan	m	m	422	2.8	419	2.8	410	4.0	m	m	m
Kyrgyzstan	m	m	322	2.9	322	2.9	301	3.4	m	m	m
Latvia	460	5.6	490	3.0	485	2.9	478	3.8	480	3.9	-2.8
Liechtenstein	476	7.1	522	4.1	516	4.0	535	4.9	m	m	m
Lithuania	m	m	488	2.8	483	2.7	492	3.5	m	m	m
Macao-China	m	m	511	1.1	505	1.0	520	1.3	527	3.7	-6.5
Montenegro	m	m	412	1.1	409	1.0	386	1.6	m	m	m
Qatar	m	m	349	.9	348	.8	312	1.5	m	m	m
Romania	m	m	418	4.2	415	4.1	414	5.6	m	m	m
Russian Federation	460	4.7	479	3.7	475	3.6	474	4.4	473	4.3	1.1
Serbia	m	m	436	3.0	432	3.0	409	4.2	m	m	m
Slovenia	m	m	519	1.1	513	1.1	511	1.7	m	m	m
Chinese Taipei	m	m	532	3.6	526	3.5	545	4.3	m	m	m
Thailand	436	3.1	421	2.1	418	2.1	391	2.9	397	3.0	-6.0
Tunisia	m	m	386	3.0	383	2.9	383	4.3	367	2.9	15.5
Uruguay	m	m	428	2.7	425	2.7	423	3.0	394	3.3	28.9

StatLink http://dx.doi.org/10.1787/142050165315

The difference in scores is then divided by the standard error to indicate statistical significance in the normal way (that is, a result greater than or equal to 1.96 indicates a significant difference at the 95% confidence level). See the *PISA 2003 Data Analysis Manual* (OECD, 2004b) or the *PISA 2006 Data Analysis Manual* (OECD, forthcoming).

As previously mentioned, for PISA 2006 a number of new items were created that reflected the development of the new science framework. Table A7.2 shows the comparison of results in science across the three cycles of PISA. Science was the major assessment area for the first time in PISA 2006 and thus the scaling led to a new scale upon which future cycles of PISA science will be based. Previously, the scaling was based on the results from PISA 2000. Table A7.2 above presents the results for the science items based on both the PISA 2000 and the PISA 2006 scales.

- *Column 1* shows the estimates of student performance for the link items based on the PISA 2000 scale.
- *Column 2* shows the PISA 2006 estimates of student performance for all science items based on the PISA 2006 scale.
- *Column 3* shows the PISA 2006 estimates of student performance for all science items based on the PISA 2000 scale.
- *Column 4* shows the PISA 2006 estimates of student performance for the link items only based on the PISA 2000 scale.
- *Column 5* shows the PISA 2003 estimates of student performance for the link items only based on the PISA 2000 scale.
- *Column 6* shows the difference between PISA 2006 and PISA 2003 science scores based on link items present in both assessments. This is calculated by subtracting column 5 from column 4. Statistically significant results are shown in bold.

371

ANNEX A8

TECHNICAL NOTES ON MULTILEVEL REGRESSION ANALYSIS

Annex A8 is available on line at *www.pisa.oecd.org*.

ANNEX A9

SPSS SYNTAX TO PREPARE DATA FILES FOR MULTILEVEL REGRESSION ANALYSIS

Annex A9 is available on line at *www.pisa.oecd.org*.

ANNEX A10

TECHNICAL NOTES ON MEASURES OF STUDENTS' ATTITUDES TO SCIENCE

Table A10.1 **Population context: proportion of students enrolled in formal education**

The percentages reported in PISA 2006 are based on valid samples of 15-year-old students enrolled in formal education. In a number of countries a significant proportion of 15-year-olds are no longer enrolled in formal education. Countries in which this proportion is less than 90% are listed below. Results in these countries may therefore be biased. Note that where data for the percentage of 15- and 16-year-olds enrolled in formal education are not available the net enrolment ratio in secondary education is provided.

A) Percentage of 15- and 16-year-olds enrolled in formal education (2005)	Age 15	Age 16
OECD Luxembourg	89	82
Mexico	66	54
Portugal	88	80
Turkey	59	55
Partners Russian Federation	84	73

Source: OECD.

B) Net enrolment ratio in secondary education (2004)	%
Partners Argentina	79
Azerbaijan	77
Brazil	76
Bulgaria	88
Chile	78
Colombia	55
Croatia	85
Estonia	90
Indonesia	57
Israel	89
Jordan	81
Kyrgyzstan[1]	88
Latvia	89
Lithuania	93
Macao	77
Qatar	87
Romania	81
Russian Federation	76
Slovenia	95
Thailand	64
Tunisia	64
Uruguay	69

1. Gross enrolment ratio.
Source: UNESCO.
StatLink http://dx.doi.org/10.1787/142050165315

Table A10.2 Psychometric quality of the PISA 2006 attitudinal measures: classical item statistics for the pooled OECD and pooled partner countries/economies

| | Cronbach's Alpha[1] | | | | |
| | Pooled samples | | Number of countries with low reliability | | |
	OECD	Partner countries /economies	OECD	Partner countries /economies	OECD countries with low reliability
Students' self-beliefs					
Index of self-efficacy in science	0.83	0.80	0	1	
Index of self-concept in science	0.92	0.89	0	0	
Support for scientific enquiry					
Index of general value of science	0.75	0.72	4	16	*Mexico, Greece, Hungary, France*
Index of personal value of science	0.75	0.72	4	16	*Mexico, Greece, Hungary, France*
Interest in science					
Index of general interest in science	0.85	0.82	0	0	
Index of enjoyment of science	0.88	0.91	0	0	
Index of instrumental motivation to learn science	0.92	0.90	0	0	
Index of future-oriented motivation to learn science	0.92	0.90	0	0	
Index of science-related activities	0.80	0.79	0	2	
Responsibility towards resources and environments					
Index of students' awareness of environmental issues	0.76	0.75	2	4	*Greece, Hungary*
Index of students' optimism regarding environmental issues	0.79	0.83	2	0	*Austria, Germany*
Index of students' responsibility for sustainable development	0.79	0.76	0	9	
Index of students' level of concern for environmental issues	0.81	0.80	1	2	*Italy*

| | Item-total correlations (number of items with r<.3)[2] | | | | |
| | Pooled samples | | Number of countries with low item-total correlations | | |
	OECD	Partner countries /economies	OECD	Partner countries /economies	Countries with low reliability
Students' self-beliefs					
Index of self-efficacy in science	0	0	0	0	
Index of self-concept in science	0	0	0	0	
Support for scientific enquiry					
Index of general value of science	0	0	0	0	
Index of personal value of science	0	0	0	0	
Interest in science					
Index of general interest in science	0	0	0	1	*Tunisia*
Index of enjoyment of science	0	0	0	0	
Index of instrumental motivation to learn science	0	0	0	0	
Index of future-oriented motivation to learn science	0	0	0	0	
Index of science-related activities	0	0	10	1	*Australia, Austria, Belgium, Finland, France, Iceland, Ireland, Netherlands, New Zealand, United Kingdom, Tunisia*
Responsibility towards resources and environments					
Index of students' awareness of environmental issues	0	0	0	0	
Index of students' optimism regarding environmental issues	0	0	0	1	*Latvia*
Index of students' responsibility for sustainable development	0	0	0	7	*Bulgaria, Colombia, Indonesia, Latvia, Russian Federation, Thailand, Tunisia*
Index of students' level of concern for environmental issues	0	0	0	1	*Tunisia*

1. Notes on Cronbach's Alpha:

High reliability	(0.80 or higher)
Moderate reliability	(0.70 to 0.79)
Low reliability	(0.60 to 0.69)
Very low reliability	(less than 0.60)

2. Notes on item-total correlations:

These correlations indicate to what extent individual items correlate with the overall score (for all other items in the index). Low item-total correlations (< 0.3) indicate items with poor scaling properties.

StatLink http://dx.doi.org/10.1787/142050165315

Table A10.3 Overview of the relationship between the attitudinal indices and science performance

	OECD countries			
	Correlation with performance across countries	Number of countries where within-country relationship with performance is		
Students' self-beliefs		Positive[1]		Negative[1]
Index of self-efficacy in science	0.33	30	0	
Index of self-concept in science	0.15	30	0	
Support for scientific enquiry				
Support for scientific enquiry scale	0.25	30	0	
Index of general value of science	0.22	30	0	
Index of personal value of science	0.12	29	0	
Interest in science				
Interest in scientific topics scale	-0.06	6	0	
Index of general interest in science	0.13	30	0	
Index of enjoyment of science	0.19	30	0	
Index of instrumental motivation to learn science	0.09	28	0	
Index of future-oriented motivation to learn science[2]	0.08	29	1	Mexico
Index of science-related activities[3]	0.04	29	1	Mexico
Responsibility towards resources and environments				
Index of students' awareness of environmental issues	0.43	30	0	
Index of students' optimism regarding environmental issues	-0.17	0	30	
Index of students' responsibility for sustainable development	0.18	30	0	
Index of students' level of concern for environmental issues[4]	0.01	17	2	Czech Republic, Iceland

	Partner countries/economies			
	Correlation with performance across countries	Number of countries where within-country relationship with performance is		
Students' self-beliefs		Positive[1]		Negative[1]
Index of self-efficacy in science	0.28	27	0	
Index of self-concept in science	-0.07	18	2	Indonesia, Kyrgyzstan
Support for scientific enquiry				
Support for scientific enquiry scale	0.23	27	0	
Index of general value of science	0.13	27	0	
Index of personal value of science	-0.05	16	6	Argentina, Colombia, Kyrgyzstan, Montenegro, Serbia, Uruguay
Interest in science				
Interest in scientific topics scale	-0.12	4	0	
Index of general interest in science	-0.02	22	2	Colombia, Kyrgyzstan
Index of enjoyment of science	-0.04	18	4	Colombia, Kyrgyzstan, Montenegro, Serbia
Index of instrumental motivation to learn science	-0.11	11	9	Argentina, Brazil, Bulgaria, Colombia, Israel, Kyrgyzstan, Montenegro, Russian Federation, Serbia
Index of future-oriented motivation to learn science	-0.13	13	10	Azerbaijan, Brazil, Bulgaria, Colombia, Indonesia, Kyrgyzstan, Montenegro, Romania, Russian Federation, Serbia
Index of science-related activities	-0.04	9	8	Argentina, Brazil, Colombia, Jordan, Kyrgyzstan, Montenegro, Qatar, Tunisia
Responsibility towards resources and environments				
Index of students' awareness of environmental issues	0.46	27	0	
Index of students' optimism regarding environmental issues	-0.19	0	26	
Index of students' responsibility for sustainable development	0.20	26	1	Israel
Index of students' level of concern for environmental issues	0.12	18	2	Hong Kong-China, Lithuania

1. Only includes countries where the association between the index and science performance is statistically significant.
2. Note that Mexico is the only OECD country where this index is negatively associated with the PISA index of economic, social and cultural status.
3. Note that in Mexico there is no association between this index and the PISA index of economic, social and cultural status.
4. Note that the Czech Republic and Iceland are the only OECD countries where there is a negative association between the PISA index of economic, social and cultural status and the index of students' level of concern for environmental issues.

StatLink ᘛᗙᣘ http://dx.doi.org/10.1787/142050165315

[Part 1/2]

Table A10.4 List of PISA science-related careers in ISCO-88

ISCO-88 Code	Occupation
1236	Computing services department managers
1237	Research and development department managers
2110	*PHYSICISTS, CHEMISTS and RELATED PROFESSIONALS*
2111	Physicists and astronomers
2112	Meteorologists
2113	Chemists
2114	Geologists and geophysicists *[incl. geodesist]*
2122	Statisticians *[incl. actuary]*
2130	*COMPUTING PROFESSIONALS*
2131	Computer systems designers and analysts *[incl. software engineer]*
2132	Computer programmers
2139	Computing professionals nec
2140	*ARCHITECTS, ENGINEERS ETC PROFESSIONALS*
2141	Architects town and traffic planners *[incl. landscape architect]*
2142	Civil engineers *[incl. construction engineer]*
2143	Electrical engineers
2144	Electronics and telecommunications engineers
2145	Mechanical engineers
2146	Chemical engineers
2147	Mining engineers, metallurgists etc professionals
2148	Cartographers and surveyors
2149	Architects engineers etc professionals nec *[incl. consultant]*
2200	*LIFE SCIENCE and HEALTH PROFESSIONALS*
2210	*LIFE SCIENCE PROFESSIONALS*
2211	Biologists, botanists zoologists etc professionals
2212	Pharmacologists, pathologists etc professionals *[incl. biochemist]*
2213	Agronomists etc professionals
2220	*HEALTH PROFESSIONALS (EXCEPT NURSING)*
2221	Medical doctors
2222	Dentists
2223	Veterinarians
2224	Pharmacists
2229	Health professionals except nursing nec
2230	*NURSING and MIDWIFERY PROFESSIONALS [incl. registered nurses, registered midwives, nurse nfs]*
2442	Sociologists, anthropologists etc professionals
2445	Psychologists
2446	Social work professionals *[incl. welfare worker]*
3110	*PHYSICAL and ENGINEERING SCIENCE TECHNICIANS*
3111	Chemical and physical science technicians
3112	Civil engineering technicians
3113	Electrical engineering technicians
3114	Electronics and telecommunications engineering technicians
3115	Mechanical engineering technicians
3116	Chemical engineering technicians
3117	Mining and metallurgical technicians
3118	Draughtspersons *[incl. technical illustrator]*
3119	Physical and engineering science technicians nec *[incl. quantity surveyor]*
3130	*OPTICAL and ELECTRONIC EQUIPMENT OPERATORS*
3131	Photographers and electronic equipment operators *[incl. cameraman, sound mixer]*
3132	Broadcasting and telecommunications equipment operators
3133	Medical equipment operators *[incl. x-ray technician]*
3139	Optical and electronic equipment operators nec *[incl. cinema projectionist, telegrapher]*
3143	Aircraft pilots etc associate professionals
3144	Air traffic controllers
3145	Air traffic safety technicians
3150	*SAFETY and QUALITY INSPECTORS*
3151	Building and fire inspectors
3152	Safety, health and quality inspectors *[incl. occupational safety inspector, inspector nfs]*
3200	*LIFE SCIENCE and HEALTH ASSOCIATE PROFESSIONALS*
3210	*LIFE SCIENCE TECHNICIANS ETC ASSOCIATE PROFESSIONALS*
3211	Life science technicians *[incl. medical laboratory assistant, medical technician nfs, physical and life science technician, technician nfs, taxidermist]*
3212	Agronomy and forestry technicians
3213	Farming and forestry advisers
3220	*MODERN HEALTH ASSOCIATE PROFESSIONALS EXCEPT NURSING*
3221	Medical assistants

[Part 2/2]
Table A10.4   List of PISA science-related careers in ISCO-88

ISCO-88 Code	Occupation
3222	Sanitarians
3223	Dieticians and nutritionists
3224	Optometrists and opticians *[incl. dispensing optician]*
3225	Dental assistants *[incl. oral hygienist]*
3226	Physiotherapists etc associate professionals *[incl. chiropractor, masseur, osteopath]*
3227	Veterinary assistants *[incl. veterinarian vaccinater]*
3228	Pharmaceutical assistants
3229	Modern health associate professionals except nursing nec *[incl. homeopath, speech therapist, occupational therapist]*
3230	***NURSING and MIDWIFERY ASSOCIATE PROFESSIONALS***
3231	Nursing associate professionals *[incl. trainee nurses]*
3232	Midwifery associate professionals *[incl. trainee midwife]*

StatLink http://dx.doi.org/10.1787/142050165315

Annex B

The development and implementation of PISA –
a collaborative effort

INTRODUCTION

PISA is a collaborative effort, bringing together scientific expertise from the participating countries, steered jointly by their governments on the basis of shared, policy-driven interests.

A PISA Governing Board on which each country is represented determines, in the context of OECD objectives, the policy priorities for PISA and oversees adherence to these priorities during the implementation of the programme. This includes the setting of priorities for the development of indicators, for the establishment of the assessment instruments and for the reporting of the results.

Experts from participating countries also serve on working groups that are charged with linking policy objectives with the best internationally available technical expertise. By participating in these expert groups, countries ensure that the instruments are internationally valid and take into account the cultural and educational contexts in OECD Member countries, the assessment materials have strong measurement properties, and the instruments place an emphasis on authenticity and educational validity.

Through National Project Managers, participating countries implement PISA at the national level subject to the agreed administration procedures. National Project Managers play a vital role in ensuring that the implementation of the survey is of high quality, and verify and evaluate the survey results, analyses, reports and publications.

The design and implementation of the surveys, within the framework established by the PISA Governing Board, is the responsibility of an international consortium, referred to as the PISA Consortium, led by the Australian Council for Educational Research (ACER). Other partners in this consortium include the Netherlands National Institute for Educational Measurement (Citogroep), the National Institute for Educational Policy Research in Japan (NIER) and WESTAT in the United States.

The OECD Secretariat has overall managerial responsibility for the programme, monitors its implementation on a day-to-day basis, acts as the secretariat for the PISA Governing Board, builds consensus among countries and serves as the interlocutor between the PISA Governing Board and the international consortium charged with the implementation of the activities. The OECD Secretariat also produces the indicators and analyses and prepares the international reports and publications in co-operation with the PISA consortium and in close consultation with Member countries both at the policy level (PISA Governing Board) and at the level of implementation (National Project Managers).

The following lists the members of the various PISA bodies and the individual experts and consultants who have contributed to PISA.

Members of the PISA Governing Board

Chair: Ryo Watanabe

OECD countries

Australia: Giancarlo Savaris and Wendy Whitham

Austria: Helene Babel and Juergen Horschinegg

Belgium: Ariane Baye, Christiane Blondin and Liselotte Van De Perre,

Canada: Satya Brink, Patrick Bussière and Dianne Pennock

Czech Republic: Jana Strakova

Denmark: Jørgen Balling Rasmussen

Finland: Jari Rajanen

France: Gérard Bonnet and Jean-Claude Emin

Germany: Hans Konrad Koch, Elfriede Ohrnberger and Botho Priebe, Alexander Renner

Greece: Panos Kazantzis

Hungary: Benő Csapó

Iceland: Júlíus K. Björnsson

Ireland: Gerry Shiel

Italy: Raimondo Bolletta, Giacomo Elias and Piero Cipollone

Japan: Ryo Watanabe

Korea: Whan-sik Kim and Mee-Kyeong Lee

Luxembourg: Michel Lanners

Mexico: Felipe Martinez Rizo and Jorge Santibáñez-Romellón

Netherlands: Jules L. Peschar and Paul van Oijen

New Zealand: Lynne Whitney

Norway: Alette Schreiner

Poland: Stanislaw Drzazdzewski

Portugal: Carlos Pinto Ferreira and Glória Ramalho

Slovak Republic: Julius Hauser and Paulina Korsnakova

Spain: Carmen Maestro Martin, Ramon Pajares Box, Enrique Roca Cobo, and Josu Sierra Orrantia

Sweden: Anita Wester

Switzerland: Heinz Gilomen, Katrin Holenstein and Heinz Rhyn

Turkey: Sevki Karaca and Ruhi Kilç

United Kingdom: Lorna Bertrand, Liz Levy, Jo MacDonald, Audrey MacDougall and Bill Maxwell

United States: Daniel J. McGrath, Mark Schneider and Elois Scott

Observers

Brazil: Reynaldo Fernandes

Bulgaria: Neda Kristanova

Chile: Leonor Cariola

Croatia: Michelle Braš-Roth

Hong Kong-China: Esther Sui-chu Ho

Indonesia: Bahrul Hayat

Israel: Michal Beller

Latvia: Andris Kangro

Macao-China: Chio Fai Sou

Qatar: Juan Enrique Froemel and Adel Sayed

Russian Federation: Galina Kovalyova

Slovenia: Mojca Straus

Chinese Taipei: Fou-Lai Lin

PISA 2006 National Project Managers

Argentina: Marta Kisilevsky (from Feb-06) and Margarita Poggi (to Oct-05)

Australia: Sue Thomson

Austria: Günter Haider and Claudia Schreiner

Azerbaijan: Emin Meherremov

Belgium: Ariane Baye and Inge De Meyer

Brazil: Sheyla Carvalho Lira (from Oct-05) and Mariana Migliari (to Oct-05)

Bulgaria: Svetla Petrova

Canada: Tamara Knighton and Dianne Pennock

Chile: Ema Lagos

Chinese Taipei: Huann-shyang Lin

Colombia: Francisco Ernesto Reyes J.

Croatia: Michelle Braš Roth

Czech Republic: Jana Paleckova

Denmark: Niels Egelund

Estonia: Imbi Henno (from Sept-06) and Kristi Mere (to Sept-06)

Finland: Pekka Arinen

France: Ginette Bourny (from Jul-06) and Anne-Laure Monnier (to Jul-06)

Germany: Manfred Prenzel

Greece: Panos Kazantzis

Hong Kong-China: Esther Ho Sui Chu

Hungary: Ildikó Balázsi (from Nov-05), Pála Károly Aug-05 to Nov-05) and Peter Vari (to Aug-05)

Iceland: Almar Midvik Halldorsson

Indonesia: Burhanuddin Tola (from Mar-06) and Bahrul Hayat (to Mar-06)

Ireland: Eemer Eivers (from Dec-05) and Judith Cosgrove (to Dec-05)

Israel: Bracha Kramarski

Italy: Bruno Losito

Japan: Ryo Watanabe

Jordan: Khattab Mohammad Abulibdeh

Korea: Mee-Kyeong Lee

Kyrgyzstan: Inna Valkova

Latvia: Andris Kangro

Lithuania: Jolita Dudaité

Luxembourg: Iris Blanke

Macao-China: Lam Fat Lo

Mexico: María-Antonieta Díaz-Gutiérrez and Rafael Vidal

Montenegro: Tanja Ostojic (from Jan-07) and Ana Grego (to Jan-07)

Netherlands: Erna Gille

New Zealand: Maree Telford

Norway: Marit Kjaernsli

Poland: Michal Federowicz

Portugal: Lídia Padinha

Qatar: Juan Enrique Froemel

Romania: Roxana Mihail

Russian Federation: Galina Kovalyova

Serbia: Dragica Pavlovic Babic

Slovak Republic: Paulina Korsnakova

Slovenia: Mojca Straus

Spain: Lis Cercadillo Pérez (from Jan-07) and Ramon Pajares Box (to Jan-07)

Sweden: Karl-Göran Karlsson

Switzerland: Huguette McCluskey

Thailand: Sunee Klainin

Tunisia: Néjib Ayed

Turkey: Müfide Çaliskan (from Oct-06) and Sevki Karaca (to Oct-06)

United Kingdom: Jenny Bradshaw and John Hall

United States of America: Holly Xie (from Mar-06) and Mariann Lemke (to Aug-05)

Uruguay: Andrés Peri (from Dec-05) and Pedro Ravella (to Dec-05)

OECD Secretariat

Andreas Schleicher (overall co-ordination of PISA and partner country/economy relations)

John Cresswell (project management and analytic services)

Miyako Ikeda (analytic services and partner country/economy relations)

Claire Shewbridge (analytic services)

Sophie Vayssettes (analytic services)

Karin Zimmer (project management)

Cécile Bily (administrative support)

Juliet Evans (administrative support)

Kate Lancaster (editorial support)

Elke Lüdemann (analytic services for the preparation of the PISA 2006 report)

Yugo Nakamura (support for the preparation of the PISA 2006 report)

Diana Toledo Figueroa (support for the preparation of the PISA 2006 report)

Susanne Salz (support for the preparation of the PISA 2006 report)

PISA Expert Groups

Science Expert Group

Rodger Bybee (Chair) (BSCS, Colorado Springs, USA)

Ewa Bartnik (Warsaw University, Poland)

Peter Fensham (Queensland University of Technology, Australia)

Paulina Korsnakova (National Institute for Education, Slovak Republic)

Robert Laurie (University of New Brunswick, Canada)

Svein Lie (University of Oslo, Norway)

Pierre Malléus (Ministère de l'Education nationale, Paris, France)

Michelina Mayer (INVALSI, Frascati, Italy)

Robin Millar (University of York, UK)

Yasushi Ogura (National Institute for Educational Policy Research, Japan)

Manfred Prenzel (University of Kiel, Germany)

Andrée Tiberghien (University of Lyon, France)

Reading Expert Group

John de Jong (Chair from Sept 2005) (Language Testing Services, Netherlands)

Irwin Kirsch (Chair to Sept 2005) (Education Testing Service, New Jersey, USA)

Marilyn Binkley (National Centre for Educational Statistics, Washington, USA)

Alan Davies (University of Edinburgh, UK)

Stan Jones (Statistics Canada)

Dominique Lafontaine (Université de Liège, Belgium)

Martine Rémond (IUFM de Créteil et Université Paris, France)

Mathematics Expert Group

Jan de Lange (Chair) (Freudenthal Institute, Utrecht University, the Netherlands)

Werner Blum (University of Kassel, Germany)

John Dossey (Consultant, USA)

Zbigniew Marciniak (University of Warsaw, Poland)

Mogens Niss (University of Roskilde, Denmark)

Yoshinori Shimizu (University of Tsukuba, Japan)

Questionnaire Expert Group

David Baker (Pennsylvania State University, USA)

Rodger Bybee (BSCS, Colorado Springs, USA)

Aletta Grisay (Consultant, Paris, France)

David Kaplan (University of Wisconsin – Madison, USA)

John Keeves (Flinders University, Australia)

Reinhard Pekrun (University of Munich, Germany)

Erich Ramseier (Abteilung Bildungsplanung und Evaluation, Bern, Switzerland)

J. Douglas Willms (University of New Brunswick, Canada)

PISA Technical Advisory Group

Keith Rust (Chair) (Westat, USA)

Ray Adams (International Project Director, ACER)

John de Jong (Language Testing Services, the Netherlands)

Cees Glas (University of Twente, the Netherlands)

Aletta Grisay (Consultant, Paris, France)

David Kaplan (University of Wisconsin – Madison, USA)

Christian Monseur (University of Liege, Belgium)

Sophia Rabe-Hesketh (University of California – Berkeley, USA)

Thierry Rocher (Ministère de l'Education Nationale, France)

Norman Verhelst (CITO, Netherlands)

Kentaro Yamamoto (ETS, New Jersey, USA)

Rebecca Zwick (University of California – Santa Barbara, USA)

Larry Hedges (Northwestern University, USA)

Steve May (Ministry of Education, New Zealand)

J. Douglas Willms (University of New Brunswick, Canada)

Pierre Foy (IEA Data Processing Centre, Hamburg, Germany)

Eugene Johnson (American Institutes for Research, Washington, D.C, USA)

Irwin Kirsch (ETS, Princeton, USA)

PISA Consortium

Australian Council for Educational Research

Ray Adams (International Project Director)

Susan Bates (Project administration)

Alla Berezner (Data management and analysis)

Yan Bibby (Data processing and analysis)

Wei Buttress (Project administration, quality monitoring)

Renee Chow (Data processing)

Judith Cosgrove (Data processing and analysis, national centre support)

George Doukas (Data processing and analysis, computer-based assessment)

Eveline Gebhardt (Data processing and analysis)

Sam Haldane (IT services, computer-based assessment)

Dewi Handayani (Data processing, field operations)

John Harding (Science instrument development)

Jennifer Hong (Data processing, sampling)

Marten Koomen (Management, computer-based assessment)

Dulce Lay (Data processing, field operations, sampling)

Le Tu Luc (Data processing)

Tom Lumley (Reading instruments, test development)

Helen Lye (Science instrument development)

Greg Macaskill (Data management and processing, sampling)

Fran Maher (Science instruments, test development)

Ron Martin (Science instruments, test development)

Barry McCrae (Science instruments, test development)

Pippa McKelvie (Project administration, data processing, quality monitoring)

Juliette Mendelovits (Reading instruments, test development)

Esther Michael (Administrative support)

Martin Murphy (Field operations and sampling)

Van Nguyen (Data processing)

Gayl O'Connor (Science instrument development)

Alla Routitsky (Data management and processing)

Wolfram Schulz (Questionnaire development and analysis)

Fionnuala Shortt (Data processing, quality monitoring)

Ross Turner (Management, mathematics instruments, test development)

Daniel Urbach (Data processing and analysis)

Maurice Walker (Sampling, questionnaire development and analysis)

Wahyu Wardono (Project administration, computer-based assessment)

Westat

Keith Rust (Director of the PISA Consortium for sampling and weighting, Chair of TAG)

Sheila Krawchuk (Sampling, weighting and quality monitoring)

Eugene Brown (Weighting)

Ming Chen (Weighting)

Fran Cohen (Weighting)

Joseph Croos (Weighting)

Susan Fuss (Sampling, weighting and quality monitoring)

Ismael Flores-Cervantes (Quality monitoring)

Amita Gopinath (Weighting)

Sharon Hirabayashi (Weighting)

John Lopdell (Weighting)

Shawn Lu (Weighting)

Christian Monseur (Consultant, sampling, weighting and quality monitoring)

Merl Robinson (Quality monitoring)

William Wall (Weighting)

Erin Wilson (Sampling and weighting)

The National Institute for Educational Research in Japan

Hanako Senuma (Mathematics instrument development)

Yasushi Ogura (Science instrument development)

Citogroep

Janny Harmsen (Project administration)

Kees Lagerwaard (Mathematics instrument development)

Ger Limpens (Mathematics instrument development)

Norman Verhelst (Technical advice, data analysis)

Jose Bruens (Science instrument development)

Joop Hendricx (Science instrument development)

Annemarie de Knecht (Management)

Educational Testing Service

Irwin Kirsch (Reading framework and test development)

Other experts

Steve Dept (cApStAn Linguistic Quality Control) (Translation and verification services)

Andrea Farrari (cApStAn Linguistic Quality Control) (Translation and verification services)

Oystein Guttersrud (ILS, University of Oslo) (Science instrument development)

Marit Kjaernsli (ILS, University of Oslo) (Science instrument development)

Svein Lie (ILS, University of Oslo) (Science instrument development)

Rolf V. Olsen (ILS, University of Oslo) (Science instrument development)

Steffen Brandt (IPN, University of Kiel) (Science instrument development)

Claus Carstensen (IPN, University of Kiel) (Science instrument development)

Barbara Drechsel (IPN, University of Kiel) (Science instrument development)

Marcus Hammann (IPN, University of Kiel) (Science instrument development)

Michael Komorek (IPN, University of Kiel) (Science instrument development)

Manfred Prenzel (IPN, University of Kiel) (Science instrument development, Questionnaire framework development)

Peter Nentwig (IPN, University of Kiel) (Science instrument development)

Martin Senkbeil (IPN, University of Kiel) (Science instrument development)

Beatrice Halleux (Consultant, Belgium) (Translation/ verification referee, French source development)

Aletta Grisay (Consultant, France) (Technical advice, French source development, questionnaire development)

Anne-Laure Monnier (Consultant, France) (French source development)

Christian Monseur (University of Liege) (Technical advice, data analysis)

Eve Recht (Consultant, Australia) (Editorial services)

Tina Seidel (Questionnaire framework development)

Alexander Wiseman (Questionnaire framework development)

Annex C

Links to the data underlying this report

Volume 2 of this report, *PISA 2006: Data/Données,* presents the data tables
underlying the analysis in Volume 1, as well as the results for regions within countries.
These data tables are also available on line via the following StatLinks:

Chapter 2   http://dx.doi.org/10.1787/142056138443

Chapter 3   http://dx.doi.org/10.1787/142102278412

Chapter 4   http://dx.doi.org/10.1787/142104560611

Chapter 5   http://dx.doi.org/10.1787/142127877152

Chapter 6   http://dx.doi.org/10.1787/142183565744

Results for regions   http://dx.doi.org/10.1787/142184405135
within countries

These StatLinks are stable and will remain unchanged over time.

In addition, all PISA data and publications are freely available on the PISA website: *www.pisa.oecd.org.*

This book has...

StatLinks

A service that delivers Excel® files from the printed page!

Look for the *StatLinks* at the bottom right-hand corner of the tables or graphs in this book. To download the matching Excel® spreadsheet, just type the link into your Internet browser, starting with the *http://dx.doi.org* prefix.
If you're reading the PDF e-book edition, and your PC is connected to the Internet, simply click on the link.
You'll find *StatLinks* appearing in more OECD books.

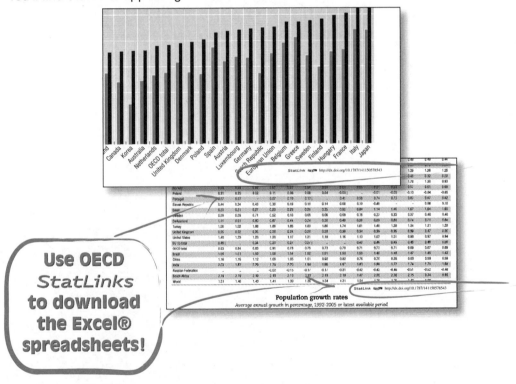

Use OECD StatLinks to download the Excel® spreadsheets!

StatLinks : another innovation from OECD Publishing.

Learn more at *www.oecd.org/statistics/statlink*

We'd like to hear what you think about our publications and services like *StatLinks*: e-mail us at oecdpublishing@oecd.org

OECD PUBLICATIONS, 2, rue André-Pascal, 75775 PARIS CEDEX 16
PRINTED IN FRANCE
(98 2007 01 1 P) ISBN 978-92-64-04000-7 – No. 55883 2007

Imprimé en France. - JOUVE, 11, bd de Sébastopol, 75001 PARIS
N° 444349G - Dépôt légal : novembre 2007